Critical Thinking in Higher Education and Labour Market

ERZIEHUNGSKONZEPTIONEN UND PRAXIS
EDUCATIONAL CONCEPTS AND PRACTICE

Edited by Gerd-Bodo von Carlsburg

VOLUME 86

PETER LANG

Valdonė Indrašienė / Violeta Jegelevičienė /
Odeta Merfeldaitė / Daiva Penkauskienė /
Jolanta Pivorienė / Asta Railienė /
Justinas Sadauskas / Natalija Valavičienė

Critical Thinking in Higher Education and Labour Market

PETER LANG

Bibliographic Information published by the Deutsche Nationalbibliothek
The Deutsche Nationalbibliothek lists this publication in the Deutsche Nationalbibliografie; detailed bibliographic data is available online at http://dnb.d-nb.de.

Library of Congress Cataloging-in-Publication Data
A CIP catalog record for this book has been applied for at the Library of Congress.

This project has received funding from European Social Fund (project No 09.3.3-LMT-K-712-01-0068) under grant agreement with the Research Council of Lithuania (LMTLT).

Reviewers :
Prof. Dr. Antonella Poce, University of Modena and Reggio Emilia, Italy.
Prof. Dr. Zanda Rubene, University of Latvia, Latvia.
Prof. Dr. Aelita Skaržauskienė, Vilnius Gediminas Technical University, Lithuania.
Prof. Dr. Irena Žemaitaitytė, Mykolas Romeris University, Lithuania.

ISSN 0723-7464
ISBN 978-3-631-83370-4 (Print)
E-ISBN 978-3-631-86147-9 (E-PDF)
E-ISBN 978-3-631-86148-6 (EPUB)
DOI 10.3726/b18636

Peter Lang – Berlin · Bern · Bruxelles New York · Oxford · Warszawa · Wien

This publication has been peer reviewed.

www.peterlang.com

Preface

In 1967, *The Society of the Spectacle* by Guy Debord was published. In this book, Debord analyses society and reveals that over history, we have come to live in an increasingly constructed society that we view as spectators. We have gradually come to live in a 'culture' that is in no way given, but in every way man-made. In the book, Debord analyses culture and the forces that play a role in its construction. In doing so, he shows what critical thinking is all about, how it can be practiced, and what it may result in. Critical thinking is about being aware that we live in a constructed world. It entails deconstruction and trying to understand why things are as they are, and it results in an opportunity to reconstruct, do it differently, and make new constructions.

Since the publication of *The Society of the Spectacle*, society has changed dramatically, with digitalisation being the most obvious case in point. The number of constructions and the awareness that we are increasingly confronted with constructions of constructions (e.g. reconstructions of constructions in virtual spaces) reveal, in my view, the enduring and growing interest in and importance of critical thinking. That is why this monograph on critical thinking in higher education and the labour market is so relevant, important and worth studying.

In addition to reconfirming important insights on critical thinking, such as the need to be as precise as possible on what critical thinking means in a specific context or for a specific group, the monograph provides a large number of insights that any critical thinker deserves to become acquainted with. Allow me to highlight three of them in this preface.

The monograph shows critical thinking to be contextual, and context to be multi-layered as well as multidimensional. While the insights brought forward in the monograph undoubtedly have global relevance, the monograph is firmly rooted in Lithuanian society. It was made possible by Lithuanian society and pertains to higher education and the labour market in Lithuania. The specific context makes specific things more or less probable, and in order to understand and critically analyse the rich set of proposals and conclusions, a good understanding of 'Lithuania', which itself is a construction, does help. By studying critical thinking in both higher education and the labour market, and even more so – in different higher education settings and labour market sectors, the monograph reveals what critical thinking is all about, how it can be practiced, and what it may result in is coloured by affordances in the general and particular context. As such, the monograph extends an invitation to other researchers and scholars to replicate the different studies in their own contexts, and to analyse how these different contexts result in new answers to the research questions. We can only hope that the invitation will be widely accepted.

The monograph documents that while critical thinking is broadly regarded to be important and even essential, it should not be taken for granted. There is a huge variety in conceptualisations on what it is, how it is shown, what it addresses, and what it requires. The use and development of critical thinking are regularly and intentionally supported both in the labour market and higher education, despite diverse and clear indications that all that supporting of critical thinking, all that teaching of critical thinking are not always equally effective. Different conceptualisations of critical thinking result in different interpretations of the value of particular interventions, and, in turn, these different interpretations result in different reactions to those interventions. In addition to that insight, the monograph also extends an invitation for more research on fostering critical thinking, both by creating situations that afford critical thinking and by developing what is needed to engage in critical thinking. Here, too, we can only hope that the invitation will be widely accepted.

The monograph highlights the importance of critical thinking, that is, why it is equally important to research it. It also highlights the complexity of critical thinking, stressing the need for research that acknowledges that complexity. The monograph recognises and illustrates that critical thinking deserves and requires multiple research approaches. Understanding critical thinking, the practice of critical thinking, the fostering of critical thinking, and the development of critical thinking requires knowledge and an in-depth understanding of the literature on critical thinking; it also requires engagement in empirical research, from qualitative and quantitative to descriptive, explanatory and interventionist. The monograph reveals that more conceptual and more empirical research need one another. Through instantiation, empirical research helps understand and validate conceptual research on critical thinking, while the use of conceptual literature is essential for deconstructing the findings in order to make them meaningful. The methodological richness and solid embeddedness in the (international) literature of this monograph might be intimidating, but extend an invitation to researchers and scholars in the domain of critical thinking to be especially critical when it comes to making methodological choices. Again, we can only hope that the invitation will be widely accepted.

In *The Society of the Spectacle*, Guy Debord invites us to be critical and not to be 'spectators', writing: 'Spectators do not find what they want, they want what they find'. This monograph helps to not become spectators – to remain critical first and foremost about (the development of) critical thinking.

Jan Elen,

Professor, KU Leuven, Belgium
Leuven, May 2021

Acknowledgement

This monograph is the result of the authors' four-year journey of scientific research and discovery. This was achieved very consistently – the team's experience in the field of the understanding and development of critical thinking presupposed the key questions raised in the monograph, as well as the path for finding answers to them. This would not have been implemented without funding from the Research Council of Lithuania – the study was financed by the European Social Fund according to the activity 'Researcher qualification development through high-level R&D projects' of Measure No 09.3.3-LMT-K-712 (grant agreement No 09.3.3-LMT-K-712-01-006). This monograph came about with the support of the Mykolas Romeris University (MRU) community. We would like to thank the MRU administrative team, especially Laura Zableckienė and Aušra Šarėjūtė, who accompanied us at all stages of the project and not only administered the project process perfectly, but also provided moral support. Sincere thanks go out to Natalija Popkova and Albertas Olechnovičius from the MRU Library, whose consultations on scientometrics strengthened us as researchers. We would also like to take this opportunity to thank associate professor Rimantas Vosylis from the MRU Institute of Psychology for his professional quantitative analysis ideas and solutions. He gave us the opportunity not only to enhance the analysis of our research results, but also to grow as researchers.

We would like to express our gratitude to everyone whose experience, ideas, encouragement and constructive criticism contributed to and enriched this book. Authors from around the world who have written about critical thinking and whose publications we read and drew inspiration from, audiences of our presentations at conferences who asked us apropos questions and encouraged us to pay attention to important aspects of critical thinking – the results presented in this book were brought about and inspired by all of you. We are especially pleased to have had the opportunity to learn from University of Gothenburg (Sweden) professors Karin Dahlberg and Margaret Lepp, who so genuinely shared the methodological principles of phenomenographic research and their professional excellence. Thanks to you, we are able to show rich phenomenographic research data about the understanding and experience of critical thinking in the contexts of higher education and the labour market. Our sincere thanks go out to University of Haifa (Israel) professors Hadass Goldblatt and Guy Enosh, whose ideas and advice on mixed methods research design provided essential insights into the links between the development of critical thinking in higher education and demand in the labour market.

We would also like to thank the higher education institution teachers and students and the organisation managers and employees who responded to our invitation to participate in the research and devoted their time, shared their experiences, and provided the material that was so necessary for this research project. Without your support and participation, this monograph would not have been possible.

For their constructive and helpful comments, without which this monograph would not have taken its current form, we are grateful to the reviewers: Professor Zanda Rubene from the University of Latvia, Professor Aelita Skaržauskienė from Vilnius Gediminas Technical University, Professor Irena Žemaitaitytė from Mykolas Romeris University, and Professor Antonella Poce from Italy's University of Modena and Reggio Emilia. We would also like to thank Professor Jan Elen from KU Leuven (Belgium) for preparing the preface to our monograph and for the thoughts and support he expressed.

In this four-year creative process, we learned from each other, and experienced both the bitterness of heated discussions and disagreements, and the indescribable feeling of discovery. We grew – both individually and together, as a team of researchers. In this extraordinary path of intense creativity, we constantly felt the support, encouragement and understanding of our friends and family. Thank you for being there for us.

The team of authors would like to thank everyone who contributed their advice, scientific insights and experience. We hope that this outcome will strengthen us and encourage us to take on new scientific challenges, and that it will inspire the readers of the monograph to foster critical thinking in both personal and professional life.

Authors

Content

Introduction

Critical thinking is an ability that is highlighted in strategic national documents, education and labour market research. Critical thinking is recognised as one of the tools for the formation and development of human and social capital, and an important global labour market competence. Critical thinking is used as a strong argument in developing missions of higher education institutions, implementing learning aims, and evaluating learning outcomes, staff abilities, organisational success and political decisions.

Critical thinking is often referred to as a higher education ideal – an aspiration which the efforts of the academic community must be directed toward. This aspiration is described as the ability of graduates to become critically thinking practitioners who are able to build a life and successfully collaborate with others in solving pressing problems, making important decisions, and contributing to the well-being of society as a whole. Researchers studying the conception and expression of critical thinking in higher education and/or the study process point to a certain discrepancy between the formulation of this ideal as an aspiration and its implementation in practice. This discrepancy could be explained by three interrelated reasons. First is the vagueness of the conception of critical thinking. It is either given many intertwined meanings (Sigurðsson, 2017) or it is reduced to a person's cognitive abilities, logical reasoning and the conclusions drawn from them, which testifies to an immature (Turner, 2005) and rather limited attitude (Walkner and Finney, 1999) towards the phenomenon of critical thinking. The second reason for the discrepancy is a lack of communication and cooperation at the higher education institution in efforts to develop critical thinking. If there is disagreement at the institutional level on what is considered critical thinking in a specifically defined context, it is unclear what critical thinking to teach and how to teach it (Noddings, 2017). There is a risk of a real deviation between programme objectives, curriculum and its implementation, the goals of teachers, and the expectations of students. The lack of naming the phenomenon and highlighting its importance not only in official rhetoric, but also in real practice, makes mutual communication very difficult not only at the institutional level, but at other levels as well – education policy, education sciences and academic practice, and education and labour market institutions. This is the third reason for the discrepancy between critical thinking as an aspiration and its implementation. One might consider whether critical thinking, being such a complex and not entirely tangible phenomenon, can go beyond the boundaries of an aspiration and become a reality of the living world at all. However, this would already be a philosophical discussion. There is ample evidence that this phenomenon is no longer the subject of philosophical reasoning alone. Critical thinking is not only clearly embedded in education policy documents (European Commission 2016; OECD, 2018) – it also thrives in educational practice (OECD 2015; 2016). One can only question what critical thinking is, and what meaning and value is given to it at what level and to what extent. Whether it is treated as a well-trained mind, a person's accumulated capital, or something else.

In 2009, UNESCO declared that the development of critical thinking and ethical thinking in graduates is becoming an objective of global higher education (UNESCO, 2009). According to Soufi and See (2019), since 2011, the development of critical thinking has become one of the most important objectives of undergraduate studies in Europe, and in the United States, critical thinking has been identified as one of the key outcomes of higher education. The European Higher Education Area (2012) has emphasised that critical thinking is an important part of student-centred teaching at many universities. The European Commission aims to equip all students with basic and professional skills so that they can establish themselves in the labour market after graduation (Council of the European Union, 2018). The document highlights critical thinking as one of the key competences and treats it as an ability manifested in other competences, such as literacy or digital competence (Council of the European Union, 2018). Discussions between university representatives (OECD, 2016) reveal that: (1) there is no clear agreement on the definition of 'critical thinking' – it is doubtful whether a consensus can be reached at all in the presence of cultural differences; (2) the assessment of critical thinking cannot be limited to one or another existing instrument – the assessment tools chosen must be appropriate for the specific context and needs; (3) higher education institutions give insufficient attention to the development of this skill; (4) teachers lack the knowledge and skills to develop critical thinking, so attention must be given to improving their pedagogical competencies. The International Bureau of Education (2019), in cooperation with social partners in the business, governmental and non-governmental sectors, identifies critical thinking as one of the key skills to be included in higher education curricula, and the European Commission (2020) identifies critical thinking as one of the student competencies that determines their success after graduation.

Critical thinking has been more than just a part of academic rhetoric and educational practice for some time now. The voice of employers is increasingly being heard, calling for attention to be paid to the importance of critical thinking skills in the labour market, as well as in the rapidly changing world of information overload and change in general. Critical thinking is considered to be one of the key 21st century skills relevant to the labour market (Rave, Guerrero and Morales, 2020; Whiting, 2020). Critical thinking is used as an important argument in analysing and evaluating employee abilities and organisational culture (Brown, 2011; World Economic Forum, 2018). It is thought that critical thinking, combined with skills such as collaboration, problem solving, leadership, creativity and self-discipline, will help employees function effectively in the organisation of today (European Commission, 2012b; Council of the European Union, 2018) and be competitive in the 21st-century labour market (Habets, Stoffers, Van der Heijden and Peters, 2020).

The labour market is characterised by uncertainty and rapid change, and this requires new competencies, the application of technology, continuous market monitoring and a focus on change. Research shows that employers have high expectations for critical thinking. According to employers, critical thinking creates preconditions for a person to constantly improve for the purpose of organisational change (Felix, 2016), encourages constant response to the challenges of the changing environment and enables employees to look for the best solutions for themselves, their customers and the organisation (Indrašienė et al., 2019), and enables employees to have self-confidence, as professionals, in dealing with difficult situations and raising questions in search of new, innovative solutions (Jiang, Gao and Yang, 2018). And not only so that employees can perform their direct functions well, but also so that they are able to raise substantiated, critical questions that lead to fair and better solutions, and know how to reflect on their own activities and those of others, correct mistakes, and perceive the importance of their personal contribution to the development of the organisation and society as a whole (Penkauskienė, Railienė and Cruz, 2019).

The World Economic Forum (2020) has ranked the most important skills in the labour market of tomorrow. Critical thinking is ranked fourth, while analytical thinking and innovation are ranked first and complex problem-solving are ranked third. The report emphasises that this demand may not be met due to the large gap between the manifestation of these abilities in practice and their declared development in the formal education system. The relevance of critical thinking skills in the labour market and education systems has become evident due to public social discourse. Researchers (Pithers and Soden, 2000; Burbach, Matkin and Fritz, 2004; Andrews and Higson, 2008) have long questioned the coherence between theory and practice in the development of critical thinking. The question is raised as to whether what is written in scientific literature about fostering and evaluating critical thinking is not just scientific wisdom without any real application (Facione, 2013), and whether existing assessment instruments are sufficient in practice (Davies, 2015; Macpherson and Owen, 2010; Schendel, 2016).

This responds to the European Commission's Communication on European Higher Education in the World (2013) and the OECD recommendations (2015) on the need to review study programmes and teaching methods that develop young people's critical thinking in a more targeted and effective way so as to achieve sustainable learning outcomes that are applicable in practice. These attitudes are also confirmed by research outcomes (Lai, 2011; Arum and Roksa, 2011; Ennis, 2016) arguing that the development of critical thinking at institutions of higher education does not have sufficient evidence of its successful application in practice, and that higher education institutions lack the effective programmes, teacher qualification and conducive academic environment needed to develop critical thinking (Abrami et al., 2015).

It is worth noting that in the empirical part of the monograph, the manifestation of critical thinking in higher education and the labour market first and foremost reflects the cultural context of the particular country (the study programmes analysed are that of Lithuanian institutions of higher education, and the qualitative and quantitative research participants are teachers and students at higher education institutions in Lithuania as well as employers and employees working at companies operating in Lithuania). However, the research findings are discussed in the context of global research. Therefore, the introduction should give at least a brief presentation of the Lithuanian higher education system and research on the development of critical thinking at Lithuanian higher education institutions.

Lithuania has a long tradition of elite higher education. The Republic of Lithuania Law on Higher Education and Research (2009) states that the mission of higher education and research is to help ensure the country's public, cultural and economic prosperity, provide support and impetus for a full life of every citizen of the Republic of Lithuania, and satisfy the natural thirst for knowledge. Lithuanian higher education is an active player in the international higher education and research. The country has a binary system of higher education consisting of university and non-university higher education institutions. In 2020, higher education was provided in Lithuania by 40 educational institutions: 18 universities and 22 colleges. Lithuanian higher education quality standards are set by Lithuanian and international higher education documents and regulations. The higher education quality system is developed and improved with regard to global and European guidelines and recommendations for quality assurance in higher education (Standards and Guidelines for Quality Assurance in the European Higher Education Area, 2015). The Lithuanian higher education and research policy makes sure that the higher education and research system is in line with the needs of society and the economy, and supports its openness and integration into the international research and higher education space.

In order for Lithuania to remain competitive, the professional competencies being developed must be relevant in the current and future labour market. The Lithuanian labour market faces similar demands in terms of employee abilities as all EU countries do. There is a growing need for highly qualified specialists who are able to act and create quickly and efficiently in changing market situations, develop high value-added products, and implement innovations (Valavičienė, 2015). Therefore, the expectations of Lithuanian employers correlate with the expectations of employers in other European countries (Penkauskienė, Railienė and Cruz, 2019).

The importance of critical thinking skills is noted in the National Progress Strategy 'Lithuania 2030' (2012), which states that imagination, creativity and critical thinking are considered important national resources. However, this strategy also points out that the current education system devotes insufficient attention to strengthening critical thinking skills not only in higher education, but in general education as well. This is in line with the provisions of the Good School Concept (2015), which note that critical, analytical and creative thinking skills, problem-solving skills, and initiative and sociality are becoming more valuable than the information stored in memory.

Lithuanian researchers are also interested in the issue of critical thinking. Nevertheless, it must be acknowledged that research on critical thinking has only been conducted here since 2000 and is not extensive. Issues of the development of critical thinking skills related to the general education school have been analysed to a greater extent. However, there is very little research about the development of critical thinking at Lithuanian higher education institutions, revealing effective tools, methods and results that testify to their further application in practice. The works of Rimienė (1998; 2006; 2013) investigating students' cognitive abilities and dispositions are worth singling out. Lithuanian educators have researched critical thinking from the aspects of collaborative learning (Klimovienė, Urbonienė and Barzdžiukienė, 2006), reflective learning (Balčiūnienė, 2006) and evaluation of a specific study subject or module (Daukilas, 2006; Kriaučiūnienė, 2010; Tolutienė, 2010). Exploratory analysis of the situation allows to state that critical thinking is studied in a fragmented and inconsistent manner (Indrašienė, Penkauskienė and Railienė, 2017) and presupposes the following conclusions: (a) the development of critical thinking has been studied in more detail in general education than in higher education; (b) most scientific publications are limited to general theoretical reasoning rather than empirical material; (c) the publications based on empirical research are fragmentary and do not provide a picture of the effectiveness of critical thinking development methods and the sustainability of results. This preliminary overview cannot be compared to an in-depth analysis, so consistent research based on specific quality indicators was and is needed.

The emphasis on critical thinking in international and national documents, the growing attention of global economic and labour organisations, the problem of defining the concept of critical thinking, and the fragmented research all contributed to the idea of the 'Critical Thinking in Higher Education: The Study and Labour Market Perspective' research project. The objective of this project is to research the correspondence of higher education studies to the need for critical thinking expressed by the labour market. The scope of the study is expressed in the following problematic questions:

- What is considered critical thinking in the contexts of higher education and the labour market? What are the constituents of the conception of critical thinking?
- How is critical thinking understood (what real significance do higher education and labour market participants attach to it) and manifested in higher education studies and the labour market?
- What are the links between the development of critical thinking competence in higher education and the needs of the labour market?
- What should the development of critical thinking look like in higher education in order to reach an agreement on the educational significance and practical value of critical thinking?

The research methodology is based on the principle of triangulation, by combining different methods of data collection, analysis and interpretation, where the data complement each other and thus neutralise and reduce the deviation and errors that result from using only one research method (Creswell, 2014). Taking advantage of the benefits of quantitative and qualitative research (Patton, 2014; Neuendorf, 2017; Creswell, 2018; Abib and Hoppen, 2019), the monograph presents four closely related studies: a systematic literature review, quantitative and qualitative content analyses of Lithuanian higher education study programme and course descriptions, a phenomenographic study of teachers, students, employers and employees, and a representative survey of these groups.

The systematic literature review was used to study of the theoretical conception of critical thinking. The selection process consisted of two stages: the selection of scientific journals and the selection of scientific articles. The scientific journals were selected from the Clarivate Analytics Journal Citation Reports database using two keywords: *education* and *educational*. During the selection, 342 journals meeting the criteria were found, which were then grouped according to four topics (Education & Educational Research; Education, Scientific Disciplines; Education, Special; and Psychology, Educational) and quartiles (Q1–Q4). Sampling of the scientific articles within the selected journals was performed in the EBSCOhost database using the following selection criteria: ISSN of the particular journal; keyword *critical thinking* in the 'Subject terms' field; full text; 1997–2017 period; English language. All 804 articles found were screened using the exclusion criteria, leaving 303 texts in the final list.

In order to reveal the expression of critical thinking in higher education, an analysis of all of the country's higher education study programme and course descriptions was performed. The study used mixed methods, including quantitative and qualitative methods of data collection, analysis and interpretation, and was based on the facilitation approach. The study consisted of four sequentially interrelated stages. In the first stage, 754 study programme descriptions were analysed. The second stage involved quantitative content analysis of the descriptions of 266 study programmes that mention the concept of critical thinking. The third stage consisted of quantitative content analysis of the seven study programme and course descriptions purposefully selected from various study fields. In the fourth stage, qualitative content analysis of the same seven study programme course descriptions was carried out.

Phenomenography was chosen as the main methodological approach to research aspects of the conception and constituents of critical thinking as perceived by representatives of higher education and the labour market. The study used purposeful sampling to select participants according to the principle of heterogeneity. Interviews were conducted with 79 research participants: 18 teachers, 16 students, 28 employers and 17 employees. For the data collection, the semi-structured interview method was chosen, which ensured the clearness of purpose of the research, and provided flexibility to present the main and follow-up questions to the research participants, respond to the course of the actual interview, and focus on the relationship between the research participant and the research phenomenon rather than on the phenomenon itself. The analysis of qualitative data consisted of the following stages: repeated reading of the text, marking the parts of the text which were relevant to the interview questions, preparation of initial descriptions, grouping the data into categories based on similarities and differences, description of categories, distinction between dominant and non-dominant categories, assigning categories to dimensions/highlighting dimensions in relation to the categories, and creating a structural picture of the manifestation of the phenomenon in the outcome space.

In order to reveal the links between critical thinking in higher education and in the labour market, a quantitative study was conducted using the written survey method. The chosen data collection method made it possible to compare the opinions of the teachers and students, employers and employees, and to reveal the links between the study groups. In order for the sample to be representative of the entire statistical population, a multistage probability sampling method was used, by surveying four groups of respondents: teachers, students, employers and employees from all regions of Lithuania. A total of 152 teachers, 1,512 students, 528 employers and 2,012 employees participated in the research. In the questionnaire, all four groups were presented with blocks of questions about the perception of critical thinking, the importance of critical thinking skills, and the importance of critical thinking dispositions. Descriptive and inferential statistical methods were used for data analysis.

All four studies followed research ethics rules, identified research limitations, and provided guidelines for further research. Efforts were also made to ensure the reliability and validity of the data in these studies.

The scientific/practical value of the monograph is based on the fact that:

- the conception of critical thinking is revealed through a systematic analysis of scientific literature published over the course of two decades;
- a detailed analysis of study programme and course descriptions in various study fields is carried out from the aspect of critical thinking development;
- the authentic attitudes of teachers, students, employers and employees towards critical thinking is revealed;
- the coherence of the development of critical thinking in higher education with the practical application of critical thinking skills in work activities is evaluated using mixed method research;
- the multifaceted approaches and methods of critical thinking research are highlighted.

The monograph consists of six chapters. The first chapter is devoted to discussion of the conception of critical thinking. It raises the question of the definition of the conception of critical thinking. A variety of attitudes, research approaches and traditions are presented. Critical thinking is described as the entirety of a person's qualities, thought processes and results. Attention is drawn to the conceptions of critical thinking and criticality as complementary and intertwined meanings. This chapter also raises the question of the value of critical thinking to the individual, interpersonal relationships and society. It talks about the impact of critical thinking and its consequences for the individual and society, and highlights the role of higher education and the influence of the cultural context on the successful development of critical thinking. The role of critical thinking in the modern labour market is also highlighted, revealing the importance of critical thinking skills for human resource management and organisational efficiency, and pointing out the relationship between personal success driven by critical thinking and the benefit to the organisation.

The second chapter is devoted to theoretical analysis of the conception of critical thinking, namely focusing on the change and dynamics of the content of the conception over two decades (1997–2017). The methodological basis of this chapter consists of a systematic literature review, which was devoted to a review of critical thinking in higher education. The diachronic analysis made it possible to better identify the intensification of research on critical thinking in higher education, while the synchronous analysis made it possible to reveal the multidimensionality and comprehensiveness of critical thinking. The growing number of publications over this period reflects the growing interest of social researchers in the role and expression of critical thinking in higher education. Critical thinking began to be more discussed in scientific publications around 2005, but this does not necessarily mean that the theory of critical thinking is intensively developed. As shown in this chapter, articles based on empirical research are beginning to dominate in comparison with articles of theoretical thought. As critical thinking is an ability relevant to all fields of science, this chapter also presents the results of the article analysis by field: IT, arts, education, social sciences, natural sciences, humanities and health sciences. Through the domain-general and domain-specific dimensions, the attitudes towards critical thinking that exist in publications in each field of science are presented, as well as how critical thinking is highlighted at the personal, interpersonal and social levels.

The third chapter of the monograph is in line with the provision declared by researchers representing European higher education institutions (Promoting Critical Thinking in European Higher Education Institutions: towards an educational protocol, 2019) that the development of critical thinking must be systematically implemented at all levels of the higher education institution, from the institution's mission to the specific course description. Therefore, this chapter presents the results of the quantitative and qualitative content analyses of Lithuanian higher education study programme and course descriptions. It shows how critical thinking is embedded in the course descriptions and what other abilities and developed qualities it is associated with. The results of this analysis provide a better understanding of how the people who compile the study programme and course descriptions see critical thinking in the context of the competencies and abilities acquired by the student. They also allow for a discussion as to how successful the development of critical thinking can be in higher education if its development is planned in a fragmented manner or not planned at all. The results of this analysis show that the study programme course descriptions do not demonstrate a systematic and consistent approach to the development of critical thinking. These results can be useful in planning the improvement of study programmes.

The fourth chapter presents, based on phenomenographic research data, how the key actors in higher education and the labour market – higher education teachers and students, employers and employees – understand critical thinking and how they experience the expression of critical thinking in the context of their studies or work. In order to make targeted changes in higher education aimed at strengthening and systematising the development of critical thinking, it is important to explore what critical thinking is to teachers and students and how they experience it, how they teach it, and how they learn it. In responding to the needs of the labour market, it is important to ascertain what the critical thinking experiences of employers and employees are, how they understand what critical thinking is, and how they recognise it in their field of activity. The value of the phenomenographic research outcomes is revealed by delving into the conceptions and experiences of the research participants and presenting them in detail, looking for similarities and differences. The attitude of the teachers towards critical thinking is more holistic than that of the students, touching upon the social level and aspects of civic responsibility. The employers' and employees' attitudes, while emphasising the person's non-stereotypical thinking, focus on the field of the organisation and meeting its interests. The phenomenographic research outcomes presented in this chapter provide practical insights on how to improve education and study policies for the development of critical thinking to become an integral and systematic part of higher education that consistently brings change to the labour market as well.

The fifth chapter presents the results of the representative quantitative research – a survey of teachers, students, employers and employees. This survey reveals the attitudes of these four groups of what critical thinking is, how they evaluate the importance of critical thinking skills and dispositions for the labour market, and how they assess the need to improve these skills. The representatives of both higher education and the labour market usually understand critical thinking as a set of abilities and dispositions through which a person makes decisions in daily and professional activities. However, the teachers, students, employers and employees have different views on the importance of individual critical thinking skills in the labour market. All of these and other identified differences and relationships are coherently presented and explained. This chapter also reveals the links between how the importance of critical thinking skills is assessed and how the need to improve those skills is expressed.

After comparing the results of the qualitative and quantitative research, insights into the understanding, experience and expression of critical thinking in higher education and the labour market are presented in the sixth chapter. The links between the development of critical thinking in higher education and demand in the labour market are also elucidated. Critical thinking is experienced in a specific context, so the work or study environment has a fundamental influence on the formation of the conception of critical thinking and the attitude towards the development of critical thinking skills. The results of both the phenomenographic study and the survey suggest that there is no unified conception of critical thinking among teachers, students, employers and employees. This situation allows for discussion about the complexity of critical thinking as a phenomenon, and also draws attention to the fact that in order to make decisions more effective in implementing policies to strengthen the development of critical thinking, it is important to agree on what is meant by this term.

The monograph concludes with recommendations for higher education and the labour market.

References

Abrami, P., Bernard, R., Borokhovski, E., Waddington, D. I., Wade, C. A. & Persson, T. (2015). Strategies for teaching students to think critically: A meta-analysis. *Review of Educational Research, 85*(2), 275–314. doi:10.3102/0034654314551063.

Andrews, J. & Higson, H. (2008). Graduate employability, "soft skills" versus "hard" business knowledge: A European Study. *Higher Education in Europe, 33*(4), 411–422. doi:10.1080/03797720802522627.

Arum, R. & Roksa, J. (2011). Limited learning on college campuses. *Society, 48*(3), 203–207. doi: 10.1007/s12115-011-9417-8.

Balčiūnienė, I. (2006). Refleksyvių metodų analizė ir įvertinimas dirbant pagal kooperuotų studijų programą [Analysis and evaluation of reflective methods in service learning classes]. *Jaunųjų mokslininkų darbai, 4* (11), 44–53.

Brown, R. (2011). *Higher Education and the Market.* London, England: Routledge.

Burbach, M. E., Matkin, G. S. & Fritz, S. M. (2004). Teaching critical thinking in an introductory leadership course utilizing active learning strategies: A confirmatory study. *College Student Journal, 38*(3), 482–493.

Council of the European Union. (2018). Council Recommendation on Key Competences for Lifelong Learning. Retrieved from https://eur-lex.europa.eu/legal-content/EN/TXT/PDF/?uri=CONSIL:ST_9009_2018_INIT&from=EN.

Creswell, J.W. (2014). *A Concise Introduction to Mixed Methods Research.* Thousand Oaks, United States: Sage Publications.

Creswell, J. W. & Creswell, J. D. (2018). *Research Design: Qualitative, Quantitative, and Mixed Methods Approaches* (5th ed.). Los Angeles: Sage Publications.

Davies, M. (2015). A model of critical thinking in higher education. In: Paulsen, M. B., ed. *Higher Education: Handbook of Theory and Research*, pp. 41–88. doi: 10.1007/978-3-319-12835-1_2.

Desjardins, J. (2018). 10 skills you'll need to survive the rise of automation. Retrieved from https://www.weforum.org/agenda/2018/07/the-skills-needed-to-survive-the-robot-invasion-of-the-workplace.

Ennis, R. H. (2016). Critical thinking across the curriculum: A vision. *Topoi, 37*(4), 165–184. doi:10.1007/s11245-016-9401-4.

European Commission. (2012a). *The European Higher Education Area. Bologna process implementation report.* Retrieved from http://www.ehea.info/media.ehea.info/file/2012_Bucharest/79/5/Bologna_Process_Implementation_Report_607795.pdf.

European Commission. (2012b). *Rethinking Education: Investing in skills for better socio-economic outcomes.* Retrieved from https://www.cedefop.europa.eu/en/content/rethinking-education-investing-skills-better-socio-economic-outcomes.

European Commission. (2013). *European higher education in the world.* Retrieved from https://ec.europa.eu/transparency/documents-register/detail?ref=COM(2013)499&lang=en.

European Commission. (2016). Review of the 2006 recommendation on key competences for lifelong learning. Retrieved from https://ec.europa.eu/education/initiatives/key-competences-framework-review-2017_en/.

European Commission. (n.d.). *Relevant and high-quality higher education.* Retrieved from: https://ec.europa.eu/education/policies/higher-education/relevant-and-high-quality-higher-education_en.

Facione, P. A. (2011). *Critical thinking: What it is and why it counts.* Millbrae, CA: Measured Reasons.

Felix, S. M. C. (2016). *Fostering criticality within neoliberal higher education: A critical action research study with first year students in Kazakhstan.* (Doctoral dissertation, University of Sussex, Brighton, England). Retrieved from https://sro.sussex.ac.uk/id/eprint/61301/.

Geros mokyklos koncepcija [Good School Concept]. (2015). Retrieved from https://www.e-tar.lt/portal/lt/legalAct/f2f65120a7bb11e5be7fbe3f919a1ebe.

Habets, O., Stoffers, J., Van der Heijden, B. & and Peters, P. (2020). Am I Fit for Tomorrow's Labor Market? The Effect of Graduates' Skills Development during Higher Education for the 21st Century's Labor Market. *Sustainability, 12*(18). doi:10.3390/su12187746.

Hayashi, P., Abib, G. & Hoppen, N. (2019). Validity in qualitative research: A processual approach. *The Qualitative Report.* doi:10.46743/2160-3715/2019.3443.

Indrašienė, V., Jegelevičienė, V., Merfeldaitė, O., Penkauskienė, D., Pivorienė, J., Railienė, A., Sadauskas, J. & Valavičienė, N. (2019). What critical thinking and for what? *Social Welfare: Interdisciplinary Approach, 1*(9), 24–38. doi:10.21277/sw.v1i9.460.

International Bureau of Education. (2019). Future Competences and the Future of Curriculum: A Global Reference for Curriculum Transformation. Retrieved from http://www.ibe.unesco.org/sites/default/files/resources/02_future_competences_and_the_future_of_curriculum_30oct.v2.pdf.

Jiang, J., Gao, A. & Yang, B. (2018). Employees' critical thinking, leaders' inspirational motivation, and voice behavior: The mediating role of voice efficacy. *Journal of Personnel Psychology, 17*(1), 33–41. doi: 10.1027/1866-5888/a000193.

Klimovienė, G., Urbonienė, J. & Barzdžiukienė, R. (2006). Developing critical thinking through cooperative learning. *Kalbų studijos, 9*, 77–84.

Kriaučiūnienė, R. (2010). Būsimų užsienio kalbų mokytojų požiūris į profesijos kompetencijas [Foreign language students' viewpoint on competencies of teacher's profession]. *Acta paedagogica Vilnensia, 24*, 114–126. doi: 10.15388/ActPaed.2010.24.3030.

Lai, E. R. (2011). Critical thinking: A literature review. *Pearson's Research Reports, 6*, 40–41.

Law on Higher Education and Research of the Republic of Lithuania. (2009). Retrieved from https://e-seimas.lrs.lt/portal/legalAct/lt/TAD/548a2a30ead611e59b76f36d7fa634f8?jfwid=i3h7wcuc6.

Macpherson, K. & Owen, C. (2010). Assessment of critical thinking ability in medical students. *Assessment & Evaluation in Higher Education, 35*(1), 41–54. doi:10.1080/02602930802475471.

Neuendorf, K.A. (2017). *The Content Analysis Guidebook*. Los Angeles: Sage Publications. doi: 10.4135/9781071802878.

Noddings, N. (2017). The search for meaning and connection. *Educational Studies, 53*(1), 1–12. doi:10.1080/00131946.2016.1269492.

OECD. (2015). *Intervention and Research Protocol for OECD Project on Assessing Progression in Creative and Critical Thinking Skills in Education*. Centre for Educational Research and Innovation (CERI) Governing Board. Paris: OECD Publishing. Retrieved from: http://www.oecd.org/officialdocuments/publicdisplaydocumentpdf/?cote=EDU/CERI/CD(2015)12&docLanguage=En.

OECD. (2016). *Fostering and Assessing Students' Creativity and Critical Thinking in Higher Education. Workshop Summary Report*. Retrieved from: http://www.oecd.org/education/ceri/EDU-CERI-CD(2016)8-ENG.pdf.

OECD. (2018). *Teaching for Global Competence in a Rapidly Changing World*. Paris: OECD Publishing.

Patton, M. Q. (2014). *Qualitative Research & Evaluation Methods: Integrating Theory and Practice*. Sage Publications.

Penkauskienė, D., Railienė, A. & Indrašienė, V. (2017). *National literature review*. Retrieved from https://sdcentras.lt/wp-content/uploads/National-literature-review.pdf.

Penkauskienė, D., Railienė, A. & Cruz, G. (2019). How is critical thinking valued by the labour market? Employer perspectives from different European countries. *Studies in Higher Education, 44*(5), 1–12. doi:10.1080/03075079.2019.1586323.

Pithers, R. T. & Soden, R. (2000). Critical thinking in education: A review. *Educational Research, 42*(3), 237–249. doi:10.1080/001318800440579.

Promoting Critical Thinking in European Higher Education Institutions: Towards an educational protocol (2019). Eds. Dominguez, C. & R. Payan-Carreira. Universidade de Trás-os-Montes e Alto Douro.

Rave, J. I. P., Guerrero, R. F. & Morales, J. C. C. (2020). Critical thinking and continuous improvement: A scientific text mining approach. *Total Quality Management*. doi:10.1080/14783363.2020.1787824.

Rimienė, V. (2006a). Studentų kritinio mąstymo dispozicijų ir įgūdžių kaitos galimybės [Possibilities for changing students' critical thinking dispositions and skills] (Lithuanian). *Acta Paedagogica Vilnensia, 17*, 78–85.

Rimienė, V. (2006b). Studentų kritinio mąstymo dispozicijų, įgūdžių bei intelekto sąsajos [Relationships between students' critical thinking dispositions, skills and intelligence]. *Educational Psychology/Ugdymo Psichologija, 24*, 6–13.

Schendel, R. (2016). Constructing Departmental Culture to Support Student Development: Evidence from a Case Study in Rwanda. *Higher Education, 72*(4), 487–504. doi:10.1007/s10734-016-0036-6.

Sigurðsson, G. (2017). Transformative Critique: What Confucianism Can Contribute to Contemporary Education. *Studies in Philosophy and Education, 36*(2), 131–146. doi:10.1007/s11217-015-9502-3.

Soufi, N. E. & See, B. H. (2019). Does explicit teaching of critical thinking improve critical thinking skills of English language learners in higher education? A critical review of causal evidence. *Studies in Educational Evaluation, 60*, 140–162. doi: 10.1016/j.stueduc.2018.12.006.

Standards and Guidelines for Quality Assurance in the European Higher Education Area (ESG). (2015). Brussels, Belgium. Retrieved from https://www.enqa.eu/wp-content/uploads/2015/11/ESG_2015.pdf.

The National Progress Strategy "Lithuania 2030". (2012). Retrieved from http://www.unesco.org/education/edurights/media/docs/2953897c103c13043bfabea84b716ae2f8c82f47.pdf.

Tolutienė, G. (2010). Andragogikos specialybės studentų kritinio mąstymo ugdymosi galimybės universitetinių studijų procese [Critical thinking self-development opportunities of andragogy speciality students in the university study process]. *Mokytojų ugdymas, 14*, 63–76.

Turner, P. (2005). Critical thinking in nursing education and practice as defined in the Literature. *Nursing Education Perspectives, 26*(5), 272–277.

UNESCO. (2009). *The New Dynamics of Higher Education and Research for Societal Change and Development*. Paris: UNESCO.

Valatkaitė-Rimienė, V. (1998). Moksleivių ir studentų kritinio mąstymo ypatumai ir lavinimo galimybės [Peculiarities of the critical thinking of students and possibilities of its development]. *Acta Paedagogica Vilnensia, 5*, 173–183. doi:10.15388/ActPaed.1998.05.9441.

Valavičienė, N. (2015). *Lietuvos fizinių ir technologijos mokslų specialistų tarptautinė migracija [International migration of Lithuanian physical and technological sciences specialists]*. (Doctoral dissertation, Vilnius University, Vilnius, Lithuania).

Walkner, P. & Finney, N. (1999). Skill development and critical thinking in higher education. *Teaching in Higher Education*, *4*(4), 531–547.

Whiting, K. (2020). These are the top 10 job skills of tomorrow – and how long it takes to learn them. Retrieved from: https://www.weforum.org/agenda/2020/10/top-10-work-skills-of-tomorrow-how-long-it-takes-to-learn-them/.

World Economic Forum (2020). *The Future of Jobs Report 2020*. Retrieved from http://www3.weforum.org/docs/WEF_Future_of_Jobs_2020.pdf.

The Concept and Context of Critical Thinking in Higher Education and Labour Market

Abstract: The importance of critical thinking is highlighted in scientific research on education and the labour market, as well as in countries' strategic documents. Critical thinking is recognised as one of the tools for the formation and development of human and social capital, and a competence important in the global labour market. However, there is no general agreement on what constitutes critical thinking in the contexts of education and the labour market and how it manifests itself in practical situations and in areas of social life.

The purpose of this chapter is to disclose the relevance of critical thinking in the contexts of higher education and the labour market and the importance of defining the concept of critical thinking. This part consists of three sections. The first section discusses the concept of critical thinking and the variety of its interpretations as determined by the period, context, and scientific attitudes and research approaches. The second section is designed to discuss the growing public awareness of the role of critical thinking in higher education, present the implications of including critical thinking in higher education for societal development and the individual, and demonstrate the influence of cultural context on the success and failure of critical thinking development. The third section analyses the importance of critical thinking in the modern labour market, discussing the importance of critical thinking skills for human resource management and organisational efficiency.

Keywords: concept of critical thinking, critical thinker, process and outcomes of critical thinking, criticality, relevance of critical thinking in higher education, value of critical thinking in labour market.

1. The Concept of Critical Thinking: A Question of Definition

So much has been written about the concept of critical thinking – from scientific and journalistic articles to monographs and dissertations – that any attempt to return to this topic again seems a bit pointless. What else can be discovered? What else can be said? Many scientists working in this field probably have these thoughts. Yet as paradoxical as it may seem, it is more important than ever to return to this concept. One of the main reasons is the multidimensionality and integrity of the concepts (Skaržauskienė, 2008), and sometimes their devaluation too (Donskis, 2009; Bauman and Donskis, 2013), as well as the personalisation and contextualisation of the concepts (Danvers, 2015), when they acquire unique meaning.

The concept of critical thinking, like many other concepts, is used ambiguously, giving it various meanings that often move away from the root concept and are sometimes misleading (Candy, 1991; Kincheloe and Steinberg, 1993; Sigurðsson, 2017; Penkauskienė, Railienė and Cruz., 2019). Critical thinking tends to be equated with good or desirable thinking (Pithers and Soden, 2000; Johnson and Hamby, 2015), honest, fair behaviour (Maloney et al., 2013), the overcoming of problems (Rodzalan and Saat, 2015), effective solutions (Ünsar and Engin, 2013), management of critical or crisis situations (Schraagen and van de Ven, 2008), and other positive phenomena. Critical thinking is directly linked to existential thinking (Ayesha and Samridhi, 2017), higher order thinking (Resnic, 1987; Helsdingen, van Gog and van Merrienboer, 2011), and liberating thinking (Apple, 1995; McLaren, 2016). Quite a few contemporary authors do not provide a clear definition of the concept. Critical thinking is referred to as 'innovative ability', 'innovative spirit' (Zhang, 2020), and a 'highly valued skill' (Aliakbari and Sadeghdaghighi, 2013). There is also a notable tendency to avoid a clear definition of the concept of critical thinking in scientific articles. Authoritative figures in the development of critical thinking concepts are often mentioned at the beginning of publications and their concepts are listed, but the authors do not clearly state what specific concept they adhere to when conducting research or teaching students (Khandaghi, Pakmehr and Amiri, 2011). Some confusion is also caused by the different terms used for critical thinking: disposition, ability, skill, competence. Therefore, the question sometimes arises as to whether it is an intrinsic personality trait, a mental operation, or a combination of everything (Dune, 2015).

Such a broad interpretation of the concept is conditioned not only by its complexity and the various scientific attitudes and traditions, but also by demand for it as a popular marketing 'brand' (Sigurðsson, 2017). Critical thinking is desirable in various spheres, sectors and strata of public life. It is considered to be one of the most important abilities that determine the well-being of the individual and society as a whole. It is used as an important argument in the development, implementation and evaluation of study goals and outcomes, missions of higher education institutions (Barnett, 1997; Brodin, 2007; Danvers, 2016; Felix, 2016; AACSB, 2017), staff skills (Brown, 2011; World Economic Forum, 2018), and political decisions (Williams, 1991; Weinstein, 2004; Sternberg and Halpern, 2020).

Because there are many concepts of critical thinking that sometimes complement each other and sometimes compete with each other, there is a need to specify what it means in a particular context, and how it is defined by its users. Otherwise, we will not be able to avoid confusion and miscommunication. Noddings (2017) emphasises that communication is necessary for two main reasons: the actual work that is being done, and the need for relationships with others. It is essential to understand what we are doing and be able to communicate it properly to anyone interested in critical thinking and working in this field. Schmaltz, Jansen and Wenckowski (2017) also point out that the complexity and vagueness of the concept can be an obstacle to agreements at the policy level of education, which would have a negative impact on the practice of developing critical thinking.

The historical development of the concept of critical thinking has been extensively explored in solid books and numerous articles. Therefore, there is no need to return to it again. However, several aspects need to be noted. First is the 'root' meaning of the concept, embedded in ancient tradition, and its interpretations in scientific publications. Second is the target of critical thinking as a value that is developed and nurtured, that is, who the addressee is and what is intended to be done with it. The root of the concept of critical thinking lies in the Greek words 'kriticos' and 'kriterion' and the Latin word 'criticus', which mean judgement based on certain measures or standards. For the ancient Greeks, this meant reasoning based on certain criteria. Faith in the power of substantiated reasoning meant faith in the possibility of getting closer to the truth and penetrating the essence of phenomena (Penkauskienė, 2016). The pursuit of truth is the fundamental goal. It has been widely used in various periods as a tool for searching for truth and clarity. However, 'kriterion' meant different things in different periods. Different approaches and methods have been used to group and classify them as certain research directions, scientific schools and traditions. The standard of critical thinking was and is used to describe a critical thinker, explain the thought process, and define the desired outcome.

1.1 The critical thinker

Dewey (1997; 2014), a leading representative of pragmatism whose name is associated with the concept of modern critical thinking and related research, describes a critical thinker as someone who is curious, open to experience, and inclined to investigate and reflect. His follower, Lipman (2003), emphasises the ability to understand one's mistakes and correct them. Ennis (1987; 2000), a representative of informal logic, describes a reflective thinker as someone who is able to form an independent opinion and decide what to believe and what not to. His colleague Siegel (1988) also adheres to a similar concept, emphasising the ability to make independent and reasoned decisions. A person's reflective thinking is the main focus of the reflective model (King and Kitchener, 1994). According to the representatives of this model, criticality is manifested in the constant rethinking of information and the assumptions that determine thinking, and in the person's ability to make reflective decisions in a certain context. Advocates of the cognitive model (Kurfiss, 1988; Halpern, 2014) also emphasise the importance and attitude of independent thinking and the ability to foster criticality in relation to oneself. 'In a cognitive perspective, critical thinking is above all a matter of being critical to one's own thoughts and, subsequently, to be critical as regards how these thoughts are enunciated' (Brodin, 2007, p. 133). For Brookfield (2005; 2012), a representative of pragmatism and critical pedagogy, a critical thinker is also associated with the assessment of presumptions that limit one's own thinking and that of others. Other representatives of critical pedagogy (Apple, 1995; Freir, 2000; 2001; McLaren, 2016; McLaren and Jandric, 2020) describe a critical thinker in a similar way, but place more emphasis on the pursuit of freedom and independence and the struggle for one's own independence and that of others, as well as the welfare of all mankind. A critical thinker can be recognised not only by analytical, metacognitive qualities, but also by certain intellectual virtues – intellectual humility and integrity. These traits singled out by Paul and Elder (2012) are associated with a responsible thinker who is fair-minded and has a strong foundation in terms of morality, ethics and values. They attribute intellectual autonomy, courage, perseverance, empathy and confidence in reason to other intellectual traits. An attempt was made to find a universal classification of personality traits/attitudes and abilities embracing many ideas. The Delphi report (Facione, 1990; Facione, Facione and Giancarlo, 2000) identified seven dispositions of critical thinking – a critical thinker is habitually open-minded, truth-seeking, inquisitive, judicious, analytical, systematic and confident in reasoning. These features essentially incorporate the ideas of many researchers. Rather than a lot of conflicting features, ones which complement one another or overlap are attributed to critical thinkers. Of mention among the ones that come up often are reflection, a tendency to consider one's own thinking and actions and that of others, and correcting oneself. It is, therefore, very common to hear that critical thinking is thinking about one's thinking and rethinking it.

A critical thinker is characterised not only by attitudes and values, but also by skills – analytical and synthetic (Liu, Mao, Frankel and Xu, 2016). Their amplitude ranges from information selection, analysis and interpretation to making informed decisions and conclusions. Analytical skills include analysis of the structure of arguments, which includes identifying the conclusions and functions of the individual elements of the argument as well as the validity of the evidence. Synthetic skills include the development of valid or meaningful arguments by selecting information that contributes to the substantiation of those arguments. Overall, critical thinking is described as a synthesis of cognitive skills and dispositions (Ku, Ho, Hau and Lai, 2014). Cognitive skills form the basis for logical thinking and argumentation and reflect a person's skill of masterfully realising a specific ability. Attitudes capture a person's conscious choice to use the skills that best meet the needs of the particular task. The value of critical thinking is seen in the ability to combine and join critical thinking attitudes and higher order thinking skills not only in the learning process (Huang, Lindell, Jaffe and Sullivan, 2016) but also in other, broader life contexts (Facione, 2011; Stupnisky et al., 2008).

The number of abilities listed differs in the same way as the attitudes, but does not differ in substance. All critical thinking skills are closely related to the desire to better recognise, ascertain and identify ill-structured problems and fallacies, and find the right answer, conclusion or solution to the problem. In summary, a critical thinker is characterised by a set of attitudes, values and skills that allow him or her to be identified as such and associated with the phenomenon of critical thinking itself.

1.2 The process of critical thinking

The process of critical thinking is defined in certain stages. Researchers list a different number of them and group them differently. Dewey (1902) associates the beginning stage with intellectual curiosity as a stimulus of thinking arising from the desire to learn, discover and understand. The next stage is raising questions and hypotheses based on one's own accumulated experience and that of others; this is followed by the search for problem-solving options, their selection, highlighting the best solution and reflection. Lipman (2003) describes the process of critical thinking in much the same way, only he emphasises the postponement of decisions when unsure of their correctness. According to Lipman, room must be left for corrections in the process of critical thinking, in the event that new facts or other evidence emerge. Facione, Facione and Giancarlo (2000) point to six stages of critical thinking: interpretation – categorisation, decoding the significance of the problem or idea and clarifying meaning; analysis – examining various data and information and analysing arguments; evaluation – logical examination of the available material and arguments; inference – querying evidence, conjecturing alternatives and drawing conclusions; explanation – how and why one or another decision was made; and self-regulation – contemplating how those decisions affected a person's thinking and taking concrete action for self-correction. Paul and Elder (2012) name eight stages: determining the purpose; raising questions related to the problem and the phenomenon under study; gathering information; interpreting it; clarifying and formulating concepts and theories; making assumptions; anticipating implications; and formulating an autonomous approach and drawing conclusions. In fact, the number of stages is not important. This does not change the essence of the process. Critical thinking emerges as an active thought process that combines the person's attitudes, values and skills and is directed towards a specific goal. In this process, many researchers see signs of research work (Beachboard, Beachboard, Li and Adkison, 2011), which include the ability to determine the reliability of sources, develop and defend one's position in relation to a specific problem, and draw conclusions (Tiruneh et al., 2017). Critical thinking is also called a process of reflection (Andrews, 2007), which challenges existing ideas and at the same time discusses with itself, doubts, and does not find an obviously correct solution (Wolcott, 2006). It is also associated with the process of logical thinking (Lim, 2011), in search of universal, correct decisions made in situations of different contexts (Cazzell and Anderson, 2016). Researchers (Rickles, Schneider, Slusser, Williams and Zipp, 2013) discern the links between critical and logical thinking in the rational evaluation of logic and empiricism. The same or very similar criteria for describing different types of thinking also cause some confusion. Perhaps this is why critical thinking tends to be equated with scientific or logical thinking.

1.3 Critical thinking outcomes

Critical thinking outcomes are often defined as the identification of fallacies or ill-structured problems (Siegel, 1988), selection of the best alternative based on evidence, decision-making and problem-solving method (McPeck, 1981; Ennis, 1962; 2003; Facione, 2011). This practical perspective points to a tangible result, which can sometimes be identified, raised and shown, or can sometimes be complicated. Of course, when it comes to products with material expression (e.g. research, publications), no problems arise. However, when we talk about outcomes as acquired critical thinking skills, reinforced attitudes, reassessed values or improved processes, it is difficult to define what the outcome is, and even more difficult to evaluate it. Even though the California (Facione, 1990) and Cornell (Ennis and Millman, 2005) critical thinking tests for evaluating attitudes and their practical application, as well as Freir's (1997) literacy programme and the critical thinking skill tests conducted by the Foundation for Critical.

Thinking (Elder, Paul and Cosgrove, 2007) and the OECD (Lancrin et al., 2019) are widely known, they do not evaluate all manifestations of critical thinking. They must also be adapted to the specific context, discipline or object of study. Doubts expressed about the tangibility of the practical outcome do not mean that it does not need to be anticipated and defined. In general, it is necessary to discuss not only the outcome of critical thinking, but also its consequences – academic or professional success, democratisation of society. But it is not easy to prove whether (and to what extent) these are the consequences of critical thinking.

Looking at the outcome of critical thinking from an idealistic perspective, one should return to the essence of critical thinking, which is termed 'the pursuit of truth'. The treatment of truth has varied from democratic to autocratic and elitist in different periods (Brodin, 2007). Antiquity speaks of a universal truth accessible to anyone who is willing and able to think, ask questions and look for answers. In the Middle Ages, truth was considered a confirmation of what is determined from above, and recognising it was considered to require exceptional wisdom. During the Renaissance, the truth lying in the perfect forms of nature was sought by inductive reasoning. In the era of rationalism, deductive, mathematical calculations had to be brought closer to objective truth. In the age of idealism, the pursuit of truth was the quest to know one's true self. The period of positivism equated truth with the search for common patterns, a testimony of objective truth. In the era of relativism, critical thinking was seen as a means of interpreting truth that could only be used by individuals with exceptional thinking skills and a strong will. In the modern, 'post-truth' period, critical thinking moved to being seen as a difficult pursuit of truth and justice, manifested in personal, but at the same time consolidated, efforts (Markowitz, 2005; Letizia, 2012; Dunne, 2015; Sinatra and Lombardi, 2020).

1.4 On the essence of criticality

Both the practical and the idealistic perspective, despite their differences, point to the essence of criticality as being the search for truth and justice. Brodin (2007), in exploring the essence of criticality, argues that critical thinking must first be understood as a dialectical connection between uncertainty and certainty, or as an attempt to dispel uncertainty in the search for justification, a confirmation of what could be real. The search for truth 'becomes the driving force for critical thinking. One does not stop thinking critically until the truth has been attained, so critical thinking becomes a meaningful activity with a certain purpose that could be concretised. On the other hand, critical thinking in this sense leads to an effacement of itself as soon as truth is thought to be found, which is not fruitful for the further development of critical thinking' (p. 58). It can, therefore, be argued that despite the fact that critical thinking has had its own definitions in different historical periods, it has always been an intellectual tool used to get closer to the truth, no matter how it is understood and in what ways it is found.

Brookfield (2012) has a similar line of thinking, arguing that despite the diversity of directions, they are united by the questioning of reality, knowledge, knowing and the assumptions that underpin them in the pursuit of justice. That is true, but the search for truth takes place at different levels and for a slightly different purpose of justice in different scientific directions. Brookfield (2005) identifies four attitudes towards criticality based on different traditions. According to the first attitude – critical theory and critical pedagogy – criticality lies in a person's ability to critically evaluate the assumptions that determine and limit thinking and see oppression, injustice and inequality. 'Criticality is the questioning of the structures and tacit assumptions of socio-political contexts while creating an awareness of self and how one's own actions maintain or counter these assumptions in order to imagine alternatives to this context in which inequity might be minimized' (Felix 2016, p. 45). Thus, socio-political goals come first for advocates of this approach (Apple, 1995; McLaren, 2003; Freire, 2005; Giroux, 2013). Personal development and interpersonal relationships are assessed in the socio-political context. Criticality is seen as a tool for discovering evils in political systems and social structures without going too deep into the individual human plane. Conversely, the second – psychoanalytic – approach is limited to the personal level. All that matters is what determines the thinking of a particular individual. The determining factors are sought in the cultural and social environment, childhood and the traumatic experiences of other periods of life that hamper a person's growth and transformation (Freud, 1927; Freud, 1936; Adler, 1991). The third approach – analytical psychology and informal logic – defines criticality as the discovery of ill-structured problems and fallacies, and the ability to put forth justified arguments and form logical justifications. Despite the focus on a person's cognitive abilities, it would not be entirely fair to say that the advocates of this approach (McPeck, 1981; Siegel, 1988; Ennis, 2000) only care about the criticality of an individual for his or her own sake. The importance of criticality for mutual relations, public welfare and democratic processes is emphasised. It has to be noted that this approach does not raise issues of power, strength or influence, and does not consider ideological problems. In the fourth tradition of pragmatism and constructivism, criticality is expressed on all three levels – personal, interpersonal and social. The essence of criticality lies in the ability to explore and reconstruct oneself, interpersonal relationships and the environment in the name of a better, fairer self, another and others (Dewey, 1997; Lipman, 2003; Brookfield, 2005;). One can also single out a fifth – feminist – tradition, which links criticality with questioning the established order and cultural, social and political constructs, and the ideas of feminist liberation (Brodin, 2007). Such an attitude clearly links this tradition to critical theory. However, there is one special feature that sets this direction apart from all others – the emphasis on the interpersonal dimension. Criticality is perceived as a phenomenon born not only in personal perception, but also in mutual community (Thayer-Bacon, 2000; Hooks, 2009), which pays no heed to racial and cultural differences (Barad, 2007; Ahmed, 2012), but at the same time does not ignore context (Danvers, 2016).

Davies (2015), in analysing the various directions of critical thinking research, highlights the contextual nature of critical thinking. In his view, critical thinking is always personally perceived, experienced and undergone in a specific context. Speaking about the expediency of critical thinking, he emphasises that everyone strives to discover basically the same thing, and the differences are only 'a matter of preference and emphasis' (p. 86). Thus, it is said that the essence of the concept of critical thinking, regardless of the various traditions, remains more or less the same. Only the emphases differ. Although Davies does not separately analyse critical thinking as the pursuit of truth and justice, he clearly advocates its service not only for personal good, but also for the public good, and notes that critical thinking is often not action-oriented. In his view, 'it should involve some actual or potential commitment to *action*. Reasonable decision-making by itself, it seems, is not sufficient for critical thinking – in other words, critical thinking in higher education is not critical judgment *in abstracto*' (p. 53). This aspect is unique in Davies' review. Other researchers pay very little attention to the action determined by critical thinking. Even in works by critical theory and pedagogy authors (Apple, 1995; McLaren, 2016), the manifestation of critical thinking is often limited to declarations, rebellion, protests or statements rather than concrete action.

The classification of criticality presented by Brookfield (2005) is based on an epistemic approach, where criticality, regardless of whether it is more practical or idealistic in nature, is attached to a very specific purpose – better knowledge, improvement and transformation of the person, relationships or society, or the search for correct answers and solutions. However, an ontological attitude is also possible, more strictly distinguishing critical thinking from criticality. 'Criticality, in contrast to critical thinking, is not something that is simply "switched on" or engaged when a specific topic that requires critical thinking emerges. Rather, criticality as critical being, is inexorably embedded in our everyday activities and experiences, regardless of how mundane they may appear' (Dunne, 2015, p. 92).

Thus, criticality is treated neither as an effort to achieve a concrete result, nor as a tool to help achieve a goal, but as a way of being, questioning, rethinking and re-creating oneself and one's relationship with oneself, the environment and the world. It is a state of constant movement characterised by Heidegger's *Dasein in action*. The ontological, existential concept of criticality encompasses the authentic existence, relationship, reactions and experiences of a person, in which knowledge and knowing, thoughts, feelings, emotions and body experiences are intertwined. In other words, the concept of criticality encompasses a person's entire lived experience. Dunne (2015), in drawing a divide between critical thinking and criticality, notes that critical thinking is instrumental thinking that is directed solely at the search for truth but forgets the person, leaving him somewhere on the side-lines with all his experiences and ordeals. Dune (2015) also makes a clear distinction between truth and reality, arguing that critical thinking cares about cognitive thinking operations to get to the truth, a 'satisfactory conclusion', ignoring the totality of life. However, he contradicts himself by stating that 'criticality internalises all that is good about critical thinking: (the search for truth, cogent reasons, inquisitiveness, prudence, willingness to reconsider, care [Sorge], creativity, imagination, etc.), and integrates them into how we live our lives and approach the world. We become criticality, and criticality becomes us' (p. 93). By focusing on the differences between critical thinking and criticality, one might get the impression that these are concepts that have little in common. However, these are the same concepts with the same root meaning. Therefore, it is worth talking about critical thinking and criticality not so much from the perspective of their differences, but more from the perspective of the qualities that connect them. Critical thinking and criticality as a single whole that is experienced is evident in the feminist tradition. Subjective feeling, emotions and experiences have a special meaning here. 'A deeper understanding of critical thinking therefore involves engaging with what critical thinking feels like and how these feelings are socially constructed, embodied and reproduced' (Danvers, 2016, p. 46). Subjective feeling is not only experienced emotionally, but it is also contemplated in order to understand the reason for its occurrence and its structure. And this also requires cognitive effort.

The epistemic and ontological meaning of criticality is organically connected in Barnett's (1997) trinomial concept of critical thinking, where the action stems from reflection, and this is derived from critical reasoning. And vice versa – thinking leads to reflection, and this leads to action. All of these epistemic chains are connected by 'critical being' – thinking and rethinking, creating and re-creating. Critical being is not just an abstractly, existentially thinking personality. Its thinking is based on specific knowledge, information and available experience, which is reflected and eventually translates into action. Critical being fosters, within itself, a critical spirit, which thrives in an intentional relationship with oneself, with another, and with the environment and the world. In his concept, Barnett clearly distinguishes only two dimensions – self and the world – but the interpersonal dimension figures in as the inevitable relationship of the person with another in the process of cognition and creation. Riley-Jones (2012), reflecting on Barnett's criticality, emphasises the complexity and totality of the concept, and defines it as the state that encompasses the lived entirety of knowledge, feelings and abilities. In Barnett's (2000) concept of criticality, a special role is played by the so-called epistemological and ontological disturbance of mind, which could also be called 'awakeness of mind'. This quality does not allow a person to get comfortable, fall into a routine, or forget that the world is changing, constantly inviting to rethink one's being. Rogoff (2006) also talks about this, emphasising that analysing and thinking critically is a necessity, but it is even more important to ensure that criticality is internalised – that it settles in each of us and becomes a part of us. According to Rogoff (2006), we can be armed with knowledge, having mastered complex patterns of reasoning, but not be critical ourselves. From the researcher's point of view, we must be vigilant towards ourselves so that when we critically analyse the environment, we do not forget ourselves and are constantly checking whether we are practicing what we preach – whether we believe and live it ourselves. This is by no means irresolution or incompetence, but rather 'a state of duality in which one is at one and the same time, both empowered and disempowered, knowing and unknowing' (Rogoff, 2006, p. 2). This is the state that is called criticality, and reflects what Barnett calls the 'disturbance of mind'. From the point of view of both researchers, the essence of criticality lies not in finding the right answer, but in the attitude of constantly pursuing it, in the position of one who is sceptical, questioning and searching. In this way, critical thinking helps a person to constantly create and re-create, improve and cultivate him or herself. For the sake of oneself and others; for the sake of a better life and a more progressive and just society (Felix, 2016). Since criticality is defined as a person's permanent and never-ending state that is also constantly questioning everything, the question may arise as to its benefits in achieving a tangible result. And does that mean that 'the concept of criticality is itself incoherent, that any decision rendered through the process of critical engagement must be labelled uncritical because it is ultimately founded on an uncritiqued, uninterrogated assertion? This is what I call the paradox of criticality, a paradox whose challenge needs to be addressed in any elaboration of criticality' (Fisherman, 2017, p. 6). Indeed, this may seem debatable and paradoxical, especially if we directly link criticality to cognitive critical thinking skills and processes and aim to demonstrate its effectiveness and usefulness.

However, it is already up to each scientific school, critical thinking approach and researcher to clearly define the concepts and show their interrelationships. In this way, Noddings' (2017) idea of the need for a definition in the name of science and mutual communication is highlighted yet again.

In summarising the concept of critical thinking, which consists of personal traits, the thought process and outcomes, several essential things emerge. *First*, the concept of critical thinking was, is, and likely will always be constantly discovered anew, depending on the periods and different contexts. In each period, in a certain context, culture, tradition or prevailing ideology, there will be attempts to rethink it, reflect it, and discover new aspects. Such a need is conditioned not only by the broader, social nature, but also by the personal nature. The human mind is curious and inquisitive – everyone personally wants to know, explore and learn anew. *Second*, the definition of critical thinking is and always will be determined by scientific attitudes and research approaches. Critical thinking is researched from psychological, pedagogical and philosophical positions; it is viewed from the perspectives of constructivism, pragmatism, critical theory, feminism, existentialism and other theories and sciences. Today, we cannot know what new directions and methods of research will be found, or what schools and traditions will be formed. *Third*, the essence of critical thinking remains unchanged – it is the desire to understand what is right and what is not, and to know the truth or at least seek towards cognition, despite different conceptions of truth and ways of exploring it. This is called criticality, no matter how it is understood and interpreted in various traditions. And today, we see the grasping to highlight the essence of critical thinking phenomena, expose fallacies and possible manipulations, and sometimes even discover recipes to avoid the misfortunes that afflict society. Criticality is defined as a person's ability to engage in quality thinking and a sign of the person's own worth. *Fourth*, critical thinking is not a phenomenon in itself – it serves the improvement of the individual, interpersonal relationships and society. Only the question of the manifestation and balance of these three levels remains open – what takes the lead where and under what circumstances, what is not visible or missing, and what the need is and how it is met. *Fifth*, the need for a definition of critical thinking is evident in various historical periods. This need is dictated by the specific period, context and necessity to communicate, agree and coordinate actions. In terms of science – to substantiate one's work and research and to disseminate and communicate it in pursuit of the response of others, academic discussion and progress in science and society. In terms of education – to foster and improve critical thinking in the academic community.

2. The Relevance of Critical Thinking in Higher Education

The 21st century differs from previous periods both in terms of technology and the nature of the knowledge generated. Along with social change, social structures are also changing, and social problems which require new approaches and new methods are diversifying. Increased mobility of the world's population, digitisation and the emergence of new professions are changing countries' lives and labour markets and creating the need for change in the education systems as well.

Education is no longer inseparable from phenomena such as globalisation, information technology inventions and international and internal migration. The answers to global challenges increasingly depend on sound scientific advice given to decision makers. The focus is on the wider context and on how research can be applied to address challenges that may ultimately threaten human existence, such as global pandemics (UNESCO, 2015). The role of higher education is crucial in these situations. In addition, some authors note that modern education systems essentially equip individuals to become 'more effective vandals of the Earth' (Orr, 2004, according to Howlett, Ferreira and Blomfield, 2016). Therefore, when it comes to the role of modern higher education in society, it is important to think not only about constant innovation, economic competition between countries and the productivity race, but also about the importance of sustainable development, social justice and sustainability in the present and future perspective. In other words, modern higher education systems need to develop individuals who think critically and reflectively and who are able to solve problems and thus contribute to sustainability (Sipos, Battisti and Grimm, 2008, according to Howlett, Ferreira and Blomfield, 2016). This position is in line with Davies' (2015) insights that critical thinking has not only a personal dimension, but also a broader social and cultural dimension.

Recently, more and more countries have been identifying critical thinking as one of the essential elements of modern education in their strategic educational documents and curricula. There is a growing recognition that one of the most important goals of higher education institutions should be developing students' critical thinking competencies (Hidayati, Zubaidah, Suarsini and Praherdhiono, 2020) by directly and indirectly including this in study programmes (Franco, 2016). Erikson and Erikson (2018) and Franco (2016) suggest linking higher education to the function of personal liberation and emancipation, and treating critical thinking as the main instrument enabling the student to act.

Why is critical thinking being taken so seriously in higher education? What is expected of critical thinking in modern society? In 2009, UNESCO declared that the development of critical thinking and ethical thinking in graduates is becoming an objective of global higher education (UNESCO, 2009). Accordingly, the ability to think critically is increasingly being included in the intended outcomes of higher education and programming documents, and is appearing in study programmes and subject descriptions. Since 2011, developing critical thinking has become one of the most important objectives of undergraduate studies in Europe, and in the United States, critical thinking has been identified as one of the key outcomes of higher education studies (Soufi and See, 2019). The European Higher Education Area (European Commission, 2012a) has emphasised that critical thinking is an important part of student-centred teaching at many universities. Based on previous studies, Shaheen (2016) claims that in Great Britain, critical thinking is not only one of the core competencies, but also the main objective of higher education.

Recognising that in the knowledge economy, memorising essential facts and knowledge is important, but not enough for progress and success, the Council of the EU issued recommendations in 2018 on key competences for lifelong learning (Council of the EU, 2018). In these recommendations, critical thinking, along with problem solving, creativity, the ability to cooperate, self-regulation and computational thinking, is referred to as a tool to make what has been learned work in real time, in order to generate new ideas, theories, knowledge and products. It is important to note that by defining competence as a set of knowledge, skills and attitudes, the Council of Europe sees critical thinking not as an individual competence, but as an ability manifested in other competences, such as literacy or digital competence (Council of the EU, 2018). This in no way diminishes the importance of critical thinking. On the contrary, it testifies to its integrity and fixedness in other competencies. We can, therefore, find elements of criticality in various competencies identified in the study process – creativity, innovation, entrepreneurship and so on. Criticality is seen as thinking from different positions, thinking that challenges existing ideas while debating with itself at the same time (Andrews, 2007).

In 2019, the International Bureau of Education (Marope, Griffin and Gallagher, 2019), in cooperation with social partners in the business, governmental and non-governmental sectors, proposed a set of competencies and abilities to prepare for the transformation of study programmes in order to get ready for future challenges and respond to technological progress and innovation. Critical thinking is also cited as one of the first skills that need to be included in higher education curricula. As declared by the European Commission (2020), it is important to ensure that higher education in the EU continuously develops and improves abilities that help maintain competitiveness. In addition, one of the key goals is to develop student competencies and abilities that will determine their success after graduation. Critical thinking is also listed among the most relevant skills, such as digital literacy and the ability to count and solve problems.

However, it is important to mention that some authors call the development of critical thinking in students one of the major ambitions of higher education (Janssen et al., 2019). In other words, there is a general consensus that strengthening and developing critical thinking is needed at all levels of study and in all subjects studied (Nedelová and Šukolová, 2017), but there is not always a consensus on how this should be done and which methods are most effective. In addition, Heijltjes, Van Gog, Leppink and Paas (2015), having reviewed a number of publications, note that studying in a higher education institution does not in itself develop a student's critical thinking skills, so we should think about targeted measures for developing critical thinking in higher education. To achieve this, the involvement of all higher education actors in the modelling, implementation and assessment of the critical thinking development process is important. Nevertheless, according to Mardis, Ma, Jones, Ambavarapu, Kelleher, Spears and McClure (2017), higher education institutions often focus on the provision and development of technical knowledge and abilities, and as a result, soft skills such as critical thinking and teamwork disappear or go unnoticed, even in the learning outcomes indicated in study programme descriptions.

It should be noted that in some cultural settings, incorporating critical thinking into formal education is a challenge. Curzon-Hobson (2003) argues that critical thinking itself does not belong to any particular locality or region, but the special social and political history of knowledge creation in Western universities has contributed most to its emergence and establishment. In this way, critical thinking became a hallmark of the 'Western' academy. The European Learning and Teaching Forum (2019) argues that it would even be difficult to imagine a Western higher education institution that does not emphasise the importance of critical thinking. Meanwhile, in certain cultures, the emergence and development of the phenomenon of critical thinking is facing challenges, because publicly disagreeing with authority – opposing or doubting it (in other words, not respecting the hierarchy) – or violating the principle of group conformism is not inherent in the cultural environment. For example, McGuire (2007) proposes that the development of critical thinking in one Asian country has not taken root because the core values implicit in critical thinking pedagogy – such as increasing one's intellectual independence and individual autonomy and improving one's linguistic skills and persuasive power – clash with the country's values. However, there are different attitudes in this aspect. Some authors claim, for example, that the ability of local students at Malaysian universities to think critically does not match the ability of students from other regions of the world (Ahrari, Samah, Hassan, Wahat and Zaremohzzabieh, 2016), while at British universities, foreign students experience considerable difficulties in demonstrating critical thinking skills because critical thinking is not an integral part of the teaching process in the education systems of their countries of origin (Shaheen, 2016).

Therefore, Danvers (2018), for example, views critical thinking as dependent on social conditions, social relationships and the processes embodied in them, and raises the question not of what critical thinking is, but what allows or prevents it from occurring. In other words, if some authors (Bailin and Siegel, 2003; Halpern, 2014; Paul and Elder, 2020) decontextualise critical thinking, Danvers (2018) actually strives to rethink and contextualise it. This view is also supported by McNamara, Sweetman, Connors, Lofgren and Greene (2020), who argue that decontextualised critical thinking embedded in curricula that does not take into account the cultural, ethical, civic and intellectual dimensions may not only be ineffective, but even harmful.

It is important to note that the situation in higher education is changing as well. To describe the changed situation, some authors, such as Danvers (2014), Davies (2015) and Camacho (2016) use the concepts of neoliberalism, commercialisation or marketisation and the university market. In a general sense, it is about a trend where higher education institutions are becoming market participants, with activities geared to responding to and serving the needs of the labour market, while students are becoming higher education institution customers. In short, some study subjects (philosophy, history) that traditionally require students to argue and present facts, thus developing critical thinking, are gradually being replaced by better-selling subjects with greater 'marketing' significance (El-Soufi, 2019).

On the other hand, as the world becomes more complicated and complex, and seeing in this context the need to better prepare students for this 'supercomplex' world, Barnett (according to Pollard, 2014) speaks of an 'ontological turn' in the education system, specifically having in mind the development of critical thinking as the ability to question truths and explain how truth became truth. To do this, he suggests using Foucault's critical ontology, which is a form of ontology that allows for a critical assessment both of oneself and knowledge about oneself.

Self-criticism can be what is needed to adapt to the rapidly changing conditions in the world and society.

Many authors agree that education must nevertheless play a role in the development of critical thinking. According to El-Soufi (2019), despite the fact that society can make mistakes and mislead, education should lead. Paul, Elder, and Bartell (1997) emphasise that the role of education is to protect human thought from bias. According to the authors, the human mind, left to itself alone, can distort thinking and lead to its bias, unless the mind is taught to understand its preconceptions. Another argument that the development of critical thinking should be purposeful is related to the meanings constructed by students. The construction of meanings is ongoing. Students do this in their daily lives based on what they experience and go through. Those values are usually affected by a limited amount of experience and are not accurate, so they are not objective. For them to be able to construct quality meanings, they need certain tools of critical thinking that allow them to assess the situation and events, and avoid distorted truths and bias. Learning as such does not guarantee the acquisition of critical thinking skills despite how diligent and responsible it may be.

2.1 Critical thinking and higher education

Higher education has a much broader mission than just preparing a person for a particular profession. Higher education is designed to prepare people to be active citizens who view life as a meaningful learning process, and whose thinking and behaviour are determined by ethical standards, freedom, personal and shared well-being (Franco, 2015). Because higher education provides more tools for a person to be free, the inclusion of critical thinking development in studies becomes particularly relevant.

Redding (2017) sees the university as an institutionalised space for the manifestation of critical thinking. Higher education has always been associated with promoting the development of society. The task of a university is to analyse and respond to the changes taking place in society. According to Redding (2017), while in the past critical thinking was exclusively an area of political speculation about higher education, today higher education teachers and employers are interested in developing critical thinking in students. Critical thinking is associated with graduates' ability to think independently and make decisions, and to argue and persuade others with their arguments. A person's ability to analyse, make a difference, and act is a guarantor, both of the person's growth, and of the progress of society itself. While everyone reiterates the importance of developing critical thinking like a mantra, the question remains as to how critical thinking can be stimulated within the framework of practical training.

At the academic and public levels, there is a consensus that the development of critical thinking should be an integral part of formal education. We might ask, is it really necessary to teach critical thinking in formal education institutions? In this case, we can answer that leaving the development of critical thinking to take care of itself and in an optional role will not ensure universality and systematicity. Given the complexity and multidimensionality nature of the critical thinking phenomenon, 'its development cannot be taken for granted' (Promoting Critical Thinking in European Higher Education Institutions: Towards an Educational Protocol, 2019, p. 25).

The significance of critical thinking in studies is emphasised for many reasons. Using a concept of critical thinking that integrates an element of higher cognitive abilities as their basis, some authors (Fahim and Masouleh, 2012; Bassham, Irwin, Nardone and Wallace, 2013) stress that critical thinking plays an important role in higher education studies because studies at this level in themselves require higher cognitive abilities, such as providing a critical assessment of a text or substantiating one's opinion with evidence. Other authors argue that critical thinking is associated with higher academic achievements as it not only helps to make information easier to understand, select and analyse, but also makes it possible to improve participation in discussions and providing logical reasoning (Stupnisky, Renaud, Daniels, Haynes and Perry, 2008), evidence and facts, and in general contributes to more effective behaviour in overcoming obstacles or dealing with ordinary situations (Ghazivakili, Norouzi Nia, Panahi, Karimi, Gholsorkhi and Ahmadi, 2014). Feng, Fan and Yang (2013) point out that students' levels of critical thinking can influence how successfully they absorb knowledge. Accordingly, knowledge acquisition has positive consequences for academic results as well. Since knowledge acquisition denotes not so much the ability to remember as the ability to understand the meaning of a text and grasp the facts and principles presented in it, knowledge acquisition becomes the outcome of understanding and reasoning using critical thinking. It enables students to select information properly, acting as a filter of sorts, it also encourages looking for the correct information in order to fully understand a phenomenon or process (Magrabi, Pasha and Pasha, 2018). Halpern (1998; 2014) argues that in a time when people are separated from information by just the click of a button, it is particularly important to train students to think critically and effectively. This is important in preparing students as participants in democratic and civil societies (Barnett, 2015) who will be able to expose fake news in the flow of information, in other words, deconstruct this fake news while also weakening the threat it poses.

Critical thinking competency is associated with better graduate readiness to compete in the global world. Critical thinking is thinking that goes beyond the canons of traditional views, enabling students adapt to everyday personal, social and professional needs (Fong, Kim, Davis, Hoang and Kim, 2017). A Renewed EU Agenda for Higher Education (European Commission, 2017) states that all post-secondary learning should train students to understand new concepts, think critically and creatively, and be entrepreneurs in order to generate and apply new ideas. Thus, critical thinking is important in the field of innovation and in the research and development activities of the universities themselves, where new products and various solutions to economic, social and environmental problems are born (Council of the European Union, 2018).

2.2 Education approaches and the institutionalisation of critical thinking in higher education

Critical thinking can be learned, and critical thinking can be taught (Niu, Behar-Horenstein and Garvan, 2013; Puig, Blanco-Anaya, Bargiela and Crujeiras-Pérez, 2019), but, as Bowell and Kingsbury (2015) argue, it takes a long time for a person to master this ability and become a great critical thinker. It is also important to remember that developing critical thinking skills is not a separate, autonomous educational goal. It is embedded in the entire education system, so it is often assumed that critical thinking is an ability that is automatically acquired through higher education (Walter, 2017). However, targeted efforts are needed to develop critical thinking, since it is not the 'by-product' of higher education that it is popularly thought to be. A group of researchers who developed the 'Critical Thinking Protocol' pointed out that the development of critical thinking must be embedded at all levels of higher education, from mission and strategy to the student audience (Promoting Critical Thinking in European Higher Education Institutions: towards an educational protocol, 2019). The protocol states that in order to achieve effective critical thinking development, all mechanisms must be activated, from institutional support and management of the study programme as a whole while seeing the contribution of each study subject to the teacher's work in the classroom with students. By understanding that critical thinking is a multifaceted phenomenon, this feature can be exploited in curriculum design so that individual subjects, depending on their specifics, can develop different critical thinking skills that, when combined into a whole at the study programme level, will result in full critical thinking fulfilment.

The key question that the entire future education strategy depends on is whether higher education institutions have to develop critical thinking. If they do, then how should it be done? Should it be a general university subject or a study area subject? Should it be a separate study subject or integrated into other subjects? Research shows that various strategies can be successful (El-Soufi, 2019). In some contexts, mixed approaches are more effective, while in other contexts, they are only effective for certain groups of students, such as, for example, native English speakers. Therefore, in looking for, developing and testing effective strategies, it is important to draw on one's own experience and that of other higher education institutions, as well as on the examples presented in literature, and to take one's cultural and social context into account.

Also, as Davies (2015) notes, it is very important to define what critical thinking is in higher education and what the scope of this concept is, and, accordingly, what specific critical thinking skills will be developed. This concreteness is necessary so that all of the actors involved in the development of critical thinking work according to the same concept and formulate the learning outcomes according to it, and select and develop adequate methods for both education and assessment. In addition, as Davies (2015) argues, the two existing 'ideological' movements – critical thinking and critical pedagogy – see the goals of developing critical thinking in higher education differently. While the critical thinking movement considers the goal of developing critical thinking in higher education to be to evoking critical thinking in students as an integral element of the learning process, and understands it as a function of student empowerment, critical pedagogy views the development of critical thinking as an instrument of indoctrination into the capitalist political system, with the emancipation of the individual left within the realm of liberation from social conditions. Thus, this author presents the idea that critical thinking is not ideologically neutral.

In discussing the development of critical thinking in higher education studies, the key issues are related to the role of universities and colleges in this process. Researchers are trying to reveal the dynamics of developing critical thinking depending on the type of higher education institution. Evens, Verburgh and Elen (2014) claim that critical thinking skills among students in professional bachelor's studies are most developed in the first year of study, with this growth slowing down later. Meanwhile, critical thinking skills among university students are only slightly developed in the first year of study, but continue to grow steadily in the following academic years, ultimately surpassing the growth of critical thinking skills achieved by students in professional bachelor's studies. When discussing how to better develop critical thinking in students – by offering students a separate subject in critical thinking studies or integrating it into a study field subject – two approaches stand out. The first is the general approach, which values critical thinking as a set of general abilities that can be transferred from one study area to another, thus avoiding the need for the student to delve into specific scientific expertise. In this respect, the development of critical thinking is organised as a general university subject, where students have the opportunity to develop general critical thinking skills, such as argumentation. Meanwhile, the explicit approach focuses on the knowledge of the subject being taught and is an integral part of the subject-specific information. For example, medical students learn how to select a treatment strategy that meets the needs of a particular patient by assessing all available information, psychology students learn how to evaluate the reliability of data in the context of theories of psychology (Duro et al., 2013), and so on. In practice, both approaches are used in combination and both can be effective. There is no unequivocal answer that either one of them is superior, because it is always necessary to take into account the context in which the studies are taking place.

Nevertheless, it is important to take into account that critical thinking is a process and takes time to acquire (Bezanilla, Fernández-Nogueira, Poblete and Galindo-Domínguez, 2019). In addition, university teachers need to know and understand which study and assessment methods are best suited for developing and evaluating critical thinking skills in their subject, and replace ones that are not suitable with more effective ones. Hence, this process requires reflection from the teachers themselves as well. LaPoint-O'Brien (2013) also points out that the effectiveness of critical thinking development is likely to be related to the concept of critical thinking held by the teachers themselves, and a study conducted by Duro et al. (2013) demonstrates that in order to apply appropriate critical thinking teaching and learning methods, it is important to 'demystify' the concept of critical thinking for students. In other words, instead of leaving the process to take care of itself and creating the context that critical thinking is very important, but what it means exactly is unclear, it needs to be explained to and discussed with students what critical thinking is, and what tasks they will perform to develop this competency. Various tasks that promote critical thinking and their discussion, according to Duro et al. (2013), can help students get rid of the polarised attitude that you are either capable of thinking critically or you aren't, and thus encourage them to become more active thinkers and analysts. Therefore, the very concept of critical thinking and the path for developing critical thinking in response to the needs of the student, the labour market and society must be discussed at the level of the university, faculty or the specific study programme. It has been discussed a bit earlier that the ability to think can be developed, although it takes quite a bit of time, and even after that this skill needs to be constantly nurtured. However, a crucial question remains: what teaching methods do teachers need to use for students to develop critical thinking skills successfully?

As Wang and Zheng (2016) explain, some education science theorists point out that critical thinking is developed through the development of skills that encourage thinking. It is mainly the ability to make assumptions, identify erroneous conclusions and logical errors of argumentation, and distinguish bias and opinions from facts and evidence. Franco (2016) notes that developing critical thinking requires clear references and instructions, examples of real problems, and constructive feedback. An experiment conducted by Ku, Ho, Hau and Lai (2014) revealed that any programme for developing critical thinking, whether it is separate critical thinking training or integrated into other study subjects, must provide students with an interactive learning environment where they can strengthen their understanding of their ideas, opinions and thought processes, thus involving them in reflection and the search for alternative solutions.

The variety of specific tasks aimed at developing critical thinking skills can be extremely large, depending on the teacher's choice and imagination. Here, Huang, Lindell, Jaffe and Sullivan (2016) report that teachers used the following methods to develop critical thinking skills in future healthcare professionals:

- promoting higher-level cognition,
- asking questions that probe the learner's understanding,
- linking discussions to the clinical context.

The authors also found in their study that teachers who were more familiar with literature on critical thinking and teachers of subjects where critical thinking was separately integrated into the subject description put the most emphasis on the value of applying direct critical thinking teaching methods. Meanwhile, teachers of subjects where the development of critical thinking skills was not singled out in the description used more indirect teaching methods, such as questioning and role-playing.

Methods for developing critical thinking can be quite diverse, especially depending on what ability is emphasised in the concept of critical thinking. For example, O'Rourke and Nussbaum (according to Lin, 2014) observe that an essential component of critical thinking is the ability to argue and defend one's position, and to formulate an argument for and against the same phenomenon. Therefore, all tasks that require both supporting and challenging the same fact, news or information are suitable for developing the ability to argue. For example, selecting a supporting argument and a counter-argument based on facts and other evidence for news published on a news portal. Another task is to justify your position. Studies conducted by Davies (2011) and Veronese, Richards, Pernar, Sullivan and Schwartzstein (2013) have confirmed that the development of critical thinking can be stimulated by a mind (idea) map, because students who have to draw connections between the mechanisms of the problem are forced to think holistically rather than superficially. This allows students to move from linear thinking to integrated thinking, and to link existing and new knowledge and identify knowledge gaps.

The natural continuation of critical thinking development methods is the topic of critical thinking assessment methods. As noted by Macpherson and Owen (2010), assessment of critical thinking skills in students is an ongoing challenge and there is still intense debate about which assessment methods are best. Students' critical thinking skills grow when unconventional, experimental training is used. For example, assessments where students have to demonstrate how they use their acquired knowledge in new situations encourage them to use critical thinking skills. However, when using innovative, experimental approaches, it is important for students to receive feedback from the teacher so that they understand the level of their thinking skills and what they should strengthen (Schendel, 2016).

In summary, it can be argued that the need, importance, purpose, content and methods of critical thinking development largely depend on the attitude chosen. However, given the intensification and abundance of debate on critical thinking and its development in higher education, as well as the inclusion of the term 'critical thinking' in regional and national programming documents for both the general economy and education, it becomes clear that critical thinking is only growing in importance and its role is increasingly understood in civic engagement, sustainable development, social justice, and other processes of civilisation progress.

3. The Value of Critical Thinking in the Labour Market

The modern labour market is characterised by uncertainty and unpredictability due to new ways of organising work, increased work intensity and a faster work pace. Increasing competition in the workplace, which encourages employees to respond more quickly to market needs and improve the quality of the organisation's activities, product or service, is also a factor. This uncertainty can be seen as both a threat and an opportunity. With the globalisation of business and the changing forms and ways of organising work, the labour market now requires flexibility from workers, and national labour market policies have sought to ensure 'flexicurity'. As a result, the picture of a successful modern employee in recent years has been created using a whole set of skills. It is emphasised that 21st-century workers need not only specific work (professional) skills but also general abilities such as communication, collaboration, problem solving and critical thinking (Habets, Stoffers, Van der Heijden and Peters, 2020). Critical thinking is named as one of the key 21st-century skills relevant to the labour market (Rave, Guerrero and Morales, 2020; Whiting, 2020).

In the context of a changing labour market, a new attitude towards the organisation is emerging in which success is largely determined by human resources. Research shows that the success of an organisation is determined by the ability of employees to respond quickly to changing situations and make reasoned, research-based decisions (Penkauskienė, Railienė and Cruz, 2019; Powley and Taylor, 2014; AMA, 2012; Phan, 2011; Fung, 2014). 'Employees need to be able to think fast and act smart – often in situations that are complex, uncertain, and where no effective policy or procedure exists' (Kreitzberg and Kreitzberg, 2011, p. 26). Thus, this era places demands on employees to look for different ways of thinking and acting in order to enable the development of the organisation and the creation of new knowledge-based products. As Elicor (2016) argues, critical thinking can be an essential tool in the management of organisations, helping to find many practical solutions when operating in modern market conditions, which require a consistently high level of competitiveness and efficacy. Analysing the importance of critical thinking in the leadership of modern organisations, Elicor (2016) also points out that the need to develop critical thinking has a strong pragmatic orientation – to help the organisation solve problems, make key decisions and direct its activities towards improvement; therefore, all employees need critical thinking, regardless of their position. He claims that 'critical thinking as a normative principle is a powerful tool that contributes to the professional arsenal of any organization particularly in crucial decision making, trouble shooting and steering the company towards holistic organizational advancement that benefit not only the few but all its members' (Elicor, 2016, p. 19).

It is believed (European Commission, 2012b; Council of the European Union, 2018) that critical thinking combined with universal abilities such as collaboration, problem solving, leadership, creativity and self-discipline will help employees to be better prepared for modern labour market issues and, at the same time, for progress. The universality of critical thinking along with other skills is not only linked to employability or staying active in the labour market, but also to the development of new products and ideas, the solution of unprecedented problems, and quick orientation in difficult situations. In short, it is critical thinking that enables us to act effectively in unusual, uncertain situations where the field of action is not defined by precise instructions (Franco, 2016). Critical thinking is thought to be particularly important when talking about crisis management and crisis leadership in business organisations (Powley and Taylor, 2014); therefore, the ability of employees to assess the challenges of various crisis situations and choose the right solution when there is no one right answer is noted (Kish-Gephart, Detert, Klebe Trevino and Edmondson, 2009; Facione, 2011; Tripathy, 2020). Hence, critical thinking is seen by employers as a necessary skill to make the right decisions while avoiding mistakes due to overconfidence or bias (Davitch and Folker, 2017).

The importance of critical thinking is highlighted when informed decisions need to be made decisively – employees need to have 'the ability to follow logical steps and arrive at a decisive and appropriate conclusion' (Subramanian, 2020, p.1179). It is perceived as a protection of sorts against possible failures, in the hope that recurring problems will be easier to overcome in the future and the organisation will acquire a certain resilience to difficulties and will be able to use 'lessons learned' in taking on new challenges understood as an adequate response to changes in the environment and risk management both inside and outside the organisation by solving problems and introducing innovations for business development (Hongas and Kuo, 1999).

Today's employee needs to be able to generate new ideas without being afraid to refute the old ones for the sake of the success of the organisation (Desai, Berger and Higgs, 2016) and competitive advantage (Subramanian, 2020). 'Companies can't have a competitive edge, particularly in a time of change, without a deep reservoir of critical thinkers' (Kreitzberg and Kreitzberg, 2011, p. 24). Critical thinking enables the employee to analyse and evaluate information (Sousa and Wilks, 2018) and consider the situation/problem being analysed from different perspectives (Wang and Zheng, 2016; Reed, 2018). According to Yanchar, Slife and Warne (2008), only employees with a set of critical thinking skills such as interpretation, analysis, evaluation, inference, explanation and self-regulation (Facione, 2011) can explain their thinking and decision-making process. Critical thinking skills enable employees to analyse complex problems with a focus on the desired outcome (Power, 2016). Thus, critical thinking is considered to be one of the most important factors in problem-solving success (Yukl, 2010).

In the context of an organisation's work, it is emphasised that only employees who are critical thinkers are motivated to seek the truth (Ku and Ho, 2010). The search for truth is defined as a kind of prosocial collective motivation that shows a person's inner desire to commit to improving the organisation objectively and honestly (Jiang, Gao and Yang, 2018). Critical thinking is perceived as a sort of guarantor of 'legitimate action'. Organisations often legitimise conflicting strategic decisions based on rationality, which has to convince stakeholders, so the ability to argue and reason properly provides grounds for 'legitimising' decisions. 'Establishing a good fit between the argumentation field and the kind of reasoning used gives decision makers more legitimacy' (Bouwmeester, 2013, p. 429).

In order to respond to today's challenges, more and more organisations are replacing old-model systems with new ones, where teamwork is the most important element of the organisation. The need for teamwork in an organisation presupposes the responsibility delegated to employees to make decisions when the solution is not obvious or requires different and new ideas. A team decision ensures the implementation of diverse information, knowledge and skills in various fields. In this context, research highlights the influence of critical thinking on the extent to which employees are involved in the creative process of developing and implementing innovation in an organisation (Natale and Ricci, 2006; Jing and Baiyin, 2015). Since critical thinking enables employees to think creatively and independently, make decisions, draw conclusions, and take action, it becomes one of the key traits that employers expect from employees (Hassan and Madhum, 2007; Piawa, 2010; Abed, Davoudi and Hoseinzadeh, 2015; Ahrari et al., 2016; Tripathy, 2020). Thus, the ability to think critically helps to grasp new ideas, make difficult decisions, dynamically engage in productive and positive activities, and link theoretical subjects with practical situations.

The importance of critical thinking at the organisational level is also displayed in the employees' ability to apply existing knowledge in new situations and disposition to test the reliability of that knowledge (Cake et al., 2016). Assessing the validity and reliability of information from a variety of unknown sources and applying that information is identified as an important transformational leader ability (Sayyadi, 2019) because it inspires members of the organisation to share knowledge and generate new ideas. Knowledge becomes a critical factor in enabling organisations to introduce innovations and compete domestically and internationally (Tang et al., 2020). The knowledge used by an individual is the basis for turning data into information and creating greater value by solving problems and developing, evaluating, making and implementing decisions (Raudeliūnienė and Račinskaja, 2014; Brix, 2017). It is important for an organisation to combine the knowledge of individuals and use it to manage business processes and create value. This is how an organisation forms its knowledge base: knowledge potential, for example, the potential of the people working in the organisation; the organisation's environment, which can increase (synergistic effect) or decrease (anti-synergistic effect) knowledge potential; and developed knowledge components (Bivainis and Morkvėnas, 2008). By being able to transform data and information into knowledge and use it to benefit the organisation, the employee becomes a member of the organisation's knowledge management process (Atkočiūnienė, 2010). Knowledge management is defined as the clear strategy, tools and practices used to make knowledge part of an organisation's resources (Tang et al., 2010). In the context of the organisation, it is the ability to collect and use what employees know in order to develop innovative products and services and implement effective and socially responsible business methods. In the context of knowledge management, critical thinking should be analysed as a precondition for knowledge creation, implementation and reflection in organisational processes and as a fundamental competence (Jou, Lin and Wu, 2014; Exnar and Pálušová, 2015).

There are certain similarities in the processes of critical thinking and knowledge management, which are undoubtedly related to the consistent, step-by-step and final processing of information. Critical thinking researchers name a different number of stages and have different ways of grouping them. Facione, Facione and Giancarlo (1997) point to these stages of critical thinking: interpretation, that is, identifying and naming the problem, constructing future research;

analysis, that is, studying and comparing various data and information, searching for connections; assessment, that is, logically examining the available material and making decisions; self-regulation, that is, justifying how and why one or another decision was made and reflecting on how those decisions affected a person's thinking – changed it, improved it. Paul and Elder (2012) name eight stages: setting a goal; raising questions related to the problem, the phenomenon under study; gathering information; interpreting it; formulating concepts, theories; making assumptions; anticipating the possible consequences, formulating an autonomous approach and drawing conclusions. The stages of the knowledge management process in an organisation are similar, referred to as finding, selecting, organising, disseminating and communicating information (Gupta, Iyer and Aronson, 2000). Selection involves analysis, synthesis and evaluation, organisation involves giving new forms and/or meaning, and communication is for the use of knowledge. The process of knowledge management is also described as knowledge creation (including both search and selection), validation, presentation, dissemination and use (Bhatt, 2001). The success of the knowledge management process in an organisation is directly related to the success of the organisation. The basis of all this is critical thinking competence with clearly identified constituents, which include the above-mentioned abilities as well as others – attention to detail, articulation and conveyance of ideas, and ensuring the sustainability of knowledge to make fundamental changes in organisations. Thus, critical thinking plays an important role in the entire knowledge management process (Wang, Woo and Zhao, 2009; Sayyadi, 2019).

In any case, in terms of both critical thinking and knowledge management, knowledge in the initial stage of processing cannot be considered 'explicit', justified and reasoned knowledge. Despite being based on past experience and available knowledge, it is initially treated as information requiring verification and validation. In order for knowledge to become a valuable product for an organisation, it must be subjected to continuous processing – being questioned, rethought, recreated, supplemented, and sometimes even rejected if its erroneousness is proven. Organisations, therefore, strive to make sure that before making decisions, their employees carry out thorough preparatory work, detecting ill-structured problems and fallacies and eliminating shortcomings by analysing, synthesising and evaluating information. Therefore, it can be argued that knowledge management processes are directly related to the renewal and growth of organisations. Critical thinking processes are also focused on an individual's intellectual growth, community maturity, and the progress of society as a whole. In this way, the processes of critical thinking and knowledge management also become a learning process – for individuals, communities and organisations. In order for learning to be effective, the processes must be well understood, communicated, interpreted and reflected.

The processes of critical thinking and knowledge management cannot be imagined without interaction – connections between people, organisations and communities. Even though it is constantly emphasised in critical thinking that this is individual and independent thinking, it is concurrently argued that this is also social thinking. There is no contradiction between these two statements. Critically thinking people think for themselves and make decisions themselves, but their thinking and decisions are influenced by the living context, social reality and interpersonal relationships. Critical thinking comes from being in an intense relationship with another, whoever that other may be. It is as individual as it is communal and social (Brookfield, 2005). Critical thinking is what people do 'most often collaboratively, while they engage in pursuing the activities and goals that fit their daily lives. Thinking rarely remains solitary activity conducted inside people's heads' (Kuhn, 2008, p. 13). Thus, critical thinking clearly has several dimensions: personal, interpersonal and communal/social.

As already mentioned, an organisation's knowledge is an accumulation of individual and community knowledge. It is created by individuals through social interaction and the use of tacit knowledge with explicit knowledge (Nonaka, Toyama and Hirata, 2008). Therefore, knowledge management in an organisation also has clear individual, interpersonal and organisational levels. Knowledge, if not shared, becomes meaningless because it does not create added value. The more knowledge is created, managed and used, the more its value grows, making knowledge sharing a key process that organisations should constantly pursue to maintain their competitiveness (Cavaliere, Lombardi and Giustiniano, 2015). To create a sustainable competitive advantage, an organisation's employees must not only share knowledge, but also put it into practice (Dalkir, 2017). One of the most important goals of knowledge management is to ensure that knowledge exchange takes place in a systematic way and creates added value. Research shows that these exchanges are particularly valuable when exchanging diverse and different knowledge, as diversity of opinions and experiences opens up wider horizons – learning takes place through interactive interaction and new organisational knowledge is created (Farhan and Muhaimin, 2019).

Looking at interaction as an opportunity to learn from each other strengthens both critical thinking and knowledge management skills. Opportunities arise when a conducive environment is created for finding them. Any organisation that values an independent but reasoned opinion, encourages research and experimentation, provides the opportunity to make mistakes and learn from them, and fosters a culture of collaboration and collegial decision-making can be called a critically thinking and functioning organisation.

Critical thinking can thus be interpreted in three ways – as a precondition for knowledge management goals, as a tool for knowledge management, and as a condition for knowledge exchange. Investing in employees' critical thinking skills and motivating them to improve their critical thinking skills and attitudes and apply them in the day-to-day decisions of the organisation will, in the long run, lead to the development of an organisation that thinks critically and applies knowledge management effectively. It is expedient for an organisation to strengthen employee critical thinking skills, enabling the creation of a competitive organisation through individual social action.

Conclusions

In summarising the concept of critical thinking, it can be argued that it is constantly being discovered anew, depending on the period and contexts, the scientific attitude, and the research approach. The need for a definition of critical thinking is obvious in order to communicate, agree and coordinate actions. In terms of science – to justify research and to disseminate and communicate it in pursuit of the response of others, academic discussion and progress in science and society. In terms of education – to foster and improve critical thinking in the academic community. On the other hand, the very essence of critical thinking remains unchanged – the desire to understand what is right and what is not, and to know the truth or at least seek for cognition, despite different conceptions of truth and ways of exploring it. This is called criticality, no matter how it is understood and interpreted in various traditions. Criticality is defined as a person's ability to engage in quality thinking and a sign of the person's own worth. Critical thinking serves the improvement of the individual, interpersonal relationships and society.

The understanding that higher education must develop critical thinking stems from the recognition that individuals who think critically and reflectively are necessary to build and maintain the sustainability of societies. Starting with the UNESCO's 2009 declaration, the development of critical thinking competencies in higher education has undergone major transformations. Even though inequalities between countries and regions exist not only because of political decisions in the education system, but also because of different cultural contexts in the broadest sense that may lead to the persistence of those inequalities, the introduction of critical thinking competence development into the higher education system still depends on the choice of the countries themselves. Research provides more and more knowledge about the various practices of developing critical thinking in higher education, so there are more and more opportunities to become acquainted with the experience of foreign countries and their decisions and results, and to have more tools to build an effective critical thinking development system in higher education.

The practical significance of critical thinking is reflected in the context of labour market. Together with universal abilities such as collaboration, problem solving, leadership, creativity and self-discipline, critical thinking enables employees to function effectively in today's organisation. It can be seen as an essential tool in the management of organisations, helping to find many practical solutions when operating in modern market conditions, which require a consistently high level of competitiveness and efficacy. Critical thinking enables employees to think creatively and independently, make decisions and conclusions, dynamically engage in productive and positive activities, and link theoretical subjects with practical situations. Investing in employees' critical thinking skills and motivating them to improve their critical thinking skills and attitudes and apply them in the day-to-day decisions of the organisation will, in the long run, lead to the development of an organisation that thinks critically and applies knowledge management effectively. It is, therefore, expedient for an organisation to strengthen employee critical thinking skills, which will subsequently develop a competitive organisation through individual social actions.

References

AACSB (2017). AACSB curriculum development: Critical thinking. Retrieved from http://www.aacsb.edu/events/seminars/curriculum-development-series/critical-thinking.

Abed, S., Davoudi, A. M. H. & Hoseinzadeh, D. (2015). The effect of synectics pattern on increasing the level of problem solving and critical thinking skills in students of Alborz province. *WALIA Journal, 31*(1), 110–118.

Adler, S. (1991). The reflective practitioner and the curriculum of teacher education. *Journal of Education for Teaching, 17*(2), 139–150. doi:10.1080/0260747910170203.

Ahmed, S. (2012). *On Being Included: Racism and Diversity in Institutional Life.* Durham, NC: Duke University Press.

Ahrari, S., Samah, B. A., Hassan, M. S. H. B., Wahat, N. W. A. & Zaremohzzabieh, Z. (2016). Deepening critical thinking skills through civic engagement in Malaysian higher education. *Thinking Skills and Creativity, 22*, 121–128. doi:10.1016/j.tsc.2016.09.009.

Aliakbari, M. & Sadeghdaghighi, A. (2013). Teachers' perception of the barriers to critical thinking. *Procedia – Social and Behavioral Sciences, 70*(1), 1–5. doi:10.1016/j.sbspro.2013.01.031.

AMA, 2010. Critical Skills Survey. Retrieved from https://docplayer.net/14250237-Ama-2010-critical-skills-survey.html.

Andrews, R. (2007). Argumentation, critical thinking and the postgraduate dissertation. *Educational Review, 59*(1), 1–18. doi:10.1080/00131910600796777.

Apple, M. W. (1995). *Education and power.* New York, NY and London: Routledge.

Atkočiūnienė, Z. O. (2010). Žinių vadybos įtaka tobulinant organizacijos kompetencijas [The Influence of Knowledge Management in Improving Organisational Competencies]. *Informacijos mokslai, 52*, 14–22. doi:10.15388/Im.2010.0.3198.

Bailin, S. & Siegel, H. (2003). Critical thinking. In N. Blake (Ed.), *The Blackwell Guide to the Philosophy of Education* (pp. 181–193). Oxford, England: Blackwell.

Barad, K. (2007). *Meeting the Universe Halfway: Quantum Physics and the Entanglement of Matter and Meaning*. Durham, NC: Duke University Press.

Barnett, R. (1997). *Higher education: A critical business.* Oxford, England: OUP.

Barnett, R. (2000). *Realizing the university in an age of supercomplexity.* Buckingham, England: Society for Research into Higher Education and the Open University Press.

Barnett R. (2015). A curriculum for critical being. In M. Davies & R. Barnett (Eds.), *The Palgrave Handbook of Critical Thinking in Higher Education* (pp. 63–73). New York, NY: Palgrave Macmillan.

Bassham, G., Irwin, W., Nardone, H. & Wallace, J. M. (2013). Critical thinking: A student's introduction (5th ed.). New York, NY: McGraw-Hill.

Bauman, Z. & Donskis L. (2013). *Moral blindness: The loss of sensitivity in liquid modernity.* Cambridge, England: Polity Press.

Beachboard, M. B., Beachboard, J., Li, W. & Adkison, S. (2011). Cohorts and relatedness: Self-determination theory as an explanation of how learning communities affect educational outcomes. *Research in Higher Education, 52*(8), 853–874. doi:10.1007/s11162-011-9221-8.

Bezanilla, M. J., Fernández-Nogueira, D., Poblete, M. & Galindo-Domínguez, H. (2019). Methodologies for teaching-learning critical thinking in higher education: The teacher's view. *Thinking Skills and Creativity, 33.* https://doi.org/10.1016/j.tsc.2019.100584.

Bhatt, G. D. (2001). Knowledge management in organisations: Examining the interaction between technologies, techniques, and people. *Journal of Knowledge Management, 5*(1), 68–75. doi:10.1108/13673270110384419.

Bivainis, J. & Morkvėnas, R. (2008). Darbuotojų žinių potencialo vertinimas [Assessing the Knowledge Potential of Employees]. *Verslas: teorija ir praktika, 9*(2), 105–115.

Bouwmeester, O. (2013). Field Dependency of Argumentation Rationality in Decision-Making Debates. *Journal of Management Inquiry, 22*(4), 415–433. doi:10.1177/1056492612469727.

Bowell, T. & Kingsbury, J. (2015). Virtue and inquiry: Bridging the transfer gap. In M. Davies & R. Barnett (Eds.), *The Palgrave Handbook of Critical Thinking in Higher Education* (pp. 233–245). New York, NY: Palgrave Macmillan.

Brix, J. (2017). Exploring knowledge creation processes as a source of organizational learning: A longitudinal case study of a public innovation project. *Scandinavian Journal of Management, 33*(2), 113–127. doi:10.1016/j.scaman.2017.05.001.

Brodin, E. (2007). *Critical thinking in scholarship: Meanings, conditions and development.* Lund, Sweden: Lund University.

Brookfield, S. D. (2005). *The power of critical theory: Liberating adult learning and teaching.* San-Francisco, USA: Jossey-Bass.

Brookfield, S. D. (2012). *Teaching for critical thinking. Tools and techniques to help students question their assumptions.* San Francisco, CA: Jossey-Bass.

Brown, R. (2011). *Higher education and the market.* London, England: Routledge.

Cake, M. A., Bell, M. A., Williams, J. C., Brown, F. L., Dozier, M., Rhind, S. M. & Baillie, S. (2016). Which professional (non-technical) competencies are most important to the success of graduate veterinarians? A Best Evidence Medical

Education (BEME) systematic review: BEME Guide No. 38. *Medical Teacher*, 38(6), 550–563. doi:10.3109/0142159X.2016.1173662.

Candy, P. (1991). *Self-direction for lifelong learning*. San Francisco, CA: Jossey-Bass.

Cavaliere, V., Lombardi, S. & Giustiniano, L. (2015). Knowledge sharing in knowledge-intensive manufacturing firms. An empirical study of its enablers. *Journal of Knowledge Management, 19*(6), 1124–1145. doi:10.1108/JKM-12-2014-0538.

Cazzell, M. & Anderson, M. (2016). The impact of critical thinking on clinical judgment during simulation with senior nursing students. *Nursing Education Perspectives (National League for Nursing), 37*(2), 83–90. doi:10.5480/15-1553.

Council of the European Union, 2018. Council Recommendation on Key Competences for Lifelong Learning. Brussels, 23 May, 9009/18. https://eur-lex.europa.eu/legal-content/EN/TXT/PDF/?uri=CONSIL:ST_9009_2018_INIT&from=EN.

Curzon-Hobson, A. (2003). Higher learning and the critical stance. *Studies in Higher Education, 28*(2), 201–212. doi:10.1080/0307507032000058091.

Dalkir, K. (2017). *Knowledge management in theory and practice.* Cambridge: MIT Press.

Danvers, E. (2015). Criticality's affective entanglements: rethinking emotion and critical thinking in higher education. *Gender and Education, 28*(2), 282–297. doi:10.1080/09540253.2015.1115469.

Danvers, E. (2016). *Re-thinking criticality: undergraduate students, critical thinking and higher education.* (Doctoral dissertation, University of Sussex, Brighton, England). Retrieved from https://www.academia.edu/26213383/THESIS_Re_thinking_criticality_undergraduate_students_critical_thinking_and_higher_education.

Danvers, E. (2018). Who is the critical thinker in higher education? A feminist re-thinking. *Teaching in Higher Education, 23*(5), 548–562. doi:10.1080/13562517.2018.1454419.

Davies, M. (2011). Concept mapping, mind mapping and argument mapping: what are the differences and do they matter? *Higher Education, 62*(3), 279–301. doi:10.1007/s10734-010-9387-6.

Davies, M. (2015). A model of critical thinking in higher education. In M. B. Paulsen (Ed.), *Higher Education: Handbook of Theory and Research* (pp. 41–88). Switzerland: Springer International Publishing.

Davitch, J. M. & Folker Jr., R. D. (2017). Operationalizing Air Force Critical Thinking. *Air & Space Power Journal, 31*(4), 62.

Desai M. S., Berger B. D. & Higgs R. (2016). Critical thinking skills for business school graduates as demanded by employers: A strategic perspective and recommendations. *Academy of Educational Leadership Journal, 20*(1), 10–31.

Desjardins, J. (2018). 10 skills you'll need to survive the rise of automation. Retrieved from https://www.weforum.org/agenda/2018/07/the-skills-needed-to-survive-the-robot-invasion-of-the-workplace.

Dewey, J. (1902). *The child and the curriculum.* Chicago, IL: University of Chicago Press.

Dewey, J. (1997). *How we think.* Mineola, NY: Dover Publications.

Dewey, J. (2014). *Demokratija ir ugdymas [Democracy and education].* Vilnius, Lithuania: Baltic Printing House.

Donskis, L. (2009). *Troubled identity and the modern world.* New York, NY: Palgrave Macmillan.

Dune, G. (2015). Beyond critical thinking to critical being: Criticality in higher education and life. *International Journal of Education Research, 71,* 86–99. doi:10.1016/j.ijer.2015.03.003.

Duro, E., Elander, J., Maratos, F. A., Stupple, E. J. N. & Aubeeluck, A. (2013). In search of critical thinking in psychology: An exploration of student and lecturer understandings in higher education. *Psychology Learning and Teaching, 12*(3), 275–281. doi:10.2304/plat.2013.12.3.275.

El Soufi, N. (2019). *Evaluating the impact of instruction in critical thinking on the critical thinking skills of English language learners in higher education* (Doctoral theses, Durham University, Durham, England). Retrieved from http://etheses.dur.ac.uk/13208/.

Elder, L., Paul, R. & Cosgrove, R. (2007). *Critical Thinking Exam. International Critical Thinking Basic Concepts & Understanding Tests: Assessing Initial Understanding of Basic Critical Thinking Concepts and Principles. Foundation for Critical Thinking.*

Elicor, P. P. E. (2016). Critical thinking and community of inquiry within professional organizations in the developing world. *Journal of Human Values, 23*(1), 13–20. doi:10.1177/0971685816673479.

Ennis, R. H. (1987). A taxonomy of critical thinking dispositions and abilities. In J. Boykoff-Baron & R. J. Sternberg (Eds.), *Teaching thinking skills: Theory and practice* (pp. 11–26). New York, NY: W. H. Freeman.

Ennis, R. (1992). Assessing higher order thinking for accountability. In Keefe, J. W. & Walberg, J. H., (Eds.), *Teaching for Thinking* (pp. 73–91) Reston, Virginia: National Association of Secondary School Principals.

Ennis, R. (2000). *A super-streamlined conception of critical thinking, critical thinking.* Illinois, IL: University of Illinois. Available from: http://www.criticalthinking.net/SSConcCTApr3.html.

Ennis, R. H. & Millman, J. (2005). *Cornell critical thinking test, Level X* (5th ed.). Seaside, CA: Critical Thinking Company.

Erikson, M. G. & Erikson, M. (2018). Learning outcomes and critical thinking – good intentions in conflict. *Studies in Higher Education, 44*(12), 2293–2303. https://doi.org/10.1080/03075079.2018.1486813.

European Commission. (2012a). *The European Higher Education Area. Bologna process implementation report.* Retrieved from http://www.ehea.info/media.ehea.info/file/2012_Bucharest/79/5/Bologna_Process_Implementation_Report_607795.pdf.

European Commission. (2012b). *Rethinking Education: Investing in skills for better socio-economic outcomes.* Retrieved from https://www.cedefop.europa.eu/en/content/rethinking-education-investing-skills-better-socio-economic-outcomes.

European Commission. (2017). A renewed EU agenda for higher education. Retrieved from https://eur-lex.europa.eu/legal-content/EN/TXT/HTML/?uri=CELEX:52017DC0247&from=EN.

European Commission. (n.d.). Relevant and high-quality higher education. Retrieved from: https://ec.europa.eu/education/policies/higher-education/relevant-and-high-quality-higher-education_en.

European University Association. (2019). European Learning & Teaching Forum. Retrieved from https://www.eua.eu/events/24-2019-european-learning-teaching-forum.html.

Evens, M., Verburgh, A. & Elen, J. (2014). The development of critical thinking in professional and academic bachelor programmes. *Higher Education Studies, 4*(2), 42–51. doi:10.5539/hes.v4n2p42.

Exnar, I. Z. & Pálušová, M. (2015). Importance of Knowledge for Critical Thinking. *System approaches'15 – Interaction of soft and hard systems 2015.* doi:10.18267/pr.2019.dvo.2316.0.

Facione, P. A. (1990). *Critical Thinking: A Statement of Expert Consensus for Purposes of Educational Assessment and Instruction. Research findings and recommendations.* Fullerton, CA: California State University.

Facione, P., Facione, N. & Giancarlo, A. (1997). *Professional judgement and the disposition toward critical thinking.* Millbrae, CA: California Academic Press.

Facione, P. A., Facione, N. C. & Giancarlo, C. A. (2000). The disposition toward critical thinking: Its character, measurement, and relationship to critical thinking skill. *Informal Logic, 20* (1), 61–84. doi:10.22329/il.v20i1.2254.

Facione, P. A. (2011) *Critical thinking: What is it and why it counts* (5th ed.). Millbrae, CA: The California Academic Press.

Fahim, M. & Masouleh, N. S. (2012). Critical thinking in higher education: A pedagogical look. *Theory and Practice in Language Studies, 2*(7). doi:10.4304/tpls.2.7.1370–1375.

Farhan, A. & Muhaimin, K. (2019). Impacts of knowledge sharing: A review and directions for future research. *Journal of Workplace Learning, 31*(3), 207–230. doi:10.1108/JWL-07-2018-0096.

Felix, S. M. C. (2016) *Fostering criticality within neoliberal higher education: A critical action research study with first year students in Kazakhstan.* (Doctoral dissertation, University of Sussex, Brighton, England). Retrieved from https://sro.sussex.ac.uk/id/eprint/61301/.

Feng, Y. H., Fan, J. J. & Yang, H. Z. (2013). The relationship of learning motivation and achievement in EFL: Gender as an intermediated variable. *Educational Research International, 2*(2), 50–58.

Fisherman, D. (2017). *Everyday criticality: Questioning, expertise, and the embodiment of critical judgment. (Doctoral dissertation,* Montclair State University, Montclair, NJ). Retrieved from https://digitalcommons.montclair.edu/etd/39/.

Fong, C. J., Kim, Y., Davis, C. W., Hoang, T. & Kim, Y. W. (2017). A meta-analysis on critical thinking and community college student achievement. *Thinking Skills and Creativity, 26,* 71–83. doi:10.1016/j.tsc.2017.06.002.

Franco, A. (2016). What do "Ode to Joy," the Nobel Peace Prize, umbrellas and cartoons have in common? Why critical thinking matters and how higher education moulds. *Higher Education for the Future, 3*(1), 108–124. doi:10.1177/2347631115610231.

Freire, P. (1997). *Education for critical consciousness* (M. B. Ramos, Trans.). New York, NY: The Continuum. (Original work published 1969).

Freire, P. (2000). *Kritinės sąmonės ugdymas [Education for Critical Consciousness].* Vilnius, Lithuania: Tyto Alba.

Freire, P. (2001). *Pedagogy of freedom: Ethics, democracy and civic courage.* New York, NY: Oxford: Rowman & Littlefield Publishers.

Freire, P. (2005). *Pedagogy of the oppressed.* New York, NY: Continuum International Publishing Group.

Freud, S. (1927). *The ego and the Id.* London, England: Hogarth.

Freud, S. (1936). *The problem of anxiety.* New York, NY: Norton.

Fung, D. (2014). The influence of ground rules on Chinese students' learning of critical thinking in group work: a cultural perspective. *Pedagogy, Culture & Society, 22*(3), 337–368. doi:10.1080/14681366.2014.899611.

Ghazivakili, Z., Norouzi Nia, R., Panahi, F., Karimi, M., Gholsorkhi, H. & Ahmadi, Z. (2014). The role of critical thinking skills and learning styles of university students in their academic performance. *Journal of Advances in Medical Education & Professionalism, 2*(3), 95–102.

Giroux, H. A. (2013). On critical pedagogy. *Series: Critical Pedagogy Today Series, 1.* New York, NY: Continuum.

Gupta, B., Iyer L. S. & Aronson, J. E. (2000). Knowledge management: practices and challenges. *Industrial Management & Data Systems, 100*(1), 17–21. doi:10.1108/02635570010273018.

Habets, O., Stoffers, J., Van der Heijden, B. & and Peters, P. (2020). Am I fit for tomorrow's labor market? The effect of graduates' skills development during higher education for the 21st century's labor market. *Sustainability, 12*(18). doi:10.3390/su12187746.

Halpern, D. F. (1998). Teaching critical thinking for transfer across domains: Disposition, skills, structure training, and metacognitive monitoring. *American Psychologist, 53*(4), 449–455. doi:10.1037/0003-066X.53.4.449.

Halpern, D. F. (2014). *Thought and knowledge: An introduction to critical thinking* (5th ed.). New York, NY: Psychology Press.

Hassan, K. E. & Madhum, G. (2007). Validating the Watson Glaser critical thinking appraisal. *Higher Education: The International Journal of Higher Education and Educational Planning, 54*(3), 361–383. doi:10.1007/S10734-006-9002-Z.

Heijltjes, A., Van Gog, T., Leppink, J. & Paas, F. (2015). Unraveling the effects of critical thinking instructions, practice, and self-explanation on students' reasoning performance. *Instructional Science, 43*, 487–506. doi:10.1007/s11251-015-9347-8.

Helsdingen, A., van Gog, T. & van Merrienboer, J. (2011). The effects of practice schedule and critical thinking prompts on learning and transfer of a complex judgment task. *Journal of Educational Psychology, 103*(2), 383–398. doi:10.1037/a0022370.

Hidayati, N., Zubaidah, S., Suarsini, E. & Praherdhiono, H. (2020). The relationship between critical thinking and knowledge acquisition: The role of digital mind maps-PBL strategies. *International Journal of Information and Education Technology, 10*(2), 140–145. doi:10.18178/ijiet.2020.10.2.1353.

Hong, J. &, Kuo, C. (1999). Knowledge management in learning organization. *The Leadership & Organization Development Journal, 20*(4), 207–215. https://doi.org/10.1108/01437739910277019.

Hooks, B. (2009). *Teaching critical thinking: Practical wisdom*. New York, NY: Routledge.

Howlett, C., Ferreira, J.-A. & Blomfield, J. (2016). Teaching sustainable development in higher education: Building critical, reflective thinkers through an interdisciplinary approach. *International Journal of Sustainability in Higher Education, 17*(3), 305–321. doi:10.1108/IJSHE-07-2014-0102.

Huang, G. C., Lindell, D., Jaffe, L. E. & Sullivan A. M. (2016). A multi-site study of strategies to teach critical thinking: 'why do you think that?' *Medical Education, 50*(2), 236–249. doi:10.1111/medu.12937.

Janssen, E. M., Meulendijks, W., Mainhard, T., Verkoeijen, P. P., Heijltjes, A. E., Peppen, L. M. V. & Gog, T. V. (2019). Identifying characteristics associated with higher education teachers' Cognitive Reflection Test performance and their attitudes towards teaching critical thinking. *Teaching and Teacher Education, 84*, 139–149. doi:10.1016/j.tate.2019.05.008.

Jiang, J., Gao, A. & Yang, B. (2018). Employees' critical thinking, leaders' inspirational motivation, and voice behavior: The mediating role of voice efficacy. *Journal of Personnel Psychology, 17*(1), 33–41. https://doi.org/10.1027/1866-5888/a000193.

Jing, J. & Baiyin, Y. (2015). Roles of Creative Process Engagement and Leader–Member Exchange in Critical Thinking and Employee Creativity. *Social Behavior and Personality: An International Journal*, 43(7), 1217–1231. doi:10.2224/sbp.2015.43.7.1217.

Johnson, R. H. & Hamby, B. (2015). A meta-level approach to the problem of defining 'Critical Thinking'. *Argumentation, 29*(4), 417–430. doi:10.1007/s10503-015-9356-4.

Jou, M., Lin, Y. T. & Wu, D. W. (2016). Effect of a blended learning environment on student critical thinking and knowledge transformation. *Interactive Learning Environments, 24*(6), 1131–1147. doi:10.1080/10494820.2014.961485.

Khandaghi, M. A., Pakmehr, H. & Amiri, E. (2011). The status of college students' critical thinking disposition in humanities. *Procedia Social and Behavioral Sciences, 15*, 1866–1869. doi:10.1016/j.sbspro.2011.04.017.

Kincheloe, J. L. & Steinberg, S. R. (1993). A tentative description of post-formal thinking: The critical confrontation with cognitive theory. *Harvard Educational Review, 63*(3), 296–320. doi:10.17763/haer.63.3.h423221226v18648.

King, P. M. & Kitchener, K. S. (1994). *Developing reflective judgment: Understanding and promoting intellectual growth and critical thinking in adolescents and adults.* San Francisco, CA: Jossey-Bass Publishers.

Kish-Gephart, J., Detert, J. R., Klebe Trevino, L. & Edmondson, A.C. (2009). Silenced by fear: The nature, sources, and consequences of fear at work. *Research in Organizational Behavior, 29*, 163–193. doi: 10.1016/j.riob.2009.07.002.

Kreitzberg, A. P. & Kreitzberg, C. B. (2011). The business case for critical thinking. *MWorld, 10*(2), 23–26.

Ku, K. Y. L. & Ho, I. T. (2010). Metacognitive strategies that enhance critical thinking. *Metacognition and Learning, 5*(3), 251–267. doi:10.1007/s11409-010-9060-6.

Ku, K. Y. L., Ho, I. T., Hau K. & Lai, E. C. M. (2014). Integrating direct and inquiry-based instruction in the teaching of critical thinking: an intervention study. *Instructional Science, 42*(2), 251–269. doi:10.1007/s11251-013-9279-0.

Kuhn, D. A. (2008). *Education for thinking.* Cambridge: Harvard University Press.

Kurfiss, J. G. (1988). *Critical thinking: Theory, research, practice, and possibilities.* ASHE-ERIC Higher Education Report No. 2. Washington, DC: Association for the Study of Higher Education.

Lancrin, V., Gonzales-Sancho, C., Bouckaert, M., de Luca, F., Fernandez-Barrerra, M., Jacotin, G, Urgel, J. and Vidal, Q. (2019). *Fostering Students' Creativity and Critical Thinking: What It Means in School. Centre for Educational Research and Innovation.*: OECD publishing.

LaPoint-O'Brien, T. (2013). Action Research: The Development of Critical Thinking Skills. Retrieved from: http://files.eric.ed.gov/fulltext/ED540359.pdf.

Letizia, A. (2012). The untruth of truth: A suggestion for teaching in information age. *The Councilor: A Journal of the Social Studies, 73*(1), 1–8.

Lim, L. (2011). Beyond logic and argument analysis: critical thinking, everyday problems and democratic deliberation in Cambridge International Examinations' Thinking Skills curriculum. *Journal of Curriculum Studies, 43*(6), 783–807. doi:10.1080/00220272.2011.590231.

Lin, S. (2014). Science and non-science undergraduate students' critical thinking and argumentation performance in reading a science news report. *International Journal of Science and Mathematics Education, 12*(5), 1023–1046. doi:10.1007/s10763-013-9451-7.

Lipman, M. (2003). *Thinking in education.* Cambridge, England: Cambridge University Press.

Liu, O. L., Mao, L., Frankel, L. & Xu, J. (2016). Assessing critical thinking in higher education: The HEIghten™ approach and preliminary validity evidence. *Assessment & Evaluation in Higher Education, 41*(5), 677–694. https://doi.org/10.1080/02602938.2016.1168358.

Macpherson, K. & Owen, C. (2010). Assessment of critical thinking ability in medical students. *Assessment & Evaluation in Higher Education, 35*(1), 41–54. doi:10.1080/02602930802475471.

Magrabi, S. A. R., Pasha, M. I. & Pasha, M. Y. (2018). Classroom Teaching to Enhance Critical Thinking and Problem-Solving Skills for developing IOT Applications. *Journal of Engineering Education Transformations, 31*(3), 152–157. doi: 10.16920/jeet/2018/v31i3/120785.

Maloney, S., Hong-Meng Tai, J., Lo, K., Molloy, E. & Ilic, D. (2013). Honesty in critically reflective essays: An analysis of student practice. *Advances in Health Sciences Education, 18*(4), 617–626. doi:10.1007/s10459-012-9399-3.

Mardis, M. A., Ma, J., Jones, F. R., Ambavarapu, C. R., Kelleher, H. M., Spears, L. I. & McClure, C. R. (2017). Assessing alignment between information technology educational opportunities, professional requirements, and industry demands. *Education and Information Technologies*, 1–38.

Markowitz, L. (2005). Unmasking moral dichotomies: Can feminist pedagogy overcome student resistance. *Gender and Education, 17*(1), 39–55. doi:10.1080/0954025042000301294.

Marope, M., Griffin, P. & Gallagher, C. (2018). *Future competences and the future of curriculum: A global reference for curricula transformation.* Geneva: UNESCO IBE.

Retrieved from: http://www.ibe.unesco.org/sites/default/files/resources/future_competences_and_the_future_of_curriculum.pdf?fbclid=IwAR1Y3Ac0dNgpHqle02-OwYQ-b-eAZfwEHJ3PwnbUZa8TXIa-PZQpTrMjnhU.

McGuire, J. M. (2007). Why has the critical thinking movement not come to Korea? *Asia Pacific Education Review, 8*(2), 224–232. doi:10.1007/BF03029258.

McLaren. (2003). Critical pedagogy. In D. Gabbard (Ed.), *Knowledge and power in the global economy: Politics and the rhetoric of school reform* (pp. 345–352). NJ: Lawrence Erlbaum Associates.

McLaren, P. (2016). *Pedagogy of Insurrection: From Resurrection to Revolution.* New York, NY: Peter Lang.

McLaren, P. & Jandric, P. (2020). *Postdigital dialogues on critical pedagogy, liberation theology and information technology.* London, New York, NY: Bloomsbury Academic.

McNamara, J., Sweetman, S., Connors, P., Lofgren, I. & Greene, G. (2020). Using interactive nutrition modules to increase critical thinking skills in college courses. *Journal of Nutrition Education and Behavior, 52*(4), 343–350. doi:10.1016/j.jneb.2019.06.007.

McPeck, J. (1981). *Critical thinking and education.* Oxford, England: Oxford University Press.

Natale, S. & Ricci, F. (2006). Critical thinking in organizations. *Team Performance Management 12*(7/8), 272–277. doi:10.1108/13527590610711822.

Nedelová, M. & Šukolová, D. (2017). Critical thinking in initial teacher education: Secondary data analysis from hello GS feasibility study in Slovakia. *New Educational Review, 49*(3), 19–29. doi:10.15804/tner.2017.49.3.01.

Niu, L., L. Behar-Horenstein, C. W. & Garvan, C. (2013). "Do instructional interventions influence college students' critical thinking skills? A meta-analysis". *Educational Research Review, 9*, 114–128. https://doi.org/10.1016/j.edurev.2012.12.002.

Noddings, N. (2017). The search for meaning and connection. *Educational Studies, 53*(1), 1–12. doi:10.1080/00131946.2016.1269492.

Nonaka, I., Toyama, R. & Hirata, T. (2008). *Managing flow: A process theory of the knowledge-based firm.* Hampshire, England: Palgrave Macmillan.

Paul, R. & Elder, L. (2012). *Critical thinking: Tools for taking charge of your learning and your life.* Boston, MA: Pearson.

Paul, R. & Elder, L. (2020). *The miniature guide to critical thinking concepts and tools.* Lanham, MD: Rowman & Littlefield.

Paul, R., Elder, L. & Bartell, T. (1997). *California teacher preparation for instruction in critical thinking: Research findings and policy recommendations.* Dillon Beach, CA: The Foundation for Critical Thinking.

Penkauskienė, D. (2016). Kritinio ir kūrybinio mąstymo sąsaja [The interface between critical and creative thinking]. *Socialinė teorija, empirija, politika ir praktika, 13*, 90–104. doi:10.15388/STEPP.2016.13.10045.

Penkauskienė, D., Railienė, A. & Cruz, G. (2019). How is critical thinking valued by the labour market? Employer perspectives from different European countries. *Studies in Higher Education, 44*(5), 1–12. doi:10.1080/03075079.2019.1586323

Phan, H. H. (2011). Deep processing strategies and critical thinking: Developmental trajectories. Using latent growth analyses. *Journal of Educational Research, 104*(4), 283–294. doi:10.1080/00220671003739382.

Piawa, C. Y. (2010). Building a test to assess creative and critical thinking simultaneously. *Procedia – Social and Behavioral Sciences, 2*(2), 551–559. https://doi.org/10.1016/j.sbspro.2010.03.062.

Pithers, R. T. & Soden, R. (2000). Critical thinking in education: A review. *Educational Research, 42*(3), 237–249. doi:10.1080/001318800440579.

Pollard, V. (2014). An ontological turn in critical thinking in higher education. In A. Kwan, E. Wong, T. Kwong, P. Lau & A. Goody (Eds.), *Research and Development in Higher Education: Higher Education in a Globalized World, 37* (pp. 266–273). Published?

Power, J. B. (2016). Has this begun to change the way they think? Moving undergraduate learners' level of reflection from where it is to where it needs to be. *Teaching in Higher Education, 21*(3), 235–248. doi:10.1080/13562517.2015.1136278.

Powley, E. H. & Taylor, S. N. (2014). Pedagogical Approaches to Develop Critical Thinking and Crisis Leadership. *Journal of Management Education, 38*(4), 560–585. doi:10.1177/1052562913519081.

Promoting Critical Thinking in European Higher Education Institutions: towards an educational protocol (2019). Eds. Dominguez, C. & R. Payan-Carreira. Universidade de Trás-os-Montes e Alto Douro.

Puig B., Blanco-Anaya P., Bargiela I. M. & Crujeiras-Pérez, B. (2019). A systematic review on critical thinking intervention studies in higher education across professional fields. *Studies in Higher Education, 44*(5), 860–869, doi:10.1080/03075079.2019.1586333.

Raudeliūnienė, J. & Račinskaja, I. (2014). Žinių įgijimo proceso vertinimas Lietuvos draudimo sektoriuje [Evaluation of the Knowledge Acquisition Process in the Lithuanian Insurance Sector]. *Verslas: teorija ir praktika, 15*(2), 149–159. doi:10.3846/btp.2014.15.

Rave, J. I. P., Guerrero, R. F. & Morales, J. C. C. (2020). Critical thinking and continuous improvement: a scientific text mining approach. *Total Quality Management.* doi:10.1080/14783363.2020.1787824.

Redding, G. (2017). *Critical thinking, university autonomy, and societal evolution; thoughts on a research agenda.* Centre for Global Higher Education

Working Paper No. 11. London: UCL Institute of Education. https://www.researchcghe.org/publications/working-paper/critical-thinking-university-autonomy-and-societal-evolution-thoughts-on-a-research-agenda/.

Reed, L. (2018). Building critical thinking skills to solve problems at work. Retrieved from https://www.business.com/articles/building-critical-thinking-skills-at-work/.

Resnick, L. (1987). *Education and learning to think.* Washington, DC: National Academy Press.

Rickles, M. L., Schneider, R. Z., Slusser, S. R., Williams, D. M. & Zipp, J. F. (2013). Assessing Change in Student Critical Thinking for Introduction to Sociology Classes. *Teaching Sociology, 41*(3), 271–281. https://doi.org/10.1177/0092055X13479128.

Riley-Jones, G. (2012). Critical thinking as an embodied criticality: The lived experiences of international art students. *Journal of Writing in Creative Practice, 5*(3), 401–421. doi:10.1386/jwcp.5.3.401_1.

Rodzalan, S. A. & Saat, M. M. (2015). The perception of critical thinking and problem-solving skill among Malaysian undergraduate students. *Procedia – Social and Behavioral Sciences, 172,* 725–732. doi:10.1016/j.sbspro.2015.01.425.

Rogoff, I. (2006), "Smuggling" – An embodied criticality. Retrieved from https://xenopraxis.net/readings/rogoff_smuggling.pdf.

Saha, A., & Ahuja, S. (2017). Critical Existential Thinking, Search for Meaning and Life Satisfaction. *Journal of Psychosocial Research, 12*(1), 187–195.

Sayyadi, M. (2019). How effective leadership of knowledge management impacts organizational performance. *Business Information Review, 36*(1), 30–38. doi:10.1177/0266382119829643.

Schendel, R. (2016). Constructing departmental culture to support student development: Evidence from a case study in Rwanda. *Higher Education: The International Journal of Higher Education Research, 72*(4), 487–504. doi:10.1007/s10734-016-0036-6.

Schmaltz, R. M., Jansen, E. & Wenckowski, N. (2017). Redefining critical thinking: teaching students to think like scientists. *Frontiers in Psychology, 8*(459). doi: 10.3389/fpsyg.2017.00459.

Schraagen, J. M. & van de Ven, J. G. M. (2008). Improving decision making in crisis response through critical thinking support. *Journal of Cognitive Engineering and Decision Making, 2*(4), 311–327. https://doi.org/10.1518/155534308X377801.

Shaheen, N. (2016). International students' critical thinking-related problem areas: UK university teachers' perspectives. *Journal of Research in International Education, 15*(1), 18–31. doi:10.1177/1475240916635895.

Siegel, H. (1988). *Educating reason. Rationality, critical thinking, and education.* London, England: Routledge.

Sigurðsson, G. (2017). Transformative critique: What Confucianism can contribute to contemporary education. *Studies in Philosophy and Education, 36*(2), 131–146. doi:10.1007/s11217-015-9502-3.

Sinatra, G. M. & Lombardi, D. (2020). Evaluating sources of scientific evidence and claims in the post-truth era may require reappraising plausibility judgments. *Educational Psychologist, 55*(3), 120–131. doi:10.1080/00461520.2020.1730181.

Skaržauskienė, A. (2008). *Sisteminis mąstymas kaip kompetencija lyderystės paradigmoje [Systems thinking as a competence in the leadership paradigm].* (Doctoral dissertation, ISM Vadybos ir ekonomikos universitetas, Kaunas, Lithuania.). Retrieved from https://www.lituanistika.lt/content/19563.

Soufi, N. E. & See, B. H. (2019). Does explicit teaching of critical thinking improve critical thinking skills of English language learners in higher education? A critical review of causal evidence. *Studies in Educational Evaluation, 60*, 140–162. https://doi.org/10.1016/j.stueduc.2018.12.006.

Sousa, M. J. & Wilks, D. (2018). Sustainable skills for the world of work in the digital age. *Systems Research and Behavioral Science, 35*(4), 399–405. doi:10.1002/sres.2540.

Sternberg, R. J. & Halpern, D. F. (2020). Conclusions: How to think critically about politics...and anything else! In R. J. Sternberg & D. F. Halpern (Eds.), *Critical Thinking in Psychology* (pp. 354–376). Cambridge, England: Cambridge University Press.

Stupnisky, R. H., Renaud, R. D., Daniels, L. M., Haynes, T. L. & Perry, R. P. (2008). The interrelation of first-year college students' critical thinking disposition, perceived academic control, and academic achievement. *Research in Higher Education, 49*(6), 513–530. doi: 10.1007/s11162-008-9093-8.

Subramanian, K. R. (2020). Organizational aspirations and critical thinking of managers. *Journal of Advances in Social Science and Humanities, 6*(4). doi:10.15520/jassh.v6i4.485.

Tang, D., Zhu, R., Tang, J., Xu, R. & He, R. (2010). Product design knowledge management based on design structure matrix. *Advanced Engineering Informatics, 24*(2), 159–66. doi:10.1016/j.aei.2009.08.005.

Thayer-Bacon, B. J. (2000). *Transforming critical thinking: Thinking constructively.* London, England: Teachers College Press.

Tiruneh, D. T., De Cock, M., Weldeslassie, A. G., Elen, J. & Janssen, R. (2017). Measuring Critical Thinking in Physics: Development and validation of a critical thinking test in electricity and magnetism. *International Journal of Science and Mathematics Education, 15*(4), 663–682. doi:10.1007/s10763-016-9723-0.

Tripathy, M. (2020). Dimensions of critical thinking in workplace management & personal development: A conceptual analysis. *Multidisciplinary Journal for Education Social and Technological Sciences, 7*(2), 1–19. doi:10.4995/muse.2020.12925.

UNESCO. (2009). *The New Dynamics of Higher Education and Research for Societal Change and Development.* Paris, France: UNESCO.

UNESCO. (2015). *Science Report: Towards 2030.* Retrieved from http://uis.unesco.org/sites/default/files/documents/unesco-science-report-towards-2030-part1.pdf).

Ünsar, A. S. & Engin, E. (2013). A case study to determine critical thinking skills of university students. *Procedia – Social and Behavioral Sciences, 75*, 563–569. doi:10.1016/j.sbspro.2013.04.061.

Veronese, C., Richards, J. B., Pernar, L., Sullivan, A. M. & Schwartzstein, R. M. (2013). A randomized pilot study of the use of concept maps to enhance problem-based learning among first-year medical students. *Medical Teacher, 35*(9), 1478–1484. doi:10.3109/0142159X.2013.785628.

Walter, T. (2017). *An Analysis of the Teaching of Critical Thinking Skills in History in Postsecondary Education.* (Doctoral dissertation, Texas Wesleyan University, Fort Worth, Texas). Retrieved from https://eric.ed.gov/?id=ED580712.

Wang, Q., Woo, H. L. & Zhao, J. (2009). Investigating critical thinking and knowledge construction in an interactive learning environment. *Interactive Learning Environments, 17*(1), 95–104. doi:10.1080/10494820701706320.

Wang, X. & Zheng, H. (2016). Reasoning critical thinking: Is it born or made? *Theory and Practice in Language Studies, 6*(6), 1323–1331. doi:10.17507/tpls.0606.25.

Weinstein, J. R. (2004). Neutrality, pluralism, and education: Civic education as learning about the tther. *Studies in Philosophy and Education, 23*(4), 235–263. doi:10.1023/B:SPED.0000028333.81199.8e.

Whiting, K. (2020). These are the top 10 job skills of tomorrow – and how long it takes to learn them. Retrieved from: https://www.weforum.org/agenda/2020/10/top-10-work-skills-of-tomorrow-how-long-it-takes-to-learn-them/.

Williams, C. H. (1991). Doing critical thinking together: Applications to government, politics, and public policy. *Political Science and Politics, 24*(3), 510–516. doi:10.2307/420101.

Wolcott, S. (2006). *College Faculty Handbook: Steps for Better Thinking. A Classroom Model for Teaching, Learning and Assessing Higher Order Thinking Skills.* Bellevue, Washington: Wolcott Lynch Associates.

Yanchar, S. C., Slife, B. D., & Warne, R. (2008). Critical Thinking as Disciplinary Practice. *Review of General Psychology, 12*(3), 265–281. https://doi.org/10.1037/1089-2680.12.3.265

Yukl, G. A. (2010). *Leadership in organizations.* Hoboken, NJ: Prentice Hall.

Zhang, N. (2020). On the Cultivation of Critical Thinking Ability in College English Class. *International Journal of English, Literature and Social Sciences (IJELS), 5*(1). doi:10.22161/ijels.51.36.

Analysing the Concept of Critical Thinking in Higher Education: Systematic Literature Review

Abstract: Researchers from different fields of science are paying more and more attention to the phenomenon of critical thinking, as evidenced by the growing number of scientific publications over the years. Nevertheless, the very concept of critical thinking is interpreted differently in both the scientific and practical contexts, giving it various meanings that sometimes differ. Such a broad interpretation of the concept also raises the question of whether critical thinking is an intrinsic personality trait, a mental operation, a thought process or all of the above. It can be assumed that the diversity of interpretations and explanations of the concept of critical thinking is determined not only by the complexity of critical thinking, but also by different scientific approaches.

The purpose of this chapter is to present, based on a systematic literature review, the dynamics of the concept of critical thinking in scientific publications from different periods in the context of higher education and to reveal the multidimensionality and comprehensiveness of critical thinking. This chapter consists of three sections. The first section describes the methodology, discussing in detail the process of systematic literature review: searching for sources, selection criteria, criteria for analysis of the selected sources. In the second section, the diachronic approach is used to discuss the growing popularity of the concept of critical thinking in higher education in the period from 1997 to 2017. The third section uses the synchronic approach to analyse domain-general and domain-specific approaches to critical thinking, aspects of critical thinking development (instructional approaches, critical thinking interventions/strategies), and the value of critical thinking to the individual, interpersonal relationships and society as a whole.

Keywords: diachronic approach, synchronic approach, critical thinking as domain-general or domain-specific, critical thinking instructional approaches, individual, interpersonal and social aspects of critical thinking, systematic literature review.

1. Research Methodology

1.1. Background for literature review

Social research methodology emphasises that literature review is a crucial step in the research process. It allows researchers to cumulate past experience (Gomersall, 2007) and summarise the earlier knowledge in the field, introduces methodological and design issues, provides data sources and opportunities to compare own research with previous work (Leedy, 1997; Edyburn, 2001), provides a rationale for further study (Badke, 2017), and leads to new insights when the literature is reviewed and each piece of relevant information is seen in the context of other information (Aveyard, 2014). At the same time, there is increasing recognition that literature review is a complicated, sometimes confusing and laborious, process (Chen, Wang and Lee, 2016), while methods of undertaking review are rigorous and time-consuming (Aveyard, 2014). Cronin et al. (2008) describe the process of literature review as selection of the topic, searching the literature, gathering, reading and analysing the literature, writing the review and providing references.

Systematic literature review is one of the 14 literature review types described by Grant and Booth (2009). It differs from a traditional or narrative review because a systematic review uses a more rigorous and well-defined approach to reviewing the literature in the specific subject area. Unlike a traditional review, the purpose of a systematic review is to provide a list as complete as possible of all published articles relating to the particular subject area. While a traditional review attempts to summarise the results of a number of studies, a systematic review uses explicit and rigorous criteria to identify, critically evaluate and synthesise literature on a particular topic (Cronin, Ryan and Coughlan, 2008).

Therefore, a systematic literature review approach (Cronin, Ryan and Coughlan, 2008) was chosen for the conceptualisation of critical thinking. Critical thinking is a vibrant topic and one of the most discussed competences, playing an important role in contemporary society, globalisation of the labour market and the creation of the welfare of the individual and community. However, there is no agreement as to what critical thinking is or how it expresses itself in practical situations and social life spheres (Facione, 1990; Lewis and Smith, 1993; Halpern, 1998; Bailin, 2002; Willingham, 2007). As Kubok (2018) states, it seems to be self-evident what critical thinking is, but when it comes to actually defining what critical thinking is, challenges arise, partly due to the fact that it is not clear how one or another author came to the definition and description of critical thinking concept. There is a lack of articles describing the methodological aspects of critical thinking conceptualisation based on a systematic literature review. Among the few existing articles, only two could be mentioned as presenting the path of conceptualisation of critical thinking: one is by Billing (2007), who describes the methodology of a survey of over 700 articles, and the other is by Bekele (2009), who revised articles about critical thinking and problem solving published from 1995 to 2006.

When it comes to the conceptualisation of critical thinking in relation to a specific topic, in this case – education, the picture becomes even more complicated. Despite the abundance of literature about critical thinking in education, most is restricted to testing existing theories, analysing cognitive skills, characteristics or attitudes, and investigating a specific study programme curriculum or students' cognitive skills (Lai, 2011). Penkauskienė (2017) stated that critical thinking in higher education was investigated inconsistently and fragmentarily, limited mostly to general theoretical reasoning (Moore, 2013; Shephard et al., 2015; Heijltjes, Van Gog, Leppink and Paas, 2015; Cake et al., 2016), and lacking a detailed methodological description; meanwhile, empirical articles are fragmented (Liu, Mao, Frankel and Xu, 2016) and do not allow for a full picture (Phan, 2008;

Slabon, Richards and Dennen, 2014). Researchers (Norris and Ennis, 1989; Silva, 2008; Ku, 2009) recognise the limitations of such studies and call for a combination of various methods, a search for new instruments, and investigation of critical thinking in specific contexts.

The importance of literature review, the obscurity of the definition of critical thinking, and the lack of analysis about methodological challenges in literature review connected with a specific topic – in this case the conceptualisation of critical thinking in higher education – all provide evidence for prioritising a systematic literature review over other types of literature review. The sampling process could be divided into two major stages: selection of journals and sampling of the articles.

1.2 Selection of journals

As the interest was in the concept of critical thinking in higher education, the first task was to identify journals of interest in the field of higher education. It was assumed that the foremost papers on critical thinking in the field of education are in journals included in Clarivate Analytics Web of Science database. This database served as a tool for identifying the most cited articles published in journals indexed in the Web of Science Core Collection database.

In the first step, the journals for higher education included in the selected database were searched for. The keywords *education* and *educational* were used. The list of journals for analysis was generated using the Clarivate Analytics Journal Citation Reports database, evaluating the journal impact factor for the 2016 period. The journal impact factors are estimated after a certain period of time, so the impact factors obtained in March 2018 covered the year 2016 and were only pertinent to June 2018. Journals under the specified keywords were divided into four themes:

- Education and Educational Research;
- Education, Scientific Disciplines;
- Education, Special;
- Psychology, Educational.

A separate list of journals for each theme was generated and the journal impact factor as a general criterion of the quality of journal was employed; in particular, quartiles by journal impact factor (Maskeliūnas, 2011; Šakytė, 2016).

In the second step, journals were grouped by quartile, a statistical indicator that shows the position of the journal in the subject category by the distribution of the citation index between the maximum and the minimum value. Quartiles are indicated by the letter Q and divide the sequence of attributes into four equal parts.

In the third step, a verification of each journal was carried out. Each journal was cross-checked on the EBSCOhost platform by typing the title of the journal and verifying its ISSN. After identifying a particular journal as matching the main criteria in terms of impact factor, authenticity and access options, the journal was included in the list of journals that were searched for articles about critical thinking.

The final distribution of the journals is presented in Table 1.

Tab. 1: *Number of journals in quartiles by journal theme*

Theme	Total	Q1	Q2	Q3	Q4
Education and Educational Research	231	58	59	56	58
Education, Scientific Disciplines	41	10	10	10	11
Education, Special	38	9	10	9	10
Psychology, Educational	32	14	15	2	1
Total	342	91	94	77	80

A similar number of journals were included in Q1 and Q2 (91 and 94 respectively), while Q3 had 77 and Q4 had 80. A total of 342 journals were examined further. The biggest share in all quartiles was in the 'Education and Educational Research' theme (231 journals).

1.3 Sampling of articles

After the selection of journals, a systematic literature review was done following the description put forth by Parahoo (2006) that a systematic literature review details the time frame within which the literature was selected, as well as the methods used to evaluate and synthesise the findings of the studies in question. In order for the reader to assess the reliability and validity of the review, the reviewer needs to present the precise criteria used to:

- formulate the research question;
- set inclusion or exclusion criteria;
- select and access the literature;
- assess the quality of the literature included in the review;
- analyse and synthesise the findings.

Four research questions were formulated:

- How does the concept of critical thinking in higher education change chronologically in the analysed publications?
- How are domain-general and domain-specific approaches to critical thinking in relation to specific study fields expressed in the analysed publications?

- What critical thinking instructional approaches and critical thinking interventions/strategies are described in the analysed publications?
- How is the value of critical thinking manifested on the personal, interpersonal and social levels?

1.4 Inclusion or exclusion criteria

Two out of the seven strategies that Barrett (1997) singled out for literature search were applied. The first of these – *a general search* – was done not due to little knowledge about the topic as the author suggests is the case, but due to a desire to capture every source containing the concept of critical thinking. In this step, the articles were searched for via the online research platform EBSCOhost (https://www.ebsco.com/). The dates of the publications covered a 20-year period (1997–2017).[1] Sampling of the articles within the selected journals was carried out using search settings with the following selection criteria:

- ISSN of the particular journal
- Keyword *critical thinking* in the 'Subject terms' field
- Full text
- 1997–2017 period
- English language

This setting produced 615 articles published in journals in Q1, 397 articles in Q2, 911 in Q3 and 1,298 in Q4. In total, there were 3,221 articles to be analysed. A preliminary review of the articles has shown that many articles were far from the subject matter under analysis, specifically – critical thinking in higher education. Therefore, *a specific search was conducted* using Boolean logic (i.e. 'AND') as a means of linking key concepts ('critical thinking' AND 'higher education') and, accordingly, reducing the number of irrelevant items. Keeping other selection criteria the same but with the keywords *critical thinking* and *higher education*, the total number of articles was 55 in Q1, 264 in Q2, 245 in Q3, and 240 in Q4 (Table 2).

1 Due to data on journal impact factors covering the period until the end of 2016 at the time of the research, it is possible that not all publications from 2017 were presented in the correct quartiles in cases where a journal was moved to another quartile after the beginning of a new period of impact factor calculation.

Tab. 2: *Number of articles in each quartile by primary and refined search parameters*

Theme	**Q1**		**Q2**		**Q3**		**Q4**	
	Critical Thinking	**Critical Thinking AND Higher Education**	**Critical Thinking**	**Critical Thinking AND Higher Education**	**Critical Thinking**	**Critical Thinking AND Higher Education**	**Critical Thinking**	**Critical Thinking AND Higher Education**
Education and Educational Research	218	31	390	264	708	227	1226	229
Education, Scientific Disciplines	347	18	0	0	122	10	63	9
Education, Special	1	0	3	0	47	4	8	1
Psychology, Educational	49	6	4		34	4	1	1
Total	615	55	397	264	911	245	1298	240

The total number of articles was 804. The number of articles was excluded due to limited access to article content. Articles with a fee were classified as articles with limited access and were therefore removed from the planned list of articles to be analysed. A total of 303 articles remained for further analysis.

1.5 Selection of and access to the literature

A total of 303 articles were analysed using a pre-designed form, which included the following items: reference, type of publication (theoretical, qualitative, quantitative); study field, definition of critical thinking (including specifying whether it is original or based on another author's paper), skills and dispositions of critical thinking, related concepts, researcher's (reviewer's) comments (see Figure 1).

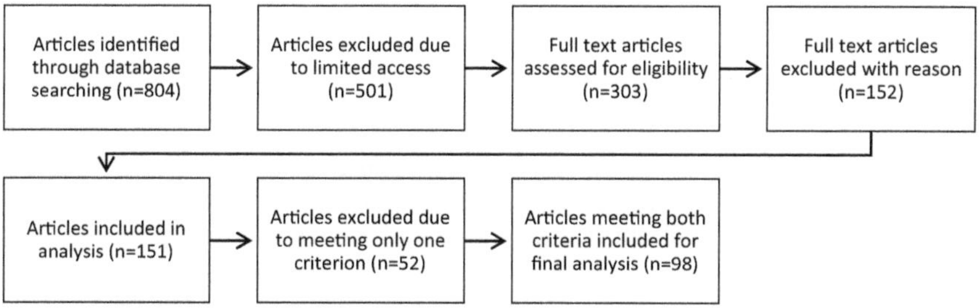

Fig. 1: *Flow chart*

After analysis of the selected 303 articles, 151 articles defining the concept of critical thinking in higher education and/or skills and dispositions were selected for further analysis, while the articles in which critical thinking was mentioned episodically were excluded from the research. Articles combining both criteria – definition of critical thinking and skills, dispositions – were left for further analysis. A total of 98 articles matching quality criteria were found.

1.6 Analysis and synthesis of the findings

The selected articles were analysed by qualitative content analysis using theoretical coding based on diachronic and synchronic approaches (Harrison, 2005; Hämäläinen, 2013). In answering the first research questions, a diachronic approach was used which made it possible to reveal the growing popularity of the concept of critical thinking in higher education in historical discourse during the 1997–2017 period. A synchronic approach was used for answering the second and third research questions. A synchronous analysis made it possible to reveal the systemic understanding of the concept of critical thinking in higher education by distinguishing similarities and differences as well as specificity. The current discussion in scientific literature is related to the analysis of the concept of critical thinking as a domain-specific or a domain-general phenomenon (Hathcoat, Penn, Barnes and Comer, 2016; Dwyer, 2017). The interpretation of the concept of critical thinking as domain-specific or domain-general is directly related to the integration of critical thinking development into higher education programmes (Tiruneh, Weldeslassie, Kassa, Tefera, De Cock and Elen, 2016). Based on Dwyer (2017), the articles were grouped into two categories: domain-general (23 articles) and domain-specific (75 articles). The next stage of the analysis examined how the concept of critical thinking is highlighted in the 98 selected articles according to different study areas, which were listed based on the Lithuanian List of Study Fields and Groups of Fields According to Which Studies Are Conducted at Higher Education Institutions (Ministry of Education and Science, 2016) and included IT, arts, education, social science, science, humanities and health. In the last stage, the publications were analysed according to critical thinking instructional approaches and critical thinking interventions/strategies.

The following methods were used to ensure the validity of the systematic literature review (Maxwell, 1992; Bowen, 2009; Creswell and Creswell, 2018):

- authenticity of sources – sources in the Clarivate Analytics Journal Citation Reports database were included; scientific journal ISSN codes, publishers, database indexing, subscriptions and access options were cross-checked during the search;
- source assessment criteria – the inclusion and exclusion criteria were clearly defined for the publications (see text above);
- period – articles published in the 1997–2017 period were included (the reference point is 2017, as scientific journal citation rates are calculated and evaluated after the corresponding period, the citation rates during the study were for 2017);
- source triangulation – articles were included that were based on quantitative, qualitative and mixed research methods;
- maximum number of sources – all scientific publications meeting the selection criteria were analysed and included in the analysis list.

The detailed results of the systematic literature review that was conducted are presented in the next chapter.

2. Expression of Critical Thinking in the Context of Higher Education: The Diachronic Approach

The diachronic cross-section made it possible to reveal the growing popularity of the concept of critical thinking in higher education in historical discourse during the 1997–2017 period. With the exception of 1998 and 2004, when not a single article on critical thinking was published in the selected scientific journals, the number of such publications grew steadily in 1997–2017 (Figure 2), which reflects the popularity of critical thinking in scientific publications. The number of publications grew steadily in 2005–2009, ranged between six and nine publications per year in 2010–2014, and dropped significantly in 2015; however, the next year, 2016, saw the maximum number of articles published per year (13) and was the only year in which the number of publications exceeded the average number of articles printed per year.

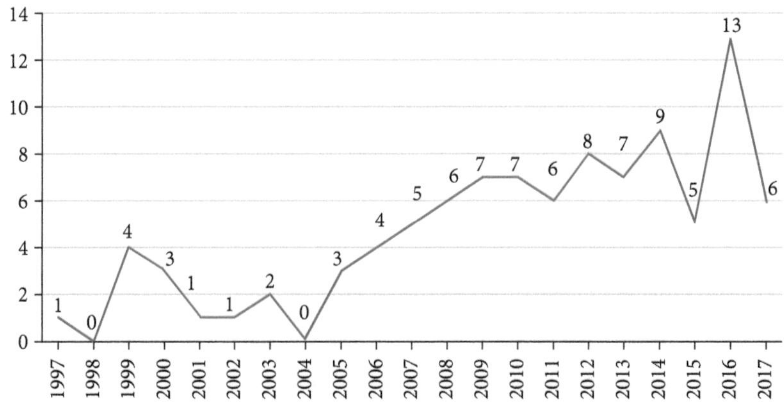

Fig. 2: *Total number of articles per year, 1997–2017*

On the one hand, the growing number of publications may be affected by the growing number of researchers. On the other hand, increasing attention to critical thinking as a general competency could be affected by globalisation processes. Higher education is also affected by these processes in terms of a need to review study programmes in order to meet the challenges of today and tomorrow (European Commission, 2017). Higher education remains one of the prerequisites contributing to the maintenance of a dialogue on national and global development (and is apparently expected to remain as such). Therefore, institutions of higher education provide conditions for learners to develop critical thinking skills, which enable them to respond adequately to national and global challenges and helps efficiently solve the problems caused by the rapidly changing, unpredictable and turbulent environments of the 21st century.

The analysis showed an obvious gap between the development of critical thinking theories and their application in empirical research, when a distinct divide becomes clear in 2014 between theoretical and empirical articles (Figure 3).

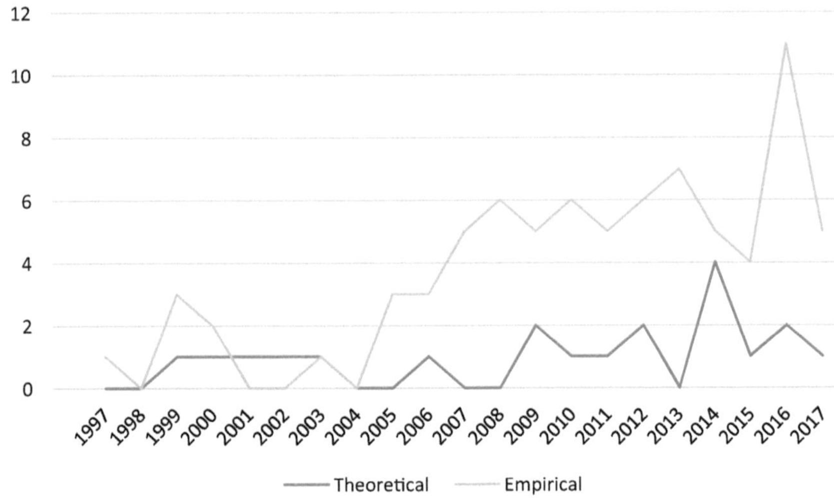

Fig. 3: *Theoretical and empirical articles, 1997–2017*

In analysing theoretical articles by year, 2014 stands out as the year that the most theoretical articles were published. No theoretical articles were published in 1997, 1998, 2004, 2005, 2007, 2008 or 2013.

With the exception of 2001–2002, the articles were dominated by empirical research. Not a single empirical article was published in 1998, 2001, 2002 or 2004, but a growth trend can be observed starting in 2005. The number remains stable in 2007–2013 (5–7 publications per year), and peaks in 2016 with 11 publications.

In 1997 and 2003, only qualitative research was published, and in 2010 – only quantitative. An inversely proportional number of publications using quantitative or qualitative research methods is observed in empirical articles – this is particularly evident in 2010, when six quantitative and zero qualitative studies were printed, and in 2013, with five and one, respectively; in 2016, it was the reverse, with eight qualitative and two quantitative studies. In 2008 and 2009, the number of articles based on quantitative and qualitative research methods was the same (three each). Three publications were found (2013, 2014, 2016) using mixed methods (Figure 4).

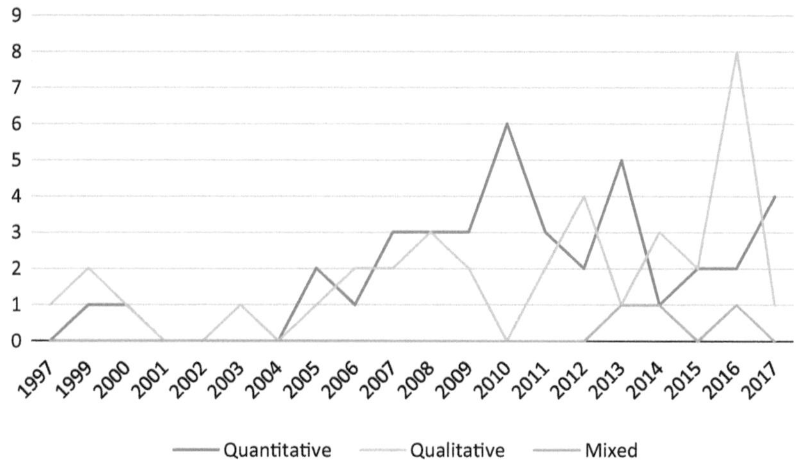

Fig. 4: *Quantitative, qualitative and mixed methods research in 1997–2017 publications*

The differences in the amount of quantitative and qualitative research and the small amount of mixed methods research possibly indicate the contrast between the positivist and post-positivist paradigms in the concept of critical thinking in higher education.

Quantitative research is dominated by questionnaires and testing using standardised tests (Classroom-Based Survey of Thinking and Interacting [CBSTI], California Critical Thinking Disposition Inventory [CCTDI], California Critical Thinking Skills Test [CCTST], Watson Glaser Critical Thinking Appraisal, the Critical Thinking subscale of the RTQ). Less common methods are quantitative analysis of students' tasks and essays.

A variety of methods can be observed in qualitative research. Phenomenography, discourse analysis, case study and grounded theory approaches are used, data are collected during interviews and in-focus groups and discussion groups, and documents, publications, student texts, reflections and essays are analysed using the content analysis method. Observation is mentioned less frequently.

Mixed methods research uses quantitative and qualitative oral student surveys and analysis of student texts, and the third article combines testing and focus group interviews.

Significant differences are observed when analysing publications that express domain-general or domain-specific approaches (Figure 5).

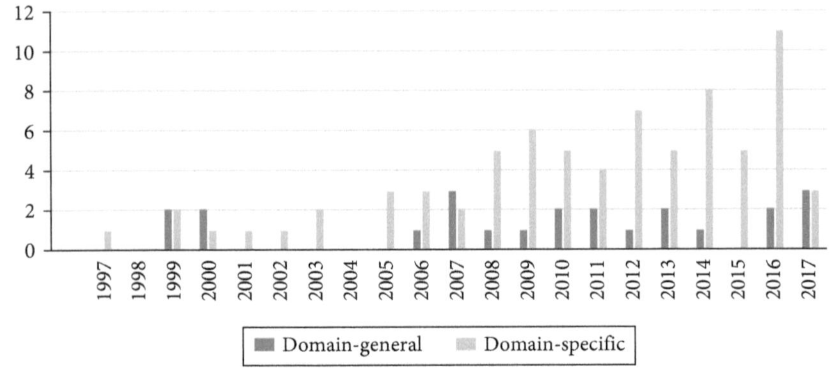

Fig. 5: *Number of publications with domain-general and domain-specific approaches*

No publications expressing domain-general or domain-specific approaches were found in 1998 and 2004. The other years during the 1997–2017 period are dominated by domain-specific publications, except in 1999–2000, when there were more domain-general publications. The year 1999 also stands out for the fact that it was the year that the largest number of domain-general publications in the analysed period was published in general. In 1997, 2011, 2002, 2005 and 2015, only articles with domain-specific approaches were published. So even though the scientific discussion about domain-general and domain-specific is bending towards merging these approaches (Grauerholz and Bouma-Holtrop, 2003; Malcom, 2006; Hassan and Madhum, 2007; Tiruneh et al., 2016), critical thinking was more often conceptualised as a domain-specific phenomenon in the publications analysed.

3. Expression of Critical Thinking in the Context of Higher Education: The Synchronic Approach

A synchronous analysis made it possible to reveal the systemic understanding of the concept of critical thinking in higher education by distinguishing between similarities and differences. In analysing the publications using the synchronic approach, it was decided to delve into the domain-general, domain-specific, and critical thinking instructional approaches, critical thinking interventions/strategies, and the personal, interpersonal and social aspects of critical thinking in the publications.

Construction of the concept of critical thinking as domain-specific or domain-general is directly related to integration of the development of critical thinking into higher education programmes (Tiruneh et al., 2016). The researchers examining the concept of critical thinking as being domain-general (Davies, 2013; De Bono, 1991; Ennis, 1989; Halpern, 1998; Kuhn, 1999) claim the existence of a certain set of critical thinking skills, which are general and applicable in various fields. These skills could be developed as a specific, independent subject of an education programme or be integrated into regular courses. On the other hand, the researchers who define critical thinking as domain-specific (McPeck, 1990; Moore, 2011) emphasise that critical thinking is dependent on domain knowledge. According to Garside (1996), critical thinking is most effectively developed in the context of a specific study area, as it is impossible to think critically without domain knowledge. Therefore, the development of critical thinking is implemented only in relation to the context of a specific field. According to Tiruneh et al. (2016), discussions regarding the generality and specificity of the phenomenon of critical thinking were directed towards a synthesis of these two approaches. Researchers (Davies, 2013; Robinson, 2011; Smith, 2002) believe that the contents and issues associated with generality and specificity differ in various areas. The ability to think critically about a certain task is perceived both as highly dependent on content knowledge and the task to be performed, as well as dependent on knowledge about critical thinking skills. This means that effective development of critical thinking has to be directed towards specific field knowledge and the respective critical thinking skills.

A systematic literature review revealed that 98 articles involve discussion related to analysis of the concept of critical thinking by associating it with a specific field (domain-specific) and by analysing it as a phenomenon independent of a specific field or discipline (domain-general) (Table 3).

There were 23 articles which presented critical thinking as domain-general and 75 which present it as domain-specific. In the domain-specific field, Social Science was the most prevalent (24 articles), followed by Education (14 articles), Science (13 articles), Humanities (6 articles), Health Science (7 articles), Arts (5 articles) and IT (6 articles).

In examining the articles according to the domain-specific and domain-general cross-section, analysis was done of whether critical thinking was the object of research or the context of research, that is, a certain assumption/factor for the object of research to be expressed. It was found that in the articles dominated by the domain-general approach, critical thinking was analysed as the object of research in 18 articles, and as the context in 5 (Table 4).

Tab. 3: *Articles analysed, domain-specific and domain-general*

No	Publication analysed	Domain-specific (study field)							Domain-general
		IT	Arts	Education	Social Science	Science	Humanities	Health	
1.	Al-Fadhli, S. & Khalfan, A. (2009)	X							
2.	Andrews, R. (2007)								X
3.	Bailin, S. (2002)					X			
4.	Bailin, S., Case, R., Coombs, J. R. & Daniels, L. B. (1999)								X
5.	Basol, G. & Gencel, I. E. (2013)			X					
6.	Beachboard, M. B., Beachboard, J., Li, W. & Adkison, S. (2011)								X
7.	Bekele, T. (2009)								X
8.	Belluigi, D. Z. (2009)		X						
9.	Bensley, D. A. et al. (2010)				X				
10.	Blessing, S. B. & Blessing, J. S. (2010)				X				
11.	Blouin, R. et al. (2009)							X	
12.	Boghossian, P. (2012)			X					
13.	Boni-Aristizábal, A. & Calabuig-Tormo, C. (2016)	X							
14.	Brodin, E. M. (2016)								X
15.	Browne, M. N. & Freeman, K. (2000)								X
16.	Bulman, Ch., Lathleanb, J. & Gobbi, M. (2014)							X	
17.	Carey, M. E. & McCardle, M. (2011)				X				

No	Publication analysed	Domain-specific (study field)							Domain-general
		IT	Arts	Education	Social Science	Science	Humanities	Health	
18.	Cisneros, R. M. (2009)							X	
19.	Colby, I. (2014)				X				
20.	Danvers, E. C. (2016)				X				
21.	Dwyer, C. P., Hogan, M. J., Harney, O. M. & Kavanagh, C. (2017)								X
22.	Eastman, C. & Maguire, K. (2016)			X					
23.	Egan, M., Neely-Barnes, S. L. & Combs-Orme, T. (2011)				X				
24.	Eisen, D. B. (2012)				X				
25.	Elander, J. et al. (2006)								X
26.	Fitzpatrick, J. J. (2006)							X	
27.	Flores, K. L. et al. (2012)								X
28.	Gambrill, E. (2014)				X				
29.	Geertsen, H. R. (2003)				X				
30.	Genc, S. Z. (2008)			X					
31.	Gliddon, C. M. & Rosengren, R. J. (2012)							X	
32.	Grosser, M. M. & Nel, M. (2013)			X					
33.	Guest, K. (2000)								X
34.	Hager, P., Sleet, R., Logan, P. & Hooper, M. (2003)					X			

(continued)

Tab. 3: *Continued*

No	Publication analysed	Domain-specific (study field)							Domain-general
		IT	Arts	Education	Social Science	Science	Humanities	Health	
35.	Halx, M. (2010)								X
36.	Hassan, K. E. & Madhum, G. (2007)								X
37.	Healey, R. (2012)					X			
38.	Heijltjes, A., Van Gog, T., Leppink, J. & Paas, F. (2015).				X				
39.	Helsdingen, A., van Gog, T. & van Merrienboer, J. (2011)				X				
40.	Howard, J. & Zoeller, A. (2007)				X				
41.	Hu, Y., Wu, B. & Gu, X. (2017)								X
42.	Huang, G. C., Lindell, D., Jaffe, L. E. & Sullivan, A. M. (2016).							X	
43.	Iskifoglu, G. (2014)			X					
44.	James, N., Hughes, C. & Cappa, C. (2010)				X				
45.	Jones, A. (2005)				X				
46.	Jones, A. (2007)								X
47.	Kilic-Cakmak, E. (2010)	X							
48.	Kim, M. & Bednarz, R. (2013)					X			
49.	Korkmaz, O. (2012)	X							
50.	Kreber, C. (2014)						X		
51.	Lai, K. (2012)						X		

No	Publication analysed	Domain-specific (study field)							Domain-general
		IT	Arts	Education	Social Science	Science	Humanities	Health	
52.	Laird, T. N. (2005)		X						
53.	Lee, A. (2008)								X
54.	Lim, L. (2011)			X					
55.	Lin, S. (2014)					X			
56.	Liu, O. L. (2016)								X
57.	Loes, C. M., Salisbury, M. H. & Pascarella, E. T. (2015)		X						
58.	Lundquist, R. (1999)				X				
59.	Maclellan, E. & Soden R. (2012)			X					
60.	Macpherson, K. & Owen, C. (2010)							X	
61.	MacPherson, K. (1999)				X				
62.	Magno, C. (2010)								X
63.	Mathias, J. (2015)				X				
64.	McCarthy, L. & Sziarto, K. (2015)					X			
65.	McLaughlin, A. A. & McGill, A. (2017)						X		
66.	Mintzes, J. J., Wandersee, J. H. & Novak, J. D. (2001)					X			
67.	Moore, T. (2013).								X
68.	Mumm, A. M. & Kersting, R. (1997)				X				

(continued)

Tab. 3: *Continued*

No	**Publication analysed**	**Domain-specific (study field)**							**Domain-general**
		IT	**Arts**	**Education**	**Social Science**	**Science**	**Humanities**	**Health**	
69.	Ng'ambi, D. & Johnston, K. (2006)	X							
70.	Pedrosa-de-Jesus, H. & Watts, M. (2014)					X			
71.	Pence, D. (2009)				X				
72.	Penningroth, S. L., Despain, L. H. & Gray, M. J. (2007)				X				
73.	Perkins, C. & Murphy, E. (2006)			X					
74.	Phan, H. P. (2011)								X
75.	Power, J. B. (2016).						X		
76.	Raveendran, A. & Chunawala, S. (2015)					X			
77.	Redmond, P., Devine, J. & Basson, M. (2014)								X
78.	Rickles, M. L. et al. (2013)				X				
79.	Rocconi, L. l. (2013)								X
80.	Roksa, J. et al. (2017)		X						
81.	Sagun, S., Ateskan, A. & Onur, J. (2016)			X					
82.	Saltmarsh, D. D. & Saltmarsh, S. (2008)			X					
83.	Samson, P. L. (2016)				X				
84.	Schendel, R. (2016)		X						
85.	Scott, M. (2000)						X		
86.	Seker, H. & Komur, S. (2008)			X					

No	Publication analysed	Domain-specific (study field)							Domain-general
		IT	Arts	Education	Social Science	Science	Humanities	Health	
87.	Sigurðsson, G. (2017)								X
88.	Soden, R. & Maclellan, E. (2005)			X					
89.	Stupnisky, R. H. et al. (2008)				X				
90.	Sziarto, K. M., McCarthy, L. & Padilla, N. L. (2014)					X			
91.	Tan, L. (2016)						X		
92.	Tiruneh, D. (2016)					X			
93.	Tiruneh, D. T. (2017)					X			
94.	Uzuntiryaki-ondakci, E. & Capa-Aydin, Y. (2013)					X			
95.	Walkner, P. & Finney, N. (1999)								X
96.	Wickersham, C., Westerberg, C., Jones, K. & Cress, M. (2016)				X				
97.	Yang, Y. C. (2008)	X							
98.	Yeh Y. (2009)			X					

Tab. 4: *Critical thinking as the object or context of research, domain-specific and domain-general*

	Study field	Number of analysed publication	Theoretical	Empirical			Critical Thinking Object (O) or Context (C)	
				Quantitative	Qualitative	Mixed	O	C
Domain-specific	IT	6	-	6	-	-	4	2
	Arts	5	-	3	1	1	3	2
	Education	14	2	5	6	1	10	4
	Social Science	24	6	10	8	-	19	5
	Science	13	3	4	5	1	6	7
	Humanities	6	2	1	3	-	6	-
	Health	7	1	2	4	-	4	3
Domain-general		23	6	8	9	-	18	5

In the articles dominated by the domain-specific approach, critical thinking was analysed as the object of research in 52 articles, and as the context of research in 23.

The most attention is given to the concept of critical thinking in social science research. In the analysed publications, critical thinking is presented as one of the higher order thinking skills. It is emphasised that critical thinking and reflective thinking are clearly different but complementary forms of higher order thinking (Geertsen, 2003). It is stressed that students' critical thinking improves by ensuring three essential features in the study subject: ensuring that students have a knowledge base of the subject, emphasising active learning through feedback, and enabling students to apply newly learned subjects (Penningroth, Despain and Gray, 2007). Stupnisky et al. (2008) emphasise the interaction of critical thinking dispositions and features of perceived academic control and their impact on academic achievement. So if they want to encourage students to think critically, higher education teachers should rethink their course structure and course instructions – they should provide students with detailed course plans, remind them of assessment dates, use a variety of study methods, and rethink the assessment system to include higher order questions and tasks (Stupnisky et al., 2008).

The analysed publications in the field of social sciences particularly emphasise that critical thinking is very strongly influenced by the teaching context in which the task was situated (Jones, 2005; Mathias, 2015; Danvers, 2016). The importance of clear critical thinking instructions and the integration of tasks into the study subject for the development of critical thinking skills (Bensley, Crowe, Bernhardt, Buckner and Allman, 2010; Heijltjes et al., 2015) was identified, as was the importance of choosing a teaching method for improving students' critical thinking skills. The inclusion of effective teaching methods in study programmes at all levels is essential for training professionals skilled in critical thinking (Mumm and Kersting, 1997; Macpherson, 1999; Pence, 2009; Blessing and Blessing, 2010; Samson, 2016). It should be noted that the importance of choosing the teaching method is also emphasised in publications where critical thinking is not the main object of research. Researchers (Lundquist, 1999; Eisen, 2012) stress that interactive educational methods not only develop the abilities necessary for students' professional activities, but also improve critical thinking. Setting study subject goals is important for the development of students' critical thinking skills, abilities and dispositions (James, Hughes and Cappa, 2010; Helsdingen, van Gog and van Merrienboer, 2011; Rickles, Schneider, Slusser, Williams and Zipp, 2013). It is emphasised that in order to develop and improve students' critical thinking, students must be given the opportunity to use theoretical knowledge in practice (Wickersham, Westerberg, Jones and Cress, 2016), because critical thinking skills are developed more effectively when students are given the opportunity to apply learning (Carey and McCardle, 2011). In publications where critical thinking was not the main object of research, the importance of critical thinking is highlighted by ensuring customer-oriented professional practice (Gambrill, 2014; Colby, 2014).

In education sciences, much attention is dedicated to models of critical thinking that could be used efficiently and easily to derive and present individual profiles of engagement in critical thinking (Perkins and Murphy, 2006). The development of critical thinking in teacher training is therefore crucial, since future teachers have an impact on the critical thinking skills of society as a whole. For this reason, professional development for educators must include the development of critical and creative thinking skills (Seker and Komur, 2008). It should be noted that educational sciences publications place special emphasis on the role of the teacher in developing critical thinking in students. The teachers themselves need to have critical thinking skills (Genc, 2008) and understand how to develop them (Yeh Yu-Chu, 2007) – when to provide information, when to demand learner accountability, when to question and challenge, and when to target. All this affects the effectiveness of teaching/learning (Maclellan and Soden, 2012). The importance of training programmes for teachers to develop their critical thinking skills is emphasised (Genc, 2008). The articles where critical thinking is analysed only as the context of the research object emphasise the need to pay additional attention to the development of critical thinking skills due to the impact of critical thinking on the development of students' academic language (Grosser and Nel, 2013) and the decision-making process (Boghossian, 2012).

The science publications that were analysed where critical thinking is the object of research stress the importance of conceptualising critical thinking and how this concept could be applied to justify the practice of science education. Applying this concept in science education requires focusing on the tasks and problems of the natural sciences programme that require or encourage critical thinking. This includes focusing on complex, scientifically significant issues, concentrating on causes rather than rules and on conceptual tools rather than procedures, and considerations in specific contexts (Bailin, 2002). According to Mintzes, Wandersee and Novak (2001), critical thinking is one of the essential factors in understanding phenomena. Those who understand scientific phenomena are able to use their knowledge to think critically about explanations offered by others, and to look for flaws in their own thinking patterns (Mintzes, Wandersee and Novak, 2001). Raveendra and Chunawala (2015) emphasise value-loaded critical thinking, one of the important components of which is the ability to form independent opinions.

In the context of the analysed articles, research that raises the issue of domain-general and domain-specific critical thinking skills stands out (Tiruneh et al., 2016; 2017). These publications highlight the efficacy of systematically designed subject matter instruction in developing students' domain-specific critical thinking skills and emphasise that systematic subject matter planning is an important component of teaching and learning in undergraduate studies if students want to demonstrate critical thinking skills in a specific area (Tiruneh et al., 2016). The development of a valid instrument to assess domain-specific critical thinking skills in a specific field is also highlighted and justified (Tiruneh, De Cock, Weldeslassie, Elen and Janssen, 2017).

The importance of applying specific strategies not only to achieve subject outcomes, but also to improve students' critical thinking skills, is emphasised (Bailin, 2002; Lin, 2014; Sziarto, McCarthy and Padilla, 2014; Tiruneh et al., 2016). It should be noted that the importance of methods is also emphasised in publications where critical thinking is expressed as the context of research. It is emphasised that such strategies may be effective for encouraging engagement and promoting critical thinking because it can provoke students to confront stark positionalities and even othering in an environment of interaction and negotiation (Hager, Sleet, Logan and Hooper, 2003; Healey, 2012; Kim and Bednarz, 2013; Pedrosa-de-Jesus and Watts, 2014; McCarthy and Sziarto, 2015).

The importance of critical thinking is also emphasised in articles in the field of health. It should be underscored that the teaching of critical thinking in medical science means the inclusion of specific components of critical thinking in the curricula for this field. Critical thinking is essential for a professional to make decisions, such as diagnosing a disease, so the ability to decide what to do or what to believe is important (Macpherson and Owen, 2010; Huang, Lindell, Jaffe and Sullivan, 2016), as is presenting an understandable intervention plan to the client (Huang et al., 2016). The publications emphasise the interaction of teachers and students and the influence of teachers' professional qualifications (Bulman, Lathleanb and Gobbi, 2014) on students' critical thinking. Cisneros (2009) also emphasises the importance of organisational culture for the development of critical thinking.

Publications that analyse critical thinking as a context for studies highlight the importance of a person's self-evaluation for critical thinking (Fitzpatrick, 2006).

In the humanities, special attention is paid to the social mission of the higher education institution (Flores et al., 2012). Emphasis is placed on the need to engage students in experiential learning by linking academic content to specific real-life issues of a social nature (Kreber, 2014). It is important that learning leads to a deeper understanding of the subject and the self, and identity based on responsibility, dedication and authenticity (Kreber, 2014). Critical thinking is not only a cognitive pursuit, but also the emotional and social axis of man (Tan, 2016).

Publications in computer science area have focused on e-learning strategies for the development of critical thinking skills (Caplan, 2004; Ng'ambi and Johnston, 2006; Grafstein, 2007; Al-Fadhli and Khalfan, 2009). Studies by other researchers in which critical thinking is not the direct object of research have found that students' communicating the information self-efficacy increases when they use metacognitive and critical thinking strategies and have control over learning dimensions of information literacy self-efficacy (Kilic-Cakmak, 2010), and emphasis is placed on the links between critical thinking skills and mathematical skills (Korkmaz, 2012).

The publications analysed in arts and sciences focus on the expression of students' critical thinking dispositions and abilities in the context of cultural experience and racial diversity. Enrolment in diversity courses and positive interactions with diverse peers are more likely to score higher on academic self-confidence, social agency and critical thinking disposition (Laird, 2005; Roksa et al., 2017). The publications analysed in this area also highlight the importance of institutional culture in the study process (Belluigi, 2009; Loes, Salisbury and Pascarella, 2015; Schendel, 2016). Clearly identified strategies for the development of critical thinking were only found in one of the analysed publications (Belluigi, 2009).

In the analysed publications where critical thinking is expressed as domain-general and is the object of research, the pedagogical uncertainty of the concept of critical thinking related to the multidimensionality of the concept of critical thinking itself is emphasised. It is stressed that any effort to simplify the meanings of difficult concepts such as critical thinking is unlikely to resolve the existing confusion with the concepts themselves. Therefore, in researching critical thinking, it is necessary to ascertain how the idea of critical thinking is actually understood and applied by teachers when teaching different disciplines. It is noted that higher education teachers and students have a sufficiently developed understanding of critical thinking. Researchers understand the diversity of critical thinking concepts (Moore, 2013). Students' critical thinking can only be encouraged when the teachers have a thorough understanding of critical thinking (Hassan and Madhum, 2007). The importance of critical thinking dispositions in developing students' critical thinking skills is emphasised. The importance of an equal understanding of students' and teachers' critical thinking dispositions is highlighted. Assessing the similarities and differences in how students and educators understand critical thinking dispositions may facilitate the development of additional and integrated models for the development of critical thinking dispositions in the university study environment (Dwyer, Hogan, Harney and Kavanagh, 2017). In analysing teachers' and students' understanding of critical thinking dispositions, it is noted that students' understanding of critical thinking dispositions is focused on utility or function rather than ideal operating principles (Dwyer et al., 2017), and that students associate critical thinking with decision-making (Bekele, 2009). The links between critical thinking and creative thinking are analysed, as are the different understandings and tensions between the two phenomena. It is emphasised that critical thinking often overshadows creative thinking in research practice (Brodin, 2016).

The need to develop validated methodologies for the assessment of critical thinking is highlighted (Liu et al., 2016), while emphasising that the assessment results of students' critical thinking depend on the methodology used (Rocconi, 2013). Publications in this area stress the need to review university curricula to include subjects designed to develop critical thinking (Hassan and Madhum, 2007).

It is underscored that highlighting critical thinking as an educational goal is more common in university practice than the actual practice of developing critical thinking. The practice of developing critical thinking is illustrated by actions such as asking questions, not foreseeing the contingency of conclusions, and active learning. The latter complement one another, and critical thinking is developed when they are applied in practice (Browne and Freeman, 2000). Critical thinking and argument correspond most closely to the outcomes of complex learning (Elander, Harrington, Norton, Robinson and Reddy, 2006). It is, therefore, very important not only what is taught, but also how it is taught. Good teaching is the key (Walkner and Finney, 1999; Guest, 2000; Elander et al., 2006), with 'good' meaning both rich content and the masterful conveyance of that content.

Publications in the domain-general group that discuss critical thinking as a context for studies emphasise that in order to improve teaching and learning processes and develop students' critical thinking skills, it is more important to know not which method to use, but how to apply individual methods and strategies (Redmond, Devine and Basson, 2014). Transformative learning (Halx, 2010) and learning in virtual communities (Beachboard, Beachboard and Adkison, 2011) have a direct impact on the development of students who are critical thinkers.

Researchers (Jones, 2005; Fitzpatrick, 2006; Kim and Bednarz, 2013; Kreber, 2014; Danvers, 2016), despite representing different fields of study, view critical thinking as a set of universal principles, abilities and attitudes unambiguously expressed in each situation and context, highlighting its different aspects. Accentuated the most are:

- the role of teachers in the development of critical thinking, their competency and individual understanding of critical thinking;
- the selection and competent application of different strategies that respond to the set goals and are designed to develop critical thinking;
- the influence of the study environment on the development of critical thinking;
- the need to put theory into practice as a condition for improving critical thinking;
- the impact of the application of assessment strategies and instruments on critical thinking, and so on.

Nevertheless, it can be argued that 'critical thinking as a domain-general skill' and 'critical thinking as a domain-specific skill' are not clearly positioned as opposing camps. There are few authors who unequivocally argue that critical thinking is only related to a specific research subject, discipline or field. It is only natural that the concepts of 'mathematical thinking', 'pedagogical thinking' or 'sociological thinking' simultaneously mean thinking critically within your field. The epistemic culture of a particular discipline influences the concept of critical thinking (Jones, 2007). However, critical thinking extends these boundaries, enabling the individual to think about everyday life phenomena and broader problems (Hassan and Madhum, 2007; Tiruneh et al., 2016). In summarising the discussions about domain-specific and domain-general, critical thinking is understood both as a transferable (general) competence and as a set of certain abilities that manifest in a particular study area.

Analysis of publications in the domain-specific and domain-general groups where critical thinking was defined as the object of research identified critical thinking instructional approaches and critical thinking interventions/strategies (Table 5).

Tab. 5: *Critical thinking approaches and critical thinking development strategies in domain-specific and domain-general groups*

	Critical thinking instructional approach					**Critical thinking interventions/ strategies (number of publications)**
	General	**Immersion**	**Infusion**	**Mixed**	**Not specified**	
Domain-specific	3	14	17	0	18	On-line forum (2) On-line discussions (5) Questioning (8) Reflective journals (3) Critical reflection (4) Critical review (6) Essay (2) Mind mapping (1) Discussion (10) Debate (1) Case studies (3) Portfolio (1)
Domain-general	0	3	4	0	11	Mind mapping (1) Critical reflection (4) Discussion (2) Debate (1) Critical review (2)

The critical thinking general approach is manifested in the fact that critical thinking abilities and dispositions are developed separately from the content of existing study subjects (Ennis, 1985). It was found that this critical thinking approach was used in three articles in the domain-specific group. Meanwhile, not a single article based on this critical thinking approach was found in the domain-general group.

The infusion approach is a '*deep, thoughtful, and well-understood subject matter instruction in which students are encouraged to think critically in the subject*' (Ennis, 1985, p. 5). With this approach, the development of critical thinking is integrated into the teaching of the subject, by explaining the general principles of critical thinking to the students. According to this approach, thinking takes place according to specific tasks; therefore, thinking teaching should be set out in specific problems and functional contexts that are embedded in disciplines rather than in individual study subjects. The application of this approach is orientated towards a change in the role of the teacher in rethinking the structure of the study programme and teaching and assessment strategies (Jones and Idol, 1990). Gardner (1993) bases the relevance of the infusion approach on the difficulties faced by students in transferring knowledge from one context to another. There is a growing awareness of the limited efficacy of applying critical thinking strategies without taking the context into account or teaching separately from the specific areas of content (Geertsen, 2003).

It was found that this critical thinking approach was used in 17 articles in the domain-specific group and in four articles in the domain-general group. It should be noted that it was this approach that was found the most frequently in the analysed articles. This is in line with the findings of other researchers calling for the development of critical thinking in all subjects of the study programme (Kirby and Kuykendall, 1991; Clarke and Biddle, 1993; Hester, 1994; Borg and Borg, 2001). Research shows that when universities integrate critical thinking development into the study programmes, it has a positive effect on the growth of students' critical thinking skills (Hassan and Madhum, 2007).

According to Ennis (1985), the immersion approach also tries to incorporate critical thinking within standard subject matter instruction. However, general critical thinking principles and procedures are not made explicit to students. It was found that this critical thinking approach was used in 14 publications in the domain-specific group and in 3 in the domain-general group.

Ennis (1985), Nickerson (1988), and Perkins and Salomon (1989), who are proponents of the mixed approach, emphasise the combination of all the above-mentioned instructional approaches (general, infusion, immersion) of critical thinking. A mixed approach is expressed in the integration of critical thinking development in all study subjects and in the study programme, with a separate subject for the development of critical thinking skills (Tiruneh, Verburgh and Elen, 2014). This critical thinking instructional approach was not found in any of the publications in the domain-specific and domain-general groups.

The critical thinking instructional approach could not be identified in the considerably large number of domain-specific (18) and domain-general (11) articles analysed. It can be assumed that this was determined by the goal chosen for the article: validation of critical thinking assessment instruments, conceptualisation of the concept, and analysis of critical thinking not in the context of education.

In the publications, a great deal of attention was paid to the teacher's preparedness to apply different critical thinking interventions/strategies that develop critical thinking skills for research (Genc, 2008). The importance of applying specific strategies not only to achieve subject outcomes, but also to improve students' critical thinking skills, is emphasised (Lin, 2014; Sziarto, McCarthy and Padilla, 2014).

Analysis of publications in the domain-specific and domain-general groups where critical thinking was defined as the object of research established, in terms of critical thinking interventions/strategies, that interventions such as discussion, critical review, critical reflection, online discussions and case studies are most often mentioned in publications. The relatively small number of publications presenting one or another critical thinking intervention/strategy and the varying attention paid to their analysis (in some cases, the intervention is only very briefly presented) make it impossible to draw deeper conclusions about the efficacy of critical thinking interventions.

Another aspect that was delved into during the systematic analysis was the highlighting of critical thinking on the personal, interpersonal and societal levels. For the most part, critical thinking is associated with fostering a person's cognitive powers and attitudes for the learner's own growth and development. This can be referred to as the strengthening of critical thinking at the individual level. This is necessary both for the maturity of the person and for the ability to later apply these skills in practice – in real life. This is emphasised by both the academic community (Kahneman, 2011; Brookfield, 2012; Halpern, 2014) and by business representatives (Burbach, Matkin and Fritz 2004; Penkauskienė, Railienė and Cruz, 2019). However, critical thinking is very often referred to as a higher education goal or ideal which the efforts of the academic community must be directed towards. This aspiration is described as the ability of graduates to become critically thinking practitioners who are able to build a life and successfully collaborate with others in solving relevant problems, making risky decisions, and contributing to the well-being of society as a whole. However, researchers studying the concept and expression of critical thinking in higher education and/or the study process are signalling a certain discrepancy between this ideal and practice. They note the 'immaturity' (Turner, 2005) and narrowness (Walkner and Finney, 1999) of the concept of critical thinking, when there is too much focus on strengthening cognitive powers and the ability to find the right solutions for oneself as a person through logical reasoning. It is feared that critical thinking will end up being just an exercise of the individual's mind – a personal asset not shared with others and not used for the broader purposes declared in higher education missions (Wang, Chao and Liao, 2011; Danvers, 2016) and education policy documents (European Commission, 2016; Teaching for Global Competence in a Rapidly Changing World,

2018). Therefore, Barnett's idea that a critical thinker is not just an intelligent being is still important. Critical thinkers can be recognised not only by what they say, but also by how they act – how they use knowledge for their own benefit and that of others (Barnett, 1997). It is more important to return to the heart of critical thinking – criticality, which is defined as the ability to question, explore, and change one's own core beliefs and that of others (Paul and Elder, 2006), order and ideologies (Brookfield, 2005), and as a set of critical thinking abilities and attitudes expressing critical reflection and critical action (Davies and Barnett, 2015). Learners need to become true critical thinkers who have a clear political orientation and contribute to the development of democracy.

It should be noted that only those publications in which critical thinking was the main object of research were analysed from a personal, interpersonal and social point of view – 52 publications from the domain-specific group and 18 articles from the domain-general group (Table 6).

Tab. 6: *Critical thinking as domain-specific and domain-general by study fields and aspects*

	Study field	**Aspect**			
		Personal	**Interpersonal**	**Social**	**Not specified**
Domain-specific	IT	3	2	1	-
	Arts	2	2	2	-
	Education	7	4	2	2
	Social Science	19	9	3	-
	Science	6	2	-	-
	Humanities	6	3	2	-
	Health	4	3	-	-
Domain- general		15	5	3	2

Most of the analysed articles talk about the cognitive abilities of a person that manifest themselves in various fields of study and professional activity. It was established that the personal level was expressed in 47 domain-specific and 15 domain-general publications, but no clear differences in how the personal level was expressed in the publications in these groups were found. It should be noted that in the publications, this level was associated with the ability to analyse and critically evaluate phenomena related to the subject being studied, argue one's opinion by providing substantiated evidence, and solve specific problems (Fitzpatrick, 2006; Genc, 2008; Kilic-Cakmak, 2010; Magno, 2010; Helsdingen, van Gog and van Merrienboer, 2011). In essence, this means trying to avoid illogicality, notice discrepancies and be as accurate and as close as possible to correct, science-based and reality-based decisions (Novak, 2001; Kreber, 2014; Mintzes, Wandersee and Raveendra and Chunawala, 2015). Critical thinking is also referred to as a person's ability to think deeply and reflectively, to see the comprehensiveness and complexity of phenomena and base assessments and decisions thereon (Howard and Zoeller, 2007; Macpherson and Owen, 2010; Huang et al., 2016), as well as to strive to improving his or her own thinking (Geertsen, 2003; Phan, 2011). Critical thinking is perceived not only as a totality of certain personal abilities, but of dispositions as well (Healey, 2012; Mathias, 2015; Dwyer et al., 2017). The articles examined do not always clearly distinguish between these two groups – they often intertwine into the same phenomenon of critical thinking. However, in some cases the differences are quite pronounced (Stupnisky, Renaud, Daniels, Haynes and Perry, 2008; Dwyer et al., 2017).

The interpersonal aspect of critical thinking is revealed in two ways: as the development of critical thinking while being with others, usually in a group of learners, and as an aspiration to contribute to the well-being of others. The first case involves the sharing of knowledge and abilities in a particular discipline, research issue or area of interest (Ng'ambi and Johnston, 2006; Jones, 2007; Yang, 2008). Group interaction aims to develop critical thinking skills and look for the best ways to solve a problem (Seker and Komur, 2008; Cisneros, 2009; Wickersham, Westerberg, Jones and Cress, 2016). Thus, the interpersonal aspect of critical thinking is expanded by the aggregate need to find a common human relationship and to be meaningful in it – by sharing thoughts, ideas, doubts, critical self-assessment and environmental assessment. Therefore, a significant number of the articles examined talk about critical reflection and self-reflection as an expression of critical thinking competency and a way to improve it in an interactive relationship with others (Jones, 2005). Special emphasis is placed on the importance of teacher-student interaction in developing critical thinking (Cisneros, 2009; Bulman, Lathleanb amd Gobbi, 2014; Boni-Aristizábal and Calabuig-Tormo, 2016). The second case concerns a much broader interpersonal relationship. The authors of the articles, who are mostly from the field of social sciences, see a need to develop social workers who are critical thinkers and can serve their clients properly (Samson, 2016). This is also evident in medical publications, which emphasise the importance of physician-client interaction through the presentation of understandable and client-oriented intervention plans (Huang et al., 2016). In their view, it is important to be able to distinguish which interventions can be harmful and which choices are wrong in order not to harm others. There are isolated examples where these two approaches – learning to think critically together and aspiring to serve others – are naturally integrated into certain study programmes. For example, Magno (2010) shares his experience working with different groups of students and argues that students' attitudes towards various phenomena are much broader and deeper when they collaborate and provide feedback together than when they work alone. Together, they learn to explore clients' problems caused by both internal and external circumstances, and look for the best solutions for the well-being of the target group.

The social level of critical thinking comes to light when trying to reveal the essence of criticality. It is argued that criticality lies not only in the ability to discover errors of reasoning, inconsistencies of facts, deviations from reality and illogical conclusions. Representatives of the social sciences (Danvers, 2016) underscore that the essence of criticality is the ability to question the assumptions on which our thinking is based, to show the tendency of knowledge and knowledge construction, and thus to raise significant questions about the promotion of ideologies and the distribution of power and influence in society. These ideas are close to the critical theory and pedagogy represented by Apple (1995, 2004, 2006), Barnett (1997), Barnett, Parry and Coate (2001), Beyer (1985, 2008), Brookfield (1995), Freire (1970), Giroux (1981), McLaren (1994, 2006), Luke (2004) and others. At the same time, the very concept of critical thinking is questioned, regretting that critical thinking is confined to the narrow framework of thinking operations and seen as nothing more than higher-order thinking, unrelated to the challenges of everyday life (Pence, 2009; Moore, 2013). The authors of the analysed articles (Pence, 2009) point out that the task of higher education is not only to provide scientific knowledge, but also to teach how to analyse and consider much more complex phenomena of public life – identity, truth, power – and to be determined to actively engage. Researchers (Yang, 2008; Raveendran and Chunawala, 2015; Schendel, 2016) argue that critical thinking is an integral part of civic thinking, so it is the duty of science not only to examine the current issues of public life, point out injustices and warn of impending dangers, but also to create future scenarios. According to Boni-Aristizábal and Calabuig-Tormo (2016), one of the missions of higher education is not to focus on what society is, but on what it should be. It is, therefore, very important to take into account the principles of justice, freedom and participation. The main critical task posed to a person is learning to be human (Sigurðsson, 2017).

Researchers (Lim, 2011) note that an instrumental understanding of critical thinking, associated solely with effective solutions, gives way to a consumerist approach and does not exploit the opportunities offered by critical thinking to see more broadly, think more deeply, and serve the wider purposes of humanity. Similar thoughts on the purpose of higher education and studies are shared by representatives of other fields – the humanities (Kreber, 2014), education (Lim, 2011), science (Raveendram and Chunavala, 2015) and the arts (Belluigi, 2009). Thus, the ability of students to analyse phenomena in broader contexts, consider issues of power and influence, and question established order gives critical thinking a political dimension.

In conclusion, the vast majority of authors, when analysing critical thinking, tend to limit themselves to the personal level focused on the targeted development of cognitive powers in order to achieve deeper knowledge and effective problem solving. The interpersonal aspect of 'I-you', 'you-we', is not clearly reflected either in learning to think critically together or in the search for the best ways to serve a particular target group. However, the interpersonal aspect revealed in scientific publications and through analysis makes it possible to refute the prevailing view in higher education that critical thinking is exclusively a problem of developing a person's cognitive powers for the sake of the learner.

Conclusions

Following a diachronic analysis of selected 1997–2017 publications, the following chronological features of the conceptualisation of critical thinking in higher education were found: the number of publications analysing critical thinking in higher education has been steadily increasing; they are more often based on empirical research than theoretical analysis; the empirical articles were based on quantitative or qualitative research methods, and mixed methods were only used in exceptional cases; critical thinking is more often analysed from a domain-specific rather than a domain-general perspective.

Synchronous analysis of the selected publications found that:

- Critical thinking is understood as a transferable (general) competence and as a set of certain abilities that manifest in a particular study area. There is no strict line between the definition of 'critical thinking as a domain-general skill' and 'critical thinking as a domain-specific skill'. Critical thinking goes beyond the borders of a particular discipline, enabling the person to think in broader contexts.
- The relatively small number of publications presenting one or another critical thinking intervention/strategy and the varying attention paid to their analysis make it impossible to draw deeper conclusions about the efficacy of critical thinking interventions. Interventions such as discussion, critical review, critical reflection, online discussions and case studies are most often mentioned in publications.
- The analysis of critical thinking is usually limited to the personal level focused on the targeted improvement of cognitive powers in order to achieve deeper knowledge and effective problem solving. Even though the interpersonal aspect is not clearly reflected, it is most evident in two ways: by learning with others and by contributing to the well-being of others. The analysis refutes the prevailing view in higher education that critical thinking is exclusively the development of a person's cognitive powers for the sake of the learner. The social level of critical thinking comes to light when revealing the essence of criticality, which is related to the ability to question assumptions, showing the tendency of knowledge and knowledge construction and raising significant questions about the promotion of ideologies and the distribution of power and influence in society. This level also manifests itself in highlighting the mission of higher education, which is related not only to the provision of scientific knowledge, but also to learning to analyse more complex phenomena of public life – identity, truth, power – and to be determined to actively engage. In essence, the conceptualisation of critical thinking from a social perspective focuses not on what

society is, but on what it should be. The main critical task posed to a person is learning to be human.

References

Abate Bekele, T. (2009). Cognitive skills in internet-supported learning environments in higher education: Research issues. *Scandinavian Journal of Educational Research, 53*(4), 397–419. doi:10.1080/00313830903043182.

Al-Fadhli, S. & Khalfan, A. (2009). Developing critical thinking in e-learning environment: Kuwait University as a case study. *Assessment & Evaluation in Higher Education, 34*(5), 529–536. doi:10.1080/02602930802117032.

Andrews, R. (2007). Argumentation, critical thinking and the postgraduate dissertation. *Educational Review, 59*(1), 1–18. doi: 10.1080/00131910600796777.

Apple, M. W. (1995). *Education and power*, 2nd eds. New York: Routledge.

Apple, M. W. (2004). *Ideology and curriculum*, 3rd ed. New York: Routledge.

Apple, M. W. (2006). Educating the 'right' way: Markets. In *Standards God and Inequality*, 2nd ed. New York: Routledge.

Aveyard, H. (2014). *Doing a literature review in health and social care: A practical guide*, 3rd ed. Berkshire: Open University Press.

Badke, W. (2017). The literature review in a digital age. *Online Searcher, 41*(3), 57–59.

Bailin, S., Case, R., Coombs, J. R. & Daniels, L. B. (1999). Conceptualizing critical thinking. *Journal Of Curriculum Studies, 31*(3), 285–302. doi:10.1080/002202799183133.

Bailin, S. (2002). Critical thinking and science education. *Science and Education, 11*(4), 361–75. doi: 10.1023/A:1016042608621.

Barnett, R. (1997). *Higher education: A critical business.* Buckingham: The Society for Research into Higher Education and Open University Press. doi:10.1108/ijem.1998.12.3.141.1.

Barnett, R., Parry, G. & Coate, K. (2001). Conceptualising curriculum change. *Teaching in Higher Education, 6*(4), 435–449. doi:10.1080/13562510120078009.

Barrett, D. J. (1997). *Net Research: Finding information online.* Sebastopol, CA: Songline Studios and O'Reilly and Associates.

Basol, G. & Gencel, I. E. (2013). Reflective thinking scale: A validity and reliability study. *Educational Sciences: Theory and Practice, 13*(2), 941–946.

Beachboard, M. B., Beachboard, J., Li, W. & Adkison, S. (2011). Cohorts and relatedness: Self-determination theory as an explanation of how learning communities affect educational outcomes. *Research in Higher Education, 52*(8), 853–874. doi:10.1007/s11162-011-9221-8.

Bekele, T. T. (2009). Cognitive skills in Internet-supported learning environments in higher education: Research issues. *Scandinavian Journal of Educational Research, 53*(4), 397–419. doi: 10.1080/00313830903043182.

Belluigi, D. Z. (2009). Exploring the discourses around 'creativity' and 'critical thinking' in a South African creative arts curriculum. *Studies in Higher Education, 34*(6), 699–717. doi: 10.1080/03075070802644911.

Bensley, D. A., Crowe, D. S., Bernhardt, P., Buckner, C. & Allman, A. L. (2010). Teaching and assessing critical thinking skills for argument analysis in psychology. *Teaching of Psychology, 37*(2), 91–96. doi:10.1080/00986281003626656.

Beyer, B. (1985). Critical thinking: What is it? *Social Education, 49*(4), 270–276.

Beyer, B. K. (2008). How to teach thinking skills in social studies and history. *The Social Studies, 99*(5), 196–201. doi:10.3200/tsss.99.5.196-201.

Billing, D. (2007). Teaching for transfer of core/key skills in higher education: Cognitive skills. *Higher Education, 53*(4), 483–516. doi:10.1007/s10734-005-5628-5.

Blessing, S. B. & Blessing, J. S. (2010). PsychBusters: A means of fostering critical thinking in the introductory course. *Teaching of Psychology, 37*(3), 178–182. doi: 10.1080/00986283.2010.488540.

Blouin, R. B., Riffee, W. H., Robinson, E. T., Beck, D. E., Green, C., Joyner, P. U. & Pollack, G. M. (2009). Roles of Innovation in Education Delivery. *American Journal of Pharmaceutical Education, 73*(8), 1–12. doi: 10.5688/aj7308154.

Boghossian, P. (2012). Critical thinking and constructivism: Mambo dog fish to the banana patch. *Journal of Philosophy of Education, 46*(1), 73–84. doi: 10.1111/j.1467-9752.2011.00832.x.

Boni-Aristizábal, A. & Calabuig-Tormo, C. (2016). Enhancing pro-public-good professionalism in technical studies. Higher education: *The International Journal of Higher Education Research, 71*(6), 791–804. doi: 10.1007/s10734-015-9916-4.

Borg, J. R. & Borg, M. O. (2001). Teaching critical thinking in interdisciplinary economics courses. *College Teaching, 49*(1), 20–25. doi:10.1080/87567550109595841.

Bowen, G. A. (2009). Document analysis as a qualitative research method. *Qualitative Research Journal, 9*(2), 27–40. doi:10.3316/QRJ0902027.

Brodin, E. M. (2016). Critical and creative thinking nexus: Learning experiences of doctoral students. *Studies in Higher Education, 41*(6), 971–989. doi:10.1080/03075079.2014.943656.

Brookfield, S. D. (1995). *Becoming a critically reflective teacher.* San Francisco: Jossey-Bass.

Brookfield, S. D. (2005). *The power of critical theory for adult learning and teaching.* Open University Press. Retrieved from http://www.arabcampaignforeducation.org/functions.php?action=files&table=files&ID=19.

Brookfield, S. D. (2012). *Teaching for critical thinking: Tools and techniques to help students question their assumptions.* San Francisco: Jossey-Bass.

Browne, M. N. & Freeman, K. (2000). Distinguishing features of critical thinking classrooms. *Teaching in Higher Education, 5*(3), 301–309. doi:10.1080/713699143.

Bulman C., Lathleanb, J. & Gobbi, M. (2014). The process of teaching and learning about reflection: Research insights from professional nurse education. *Studies in Higher Education, 39*(7), 1219–1236. doi:10.1080/03075079.2013.777413.

Burbach, M. E., Matkin, G. S. & Fritz, S. M. (2004). Teaching critical thinking in an introductory leadership course utilizing active learning strategies: A confirmatory study. *College Student Journal, 38*(3), 482–493.

Cake, M. A., Bell, M. A., Williams, J. C., Brown, F. J., Dozier, M., Rhind, S. M. & Baillie, S. (2016). Which professional (non-technical) competencies are most important to the success of graduate veterinarians? A best evidence medical education (BEME) systematic review: BEME guide. *Medical Teacher, 38*(6), 550–563. doi:10.3109/0142159x.2016.1173662.

Caplan, D. (2004). The development of online courses. In T. Anderson and F. Elloumi, *The Theory and Practice of Online Learning* (pp. 174–177). Alberta: Athabasca University.

Carey, M. E. & McCardle, M. (2011). Can an observational field model enhance critical thinking and generalist practice skills? *Journal of Social Work Education, 47*(2), 357–366. doi:10.2307/23044456.

Chen, D., Wang, Y. & Lee, W.C. (2016). Challenges confronting beginning researchers in conducting literature reviews. *Studies in Continuing Education, 38*(1), 47–60. doi:10.1080/0158037x.2015.1030335.

Cisneros, R. M. (2009). Assessment of critical thinking in pharmacy students. *American Journal of Pharmaceutical Education, 73*(4), 1–7. doi: 10.5688/aj730466.

Clarke, John H. & Biddle, Arthus, W. (1993). *Teaching critical thinking: Reports from across the curriculum.* Englewood Cliffs, NJ: Prentice Hall.

Colby, I. I. (2014). Challenging social work education's urban legends. *Journal of Social Work Education, 50*(2), 206–218. doi:10.1080/10437797.2014.885239.

Creswell, J. W. & Creswell, J. D. (2018). *Research design: Qualitative, quantitative, and mixed methods approaches*, 5th ed. p. 304. Sage Publications.

Cronin, P., Ryan, F. & Coughlan, M. (2008). Undertaking a literature review: A step-by-step approach. *British Journal of Nursing, 17*(1), 38–43. doi:10.12968/bjon.2008.17.1.28059.

Danvers, E. C. (2016). Criticality's affective entanglements: Rethinking emotion and critical thinking in higher education. *Gender & Education, 28*(2), 282–297. doi: 10.1080/09540253.2015.1115469.

Davies, M. (2013). Critical thinking and the disciplines reconsidered. *Higher Education Research & Development, 32*(4), 529–544. doi:10.1080/07294360.2012.697878.

Davies, W. M. & Barnett, R. (2015). *The Palgrave handbook of critical thinking in higher education.* New York: Palgrave.

De Bono, E. (1991). The direct teaching of thinking in education and the CoRT method. In Maclure, S. & Davies, P. (Eds.), *Learning to Think: Thinking to Learn,* 3–14. Oxford: Pergamon Press.

Drayton, B. E. (2014). Book Review: Teaching for critical thinking: Tools and techniques to help students question their assumptions by Brookfield, S. *Adult Learning, 25*(4), 169–170. https://doi.org/10.1177/1045159514546210.

Dwyer, C. P., Hogan, M. J., Harney, O. M. & Kavanagh, C. (2017). Facilitating a student-educator conceptual model of dispositions towards critical thinking through interactive management. *Educational Technology Research and Development, 65*(1), 47–73. doi: 10.1007/s11423-014-9360-7.

Eastman, C. & Maguire, K. (2016). Critical autobiography in the professional doctorate: Improving students' writing through the device of literature. *Studies in Continuing Education, 38*(3), 355–372. doi: 10.1080/0158037X.2016.1180510.

Edyburn, D. (2001). Research and practice: Scholarly endeavors: Conducting a comprehensive review of the literature using digital resources. *Journal of Special Education Technology, 16*(1), 49–52 doi:10.1177/016264340101600410.

Egan, M., Neely-Barnes, S. L. & Combs-Orme, T. (2011). Integrating neuroscience knowledge into social work education: A case-based approach. *Journal of Social Work Education, 47*(2), 269–282. doi:10.5175/JSWE.2011.200900109.

Eisen, D. B. (2012). Developing a critical lens: Using photography to teach sociology and create critical thinkers. *Teaching Sociology, 40*(4), 349–359. doi: 10.1177/0092055X12448322.

Elander, J., Harrington, K., Norton, L., Robinson, H. & Reddy, P. (2006). Complex skills and academic writing: A review of evidence about the types of learning required to meet core assessment criteria. *Assessment & Evaluation in Higher Education, 31*(1), 71–90. doi:10.1080/02602930500262379.

Ennis, R. H. (1985). A logical basis for measuring critical thinking skills. *Educational Leadership, 43*(2), 44–48.

Ennis, R. H. (1989). Critical thinking and subject specificity: Clarification and needed research. *Educational Researcher, 18*(3), 4–10. doi:10.3102/0013189x018003004.

European Commission (2016). Review of the 2006 recommendation on key competences for lifelong learning. Retrieved from https://ec.europa.eu/education/initiatives/key-competences-framework-review-2017_en/.

European Commission. (2017). *A Renewed EU Agenda for Higher Education.* Retrieved from https://eur-lex.europa.eu/legal-content/EN/TXT/?uri=CELEX%3A52017DC0247.

Facione, P. A. (1990). *Critical Thinking: A Statement of Expert Consensus for Purposes of Educational Assessment and Instruction. Research Findings and Recommendations.* Retrieved from https://files.eric.ed.gov/fulltext/ED315423.pdf.

Fitzpatrick, J. J. (2006). An evaluative case study of the dilemmas experienced in designing a self-assessment strategy for community nursing students. *Assessment & Evaluation in Higher Education, 31*(1), 37–53. doi:10.1080/02602930500262361.

Flores, K. L., Matkin, G. S., Burbach, M. E., Quinn, C. E. & Harding, H. (2012). Deficient critical thinking skills among college graduates: Implications for leadership. *Educational Philosophy and Theory, 44*(2), 212–230. doi: 10.1111/j.1469-5812.2010.00672.x.

Freire, P. (1970). *Pedagogy of the oppressed.* New York: Continuum.

Gambrill, E. (2014). Social work education and avoidable ignorance. *Journal of Social Work Education, 50*(3), 391–413. doi: 10.1080/10437797.2014.916937.

Gardner, H. (1993). *Multiple intelligence: The theory in practice.* New York: Basic Books.

Garside, C. (1996). Look who's talking: A comparison of lecture and group discussion teaching strategies in developing critical thinking skills. *Communication Education, 45*(3), 212–227. doi:10.1080/03634529609379050.

Geertsen, H. R. (2003). Rethinking thinking about higher level thinking. *Teaching Sociology, 31*(1), 1–19. doi: 10.2307/3211421.

Genc, S. Z. (2008). Critical thinking tendencies among teacher candidates. *Educational Sciences: Theory and Practice, 8*(1), 107–116.

Giroux, H. (1981). *Ideology, culture and the process of schooling.* London: Falmer.

Gliddon, C. M. & Rosengren, R. J. (2012). A laboratory course for teaching laboratory techniques, experimental design, statistical analysis, and peer review process to undergraduate science students. *Biochemistry and Molecular Biology Education, 40*(6), 364–371.doi:10.1002/bmb.20645.

Gomersall, A. (2007). Literature searching: Waste of time or essential skill? *Evidence & Policy: A Journal of Research, Debate and Practice, 3*(2), 301–320. doi:1332/174426407781172243.

Grafstein, A. (2007). Information literacy and technology: An examination of some issues. *Libraries and the Academy, 7*(1), 51–64. doi:10.1258/ijsa.2010.010160.

Grant, M. J. & Booth, A. (2009). A typology of reviews: An analysis of 14 review types and associated methodologies. *Health Information & Libraries Journal, 26*(2), 91–108. doi:10.1111/j.1471-1842.2009.00848.x.

Grauerholz, L. & Bouma-Holtrop, S. (2003). Exploring critical sociological thinking. *Teaching Sociology, 31*(4), 485–496. doi:10.2307/3211372.

Grosser, M. M. & Nel, M. (2013). The relationship between the critical thinking skills and the academic language proficiency of prospective teachers. *South African Journal of Education, 33*(2), 1–17. doi:10.15700/saje.v33n2a639.

Guest, K. (2000). Introducing critical thinking to 'non-standard' entry students. The use of a catalyst to spark debate. *Teaching in Higher Education, 5*(3), 289–299. doi:10.1080/713699139.

Hager, P., Sleet, R., Logan, P. & Hooper, M. (2003). Teaching critical thinking in undergraduate science courses. *Science & Education, 12*(3), 303–313.

Halpern, D. F. (1998). Teaching critical thinking for transfer across domains: Disposition, skills, structure training, and metacognitive monitoring. *American Psychologist, 53*(4), 449–455. doi:10.1037/0003-066x.53.4.449.

Halpern, D. F. (2014). *Thought and knowledge: An introduction to critical thinking*, 5th ed. New York, NY: Psychology Press.

Halx, M. (2010). Re-conceptualizing college and university teaching through the lens of adult education: Regarding undergraduates as adults. *Teaching in Higher Education, 15*(5), 519–530. doi:10.1080/13562517.2010.491909.

Hämäläinen, J. (2013). Comparative research in social work: Methodological considerations using the 'diachronic–synchronic' distinction in linguistics. *European Journal of Social Work, 17*(2), 192–205. doi:10.1080/13691457.2013.777333.

Harrison, S. P. (2005). On the limits of the comparative method. *The Handbook of Historical Linguistics*, 213–243. doi:10.1002/9780470756393.ch2.

Hassan, K. E. & Madhum, G. (2007). Validating the Watson Glaser critical thinking appraisal. *Higher Education, 54*(3), 361–383. doi:10.1007/s10734-006-9002-z.

Hathcoat, J. D., Penn, J. D., Barnes, L. L. B. & Comer, J. C. (2016). A second dystopia in education: Validity issues in authentic assessment practices. *Research in Higher Education, 57*(7), 892–912.

Healey, R. R. (2012). The power of debate: Reflections on the potential of debates for engaging students in critical thinking about controversial geographical topics. *Journal of Geography in Higher Education, 36*(2), 239–257. doi:10.1080/03098265.2011.619522.

Heijltjes, A., Van Gog, T., Leppink, J. & Paas, F. (2015). Unraveling the effects of critical thinking instructions, practice, and self-explanation on students' reasoning performance. *Instructional Science, 43*, 487–506. doi: 10.1007/s11251-015-9347-8.

Helsdingen, A., van Gog, T. & van Merrienboer, J. (2011). The effects of practice schedule and critical thinking prompts on learning and transfer of a complex judgment task. *Journal of Educational Psychology, 103*(2), 383–398. doi: 10.1037/a0022370.

Hester, J. P. (1994). *Teaching for thinking*. Durham, NC: Carolina Academic Press.

Howard, J. & Zoeller, A. (2007). The role of the introductory sociology course on students' perceptions of achievement of general education goals. *Teaching Sociology, 35*(3), 209–222. doi:10.1177/0092055x0703500301.

Hu, Y., Wu, B. & Gu, X. (2017). An eye tracking study of high- and low-performing students in solving interactive and analytical problems. *Educational Technology & Society, 20*(4), 300–311.

Huang, G. C., Lindell, D., Jaffe, L. E. & Sullivan, A. M. (2016). A multi-site study of strategies to teach critical thinking: 'why do you think that?' *Medical Education, 50*, 236–249. doi: 10.1111/medu.12937.

Iskifoglu, G. (2014). Cross-cultural equivalency of the California critical thinking disposition inventory. *Educational Sciences: Theory and Practice, 14*(1), 159–178. doi: 10.12738/estp.2014.1.1840.

James, N., Hughes, C. & Cappa, C. (2010). Conceptualising, developing and assessing critical thinking in law. *Teaching in Higher Education, 15*(3), 285–297. doi:10.1080/13562511003740858.

Jones, A. (2005). Culture and context: Critical thinking and student learning in introductory macroeconomics. *Studies in Higher Education, 30*(3), 339–354. doi:10.1080/03075070500095788.

Jones, A. (2007). Multiplicities or manna from heaven? Critical thinking and the disciplinary context. *Australian Journal of Education, 51*(1), 84–103. doi: 10.1177/000494410705100107.

Jones, B. F. & Idol, L. (1990). *Dimensions of thinking and cognitive instruction.* Hillsdale, NJ: Lawrence Erlbaum Associates.

Kahneman, D. (2011). *Thinking, fast and slow.* New York, NY: Farrar, Straus and Giroux.

Kilic-Cakmak, E. (2010). Learning strategies and motivational factors predicting information literacy self-efficacy of e-learners. *Australasian Journal of Educational Technology, 26*(2), 192–208. doi: 10.14742/ajet.1090.

Kim, M. G. & Bednarz, R. (2013). Development of critical spatial thinking through GIS learning. *Journal of Geography in Higher Education, 37*(3), 350–366. doi:10.1080/03098265.2013.769091.

Kirby, D. & Kuykendall, C. (1991). *Mind matters.* Portsmouth, NH: Boynton/Cook Publishers.

Korkmaz, Ö. (2012). The impact of critical thinking and logico-mathematical intelligence on algorithmic design skills. *Journal of Educational Computing Research, 46*(2), 173–193. doi:10.2190/ec.46.2.d.

Kreber, C. (2014). Rationalising the nature of 'graduateness' through philosophical accounts of authenticity. *Teaching in Higher Education, 19*(1), 90–100. doi: 10.1080/13562517.2013.860114.

Ku, K. Y. (2009). Assessing students' critical thinking performance: Urging for measurements using multi-response format. *Thinking Skills and Creativity, 4*(1), 70–76. doi:10.1016/j.tsc.2009.02.001.

Kubok, D. (2018). Critical thinking and philosophical criticism – an outline of the problem. In D. Kubok (Ed.), *Thinking Critically: What Does It Mean? The Tradition of Philosophical Criticism and Its Forms in the European History of Ideas* (pp. 1–10). Berlin: De Gruyter.

Kuhn, D. (1999). A developmental model of critical thinking. *Educational Researcher, 28*(2), 16–46. doi:10.3102/0013189x028002016.

Lai, K. (2012). Assessing participation skills: Online discussions with peers. *Assessment & Evaluation in Higher Education,* 37(8), 933–947. doi:10.1080/02602938.2011.590878.

Laird, T. N. (2005). College students' experiences with diversity and their effects on academic self-confidence, social agency, and disposition toward critical thinking. *Research in Higher Education, 46*(4), 365–387. doi: 10.1007/s11162-005-2966-1.

Lee, A. (2008). How are doctoral students supervised? Concepts of doctoral research supervision. *Studies in Higher Education, 33*(3), 267–281. doi:10.1080/03075070802049202.

Leedy, P. D. (1997). *Practical research: Planning and design,* 6th ed. Upper Saddle River, NJ: Prentice Hall/Merrill.

Lewis, A. & Smith, D. (1993). Defining higher order thinking. *Theory into Practice, 32*(3), 131–137. doi:10.1080/00405849309543588.

Lim, L. (2011). Beyond logic and argument analysis: Critical thinking, everyday problems and democratic deliberation in Cambridge International Examinations' Thinking Skills curriculum. *Journal of Curriculum Studies, 43*(6), 783–807. doi:10.1080/00220272.2011.590231.

Lin, S. (2014). Science and non-science undergraduate students' critical thinking and argumentation performance in reading a science news report. *International Journal of Science and Mathematics Education, 12*(5), 1023–1046. doi:10.1007/s10763-014-9524-2.

Liu, O. L., Mao, L., Frankel, L. & Xu, J. (2016). Assessing critical thinking in higher education: The HEIghten™ approach and preliminary validity evidence. *Assessment & Evaluation in Higher Education, 41*(5), 677–694. doi:10.1080/02602938.2016.1168358.

Loes, C. M., Salisbury, M. H. & Pascarella, E. T. (2015). Student perceptions of effective instruction and the development of critical thinking: a replication and extension. *Higher Education, 69*(5), 823–838. doi:10.1007/s10734-014-9807-0.

Luke, A. (2004). Two takes on the critical. In B. Norton & K. Toohey (Eds.), *Critical Pedagogies and Language Learning* (pp. 21–30). Cambridge: Cambridge University Press.

Lundquist, R. (1999). Critical thinking and the art of making good mistakes. *Teaching in Higher Education, 4*(4), 523–530. doi: 10.1080/1356251990040408.

Maclellan, E. & Soden R. (2012). Psychological knowledge for teaching critical thinking: the agency of epistemic activity, metacognitive regulative behavior and (student-centred) learning. *Instructional Science, 40*, 445–460. doi:10.1007/s11251-011-9183-4.

Macpherson, K. (1999). The development of critical thinking skills in undergraduate supervisory management units: Efficacy of student peer assessment. *Assessment & Evaluation in Higher Education, 24*(3), 273–284. doi:10.1080/0260293990240302.

Macpherson, K. & Owen, C. (2010). Assessment of critical thinking ability in medical students. *Assessment & Evaluation in Higher Education, 35*(1), 41–54. doi:10.1080/02602930802475471.

Magno, C. (2010). The role of metacognitive skills in developing critical thinking. *Metacognition and Learning, 5*(2), 137–156. doi:10.1007/s11409-010-9054-4.

Malcom, N. L. (2006). Analyzing the news: Teaching critical thinking skills in a writing intensive social problems course. *Teaching Sociology, 34*(2), 143–149. doi:10.1177/0092055x0603400204.

Maskeliūnas, S. (2011). Lietuvos mokslo produkcijos vertinimo įtaka Lietuvos mokslo žurnalų leidybai. *Mokslo ir technikos raida, 3*(2), 129–138. doi:10.3846/est.2011.11.

Mathias, J. (2015). Thinking like a social worker: Examining the meaning of critical thinking in social work. *Journal of Social Work Education, 51*(3), 457–474. doi:10.1080/10437797.2015.1043196.

Maxwell, J. (1992). Understanding and validity in qualitative research. *Harvard Educational Review, 62*(3), 279–301. doi:10.17763/haer.62.3.8323320856251826.

McCarthy, L. & Sziarto, K. (2015). Zombies in the classroom: A horrific attempt to engage students in critically thinking about Turkey's undead application to join the European Union. *Journal of Geography in Higher Education, 39*(1), 83–96. doi:10.1080/03098265.2014.1002078.

McLaren, P. L. (1994). Foreword: Critical thinking as a political project. In: K.S. Walters (Ed.), *Re-thinking Reason: New Perspectives in Critical Thinking* (pp. 9–15). New York: State University of New York Press.

McLaren, P. L. (2006). *Life in schools: An introduction to critical pedagogy in the foundations of education.* Boston, MA: Allyn & Bacon.

McLaughlin, A. A. & McGill, A. (2017). Explicitly teaching critical thinking skills in a history course. *Science & Education, 26*(1/2), 93–105. doi:10.1007/s11191-017-9878-2.

McPeck, J. (1990). *Teaching critical thinking: Dialogue and dialectic.* New York: Routledge. doi:10.4324/9781315526492.

Ministry of Education and Science. (2016). *Dėl studijų krypčių ir krypčių grupių, pagal kurias vyksta studijos aukštosiose mokyklose, sąrašo, jo keitimo tvarkos, kvalifikacinių laipsnių sąrangos ir studijų programų pavadinimų sudarymo principų patvirtinimo* [Approval of the List of Study Fields and Groups of Fields According to Which Studies Are Conducted at Higher Education Institutions and the Procedure for Amending It, the Framework of Qualification Degrees and the Principles of Compiling the Names of Study Programmes]. Retrieved from https://www.e-tar.lt/portal/lt/legalAct/ae5d5730b7c211e693eea1ef35f20da9.

Mintzes, J. J., Wandersee, J. H. & Novak, J. D. (2001). Assessing understanding in biology. *Journal of Biological Education, 35*(3), 118–24. doi:10.1080/00219266.2001.9655759.

Moore, T. J. (2011). Critical thinking and disciplinary thinking: A continuing debate. *Higher Education Research & Development, 30*(3), 261–274. doi:10.1080/07294360.2010.501328.

Moore, T. (2013). Critical thinking: Seven definitions in search of a concept. *Studies in Higher Education, 38*(4), 506–522. doi:10.1080/03075079.2011.586995.

Mumm, A. M. & Kersting, R. (1997). Teaching critical thinking in social work practice courses. *Journal of Social Work Education, 33*(1), 75–84. doi:10.1080/10437797.1997.10778854.

Ng'ambi, D. & Johnston, K. (2006). An ICT-mediated constructivist approach for increasing academic support and teaching critical thinking skills. *Journal of Educational Technology & Society, 9*(3), 244–253. doi:10.4324/9780203065341-13.

Nickerson, R. S. (1988). On improving thinking through instruction. *Review of Research in Education, 15*, 3–57. doi:10.2307/1167360.

Norris, S. & Ennis, R. H. (1989). *Evaluating Critical Thinking*. Pacific Grove, CA: Midwest Publications.

Parahoo, K. (2006). *Nursing Research – principles, process and issues*, 2nd ed. Houndmills: Palgrave.

Paul, R. & Elder, L. (2006). *The miniature guide to critical thinking: Concepts and tools*. Tomales, CA: The Foundation for Critical Thinking.

Pedrosa-de-Jesus, H. & Watts, M. (2014). Managing affect in learners' questions in undergraduate science. *Studies in Higher Education, 39*(1), 102–116. doi:10.1080/19415257.2016.1194877.

Pence, D. (2009). "I'll Take Ideology for $200, Alex": Using the game show "jeopardy" to facilitate sociological and critical thinking. *Teaching Sociology, 37*(2), 171–176. doi:10.1177/0092055X0903700204.

Penkauskienė, D. (2017). *A pedagogical provocation and rethinking learning: An experience from university studies*. In D. Jakavonytė-Staškuvienė & E. Sakadolskienė (Eds.), *Towards research-based education* (pp. 501–510). Villnius: Lietuvos edukologijos universiteto leidykla.

Penkauskienė, D., Railienė, A. & Cruz, G. (2019). How is critical thinking valued by the labour market? Employer perspectives from different European countries. *Studies in Higher Education, 44* (5), 1–12. doi:10.1080/03075079.2019.1586323.

Penningroth, S. L., Despain, L. H. & Gray, M. J. (2007). A course designed to improve psychological critical thinking. *Teaching of Psychology, 34*(3), 153–157. doi:10.1080/00986280701498509.

Perkins, C. & Murphy, E. (2006). Identifying and measuring individual engagement in critical thinking in online discussions: An exploratory case study. *Journal of Educational Technology & Society, 9*(1), 298–307.

Perkins, D. & Salomon, G. (1989). Are cognitive skills context-bound? *Educational Researcher, 18*(1), 16–25. doi:10.3102/0013189x018001016.

Phan, H. P. (2008). Predicting change in epistemological beliefs, reflective thinking and learning styles: A longitudinal study. *British Journal of Educational Psychology, 78*(1), 75–93. doi:10.1348/000709907x204354.

Phan, H. P. (2011). Deep processing strategies and critical thinking: Developmental trajectories using latent growth analyses. *Journal of Educational Research, 104*, 283–294. doi: 10.1080/00220671003739382.

Power, J. B. (2016). Has this begun to change the way they think? Moving undergraduate learners' level of reflection from where it is to where it needs to be. *Teaching in Higher Education, 21*(3), 235–248. doi:10.1080/13562517.2015.1136278.

Raveendran, A. & Chunawala, S. (2015). Values in science: Making sense of biology doctoral students' critical examination of a deterministic claim in a media article. *Science Education, 99*(4), 669–695. doi:10.1002/sce.21174.

Redmond, P., Devine, J. & Bassoon, M. (2014). Exploring discipline differentiation in online discussion participation. *Australasian Journal of Educational Technology, 30*(2). doi:10.14742/ajet.624.

Rickles, M. L., Schneider, R. Z., Slusser, S. R., Williams, D. M. & Zipp, J. F. (2013). Assessing change in student critical thinking for introduction to sociology classes. *Teaching Sociology, 41*(3), 271–281. doi:10.1177/0092055X13479128.

Robinson, S. R. (2011). Teaching logic and teaching critical thinking: Revisiting McPeck. *Higher Education Research & Development, 30*(3), 275–287. doi:10.1080/07294360.2010.500656.

Rocconi, L. (2013). Analyzing multilevel data: Comparing findings from hierarchical linear modeling and ordinary least squares regression. *Higher Education, 66*(4), 439–461. doi:10.1007/s10734-013-9615-y.

Roksa, J., Trolian, T., Pascarella, E., Kilgo, C., Blaich, C. & Wise, K. (2017). Racial inequality in critical thinking skills: The role of academic and diversity experiences. *Research in Higher Education, 58*(2), 119–140. doi:10.1007/s11162-016-9423-1.

Sagun, S., Ateskan, A. & Onur, J. (2016). Developing students for university through an international high school program in Turkey. *Educational Sciences: Theory and Practice, 16*(2), 439–457. doi:10.12738/estp.2016.2.0313.

Saltmarsh, D. D. & Saltmarsh, S. (2008). Has anyone read the reading? Using assessment to promote academic literacies and learning cultures. *Teaching in Higher Education, 13*(6), 621–632. doi:10.1080/13562510802452343.

Samson, P. L. (2016). Critical thinking in social work education: A research synthesis. *Journal of Social Work Education, 52*(2), 147–156. doi: 10.1080/10437797.2016.1151270.

Schendel, R. (2016). Constructing departmental culture to support student development: Evidence from a case study in Rwanda. *Higher Education, 72*(4), 487–504. doi:10.1007/s10734-016-0036-6.

Scott, M. (2000). Student, critic and literary text: A discussion of 'critical thinking' in a student essay. *Teaching in Higher Education, 5*(3), 277–288. doi:10.1080/13562510050084686.

Seker, H. & Komur, S. (2008). The relationship between critical thinking skills and in-class questioning behaviours of English language teaching students. *European Journal of Teacher Education, 31*(4), 389–402. doi:10.1080/02619760802420784.

Shephard, K., Harraway, J., Lovelock, B., Mirosa, M., Skeaff, S., Slooten, L., Deaker, L. (2015). Seeking learning outcomes appropriate for 'education for sustainable development' and for higher education. *Assessment & Evaluation in Higher Education, 40*(6), 855–866. doi:10.1080/02602938.2015.1009871.

Sigurðsson, G. (2017). Transformative critique: What Confucianism can contribute to contemporary education. *Studies in Philosophy and Education, 36*(2), 131–146. doi:10.1007/s11217-015-9502-3.

Silva, E. (2008). Measuring skills for the 21st century. Education Sector Reports. Retrieved from: http://elenamsilva.com/wp-content/uploads/2013/05/MeasuringSkills.pdf.

Slabon, W. A., Richards, R. L. & Dennen, V. P. (2014). Learning by restoring. *Instructional Science, 42*(4), 505–521. doi:10.1007/s11251-014-9311-z.

Smith, G. (2002). Are there domain-specific thinking skills? *Journal of Philosophy of Education, 36*(2), 207–227. doi:10.1111/1467-9752.00270.

Soden, R. & Maclellan, E. (2005). Helping education undergraduates to use appropriate criteria for evaluating accounts of motivation. *Studies In Higher Education, 30*(4), 445–458. doi:10.1080/03075070500160145.

Stupnisky, R. H., Renaud, R. D., Daniels, L. M., Haynes, T. L. & Perry, R. P. (2008). The interrelation of first-year college students' critical thinking disposition, perceived academic control, and academic achievement. *Research in Higher Education, 49*(6), 513–530. doi:10.1007/s11162-008-9093-8.

Sziarto, K. M., McCarthy, L. & Padilla, N. L. (2014). Teaching critical thinking in world regional geography through stakeholder debate. *Journal of Geography in Higher Education, 38*(4), 557–570. doi:10.1080/03098265.2014.958658.

Šakytė, M. (2016). Lietuvos aukštojo mokslo institucijų leidžiamų mokslinių periodinių leidinių kokybės problemos. *Knygotyra, 67*, 191–205. doi:10.15388/knygotyra.67.10182.

Tan, L. (2016). Confucius: Philosopher of twenty-first century skills. *Educational Philosophy and Theory, 48*(12), 1233–1243. doi:10.1080/00131857.2016.1182416.

Teaching for Global Competence in a Rapidly Changing World. OECD (2018). Paris: OECD Publishing.

Tiruneh, D. T., De Cock, M., Weldeslassie, A. G., Elen, J. & Janssen, R. (2017). Measuring critical thinking in Physics: Development and validation of a critical thinking test in electricity and magnetism. *International Journal of Science and Mathematics Education, 15*(4), 663–682. doi:10.1007/s10763-016-9723-0.

Tiruneh, D. T., Verburgh, A. & Elen, J. (2014). Effectiveness of critical thinking instruction in higher education: A systematic review of intervention studies. *Higher Education Studies, 4*(1). doi:10.5539/hes.v4n1p1.

Tiruneh, D., Weldeslassie, A., Kassa, A., Tefera, Z., Cock, M. & Elen, J. (2016). Systematic design of a learning environment for domain-specific and domain-general critical thinking skills. *Educational Technology Research & Development, 64*(3), 481–505. doi:10.1007/s11423-015-9417-2.

Turner, P. (2005). Critical thinking in nursing education and practice as defined in the Literature. *Nursing Education Perspectives, 26*(5), 272–277.

Uzuntiryaki-ondakci, E. & Capa-Aydin, Y. (2013). Predicting critical thinking skills of university students through metacognitive self-regulation skills and chemistry self-efficacy. *Educational Sciences: Theory and Practice, 13*(1), 666–670.

Walker, M. (2015). Higher education and the public good. In: McGrath, S. & Gu, Q. (Eds.), *Routledge Handbook on International Education and Development.* Routledge, London.

Walker, P. & Finney, N. (1999). Skill development and critical thinking in higher education. *Teaching in Higher Education, 4*(4), 531–547. doi: 10.1080/1356251990040409.

Wang, Y., Chao, C. Y. & Liao, H. (2010). Poststructural feminist pedagogy in English instruction of vocational-and-technical education. *Higher Education, 61*(2), 109–139. doi:10.1007/s10734-010-9327-5.

Wickersham, C., Westerberg, C., Jones, K. & Cress, M. (2016). Pivot points: Direct measures of the content and process of community-based learning. *Teaching Sociology, 44*(1), 17–27. doi:10.1177/0092055X15613786.

Willingham, D. T. (2007). Critical thinking. *American Educator, 31*(2), 8–19. doi:10.3200/AEPR.109.4.21-32.

Yang, Y. C. (2008). A catalyst for teaching critical thinking in a large university class in Taiwan: asynchronous online discussions with the facilitation of teaching assistants. *Educational Technology Research & Development, 56*(3), 241–264. doi: 10.1007/s11423-007-9054-5.

Yeh, Y. (2007). Integrating E-lEarning into the direct-instruction model to enhance the effectiveness of critical-thinking instruction. *Instructional Science, 37*(2), 185–203. doi:10.1007/s11251-007-9048-z.

Yeh, Y. (2009). Integrating e-learning into the Direct-instruction Model to enhance the effectiveness of critical-thinking instruction. *Instructional Science, 37*(2), 185–203. doi: 10.1007/s11251-007-9048-z.

Critical Thinking as a Unique Competence: Evidence from Higher Education Studies

Abstract: Higher education plays an important role in promoting personal development and social progress; it promotes innovation-based research, and thus makes a considerable contribution in training the highly qualified employees needed for knowledge-based economic growth and prosperity. Hence, higher education is expected to do more than just provide training – it needs to contribute to the development of an economically sustainable, integral, progressive society and mature individuals, respond to the changing needs of the specific time period, and predict and model these needs. International organisations recognise critical thinking as an essential competence that is one of the best tools for achieving these goals. Higher education, therefore, faces the need to ensure the development of critical thinking skills at all cycles of study. European researchers from higher education institutions agree that critical thinking has to be a goal of education, integrating it on three interrelated levels: institutional, teaching programme/curriculum and course. However, for the development of critical thinking to be successful and sustainable, it must be systematic, consistent, uninterrupted, and present in all parts of the educational content and studies.

The purpose of this chapter is to reveal the manifestation of critical thinking in higher education by analysing higher education study programme and course descriptions. This chapter consists of three sections. The first section describes the methodology of the analysis of higher education study programme and course descriptions, and presents the selected strategy of mixed methods research. The second section discusses the manifestation of critical thinking in the selected study programme and course descriptions. The findings of the quantitative and qualitative content analyses are presented. Based on the research outcomes, the third section discusses how critical thinking is integrated into study programme and course descriptions at Lithuanian higher education institutions.

Keywords: study programme descriptions, study course descriptions, constituents of critical thinking, disposition, ability, skill and competence, mixed methods research.

1. Research Methodology

1.1 Research design

In order to reveal the manifestation of critical thinking in higher education, an analysis was performed of the descriptions of the higher education study programmes that were registered in the AIKOS[2] system in 2019. A mixed methods research approach was used, that is, quantitative and qualitative methods of data collection and analysis were employed. Creswell (2014) defines mixed methods research as an approach to research in which the investigator gathers quantitative and qualitative data, integrates the two, and then draws interpretations based on the combined strength of both sets of data to understand the research problem. This collective strength provides a better understanding of the research problem than either form of data alone.

The philosophical foundation most often associated with mixed methods methodology is pragmatism (Teddlie and Tashakkori, 2008; Creswell and Poth, 2017). Teddlie and Tashakkori (2008) define pragmatism as a deconstructive paradigm that debunks concepts such as 'truth' and 'reality', and focuses instead on 'what works' as the truth regarding the research questions under investigation, that is, it looks for answers to the questions of *what and how*, and truth is considered to be what is found in the study *here and now*. Pragmatism rejects the 'either/or' choices associated with the paradigm wars. It acknowledges that the values of the researcher play a large role in the interpretation of the results. Pragmatism highlights the researcher's role, initiative and freedom to make the decisions at each stage of the research that he or she feels best responds to the research problem.

In order to keep in line with this mixed methods research (pragmatism) perspective, the research team constantly discussed the course of the research and was flexible in the research process when it was necessary to return to the previous stage and make new decisions that would better respond to the problems raised in the study. In the pragmatism perspective, there is emphasis on the research outcomes, but not on the causes that determine these outcomes, that is, the manifestation of critical thinking in the study programme and course descriptions is analysed, but without delving into the reasons or motives for the inclusion of critical thinking in the study process. The social, cultural, political and other contexts are important for understanding the research findings, so Lithuanian higher education studies are described in this part. Pragmatism advocates for the use of mixed methods in research, so the research team employed multiple sources (study programme descriptions and course descriptions) of data collection and used multiple methods of data analysis (quantitative and qualitative content analysis) in order to best answer the research questions. This perspective encourages providing the practical implication of the research, which can be found in the Recommendations part.

---

2 AIKOS is an open vocational information, counselling and guidance system providing a wide range of users with information based on public, departmental and other databases and registers. The main activities of AIKOS are to provide qualitative information on the possibilities of distant learning; to inform and consult a wide range of users, irrespective of their age, helping them to choose their own path in the sphere of education, training and occupation and building their professional career; to provide internet services to the users of data obtained from the databases used by AIKOS.

The choice of mixed methods research is based on general and specific rationale (Creswell, 2014). The general rational for mixed methods research is based on an insufficient understanding of the problem with quantitative or qualitative research alone, so the advantages of quantitative and qualitative research are used for the analysis of the study programmes: quantitative data and their analysis made it possible to form a broad and comprehensive picture of critical thinking in Lithuanian higher education, and qualitative data and their analysis made it possible to look deeper into the phenomenon under study. The specific rationale for using a mixed methods research approach in this study was based on the desire to obtain a more comprehensive view and more data about the research problem (Creswell, 2014), and to provide better (stronger) inferences (Teddlie and Tashakkori, 2008). The specific rationale led to the choice of a method for combining quantitative and qualitative data collection and analysis. Of the three multi-strategy approaches (triangulation, facilitation and complementarity) suggested by Hammersley (1996), this study uses the facilitation method, which stresses the supporting function of each approach, rather than seeking mutual validation of the results like in the triangulation method, or using quantitative and qualitative data together like in the complementarity method. Facilitation uses an explanatory sequential design, in which the intent is to find and use quantitative methods and then use qualitative methods (Creswell, 2014); the questions and procedures of one method emerge from or are dependent more on the previously applied method (Teddlie and Tashakkori, 2008).

In conducting the quantitative research, it is assumed that critical thinking is integrated into the study programme descriptions at Lithuanian higher education institutions. The aim of the qualitative research is to investigate the manifestation of the conception of critical thinking and the constituents of critical thinking by raising three research questions: (1) What meaning is given to the conception of critical thinking?; (2) What are the key elements of this conception?; (3) How are they reflected in the aims and outcomes of the programme subjects? In the facilitation of both methods, the mixed methods question is formulated as: How does the critical thinking declared in the study programme descriptions manifest itself in the course descriptions?

Research process. The study consisted of four sequentially interrelated stages to identify the extent to which critical thinking manifests itself in the study programme descriptions and how it is expressed in the course descriptions: (1) selection of study programmes; (2) quantitative content analysis of the study programme descriptions; (3) quantitative content analysis of the course descriptions; (4) qualitative content analysis of the course descriptions (Figure 6).

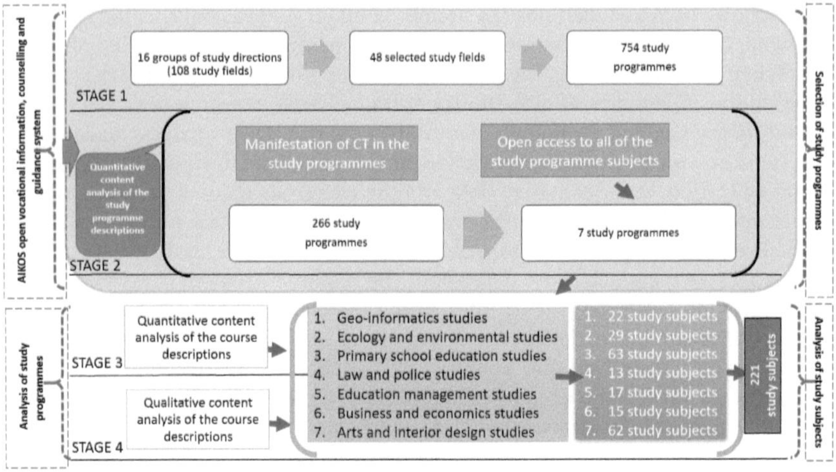

Fig. 6: *Logic diagram*

Quantitative research methods were used in the first three stages and qualitative research methods were used in the fourth:

- Stage 1. Selection of study programmes at Lithuanian higher education institutions, ensuring representation of the study field groups. A total of 754 study programme descriptions were selected for the analysis, of which 266 mentioned the concept of critical thinking.
- Stage 2. Quantitative content analysis of the 266 study programme descriptions, which made it possible to single out seven study programmes for more detailed analysis.
- Stage 3. Quantitative content analysis of the seven study programme and course descriptions, which led to a qualitative content analysis of the course descriptions.
- Stage 4. The qualitative content analysis of the seven study programme course descriptions made it possible to reveal the manifestation of critical thinking and its elements in the aims and outcomes of the study programme subjects.

1.2 Data analysis methods

Two data sets were used in the research: the texts of the publicly presented study programme[3] descriptions were analysed in the second stage, and the texts of the

3 Study programme – the totality of the implementation of a study field(s) at an institution of higher education and its description, which foresees the learning outcomes

course descriptions for the selected study programmes were analysed in the third and fourth stages. The study used data content analysis by joining both data sets, that is, by combining the quantitative content analysis of the study programmes and their descriptions with the qualitative content analysis of the course descriptions of the study programmes selected for further analysis.

Content analysis was chosen because it can be applied to both quantitative and qualitative data when they are intertwined in the research field; as Mudde and Schedler (2010, p. 418–419) argue, ‘even the most sophisticated piece of quantitative research remains dependent on natural language (words), while most qualitative studies do contain some kind of quantitative information (numbers)’. The phenomenon under investigation, or the constructs being examined, might be very qualitative in nature, and the analyses applied might be indisputably quantitative. The reverse is also possible, in which quantitative events might be interpreted in a qualitative fashion (Neuendorf, 2017).

Quantitative content analysis may be briefly defined as the systematic, objective, quantitative analysis of message characteristics. A quantitative content analysis has as its goal a numerically based summary of a chosen message set. Content analysis summarises rather than reports all details concerning a message set. This is consistent with a nomothetic approach to scientific investigations (i.e. seeking to generate generalisable conclusions from an aggregate of cases), rather than an idiographic approach (i.e. focusing on a full and precise conclusion about a particular case, as in a case study). The nomothetic approach implies conclusions that are broadly based, generalisable, objective, summarising and inflexible (Neuendorf, 2017). Therefore, the quantitative content analysis in this study is based on two main assumptions:

- the parts of the text reflect the contexts behind the text, the analysis of which is the main research aim, that is, it is possible to talk about the manifestation of critical thinking in higher education studies based on the word combination ‘critical thinking’ found in the study programme descriptions;
- the frequency of repetition of certain parts of the text reflecting a particular topic reflects the importance of that topic in the text: the more frequent a certain piece of text reflecting a particular topic occurs in the text, the more important that topic is to the person who created the text, that is, the frequency of repetition of the word combination ‘critical thinking’ reveals the manifestation and importance of critical thinking in higher education studies.

Qualitative content analysis relies on sequential steps, thus ensuring depth of data interpretation (Hennink, Hutter and Bailey, 2020; Silverman, 2020). This is a

---

and the study content, learning activities, methods, tools, and human and other resources required to achieve them (Law on Higher Education and Research of the Republic of Lithuania, 2009).

technique that allows reliable conclusions to be drawn after objective and systematic examination of the text (Maxwell, 2008; Cohen, Manion and Morrison, 2013).

The research sought to understand the meaning given to the conception of critical thinking, what the key constituents of this conception are, and how they are reflected in the aims and outcomes of the study programme subjects.

The word 'critical' was chosen as the semantic unit of analysis. In the first stage of the analysis, there was repeated reading of the text/selected study programme descriptions in order to understand all the data obtained and reveal the deep manifestation of the semantic unit. In the second stage, the data were grouped into two main categories: study subject aims and study subject outcomes. This data grouping was used to reveal the manifestation of critical thinking in the study subjects. The third stage of the analysis – interpretation – involved giving meaning to the data and substantiating it with evidence extracted from the text. These illustrations from the course description form the basis for assessing the validity and reliability of the conclusions. The interpretation of the data is based on an inductive attitude, moving from individual, isolated cases to general conclusions and summarisation, that is, describing the manifestation of critical thinking constituents in the aims and outcomes of the study subjects.

1.3 Reliability and validity

Mixed methods research calls for ensuring the reliability and validity of each quantitative and qualitative study separately, and has specific requirements for combining them.

The reliability of the quantitative content analysis (Neuendorf, 2017) of the study programme descriptions at Lithuanian higher education institutions is ensured by the following methods:

- all decisions on variables, their measurement, and coding rules were made before the final measurement process;
- the coding scheme was developed by three researchers and then discussed and approved by all eight participating researchers.

The validity of the quantitative content analysis (McCulloch, 2004; Creswell and Creswell, 2018) of the study programme descriptions at Lithuanian higher education institutions is ensured by the following methods:

- authenticity of sources, which ensures that the source version of the document is the real one, that is, all of the analysed programmes are registered in the State supported system AIKOS, which contains official information about all study programmes in Lithuania;
- reliability of sources, which defines the importance and/or weight of the document in the context of similar sources, that is, all of the analysed programmes are in AIKOS, which means that the analysed programmes are registered and have a state code;

- time period, that is, only study programmes with valid accreditation are included;
- maximum number of sources, that is, college and university bachelor's and master's degree programmes from all study fields are included; all study programmes that meet the selection criteria are included in the analysis list and analysed.

During the quantitative analysis of the study programmes at Lithuanian higher education institutions, the following factors affecting validity and reliability were encountered: the programmes presented in the AIKOS system had different description forms, so the content of the information differed and/or part of the information was not provided; active links were provided, but electronic access to the study programme was not always possible. Moreover, reliability in quantitative content analysis is defined more specifically as intercoder reliability, or level of agreement among two or more coders (Neuendorf, 2017). Intercoder reliability in this research was ensured during the data collecting and analysis process, when eight researchers worked in smaller subgroups, reached a consensus, and then brought the analysed text for discussion with the entire group of investigators.

The methods ensuring the internal validity of qualitative content analysis of the course descriptions (Maxwell, 1992; Miles and Huberman, 1994; Hayashi, Cohen, Manion and Morrison, 2013; Patton, 2014; Abib and Hoppen, 2019) were as follows:

- correspondence of the research outcomes to the actual situation under investigation, when questions were regularly raised in the course of the research: whether an authentic picture of the field under analysis – that is, critical thinking in higher education – is being depicted, and whether the summaries/conclusions of the findings have meaning to stakeholders;
- detailed and comprehensive description and interpretation of the data.

External qualitative data validity (Bitinas, Rupšienė and Žydžiūnaitė, 2008) was ensured using the investigator triangulation method, when intermediate insights, planned analytical actions, possible solutions, interpretations, summaries and conclusions were discussed at each stage of data selection and analysis in pursuit of a conceptual and substantiated solution.

During the qualitative content analysis of the course descriptions, the following factors threatening research validity were encountered:

- only some of the study programmes were selected for analysis, so there is a lack of deeper insights into the manifestation of critical thinking in study field groups such as informatics, engineering, mathematics, health, technology, veterinary, business and public management;
- the content of the descriptions studied does not make it possible to judge the uniqueness of the programmes by conceptualising the concept of critical thinking and highlighting specific skills and dispositions. It was, therefore, decided to proceed without a study programme comparison and generalising conclusions.

In mixed methods research, it is not enough to separately ensure the validity of quantitative data alone and qualitative data alone – validity must be increased in the coherence of both methods. For ensuring mixed methods research validity, Teddlie and Tashakkori (2008) suggest using the term 'inference quality', which incorporates the term 'internal validity and trustworthiness'. Inference quality refers to the standard for evaluating the quality of conclusions that are made based on both quantitative and qualitative findings. In this study, it was ensured by investigator triangulation and methodological triangulation. It is also proposed (Teddlie and Tashakkori, 2008) to use the term 'inference transferability', which incorporates external validity and transferability. In this study, it was ensured by analytical generalisation. Inference transferability is the degree to which the conclusions from mixed methods research may be applied to other settings, people, time, periods and contexts.

2. The Embeddedness of Critical Thinking in Higher Education Curriculum

Higher education is the main tool for ensuring public welfare, fostering personal development and social progress, and influencing innovation and research in training the highly qualified employees needed to ensure the well-being of society. The aim of higher education studies is to help a person acquire a modern level of knowledge and technology and a higher education qualification that meets the needs of the economy, and prepare for active professional, social and cultural activities (Mačerinskienė and Kučaidze, 2019).

The changing needs of the business world, the market economy and the development of an information society have led to higher education becoming mass. And even though Lithuania has a long tradition of elite higher education (Vilnius University, one of the oldest universities in Europe, was established in the country's capital in 1579), this phenomenon affected not only the European educational system but Lithuania's as well. In order to better understand the outcomes of the presented research, the higher education system in Lithuania is introduced.

Before the phenomenon of mass higher education became widespread, a binary system of higher education was established by the Republic of Lithuania Law on Higher Education (2000). This system consists of university (universities, academies, seminaries) and non-university (colleges, higher education schools) higher education institutions. University higher education institutions carry out research and experimental development and/or high-level professional art, while non-university higher education institutions carry out applied scientific research and/or professional art. According to data from the Ministry of Education, Science and Sport of the Republic of Lithuania (Educational and scientific institutions by group, type and affiliation, n.d.), higher education was provided in Lithuania in 2020 as full-time or part-time studies by 40 educational institutions: 11 state universities,

7 private universities, 10 state colleges and 12 private colleges. The Ministry of Education, Science and Sport, when presenting the higher education system (Higher education system, n.d.), singles out the three-cycle degree programmes and non-degree programmes designed for acquiring a qualification or preparing for independent activities.

Degree-awarding university studies are first-cycle studies offered at university and non-university higher education institutions to develop general erudition, convey the theoretical foundations of the study field, and form professional skills. The study programmes offered at non-university higher education institutions are focused on preparation for professional activities, and academic university study programmes provide universal general education and are focused on theoretical preparation and the highest level of professional skills.

Second-cycle study programmes are offered at university higher education institutions and prepare the student for independent scientific, artistic or other work. Some higher education institutions offer integrated studies leading to a master's degree.

Third-cycle studies are doctoral studies in science and art. Institutions of higher education may offer joint study programmes leading to a joint qualification degree, as well as programmes leading to a double qualification degree. Upon completion of non-degree residency or pedagogy study programmes for the acquisition of a qualification or preparation for independent practice, a certificate is issued. A university study programme is approved by the Senate, while a college study programme is approved by the Ministry of Education, Science and Sport.

The main document regulating Lithuanian higher education – the Law on Higher Education and Research (2016) – establishes the state regulation of higher education and research, the principles of quality assurance, the legal bases for the establishment, termination and reorganisation of institutions, the award and recognition of higher education qualifications and degrees, the management of research and higher education institutions, the organisation and supervision of activities, the rights and obligations of teachers, researchers and students, higher education and research funding, and the principles of management, use and disposal of the property of state higher education institutions. The General Requirements for Study Implementation (2016) establish the basic principles of the organisation of cycle (except doctoral) studies needed to create a learning environment and ensure the quality of studies. Master's studies are regulated by the Description of General Requirements for Master's Study Programmes (2010).

Lithuania has a national higher education quality assurance system. The Qualifications and Vocational Education and Training Development Centre organises quality assessment of college activities. The Centre for Quality Assessment in Higher Education (SKVC) organises partial and comprehensive assessment of study programmes and evaluation of scientific research and development. Accredited study programmes are registered in the AIKOS database.

2.1 Research process

The study consisted of four interrelated stages. Study programmes were selected for analysis during the first stage, and the study programme and course descriptions examined using quantitative and qualitative content analysis during stages two through four.

In the first stage, the selection and analysis of study programmes at Lithuanian higher education institutions was carried out using the data of the Open Information, Counselling and Guidance System (AIKOS), which includes registers and databases of the educational system of Lithuania. The educational system in Lithuania is based on 108 study fields,[4] which consist of 16 study field groups:[5]

- Mathematical Sciences (A) (A01 Mathematics; A02 Applied Mathematics; A03 Statistics).
- Informatics Science (B) (B01 Informatics; B02 Information Systems; B03 Software Engineering; B04 Informatics Engineering).
- Physical Sciences (C) (C01 Chemistry; C02 Physics; C03 Geology; C04 Environmental Sciences; C05 Physical Geography).
- Life Sciences (D) (D01 Biology; D02 Genetics; D03 Microbiology; D04 Molecular Biology; D05 Biophysics; D06 Biochemistry; D07 Ecology).
- Engineering Sciences (E) (E01 Safety Engineering; E02 Bioengineering; E03 Environmental Engineering; E04 Measurement Engineering; E05 Civil Engineering; E06 Mechanical Engineering; E07 Maritime Engineering; E08 Electrical Engineering; E09 Electronics Engineering; E10 Production and Manufacturing Engineering; E11 Chemical Engineering; E12 Transport Engineering; E13 Power Engineering; E14 Aerospace Engineering).
- Technological Sciences (F) (F01 Natural Resource Technology; F02 Polymer and Textile Technology; F03 Materials Technology; F04 Maritime Technology; F05 Biotechnology; F06 Food Technology; F07 Public Catering).
- Health Sciences (G) (G01 Medicine; G02 Dentistry; G03 Professional Oral Hygiene; G04 Public Health; G05 Pharmacy; G06 Rehabilitation; G07 Nutrition; G08 Nursing and Midwifery; G09 Medical Technology; G10 Cosmetology).
- Veterinary Sciences (H) (H01 Veterinary).
- Agricultural Sciences (I) (I01 Agriculture; I02 Agronomy; I03 Forestry; I04 Animal Husbandry; I05 Fishery; I06 Food Studies).
- Social Sciences (J) (J01 Economics; J02 Political Sciences; J03 Sociology; J04 Social Work; J05 Anthropology; J06 Human Geography; J07 Psychology; J08

4 Field of study – an academic, professional or research field, which is united by a common concept, study outcomes and methods for their achievement (teaching, studying, assessment) (Law on Higher Education and Research of the Republic of Lithuania, 2009).

5 The list of study fields and groups of fields according to which studies are conducted at higher education institutions and the framework of the degrees awarded Approval of the List of Study Fields and Groups of Fields, 2016.

Public Security; J09 Information Services; J10 Communication; J11 Publishing; J12 Journalism).
- Law (K) (K01 Law).
- Business and Public Administration (L) (L01 Business Studies; L02 Management Studies; L03 Finance; L04 Accounting; L05 Marketing; L06 Human Resource Management; L07 Public Administration; L08 Tourism and Leisure).
- Education Sciences (M) (M01 Pedagogy; M02 Educology/Education; M03 Andragogy).
- Humanities (N) (N01 Linguistics; N02 Literary Studies; N03 Classical Studies; N04 Philology (by language); N05 Translation Studies; N06 Area Studies; N07 Lingual Studies; N08 History; N09 Archaeology; N10 Philosophy; N11 Theology; N12 Heritage Studies; N13 Religious Studies; N14 Cultural Studies; N15 History of Art).
- Arts (P) (P01 Fine Art; P02 Design Studies; P03 Music; P04 Theatre; P05 Film; P06 Dance; P07 Media Art; P08 Artworks Restoration; P09 Architecture; P10 Landscape Architecture).
- Sport (R) (R01 Competitive Sport; R02 Recreational Sport).

The selection of study programmes was aimed at ensuring the diversity of study field groups (n=16) and study fields (n=108) at Lithuanian higher education institutions.

It should be noted that each study field group has a different number of study fields. There are groups that consist of only 1 field of study (e.g. Veterinary Sciences), and there are groups that consist of as many as 15 study fields (e.g. Humanities). Therefore, multistage sampling was used for the selection of study fields. Taking into account the number of study fields and in order to ensure representation of the study field groups, the following principle was applied: if the study field group consists of one to six study fields, the first four study fields participate in the analysis; if there are more than six study fields, systematic sampling is applied. Systematic sampling was slightly modified depending on the number of study fields in the group, so the sampling interval ranged from three to four. This allowed ensuring that three or four study fields from each study field group participated in the analysis, except for cases where the study field group consists of one or two study fields. Of the 108 study fields, 48 study fields were selected, in which 754 study programmes were registered:

- A01 Mathematics (8 study programmes); A02 Applied Mathematics (7 study programmes); A03 Statistics (8 study programmes).
- B01 Informatics (36 study programmes); B02 Information Systems (12 study programmes); B03 Software Engineering (10 study programmes); B04 Informatics Engineering (26 study programmes).
- C01 Chemistry (8 study programmes); C02 Physics (14 study programmes); C03 Geology (4 study programmes); C04 Environmental Sciences (5 study programmes).
- D01 Biology (10 study programmes); D04 Molecular Biology (3 study programmes); D07 Ecology (9study programmes).
- E01 Safety Engineering (3 study programmes); E05 Civil Engineering (38 study programmes); E07 Maritime Engineering (9 study programmes); E11 Chemical Engineering (4 study programmes).

- F03 Materials Technology (15 study programmes); F05 Biotechnology (8 study programmes); F07 Public Catering (2 study programmes).
- G04 Public Health (13 study programmes); G07 Nutrition (3 study programmes); G10 Cosmetology (10study programmes).
- H01 Veterinary (18 study programmes).
- I01 Agriculture (12 study programmes); I03 Forestry (7 study programmes); I05 Fishery (1 study programme).
- J04 Social Work (26 study programmes); J07 Psychology (23 study programmes); J10 Communication (34 study programmes).
- K01 Law (57 study programmes).
- L01 Business Studies (72 study programmes); L04 Accounting (4 study programmes); L06 Human Resource Management (6 study programmes).
- M01 Pedagogy (82 study programmes); M02 Educology/Education (34 study programmes); M03 Andragogy (4 study programmes).
- N02 Literary Studies (2 study programmes); N06 Area Studies (6 study programmes); N10 Philosophy (11 study programmes); N14 Cultural Studies (3 study programmes).
- P01 Fine Art (27 study programmes); P05 Film (4 study programmes); P08 Artworks Restoration (3 study programmes).
- R01 Competitive Sport (4 study programmes); R02 Recreational Sport (1 study programme).

This choice of programmes ensured representation of the study field groups and study fields.

In order to determine the extent to which critical thinking manifests in study programmes, a quantitative content analysis of 754 study programme descriptions was performed *in the second stage of the research.*

For systematising the study programmes, a form was prepared by the researchers. It included study field group, study field code and name, programme name, level (college/university; bachelor's/master's), credits, form and duration, programme summary, aim and learning outcomes.

The analysis of the study programme descriptions at Lithuanian higher education institutions showed that out of all the 754 study programmes selected, the descriptions for 266 study programmes mentioned the concept of critical thinking: 89 times in goals and 177 in learning outcomes.

Evaluation of the registered study programmes selected (n=754) and the programmes that mention critical thinking (n=266) found that critical thinking is most often mentioned in the aims and learning outcomes for programmes belonging to the Engineering Sciences group of study fields; to a lesser extent, critical thinking is mentioned in the study field programmes in Life Sciences, Technology Sciences, Social Sciences, Health Sciences and Business and Public Management. In study field groups such as Mathematics Sciences and Veterinary Sciences, critical thinking is mentioned extremely rarely (Table 7).

Tab. 7: *Relationships between the number of study programmes and critical thinking by type of higher education institution and cycle of study*

Group of study fields	Total number of progra-mmes	Number of study programmes that mention critical thinking	College	University		Number of available programmes that mentioned critical thinking
				Bachelor's	Master's	
Mathematical Sciences (A)	223	13	0	7	6	8
Informatics Science (B)	84	23	5	11	7	11
Physical Sciences (C)	31	9	0	3	6	5
Life Sciences (D)	22	10	0	6	4	6
Engineering Sciences (E)	54	25	1	8	16	13
Technological Sciences (F)	25	11	0	4	7	9
Health Sciences (G)	26	10	7	0	3	1
Veterinary Sciences (H)	18	2	0	2	0	0
Agricultural Sciences (I)	20	8	2	3	3	0
Social Sciences (J)	127	52	13	20	19	34
Law (K)	57	20	6	3	11	11
Business and Public Administration (L)	82	31	9	15	7	11
Education Sciences (M)	120	36	3	26	7	8
Humanities (N)	26	7	0	4	3	4

Group of study fields	**Total number of progra-mmes**	**Number of study programmes that mention critical thinking**	**College**	**University**		**Number of available programmes that mentioned critical thinking**
				Bachelor's	**Master's**	
Arts (P)	34	6	4	1	1	4
Sport (R)	5	3	0	3	0	0
Total:	754	266	50	116	100	125

In all of the fields of study analysed, the *Engineering Sciences* study field is a leader of sorts: almost half (n=25; i.e. 46.3 %) of the study programmes registered in this field of study have the concept of critical thinking in their descriptions (9 programmes at the bachelor's level [1 college + 8 university], and 16 at the master's level). A similar ratio of study programmes was found for *Life Sciences* (10 programmes out of 22; i.e. 45.5 %), with 6 programmes at the bachelor's level and 4 at the master's level; *Technological Sciences* (11 out of 25; i.e. 44 %), with 4 programmes at the bachelor's level and 7 at the master's level; *Social Sciences* (52 out of 127; i.e. 40.9 %), with 33 programmes at the bachelor's level (13 college + 20 university) and 19 at the master's level; *Health Sciences* (10 out of 26; i.e. 38.5 %), with 7 programmes at the bachelor's level (college) and 3 at the master's level; and *Business and Public Administration* (31 out of 82; i.e. 37.8 %), with 24 programmes at the bachelor's level (9 college + 15 university) and 7 at the master's level. In other fields of study, this ratio is much lower; of mention is *Mathematical Sciences*, where a large number of programmes are recorded (223 programs), but the number of programmes that mention the concept of critical thinking is particularly small (13 programmes; i.e. 5.8 %).

In the third stage, the aim was to investigate how the critical thinking mentioned in the study programme description is transferred to the course descriptions for the respective study programme, that is, how the continuity of the developed critical thinking competence is maintained. Open access study programmes prepared in accordance with ECTS requirements and representing different groups of study fields were selected for the analysis at this stage.

In the seven study programmes selected (master's: Law and Police Studies, Education Management, Ecology and Environmental Studies, Business and Economics, Geoinformatics; bachelor's: Primary School Education, Arts and Interior Design), 221 course descriptions were found; they were all analysed based on the form used for systematising in Stage 2 (study field group, study field code and name, programme name, level [college/university; bachelor's/master's], credit, form and duration, programme summary, aim and learning outcomes), supplementing it with new criteria: study methods, assessment methods, generic and subject-specific competences developed. The analysis revealed that the concept of critical thinking is found in the vast majority (199 of 221) of the course descriptions analysed:

- Law and Police Studies (master's studies) – 10 subjects where critical thinking was mentioned;
- Primary School Education (bachelor's studies) – 50 subjects where critical thinking was mentioned;
- Education Management (master's studies) – 17 subjects where critical thinking was mentioned;
- Ecology and Environmental Studies (master's studies) – 29 subjects where critical thinking was mentioned;

- Business and Economics (master's studies) – 15 subjects where critical thinking was mentioned;
- Arts and Interior Design (bachelor's studies) – 62 subjects where critical thinking was mentioned;
- Geoinformatics (master's studies) – 22 subjects where critical thinking was mentioned.

The content analysis of the course descriptions revealed that critical thinking is manifested in the programmes aims/learning outcomes through the generic and subject-specific competences singled out in the descriptions. In terms of generic competences, critical thinking was listed as an independent concept in five of the seven study programmes analysed. It is usually detailed as evaluation (*critically evaluate their own professional practice and that of others; critical evaluation of scientific knowledge and experience; critically evaluate; critically evaluate scientific information; critically evaluate information sources; critically evaluate and apply theoretical and practical innovations*). Critical thinking is also listed through skills such as argumentation, constructive criticism, self-criticism, reflection, generalisation and analysis. It is mentioned that the student must be proactive, fair, independent, self-critical, self-confident and an optimist.

In subject-specific competences, critical thinking is usually defined as the ability to analyse (*is able to critically and systematically analyse basic economic theories; systematically analyse and explain business economic theories; critically analyse information ... on a specific topic in the context of all possible sources of information; will have multidimensional environmental protection and environmental sciences data analysis skills*). Also mentioned is argumentation (*provide critical economic argumentation in the chosen topic; provide critical economic argumentation in solving economic problems*), generalisation, interpretation (*will be able to summarise and interpret information on a specific topic; will be able to critically interpret and present the results of the analysis correctly*) and evaluation (*critically evaluate and apply modern emerging technologies ... in the field of geoinformatics and geoinformation systems*). It is stated in the programmes that the student *will be able to formulate, in a clear and argued manner, both subject-specific and summary conclusions in resolving environmental management, marine area and the coastal zone ecological problems, and will be able to create ... an educational environment that promotes critical thinking and creativity.* Critical thinking was mentioned as a concept *per se* in one study programme: *will be able to demonstrate developed logical, creative and critical thinking, making it possible to understand the role, place and relationship of national and international law enforcement actions with the domestic law of states.*

The results of the third stage consistently led to the *fourth stage of the research* – qualitative content analysis, in order to explore the manifestation of the concept of critical thinking and the constituents of critical thinking in the study subjects of study programmes selected. Qualitative content analysis was used. The main aim was to understand what meaning is given to the concept of critical thinking, what the key elements of this concept are, and how they are reflected in the goals and outcomes of the study programme subjects.

2.2 Results of content analysis

It was revealed that the term 'critical' is used in most course descriptions as an abstract description of the intended outcome – the manifestation of a person's critical thinking, without specifying the individual constituents of critical thinking that explicate this conception. However, some course descriptions also identified the constituents of critical thinking that explain and develop the conception of critical thinking.

The qualitative content analysis revealed the following key constituents of critical thinking: critical analysis, critical evaluation and critical interpretation. They are singled out in the course descriptions in describing the learning outcomes, and in rare cases – in the learning aims of a specific subject.

Critical analysis skills are singled out as a constituent of critical thinking in learning outcomes, linking them to the specific context of the study subject or study programme. That is, the learning outcomes singled out in the course descriptions focus on what students should be able to critically analyse while studying the specific subject:

> *Will be able to ... critically analyse family conflicts ...* (Primary School Education).
> *... to critically analyse anaerobic environmental conditions ...* (Ecology and Environmental Studies).

Or they are focused on the ability to critically analyse certain information specific to a particular subject:

> *... information, and critically analyse it in resolving environmental management, marine area and coastal zone ecological problems* (Ecology and Environmental Studies).
> *...information related to the subject of biological oceanography, and critically analyse it in the context of all possible sources of information ...* (Ecology and Environmental Studies).

This suggests that in this case, critical analysis skills are manifested in learning outcomes as specific skills related to the specifics of the studied subject or programme.

The study also revealed that critical analysis skills are associated with the analysis of information/information sources or research data, without naming or specifying the topic:

> *... to critically analyse the research outcomes obtained in the context of all possible sources of information ...* (Ecology and Environmental Studies).

Hence, the ability to critically analyse is treated in these cases as independent of the subject taught and is considered a universal skill.

The ability to critically analyse is also expressed in course descriptions as a prerequisite for the ability to evaluate:

> ... *critically analyse and perform ... evaluation* ... (Ecology and Environmental Studies).

Critical analysis is also linked to reflexive analysis:

> *To perform a critical and reflective analysis of the result data* ... (Primary School Education).

Thus, in this wording of the learning outcome, the conception of critical thinking is treated as coherence between critical analysis and evaluation.

The ability to critically analyse is associated exclusively with the ability to collect data/information and link it to other data/sources:

> ... *to critically analyse it [information] in the context of all possible sources of information, and use legal and normative documents* ... (Ecology and Environmental Studies).
> ... *to independently, comprehensively and critically examine the chosen scientific or topical practical problem* ... (Law and Police Studies).

The essence of critical analysis skills in the wording of learning outcomes is also defined by linking it to evaluation and noting that the analysis must not only be substantiated and argued, but must also take into account various approaches/phenomena:

> *The student will be able to analyse and evaluate various intersections of art and technology and related phenomena and trends in a critical, constructive and argued manner* (Arts and Interior Design).

Other constituents of the critical analysis skills group, such as the ability to reveal connections between statements/facts/concepts or to find connections between the whole and its parts, are not identified in the course descriptions.

Analysis of the research data revealed that critical analysis skills are more highlighted from a personal aspect. Critical analysis is first and foremost treated as a benefit to the individual – students will learn/be able. The interpersonal aspect, which is understood as the 'I-you', 'I-other', 'we-you' relationship, was not observed in the manifestation of critical analysis skills in the study programme and course descriptions analysed. The social aspect is highlighted in a comprehensive context that goes beyond the professional field:

> ... *information, and critically analyse it in the context of all possible sources of information* ... (Ecology and Environmental Studies).

However, the significance of critical analysis for society or the wider professional community is not further developed.

It is important to note that the analysis of the data revealed another constituent of critical thinking – **critical reasoning**, which, without exception, is associated with the ability to analyse:

Will be able to analyse and critically reason ... (Education Management).
... *will be able to analytically and critically reason* ... (Education Management).

Critical reasoning skills are presented abstractly, as an intended learning outcome or part thereof:

... *analytically and critically reason* ... (Education Management).
To analytically, creatively and critically reason, and independently solve the problems of language teaching and learning (Education Management).

Or linked to the context of the specific study subject:

...*critically and analytically reason* ... *in resolving education management problems* (Education Management).
... *analytically and critically reason in assessing the social education resources in the community* (Education Management).

Strong links between critical and analytical reasoning emerged in the wording of learning outcomes. This testifies to the importance of developing analytical skills.

Critical evaluation skills are expressed less in the analysed programmes than critical analysis.

Like critical analysis, critical evaluation skills are linked in learning outcomes to the specific context of the study subject:

... *to critically and objectively evaluate the organisational, structural and functional system of police activities* (Law and Police Studies).
... *to critically evaluate the processes taking place in seas and oceans* ... (Geoinformatics).

Or it is presented abstractly:

... *to critically evaluate scientific information* ... (Ecology and Environmental Studies).
... *to develop students' analytical thinking and critical evaluation* ... (Ecology and Environmental Studies).
... *be able to independently expand and enrich empirical and theoretical knowledge by critically evaluating it* ... (Arts and Interior Design).

The ability to critically evaluate is situation-oriented:

... *to evaluate a person's behaviour and activities* (Law and Police Studies). And information/data-oriented:
.... *to critically evaluate and apply modern emerging technologies and new research outcomes and achievements* (Geoinformatics).

Meanwhile, the ability of self-evaluation is focused on the self-evaluation of personal skills:

... *critically self-evaluate their personal language skills* <...> (Primary School Education).
Critically evaluate their own professional practice and that of other restorers (Arts and Interior Design).

Analysis of the course descriptions revealed that the dominant skill in the critical evaluation skills group is to evaluate data/information taking various opinions/ situations into account:

> *... to critically evaluate family policy issues by analysing various situations in the family, the educational institution, the classroom, etc.* (Primary School Education).
> *To critically evaluates the theoretical provisions of various authors ... ...* (Business and Economics).

Critical evaluation skills are contextualised by linking them to evaluation without prejudice:

> *Will be able to critically and objectively evaluate a person's behaviour and activities* (Law and Police Studies).

Manifestation of the ability to evaluate a situation based on data or information was not found in the study programmes analysed.

Like critical analysis, critical evaluation is most highlighted from a personal aspect; however, evaluation, unlike analysis, is also highlighted from an interpersonal aspect. Students must be able to evaluate not only their own behaviour, but also that of others, and make a critical evaluation taking the opinions and views of others into account. The social aspect of critical evaluation is revealed as the ability to evaluate a broad professional field or system.

Critical interpretation as a constituent of critical thinking is considered to be a specific skill, which is expressed in the wording of learning outcomes in the context of the specific subject:

> *... carry out multidimensional analysis of environmental protection and environmental sciences data using modern software and methods, will be able to critically interpret ...* (Ecology and Environmental Studies).

Unambiguously, critical interpretation is associated only with the results of the analysis and the ability to present them properly:

> *... will be able to critically interpret and correctly present the results of the analysis* (Ecology and Environmental Studies).

Thus, it can be argued that two aspects of critical interpretation are emphasised in this context: understanding the content of the data and conveying the data in one's own words. Critical interpretation is highlighted from a personal and interpersonal aspect. The personal aspect manifests itself as an individual valuable skill to understand and interpret information for oneself, while the interpersonal aspect manifests itself as the conveyance of data and analysis to others.

The content analysis of the course descriptions revealed that critical thinking is stressed without detailing specific skills, but by emphasising their relationship with analytical, creative or reflective thinking.

The coherence of **critical and analytical** thinking is only highlighted in study programme course descriptions at the master's level and is presented abstractly:

> *Be able to analytically and critically think* … (Education Management).
> *Be able to think analytically and critically* … (Education Management).

The relationship between **critical and creative** thinking is linked to a person's professional development:

> … *to think critically and creatively in reflecting on their professional activities and designing professional development* (Primary School Education).

Or to the development of professional activities:

> … *to think critically and creatively in designing their professional career and planning educational activities and guidelines for their improvement* (Primary School Education).

The relationship between **critical and creative** thinking is also revealed as a precondition for decision-making in professional activities:

> *Be able to make strategic and tactical economic decisions by thinking critically and creatively* … (Business and Economics).

The content analysis of the course descriptions revealed that in designing learning outcomes, attention is given not only by abstractly listing critical thinking skills, but also by providing that this skill requires certain conditions. The teacher training study programme highlights the preparation of suitable subject material for the development of critical and creative thinking:

> *Will be able to prepare … teaching/learning material that promotes not only problem solving, but also critical thinking and creativity* … (Primary School Education).

A prerequisite for critical and creative thinking – a safe environment – is also programmed in the learning outcomes for the aforementioned study programme. The aim is for a graduate of the study programme to be able to create an environment that encourages critical and creative thinking:

> *Will be able to create a safe teaching/learning environment that promotes the pupil's creativity and emotional, social and critical thinking.* (Primary School Education).
> *Will be able to create … an educational environment that encourages critical thinking and creativity, taking into account the special and social needs of the pupils.* (Primary School Education).

The relationship between **critical and reflexive** thinking is revealed in the context of knowledge application:

> *Will be able to apply knowledge forming the basis for the development of critical and reflexive thinking*… (Primary School Education).
> … *to organise and lead the process of developing critical and educational reflexive thinking* … (Primary School Education).

The content analysis revealed that the **dispositions of critical thinking** are extremely weakly expressed in the course descriptions of the analysed study programmes. There is fragmented mention of the following dispositions: open-mindedness, flexibility, rightness, self-confidence, rightness.

Open-mindedness and flexibility are linked to critical evaluation in the context of the particular subject:

> *Will be able to openly, flexibly and critically evaluate family policy issues...* (Primary School Education).

Fairness and self-confidence are expressed abstractly:

> *Will be able to be proactive, fair, independent, self-critical, self-confident, an optimist, etc.* (Education Management).

Rightness, meanwhile, is highlighted in the context of the particular subject and linked to evaluation:

> *Will be able to fairly evaluate the meaning of values with respect to people of different cultures, social status, age and views* (Education Management).

Or correct knowledge application:

> *Understand the conception of business competitiveness, be able to use and analyse it correctly in the broader context of the subject, and interpret and integrate it with knowledge from other study subjects* (Business and Economics).

The listed dispositions are considered valuable for the individual him or herself, for interpersonal relationships, and for the broader social context.

A detailed comparison of the descriptions for the study programmes and their subject descriptions was not possible due to the fragmented nature of the research subject. The investigated descriptions and their content do not make it possible to judge the uniqueness of the programmes in the development of critical thinking skills and dispositions. In terms of the theoretical conceptualisation of critical thinking, the Arts and Interior Design bachelor's programme is unique. The description for 'Introduction to Contemporary Art and Theories' lists one of the learning outcomes as acquainting students with the most important ideas of contemporary art by revealing their relationships with contemporary philosophy and critical theories. Queer theory is specified in the description of another subject – 'Queer Images in Art and Pop Culture'. The names of Michel Foucault, Judith Butler, Adrienne Rich, Teresa de Lauretis and Elizabeth Grosz are mentioned in highlighting the importance of their texts for the critical analysis of works of art and phenomena of popular culture. It is expected that students will not only be able to define, interpret and explain the key ideas of queer studies, but will also be able to apply the methodological approaches of this theory in art and popular culture, and detect manifestations of this theory in different cultural and political contexts. In this particular case, it is possible to make assumptions about the conceptual relations between the subject studied and the development of critical thinking. No other analysed study programmes and/or course description even hints at a theory or methodology that would underpin the development of critical thinking and/or the teaching of the subject being studied.

3. Critical Thinking in Higher Education Curriculum: Between Ambition and Reality

Critical thinking is one of the most central concepts for teaching and learning in higher education, and it is difficult to imagine a Western institution of higher education not endorsing its importance. Critical thinking has to be a goal of education, integrating it on three interrelated levels: institutional, teaching programme/curriculum and course. In the broadest sense, the curriculum can also be understood as a political and social agreement that reflects a society's common vision while considering local, national and global needs and expectations. It is in and through the curriculum that key economic, political, social and cultural questions about the aims, purposes, content and processes of education are resolved. The policy statement and technical document that represent the curriculum reflect also a broader political and social agreement about what a society deems of most worth – that which is of sufficient importance to pass on to its learners (UNESCO International Bureau of Education, 2016).

Critical thinking is also highlighted in national documents. The National Progress Strategy 'Lithuania 2030' (2012) notes that critical thinking is one of the skills that is attributed to important national resources. This is based on the fact that Lithuania has made commitments to direct more attention to the quality of studies and development of the competencies needed for future jobs, and to adapt the higher education system to respond flexibly to changes in the labour market (National Programme for the Development of Studies, Scientific Research and Experimental [Social and Cultural] Development for 2013–2020, 2012).

The quantitative content analysis of the study programme descriptions revealed that the concept of critical thinking is mentioned in approximately one-third (266 out of 754) of the study programme descriptions. It can therefore be stated that critical thinking manifests itself in one-third of the Lithuanian higher education context. These findings should be interpreted ambiguously. On the one hand, with Lithuania's involvement in the Bologna Process from the very beginning, the 20-year period may have been enough to ensure the manifestation of critical thinking in Lithuanian higher education, as well as to respond to key European Commission education policy provisions (European Commission, 2012). The European Commission aims to equip all students with advanced transversal skills and key competences so that they can establish themselves in the labour market after graduation (European Commission, n.d.), and in this context, critical thinking is highlighted as one of the core competences (Council of the EU, 2018). On the other hand, research data show that in terms of the manifestation of critical thinking in Lithuanian higher education, it is given insufficient attention. It is also emphasised in the National Progress Strategy 'Lithuania 2030' (2012), which points out that the current education system gives insufficient attention to strengthening critical thinking skills.

Critical thinking is recognised as a complex phenomenon. 'The field of developing critical thinking is characterised by a lack of consensus on three major and closely interrelated issues: the meaning of critical thinking, the assessment of critical thinking, and the methods to foster its development. That absence of consensus reflects the multidimensionality, the complexity, the domain-specificity as well as the richness of critical thinking (Promoting Critical Thinking in European Higher Education Institutions: towards an educational protocol, 2019). Thus, in this context, the research outcomes suggest that the achievements of 20 years in Lithuanian higher education can be assessed positively.

In analysing the manifestation of critical thinking more specifically by study field group as a domain-specific phenomenon, the highest frequency of critical thinking concepts was found in Engineering Sciences (46.3 %), Life Sciences (45.5 %) and Technology Sciences (44.0 %). Based on the methodological provision of quantitative content analysis that the frequency of repetition of certain parts of the text reflecting a particular topic reflects the importance of that topic in the text (i.e. the more frequent a certain piece of text reflecting a particular topic occurs in the text, the more important that topic is), it can be argued that the frequency of repetition of the word combination 'critical thinking' in the study programmes of the aforementioned study field groups prioritises the manifestation of critical thinking in the aforementioned study fields.

Responding to the assumption made in the quantitative research that critical thinking is integrated into the study programme descriptions at Lithuanian higher education institutions, it can be argued that in terms of higher education policy, the manifestation of critical thinking could be greater, as only one-third of the study programmes had this feature. Lithuanian higher education is in the critical thinking integration process, which is more evident in Engineering, Life and Technology Sciences.

Quantitative analysis of the course descriptions revealed that the concept of critical thinking mentioned in the descriptions of the selected study programmes is expanded and detailed in almost all of the course descriptions, that is, in 199 out of 221. Critical thinking as a concept *per se* is more often mentioned in relation to generic competences than to subject-specific competences. Generic competencies stress the ability to evaluate, while subject-specific competences stress the ability to analyse. It should be noted that the evaluation and analysis skills listed in the course descriptions for different study programmes can be assigned to generic competences in some cases, and to subject-specific competences in others. This can be explained by the fact that the allocation of a skill to one or another group of competences depends on the specifics of the study programme.

The quantitative content analysis is deepened by qualitative findings. The qualitative content analysis revealed that in terms of generic competences, critical thinking was listed as a concept *per se*, and usually detailed as evaluation (e.g. *critically evaluate scientific information; critically evaluate and apply theoretical and practical innovations*). Critical thinking is also listed through skills such as argumentation, constructive criticism, self-criticism, reflection, generalisation and analysis.

In subject-specific competences, critical thinking is usually defined as the ability to analyse (e.g. *is able to critically and systematically analyse various theories and/or information sources*). Also mentioned is argumentation (e.g. *provide critical economic argumentation)*, generalisation, interpretation (e.g. *will be able to summarise and interpret information on a specific topic*) and evaluation (e.g. *critically evaluate and apply modern technologies)*.

The analysis showed that some course descriptions identify constituents of critical thinking that explain and develop the conception of critical thinking. However, in most course descriptions, the term 'critical' is used abstractly as a concept *per se*, in describing of the intended outcome – the manifestation of the person's critical thinking, without revealing or detailing the constituents of critical thinking that explicate this conception.

The qualitative content analysis revealed the following key constituents of critical thinking: critical analysis, critical evaluation and critical interpretation. They are singled out in the course descriptions in describing the learning outcomes, and in rare cases – in the learning aims of a specific subject.

The content analysis of the course descriptions revealed that critical thinking is stressed without detailing specific skills, but by emphasising their relationship with analytical, creative or reflective thinking.

The research has revealed that the individual dimension is dominant in study programmes. In the majority of cases, critical thinking is treated as a cognitive skill related to the development of students' reasoning skills for personal purposes – better learning results and intellectual growth. In rare cases, evidence of a social dimension was also found. However, this was limited to interpersonal relationships. Other people are important for listening to reasoned arguments, understanding how and why a certain decision is made, finding agreement in solving problems, and responding to the challenges of a specific study field. The importance of others also manifests itself through empathetic relationships: openness to different opinions, cultures or/and contexts. Nothing was found about social dimensions in terms of questioning authorities, raising social problems, fighting for rightness, or contributing to the welfare of society. Therefore, Davies' (2015) question – 'Can we say then, that critical thinking is a social aspiration as well, i.e., that it has a social dimension?' (p. 44) – remains unanswered.

Conclusions

The quantitative content analysis of the study programme descriptions revealed that the concept of critical thinking is mentioned in approximately one-third of the study programme descriptions. The highest frequency of the critical thinking concept was found in the Engineering Sciences, Life Sciences and Technology Sciences study field groups.

The concept of critical thinking mentioned in the descriptions of the selected study programmes is expanded and detailed in almost all of the course descriptions. Critical thinking as a concept per se is more often mentioned in relation to generic competences than to subject-specific competences. Generic competencies stress the ability to evaluate, while subject-specific competences stress the ability to analyse.

Both the quantitative and qualitative analyses of the course descriptions revealed that critical thinking tends to be conceptualised as a skill, without specifying its nature – personal, professional (special), general or other. In most cases, critical thinking is highlighted as a significant personal skill in a particular professional field. It is also seen as a generic competence that unfolds in the broader – social – context. The significance of critical thinking for interpersonal relationships is poorly reflected.

The revealed constituents of critical thinking are related to the context of the specific subjects or presented abstractly. Critical thinking is most commonly associated with creative, analytical and reflexive thinking.

References

AIKOS. (n.d.). Retrieved from https://www.aikos.smm.lt/en/Pages/About-AIKOS.aspx

Approval of the List of Study Fields and Groups of Fields. (2016). Retrieved from https://www.e-tar.lt/portal/lt/legalAct/ae5d5730b7c211e693eea1ef35f20da9/asr.

Bitinas, B., Rupšienė, L. & Žydžiūnaitė, V. (2008). *Kokybinių tyrimų metodologija.* Klaipėda: S. Jokužio leidykla.

Cohen, L., Manion, L. & Morrison, K. (2013). *Research methods in education.* London: Routledge. doi:10.4324/9780203720967.

Council of the European Union. 2018. Council Recommendation on Key Competences for Lifelong Learning. Retrieved from https://eur-lex.europa.eu/legal-content/EN/TXT/PDF/?uri=CONSIL:ST_9009_2018_INIT&from=EN.

Creswell, J. W. (2014). *A concise introduction to mixed methods research.* Thousand Oaks: Sage Publications.

Creswell, J. W. & Creswell, J. D. (2018). *Research design: Qualitative, quantitative, and mixed methods approaches,* 5th ed. Los Angeles: Sage Publications.

Creswell, J. W. & Poth, C. N. (2017). *Qualitative inquiry and research design choosing among five approaches,* 4th ed. Thousand Oaks, CA: Sage Publications.

Davies, M. (2015). A model of critical thinking in higher education. In: Paulsen, M. B. (Ed.), *Higher Education: Handbook of Theory and Research,* pp. 41–88. doi: 10.1007/978-3-319-12835-1_2.

Educational and scientific institutions by group, type and affiliation. (n.d.). Retrieved from https://www.aikos.smm.lt/Puslapiai/Ataskaitos.aspx.

Erikson, M. G. (2019). *Supporting critical thinking in higher education – considerations for strategic discussions.* Learning & Teaching Forum paper. Retrieved from https://eua.eu/downloads/content/2019.29_erikson.pdf

European Commission. (2012). *The European Higher Education Area. Bologna process implementation report.* Retrieved from http://www.ehea.info/media.ehea.info/file/2012_Bucharest/79/5/Bologna_Process_Implementation_Report_607795.pdf.

European Commission. (n.d.). Relevant and high-quality higher education. Retrieved from: https://ec.europa.eu/education/policies/higher-education/relevant-and-high-quality-higher-education_en.

Hammersley, M. (1996). The relationship between qualitative and quantitative research: Paradigm loyalty versus methodological eclecticism. In: Richardson, J. T. E. (d.), *Handbook of research methods for psychology and the social sciences.* Leicester, UK: BPS Books. 159–174.

Hayashi, P., Abib, G. & Hoppen, N. (2019). Validity in qualitative research: A processual approach. *The Qualitative Report.* doi:10.46743/2160-3715/2019.3443.

Hennink, M., Hutter, I. & Bailey, A. (2020). *Qualitative research methods.* London: Sage.

Higher education system. (n.d.). Retrieved from https://www.smm.lt/web/lt/smm-studijos/aukstojo-mokslo-sistema.

Law on Higher Education and Research of the Republic of Lithuania. (2009). Retrieved from https://e-seimas.lrs.lt/portal/legalAct/lt/TAD/548a2a30ead611e59b76f36d7fa634f8?jfwid=i3h7wcuc6.

Mačerinskienė, I. & Kučaidze, N. (2019). *The evaluation of the impact of higher education funding models on access to higher education in European Union member states: methodological approach Adam P. Balcerzak & Ilona Pietryka (Eds.), Proceedings of the 10th International Conference on Applied Economics Contemporary Issues in Economy*: Economics Olsztyn: Institute of Economic Research, 244–252.

Maxwell, J. (1992). Understanding and validity in qualitative research. *Harvard Educational Review, 62*(3), 279–301. doi:10.17763/haer.62.3.8323320856251826.

Maxwell, J. (2008). Designing a qualitative study, 2nd ed. *The SAGE Handbook of Applied Social Research Methods,* 214–253. Los Angeles; London: Sage.

McCulloch, G. (2004). *Documentary research in education, history, and the social sciences.* Psychology Press. London: Routledge.

Miles, M. B. & Huberman, A. M. (1994). *Qualitative data analysis.* Thousand Oaks, CA: Sage.

Mudde, C. & Schedler, A. (2010). Introduction: Rational data choice. *Political Research Quarterly, 63*(2), 410–416. doi: 10.1177/1065912910371286.

National Programme for the Development of Studies, Scientific Research and Experimental (Social and Cultural) Development for 2013–2020. (2012). Retrieved from https://e-seimas.lrs.lt/portal/legalAct/lt/TAD/TAIS.439448.

Neuendorf, K. A. (2017). *The content analysis guidebook*. Los Angeles: Sage Publications. doi: 10.4135/9781071802878.

Patton, M. Q. (2014). *Qualitative research & evaluation methods: Integrating theory and practice*. Sage Publications.

Promoting Critical Thinking in European Higher Education Institutions: Towards an educational protocol (2019). Eds. Dominguez, C. & R. Payan-Carreira. Universidade de Trás-os-Montes e Alto Douro.

Republic of Lithuania Law on Higher Education. (2000). https://e-seimas.lrs.lt/portal/legalAct/lt/TAD/TAIS.97866.

Silverman, D., ed. (2020). *Qualitative research*. Sage Publications.

Teddlie, C. & Tashakkori, A. (2009). *Foundations of mixed methods research. Integrating quantitative and qualitative approaches in the social and behavioral sciences*. Los Angeles: Sage Publications.

The Description of General Requirements for Master's Study Programmes (2010). Retrieved from https://e-seimas.lrs.lt/portal/legalAct/lt/TAD/TAIS.374821.

The General Requirements for Study Implementation. (2016). Retrieved from https://www.e-tar.lt/portal/lt/legalAct/739065a0ce9911e69e09f35d37acd719.

The National Progress Strategy "Lithuania 2030". (2012). Retrieved from http://www.unesco.org/education/edurights/media/docs/2953897c103c13043bfabea84b716ae2f8c82f47.pdf.

UNESCO International Bureau of Education (2016). *What makes a quality curriculum? In-Progress Reflection No. 2 on Current and Critical Issues in Curriculum and Learning*. 41.

Critical Thinking in Study Process and Labour Market: Phenomenographic Study

Abstract: In many countries, higher education has similar goals – contributing to personal development and preparing students for the labour market and for life as active citizens in democratic societies. Critical thinking is a competence that is considered equally important for both personal growth and professional and social life. This is recognised not only by academia, but also by the world of labour.

The purpose of this chapter is to reveal how teachers, students, employers and employees understand critical thinking, and how critical thinking manifests itself in the specific context of studies and the labour market. This chapter consists of three sections. The first section discusses the research methodology of phenomenography. The choice of the phenomenographic research method, the characteristics of the research participants, the research performance and data analysis processes, and research ethics and validity are discussed in detail. The second section presents an analysis of the manifestation of critical thinking in the higher education study process. The understanding of critical thinking and teaching and learning experiences of higher education participants – teachers and students – are discussed. The third section presents the manifestation of critical thinking in the labour market. The understanding of critical thinking and the experience of critical thinking in real professional practice of the participants of the labour market process – employers and employees – are revealed.

Keywords: manifestation of critical thinking, understanding of critical thinking, experience of critical thinking, phenomenographic research.

1. Research Methodology

1.1 Research design

Phenomenography was chosen as the main methodological approach to research aspects of the concept of critical thinking among representatives of higher education institution and the labour market and its components. Phenomenography is based on the assumption that the world is perceived and experienced in a variety of ways. In order to reveal the diversity of experiences and conceptions, the researcher uses the so-called 'second-order' perspective (Marton, 1981), which makes it possible to look at the phenomenon under study 'from the inside', through the eyes of the person who experienced it. Researchers do not question why phenomena are understood in one way or another. They ask how they are understood and experienced, what they are, and what content and meaning are given to them.

As a method for qualitative research, phenomenography was developed by Swedish educational researchers in the 1960s. Its pioneer is considered to be Ference Marton, who applied this method to explore attitudes towards learning (Marton and Saljo, 1976; Dahlgren and Marton, 1978; Francis, 1993; Entwistle, 1997). It should be noted that phenomenography is widely used in Health Sciences (Lepp and Ringsberg, 2011), IT (Hsieh and Tsai, 2017; Khan and Markauskaitė, 2017), Environmental Protection (Teeter and Sandberg, 2016), Engineering (Gibbings, Lidstone and Bruce, 2015), and many other fields of science (Tight, 2016). In Education Sciences, phenomenography has begun to be used to explore attitudes towards learning (Marton and Saljo, 1976; Dahlgren and Marton, 1978; Francis, 1993; Entwistle, 1997).

Phenomenography is a research method to study peoples' perceptions and conceptions of a given phenomenon in the surrounding world (Dall'Alba, 2000; Limberg, 2008; Marton and Booth, 2007). It aims to reveal different ways of understanding, describe variations of conceptions, and discover interconnections between them. That is, phenomenography research is characterised by an interpretive paradigm, based on which the reality that comes from the data can be interpreted in a variety of ways.

> *Differences in conceptions are explained by the fact that different people have different experiences because of their different relations to the world.* (Lepp and Ringsberg, 2011, p. 109)

According to researchers, even the same phenomena or aspects thereof can be understood differently, leading to different conceptions of the same phenomenon (Han and Ellis, 2019). Those differences constitute peoples' knowledge, understanding and models of behaviour in various life situations. To be aware of those differences means to be aware of ourselves and reality (Barnard McCosker and Gerber, 1999). Differences of conceptions are called 'categories' (Marton, 1994).

The phenomenographic research method was chosen because of its suitability for revealing the research subject and the main research questions formulated. The study aimed to answer two research questions: (1) What do the research participants consider to be critical thinking?; (2) How does critical thinking manifest itself in the specific context of studies and work? The first research question is intended to reveal the subjective conceptions of the concept of critical thinking among higher education teachers and students, as well as employees and employers. The second question is designed to learn about the manifestation of critical thinking in the study process and in daily professional activities through the experiences of the research participants. The research is focused on the search for qualitatively different ways of understanding the concept of critical thinking in the broad contexts of higher education and the labour market. For this purpose, the research data are analysed and grouped into appropriate categories, the key generalisations are presented, and the outcome space is described, revealing the overall picture of the phenomenon under study. The outcome space reflects both the phenomenon and the ways in which it is experienced.

The phenomenographic research method was also chosen for a clear scientific interest/goal – finding differences in attitudes towards critical thinking, and investigating the conception of the same phenomenon in different study groups and finding its variations. It should be noted here that it is precisely the use of phenomenography that makes it possible to reveal the full variety of conceptions with its different variations. On the other hand, this research method was chosen due to its innovativeness in research conducted in Lithuania. In the national context, phenomenography is used in the preparation of doctoral dissertations related to the development of entrepreneurial competences (Bortkevičienė, 2015) and dignity of the disabled (Ruškė, 2014), as well as in researching the development of professional competences (Sabaliauskas, Poteliūnienė, Česnavičienė and Juškevičienė, 2018). Nevertheless, renewed interest in the phenomenographic research method is being observed worldwide. It is used fairly broadly in various fields of higher education (Blimling, 2013; Bresciani, 2013; 2015; Rands and Gansemer-Topf, 2016; Khan and Markauskaitė, 2017; Vermunt and Donche, 2017; Zou et al., 2019; Baysen and Baysen, 2020). A no less significant factor in the choice of this method is the possibility to learn from students of Ference Marton (Dahlberg and Lepp), the pioneer of phenomenography.

1.2 Participants

Targeted selection of participants was used for the phenomenography research, as this is the main selection method in the application of the phenomenographic research method (Han and Ellis, 2019). Therefore, those representing higher education and the labour market were invited to participate in the study, that is:

- university teachers;
- students;
- employers;
- employees.

The research participants were selected using the purposeful sampling technique. The specific selection criteria are provided in the description of each group of research participants.

The phenomenographic approach does not require large numbers of research participants. Having from 10 to 20 research participants is recommended so that the data can be managed while also providing enough variations of experiences (Trigwell, 2000; Larson and Holmstrom, 2007).

A total of 79 interviewees participated in the phenomenographic study, of which 18 were teachers, 16 were students, 28 were employers and 17 were employees. Before beginning the study, interviews were planned with 20 research participants from each target group. The collection of empirical data was suspended due to the saturation of qualitative data for teachers, students and employees, and was extended in the case of employers due to insufficient data saturation.

1.2.1 University teachers

When inviting university teachers to participate in the study, the aim was to ensure that the sample of teachers was in line with the principle of heterogeneity in terms of gender, subject, study area and institution represented. The study involved teachers who had at least five years of teaching experience in higher education and who held different positions, with a total of ten male teachers and seven female teachers from eight institutions of higher education. The research participants ranged from 40 to 60 years of age. Their teaching experience in higher education ranged from 10 to 28 years. There were three research participants each from the fields of Medicine, Arts, Engineering and Humanities, and five from Social Sciences. These teachers teach study subjects in their area. Two research participants were lecturers at the time of the study, ten were associate professors, and five were professors. The main characteristics of the university teacher research participants are presented in Table 8.

Tab. 8: *Social and demographic characteristics of the university teachers*

Code	Study field	University	Position	Sex	Age
C1	Arts	University 1	Assoc. prof.	Female	52
C2	Humanities	University 2	Lecturer	Male	42
C3	Social Sciences	University 3	Assoc. prof.	Male	42
C4	Engineering	University 4	Prof.	Male	60
C5	Medicine	University 5	Assoc. prof.	Female	53
C6	Engineering	University 6	Assoc. prof.	Male	42
C7	Engineering	University 4	Prof.	Male	60
C8	Arts	University 8	Prof.	Female	55
C9	Arts	University 8	Lecturer	Male	44
C10	Social Sciences	University 4	Assoc. prof.	Male	52
C11	Social Sciences	University 7	Assoc. prof.	Male	43
C12	Medicine	University 6	Assoc. prof.	Female	52
C13	Medicine	University 5	Prof.	Male	45
C14	Humanities	University 6	Assoc. prof.	Male	44
C15	Social Sciences	University 3	Assoc. prof.	Female	41
C16	Humanities	University 6	Assoc. prof.	Female	40
C17	Social Sciences	University 3	Prof.	Female	53

None of the research participants have taught critical thinking as a separate subject. Critical thinking is considered to be an integral part of their professional practice.

1.2.2 Students

When inviting students to participate in the study, the aim was to ensure that the sample of students was in line with the principle of heterogeneity in terms of gender, age, university, field of study and years of study. The study involved eight male students and eight female students aged 19–49 from six Lithuanian higher education institutions.

The sample consisted of students from eight study areas: Arts, Health Sciences, Social Sciences, Humanities, Informatics Science, Mathematical Sciences, Technological Sciences and Physical Sciences. In terms of the study areas, there were three research participants each from the fields of Physical Sciences, Engineering Sciences and Social Sciences. There were two research participants each from the fields of Health Sciences and Informatics Science. There was one research participant each from the fields of Arts, Humanities and Mathematical Sciences. The research participants were in different cycles of study and different years of study. In terms of study cycle, 12 research participants were bachelor's students (three first-year, four second-year, three third-year and two fourth-year), three were master's students (two first-year, one second-year), and one was a second-year doctoral student. The main characteristics of the student research participants are presented in Table 9.

Tab. 9: *Social and demographic characteristics of the students*

Code	Study field	University	Study level	Year	Sex	Age
D1	Physical Sciences	University 6	BA	3	Male	26
D2	Engineering Sciences	University 4	BA	2	Male	21
D3	Health Sciences	University 6	BA	3	Female	22
D4	Humanities	University 6	BA	1	Male	
D5	Informatics Science	University 6	BA	1	Male	19
D6	Engineering Sciences	University 4	BA	3	Male	24
D7	Mathematical Sciences	University 6	MA	1	Female	24
D8	Physical Sciences	University 6	BA	2	Male	21
D9	Physical Sciences	University 6	BA	2	Male	21
D10	Social Sciences	University 3	BA	4	Female	49
D11	Health Sciences	University 6	MA	1	Female	24
D12	Engineering Sciences	University 4	BA	4	Male	23
D13	Informatics Science	University 2	BA	1	Female	20
D14	Social Sciences	University 6	MA	2	Female	41
D15	Social Sciences	University 8	BA	2	Female	22
D16	Arts	University 1	PhD	2	Female	32

1.2.3 Employers

When inviting employers to participate in the study, the aim was to ensure that the sample of employers was in line with the principle of heterogeneity in terms of gender, age, area of activity, management experience and sector. The study included 11 women and 17 men aged 32–60. In terms of the type of organisation, there were managers from 15 public institutions, 11 private organisations, and 2 non-governmental organisations. In terms of the type of economic activity, there were managers from six social services, five educational enterprises, three information technology enterprises, two public health enterprises, two pharmacies, two construction enterprises, two ecology enterprises, two commerce enterprises, one real estate enterprise, one transport and logistics enterprise, one accounting firm, and one insurance enterprise. Their managerial experience ranged from 5 to 30 years. The main characteristics of the employer research participants are presented in Table 10.

Tab. 10: *Social and demographic characteristics of the employers*

Research participant ID	Economic activity	Sector	Managerial experience	Sex	Age
A1	Social services	Non-governmental	20	Male	46
A2	Education	Public	15	Male	49
A3	Commerce	Private	12	Female	48
A4	Pharmacy	Private	20	Male	50
A5	Ecology	Public	30	Male	60
A6	Public health	Public	30	Male	60
A7	Construction	Public	12	Male	50
A8	Insurance	Private	25	Male	57
A9	Education	Public	20	Female	56
A10	Social services	Public	15	Male	41
A11	Information technology	Public	19	Male	41
A12	Pharmacy	Private	15	Male	50
A13	Social services	Public	3	Female	32
A14	Information technology	Public	10	Female	55

Tab. 10: *Continued*

Research participant ID	Economic activity	Sector	Managerial experience	Sex	Age
A15	Commerce	Private	23	Male	41
A16	Real estate	Private	15	Male	43
A17	Education	Public	10	Female	51
A18	Social services	Public	10	Female	54
A19	Transport and logistics	Private	14	Male	45
A20	Construction	Private	22	Male	53
A21	Social services	Public	12	Female	54
A22	Education	Public	2	Female	45
A23	Education	Non-governmental	6	Female	35
A24	Social services	Public	15	Female	56
A25	Accounting	Private	9	Male	40
A26	Public health	Public	10	Female	47
A27	Information technology	Private	9	Male	42
A28	Ecology	Public	15	Male	48

1.2.4 Employees

When inviting employees to participate in the study, the aim was to ensure that the sample of employees was in line with the principle of heterogeneity in terms of gender, age, professional experience, economic activity and sector of activity. Eight women and nine men participated in the study. The interviewees were between 26 and 56 years old, with professional experience ranging from 3 to 37 years. In terms of the area of economic activity in which they operate, the research participants were distributed as follows: three in medicine, two each in education and music, and one each in ecology, commerce, public health, military, advertising, information technology, construction, law, public management and publishing. In terms of the sector, 12 participants were working in public sector organisations and 5 were in private organisations. The main characteristics of the employee research participants are presented in Table 11.

Tab. 11: *Social and demographic characteristics of the employees*

Code	Economic activity	Sector	Job experience	Sex	Age
B1	Education	Public	37	Female	56
B2	Ecology	Public	20	Male	49
B3	Public management	Public	12	Male	36
B4	Commerce	Private	15	Male	35
B5	Medicine	Public	19	Male	44
B6	Medicine	Public	27	Female	53
B7	Public health	Public	17	Female	49
B8	Education	Public	31	Female	52
B9	Military	Public	17	Male	45
B10	Advertising	Private	3	Male	26
B11	Information technology	Private	3	Female	26
B12	Construction	Public	30	Male	52
B13	Music	Public	24	Male	44
B14	Publishing	Private	6	Female	45
B15	Music	Public	13	Male	44
B16	Medicine	Private	20	Female	46
B17	Law	Public	25	Female	48

1.3 Data collection

Application of the phenomenographic research approach is associated with a variety of data collection methods: observation, open-ended questions, thinking aloud, semi-structured interviews (Han and Ellis, 2019), as well as diaries, drawings and videos (Lepp and Ringsberg, 2011). The semi-structured interview method was chosen to find answers to the research questions. Semi-structured interviews ensure the clearness of purpose of the research, and provide flexibility to present the main and follow-up questions to the research participants and respond to the course of the actual interview. It should be noted that in order to ensure the reliability and validity of the data, the follow-up questions asked by the researchers during the interviews were permitted from prompting answers, suggesting ideas, offering opinions, and so on. Following the phenomenographic research method, the research instrument was prepared: a semi-structured open-ended questionnaire for each group of research participants: higher education teachers, students, employers and employees. A very important feature of phenomenography is that the focus is not on the phenomenon as such, but on the relationship between the research participant and the phenomenon of interest. For example, when using phenomenography, the question 'What is critical thinking?' is inappropriate because it is a question about the phenomenon of critical thinking as such, but not about the experience of the research participant. Therefore, when using a phenomenographic research approach, the questions must be 'phenomenographic' – worded with the utmost care, so that the research participants have the opportunity to share their experiences, for example, '*How do you understand critical thinking?*', '*How do you understand that you are thinking critically?*'. The interview started with an open-ended question: 'What does critical thinking mean to you?' During the interviews, this question was reworded and various questions were used depending on the specific situation, for example, '*What do you think critical thinking is about?*', '*What meaning do you attach to critical thinking?*', '*What is critical thinking to you?*' These variants emerged naturally in talking about the critical thinking experiences of the interviewees. Open-ended questions are directed at the unique experiences of the subjects born in different contexts and do not allow the research participants to present a uniform, scientifically correct concept of critical thinking. It was the personal position of the interviewees on this issue that was important – how each person perceives, understands and interprets it. Additional questions were asked for clarification or illustration of thoughts: '*Are you saying that …?*', '*Does this mean that …?*', '*Could you give an example?*'

In response to the principles of constructing phenomenographic research questions, the teachers were asked during the interview to tell about how they teach critical thinking, and what this process looks like in the study process. They were also asked to share their experiences of how they personally learn and/or improve critical thinking skills. The students were asked to tell about how they are taught critical thinking. From a methodological point of view, it is important to note that during the analysis and presentation of the data, this question was reworded from '*How is it taught?*' to '*How is it learned?*' This was done in response to the authentic narrative style and content, as students positioned their experiences from a personal 'I' perspective. Therefore, in order to maintain and ensure the validity of the data collected and reflect their meaning as accurately as possible, students' experiences are presented from the '*How is it learned?*' position.

The main interview question for employers and employees was: '*How important is critical thinking in your professional activities and how does it manifest itself?*' The interview questions are presented in Table 12.

Tab. 12: *Interview questions*

Interview Questions for Teachers
Introductory question: The development of critical thinking is an important part of higher education and studies. Critical thinking is also mentioned in the programme/subject you teach. We would be interested in knowing how you teach critical thinking. Tell us *what it looks like in your lectures?*
• What do you anticipate? What expectations do you have for the development of critical thinking? • How are you faring with meeting those expectations? • How do you understand/sense that students have improved their critical thinking skills? • What is the most striking example of your expectations and efforts? • How do you improve your own critical thinking skills?
Interview Questions for Students
Introductory question: The development of critical thinking is an important part of higher education and studies. Critical thinking is also mentioned in the programme/subject you are studying. We would be interested in knowing how you are taught critical thinking. Tell us, *what does it look like?*
• How do you understand that you are being taught to think critically? • How do you learn/sense that you have learned/improved your critical thinking skills? • What is the most memorable/vivid example of critical thinking learning? • Why is critical thinking important to you?
Interview Questions for Employers
Introductory question: The World Economic Forum has identified the ability to think critically as one of the most important employee skills. *How is this ability important to you in your professional area?*
• How do you understand that your employees think critically? • What is your most memorable/vivid example of critical thinking? Why? • How do you personally promote critical thinking among your employees? • How do you use critical thinking skills in your own work?
Interview Questions for Employees
Introductory question: The World Economic Forum has identified the ability to think critically as one of the most important employee skills. *How is this ability important to you in your profession/job?*
• What critical thinking skills are best/most evident in your work? • How are you faring in applying them? Provide specific examples. • How do you understand that you are applying critical thinking skills? Provide specific examples. • How are you encouraged to use critical thinking in your work?

The interviews took place in a comfortable and friendly environment (outside the interviewee's place of work/study), where the research participant could freely express his or her independent opinion. The interview lasted from 15 to 47 minutes. Interviews were recorded on audio recording media (including voice recorders on mobile phones) and transcribed. Each research participant was assigned a code in the interview transcription according to the research participant group that he or she belonged to (e.g. employers A1, A2 ...; employees B1, B2 ...; teachers C1, C2 ...; students D1, D2 ...).

It is important to note that due to the specifics of the interview questions – namely, the need to reflect, think over and remember one's experiences on the research topic – it became clear during the first interviews that it was much more productive to present the interview questions to the participants in advance. The study participants were, therefore, familiarised with the interview questions before the interview.

1.4 Data analysis

Considerable time is required to collect, analyse and look into phenomenographic research data. Initial analysis of the data is only performed after repeatedly reading the texts in an effort to understand their content. Categorising meanings cannot be rushed. The meaning of a phenomenon is revealed not from one, but from the source of all data. Variations in the perception and experience of a phenomenon are listed as categories that describe different aspects of the same phenomenon under study. More frequently recurring categories of meanings are considered to be dominant, while less frequently recurring categories are considered to be non-dominant. The relationships between the categories are then revealed and described. They can be listed differently, but, in any case, reveal the connecting referential and structural aspects (Marton and Pong, 2005). Finally, a summary picture of the phenomenon under study is presented, reflecting the diversity of its meanings in a hierarchical structure (Marton and Booth, 1997).

There are no clearly defined methodological analysis algorithms that are uniform for all (Yates, Partridge and Bruce, 2012). Researchers are free to choose how many research stages they will have and how they will be named, what they will call the singled-out categories of meanings, and how they will illustrate the research outcomes. Some single out more detailed stages and choose metaphoric category names (Larson and Holstrom, 2007), while others tend to amalgamate the stages and use simple, abstracted category names (Stamouli and Huggard, 2007). The interrelationships of the categories and the general outcome space of the phenomenon are depicted by using various diagrams and figures and by selecting the display logic – based on hierarchical relations and reflecting the history of experiences or the process of their acquisition (Laurillard, 1993).

The stages of the data analysis process were close to the research stages specified by Larson and Holmström (2007). Only in this case, category names generalising the experience were chosen in lieu of metaphoric category names. The results of the analysis are reflected in the descriptions of the categories and the dimensions assigned to the categories, as well as in the displayed general outcome space. Hence, analysis of the research data took place in the following stages:

- Repeated reading of the text.
- Marking the text where the interviewee gave answers to the interview questions.
- Preparation of initial descriptions.
- Grouping the data into categories, based on similarities and differences.
- Description of categories.
- Distinction between dominant and non-dominant categories.
- Assigning categories to dimensions/highlighting dimensions in relation to the categories.
- Creating a structural picture of the manifestation of the phenomenon in the outcome space.

Data analysis started right after all of the data had been collected and transcribed. This method was selected for a few reasons. First, the idea was to become familiar with all of the ideas and compare different perceptions. This was only possible with all of the data at hand. Second, the large team of researchers was able to share the workload. Eight authors worked in two groups of four researchers each. Each group had a lead researcher who was more knowledgeable in phenomenography and/or had practical experience. Each group member had to: (1) read to the entire transcribed text several times to get an overall impression; (2) read the text again and mark answers to the interview question. After these two steps were completed, the groups gathered to discuss individual findings and verify the preliminary results of the analysis. These discussions were valuable for getting an in-depth understanding of the phenomenon under investigation – they made it possible to argue, reason and go back to the transcribed text (or in some cases – audio material) to check the meaning. All of the group members had to reach an agreement on the answer to the research question. Where the group members were in disagreement, a more qualified opinion was sought by contacting knowledgeable experts outside of the team. The work was then continued by: (3) noting the similarities and differences of the experiences in interview texts; (4) deciding on descriptive categories of the conceptions; (5) determining the interrelations between the categories of conceptions. The groups then gathered again to discuss individual findings, which were checked, approved or corrected within the group. One member of the group was in charge of preparing the final version of the categories with illustrations of their meanings. The final stage of analysis included: (6) looking for and describing non-dominant ways of understanding; (7) assigning a name to each category of description; (8) finding structure in the outcome space.

The two groups of researchers had regular weekly meetings to discuss the results of the analysis process and consult with each other. All of the final decisions (on descriptive categories, dimensions of variations and the structure of the outcome space) were made by all of the researchers collectively. In this way, the validity of the research was ensured.

1.5. Research ethics

Ethical researcher behaviour is an important indicator of research quality (Sin, 2010). Participation in the study was voluntary. The research participants were introduced to the research project and its objectives were explained how the data collected during the interviews will be used, and were guaranteed confidentiality. The research participants were also informed that they could, at any time, terminate their participation in the study or refrain from answering any question. The principles of research ethics were also followed in the processing of the research data. Data related to individual research participants are described in detail, but personal information that could be used to identify the research participants has been eliminated. The transcripts of the interviews were member-checked with the interview participants, and, as recommended in methodological literature for social research (Merriam, 2002; Karnieli-Miller, Vu, Holtman, Clyman and Inui, 2010), consents were obtained to cite their interview in presenting the research data. The research information obtained is protected and only accessible to the researchers.

1.6 Validity and limitations of the study

In phenomenography, just as in all qualitative research, objectivity and validity are essential features of scientific rigorousness which are manifested in the researcher's bridling and openness to the phenomenon being studied, careful data analysis avoiding hasty and unfounded generalisations, and the researcher's reflexivity throughout the research process, as well as the recognition of objective reality in subjectively experienced experiences (Penkauskienė, 2019). Researchers often use so-called 'trustees' in the research process in order to achieve the highest possible quality and reliability of analysis. These can be members of the research team or more experienced colleagues or experts. The ideal situation is for several researchers to work in a team and devote sufficient time to discussions in the process of data analysis and interpretation. Joint consultations help to avoid unilateral opinions and erroneous conclusions, and contribute to ensuring validity, which is called a 'communicative validity check' in literature (Kvale, 1994; Akerlind, 2005). Another type of validity is singled out in phenomenographic literature: pragmatic validity check (Mann, Dall'Alba and Radcliffe, 2007). This signifies the importance and applicability of the research outcomes in practice. In discussing the problem of validity in phenomenographic research, Cope (2004) emphasises the need to devote more space to the description of the entire research process. It must reflect the researcher's experience and relationship with the research phenomenon, the selection criteria for subjects, the principles of compiling the interview questionnaire, ways to avoid preconceptions, assurance of openness to research data, the data analysis methods, completeness of the data description, and the form in which the outcomes are presented and their clarity.

In this study, the main ways by which validity was ensured were: (a) openness to the phenomenon being studied – the study field was entered without a specific definition of the research phenomenon so as not to thrust it on the research participants; (b) open-ended interview questions that encourage subjective experience and understanding of the phenomenon; (c) teamwork in collecting, analysing and interpreting the research data, allocating sufficient time for discussion; (d) consultation with experienced external experts on research methodology; (e) a detailed description of the data, revealing variations in the conceptions and experiences of the research phenomenon; (f) a consolidated, generalised presentation of the outcome space. The qualitative research data also served to form a quantitative research instrument. It can, therefore, be argued that both communicative validity and pragmatic validity were ensured.

One of the limitations of the study was the time constraint. There is usually a time limit for conducting a study, and phenomenographic qualitative research is very time-consuming. Another limitation was the large volume of data collected that was a challenge to manage, that is, analyse and interpret.

Despite these potential limitations, phenomenography was an appropriate tool for investigating the conceptual understanding of critical thinking in higher education and the labour market. By using the right techniques and allocating enough time, the above-mentioned limitations were managed.

2. Manifestation of Critical Thinking in the Study Process: How Critical Thinking Is Understood

One of the aims of the phenomenographic research was to find out how participants in higher education studies – teachers and students – understand critical thinking. This section discusses phenomenographic research findings reflecting the subjective understanding of critical thinking among higher education teachers and students.

2.1 How university teachers understand critical thinking

Our analysis revealed eight qualitatively different ways of understanding the concept of critical thinking. Six of them were grouped into the following dominant categories: (1) critical thinking as self-improvement; (2) critical thinking as the development of an open relationship with the environment; (3) critical thinking as a decision-making instrument; (4) critical thinking as learning to doubt and recheck knowledge; (5) critical thinking as learning to choose; (6) critical thinking as learning to ask questions and express thoughts. The remaining two were grouped into the following non-dominant categories: (7) critical thinking as a creative capacity; (8) critical thinking as an attribute of civil, democratic society.

Dominant categories include the most common, frequently repeated meanings, while non-dominant categories include singular meanings that are not repeated.

2.1.1 Description of dominant categories of critical thinking

Category 1: Critical thinking as self-improvement. University teachers recognise critical thinking as the ability to know oneself better – to see and acknowledge one's weak and strong points, and to identify traits that need improvement, beliefs that need to be revisited, and actions that need to be corrected. *The most important thing in critical thinking is to change the established rules and steadfast attitudes* (C7). It means the personal inclination and readiness to practice a critical approach to oneself – the ability to raise open-ended questions that are often awkward: *is everything correct? Am I in the right place with the right people?* (C1). Open-ended and authentic questions like these lead to *personal freedom and the courage to tackle serious problems* (C16) and *move on in life* (C13). In summary, critical thinking as self-improvement is a process of active thinking and rethinking, changing habits and modes of behaviour for one's own good and the good of others. 'For one's own good' means *awareness of one's strong points in order to compete and make the most of one's capacities* (C1), as well as the improvement of personal character as such. 'For the good of others' means one's ability *to understand others better* (C13), and to improve oneself in respect to others. In many cases, the personal and interpersonal aspects are interconnected.

Category 2: Critical thinking as the development of an open relationship with the environment. An open relationship with the environment can come about in several ways. One way is *to look at reality with an open attitude and wonder* (C14). This helps break free from assertiveness and make space for the search for answers, both alone and with others:

> *We might be very critical about our reality, but it is not in our power to search for answers on our own. We need to trust the other side of the dialogue, and keep both presence of mind and critical distance at the same time.* (C14)

Presence of mind does not confront empathy – on the contrary. One can be open to other's feelings and thoughts while remaining calm. This is considered to be a critical ability, especially in an emergency, when someone needs help. Another way to nurture an open relationship with the environment is to study it. This means observing social processes and trends, and identifying problems for the common good. In this case, critical thinking means the ability *to swim against the current, according to what your heart feels and your mind tells you* (C8). It is not an easy task, but it is a necessary one if one is striving for the truth. Critical thinking as the development of an open relationship with the environment contains two 'opposing' features – openness and distance. One has to be open and also a bit distanced in order to understand reality and control oneself in it for the benefit of others and social well-being. In this respect, this category is slightly different from the one described above. It also embraces an interpersonal aspect, that is, *showing empathy* (C5) *and demonstrating trust* (C14) in another person, but this aspect is in many cases associated with a strong social concept – collegiality, alliance, humanity and a holistic world-view. In general, the 'Open relationship with the environment' category indicates strong philosophical concepts – the search for truth, trust and wonder.

Category 3: Critical thinking as a decision-making instrument. As a decision-making instrument, critical thinking is considered to be very practical. First, for making decisions in everyday situations: what to buy and what not to buy, what course of action to choose, what to give up, what problem to solve first and what to leave for later. Second, for making the right decisions in ambiguous, complex situations that do not happen often. For example: *Is it right to turn off life support if a person is brain-dead?* (C5). Complex situations always involve ethical aspects and morality. Making the right decision is not easy, and sometimes nobody knows what decision is really right. Critical thinking is a practical tool for finding one's niche in a competitive environment:

> *Critical thinking has an organic relationship with economics. A person has to compete in everyday life. This means thinking about how to use your time effectively, tailoring your abilities, and selling yourself.* (C10)

Competitiveness is seen as a reality that everyone needs to adjust to, and critical thinking helps you not to get lost or frustrated, but to find the best place for yourself instead. Critical thinking helps to see, name and interpret reality, and make practical, informed decisions. Sometimes they are made after a certain period of time rather than immediately.

This category includes personal and interpersonal aspects. The personal aspect means the ability to make the right choice for yourself, and the interpersonal aspect means the ability to make the right choice for the benefit of others. The social aspect is not reflected in this category.

Category 4: Critical thinking as learning to doubt and recheck knowledge. University teachers understand education as the cultivation of independent thinkers. Independence manifests itself in learning to be a healthy sceptic – *not to trust everything that is written in scientific articles* (C12), because things change, both in life and in science. Scientific knowledge must be revisited and rediscovered by the students themselves. They have to look at the same phenomenon from different perspectives of time, space and context, and find answers to questions based on sound arguments. This means that students must learn that there is no single 'correct' answer in either theory or practice:

> *There is no definite definition in economics of anything that can be learned as a completed poem ... '2 x 2 = 4' is not an answer that requires critical thinking. We teach students to think for themselves ... if they can find their own way to solve the task and get closer to the truth, then we are happy.* (C10)

University teachers feel committed to teaching not to take everything that is said and written by others as a given. They see critical thinking as a tool of provocation to look into a topic or a question, and not to be satisfied with the answers already given. University is considered to be a place where critical minds learn to rethink and rebuild knowledge without fear of authorities.

This category embraces two aspects – personal and social. The personal aspect is reflected in the individual's efforts not to be fooled or manipulated, and to become more critical in order to protect him or herself and become wiser. The social aspect unfolds as an attempt to demonstrate the importance of non-uniform thinking, watchfulness and accuracy as a social value for all, and as a precondition for the development of science and humanity.

Category 5: Critical thinking as learning to choose. Critical thinking is learning to choose a point of view, position, values, a topic to study and its interpretation. Teachers say choosing a topic for an independent assignment or thesis is not an easy task. Students have to do a lot of work – look for information, think about its appropriateness, organise it, and decide what is meaningful to them. And then *students must choose their position, their truth, and prove their choice* (C11).

Making choices takes time, effort, persistence and a willingness to work with details:

> *One learns to look for nuances and accents, understand where the problem is, and then choose a course of action.* (C8)

University teachers say that it is important to choose the method of interpretation – results, scientific findings or a piece of artistic production. They argue that the ability to choose a method of interpretation indicates a student's ability to think critically. In other words, the ability to use basic knowledge, apply it to in-depth analysis and make informed choices:

> *Critical thinking is directly connected with interpretation. Musical works can be presented in different ways … Students have to know different styles and understand the features of a certain era … and choose the logical method of interpretation.* (C1)

Critical thinking as learning to choose is understood as a final decision that is made by oral or written reasoning, performed in an artistic or scientific form. Learning to choose is seen as a personal ability for personal benefit. Critical choices are beneficial in proving one's ideas and actions in learning and everyday life situations.

Category 6: Critical thinking as learning to ask questions and express independent thoughts. Critical thinking is recognised through the student's ability to formulate questions and express independent thoughts. University teachers emphasise that this ability must be developed throughout life, starting in childhood:

> *Working, researching, searching and solving tasks is common practice. Regularity trains the mind. As a scientist, I am not afraid of getting stuck in a certain place – I interrogate and take risks, as science is a risky business.* (C7)

At the very beginning, students are not able to demonstrate this kind of critical thinking – they just reiterate what they have read. Later, they start wondering *whether it is correct or not, whether it is positive or negative* (C11). Independent thought comes as a result of interrogation and investigation. If a student dares *to question, disagree, fight for independent ideas, and support them with evidence, it means that he or she has achieved a high level of criticality* (C11). And vice versa – if a student asks *what he or she has to do, or whether it is correct or not* (C9), it indicates an absence of critical thinking. University teachers acknowledge the importance of learning how to ask critical questions at university. And not just for cognitive training:

> *It is very important to learn to ask questions, sometimes even awkward ones, as they can help shorten the work process. If you perform the task obediently according to the instructions, you can only achieve a satisfactory result. But if you are looking for original solutions, you need to learn to ask critical questions.* (C9)

A patient's health may depend on the ability to question, disagree and look for unconventional solutions. Students training to become doctors should ask themselves questions:

> *... what's happening in the body ... why do I resuscitate or not resuscitate a patient, where should I stop and where should I proceed ... these are complex things that are not easy to combine into one algorithm.* (C5)

The courage to ask is required in any professional field. Employers value those who ask authentic questions which *sometimes no one knows the answers to* (C9).

The concept of critical thinking in this category manifests itself as questioning and independent thinking, which results in intellectual and/or practical ability. Intellectual ability is related to scientific or academic work at university, while practical ability is related to mastering a profession outside of university. This ability is personally beneficial – it develops the mind and makes a person stronger. But it is also beneficial for others. If a teacher or a student acts as a 'provocative agent', questioning reality and expressing independent thoughts, he or she models the desired way of teaching and learning and creates a broader critical discourse. Social benefits lie in the results of independent thinking – new, original solutions and innovations, as well as responsible professionals and honest citizens.

2.1.2 Description of non-dominant categories of critical thinking

Category 7: Critical thinking as a creative capacity. Though few in number, there were very strong notions about critical thinking as a creative capacity in the research data. One respondent expressed a firm belief that *creativity is a very important part of critical thinking* (C7). He sees an interrelation between criticality and creativity in many respects: refusal to follow models, and freedom to think and decide, to approach problems in an unconventional manner, to think about and try 'impossible' solutions, and to create new rules and reality:

A critical thinker creates him or herself ... it is the only way to come up with a new quality ... the more creative you are, the more critical thinking skills you have ... It is key. I don't care about other components – analysis, synthesis, and so on. That is for special literature. (C7)

In short, a critical thinker is the creator/discoverer of something new, at least for him or herself.

Another idea about the interrelation between creativity and critical thinking is about the critical message embedded in a work of art:

Critical thinking is not necessarily reflected in words. It can be reflected in piece of art ... a creative person cannot do without critical thinking. Because artistic ideas are born after a careful investigation of the environment, material and personal abilities ... a piece of art must bring a critical message, an idea originating from the environment. (C8)

These examples indicate that critical thinking and creativity are two halves of the same apple. Creative solutions require a critical mind. Criticism is reflected in the final product, whether it is a work of art, an engineering solution or a mathematical formula. Critical thinking and creative thinking are about bringing new, qualitatively different and significant messages to oneself and others, as well as to society as such. Personal significance is concerned with educating one's mind and finding original ways of acting. The interpersonal aspect is concerned with the modelling of criticality as part of the creative thinking process with and among others in the academic setting. Other students are inspired to think 'out of box' and look for unconventional solutions. Social significance lies in the creative products to be used by a wide audience and for scientific progress.

Category 8: Critical thinking as an attribute of civil, democratic society. University is considered a very special educational institution that differs from others in that it offers a broad approach which is not necessarily limited to subject knowledge:

Students have to know what is being done for humanity and what needs to be done ... in this respect, university and critical thinking are closely connected. Critical thinking is a basic competence acquired at university. (C10)

University broadens your horizons and allows you to see yourself as a part of society, connected with others by the past, present and future. Critical thinking helps to nurture *an honest person with clear values who contributes to civil society* (C17). Civil, democratic society is understood as an open space for thinking without boundaries and speaking without fear (C17). A broadly educated, free and responsible person is always committed to the social good, is always ready *to make a meaningful contribution through his or her work* (C8), and always acts for the benefit of humanity. In this respect, critical thinking is characterised as a socially oriented competence.

2.1.3 Relationships between categories of description

The eight different ways of understanding the concept of critical thinking fall into the following dimensions: critical thinking as a relationship; critical thinking as a practical result; critical thinking as a learning process; and critical thinking as an integral part of another phenomenon.

Dimension I: Critical thinking as a relationship. This dimension is made up of two categories: 'Critical thinking as self-improvement' (Category 1) and 'Critical thinking as the development of an open relationship with the environment' (Category 2). It represents the concept of critical thinking as a value-based competence. On the one hand, it has to do with the value of personal development for one's own good (Categories 1 and 2). Critical thinking helps to reshape one's relationship with oneself and improve oneself – to make oneself better. This means being more open, bolder, wiser and self-critical. On the other hand, it is about bringing value to others (Categories 1 and 2). Critical thinkers are more sensitive to others and can respond appropriately to a person's needs. However, this dimension also concerns the wider community and society as a whole (Category 2). It means the disposition to respect diversity, to be open to the outside world and to wonder, and to look for the unknown and seek the truth. Critical thinkers foster a holistic approach to the environment, and are willing to build relationships with others, despite differences; they try to see more than a specific moment gives, and connect the past, present and future.

Dimension II: Critical thinking as a learning process. This dimension is made up of three categories: 'Critical thinking as learning to doubt and recheck knowledge' (Category 4), 'Critical thinking as learning to ask questions and express thoughts' (Category 5) and 'Critical thinking as learning to choose' (Category 6). Critical thinking is treated as a process of developing intellectual abilities. This process begins with learning healthy scepticism and not taking any information or scientific truth as a given. Students are taught to check and recheck knowledge, and look for claims and reasoned justifications. This is closely related to learning to ask open, critical questions, leading to purposeful and thorough research and verification of theories and concepts. This process teaches a person to make informed, independent decisions and choices for personal (Categories 4, 5, 6), interpersonal (Category 6) and social (Categories 4 and 6) benefit. Critical thinking as a learning process encompasses the person as a whole, that is, his or her cognitive, emotional and emotional abilities. Critical thinkers learn to become cognitively proficient, accurate and cautious, emotionally resilient, and confident in their ability to become critical, independent thinkers.

Dimension III: Critical thinking as a practical result. This dimension is made up of a single, but largely represented category: 'Critical thinking as a decision-making instrument' (Category 3). This dimension reflects the concept of critical thinking as being practical, positive and goal-oriented. Its practicality has very specific forms – problem solving or finding ways out of complex situations, resolution of conflicts, making the right decisions, risk management. Critical thinking helps to make the right selection and to select the right thing. This means that in some cases, it is not only the end result that is important, but also the way it is achieved. In many cases, correct decisions involve a process of critical analysis, consideration of different solutions, and making difficult – even risky – choices in the event of uncertainty and ambiguity. A result found critically has value on a personal and interpersonal scale. This means that a critical decision has a positive impact on both the person who makes it and others in the academic or professional setting.

Dimension IV: Critical thinking as an integral part of another phenomenon. This dimension is made up of two non-dominant categories: 'Critical thinking as a creative capacity' (Category 7) and 'Critical thinking as an attribute of civil, democratic society' (Category 8). Critical thinking is understood as a natural, integral part of other concepts – creativity and civil society. Critical thinking is understood as an attribute of another phenomenon, without giving priority to what is primary and what is secondary. Critical thinking belongs to creativity, and creativity entails criticality. Both are equally important for the person (Category 7), other people (Category 7) and society (Categories 7 and 8). Both are related to originality and innovation, and the evolution of the world of science and life. Critical thinking is also a precondition and one of the key features of civil society. The more critical thinkers a society has, the more democracy it has.

2.1.4 Outcome space

The detected categories and variations of the dimensions form the outcome space. It is a summary of our study that reflects the perception of critical thinking (what is it?) and indicates its significance (what is it for?). Table 13 presented shows the outcome space of our study. It connects the conceptual (what is it?) and structural/value (what is it for?) components. The conceptual part is represented by the categories and variations of dimensions, as inter-conceptual units. The value component consists of three different aspects – personal, interpersonal and social, which represent different levels of importance.

Tab. 13: *Outcome space: Conceptual and value components of perceptions of critical thinking among university teachers*

Conceptual component		Structural/value component
Variations of dimensions (interrelations between categories)	Categories (concepts)	Level of importance
Critical thinking as a relationship	Critical thinking as self-improvement (1)	Personal, interpersonal
	Critical thinking as a relationship with the environment (2)	Interpersonal, social
Critical thinking as a learning process	Critical thinking as learning to doubt and recheck knowledge (4)	Personal, social
	Critical thinking as learning to ask questions and express thoughts (5)	Personal
	Critical thinking as learning to choose (6)	Personal, interpersonal, social
Critical thinking as a practical result	Critical thinking as a decision-making instrument (3)	Personal, interpersonal
Critical thinking as an integral part of another phenomenon	Critical thinking as a creative capacity (7)	Personal, interpersonal, social
	Critical thinking as an attribute of civil, democratic society (8)	Social

It is interesting to note that there is no significant gap between the levels of importance indicated. Six categories represent the personal value of critical thinking, while five represent the interpersonal value and five represent the social value. Some categories/concepts indicate two or even three levels of importance, with the exception of the fifth category. In fact, all three levels of importance are interrelated because they are equal parts of the same process that follow and support each other. Critical thinking as a relationship starts as personal efforts for one's own benefit, but then it steps out of the private space and touches others and society as a whole. Critical thinking as a learning process also begins at the personal level, but continues as a process with a clear understanding of critical thinking as entailing a broader sense of value. Even the instrumentality of critical thinking, which is conceptually result-oriented, is accepted as having more than just singular value. The last dimension, which consists of two non-dominant categories, indicates all three levels of importance in Category 7 and only the social level in Category 8. The latter clearly advocates critical thinking as having unquestionable social value. Figure 7 shows the hierarchical relationship between the value components and the categories of conceptions.

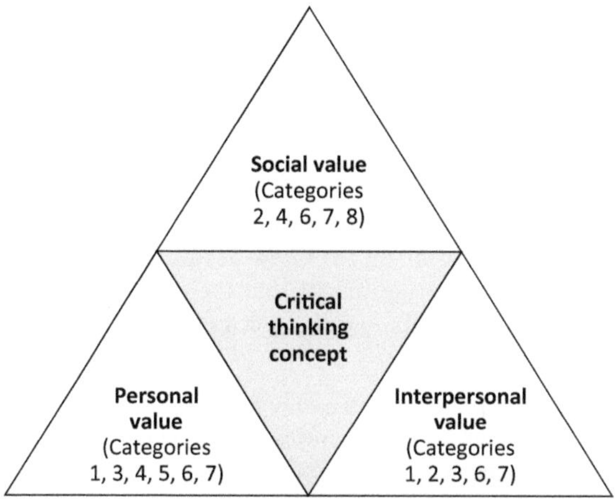

Fig. 7: *Hierarchical relationship between the value components and the categories of conceptions*

There are two ways to interpret the hierarchical order of concepts and value components. One way is to look at the size of three triangles and discover that they are equal. This means that all three components are given qualitatively equal attention by the research participants. Another way is to look at the top and bottom of the whole figure. The personal and interpersonal value components are placed at the bottom for two reasons. First, because they concern person-to-person contact and individual interrelations, either between the same person (internally), or between two persons or a relatively small, homogeneous group (externally), for example, teachers, students, employees. Second, because of the common space that the individual and others share in the context of the story. This space is either an academic community or a specific professional field where the individual meets and shares the value of critical thinking. The social value component is placed on top because it is more distant in terms of space (neither the academic nor the professional field) and does not indicate any specific group sharing the value of critical thinking.

This hierarchical relationship represents a summarised, generalised perception of critical thinking and its value. The picture of individual perceptions may be different. However, the aim of our study was not to assess the personal, interpersonal and social value of critical thinking.

2.2 How students understand critical thinking

Four categories were singled out which reveal the students' understanding of critical thinking: (1) critical thinking as the ability to engage in a multi-perspective approach; (2) critical thinking as an evaluation tool; (3) critical thinking as the ability to find the right solution; and (4) critical thinking as empowerment to become independent. All of the categories are dominant. Before starting a more detailed presentation of the categories, it is important to note that some of the students had difficulty describing how they understand what critical thinking is, or what qualities they attribute to it. This was due, in their view, to the naturalness of the concept of critical thinking – the concept of critical thinking was so self-evident to them that it was difficult for them to choose accurate descriptions and put their thoughts into words. It is also significant that the students said that throughout their studies, the teachers never talked about critical thinking and its development in any class:

> *This word was never specifically used in all my five years of training. Actually, I never heard the word 'critical thinking' in all those five years. ...no one ever clearly said or mentioned that now we're going to learn critical evaluation. ... It was like you were supposed to realise it yourself.* (D10)

However, this does not limit the ability to explore how students understand what critical thinking is, how they describe it, and what qualities they attribute to it, as this question touches on the students' perception, which can also be based on indirect experiences. These examples reaffirm that critical thinking is a complex and multifaceted phenomenon, which only further arouses scientific curiosity about it.

Category 1. Critical thinking as the ability to engage a multi-perspective approach. In this category, the conception of critical thinking unfolds as a personal quality. Critical thinking is interpreted as a person's ability to adopt a manifold attitude:

> *I perceive and accept critical thinking as the ability to see any situation or any issue, choice or solution more broadly; to have several versions of how it could be.* (D11)

Two aspects can be distinguished in the manifold nature that unfolds. The first is the ability to examine a problem or topic from different perspectives, that is, to see its multidimensionality and, possible interpretations in a broader context. For students, critical thinking is the ability to evaluate a phenomenon from different perspectives and see the diversity of a particular subject:

> *... there were GUSes – general university studies elective subjects. So stuff that isn't really even related to our studies. I was choosing something along those lines, so my GUS was Physical Image of the World. It's a subject that's more for relaxation, to give you more knowledge before physical phenomena, like what fractals or the Big Bang Theory are. It's to know those theories and maybe see what's bad about them, what's good, and what can be used. Then I chose Biological Evolution for another GUS. So in those GUSes, there was a*

pretty strong emphasis on critical thinking – looking at things from a different angle, and critically evaluating theories, what's applicable in them and what's not. (D8)

Showing different positions in some cases means not just a simple consideration, but a search for arguments for each position that would substantiate them:

When I can let myself think – maybe it is different after all, and then maybe rewind a little and see those arguments that were put forward, and ones that might not have been arguments at all, where some conclusion was presented without any reasoning, but just drifted off like that with that talk. (D14)

... always substantiate your answer, why that's what you think, not that I just launched some thought because I think it's the best solution or something. Always have arguments. (D3)

Students associate contemplation from different perspectives with the practice of not linking one's beliefs and opinions as the only ones that are right, and acknowledging that each situation may be different than you think. The ability to look at things from a different angle also means to evaluate the applicability of theoretical information in practical situations, where there is a need to include the contextual aspects of the problem, and the ability to think beyond the confines of a particular problem by including information from the full context:

... critical thinking here would be like some kind of sharp thinking. A person does not rely solely on his intuition, but bases himself on various factors in life that can have factors for someone. (D5)

So, from the point of view of the students in this category, critical thinking is the ability to see the subject from different perspectives and identify it in the context of the whole.

The second aspect of the manifold nature that unfolds in this category is the ability to look more broadly, taking the context into account:

I perceive and accept critical thinking as the ability to see any situation or any issue, choice or solution more broadly; to have several versions of how it could be. I won't deny that when we come to study critical thinking, we're tousled anew, because the specialty of a social worker itself obliges you to be able to see more broadly and look for those solutions and options in a very wide range of situations. (D11)

Analysis of the research data revealed that broad vision is not necessarily limitless possibilities of action. On the contrary – in the students' conception of critical thinking, it came to light that although it is equated with broad vision, it is also recognised as the acknowledgement of certain limitations, which only become possible with a broad outlook:

Critical thinking makes life more interesting, it lets you notice cracks in a story and maintain a certain distance with existing narratives. In general, critical thinking is the recognition of the limitation of your own and other people's attitudes and constructed narratives. (D16)

It can be concluded that students understand critical thinking as the personal ability to adopt a multidimensional attitude and pluralism of opinions, as well as the ability to identify possible process trajectories, see the full context, and, accordingly, have a wider range of possibilities for action by perceiving their limits.

Category 2. Critical thinking as an evaluation tool. This category consists of meanings which are unified by the students' instrumental attitude towards critical thinking as a tool used when there is a need to evaluate something. They describe critical thinking as an evaluation that they can use to achieve certain goals – evaluate a situation or organise their thinking.

Critical thinking as a tool for evaluating a certain situation includes not only a thorough analysis of the issue being analysed, but also synthesis and the formulation of conclusions. From the students' point of view, detailed analysis of the situation or problem and examination and evaluation of its various aspects mean critical thinking:

> *... it's not enough to solve tasks according to those usual methods, where you have to make your own decisions, analyse the situation yourself, and based on that, look at the task critically yourself and devote more of your thinking than use information from books.* (D5)

Another aspect that unfolded in this category is that critical thinking is understood as a kind of tool for organising your thinking that allows you to arrange the abundance of information, diversity of attitudes and contradictions into a coherent and logical picture:

> *Critical thinking is important in that it's like a tool that polishes all of the content in your mind and arranges it into a mosaic. A tool that helps you put together the content of your thoughts in a nice, intelligent and logical way, so that your thoughts aren't cluttered, where one of your opinions contradicts another opinion.* (D4)

Another aspect that came to light in this category of the conception of critical thinking is related to self-evaluation of the situation in order to have a reasoned and substantiated position on a specific issue:

> *... so that you know how to self-evaluate the environment both logically and emotionally from various areas and have your own position on the subject, not only because others think so, but so that you know why yourself. Or if others think so too, to be able to name why you think so or believe in something, do something, make some decision.* (D7)

Thus, the category of the conception of critical thinking as a tool for evaluation unfolds as the ability to deconstruct a problem, understand each of its parts, understand the meaning and role of each part in the whole, perceive and resolve contradictions between the parts, and put it all back into a coherent picture, already comprehending its mechanism and logical structure. It can be argued that critical thinking is understood here as a means – a tool – that provides analytical powers to thoroughly evaluate the phenomenon or situation in question while also self-evaluating your position in the relevant context.

Category 3. Critical thinking as the ability to find the right solution. Analysis of the student interviews revealed that when thinking about what critical thinking is, the students single out the meanings of critical thinking that indicate the ability to find the right solution. This is the ability not only to come up with a way out, but also to accurately choose a certain version of the way out. In this category, critical thinking unfolds at the personal level as the ability to find an adequate solution to a specific or complicated problem or situation.

The research data also reveals an aspect of the conception of critical thinking as the ability to find an adequate solution to a specific problem. That is, the students' conception of critical thinking is focused on the ability to select the right key for solving this particular problem:

> *... the ability to find exactly the solution needed to solve that problem, rather than some careless programme writing, without assessing the situation at all. I'd say critical thinking is precisely the detailed evaluation of situations and problems.* (D5)

From the students' point of view, critical thinking is the ability to select fact-supporting information on the basis of which a decision can be made effectively:

> *We always have some facts, we have information that we rely on so that we can substantiate it. I think that's what critical thinking is.* (D3)

The second aspect of the conception of critical thinking revealed in this category is related to the ability to find the right solution to a problem situation. The students value critical thinking as an ability that helps find a way out in problematic, stressful, highly emotional situations. In the context of these situations, the students attribute the quality of an empathic mind and rational thinking to critical thinking:

> *... there are difficult situations, how can you think soberly when you need to provide help, especially when there's some sort of disagreement between the patient and the loved ones? That's how I imagine critical thinking, that if there are people who are unhappy with the hospital's work, and how you have to think critically and not offend one or the other, and explain what the situation is, and what the solutions are. For me, critical thinking is sober thinking about how to communicate with the same patient and his loved ones, and how to present the fact of the illness.* (D10)

This category includes students' conceptions of critical thinking as the personal quality of being able to solve problems properly. It can be argued that students associate the right way to solve problems with the ability to choose adequate solution paths and maintain an optimal combination of rationality and empathy in stressful and complicated situations.

Category 4. Critical thinking as empowerment to become independent. Analysis of the research data revealed yet another direction of students' thinking about the conception of critical thinking, where critical thinking is associated with empowering a person to become independent. In this category, three aspects of the conception of critical thinking are revealed, where critical thinking is understood as empowerment to independently: think, make decisions and act.

The research data revealed that critical thinking as empowerment to think independently includes the students' conceptions of critical thinking as independent thinking. Independent thinking empowers you to comprehend your power to think for yourself, and provides freedom of thought:

> *... a person is able to independently create something, evaluate a situation, make decisions. For me, critical thinking is associated with the detail of independence, analysis of the situation.* (D5)

In this aspect of the conception of critical thinking, independence emerges at the personal level as an individual, personal and independent thought process, taking responsibility for one's own thinking and decisions. The explanation of the students' conceptions of critical thinking is related to the perceived power to make independent decisions:

> *First of all, it's an autonomous thinking that doesn't depend on anything, because usually at school there's this herd, mass thing when everyone says the answer 'yes' and there's always that one person who answers 'no'. But he usually hesitates for a really long time, thinks, weighs all the arguments for and against, makes up his mind, and only then says it.* (D3)

From the students' point of view, only by being able to think autonomously do you become independent, and once you are independent, you can gather the necessary information and make decisions, such as solving problems independently, deciding independently what subjects to study, and so on:

> *When you can think independently of others, you're completely independent, and can make decisions with of all the information and facts.* (D3)

In this category, the students' conception of critical thinking is associated with independence, which enables you to add the result of your thinking to the task at hand:

> *... that whole choice, when you don't have to put it together the same like a puzzle, when you have some sort of choice, that's when critical thinking starts to work. Because otherwise you just put it together any old way, the way it should be, instead of trying to incorporate your own colours into the whole creation.* (D12)

It can be argued that the conceptions of critical thinking in this category focus on empowerment, the perception of independence, and learning to use that perceived independence in creating your own ideas, creating your own content in its various forms.

2.2.1 *Relationships between the categories*

The two qualitatively different conceptions of critical thinking can be explained by the differences in the interrelated variations (dimensions). These differences reveal relationships between the categories: critical thinking is understood as a personal cognitive quality and disposition, and critical thinking is a practical tool or factor for achieving the intended goals. The main relationships between the categories are presented in Table 14.

Tab. 14 *Relationships between the categories*

Category / Dimension	**Critical thinking as the ability to engage a multi-perspective approach**	**Critical thinking as an evaluation tool**	**Critical thinking as the ability to find the right solution**	**Critical thinking as empowerment to become independent**
Personal cognitive quality and disposition	Examination from different perspectives, ability to see more broadly, acceptance of different views	Ability to analyse the situation, link individual elements into a whole, prepare arguments	Combining rationality and empathy	Courage to disagree with the dominant opinion and to think autonomously
Practical tool	The search for truth, the search for arguments to support different opinions, thinking beyond the boundaries of a particular problem	Deconstruction of the problem, understanding and evaluation of the (complex) situation	Application of appropriate measures in a given situation, appropriate solution to the problem	Independent problem solving, becoming a thinking and autonomous individual

This reveals a broadening of the understanding of the research participants in both dimensions across all of the categories singled out.

Dimension I: Critical thinking as a personal cognitive quality and disposition. This dimension reveals critical thinking as a feature of a person's thinking and actions. In the students' conception, critical thinking as a personal quality and internal disposition denotes a certain benchmark, that is, a quality worth noting that provides additional abilities.

In the first category, critical thinking as a person's cognitive quality is expressed as active thinking in a multifaceted examination of the situation, from different perspectives. It also manifests itself as a disposition not to hold to one's opinion as the only one that is right, and to accept a variety of thinking and decisions and see any situation more broadly:

> *Be able to see more broadly and look for those solutions and options in a very wide range of situations. ... That's what critical thinking is to me – going down a much wider corridor.* (D11)

In the second category, critical thinking as a person's cognitive quality indicates open-mindedness and flexibility of thinking, which in turn is associated with the ability to evaluate – for example, *critically evaluating theories, what's applicable in them and what's not* (D8). Evaluation is partly related to the meanings of 'broader vision' and the opportunity to choose and find a solution:

> *[you have to have] a choice, a solution, have several versions of how it could be ... thanks to critical thinking, a person can see more broadly, and by seeing more broadly, he simply has more choices, options, because there's always more than one way out of a situation.* (D11)

In the third category, the cognitive abilities of critical thinking are also manifested in the analysis of complex, complicated situations, when it is necessary to *think soberly* (D10) and make the best possible decisions. The search for choices in difficult situations is also related to ethical decisions – feeling for others, being empathetic, knowing how to convey information to other people:

> *Critical thinking really gives a person a lot of rationality. Being rational is very important just in talking to other people and being able to communicate what's being asked of you. Critical thinking gives students not only in professional life, but also in communicating with people, not to give in to emotions, and to ask of other people exactly what you want or to understand what they want.* (D9)

In this respect, the search for solutions is also related to the application of a solution in specific life situations, and is valuable not so much to the actual decision-maker as to the other people involved in the decision. It should be noted that this partly reflects a certain instrumentality of critical thinking.

In the fourth category, critical thinking as a person's cognitive quality also manifests itself in the freedom to *think independently of others* (D3), which enables independent decision-making, as well as to disagree with the dominant opinion. Critical thinking is free thinking that does not depend on anything and is characteristic of an independent and self-confident individual.

Dimension II: Critical thinking as a practical tool. Unlike the first dimension, this dimension reveals that in the students' conception, critical thinking is perceived as a means that can be used in a wide variety of situations as needed. By understanding critical thinking as a practical tool and seeing it as something that creates added value, the students understand that critical thinking is precisely what can be used to achieve defined goals.

In the first category, critical thinking emerges as a practical tool to explore and better understand a problem, phenomenon or situation. It is used to look for additional information and arguments to support different positions, as well as to go beyond the boundaries of a particular situation.

> *... to explain why some factors were chosen, and why others weren't necessary. It wasn't as important what factors you chose as it was how you justified your choice. There was no one right solution to the problem, but it was important how you were able to explain why you chose it. All attention was focused on the selection of factors rather than on simulating everything like it's written in the textbook.* (D5)

In the second category, critical thinking as a practical tool manifests itself in the evaluation of situations and problems – especially when they are ambiguous or complex. Critical thinking then helps to open up and see the internal structure of that situation or problem and their place in the broader context, and at the same time to better understand and evaluate the problem or situation under consideration:

> *I'd say critical thinking is precisely the detailed evaluation of situations and problems.* (D5)

In the third category, critical thinking is used as a practical tool for solving problems, finding ways out of problem situations, and selecting adequate problem-solving tools. The instrumentality of critical thinking is also manifested in creative activity, when a person is able to actively act and create independently:

> *You have to make your own decisions, analyse the situation yourself, and based on that, look at the task critically yourself and devote more of your thinking than use information from books.* (D5)

In the fourth category, critical thinking as a practical tool manifests itself in its quality of giving students the courage, strength and other internal resources to become autonomous thinkers:

> *Having a reasoned opinion, feeling self-confident, having an opinion, being able to defend it, having arguments.* (D4)

In the students' conception, without critical thinking, the possibility of becoming free-thinking individuals is of little promise.

2.2.2 Outcome space

Analysis of the outcome space reveals that the students understand critical thinking as a person's cognitive quality and disposition and as a practical tool that can be used to achieve certain goals, both individually and in interaction with others. The most pronounced is the personal aspect, which is found in all categories (Table 15).

Tab. 15: *Outcome space. Referential and structural components: How students understand critical thinking*

Referential component (what it is manifested as)	**Structural component (what is it for)**
Critical thinking as the ability to engage a multi-perspective approach	Personal Interpersonal
Critical thinking as an evaluation tool	Personal
Critical thinking as the ability to find the right solution	Personal Interpersonal
Critical thinking as empowerment to become independent	Personal Interpersonal/ Social

Critical thinking is mainly defined by students at the personal and interpersonal level. In describing what critical thinking is to them, they use situational examples, and also give its value weight over a very wide range, from its impact on confidence in one's power to active use in solving various problems. However, the students are not much inclined to talk about critical thinking with regard to its role in social or global processes.

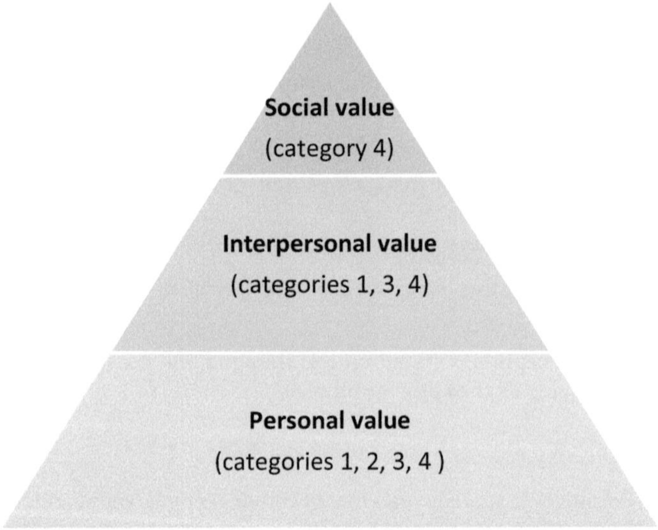

Fig. 8: *Hierarchical relationship between the value components and the categories of conceptions*

Figure 8 shows how the hierarchical relationships between the categories are manifested.

It should be noted that in all of the singled-out categories, the conception of critical thinking among students is very sharply focused on the personal level. It is associated with both studies and future perspectives, as well as forthcoming professional activities. The students' statements suggest that critical thinking skills and dispositions open up wider opportunities for them to grow and improve.

No less pronounced is the interpersonal level, at which the conception of critical thinking is explained. The students note that the possession of critical thinking as a broad view of a phenomenon or a specific situation is born only in an interpersonal relationship. Moreover, in each case, it is important to communicate one's position properly, so only by interacting with each other do they learn to substantiate their decisions.

The social value of critical thinking is only mentioned when it comes to critical thinking as empowerment to be independent. And it is associated not only with the ability to make a decision independently – the benefits and effectiveness of the decision made in the organisation are also noted.

3. Manifestation of Critical Thinking in the Study Process: How Critical Thinking Is Taught and Learned

The manifestation of critical thinking in higher education studies is also revealed by how teachers teach and learn critical thinking, and by how students learn critical thinking. This section will discuss how participants in the study process experience critical thinking when teaching and learning.

3.1. How teachers teach critical thinking

An analysis of teachers' learning experiences revealed that they teach critical thinking in seven qualitatively different ways, which are identified as dominant categories and non-dominant categories. The following dominant categories have been singled out: (1) assigning independent tasks; (2) teaching how to analyse a problem; (3) teaching how to analyse and evaluate texts; and (4) teaching by personal example. The following non-dominant categories have been singled out: (5) teaching how to compare; (6) organising group work; (7) assigning non-traditional tasks. The dominant categories consist of the most abundant experiences, and the non-dominant categories consist of statements illustrating individual experiences. The qualitative differences in the experiences lie in the way, approach and relationship of how critical thinking is developed. The 'way' is *how* teachers teach, and they are reflected in the category titles. In each of them, a certain teaching approach is revealed. That is, a view of critical thinking *as* an applied competency or *as* a holistic competency. Whether critical thinking is developed *as* a specific ability or *as* a set of abilities is also discussed. Differences in the relationships open up, answering the question of whether critical thinking is taught *as* an individual ability and/or *as* an interpersonal competence and/or *as* a social competence.

3.1.1 Dominant categories

Category 1: Assigning independent tasks. This category includes the most abundant critical thinking teaching experiences. They unfold through independent tasks that are assigned, which are of two kinds: short tasks that highlight the content being taught and help understand it better, and complex practical tasks – situation solutions, simulations, case analysis, internships and laboratory work that deepen the understanding of the subject being studied and provide practical professional skills. Short tasks are assigned to think over, consider and reconsider the teaching material, suggest the best way to solve the problem, and evaluate one's choices. The teachers assign the task themselves or allow the students to choose it:

> *My principle is this. I have quite a few tasks prepared, and I try to develop that critical thinking like this – I present the task and wait for questions. And then I work with each student. Whatever the question is, I'll always be interested and happy to answer that student's question, because I see that he has already begun to go into the heart of the matter and think about what he knows and doesn't know. Before receiving the task, the student usually thinks that he knows – you can see it from the self-confident look in his eyes. But as soon as he receives the task, that look becomes less self-confident, because the student often sees that he can't solve the task himself. And he has certain questions that I'm happy to answer. I think that this is the best way to develop critical thinking. (C10)*

Independent tasks help students understand what they know and understand, and what they do not. It teaches them to dare to ask questions, search for answers independently, model and substantiate the ways of solving the problem, and apply theoretical material to a specific practical case:

> *... say, the use of media – which media is most effective for this or that product? Let's say you don't have the money for TV or radio, which is the most expensive, and you understand that it would be ineffective because it's totally not the niche, not the consumers who watch TV and hang out online.* (C9)

Tasks like this encourage you to *use your head* (C10) and figure out how to use theory to solve a specific problem. Students learn to understand *how the laws and principles that they are analysing work ... by providing evidence of how it works in their lives and on what reasoning it could be proven that it works* (C11). The students provide reasoned answers to questions and theory-based solutions illustrated by practical examples. Independent student solutions do not necessarily have to be identical, as each task provides enough freedom for creative decisions. The teachers claim they formulate tasks that help everyone to gradually *climb the ladder of cognition, when one thing opens up, then another, and then another* (C8).

Instead of narrow, topic-specific tasks, some teachers like to give broader tasks. In this case, students have more freedom of individual choice. Then *you see that the person raises something very relevant and immediately gets the entire audience involved in the discussion* (C14). Freedom of choice is associated not only with the raising of interesting, relevant topics and engaging discussion, but also with the promotion of non-cookie-cutter thinking, which is seen as a certain manifestation of critical thinking.

The development of critical thinking is not limited to purely theoretical tasks. Teachers also assign personal tasks that require open-mindedness and a critical look at oneself:

> *And they have to choose a case when I was hesitant, describe it, and then give it some thought and describe how my friend, who is determined and persistent, would have behaved. And then they again see that diversity of ideas, diversity of solutions, that I can make a different decision or could have acted differently. That possibility, that we call reflection.* (C 17)

Tasks like this promote adequate self-assessment in a specific situation and teach you how to see alternatives and model other possible behaviours in the personal and professional field space.

Complex practical tasks are also designed for independent student work, but differ from those described above in their scope, nature and time allocated. They are called 'practical' because they go beyond lectures or seminars. Part of the work is performed in the classroom, and part is performed in a practical professional workspace, such as laboratories or various organisations or institutions. The tasks are called 'complex' both because of the variety of learning locations and because of the nature of the tasks themselves. Students have to look into scientific literature, experiment, model situations, take on various roles, and perform research. Often, students deal with clinical situations, where they collect all possible data from different sources, evaluate them in the broad context of the specific situation, make a diagnosis, analyse possible treatment options and decide on the best one, and draw up an individual treatment plan:

> *Students receive clinical situations right from the first year. Previously, there was only theoretical training, and after three years of learning theoretical material, they were prepared for clinical situations. Now they immediately get clinical situations and have to analyse them. I mostly teach 5- and 6-year residents, and they already come in with certain developed critical thinking skills, so we then work more on skills development – again, they work mostly with clinical situations and algorithms. Certain questions are given and they then solve them using algorithms. There are also hybrid laboratories where they divide into roles – there is the patient who has a task, as well as a medic and an observer. This is this sort of preparation, because everything is different with a live patient.* (C5)

Students are encouraged to look not only into theoretical, but also into practical, tangible things, such as product composition and service quality. It is this deepening that helps to compare and evaluate the value of each item, rejecting ones that are false, pushed by others, or advertised:

> *For example, toothpaste. It says it whitens teeth and there's not a single ingredient that whitens teeth, and they examined it and say to me, this and that, this is just advertising, there's nothing in that toothpaste. This is also like critical thinking.* (C12)

Working with clinical situations requires independent, case-based critical thinking. Students are taught to critically evaluate available methodologies and algorithms and decide if they can be applied, and if so – in what way. The teachers claim to develop *critical thinking with additions to the Hippocratic Oath* (C12). That is, they teach not to blindly follow rules and norms and not to be selfish, but to do the job honestly and diligently. To be open and focused on someone else – able to hear and listen:

> *Because it's very important for medics ... to word questions for the patient. And not any old way, but so as to encourage them to open up and tell all, so that the medical student can feel what problems the patient came in with, systematise this and make a diagnosis and conclusions, and prescribe appropriate treatment.* (C5)

Complex tasks require demonstrating the ability to apply theoretical knowledge in practice, a disposition to adhere to the highest standards of professional ethics and morals, interest in professional innovation, and seeing the specific task in a broader professional context. Complex tasks are designed to look into a specific situation and model independent, reasoned decisions. This is a research process that includes analysing and evaluating various sources of information, disclosing cause-effect relationships, looking for and evaluating alternative solutions, and selecting the best solution for the specific person or specific situation. In both complex and short tasks, the learning initiative is transferred to the students themselves. The teacher's role is that of observer and evaluator.

Category 2: Teaching how to analyse a problem. This category includes experiences where critical thinking is taught by analysing problems arising from theoretical material directly related to the subject being studied or the future profession. Students are taught to perform a broad analysis of the problem, getting acquainted with various sources and work done by others, studying analogues and possible ways of solving problems, and comparing and critically evaluating them. Despite the fact that teachers refer to teaching critical thinking as teaching how to analyse a problem, it could not be described as one-dimensional. Problem analysis includes teaching that is much broader in nature – source searching and selection, analysis and comparison, interpretation of content, inference and evaluation.

Problem analysis is taught for several reasons: to learn not to trust a single truth and to evaluate problems critically; to learn to solve problems, independently model their solution options and look for the best ones; and to know how to substantiate the chosen way of solving a problem. Problem analysis helps to understand that there are many attitudes towards the same phenomenon, so it is not appropriate to trust any one of them as being the most correct:

> *The student is advised not to trust one research source in the work process. Students have to perform a problem analysis, look at analogues, and read about what has been done in that sphere, and we always try to ensure that they don't trust one single opinion. Because there is this tendency, out of laziness perhaps, to find one source and do everything based on it. We urge them not to trust not just one source, but also the sole opinion of the teacher. That doesn't satisfy us.* (C9)

The teachers teach students to reasonably doubt one solution to the problem by 'delving deep into the problem', that is, by exploring it from all possible angles, trying to understand how others see the same phenomenon, starting with the specific target groups on whose behalf the problems are being solved. Problem analysis requires students to do a great deal of in-depth study and demonstrate openness to the phenomenon under study, because this is precisely what determines the level of critical thinking:

> *... understand the same phenomenon as much as possible, namely, its reasoning, its conception itself, and its evaluation is much more critical with respect to one phenomenon or another.* (C11)

Problem analysis corresponds to the conception of teachers' problem-based teaching and research work, because students learn to raise a scientific problem, perform situation analysis, model possible solutions and substantiate their choice: *these people tried to solve the problem, others solved it one way or another, but I'm choosing my own path and that path of mine is as follows* (C16). Problem analysis is easier when dealing with fairly common, familiar situations, but when learning a new topic, more time and effort is required. The teachers argue that it is precisely the exploration of an unknown field that opens up wider opportunities for developing critical thinking. Students *dig longer and deeper and prepare insights and decisions* (C3). In-depth and thorough analysis not only teaches research basics and problem-solving methods – it also teaches independent, autonomous thinking, which is useful for various professional fields.

The experiences described in this category include teachers' direct teaching of one subject or another. The role of the teacher is fairly active. They assign tasks, direct, suggest, advise, explain and evaluate, and the students analyse the problems given by the teachers. Teaching takes place in the space of the higher education institution.

Category 3: Teaching how to analyse and evaluate texts. This category includes experiences where the teacher teaches critical thinking through the analysis and evaluation of texts during lectures. The students analyse texts related to a specific profession for two purposes – to develop professional and personal competencies. The teaching of critical thinking is perceived as the development of analytical skills, which, in the opinion of teachers, are best developed by working *with texts* *in a broad sense. A text can be more than just read. It can be watched as a television programme or film* (C14).

Professional competencies are developed by delving into the latest research and scientific articles, by evaluating *whether the number of subjects was collected correctly, or whether the statistical methodology was chosen correctly … because anyone and everyone writes, prints and asserts his or her own truths* (C12). Scientific truth is not considered to be material based on one-off, one-dimensional evidence, but rather, time-tested and verified information, so students are encouraged *to look at each hypothesis, theory or research output from a variety of perspectives* (C13). Students are taught to distinguish between *what is proven … and what needs more research* (C12).

Professional goals are complemented by personal ones, which are associated with developing students' personalities and broadening their outlook. The teachers introduce students to important texts that highlight not only the present, but also the past. The aim is for students to learn to understand what a good, valuable text is, and what the relationships are between the past and the present.

The teachers assign texts that are related to current affairs of public life, which often remain untouched in the academic environment. The students are invited to express their opinion and engage in discussion. In this way, the events of public life are highlighted, a vigilant, watchful eye is developed, and the field of professional studies is enriched.

The teachers also try to select topics that are of personal relevance to the students and *that would develop that critical attitude toward both the phenomenon and the text …* (C14). Topics of personal relevance increase interest in the topic and the curriculum and actively engage students in the learning process.

The experiences attributed to this category highlight the curriculum as valuable material for the development of critical thinking. The teachers devote considerable attention to the selection of texts and their analysis and evaluation. The students analyse the texts both independently and with the entire group. The teacher initiates and leads general discussions. The analysis of texts develops analyticity and objectivity, and expands professional and personal horizons.

Category 4: Teaching by personal example. This category stands out for highlighting the role of the teacher in teaching critical thinking. The teachers teach critical thinking by their own personal example – the thoughts they express, the convictions and values they declare, and the behaviour they model. The teachers manifest themselves as critical thinking educators in their individual relationships with individual students or the entire group of students. Critical thinking is taught for professional mastery and for personal growth. Professional mastery is associated with independent thinking in making professional decisions, with the ability to understand cause-effect relationships, with seeing the totality of phenomena, and with the development of creativity. Students are told strongly that they should never trust one opinion, even if it is that of the teacher:

> *If the result shows that you did much better without relying on my opinion, that's just fantastic ... I don't want everything to be in my hands alone ... my suggestion is just one of a thousand suggestions.* (C9)

In this way, teachers demonstrate by their words that authorities can and should be questioned, because they are also not omniscient. The world is a living organism, and all of its phenomena are moving and changing. Therefore, blind repetition of what others say and think is not only of no interest, but also has no prospects. By inviting students to doubt and question, to not be afraid of making mistakes, and to look for answers, the teachers are encouraging professional courage, initiative and independence.

When speaking about their teaching method, the teachers claim that they try to teach each subject *as incomplete from the critical side ... to say that this has not been done, that is unknown, here we are making this error ...* (C7). The professional field is presented as not yet fully discovered and explored, and scientific knowledge is presented as contextual and relative. The teachers, therefore, believe that it is critical to educate not obedient executors, but *the creators of the norms and rules of life* (C7) who are committed to new searches and investigations. In encouraging creative work and independent discoveries, teachers value not the humble but those who have matured to an autonomous opinion and are *audacious in a good way* (C9). This is because such students are not afraid to notice and bring up what is wrong or inaccurate, and are brave enough to make a statement or disagree. Such students are a joy because the teacher understands that *the person is thinking and that critical thinking is activated* (C9).

In their lectures, the teachers teach the students to evaluate not a single phenomenon, but the totality of phenomena – to see the cause-effect relationship in it and to understand its significance in science. When assigning tasks, they try to leave them not for students' independent work, but for collegial research. The students explain, discuss and analyse together with the teacher. However, the role of the teacher is central in this case as well – he or she leads the learning process.

Teacher and student joint learning is considered valuable, because this is the best way to see what knowledge the student lacks, what skills need to be developed, and how the teacher can best contribute to the student's education. But not just because of that. The teachers list obvious benefits for themselves. Such teaching and learning is considered a great privilege, because *the teacher and the student can ... analyse the theme, idea, work, creative process, the object itself or the result, analyse the works of other artists, and generate new ideas* (C8). The generation of new ideas is associated with both the creative process and the development of critical thinking. This process involves an exchange of thoughts, deep analytical work, and synthesis and evaluation of existing experience and newly acquired experience. At the same time, the teacher demonstrates professional culture and an equal relationship, and cultivates the student's confidence in his or her own powers. It can, therefore, be argued that the student's personality is also developed in parallel.

The experiences attributed to this category highlight the meaning of relationships in creating an environment conducive to critical thinking and revealing the value of critical thinking. The teachers model situations in which the students are convinced of the importance of critical thinking and gain critical thinking experience. The value of critical thinking is revealed by the questioning of authorities, the courage to err and to create, fairness, and faithfulness to the truth. In this way, the teachers stress what is socially significant.

3.1.2 Non-dominant categories

Category 5: Teaching how to compare. This category includes experiences that illustrate the teaching of critical thinking as a specific ability. The teachers teach the students to compare the content of the material being taught, phenomena and to understand beter themselves. It is important for the teachers that ... *the students understand what the basis for comparison is and if it exists* (C14), *see more general things [distinguish them] in concreteness, and be able to compare* (C1). The teachers name specific methods – Venn diagram, cinquain – which, in their opinion, not only help learn comparison, but also engage in learning and help think deeper:

> *The family is assisted by both a social educator and a social worker. So what's common between them and what's different. Write it down. For them, they're very engaging. On the one hand, they take them as a game, but then they think very deeply. And I like that. Of course, if I see that they're tired or not in the mood, then they do a cinquain. This is a good way to engage in learning so that they read deeply and understand deeply and then write that cinquain.* (C 17)

Despite the fact that comparison is not treated as being particularly complex, it takes a long time to learn. It is defined as a job and a process during which the students perceive the reference points of comparison and certain criteria that they can also use for themselves: ... *yes – I work well, yes – I cheat, yes – I pretend, yes – I plagiarise* (C8).

In this way, students learn to look at themselves objectively and evaluate themselves adequately. Teaching to compare manifests itself as a valuable skill developed for both professional and personal life.

Category 6: Organising group work. In order to develop critical thinking, teachers organise group work during which the students teach each other. Learning takes place in two ways – everyone teaches everyone and a few teach everyone. Everyone teaches everyone in cases where the teacher asks the students to share ideas and express their autonomous opinions and attitudes. The students learn to *hear one another, hear someone else's position* (C17) and respect it. They also learn to analyse material related to the study subject, formulate thoughts and suggestions, and choose – together. A few teach others in cases where the teacher is having difficulty engaging all of the students in the learning process. The teacher then assigns the active ones to certain groups *so that the other also take a bit of interest and follow* *their example* (C3). The active students are called 'ambassadors' of critical thinking, capable of *inspiring others ... to catch ... the pace and speak the language of arguments more, not just what they find on Wikipedia or Google and copy and replicate that material* (C3).

These individual experiences of teaching critical thinking are revealed as learning by students in an active relationship with each other. The role of the teacher is organisational. The teacher creates conditions to learn from each other, and organises and monitors the learning.

Category 7: Assigning non-traditional tasks. Non-traditional tasks are considered to be unusual, non-standard tasks that require a closer look, deeper research and original thought. They are aimed at learning reasonable doubt, learning from mistakes, and learning conceptuality and creativity. Tasks that teach reasonable doubt are also called *tasks with a catch* (C16) because they are deceptive:

> *At first glance, it would seem as if everything is fine ... You take texts written by professionals ... but even the professional may not have recognised some concept in that context or underestimated some things, there's a catch somewhere. We always try to motivate them not to trust blindly. The first answer is: 'That's what I found in the book, that's what I found in the dictionary, or that's what Google said.' So we don't want there to be answers like that. There is a lot of everything in the dictionary, but not all situations are in there.* (C16)

It can be said that teachers, by assigning non-traditional tasks, purposefully provoke students' critical thinking: ... *we say nonsense on purpose and watch to see if the student reacts or not to what is being said* (C9).

In this way, students are taught not to trust the 'obvious truth', to evaluate the wider context, to look for mistakes and recognise them, to *trace why it happened that way* (C6), and to explain and substantiate.

Non-standard tasks also include Olympic tasks, which the teachers think up themselves – these are considered *'unexpected'*, formed *not according to one shoe last* (C7), and encourage original thinking. Original, creative thinking is also developed by complex research tasks:

> *Let's say there was one student this year who was researching the concept of temporality ... the topic of 'kairos' that is another time. Not 'chronos' time, not the one that ticks in seconds, but the time where qualitative change takes place. So she read, researched, formulated, searched for what artistic manifestation could convey that sense of temporality, so that the viewer would not only have a beautiful piece of jewellery, but could also feel that in our environment, in our lives, there is also a criterion or concept of temporality. She created jewellery from sea salt, from metal that melts in the palm of your hand. So if you put a piece of jewellery like this on, it melts from your body temperature and disappears. So she explores processes, from philosophy to matter, through certain pieces of jewellery and metal forms.* (C8)

Tasks of this nature, when an abstract idea needs to be turned into a concrete substance or product, are considered a manifestation of conceptual thinking, of teachers identifying with critical thinking.

The teaching experiences in this category reveal the efforts of teachers to develop critical thinking atypically, with more complex, unusual and challenging tasks. The students have to put in more effort, and work diligently and attentively. The teacher is a provoker of sorts, giving the students challenges and observing how they handle them.

3.1.3 Relationships between the categories described

The seven qualitatively different ways of teaching critical thinking can be explained by the differences and similarities between the two interrelated variations (dimensions), which help to reveal the interrelationships. In the experiences described, the dual role of the teacher is revealed. The teacher as an active teacher and the teacher as a passive teacher. The division of the categories into dimensions is reflected in Table 16, which depicts the overall outcome space.

Dimension I: The teacher teaches critical thinking actively. The first dimension includes the experiences described in Categories 2, 3, 4 and 5. Their unifying feature is that the teacher manifests as an active teacher of critical thinking. The active role of the teacher is revealed in a higher degree of engagement in the teaching and learning process. The teacher actively takes on the modelling and construction of critical thinking, explaining, showing, demonstrating and asking. By teaching to analyse a problem and compare, analyse and evaluate texts, and by showing a personal example, the teacher is working towards these main goals: not to believe one truth, to be able to evaluate critically, and to think deeper. These goals recur more frequently. The teachers also try to teach students to look at the phenomenon from different perspectives, broaden their horizons of thinking, learn to understand the relationship between cause and effect, distinguish the essence of phenomena, and be open, honest and faithful to the truth. It can, therefore, be argued that teachers not only develop cognitive abilities – they also develop critical thinking dispositions and foster criticality. They do this by developing specific abilities and a set of abilities. The development of specific abilities is related to specific tasks, such as comparing, collating and recognising differences:

> *The family is assisted by both a social educator and a social worker. So what's common between them and what's different.* (C17)

The development of a set of abilities is related to the attitude towards critical thinking as a complex competence and manifests itself in teaching to collect and select information, analyse various aspects of the phenomenon, look into the problem, solve various cases, and make independent decisions and substantiate them. Students are taught to ask questions, doubt, search and examine *what has been done in that sphere, and we always try to ensure that they don't trust one single opinion* ... (C9). Critical thinking is taught not only for professional, but also for personal purposes – so that students are not blind executors of instructions, but *the creators of their own norms and rules of life* (C7). The teachers believe that their own active involvement in the learning process is an appropriate way to highlight the importance of critical thinking, by demonstrating its value in the spheres of personal, professional and public life.

Dimension II: The teacher teaches critical thinking passively. In Categories 5, 6 and 7, the teacher manifests as a passive teacher of critical thinking. The teachers do not teach as much as they specify what to learn, and lead and control learning, assigning task and organising the learning process. However, passivity does not have a negative connotation. It simply means that the teacher 'transfers' the active role, delegating it to the students themselves. The equivalence of the active and passive roles is revealed in the outcome space, by discussing the expediency and value of teaching critical thinking. The passive way of teaching is explained by the desire to enable students to find their own answers to questions and thus *climb the ladder of cognition, when one thing opens up, then another, and then another* (C8). Passive teaching means that the teacher is well prepared for teaching – thinks through the course of the lecture, prepares tasks:

> *... I have quite a few tasks prepared, and I try to develop that critical thinking like this – I present the task and wait for questions.* (C10)

Teachers do not just assign individual assignments or work with individual students. They also organise group work by transferring the initiative of teaching and learning to the members of the groups. The students themselves take on the role of teacher and learning facilitators – *inspiring others ... to catch ... the pace and speak the language of arguments more ...* (C3). Like in the first dimension, the teachers in this one also develop both cognitive critical thinking skills and dispositions – open-mindedness, curiosity, self-reflection. The teachers believe that their passive participation in the teaching process creates more opportunities for deep and responsible learning. In their view, this way of teaching develops long-term, sustainable abilities that are useful in the spheres of personal, professional and public life.

3.1.4 Outcome space

The outcome space for this part of the study summarises the referential and structural components and their interrelations. The referential component answers the conceptual questions of how and what is taught. It describes the experience reflected in the categories described. There are two structural components. The first – value level I – shows the values that describe what is being taught and for what purpose. The second – value level II – indicates three levels of meaning: personal, interpersonal and social significance. Both structural components reflect the expediency and value of the experience. Value level I is depicted in Table 16.

Tab. 16: *Outcome Space. Conceptual and structural component: Value level I*

Structural component: Value level I (what)	**Categories (concepts) (how)**	**Dimensions of categories**
Not to believe in one truth	The teacher teaches how to analyse problems	Active teaching
	The teacher teaches how to analyse and evaluate texts	
	The teacher teaches by personal example	
	The teacher assigns non-standard tasks	Passive teaching
To think deeper/broaden your horizons	The teacher teaches how to analyse and evaluate texts	Active teaching
	The teacher teaches how to compare	
	The teacher assigns non-standard tasks	Passive teaching
To make reasoned decisions	The teacher teaches how to analyse problems	Active teaching
	The teacher gives independent tasks	Passive teaching
	The teacher assigns non-standard tasks	
To reason	The teacher gives independent tasks	Passive teaching
	The teacher organises group work	
	The teacher assigns non-standard tasks	
To interrelate theory and practice	The teacher teaches how to compare	Active teaching
	The teacher gives independent tasks	Passive teaching
To understand the interrelationship between reason and consequence	The teacher teaches by personal example	Active teaching
	The teacher gives independent tasks	Passive teaching
To search for decisions independently	The teacher teaches how to analyse problems	Active teaching
	The teacher gives independent tasks	Passive teaching
To evaluate critically	The teacher teaches how to analyse and evaluate texts	Active teaching
	The teacher teaches how to analyse problems	
To become creative	The teacher teaches by personal example	Active teaching
	The teacher assigns non-standard tasks	Passive teaching

Tab. 16: *Continued*

Structural component: Value level I (what)	**Categories (concepts) (how)**	**Dimensions of categories**
To learn to look from different perspectives	The teacher teaches how to analyse and evaluate texts	Active teaching
To learn to reflect	The teacher teaches how to compare	
To engage in the learning process	The teacher teaches how to compare	
To be able to generate new ideas	The teacher teaches by personal example	Active teaching
To distinguish the essence of phenomena		
To be honest/faithful to the truth		
To be open		
To learn to analyse		
To learn to ask questions	The teacher gives independent tasks	Passive teaching
To solve problems		
To take responsibility		
To learn to understand		
To make inferences		
To learn to hear others	The teacher organises group work	Passive teaching
To learn from others		

It should be noted that in the outcome space depicted above, the hierarchical relationships of meanings are clearly visible when answering the question of 'What is taught?' The most frequently recurring meanings are: (a) one meaning across four categories – 'not to believe in one truth'; (b) three meanings across three categories – 'to think deeper/broaden your horizons', 'to make reasoned decisions', 'to reason'; (c) five meanings across two categories – 'to interrelate theory and practice', 'to understand the interrelation between reason and consequence', 'to search for decisions independently', 'to evaluate criticism', 'to become creative'. All other meanings are repeated once in one specific category. Of the seven meanings in four categories, the two recurring meanings of 'not to believe in one truth' and 'to think deeper/broaden your horizons' indicate the significance of critical thinking dispositions. All other meanings are associated with the development of critical thinking skills. In terms of the significance of the dispositions, attention should be paid to the 'teacher teaches by personal example' category. The teachers confirm the value of open-mindedness, fairness, creativity and the pursuit of truth by demonstrating that dispositions are no less important than cognitive and/or practical abilities.

Analysis of the outcome space at the next level reveals that critical thinking is primarily taught for personal/professional purposes. Students look into specific study material and are prepared for a specific profession. The professional purpose is related to expanding the field of professional knowledge and improving on the competencies required for the future profession. However, the teachers also recognise the value of critical thinking for the student as a person, for cultivating his or her personality. The personal purpose is perceived as broadening one's outlook, education, self-education and improvement. The interpersonal value of critical thinking is revealed through mutual learning experiences in developing professional abilities and an empathic relationship. The social purpose includes the pursuit of truth and rightness that goes beyond the professional and personal field. Figure 9 below illustrates how the hierarchical relationships between the categories are revealed at the personal, interpersonal and social levels.

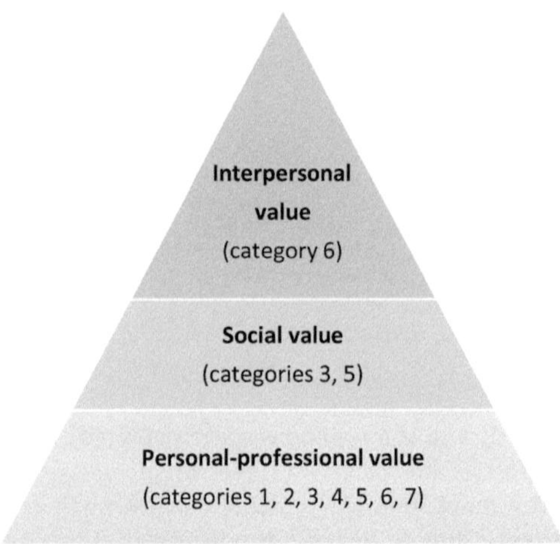

Fig. 9: *Outcome Space. Conceptual and structural component*

It should be noted that the perceived benefits for the person as such and for the person as a future professional and a participant in the labour market often merge into one picture. The boundaries separating these meanings are permeable. If students are taught to doubt and not believe in one truth, it is seen as beneficial both for cultivating their personality and for their professional development. If analysing and evaluating professional literature is taught, it is thought that it will be useful in evaluating any texts of a personal nature. The analysis of professional cases is considered valuable in analysing life situations as well. These meanings are, therefore, at the widest lower level of the triangle in this figure. It contains the meanings of all categories.

The social value of critical thinking is only mentioned in two cases – when the teacher teaches how to analyse and evaluate texts and when the teacher teaches by personal example. In the first case, text analysis is related to the ability to read, interpret and deeply understand socially significant knowledge, in whatever format it is presented. In the second case, personal example is understood as a role model to follow – to question, to not be afraid of making mistakes, to create, and to remain honest and faithful to the truth in various situations of public life. Meanings with social value are shown in the middle of the triangle, as there are less of them than at the lower level and more of them than at the upper level.

The interpersonal value of critical thinking is only revealed in one case – when students teach each other and learn from one another when the teacher organises group work. In this case, critical thinking is expressed in the interpersonal relationship of perceiving the benefits of such learning for one another. Meanings with scarce interpersonal value are shown at the top of the triangle – in the narrowest part.

3.2. How teachers learn critical thinking

Analysis of the teachers' learning experiences revealed that critical thinking is learned in three qualitatively different ways, which fall into three dominant categories: (1) learning critical thinking independently; (2) learning critical thinking with others; and (3) learning critical thinking from others.

3.2.1 Categories

The qualitative difference lies in the relationship. The first category includes statements that illustrate the teachers' learning while in an open relationship with themselves – by asking themselves questions, analysing themselves and the environment, reflecting on their thoughts and attitudes, and rethinking their experience and behaviour. The second category includes statements that illustrate the teachers' learning while in direct contact with others – in the personal or professional field. The third category includes statements that illustrate the teachers' learning from others by experiencing an indirect relationship –by observing the professional and wider environment as well as social processes.

Category 1: I learn critical thinking by myself. This is the broadest category, encompassing learning experiences that can be defined as the use of the resources within oneself (thoughts, feelings, emotions, accumulated experience) in order to enrich, improve and renew oneself while in a dialogical relationship with oneself. The main prevailing conviction is that critical thinking lies within (although you may not be aware of it) and needs to be aroused, improved and fostered.

The teachers claim that they analyse themselves, ask themselves questions, weigh how best to proceed in one case or another, compare their own attitudes and those of others, and draw conclusions. Despite the use of other resources such as books and other people's experiences, the main resource remains the person him or herself. He or she analyses, reflects, and makes decisions and conclusions by devoting time to that:

> *You improve through everyday events and situations, when you learn from them, rethink, and reflect on what happened; maybe not every day or every evening, but once in a week. You just dedicate some time to it in the morning or evening, depending on the occasion. Sometimes you rethink when you are walking or doing something. As well as when you're reading or collecting information from different sources.* (C3)

Self-improvement is also associated with personal growth and development, but most often to the desire to keep up with professional innovations and expand one's field of knowledge so that it can be shared with other colleagues and conveyed to students. The teachers claim that they want students to not limit themselves to textbook knowledge; to understand that there are live processes in every specialty and that everything changes. They also want teachers to be seen not as stagnant individuals stuck in their narrow profession, but as individuals who are constantly learning and deepening their knowledge. They, therefore, consider it very important to remain *in the horizontal plane* (C2), that is, not to get caught up in a narrow field, and to be able to combine several professional fields such as *law, medicine, ethics, bioethics and many other subjects* (C13).

However, learning critical thinking takes place not only as an internal incentive for personal or professional development, but also as an everyday necessity arising in a specific professional situation:

> *Every time, you're forced to think, reappraise the boundaries of professional ethics, the boundaries of your activities, how much you have to bow to your customers, how much you have to adhere letter for letter to your code of ethics, or how much of that interpretation you can provide. So you're forced to think every day because you're not standing at a machine, you're not arranging loaves of bread – you're working with people. It's a living matter. You don't know where a given situation can take you. And then there are new situations not only from professional ethics, but also from certain choices – how I should have done it, whether I did the right thing – or you see that some responses aren't the best, then you're forced again to somehow justify why you did it what you did.* (C2)

Although this situation is described as 'forced', it has no negative connotation. On the contrary, it testifies to live learning by rethinking professional choices and re-evaluating and substantiating them. Critical thinking learning in this category manifests itself in a natural way – through self-education and self-development. They include these dimensions of critical thinking: self-analysis, self-reflection and rethinking. The latter dimension has manifestations not only of active thinking, but also of changes in one's behaviour, 'correction'. The teachers learn by leaning inwards and looking back at themselves – there, they look for answers to questions, contemplate professional competencies, and rethink their behaviours. The main methods of self-development are reading, observation and thinking.

Category 2: I learn critical thinking with others. This category includes learning experiences that teachers have from a direct relationship with others, most often their colleagues. The teachers claim that being with others in training courses, seminars or conferences related to a specific profession or area of interest provides opportunities to discuss and share experiences, and thus learn:

> *My colleagues and I try to share our experience and have had the chance to attend a few seminars abroad. It seems to me that the team and the people alongside you are very important for critical thinking. They encourage you because you weigh things critically on your own, one way or another, but it's actually very hard to find a solution. And when you're on a team, you learn to take a detached view and step back from everything, you learn not to identify with what you've done and to evaluate critically.* (C16)

Learning critical thinking is treated as considering different attitudes and opinions together – an incentive to look at yourself from the outside and evaluate yourself more adequately. Being in an active relationship with others not only helps to re-evaluate yourself and your attitudes – it also teaches you how to convey them to others and *justify and defend your position* (C11). Despite the fact that learning takes place in smaller or larger groups, the content of learning is considered independently. The teachers stress that what is learned collectively must be rethought individually and tested in a specific context:

> *When I worked for advertising agencies, all types of courses were hired, some lecturer presents some sort of methodology, and at first it seems like it's something special, that it works, but it only works as long as you're with that lecturer. Then you go back to your environment, which is not, say, London, there are no London clients – these are completely different contexts. And you start to think – hold on, in my opinion this method doesn't work in this context, even though it was presented to me as a network methodology of our company, which I kind of have to use. I do better with a completely different methodology that I used before that or discovered myself. But at the same time, you can take advantage of what seems to you to be appropriate in the proposed methodology. Ultimately, you investigate a few methodologies, connect them with your own and see what result it gives you. Again, the result is usually evaluated by clients, the consumers, you check to see if it works or not.* (C9)

In this exceptional case, learning critical thinking is revealed as a specific learning experiences with others that has been checked in the professional field. All other examples are more concerned with personal contemplations and reflections.

Learning with others in all cases opens the horizons for a broader, more diverse attitude; it creates opportunities to look at common phenomena and situations through the eyes of others and reconsider your convictions and beliefs or – vice versa – strengthen them.

Learning critical thinking in this category is manifested in an organised, collective way. Like in the first category, learning in this category also includes three essential dimensions of critical thinking: self-analysis, self-reflection and rethinking. Teachers learn with others and only thanks to others are they able to improve their critical thinking skills and review their convictions. The main ways of learning are discussion and thinking.

Category 3: I learn critical thinking from others. This category is characterised by the fact that learning takes place through active and purposeful observation and evaluation of the environment, both professional and social, and the processes that develop in it. If, in the first case (Category 1), the component 'I' is raised, then here, the 'other'/'others' component becomes more important. The incentive to learn comes not from within, but from the outside, while in an indirect relationship with other people, with events in the external environment. The main way of learning becomes observation: *I watch and do an analysis* (C9), *I drive and observe* (C8); *I watch and compare* (C14). The goals of such learning are threefold. The first case involves delving into the learning content in order to better comprehend it and convey it to others:

> *First I did an analysis of what's been done for this film, I watch what people are doing that it's already becoming something of a cliché. Since I want to be original, I try to avoid clichés as much as possible when still communicating that film so that people somehow get the gist, to read my metaphor, so I can tell the message through the metaphor rather than straightforwardly. Then I review the standpoint of film critics who see all kinds of angles about that film, I watch the film many times, I try to understand what the director wanted to say, how he interpreted some piece of literature, and then I read that piece of literature. In a word, I approach it from all sorts of angles. It doesn't guarantee the best result, but it is, in a sense, again 'putting yourself in [someone else's] shoes'. I try to put myself into that problem every time, put myself into the film.* (C9)

Getting a grasp is metaphorically referred to as an attempt to *put yourself in someone else's shoes* (C9), that is, to become accustomed to the content in question and look at it through someone else's eyes. Learning criticality manifests itself in examining different attitudes and perspectives and looking for an original, non-cliché evaluation.

In the second case, the truth is sought. The teacher observes the environment, follows public debates on topical public issues, and tries to figure out *what's right here and what isn't* (C14). Comparing, considering and rethinking different opinions and attitudes helps figure this out.

In the third case, an objective perception of reality is sought, which is achieved through close observation of society, the environment and processes, and being in an open relationship with people:

> *And I tell students – the greatest teacher is reality. If you're soldering metal and it doesn't melt, then you observe what's wrong, where it's stuck. I'd say to remain active in observing that environment, and exactly the same with loved ones, exactly the same with*

> *more distant people, colleagues, co-workers, artists, with what is going on in the exhibition halls, in cultural policy. This is fairness. You still have to look for certain criteria.* (C8)

Objective reality is perceived as the tangibility of a 'living' phenomenon in the professional or social field, achieved by *remaining active in observing* (C8), that is, a vigilant practicing observer. It is in this way that critical thinking is learned, which manifests itself in various forms of objective reality. In objective reality, a specific reference criterion is sought – fairness, which could be interpreted as rightness.

Critical thinking learning in this category manifests itself in purposeful observation of the environment, encompassing dimensions of critical thinking such as analysis, synthesis, interpretation and conveyance, and evaluation. The teachers learn from environmental phenomena and processes that occur in both the professional context and the wider social context. The main ways of learning are observation and comparative analysis.

3.2.2 Relationships between the categories described

The three qualitatively different ways of learning critical thinking can be explained by the differences and similarities between the two interrelated variations (dimensions), which help to reveal the interrelationships. Critical thinking is learned either individually or in an organised way. The individual way can also be called self-regulated because it stems from a person's internal or external need and is self-managed. The organised way means that learning takes place as an activity planned by others.

Dimension I: The individual (self-regulated) way of learning. This dimension includes all three categories and the vast majority of the meanings listed in them. The teachers usually learn critical thinking individually. Whether they are learning on their own, with others, or from others, in all cases, this learning takes place within them. The teachers think and ask questions, and mentally weight, compare, analyse, evaluate, reflect and draw conclusions. The active learning process takes place as an internal and constant conversation with oneself:

> *... you rethink and reflect on what happened; maybe not every day or every evening, but once in a week. You just dedicate some time to it ...* (C3)

The need for learning is twofold. It is an inner incentive to improve, to have an original manifestation or a unique way of thinking: *I want to be original, I try to avoid clichés* (C9), or a necessity dictated by the professional environment: *you're forced to think, reappraise the boundaries of professional ethics, the boundaries of your activities ...* (C2). No clear divide between these two needs has been established. The teachers are more likely to combine these two needs into one than to set them in opposition. Learning takes place by learning from both professional literature and material from the living environment. The research data allow this way of learning to be considered self-regulated. Teachers set learning tasks for themselves, organising, evaluating and contemplating them themselves.

Dimension II: The collective (organised) way of learning. This dimension consists of several meanings from the second category that describe a collective way of learning. Teachers learn critical thinking by being in an intense open relationship with others, usually with members of the same profession. Learning takes place on outings outside of the institution, such as conferences and seminars. There, knowledge and experience is shared, which in turn teaches the teachers *to take a detached view and step back from everything ... not to identify with what you've done and to evaluate critically* (C16). In this way, they learn self-reflection, open-mindedness, respect for different opinions, as well as the ability to convey your opinion and *justify and defend your position* (C11).

Despite the fact that learning is organised and collective, the content of learning is considered independently. The teachers rethink it in order to adapt the lessons learned to their own working environment and context:

> *... you start to think ... in my opinion this method doesn't work in this context ... you investigate a few methodologies, connect them with your own and see what result it gives you ...* (C9)

It can, therefore, be argued that the independence of the values of this dimension is conditional. Learning takes place both in the interpersonal collective space and in the personal inner space. However, it is noteworthy that the organised, collective way of learning creates more opportunities to look at phenomena and situations through the eyes of others, and to reconsider and/or reinforce your beliefs and decisions.

3.2.3 Outcome space

Table 17 presents the outcome space for this part of the study, reflecting the dimensions listed and the categories assigned to them. It also reveals the general outcome space, its referential and structural components, and their interrelations. The referential component answers the question of 'what' and describes the experience reflected in the described categories. The structural component answers the question of 'what is it for' and reflects the expediency and value of the experience.

Tab. 17: *Outcome space: Conceptual and value components of critical thinking learning for teachers*

Conceptual component		**Value component**
Variations of dimensions (interrelations)	Categories (concepts)	Level of importance (value)
Individual (self-regulated) learning	I learn critical thinking by myself	Personal/professional
	I learn critical thinking from others	Professional/social
Collective (organised) learning	I learn critical thinking with others	Personal/professional

In summary, it can be said that the individual (self-regulated) way is the main way of learning in learning independently and from others. It also applies to learning with others, but is secondary to collective learning in a larger professional group. The collective (organised) way of learning does not apply to learning independently and from others when the person is alone with him or herself, that is with his or her thinking, regardless of whether there are other people around or not. There is one aspect that unites all three different categories: comparing and evaluating different attitudes and drawing one's own conclusions. Regardless of the way of learning, in all cases, the teachers stress the importance of evaluating the same phenomenon, event or situation in the context of multifaceted attitudes.

Personal and professional meaning is attributed to both individual and collective learning. Personal significance is perceived as broadening one's outlook, education, self-education and improvement. Professional significance is perceived as expansion of the field of specific knowledge and improvement of professional competencies. The social value of learning is found in learning from others. It includes the pursuit of truth and rightness that goes beyond the professional and personal field. However, the most striking is the professional aspiration, which encompasses the meanings of all three categories. Teachers learn out of professional interest, in order to keep up with innovations, highlight them and convey them to students.

Despite the variations in the categories listed, there are also significant aspects that recur in each category. They are reflected in Figure 10.

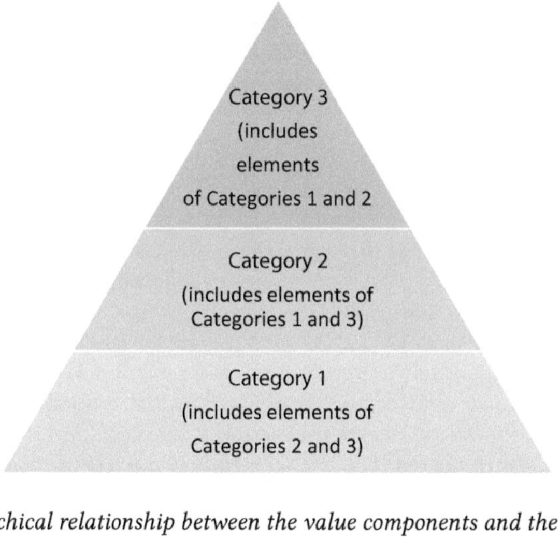

Fig. 10: *Hierarchical relationship between the value components and the categories of conceptions*

The first category – I learn critical thinking by myself – has the greatest abundance of experiences and is depicted at the bottom. It contains similar elements as the other two categories. Learning is done independently and through self-development and self-education, but is for the same purposes as in other categories – personal and professional. The second category – I learn critical thinking from others – is second in terms of abundance of experiences. It is therefore depicted in the middle. Learning with others fulfils the same personal and professional purposes as in the first category. The only difference is that learning takes place not just in the personal space, but in the active interpersonal space as well. At the top of the figure is the third category – I learn critical thinking with others – with the lowest manifestation of experiences. It includes the professional interest that is also pronounced in the other categories. It is also linked to the second category by the interpersonal aspect, which here acquires a slightly different meaning. Learning with others helps to accumulate personal and professional capital. Learning from others provides more than just that. This kind of learning also contributes to the understanding of how to better serve other people and society. So unlike the others categories, this category also includes the social aspect of learning critical thinking.

3.3. How students learn critical thinking

Analysis of the student interviews revealed the students' experiences of how they learn critical thinking while studying at institutions of higher education. The qualitatively different ways were divided into two dominant categories: (1) learning critical thinking through discussion; (2) learning critical thinking by performing tasks simulating real situations; and two non-dominant categories: (3) learning critical thinking from the teacher's questioning; (4) learning critical thinking by working with multiple sources of information. Each category is presented in detail below.

3.3.1 Dominant categories

Category 1. Learning critical thinking through discussion. This is the broadest category, encompassing the students' experiences of participating in discussions, which they attributed to learning critical thinking. The students referred to discussion as a way in which they were encouraged by teachers to think critically and reveal and demonstrate their critical thinking during classroom sessions. The interview material also showed that in the context of critical thinking learning, discussion is a fairly versatile tool that is used across different study fields and cycles. The students indicated that in their studies, discussion was for expressing different attitudes, examining problems, formulating arguments, and substantiating one's position.

In this category, it comes to light that critical thinking is learned in discussions that present different, diverse attitudes to the same phenomenon or process. In discussion, not only does one become more familiar with the topic and better acquainted with the very subject of discussion – doubt is also aroused as to whether what is known is the only possible knowing:

> *... actually encourages you think about whether what is presented one-sidedly really is the real truth. Or maybe there's another way and that there really can be another way. This type of teaching kind of encourages you to think and ask the question, that there are two sides to every situation and that there can be different attitudes.* (D14)

Besides the fact that general discussion allows you to get to know the topic or problem better, the students value discussion as a way to reveal different attitudes towards the topic first and foremost to yourself, and as a way to discover new points of view that would not be discovered without discussion with others:

> *... that exchange of knowledge and that promotion of shared communication, I think it contributed a lot to that critical thinking, since everyone sees from very different viewpoints.* (D1)

By discussing and, for example, analysing a case, students can hear the opinions of their group colleagues, evaluate them in the general context, supplement them with their own information, and use the synergy of group knowledge to come up with new solutions:

> *There are some situations, let's say a case study or situation, that you have to describe and propose solutions. Even yesterday, for example, we did that, and there are very different variants and I already recognise this as a manifestation of critical thinking. You need to turn on your entire library that you know and how you would do it. And the other thing is that I hear how someone else thinks. So there are already options then, and in this way we learn and complement each other. I think it's about developing critical thinking.* (D11)

In sharing their experiences, the students showed that the qualities of discussion that lead to or reinforce critical thinking learning are revealed in the relationship with the teacher, with the group colleagues, and with themselves. The teacher-student, teacher-group and student-student interaction during the discussion is important in creating an open culture where you can safely speak your mind and hear someone else out:

> *We would watch films and try to interpret them in our own way. So I think that was the thing that was most revealed there, because you just don't have to do it according to some manual or book, but you interpret those things based on how you understand them. ... there's a film that you have to understand, and there are no other requirements. You understand it how you understand it. It's not like you understood it wrong here; there's just a discussion and you discuss which place seems more important to you and which is not as important. There's no end result that you have to come to like in a mathematical problem. It's just a broad thing where there's no right answer. Everyone sees it in their own way from their own position.* (D12)

However, creating this open environment in terms of critical thinking has much greater significance than just the opportunity to speak out or share your thoughts. It encourages thinking, creating new ideas, and discovering what the student has not come up with thus far:

> *It all starts with the fact that questions are usually asked that don't require a 'yes' or 'no' answer, that develop thinking and reveal attitudes through the prism of our ideas, thoughts and beliefs, and we're encouraged to think in this way. He doesn't immediately present a stereotypical opinion – he lets us express ourselves and doesn't critically evaluate everyone's opinion and ideas.* (D3)

In addition, the teacher encourages the students to think more by not giving an unequivocal answer to the discussion question, so they have to look for the necessary information themselves:

> *One really striking example was that there are teachers that you can just ask and that question will be ordinary, where you want to clarify the answer, and the answer will always be 'yes', but 'no' and then 10 minutes of extra speech where it can be one side or the other ... So from things like that we have to know how to collect what we need, and a lot of times those answers are ... about what is harder to find. So this is exactly from where we learn to think even more and select the things that we really need.* (D13)

Another aspect of discussion that came to light and which is important in terms of critical thinking is the students learning to argue. The students claim that by discussing, they learn not just to express their attitude towards the problem at hand, but also to formulate arguments and substantiate their opinions and insights about the text read, the film watched, or the work done. As the students point out, they are encouraged to argue by teachers, so the interaction between the teacher and the student is also important here:

> *The teachers ask our opinion. If they also have their own opinion, they often correct us, but they still listen to what the students' opinion is, what their insights are, asking to substantiate the insights so that it's not just utterances without any argumentation. If you say something, you have to argue and say why you think that way, why that is your insight* (D4).
> *... but always ask to argue why you think so, what led to your making that decision. I think that's one aspect of critical thinking. ... never criticised, wanted to extract information about why we think that way, what basis we're making the decision on. ... taught us to argue.* (D3)

The opportunity to speak out on discussion questions encourages students to contemplate the material read and evaluate it in order to choose their position in the discussion, present it, and substantiate it with the arguments they have formulated and selected:

> *When we get some sort of content during lectures and then develop critical thinking during seminars, then you can notice that you have an opinion on certain issues, you*

> *hold some sort of position and then you know some sort of arguments and have your own arguments and appreciate which ones are smarter, which ones are more rational. You can speak out on certain issues, you have a reasoned opinion.* (D4)

However, there are also experiences in which the opportunity to learn to think critically in support of one's opinion or position is not typical:

> *Sometimes I hear a question from teachers, what's your opinion, what would you choose, but more often they tell you how it should be done and don't ask what you would choose.* (D10)

The third aspect that emerged in this category characterises the students' experiences in which discussion is a way to think critically together and contribute to finding a solution to a problem or information on how that problem can be solved. They indicated that one of the problems to be addressed is the different sources of information that they learn to compare by starting a discussion:

> *It's precisely from those discussions, because it's by initially getting different sources and seeing different options for how things work that discussions begin on how it really should be.* (D13)

Thus, when analysing a problem, the *different arguments and different primary data* available (D14) encourage critical thinking and looking for different solutions to the problem:

> *It's precisely from here that I understand that it's not the only ways to get to a solution to the problem that are being taught.* (D13)
> *She [the teacher] also encouraged us a lot – so how would you get out of a situation like this? How about one like this? We ... purely from life had to try to find ways out and this also arouses critical thinking.* (D11)

In addition, the students realise and appreciate that by learning to look for different solutions in discussions, they can also open up to themselves more new, different attitudes, and *then look for even more answers that may be even more different* (D13).

As the students' experiences show, discussion is a tool and space for learning to think critically. It can be argued that this is one of the most common paths in which the process of learning critical thinking takes place. The students point to several attributes of discussion in learning critical thinking: discussion allows you to get to know the topic better, reveal different attitudes first and foremost to yourself, discover new points of view that would not be discovered without group discussion, present your position, and learn to support your statements with arguments while discussing. The students single out the role of the teacher in discussion, who chooses the teaching method, is responsible for the atmosphere in the classroom, creates or does not create an open discussion environment without preconceptions, and encourages and engages students in the search for critical thinking and its development during the study process.

Category 2. Learning critical thinking by performing tasks simulating real situations. This category includes critical thinking learning experiences that students had by performing tasks that mimic a real situation or real-life problems. Such tasks require students to understand the full context of the situation specified in the task, see ways of solving it, grasp cause-effect relationships, make a reasoned decision on how it will be implemented, and then implement and evaluate how it turned out.

The first aspect that came to light of what the students experience in performing tasks of a similar nature is the need to narrow down a great number of solutions and select their own way:

> *We have to learn to think, first and foremost to understand ourselves what kind of task it is, not everything is easy, nicely explained, you still have to put some of your work into it and think about what this is, what tools you'll need, what formulas you'll need, because you're not given a list.* (D1)

When deciding how a task will be performed, students point out that this requires looking deeper into the situation, seeing and understanding the entire context in which the task is performed, and taking into account the factors that influence that context and very many different circumstances:

> *In my organic synthesis, there are different ways to synthesise a molecule. There are a few more practical tasks where you have to weave logical thinking into a specific global situation, where it then comes out more, because there are various assumptions you have to define or evaluate and logic alone is not enough because you have to examine more things. Those tasks were ones that develop critical thinking* (D7).
> *Factors that may be important in generating profits from the grain trade were presented, but we had to evaluate for ourselves which factors are important and which to ignore, because there were quite a few of them. We had to find links between those factors that affect profits and those that don't. Then we had to randomly generate those factors ourselves and simulate the development of that company based on that. ... A lot of different circumstances had to be taken into account when creating the simulation, and I'd say it required pretty strong critical thinking, because those aspects that a company's profits depend on, there were a lot of them, so everything had to be put into that programme, everything had to be critically thought over.* (D5)

Also, in order to perform a task with a practical, applied nature, students not only have to take into account the entire context, but also learn to use the acquired theoretical knowledge and apply it in solving the task:

> *We come to the lab one day and she tells us: 'You'll need to make menthol pills.' We've been learning all semester; we have accumulated information. But she didn't give us any formula, any example of how we should do it; she didn't tell us what materials we should use, wet granulation or dry. But you, with that whole baggage of knowledge, you try to adapt.* (D3)

Real-situation tasks that require using scientific information, applying acquired knowledge and proposing a solution are also given during assessments. In the context of critical thinking learning, the students evaluate these tasks as ones that develop critical thinking:

> *There was a very interesting exam where a short film was shown and you had to recognise what we had theoretically learned. Without critical thinking, without the ability to understand what's going on here now, what model this is – there was no way. This was a really impressive exam for me, I like tasks like that, that way of learning – not theoretical, but when they make you think right there. … And the teacher said: 'Write what you feel, not what you took notes on somewhere, but how you would really deal with that situation yourself.' So this is absolutely your critical thinking turning on and you evaluate the situation, and based on that you set out what I know from my experience, how I think I would deal with it. And of course, there's also your baggage of knowledge, in theory we already have some reference points as well.* (D11)

According to the students, those tasks that require understanding the situation, defining the problem in it, analytically breaking it down, and rejecting cookie-cutter solutions are at the same time very effective in promoting personal responsibility and engaging critical thinking:

> *Practical tasks consist of first looking critically at the problem, I mean, not just using formulas, but understanding the situation, and then, based on the knowledge available, placing it into certain metaphorical boxes of the solution and deciding based on them. … You're given the tools to solve a particular problem, but you have to see the problem in that task yourself, know what tools to use in solving it, and solve it. And I think that's where that critical thinking distinguishes itself – being able to look at a problem coolly and knowing what has to be used there in solving it.* (D9)

Another important aspect is the nature of the task itself. The trial-and-error method and evaluation and modification of the task parameters encourage students to think about their task and look into its essence. An important role is also played by the task itself – whether it is strictly regulated or provides for freedom of action. From the students' point of view, tasks with freedom of action that cannot be solved according to a simple scheme *encourage you to think and narrow things down the most* (D1). When performing this type of task, students choose the way of solving it themselves and analyse the situation of the task on their own, so they have to put more effort into delving into it, which, in their opinion, contributes greatly to the development of critical thinking:

> *You see how drastically things change when you have to think for yourself. It really felt like university is not just the next textbook, but a completely different thing. You actually start evaluating those problems, especially physics problems, where you don't have some kind of framework, where it's not that there's a task and you have the method and you have to apply it. It's up to you to come up with the method and choose the tools, how*

you're going to approach that task, what formulas you're going to use, what methods, how you're going to explore it. (D1)

Solving such pseudo-free tasks teaches students to act independently and harness creativity while also doing everything according to the requirements and covering the entirety of the task and its process, from start to finish. So it is as if tasks like these liberate and provide space while also disciplining:

This is probably most felt when the tasks aren't really specifically formulated, when they're fairly loose in content and you have to choose things yourself. So it seems like a lot of fun, you have freedom for creativity, but on the other hand, the evaluation is pretty strict and you can't do just anything, you really have to figure out for yourself what's basically the most important thing here and pick out the things that are important to you, that you want to present, and of course you have to do stuff from the technical side. So I think it's this pseudo-free presentation of tasks that encourages the most thinking. ... there was a lot of critical thinking there, because first of all, you had to come up with a task within the framework of that area, basically something with images and data and their processing. ... either in some sort of practical tasks, or a lot of times various creative tasks are assigned, like creating some kind of message or short piece of news about some specific thing. And then the first thing you do is pick out the information – so for that, I think, critical thinking is used very heavily. (D1)

In addition, tasks that provide freedom and at the same time do not have one correct answer, according to the students, encourage choosing arguments to support decisions, develop the ability to formulate one's position using facts and evidence, and thus teach critical thinking:

Tasks where more freedom is given and there isn't one correct answer, it seems to me that they're the ones that develop critical thinking. Because you have to take into account, think over and evaluate the situation from your standpoint, from your point of view. When there are tasks where you have to defend your position, not just get the right answer. That's where critical thinking is developed. (D7)

The students pointed out that tasks that are intended not just to be performed mechanically, but to develop certain abilities, such as making independent decisions to solve a real problem, develop their critical thinking:

... students are given some programming problems that they can even encounter in real life that need to be solved, when the students have to find a way to solve them themselves. It's not enough to show that you know how to programme – you have to show that you know how to make your own decisions on how to solve the problem. ... Critical thinking in programming manifests itself as the evaluation of a problem and the ability to find exactly the solution needed to solve that problem, rather than some careless programme writing, without evaluating the situation at all. (D5)

Another important aspect of critical thinking that came to light in these simulation tasks is learning to identify the cause-effect relationships of the process and justify the decisions you make in performing the task based on them, sometimes without even taking the response received or the result achieved into account. According to the students, teachers use problematic tasks to develop their understanding of cause-effect relationships and their ability to formulate and substantiate their position:

> *It wasn't as important what factors you chose as it was how you justified your choice. There was no one right solution to the problem, but it was important how you were able to explain why you chose it.* (D5)

Students are encouraged to learn to notice the cause-effect relationships of a process in a variety of ways. One of them is when the teacher presents a problem and invites the students to actively engage in its analysis to understand the principles of how the process works:

> *Usually teachers just bring up a problem and ask the students to solve it. If the students have trouble, they give them a tiny bite that they can hook onto, and that's how we rise. It's really important to them that the students understand what and why. ... He didn't ask you to cram anything at all, but with each process all of those phenomena were really true-to-life. He wanted to instil an understanding into us of roughly how things work, that everything works according to its own formula, that it doesn't really matter exactly how things work, the important thing is that they have a certain cycle that they revolve around, and in particular to have an attitude toward things, that you understand more or less how things work and you're not some lost sheep who doesn't know where it is.* (D9)

Another way to learn to notice the cause-effect relationships of a process, according to the students, is to do laboratory work, during which experiments are performed, tests are carried out, and real materials are used. This laboratory work incorporates a full range of aspects that are important for learning critical thinking, such as the need to show the cause-effect relationships of a process, orient oneself in a large amount of information, understand the entire process, be able to specify a goal, and not memorise the study material:

> *A really big part of critical thinking is in defending lab work. ... I think that critical thinking here is one of the aspects, so you don't get lost, so you see the big picture, what that chain is capable of, not to get lost in individual devices. During labs, the teachers don't ask you to learn everything by heart, they just try to get it into your head what the purpose of this chain was and you have to answer it. I think critical thinking is developed really well this way.* (D9)

When learning to identify cause-effect relationships, as noted by the students, it sometimes does not matter to the teacher whether the task is performed correctly because the entire chain of actions performed is evaluated. Here, the student is encouraged to carefully review his or her path of performing the task and identify key points that could tilt cause-effect relationships into other trajectories:

> *A lot of times those syntheses you're doing don't work out, so then you have to run through what you could change, what conditions you could modify. To achieve the goal in my work, critical thinking is very important.* (D8)

The fact that specifying the cause-effect relationship or connection of the elements is important is shown by the students' experiences, when a reference to this relationship is missing for the student to answer in detail. And by additionally asking for an explanation of the relationship, the teacher draws the student's attention to the importance of understanding and demonstrating deterministic relationships:

> *Other teachers sometimes ask you to explain some concept, but then say: 'I wanted you to also write why and where that comes from.'* (D8)

One more important aspect that came to light in this category is the skill formed to evaluate how you succeeded or failed in performing the task:

> *I wrote my game in different six ways in half a year. So those different ways, searching for how to do something, that's the search for that critical thinking, which option is better in certain aspects. Because nevertheless, certain aspects are evaluated. So this lets you not only do it once you find it, but also evaluate for yourself what's better.* (D13)

or what else can be changed:

> *... so critical thinking is more visible in application – you think about how you could change something more effectively – like saving space, weight.* (D12)

According to the students, they learn critical thinking when performing tasks in a real-life context where they have to integrate the problem situation to be solved with the whole. The students singled out that when performing tasks where the teachers looked into the students' thinking trajectories, decision-making logic, and chain of action with the process itself rather than assessing knowledge and results, they learned critical thinking intensively. Laboratory work as assessment tasks, in the opinion of the students, is of great importance for the development of critical thinking both because of the content of the task and because of the extent to which students are enabled in a practical trial to combine their acquired theoretical knowledge, activate their thinking abilities, and create a result that gives them discoveries both about the subject being studied and about themselves as actors who can make a difference. In summarising what the students said, one could say that all of the assessments that they singled out as ones that made a significant contribution to the development of their critical thinking are based not on the repetition of knowledge, but on the use of knowledge in solving real or imaginary problematic situations that encourage the practical application of knowledge.

3.3.2 Non-dominant categories

Category 3. Learning critical thinking from the teacher's questioning. The students indicated that they learn critical thinking from teachers questioning them in such a way that teaches them reflexive and reasoned speaking. This speaking is not necessarily a discussion of a topic, picture or event during a direct activity, but can be speaking as writing or laying out thoughts where, in recognising that a student's social status, demographic characteristics and time context may influence his or her own way of thinking, the perception of the phenomenon is objectivised and explained:

> *When you don't reflect on what and how you speak, that speaking is hanging in the air. Self-reflection gives you self-knowledge, an understanding of how you're affected by context, the country you were born in, the gender relations that you live in. The predominant faith that you live in, the experience brought from the family, the circle of people you interact with, your age ... aha ... and in a sense objectivises my own speaking, I realise that I won't be able to speak objectively because objective speaking hardly exists, but I understand what circumstances affect my speaking, but after naming it in the text ... speaking acquires a certain validity, it's easier to agree or oppose others, you define what point you're speaking from and opportunities open up for the other speaker to supplement and thus move for a possibly more objective perception of the phenomenon.* (D16)

Speaking in writing is important from the point of view of critical thinking and in that it teaches students to doubt, to begin to distrust the knowledge they have, and to strengthen the thought processes that the students feel awaken critical thinking:

> *... thinking, at least for me, is most needed for assessment ... when every one of your decisions, every one of your statements in answering the question, is questioned again: 'Why this way, why not that way?' And then you're forced to think. You can't just memorise or learn something – then you have to think. At least for me, that's when it feels the most like critical thinking.* (D1)

Questioning on the part of the teacher can also be passive, without taking the form of dialogue or discussion. For example, when formulating an exam question, the student must establish that the question has a certain gap or catch, the task of which is to encourage the student to ask, request an explanation:

> *... a lot of times during assessments it's like there are gaps left in the questions, where the point is to ask and clarify a certain detail based on which they want it to be resolved. Since some things are just a matter of agreement. Because of that agreement, these sort of gaps are left, that you have to know that you're missing information and based on that let things be unified somehow.* (D13)

Questioning can also be active, which causes students to learn to use terminology in a certain way and replace relative concepts with more precise ones that have a certain degree of certainty. Students attribute this kind of questioning to critical thinking learning:

> *Especially during assessments, it's already commonplace for us, during various term paper defences or even final defences, you really think through each one of your statements. And this is where critical thinking is already pounded into your head that*

you don't say just anything anymore. You also think through all of the terms really well, and not just the complex terms, but also when you say the words 'a lot' or 'a little', you understand that this is not some defined thing, that it's a very, very relative thing, and you try to put numbers into the context, that you say 'approximately this much or this much'. (D1)

So for critical thinking to emerge, in the opinion of the students, it is enough to eliminate the option of memorising the material required for the assessment. Through the questioning that emerges in teacher-student interaction, teachers encourage students' thinking as such, as well as the ability to construct logic and argue, which students feel to be critical thinking.

Category 4. Learning critical thinking by working with multiple sources of information. This category reveals the students' experiences where students attribute work with different sources of information to critical thinking learning. In this category, an important aspect came to light that by delving into the topic under analysis and reading more and more literature, students experience that the task can be solved in various ways, and that a single answer is no longer the norm. This experience shakes the foundations of standard, usual thinking and, according to the students, creates preconditions for the development of critical thinking:

First of all, attention is always paid to very different sources from which you understand that the same task, even though this is the exact sciences, can be solved in completely different ways. It's not that there's just not one answer – there's also not one way. The same tasks can't be seen as done or not done. There always has to be a delving into our perception, how we're going toward the goal. This is precisely where critical thinking comes from. (D13)

That critical thinking learning stems primarily from the experience that by getting to know the problem situation of the task and reading more about it, different ways of solving that task are discovered and there is no single set path. Delving into the material being studied includes not only learning to gather information about the research phenomenon, but also to carefully evaluate the information provided, check it, compare empirical data from different studies on the same topic, generalise them, and understand that the answer obtained is not necessarily the only one:

We've already been taught a bit in these studies that there has to be a few sources that you can derive some common denominator from, and that's still not the ultimate truth. (D11)

So delving into the material being studied is in principle perceived as endless, and this perception comes from the text analysis and source analysis process that takes place at the personal level of the student.

In summary, it can be stated that several different sources of information reveal to the students the diversity of the topic they are analysing, which they have to immerse themselves in, look into and read more about, and which they have to understand and accept as a reality in which the same task can be solved in different ways, so it is important to understand the consequences of those different solutions for the development of the problem itself.

3.3.3 *Relationships between the categories of description*

The four qualitatively different ways of learning critical thinking can be explained by the differences between the two interrelated variations (dimensions). These dimensions are theoretical learning and practical learning, and the relationships are summarised in Table 18.

Tab. 18: *Relationships between the categories*

Category / Dimension	**Learning critical thinking through discussion**	**Learning critical thinking by performing tasks simulating real situations**	**Learning critical thinking from the teacher's questioning**	**Learning critical thinking by working with multiple sources of information**
Theoretical learning	Deeper disclosure of the topic, discovery of new directions of attitude, perception of the limitations of subjective knowledge	Reflecting on an individual path to solve a task by thinking through the context, its factors, the advantages and disadvantages of the chosen method, and the possible consequences	Perception of oneself as an active subject in the process of cognition – the skill of reflection, self-observation	Determining the reliability of information, recognising and managing conflicts between different information sources
Practical learning	Participating in open dialogue, presenting one's attitude, improving oral argument, looking for solutions	Implementing a solution to a problem, developing responsibility for the results of the solution, studying the cause-effect relationship and its factors	The skill of speaking accurately (orally or in writing), giving clarity and precision to speaking	Active verification of information, searching for reliable information

Dimension I: Theoretical learning. This dimension reveals the learning of critical thinking as a theoretical aspect of cognition. Theoretical learning provides fundamental knowledge and helps link it to the overall picture and better understand why things work. There are various ways of theoretical cognition, but the main ones are reading educational material, contemplation, reflection and writing. Theoretical learning is not decoupled from practical learning – it provides a rationale for practical tasks, and helps to better understand and explain the results.

In the first category, theoretical learning manifests itself as a kind of continuous knowledge-shattering event where, by discussing, students reveal to themselves new, hitherto unknown angles of attitude, and realise that the reality being analysed is more diverse and complex than they previously thought. However, it is also a way to become acquainted more deeply and systematically understand the underlying processes of phenomena: *A skill is formed to see hidden things that are taken for granted* (D16).

In the second category, theoretical learning manifests itself as readiness to perform a practical task, and the careful planning of actions, considering the operating conditions, necessary tools and their properties that may affect the result, and evaluating the success of the result after the task is performed:

> *... you have to critically choose which path is better, which is cheaper, which is faster. One path is longer, but it's cheaper, but that means you're going to lose a lot of time. You have to either buy more expensive reagents, but that means you'll reach your goal faster.* (D8)
> *... because you think and the faster you come up with an idea, how to solve it, the faster that decision comes to mind, then all that's left are calculations, and calculations depend on the person's speed. But all that putting together a plan, how you're going to solve the task given to you, depends on the person's ability to come up with how to break down that task.* (D12)

In this category, theoretical knowledge connects aspects of practical work into the whole and makes it possible to better understand and explain practical processes:

> *In engineering, you need a lot of knowledge, you have to link it all together. I think that linking is sometimes missing. I think I'm pretty good at understanding causes and consequences ... If you don't really know why that theory is right, then it's much harder.* (D2)

The third category stresses the skill formed by theoretical learning to reflect and observe the influence of one's subjectivity on the cognitive process and the interpretation of results. This skill arises in the relationship with the teacher who, through questioning, provokes students' self-reflection and teaches them to pay attention to the influence of their way of thinking on everything that they are trying to become acquainted with, interpret and perceive.

> *The most memorable was the encouragement of teachers to understand our influence as the subject on the way we think about a work of art or a political phenomenon. The way I accept and interpret a painting depends on my gender, age and race, and the social and*

> *historical context that I live in. In other words, during lectures and seminars, I realised the importance of self-reflection.* (D16)

In the fourth category, theoretical learning is related to the students' skills being formed to work with several different sources, recognise conflicts of information in them, and resolve them. Students are taught that when analysing a problem, verifying information and looking for multiple sources is an integral part of the work.

> *You just know what sources you should rely on, not an article that you read in* Delfi, *not the opinion of a* Lietuvos rytas *journalist, not* Dviračio žinios. *I observe how people don't have critical thinking – out of inertia, they hear something on the television or radio and immediately settle on that opinion.* (D11)

Dimension II: Practical learning. This dimension reveals the learning of critical thinking as a practical aspect of cognition. Practical learning allows you to experience, test and check processes and thus better understand them; it allows you to make mistakes and learn from them.

In the first category, practical learning manifests itself through the active formation of one's position in a discussion, the application of the ability to present one's ideas and attitudes to an audience, and the selection of appropriate arguments to support one's personal position. Practical opportunities to participate in a discussion where an open and ethical environment is created are something of a turning point for students, from which they not only engage in discussions more confidently, but also acquire increasingly strong critical thinking skills:

> *... we discuss, talk, read texts, talk over some topic or the problems of those texts. Everyone has to prepare something for each seminar from themselves and then there's a discussion, consideration, presentation of your insights.* (D4)

In this category, practical learning also manifests itself as looking for solutions to a problem during a discussion:

> *... prompted: 'So how would you get yourself out of a situation like this? And one like this?' We didn't have any basic knowledge yet, and purely from life had to try to find ways out and this also arouses critical thinking.* (D11)

In the second category (implementing a solution to a problem, developing responsibility for the results of the solution, studying the cause-effect relationship and its factors), practical learning manifests itself through the solution of real problems, starting with its analysis, designing a solution and implementing it.

> *... we get a lot of complex tasks to solve that really need critical thinking, that can't be solved by those banal algorithms ... by those usual methods ... that you have to take a deeper look at the problem for and make your own decisions on how to do what ... analyse the situation yourself, and based on that, look at the task critically yourself and devote more of your thinking than use information from books.* (D5)

Of no less importance to students in practical tasks is to feel a responsibility for their choices in solving the problem, which somehow mobilises them and encourage them to devote more attention to solving the problem and try harder. Practical tasks allow students to test how effective and purposeful their choices and solutions are, and to check how the method works in practice, what could be improved, and what other planning steps to take:

> *... you look at the situation yourself, if you were an employee, what the customer might need more, to look at the situation, what market the programme will be offered to, what problems to solve or maybe the programme will have to be improved in the future, to evaluate what will be needed from that programme later, and based on that, to make some important architectural programming decisions that would let the programme be a better fit afterwards.* (D5)

In the third category (the skill of speaking accurately [orally or in writing], giving clarity and precision to speaking), practical learning unfolds through the students' experiences where the teachers give particular attention to the terminology used by students, both in writing and orally. This draws students' attention to the importance of the word and the monitoring of language. In this way, students learn in practice how to observe, analyse their language, and strive for maximum accuracy:

> *And this is where critical thinking is already pounded into your head that you don't say just anything anymore. You also think through all of the terms really well, and not just the complex terms, but also when you say the words 'a lot' or 'a little', you understand that this is not some defined thing, that it's a very, very relative thing, and you try to put numbers into the context, that you say 'approximately this much or this much', you don't say 'a lot or a little' in general ... You already feel that you have to think about what you're saying and you catch yourself if you say something, and then you immediately clarify yourself.* (D1)

In the fourth category (verification of information, searching for reliable information), practical learning involves checking the information used to perform a task, collating information from several sources, and searching for reliable information:

> *... either in some sort of practical tasks, or a lot of times various creative tasks are assigned, like creating some kind of message or short piece of news about some specific thing. And then the first thing you do is pick out the information – so for that, I think, critical thinking is used very heavily.* (D1)

3.3.4 Outcome space

Analysis of the outcome space reveals that students learn critical thinking both individually and in interaction with others. The most pronounced is the personal aspect, which is found in all categories (Table 19).

Tab. 19: *Outcome space. Referential and structural components: How students learn critical thinking*

Referential component (what the experience is, how it is manifested)	**Structural component (what that experience is for)**
Learning critical thinking through discussion	Personal Interpersonal
Learning critical thinking by performing tasks simulating real situations	Personal Interpersonal
Learning critical thinking from the teacher's questioning	Personal Interpersonal
Learning critical thinking by working with multiple sources of information	Personal

Students learn critical thinking both individually and in interaction with others. The significance of the interpersonal (student-teacher) relationship is related to how contact sessions are implemented, and what the student has to do, what tasks assigned by the teacher to perform both in the classroom and beyond. Critical thinking learning also takes place at the individual level, when the students think and learn from their own thinking or work on their own. Thus, critical thinking learning could be examined as a two-way street, where the imperative coming from the learning environment of what and how to study is important, but also of importance are the personal response and the personal action and effort, without which critical thinking cannot be developed.

4. Manifestation of Critical Thinking in the Labour Market: How Critical Thinking Is Understood

This section aims to answer the question of what the research participants consider critical thinking. This research question was designed to reveal the subjective conceptions of the concept of critical thinking among employees and employers.

4.1. How employers understand critical thinking

The conception of critical thinking in the thinking of employers is revealed as certain abilities and as a person's qualities. The following were singled out as dominant categories: (1) analysis; (2) evaluation; (3) argumentation; (4) independence. There was also one non-dominant category: (5) self-confidence.

4.1.1 Dominant categories

Category 1: Critical thinking is analysis. In this category, the conception of critical thinking is revealed as a process of analysis organised by the person him or herself – by asking him or herself questions. Asking yourself questions is manifested as a motivator that encourages you to look deeper into a specific problem or topic, and forces you to think when looking for or making a decision. In some cases, asking questions is a prerequisite for analysing and delving into the essence of a phenomenon or information:

> *So that critical thinking is still to ask yourself questions, you can find information, you can come to me, ask – I'll tell you, I'll answer, but to ask a question.* (A7)

In other cases, constantly asking yourself questions is seen as a prerequisite for analysing possible solutions or problems, or in evaluating risk:

> *... but it's also very important how you communicate, how you ask questions. And in that place, too, I'd say, the skill of critical thinking, not just knowledge. Because knowledge is a technical thing with us. For example, the internet is down, there's no internet, but what does that mean is missing – is it a computer, a line, or so on. So a person has to ask himself questions in a very logical, purposeful way so that he can reject certain problems, or discover.* (A15)

Another aspect revealed in this category, continuous analysis, is understood as the detailed examination of a subject or phenomenon, and looking at it from different angles. In this regard, the analysis process is associated with all-inclusive thinking:

> *... If I see that the question is presented without an analysis that uses critical thinking, without looking at it from different angles, that annoys me and I don't make a decision. ... For me, critical thinking is looking at a situation from different angles, the ability to discuss a phenomenon from the outside, the ability to see intention, why that phenomenon is what it is and its influences.* (A10)

Multifaceted analysis as a component of critical thinking is associated with self-evaluation:

> *You're constantly thinking and analysing, finding something new on the one hand, seeing on the other hand that I didn't know that, that didn't occur to me, and, maybe, that critical thinking of yours is limited because you don't have some basic knowledge.* (A8)

And also – with making a substantiated and optimally selected decision. According to the employers, the analysis process provides a broad understanding of the entire phenomenon, which helps to choose the most appropriate solution to the problem. Analysis encourages not to give in to impulsive decision-making, but to rethink various alternatives and the consequences of one or another decision more broadly:

... and not to give in to the first instinct, the first thought, and to really think about those important decisions, right. Why you're leaning toward one decision or another, what it'll give you. (A25)

... the most important thing in making decisions is the facts: what are the facts that have been identified and then from all that you try to form a complete picture of what's really going on, then you identify the problem and make a decision. I don't know how critical thinking is theoretically defined, but this is something like that here. (A16)

It should be noted that continuous analysis reveals itself the most in the personal context, both at the level of the employees and at the level of the employers themselves. The conception of critical thinking as an analysis process manifests itself in the employers' statements as an employee-initiated process:

... critical thinking is necessary, this is first and foremost analytical skills. A person has to constantly check himself on the qualitative and quantitative indicators of his work. He has to collect the data himself, analyse them, process them himself, sort, group, and check within those broad tasks what goals he has to set for himself ... (A28)

The research also revealed another aspect of the conception of critical thinking related to the self-analysis process initiated by the employers themselves, which leads to self-reflection. The study revealed that employers promote the analysis of their activities as a manifestation of critical thinking by initiating certain self-analysis questionnaires, personal interviews or self-analysis discussions:

After that, like it or not, I replay all of the possible options in my head, analyse what I could have done differently, how I could have done even better, how I could have avoided something, and so on. This is partly tiring, because there's no longer any rest. Even in personal relationships, like now I got together with you, so a while later, I'll probably replay in my head how I could have done it differently. ... If I were a psychologist, I'd say that to a limit, that critical thinking is like a positive thing, because I analyse myself. (A4)

Self-analysis is seen as a guarantor of each person's professional development. And the experience of each employee is useful and applicable in activities if it is analysed.

Category 2: Critical thinking is evaluation. Analysis of the employers' interviews revealed that when thinking about what critical thinking is, the employers note the ability to evaluate information or a situation. Evaluation as a feature of critical thinking is revealed in different contexts. First of all, evaluation appears in relation to the verification of information or facts:

You have to pass through your perception, through your level of knowledge. You have to evaluate every phenomenon or human statement. The information you receive is never a hundred per cent true. That's how I understand critical thinking. You have to evaluate every phenomenon or human statement. (A5)

According to the employers, critical thinking is when each phenomenon or fact is checked and evaluated without reservation:

> *We never make decisions on the basis of assumptions, we have to check the facts and evaluate – we can only rely on the facts.* (A8)

Another aspect that emerged in this category is the link between evaluation and foresight or forecasting. To evaluate so that you can foresee possible alternative solutions or actions. The ability to evaluate is necessary in professional activities, regardless of their nature, in order to provide an optimal solution:

> *... to choose from what is on the market, from what we, say, have from strategic suppliers, we find a part through exhibitions, through items. Yeah, so first of all, to critically choose the right solution for ourselves, the one that'll be able to be successfully sold later, in terms of quality, both as far as price and so that the customer is satisfied.* (A27)

The latter ability is also necessary in anticipating the path to achieving the result:

> *This seems like a meaningless, monotonous job, but on the other hand, when you do that job, you're trying to evaluate some suppliers, look to see if they're doing a good job, if you'd buy from them next time. You're trying to evaluate something.* (A11)

Evaluation is linked to the need to choose the right decision, arguments and information:

> *... in the current world, we get a lot of information and you have to know how to evaluate and filter that information, where it's true, and where it's fake news or manipulation* (A17);
> *When there's such a large team, information isn't usually passed on face-to-face, so you have to evaluate it very adequately, correctly, so you can make the right decision.* (A13)

Another aspect that emerges in the topic being analysed is the link between evaluation and analysis. The emphasis is not on the use of evaluation as a separate ability, but on evaluation as a result of the analysis process. Critical thinking is understood as a combination of analysis and evaluation, highlighting the importance of both elements:

> *... we evaluate and have certain evaluation criteria. In every job, in every group, it's always different ... critical thinking in our team is perpetuum mobile. Evaluation, analysis, purposeful presentation and knowledge. How can a unit recommend something to scientists without going through it, without making sure of it, without evaluating it? Every item in our work has to be both evaluated and analysed, and strongly measured on all sides.* (A14)
> *By hearing and analysing who thinks what on some issue and taking what the other side wants to say correctly, if you have to coordinate a position, document or something. Even by elementarily participating in some meetings or committees. Well, even in the Seimas when they're somewhere if there's some invitation. So you just have to listen to who says what, filter it and evaluate it* (A26).

> *... so I have to evaluate a lot of factors to make a decision, but by looking at each factor very analytically. I have to evaluate the X factor from A to Z, but you analyse each factor, they complement each other.* (A8)

The research data reveal the element of evaluation without preconceptions as a manifestation of critical thinking; according to the research participants, *critical thinking is that doubt everything, think ahead* (A23). According to the employers, evaluation should be done without assumptions, distancing oneself from existing stereotypes or beliefs:

> *Distancing yourself from assumptions is probably one of the strongest components of critical thinking, because we make a lot of assumptions and then to distance yourself and look at the facts, evaluate them. We all tend to live by and follow assumptions in both personal life and professional life, 'I think that'.* (A9)
> *That critical thinking, if I understand correctly what it is, is, in my view, to look, check and not immediately accept everything as the truth.* (A18)

Thus, one of the dispositions of a person is highlighted – the importance of scepticism. According to the employers, critical thinking is a certain position based on doubts about the existence of any pre-existing monopoly on absolute truth. It is noted that critical thinking manifests itself through constant searches for the truth, doubting, and the accompanying questions of 'Why? How else?' The research participants explain that doubting is part of critical thinking. This is because checking doubts and looking for solutions by comprehensively analysing the problem help make the best decision for the organisation, no matter what it is related to – crisis management, product sales or the provision and development of a service.

Thus, the most important emphasis in this category is on healthy scepticism. Employees who are critical thinkers must have curiosity and a desire to explore problems by raising various hypotheses and looking for sound arguments:

> *He [the employee] has to choose, I mean, I don't know what you describe as critical thinking, of course, the question is for me, maybe we look at it differently. I'm talking about that this, this is probably some evaluation, I don't know, maybe it means a scientific format – doubt everything, or ask questions, or check, don't accept everything blindly. What's written in a book, or even more so shown now on television, that's not necessarily the absolute truth.* (A23)

The need to evaluate information without accepting it as an indisputable truth points to the fact that 100 % truth does not exist:

> *I have to critically accept what they noticed, what they saw, what information they provide me with. I can't accept it as the absolute truth, you have to evaluate.* (A5)

Thus, the research data revealed that the employers distinguish the aspect of critical thinking as the ability to evaluate by linking it to certain situations that require evaluating or checking information, arguing a choice, or forecasting a possible way to solve the problem.

Category 3: Critical thinking is argumentation. Analysis of the research data revealed yet another direction of employers' thinking about the conception of critical thinking, where critical thinking is associated with the argumentation of choices and decisions. In this category, critical thinking manifests itself as argumentative decision-making. The employers value decisions that are substantiated, based on existing practice or an independent analysis of the problem. Employees who are critical thinkers develop their own solutions to problems, substantiating them with strong arguments and compelling reasons. Critical thinking occurs when an employee understands that more than one solution exists and tries to demonstrate why his or her decision is more beneficial to the organisation. Critical thinking occurs when an employee is able to argue why he or she has made a certain decision and demonstrates that the decision made is based on an analysis performed or substantiates the arguments with facts:

> *... all decisions have to be argued, because in any case, that argument, both in the company's activities and as I mentioned, the client who, let's say, we bring a certain decision, a certain proposal to, still most of all asks questions like 'What if?' So we have to prepare answers before and already have a client, so yeah, the employee has to do that homework.* (A27)

Argumentation is interpreted here as a reasoning of the rightness of a statement in the context of other statements, by certain arguments, and related to a specific professional field in the interpersonal context:

> *You have to argue in your everyday work, because you have to make decisions. Decisions should only be made on the basis of arguments, after listening to the arguments of others and consulting with the team.* (A21)
> *It's important not to criticise, but to argue, if, say, we're going to talk about monitoring open activities, because educators are very sensitive to this, so for it not to sound like criticism or a discussion of open activities, but as advice based on certain theoretical knowledge.* (A22)

Argumentation is also interpreted as argument in broader or social contexts:

> *... the ability to reject what may be being pushed but is unacceptable, but by presenting arguments as to why that is. I'd think one of the components of critical thinking is the ability to present arguments and the ability to formulate them.* (A9)

Argumentation manifests itself as a process – the presentation of evidence by substantiating the statements about the chosen solutions and the identified problems. This is explained by the fact that in this process, in order to manage the argumentation process, the critical thinker must be able to use the material accumulated and clearly project the objectives:

> *... is thinking based on evidence, in other words, in making decisions and carrying out activities, the employee has to be able to follow evidence – not intuition, not preconceptions or assumptions – but evidence.* (A9)

Argumentation in this category also manifests itself as a manifestation of communication based on reasoning – *a person is able to present his or her opinion with arguments* (A9). In other words, critical thinking is understood as a certain communicative activity in order to convince yourself of the rightness of your choices, or to influence other people's beliefs, values and/or behaviour. The employers note that critical thinking is first and foremost the ability to use certain statements or evidence to persuade an interlocutor or opponent to change their position or beliefs and to take a different position:

> *This is the key to that critical thinking. It doesn't only have to seem that it's right to you – you also have to be able to convey that to another person and convince him that it is. But in the good sense, not the bad.* (A20)

The research data suggest that argumentation is also seen as a rational activity based primarily on the search for substantiated explanations and assertions, and not on the weight of emotions. This does not mean that the emotional factor is not important in arguing, but that rationally perceived arguments are presented for evaluation. According to the employers:

> *... to find argumentation for some things, why I act that way. That I act not only from my feeling, but I have to choose arguments. We have to acquire arguments somewhere, understand, comprehend, find information that can help me.* (A17)

The rational nature of argumentation, recognition of the indisputability of arguments, or the presentation of weightier arguments are based on the criteria of validity, reliability and efficiency and are the employee qualities that employers see as a manifestation of critical thinking.

Category 4: Critical thinking is employee independence. In this category, critical thinking is associated with an individual's autonomous and independent action in the professional field in solving the problems that come up. It is important for employers that employees are able to make immediate decisions in the event of a problem or an unforeseen event. Employees need decision-making skills not only in crisis situations, but also in their daily activities, when faced with any deviation from normal operations. The research participants revealed that critical thinkers develop their own ideas using experience and facts, and that courage in employees is a powerful charge for an organisation. Therefore, when reasoning about the conception of critical thinking, employers use examples of specific situations in which employees demonstrate courage and determination to make a decision:

> *... to quickly be able to make all kinds of critical decisions that you can have every day, every week, because there are fires and problems everywhere, everyone goes to the manager if the situation is non-standard. So in all these years, I can just say that the biggest*

challenge is – and this is a skill – to make quick decisions. Determination, whether you'll make the right or the wrong decision – it doesn't matter. You turn on critical thinking, all [your] experience, knowledge and you make a decision. ... You say: 'Whatever the other is, I'm taking this one, that's my decision.' Whether it's right or not is no longer important, because I made the decision after evaluating all the circumstances. (A19)

This category also includes the ability of employees to make independent decisions. Independence is seen by employers as the ability to decide what actions need to be taken and what alternative solution should be proposed. According to the research participants, a good employee must strive for the best results and be able to make final decisions, which means that he or she must be independent.

No kind of special advice or help was asked for. There is a basic measure in our lives – time. You understand that the manager was not burdened with what he shouldn't be burdened with. And he up and solved it. The result was achieved without your interference. There could be no better identification that critical thinking was used. (A2)
Independent thinking, so they don't run to ask every time what to do with this or with that, now I don't know anything here, now a client came in and he's aggressive, here mum is making big demands, and now come up with what to do. (A21)

Based on this finding, it can be assumed that the modern labour market needs employees who are independent in their professional activities and who have the ability to assume responsibility. Responsibility, which is understood as a sign of a person's moral maturity and self-control. Thus, employees who are critical thinkers clearly know the limits of their responsibility and the results that are expected of them:

In our work, we don't use terminology like 'critical thinking'; we say 'lack of responsibility', an unwillingness to take responsibility, because it's easier that way ... each time it's a bit unique, but it's repetitive and people don't take responsibility, they pin it on the head of the department, rid themselves of responsibility. (A9)

It is worth noting that the aspect of taking responsibility is especially pronounced when the employers reason about problematic or crisis situations arising in professional activities. Each of these situations is specific, so here, according to the employers, it is important to act and take responsibility for your actions:

For me, it has to do with taking responsibility, because they usually say: 'I thought about it, but I was afraid to take responsibility.' In the event of a crisis, you always ask, what if it had happened to you as a person, and not as an employee of the establishment, so then, they say, I would have known what to do, that and that. Well, I say, it would have been completely right if you had done that here too. So a lot of times the person somehow separates his own self from the responsibilities and positions of people working at the establishment. Because as a person he would act in the relationship of his responsibility. (A1)

In the conception of the employers, critical thinking manifests itself not only as taking responsibility, but also as autonomous thinking in a specific professional activity. According to the employers, critical thinking manifests itself in a person's autonomy, when the person him or herself solves important issues here and now by taking responsibility here and now, regardless of the influence of others and without relying on anyone's opinion or guarantee.

> *... when you have to react lightning fast and act not in accordance with the instructions, what's really important for every manager in their relationship with those who carry out the tasks you have given, is the ability to make decisions that are as autonomous as possible, with the knowledge available here and now. Having critical thinking is especially important for an employee in that, as a manager, you can be guaranteed about the effectiveness of certain processes, that certain disruptions won't be critical in the end result.* (A2)

Professional independence as a manifestation of critical thinking is revealed in the thinking of employers as an employee's freedom to act in making decisions that are important to the organisation. On the other hand, independence in professional activities includes more than the delegation of powers – it includes employees' freedom of choice.

4.1.2 Non-dominant category

Category 5: Critical thinking is self-confidence. The manifestation of the conception of critical thinking in this category is revealed by another aspect – self-confidence. Self-confidence is equated with a person's attitude that determines his or her behaviour. So, according to the employers, believing in yourself and your powers enables the organisation to change:

> *... that he'll be able to question what has been done for many years, in a large company and the like, and be confident and not afraid to look for ways, what would happen if we did something differently, is that process necessary, does it create added value, can we not do it, save time and focus on another, another task that basically creates more of that added value. So it's this kind of person that fulfils the standard of critical thinking when he is able to question the processes of a large company, an established company, and think, suggest how to do things differently.* (A25)

Not only does how a person evaluates a situation depend on self-confidence – his or her ability to resist the influence and pressure of others does as well. A self-confident person always has an easier time overcoming difficulties and solving problematic situations. Self-confidence creates a positive and at the same time realistic picture of the case, which enables you to control and manage the situation:

> *This is where a package of qualities is also required. You can have whatever critical thinking you want, and sit there and troll all those* Delfi *messages. You're really critical,*

but what's in it for the person's organisation? If you have self-confidence, then this is a powerful charge for the person and the organisation. (A9)

Even if they sometimes fail, such individuals remain positive and evaluate themselves positively, so in problems they see opportunities, not the other way around:

I mean, there wasn't even such a practice. He came up with it, filled it out, showed it and everything was fine. And then I came and found out that there were and they swapped and I already wanted to blast them, but he says – nothing, I wrote it. Well, I say, I didn't want to either praise or reprehend. I smiled, you rascals, I say, well and that's it. It ended well. You just try to come up with that in such a flash and sign it so accurately. He signed everything according to his visual memory in that stress. (A1)

Self-confidence as a manifestation of critical thinking manifests itself in employers' thinking through situations in which employees' belief in their power to carry out transformation and change within the organisation comes to light. In other words, employees who are critical thinkers are independent makers of bold decisions due to the fact that they are self-confident.

4.1.3 Relationships between the categories of description

The two qualitatively different conceptions of critical thinking can be explained by the differences in the interrelated variations (dimensions). These differences reveal relationships between the categories: critical thinking is a guarantor of an organisation's efficiency and critical thinking is a factor in solving problems in professional activities. The main relationships between the categories are presented in Table 20. This reveals a broadening of the understanding of the research participants in both dimensions across all of the categories singled out.

Tab. 20: *Relationships between the categories*

Category / Dimension	**Analysis**	**Evaluation**	**Argumentation**	**Autonomy**	**Self-confidence**
Guarantor of professional operational efficiency	Performance engine	Direction of progress	Choosing the optimal solution	Fast action	Original solutions, suggestions
Problem-solving factor	Risk identification	Basis of action	Interpersonal interaction	Responsible action	Situation control

Dimension I: Critical thinking as a guarantor of professional operational efficiency. In the first category, employees' analytical skills are associated with the conditions to look into the essence of action, information or a situation. Questions should raise questions – only then will there be progress:

So in this place, I think, critical thinking is that you ask yourself questions, then see that you're missing information, go in deeper and answer something, but new questions come up. (A4)

Constantly asking oneself questions is inspired by the person's inner mood and desire to look into professional activities:

And you ask yourself questions, you ask the question: 'Which would work best, what combination would work best?' And that's how that search goes. Maybe that critical thinking is less in the first place here, but it's there, because it's important not only to find for yourself how to say one of the possible solutions, because there are usually a lot of them, but you have to find the best one. (A27)

According to the employers, critical thinking manifests itself through constant searches for the truth, doubting and the accompanying questions of 'Why? How else?', because doubting is part of critical thinking. Because checking doubts and looking for solutions by comprehensively analysing the problem help make the best decision for the organisation, no matter what it is related to – crisis management, product sales or the provision of a service:

A person shouldn't do some job like it was a template or just strive for some amount – he should strive for quality too. I call that analytical thinking, the ability to work with information, with data, to collect, process and use it accordingly. (A28)

In the second category, evaluation and self-evaluation as a feature of critical thinking emerge through the employee's ability to evaluate a situation or information and forecast further actions. That is, critical thinking is manifested not only in the ability to evaluate, but also to predict how to behave in one situation or another, how to solve a problem by improving activities and striving for better results:

... to manoeuvre in a situation, evaluate how beneficial it'll be for you to act one way or another. This isn't necessarily a financial benefit, it can be a moral benefit, a time benefit, it can be more expensive, but more likely – depending on what's needed in that situation. ... avoiding unnecessary conflicts and an opportunity for smoother operations. ... try to evaluate why it turned out that way and achieve better results. (A20)

... he evaluates what materials he'll needs, about how much time it'll take him, where he needs to go. But if there's critical thinking, it'll solve other issues as well – how to do it easier, if mistakes have been made, if you shouldn't immediately do something differently to avoid mistakes in the further process. (A7)

The importance of evaluation and self-evaluation as a guarantor of professional activities is especially singled out when the employers think about the need for continuous improvement of the organisation. The employers note that it is important for a modern organisation to strive for the development of innovative products and services, and the implementation of efficient and socially responsible operating methods:

> *... critical thinking is also the kind of thing that there is a real evaluation of the situation. You can think really well of yourself, but if there are ... some changes in life, new things. I think that the manager has to have that critical thinking and adapt, because there are new things, there are changes, you have to march in step.* (A24)

In other words, continuous professional evaluation and self-evaluation create conditions to understand the real situation, plan your next steps, and suggest how to act at the organisational level. According to the employers, self-evaluation of one's activities as a feature of critical thinking is necessary for every manager:

> *So that constant evaluation of reality is very important. It's really important to evaluate and admit where you're sleeping, where you have problems, because it's easy to justify yourself – the results are good, everything is fine – and rest on your laurels. Even when things aren't going well, you'll still find an excuse. I'd say the greatest need for a manager of critical thinking is that constant evaluation of the current situation and then the direction in which they want to move forward.* (A16)

In the third category, critical thinking as a guarantor of professional activity manifests itself in a person's ability to argue decisions in search of the most optimal option:

> *... and the employee says, but director, we can make better forms. But maybe let's search differently, flexibly here. No, I can't work in these forms, this is a waste of time. Then come arguments, so we still have to offer them somehow, we have to improve, we've worked this one out better, so we can't go back, so what good experience are we going to give back? No, no, director, I won't do that.* (A26)

The employers pay attention to the individual work of each person, because the main concern of the employees is to make a decision themselves in the workplace when there is a problem. It is stressed that critical thinking occurs when urgent decisions are substantiated and reasoned. According to the employers, this determines the success of the organisation:

> *If employees make reasoned job-related suggestions, if they see shortcomings and can declare them publicly, then I'd say that they think critically. ... Through the manifestation of their thoughts with statements like this, they kind of stimulate the establishment's work and its quality.* (A24)

In the fourth category, critical thinking is revealed through a person's independence, which enables them to act quickly. Employee independence is seen as a prerequisite for fast action when making decisions in various situations:

> *Because you can't list all the places that you'll fall so that you can put a pillow down everywhere. This unique solution is the freedom for a person to create at that time. Then you need to create and make a decision in a flash.* (A1)

Independence enabling one to act decisively and quickly strongly influences the successful functioning and development of an organisation. Speed in decision-making is unequivocally recognised as one of the main factors determining the efficiency of an organisation:

> *Maybe that critical thinking is less in the first place here, but it's there, because it's important not only to find for yourself how to say one of the possible solutions, because there are usually a lot of them, but you have to find the best one. ... Yeah, so first of all, to critically choose the right solution for ourselves, the one that'll be able to be successfully sold later, in terms of quality, both as far as price and so that the customer is satisfied.* (A27)

In the fifth category, self-confidence as a feature of critical thinking is revealed through initiative in putting forth original proposals that enable the organisation to create added value. The success of an organisation in the modern labour market is greatly influenced by original proposals. The research participants, therefore, monitor the manifestation of critical thinking through the original/innovative suggestions put forth by employees:

> *... A person came in and looked at it not only structurally, but also from very different angles, said what's bad now and what would be good to have already resolved in the new system, what the tmhreats were if it's not fixed and which ones should just be accepted, and listed how much more money should be invested in certain things to address this and how much it'll save the company. That surprised me because I just wasn't expecting it.* (A15)

Organisations that want to succeed must strive for progress by introducing scientific and technological innovation. Therefore, the employers see a completely different employee attitude, a vision detached from the hierarchy, and the self-confidence that enables that vision to be expressed, as a benchmark for critical thinking:

> *After all, there are processes, we have a quality management system, everything is going along and suddenly this person shows up who says: 'Look, this is nonsense, a redundant step, it can be done this way and that.' So what is this? So this is definitely critical thinking. He took those processes that worked for years and he reconsidered it. He makes an argument and we really accept it and say really – why not?* (A9)

With the rapid development of the country's economy and the increasing technical and financial capacity of companies, one of the most relevant areas in a company's activities is the evaluation of its operational efficiency, which provides information about a particular organisation, but also obligates it to look for tools and ways to improve operational efficiency. The research data revealed that the employers value employees' critical thinking skills as one such option.

Dimension II: Critical thinking as a problem-solving factor. In this dimension, it came to light that critical thinking is associated with solving the problems that arise in daily activities. In the first category, the dimension of critical thinking as a problem-solving factor manifests itself through the manifestation of analytical skills in identifying the various risks that are likely to be encountered in professional practice:

> *So let's say that critical thinking probably is that looking at a project, not just that 'hurrah, good, what a good job we're going to do here, the very fastest, in the most optimistic time' and so on, but looking at it critically – what would happen if there are certain conditions that, say, depend on the company's internal processes, or vice versa, that don't depend, on some sort of external ones.* (A27)

According to the employers, risk identification starts with the ability to go into the heart of the matter and analyse:

> *Critical thinking is also recognising risks, because sometimes you have a hunch, then you start to look and delve into it deeper. ... You have to have critical thinking and anticipate risks, that there may be this kind of risk here, there may be another risk there, the manager may not like this, we may not manage to send this to the European Commission on time. So wait, so maybe I don't just go with 'Eh, it'll be fine' after all. Maybe I do clarify after all.* (A9)

By encouraging analysis, employers create the conditions that enable employees not to just act, but to act in anticipation of opportunities and threats:

> *So we have this rule that you can never say if someone asks you why things need to be done one way or another. You can't use the word 'because someone told me so, because it was done that way'. You basically everything when you get a project to work on, you basically have to understand over a period of two to three years the reasons why it's done this way and what the reasons would be if it had to be done in one way or another. What the consequences would be, what would be, what risks, what the benefits would be, that you and that people would actually work with each other as equals, who could, could advise and help one another, but by no means, not do so because that's how it was done before. That's the rule.* (A9)

In the second category, critical thinking as a problem-solving factor manifests itself as the ability to evaluate the situation and decide what actions need to be taken. The employers say that in order to make a decision, it needs to be evaluated quickly, here and now:

> *Or you get threatening letters that they'll do something bad to you – you have to critically evaluate if there's a threat in it or if it's just a joke. You have to evaluate information critically, and this is important not only in my field, but in general for all people in the age of technology, because there are a lot of letters, large quantities. Attacks against companies are specially designed. You have to evaluate what comes to you through those technological channels really critically, because you can't verify that other source that it came from, whether it's a reliable person or a saboteur.* (A11)

The employers note that critical thinking occurs when employees are able to evaluate the entire process of a decision or decisions and their role in it when self-evaluating the end result:

> *... in presenting the report on how it was done, the employee evaluates his activities: presents certain obstacles, certain processes that were performed in carrying out the tasks, that he encountered. In the presentation, you fully understand that certain problems were unplanned, unforeseen, and he dealt with them.* (A2)

In the dimension under analysis, critical thinking as a problem-solving factor manifests itself through the promotion of interpersonal interaction. When arguing for one decision or another, the employees discuss a decision that is acceptable to everyone:

> *So they had to discuss among themselves and find a certain solution so that one project could be presented with a specific description of activities, with an estimate. So obviously they had to both discuss and find a compromise ... I think this required critical thinking and an attitude both toward what he himself was proposing, and toward what the team members were proposing. This ability to hear another person, the ability to present your opinion and not just present it, but to wrap it in a certain form, because the form was prepared.* (A6)

Interpersonal interaction and diversity of opinion are extremely important when taking decisions or putting forth proposals – through discussion, learning takes place, experiences are shared, and knowledge is gained. The employers note that the ability to choose and present arguments and defend one's opinions encourages employees to share knowledge and create new knowledge:

> *... goodness should be with boxing gloves. What I was trying to say with that metaphor is that if you're capable of thinking critically, then you're a national treasure, but you have to be able to argue and express it properly. Then it becomes goodness, then we could connect the potential.* (A9)

The fourth category in this dimension is revealed as responsible action. By acting independently, the employee is assured of his or her choice of a decision and assumes responsibility for the consequences:

> *Critically minded people, mature people, who know the limits within which they can act, I think they're also more decisive, able to assume responsibility for their area, the decision made, to lead in that area.* (A9)

According to the employers, taking responsibility emerges at the personal level, when decisions important to the organisation need to be made: *... personal, because when you kind of raise it, it's yours, not someone else's. As a manager, I can say that this saves a lot of expenses.* (A4)

In the fifth category, self-confidence as a feature of critical thinking is expressed through the employee's ability to control the situation at any time, even in a crisis situation:

> *So the employees swapped without me knowing about it, they thought everything would be fine, and bam – an inspection. So another employee suddenly devised that there's a paper upstairs – you wait here, I'll go. He went and quickly wrote this sheet for the other employee and signed it, and brought it to show them. Doing that was possible. They agreed verbally but forgot to fill it out.* (A1)

The employers revealed that self-confident employees tend to take risks, but that this is seen as an engine for the organisation's progress.

Critical thinking as a problem-solving factor is highlighted through the ability of employees to evaluate the situation and provide a reasoned solution. It is equally important to note here that the employers highlight the importance of critical thinking not only at the personal level. This dimension emphasises the interpersonal context – making a decision in consultation with others.

In general, it was revealed that the thinking of the research participants (employers) about the manifestation of critical thinking in employees is developed from simpler to more complex reasoning. The research participants develop the conception of critical thinking from individual abilities to analyse, evaluate and argue so that you can act before acting independently and with confidence. The third and fourth categories reflect the main direction of the employers' understanding of critical thinking, as the main focus here is on reasoned and independent decision-making. The first and second categories reflect a narrower thinking space, where the research participants explain critical thinking as a process of analysis and evaluation, serving to gather facts and arguments. The fifth category is expanded: the research participants associate critical thinking with self-confidence in making innovative suggestions and controlling a situation, which are seen as an organisation's progress.

4.1.4 Outcome space

Analysis of the research outcome space reveals that employers understand critical thinking as the manifestation of an employee's abilities and qualities/traits in terms of the personal, organisational and social aspects (Table 21; Figure 12).

Tab. 21: *Referential and structural components: How employers understand critical thinking*

Referential component (what critical thinking is)	Structural component (how critical thinking is understood)
Critical thinking is analysis	Personal Organisational
Critical thinking is evaluation	Personal Organisational
Critical thinking is argumentation	Personal Organisational Social
Critical thinking is employee independence	Personal Organisational
Critical thinking is self-confidence	Personal Social

The most pronounced is the personal aspect, which is found in all categories. The organisational aspect, which covers four of the five categories, is somewhat less pronounced. The least pronounced is the social aspect, which covers two of the five categories.

The hierarchical relationships between the structural components and the categories are illustrated in Figure 11.

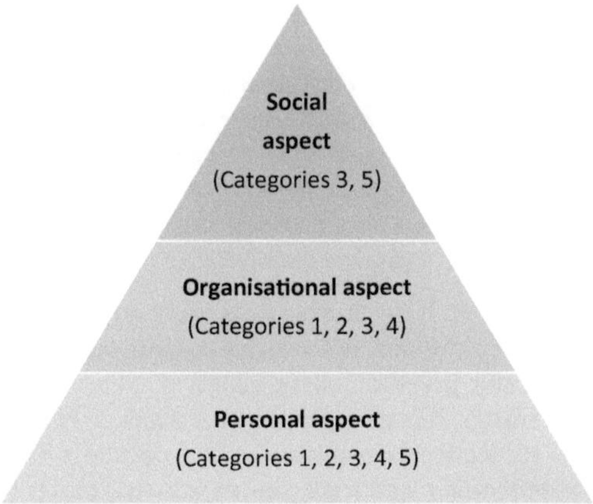

Fig. 11: *Hierarchical relationships between the structural components and the categories*

In explaining how they understand critical thinking, the employers note that each employee must be able to analyse and evaluate a problem situation, and present a reasoned decision on their own. However, it also comes to light that the personal level alone in this case is not a guarantor of an organisation's efficiency. They, therefore, note that arguments need to be considered and presented within the organisation by communicating them with other employees or managers. The social aspect is the least pronounced, and only comes to light when talking about making innovative decisions that guarantee a breakthrough in the organisation.

4.2. How employees understand critical thinking

In order to reveal what critical thinking is to employees, two dominant categories were singled out: (1) critical thinking is the search for truth; and (2) critical thinking is bold thinking.

4.2.1 Categories

Category 1: Critical thinking is the search for truth. The employees describe critical thinking as the search for truth in professional situations, where the aim is to have as true an understanding of what is being done as possible and find a point of view that would help to evaluate the solution or subject of analysis rationally. The search for truth is like not only following a personal, individual attitude, but the ability to look at the situation, solution or subject of analysis more broadly, distancing oneself from preconceived notions and authorities. An unbiased view of a situation allows substantiated decisions to be made. Critical thinking as the search for truth is first and foremost understood through the desire to not be subjective. This is associated with *a departure from standards* (B9) and the questioning of absolute truth, when a situation is viewed with open eyes, without preconceptions, despite the authorities:

> *It's a certain caution with respect to the information received, a caution with respect to your own preconceptions, a caution with respect to your own vision of how processes work. You have it, you shape it, your goal is to have that vision, but at the same time you realise that you can be wrong, that that vision is not absolute truth ... The second thing is that you understand that the other team members also have their own visions, and you don't accept them as self-evident absolute truth either.* (B3)

Critical thinking, as the search for truth, is also recognised as a precondition for performance quality when the aim is to correctly and reasonably evaluate a certain situation or task and present substantiated conclusions by evaluating the totality of objective findings. It is noted that in the absence of critical thinking, one becomes attached to subjective circumstances and opinions, which leads to erroneous decisions and *potboiling, nescience and unreasoned things* (B14).

The understanding of critical thinking as the search for truth places great emphasis on the sense of context. This is linked to a person's erudition and understanding of the situation in which he or she is acting, the environment in which he or she lives, and *the knowledge and practice required to substantiate cases* ... (B17). One of the obstacles in the search for truth is getting stuck in your past and your experience, and the inability to grasp the context of the present:

> *It seems to a person that this is his experience, his self, that he's so well-read here. But that these are complete Soviet delusions of a limited world, as it seems to us now, that he doesn't grasp. He has absolutely no understanding of the context, how can you quote Soviet aesthetics authors now, that now we've abandoned them altogether or are now all reading the originals. But this is his baggage. Yes, this is a certain lack of a sense of context, and that is the absence of critical thinking. You have no idea where you live now and what you can put forward.* (B14)

In search for truth, grasping the context is also associated with *stirring up silt* (B4), when the aim is to evaluate all the circumstances, *what could be bad, what could go wrong, or where it needs to be done better, and so on* (B4). This is like a broader view of the field, when the aim is to look at a specific situation from different perspectives, anticipating risks and coping measures, and presenting several solutions and arguments why this could or could not be, what benefits it would bring, what harm it would cause, and what the strengths would be:

> *You always want to take a broader look, what will be around that corner too, than we see – that's all. So that criticality is to look from as many angles as possible what will be waiting there.* (B4)

The employees' conception of critical thinking as the search for truth stresses the ability to identify the main problem by looking for certain signs, interpreting them, evaluating them within the limits of your competencies and responsibilities, and drawing conclusions:

> *I think that critical thinking in my case is most necessary on a daily basis, when a person comes with his or her disability and expectations, and I, as a doctor, have to decide which is the main problem at that time, and whether that problem is within my competence at all ... Since there are a lot of teeth in the mouth, there's usually more than one job, so you have to decide where to start. You try to start with the most severe cases ...* (B16)

Critical thinking in this context is understood as the language of arguments: *for me, a critical thinker is again someone who is capable of basing his decisions on certain arguments* (B4).

Thus, it is important that the most optimal decisions are made in a particular situation. The employees refer to such reasoned thinking as *'cooler'* (B10), when decisions are made not based on emotions, but by keeping a cool head so that thinking remains thinking and not emotions. *Peace* (B16). It is not an emotional response, but a rational, perspective-oriented contemplation of another opinion or suggestion.

The employees stress that in the understanding of critical thinking as the search for truth, a very important aspect is empathy. This element of the search for objectivity is revealed in the interpersonal relationship when trying to empathise with someone else's needs:

> *For me, somehow, that critical thinking is first and foremost seeing the child, seeing his needs, trying to feel for him.* (B8)

The employees associate critical thinking as the search for truth with understanding someone else, feeling someone else's situation:

> *... critical thinking – you try to understand how they live. ... As for gays, we all understand that this is abnormal, that has to be acknowledged, that's not how nature created us, but if love is put in there, if they want to take care of each other, have some sort of common property, then it's not for us to decide. If you have critical thinking, you look at those things differently, it'll be useful and very effective.* (B9)

The understanding of critical thinking as the search for truth is described as a necessary tool in professional activities. It is a condition that enables the employee to act professionally – to make rational, reasoned, objective decisions by thinking over the various circumstances, context and possible alternatives, and predicting the intended benefits.

Category 2: Critical thinking is bold thinking. The employees refer to critical thinking as bold thinking. Bold thinking is characterised by determination, initiative and self-confidence. Critical thinking is described by the employees as the ability to take initiative and act independently:

> *Not to wait for orders from above, but to find ideas and realise them either alone or working in a team.* (B15)

Bold thinking is also interpreted by the employees as free thinking, when, in making decisions, they freely generate ideas, when they are not afraid *to think outside the box, to be in frames ... to discover something outside the box* (B10).

Another aspect of the perception of critical thinking as bold thinking is not being afraid to make mistakes. Employees understand the courage to err as an integral part of critical thinking, and associate it with not being afraid to take risks, thus exploiting their full creative potential:

> *If we don't make mistakes, it means we're not taking risks, if we don't take enough risks, it means we're not doing anything important enough, we're not using all of our creative capacity. You shouldn't be afraid of making mistakes, because the one who makes the most mistakes wins.* (B15)

By describing critical thinking as bold thinking, employees associate it with an internal disposition that allows the employee to act decisively in a specific professional situation, to achieve a goal.

A qualitative difference was found between the categories. The conception of critical thinking described in the first category is interpreted as a precondition for an employee to act professionally. The conception described in the second category stresses the internal disposition of how to act.

4.2.2 Relationships between the categories of description

The two qualitatively different conceptions of critical thinking can be explained by the differences in the interrelated variations (dimensions). These differences reveal relationships between the categories: critical thinking is a condition for acting professionally, and critical thinking is an internal disposition of how to act in a professional environment. The main relationships between the categories are presented in Table 22, which puts forth the research participants' understanding of critical thinking in the different dimensions of variations in both categories.

Tab. 22: *Relationships between the categories*

Category / Dimension	**Critical thinking is the search for truth**	**Critical thinking is bold thinking**
Critical thinking is a condition for acting professionally	Questioning absolute truth, argumentation, sense of context, drawing substantiated conclusions, seeing a wider field.	Ability to take the initiative and act independently
Critical thinking is an internal disposition of how to act in a professional environment	Unemotional, cool thinking; empathy.	Courage to make mistakes and free generation of ideas.

Dimension I: Critical thinking is a condition for acting professionally. This dimension reveals a perception of critical thinking that describes the topic as a condition for acting professionally. In the first category, the employees' understanding of critical thinking is interpreted as a reasoned, rational, contextual contemplation of activities and/or solutions from various perspectives in order to ensure their validity and objectivity.

> *I might associate critical thinking with prudence. You just don't accept things as a matter of course, you weigh what's important. On the one hand, there are things where you have to look deeper, consider them yourself, and there are a lot of times when you have to react to a situation lightning fast, give a critical attitude toward the situation. In the end, you have to recognise the situation, that here you already have to react, or you don't have to react, or now you'll just analyse, or now you have to react.* (B3)

In the second category, the conception of critical thinking stresses the aspects of independent action and initiative related to the employee's self-confidence. This interpretation of the conception of critical thinking is revealed by acting with others.

Dimension II: Critical thinking is an internal disposition of how to act in a professional environment. This dimension reveals critical thinking that describes the topic as an internal disposition to act. In the first category, the employees' understanding of critical thinking is interpreted as an empathic response to those around them (the personal aspect). On the one hand, this is understood as the ability to identify oneself with others, and to understand other people's feelings, intentions and behavioural prospects. On the other hand – as impartial and professional action with others that manifests itself in a specific situation (the organisational aspect). This element of the conception is also revealed at the social level, stressing an emotional response to other people's experiences, encouraging them to help or otherwise change their situation, as a prerequisite for the creation of social justice in society:

> *... as for gays – no, the church doesn't approve. Wait, but they're people who sincerely love. And here's that critical thinking again – you try to understand ... Let's say one day everything in society changes, they become the majority and we're the minority, and now I'm not allowed to live with a woman, legalise marriage and so on. And we would feel how hard it would be when you can't live with the person you love. ... but we can help so they can live together, share property, help each other. If you have critical thinking and look at those things differently, it'll be useful and very effective.* (B9)

Another element of the conception is keeping cool and unemotional when thinking over arguments, alternatives, solutions and opinions. An unemotional response is necessary to avoid problem-solving mistakes and a non-constructive response to the environment. Keeping cool and unemotional gives you time to think out the optimal solution strategy – *you give in not to feelings, but to thinking* (B11).

In the second category, the employees' understanding of critical thinking stresses not being afraid to make mistakes, which is associated with the courage to take risks and challenge the established order in order to fully express your creative potential and the free generation of ideas:

> *... critical thinking is like this free, like idea generation, when you're free to express your ideas without being afraid of getting not only negative feedback, but also a negative emotional evaluation or even humiliation.* (B7)

In this aspect, the personal aspect is tangible as the courage to go *from the known to the unknown despite all of your fears and the reaction of the environment* (B7).

4.2.3 Outcome space

The research outcome space, which summarises the referential and structural components of the outcome and their relationships, is given in Table 23.

Tab. 23: *Referential and structural components: How employees understand critical thinking*

Referential component (what critical thinking is)	**Structural component (how critical thinking is understood)**
Critical thinking is the search for truth	Personal Organisational Social
Critical thinking is bold thinking	Personal Organisational

The referential component describes what critical thinking is. It corresponds to the categories described above. The structural component describes how (in what aspects) that understanding manifests itself.

Analysis of the outcome space does not reveal a large gap in the understanding of critical thinking in employees. In both the first and second categories, the emphasis in defining critical thinking is placed on both personal efforts to act as a professional, and attention to organisational outcomes. The variation is that in the first category, there is a very clear and social focus, which is stressed through the creation of social justice (Figure 12).

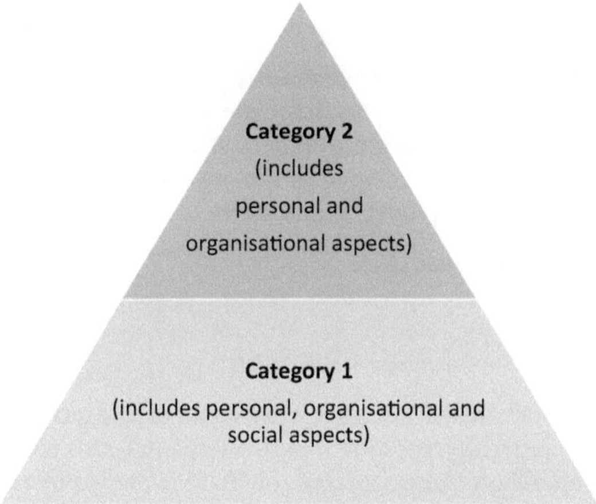

Fig. 12: *Hierarchical relationships between the categories and the structural components*

Hierarchical data analysis suggests that the conception of critical thinking is formed by contemplating the experience of this phenomenon. The employees' subjective understanding of critical thinking corresponds to their experience of critical thinking in their daily professional activities.

5. Manifestation of Critical Thinking in the Labour Market: How Critical Thinking Is Encouraged and Experienced

An important aspect of the phenomenographic research was to clarify how critical thinking manifests itself in specific labour market contexts. The study aimed to learn about the manifestation of critical thinking in daily professional activities through the experiences of the research participants: how employers promote critical thinking and how employees experience critical thinking in daily professional situations.

5.1. How employers encourage critical thinking in employees

Seven qualitatively different directions of employers' actions in promoting critical thinking were singled out. Three of these are dominant categories: (1) fostering open-mindedness; (2) using organisational measures; (3) using motivational measures; and four are non-dominant categories: (4) promoting independence; (5) asking questions; (6) showing personal example or someone else's; (7) challenging.

5.1.1 Dominant categories

Category 1: Critical thinking is promoted by fostering open-mindedness. The study revealed that the employers associate the promotion of critical thinking with the creation of a stimulating environment within the organisation. First of all, trust-based relationships are developed in the organisation, where the manager is open and ready to see the employee at any time:

> *... come, the door is always open.* (A13)
> *... any employee who want to express their opinion is heard out. They can come see me at any time. Sometimes you come to work at 7 a.m. and there's a person sitting there waiting. With observations, with everything.* (A24)

Equally important for critical thinking is whether an organisational culture is being developed that not only interpersonal relationships but also employee behaviour and interaction depend on. An important role here is played by the manager, who *has to find common ground with the staff* (A22), so that there is *this open ... relationship* with the employees (A23). In the analysed category, it came to light that the promotion of critical thinking in employees is associated with an organisational culture that promotes diversity of opinions and fosters respect for each opinion:

> *... that all those points of view be respected equally, that they're not chopped off, especially in all kinds of crisis situations, tense situations, and the tension is almost constant,*

> *because there's always some kind of reform going on, that every point of view has the right to be on the table. Creating this kind of respect for someone else's vision, to my mind, contributes to personal critical thinking, that I can accept someone else's attitude, someone else's point of view, I can also think critically about my own point of view. Creating a space so that everyone has the right and opportunity to have a say and also to ensure that opinion is respected, even if it is confronted.* (A10)

Another aspect that is tangible in this category is related to fostering open-mindedness through the provision of feedback. The employers note that in order to obtain a quality result, when they are not satisfied with the work done or the task performed, they initiate the provision of feedback ... *so that they get together and re-do that job* (A10):

> *Say like in our department: he does a needs assessment, he determines how many services we'll give the person, what his basket will be. He has to think critically; he has to see if all the circumstances have been investigated or if something else is missing. In order for us to help him, we came up with various forms to cover all areas, so he could have it as a template, so he doesn't miss anything. But sometimes we look into it and return it, because it seems to us that he gave in to emotion, there was no critical point, maybe he didn't see something negative, even though he could have. For there to be that social justice after all.* (A17)

Hence, by providing feedback, it is as if employers mark the guidelines for the expected result – how the task should be performed and what result they expect from the employee. Through the provision of feedback, they are also encouraging re-analysis and re-evaluation of the situation, problem or task so that everything is done correctly and well – they are developing responsibility.

In other cases, feedback is provided in order to encourage the employee to look for alternative solutions, or to *change activities, direction* (A14) in order to achieve a quality result. In this way, employers encourage open-mindedness and sharing among employees:

> *... but in this case, I'd say, by publicising the company's operating results, each contribution to those results, then they begin to believe it, because I'd like to be treated that way and I imagine that people want to be treated that way.* (A19)

The employers look for opportunities and take advantage of a variety of situations in which they take the initiative to discuss work situations and tasks that have been or are being performed. A specific time is allocated for this, when employees can come to the employer with certain suggestions or questions and get feedback:

> *... I've even set aside time at work from 15:30 to 16:00 when all interested parties, since they finish work at 15:30 and I work until 16:00, can come in with suggestions. Obviously, there are suggestions that are defined, I have to be sure to give them feedback within 10 days, what I can do, what I can't do, and whether that suggestion can be submitted for evaluation at all.* (A3)

Or an informal environment is used, when the employer first takes the initiative to reflect on the decisions made and tasks performed, thus creating conditions for the employees to express their opinion or evaluation:

> *Sometimes I also like to [give feedback] especially when travelling, because sometimes I travel with one employee or another, and sometimes with the whole team, especially when we go to municipalities, when we fly abroad, to scientific conferences or representative councils, so usually I'd do the reflection part, so we'd exchange our evaluation, how each of us evaluate what happened, what we have to improve, develop.* (A10)

Hence, by initiating feedback, the employers create an open space for sharing opinions and show that manifestation of the employees' personal opinions is valuable and desirable.

Category 2: Critical thinking is promoted using organisational measures. This category reveals the organisational measures taken by employers to promote critical thinking that are related to the opportunity to express one's opinion on a specific issue and evaluate the situation or problem. One such measure is the initiation of regular meetings by the employers to help prepare for the week's work and discuss emerging problems or situations:

> *There are weekly meetings and then you sit down and solve those problems. ... Just the most important thing is to let people speak the facts. When they begin speaking facts, squaring of the facts really relaxes the situation. It comes together even for the one who is taking a conflicting position, who by speaking loudly and thinking somehow sees that reality.* (A16)

Meetings are *accepted as part of the establishment's culture* (A21), where employees can not only hear each other's thoughts, ideas and suggestions, but also actively share their own experience. In this way, employees are encouraged to reason critically and use critical thinking skills such as analysis, interpretation, explanation, inference and evaluation.

Another aspect that is highlighted in the category under consideration is consultations to evaluate specific problems, situations or information. These meetings are organised to discuss and present each stage of activity, intermediate product or result. The key to these meetings is to create conditions for each employee to express his or her thoughts and thus encourage critical thinking:

> *And would have the opportunity to speak out. What they think, what they suggest, what could be different. Or at the idea level, let's say. Like here, for example, the lecturer has to prepare some kind of theoretical publication. We could just shut her up alone and that's it. But the encouragement is that at least who encounters that area, that at least a few of them sit down and discuss it before that methodological publication comes out, and this is done normally. What we always try to implement. Not criticising, but waking up critical thinking.* (A26)

Consultations are also organised to discuss specific cases, when a problem is overcome or a decision is made. During these meetings, employees are given the opportunity to hear the manager's evaluation:

> *After each crisis, to discuss feelings, to discuss actions, to say how I evaluate it as the manager – it's necessary for that person to hear. If he doesn't hear it, that fear of his of whether I did the right or wrong thing adds to this paranoia, and the next time he'll avoid that critical thinking even more. ... You take specific cases and analyse them, and you say, look – if that factor hadn't been turned on at all, the result would have been completely different to this day.* (A2)

The meetings that are organised allow the employees to analyse their actions and decisions themselves in order to obtain a better result:

> *... how he did it, why he did it, and why he changed it here now. It's this ongoing interaction. Maybe that's what leads to an educational situation, that each time we decide. This is what interaction comes from. Like you and I are interacting now: you say this, that, another one of my customers says lay the tiles here or do something else. So you immediately tell him that it can't be done like that. ... Some object is being made, that's his discussion – why someone drew it that way. And if there are any problems, why he drew it like that, and that didn't work for someone else. But this isn't tied to encouraging critical thinking, but to making the process easier.* (A7)

Through regular organisational measures, the employers operate by trying to stimulate the employees' habit of analysing, evaluating the situation and information, and making decisions. Meetings, consultations and conferences are organised to encourage employees to exchange views and listen to and hear one another, and to create an environment where weighed and thought-out action is important.

Category 3: Critical thinking is promoted using motivational measures. The development of critical thinking in this category is revealed as the activity of applying motivating measures. Encouragement and support in this context are understood as material and moral means that motivate employees to seek optimal solutions and encourage them to look into their professional activities. The most important motivator for encouraging critical thinking in employees is considered to be material incentive:

> *... the prize fund was 2,500 euros. And since the staff is large, there are a lot of those teams, brigades. And again, the question came up as to which brigade, which thought most critically, to give that prize to. And the task was how each group will present itself, what they'll suggest, how they'll implement it and in how much time, and then the prize will be distributed. So I really liked that and it really encouraged people.* (A3)

This is explained by the fact that the salary depends on the goals set and results achieved – *... the bonus system depends directly on the result. People see that it exists, that it works, that it works well and that it can affect ...* (A19), employee commissions, because *there's no salary, just commissions* (A16). Financial reward is thus an important factor that affects most people's living standards, social status and recognition inside and outside the organisation. Therefore, according to the employers, reinforcement with a reward for achieving a result that is significant for the organisation affects employee self-motivation:

> *If everyone was business-minded and had critical thinking, they would think – what should I do for it to benefit the company, and I'll also benefit through the company, because companies share their profits by paying salaries and bonuses, giving incentives ... If a person gets a salary, then another third of the salary as a bonus, and sees that it depends on his result, on his ability to act, then business-mindedness is activated.* (A19)

Nevertheless, employers are cautious about financial motivation as a factor in creating conditions for critical thinking:

> *Financial incentive is very limited in practice, although, on the other hand, we know that it's effective in the short term.* (A6)

Moral encouragement is also used to promote critical thinking, that is, praise, thanks or an opportunity for employees to improve their competencies:

> *I personally thank those people who, when I say we're doing it like this, they say, maybe there's another way? Look, we can do it like this, or not, and there will be those consequences, and for me, as a manager, these insights are really valuable and I really thank people who make suggestions rather than just accepting some of my suggestions at face value.* (A25)

The employers note that they verbally provide praise, encouragement and incentive for ideas, for thinking at work, and also give certificates of appreciation. According to the employers, this is a way *not only to praise, but also to suggest how to improve, how to develop in order to move forward* (A13).

Motivation is used as a means of promoting critical thinking through special professional development events – trips and outings to gain professional experience – and by organising targeted training or delegating employees to go to international events:

> *... I encourage it by organising outings where we can gain some professional experience and re-evaluate, maybe we can do it that way too. Sometimes there is a lack of examples of what activities we could do, and when you can go and see how other specialists do it, not sit around and philosophise, it's better to go, see and evaluate once you get back* (A14). *Well, and I always try to let people go to various courses and training sessions, and to business trips abroad as far as possible. As an example, there are people who regularly go to Lithuanian language courses. It would seem, who needs that, but if a person wants to, is interested ... But afterwards there's a certain result ... I want everyone in their area, which we supervise, that if there is some training or representation abroad in that area, that they go, represent, talk.* (A6)

Employees are motivated by various factors, so it is the task of the employers to regulate the factors in such a way that they encourage employees to strive for efficiency. The employers, therefore, choose different motivational measures related to external or internal motivational stimuli.

5.1.2 Non-dominant categories

Category 4: Critical thinking is promoted by creating conditions for employee independence. The study revealed that when thinking about how they encourage critical thinking in employees, employers single out a variety of initiated activities that not only create conditions for employees to express their thoughts, but also promote their independence. The employers stress the delegation of certain work tasks that give freedom of thought and action. By delegating tasks, the employers encourage employees to think independently and look into the problem:

> *I occasionally say: 'Think about it, look into that problem.' The first impression, the emotional impression, can't be right. ... The same is true in our work, we have to work on those things. Like if a forester goes out and his car breaks down – let's look into the problem, do we call a mechanic, or maybe he can solve something on his own.* (A5)

It also enables the employee to solve the problem, analyse the situation, by giving full responsibility for the performance of a certain task: ... *you say – here are your authorisations, you work, you make the decision* (A8).

The data reveal that in order to encourage critical thinking, employers delegate tasks according to the employee's level of independence or self-confidence. For some, the task is simply assigned and the expected result is given; for others, the task is divided into certain stages, discussing the performance of the task:

> *I have this one manager, you tell him: 'There's this task and you have to complete that task by that day.' And I know that this is a person who has his own opinion, critical thinking – he'll do it. But knowing this, I don't even dare tell him how to do it. There's another manager who's not as self-confident. I even delegate tasks to him differently. I tell him: 'Look, we've got until then, right, but look, in a week you'll bring that in, the second week you'll bring that in, then we'll talk.' If I were to tell him the way I tell that first manager, he'd be paralysed, he wouldn't be able to move for a week.* (A9)

By enabling employees to take responsibility for the decision made or the work done, the employers hope that they are encouraging the employees to be more self-confident, to look more responsibly into their activities or the problem or situation they are solving, and to act independently:

> *When a person has to present the activities that they're responsible for, they're still somewhat forced to prepare beforehand, to find arguments.* (A21)

It is also revealed in this category that employers assign tasks by specifying certain criteria for how that task is to be performed. By providing indicators for the performance of specific tasks, employers create conditions for employee self-control, as the employees must check themselves how they achieved those goals according to certain criteria:

> *If a person doesn't know how to think critically, he can at least start by comparing his activities with certain standard indicators, with standards of conduct, rules, and so on. So I give indicators for the entire unit. Some indicators are really formalised and linked to individual tasks, while others are common – all employees have to make some contribution to the achievement of common indicators.* (A28)
> *So we have the ISO 9001 quality management system, one of the procedures in it is also, let's say again, to check certain incoming data from third countries, again, if we say proposals, so to compare them with possible other proposals in order to select the best one according to the conditions.* (A27)

Thus, the employers are increasingly asking the question: What else can we do to encourage our employees to find solutions on their own and to improve, and what would guarantee the organisation a competitive advantage? And they note themselves that they solve this situation by developing employee independence: by teaching them to perform as many tasks as possible without the help of a manager, to take the initiative in new, difficult situations, and to find the best solutions.

Category 5: Critical thinking is promoted by asking questions. This category includes promoting critical thinking by asking employees questions. The employers see the benefits of questioning as a motivation to think about a particular situation, problem or solution. By asking questions, they encourage employees to think over and evaluate the situation or information, and to consider the possible alternatives and priorities:

> *You want to direct, help the person – he might not think, but if you ask a question, then he starts thinking. We try to ask the person questions so that he can think critically, evaluate his work, what new goals emerge.* (A17)

The employers note that asking questions in their daily professional activities is necessary, because as you work, various problems come up, and you have to evaluate the risks and make the most optimal decisions, so it is important for employees to think for themselves, for them to evaluate their own decisions:

> *I talk to them, I really like talking to them, I listen to them, we discuss, I ask questions, sometimes these awkward questions, 'Why?' 'Why?' is a common one with me. Like a child. 'But why?' So yeah, I do that. ... Questions can't not come up at work, they can't.* (A23)

Questions are asked in order for the employee to put forth thought-out suggestions or make reasonable decisions that have been coordinated in the team or group:

Then they ask the employee: aha, something happened, what do you suggest, what will happen if we do it like this, we think, we model what we can say to a loved one because this and that happened. If he asks this, if he asks that, how will we answer him? So maybe let's do it differently then, then maybe it'd be like this, or maybe like that, what do you think, do you agree? And then something comes out of it, we usually glue it together from little parts, because very different professionals from different areas are working, and you can't come up with it on your own, everyone has to think and make suggestions from their area, what they think is best from their profession. You put it together and the solution comes out. (A13)

Constant questioning manifests itself as a certain process during which critical thinking is stimulated in employees.

Category 6: Critical thinking is promoted by showing personal example or someone else's. In this category, another aspect of promoting critical thinking is revealed – personal example. When thinking about how they promote critical thinking in employees, the employers reveal their role as a manager/authority:

The best is by your own example. You take specific cases and analyse them, and you say, look – if that factor hadn't been turned on at all, the result would have been completely different to this day. So when interacting with the staff the best is a concrete example of how applying critical thinking changed your life. This is the most effective method because you can show progress, the stages and the end results. ... because by going to work with the staff you can then show those changes by your own example. And you make progress yourself, because when you give your examples to the staff, to other people, they watch you and you have to make progress yourself, show those examples yourself. (A2)

The data reveal that the position of managers, when they use their own example to present a personal thought process during action, obliges them to improve themselves and at the same time to make progress in their professional activities.

By relying on their achievements as an example to illustrate the impact of critical thinking on outcomes, the employers seek to substantiate the importance and benefits of critical thinking in achieving professional results:

I know the entire job from the very bottom, I went through that entire chain to the current level, to the international level. And by my example, I try to convey the whole thing to employees during interaction. (A28)

When presenting their thought process about the way to solve a problem or when analysing a situation, it is as if the employers demonstrate how the situation should be thought out, what the stages of thinking are, and what questions can and should come up. According to the employers, when you demonstrate critical thinking yourself, show by your own example, it becomes acceptable for employees as well.

In other words, the employees get used to thinking and asking themselves and others questions:

> *When thinking critically yourself, you also try to force that person to think critically, that he's not quite right in what he's saying. Maybe his expectations aren't what we can meet, maybe he's imagining the situation in completely the wrong way. You try to explain to him why this is. You go deeper and deeper and somehow people come to an understanding, they start to think themselves that maybe it's not quite the way I think here. But it takes a lot of work, determination; you have to want to do it, because you can say – everything is fine, so what are you getting on my case for.* (A13)

On the other hand, efforts are made to promote critical thinking by providing the best examples from the employees' professional activities:

> *... this is even the standard – sharing good practice. The best person ... simply tells everyone, without any plan, without any slides, without anything, how he does it, because he does it best. It can be a driver and he doesn't have any points that he didn't visit, or an industrial worker who also did something. So he just explains how he does it, and since the people who are listening are just like him, well, for example, I can explain that there's this process, this model that is used, and everyone steps back, scared; but he just explains without anything, everyone's just sitting there drinking coffee.* (A4)

The research data show that in the employers' thinking, the promotion of critical thinking manifests itself as the role of a certain teacher in various professional situations, when the example of the manager as an inspirer, encourager and helper is seen.

Category 7: Critical thinking is promoted by challenging. This category reveals the promotion of critical thinking as the employer challenging the employee, as a kind of provocation to arouse their critical thinking:

> *And I'll get their attention, when I come in I say: 'I want blood.' Me saying that, it's not that it's bad for someone, but to a person blood is something special, like life, and I want that kind of conversation, that kind of vision that is risky, with deep trembling, well, one that's changing, deep, and not like spending that time and sitting there on the outside.* (A1)

By challenging, by provoking, the employers create work situations that force employees to contemplate one or another aspect of a decision ... *think about it, look into that problem. The first impression, the emotional impression, can't be right* (A5), to harness creativity in the thought process and show initiative, *not to do the work, but what more can be done, if that person was happy with your work, to take more initiative* (A11).

The employers also note that in order to promote critical thinking in employees, they allow them to make mistakes and learn from their mistakes, that is, *to also give an element of error culture – the fact that he has the right to make mistakes* (A8). This means that employers empower employees not to be afraid of making mistakes, and if they do make a mistake, to think about how to correct those mistakes for optimal results:

> *In this way, I let a lot of people make mistakes so that they think more next time when they push those kind of thoughts and ideas or spend more time thinking about theoretical models instead of just rushing to do it.* (A4)

In this way, employees are also expected to take responsibility in the thinking process and look more into the specific situation or the proposals being made.

5.1.3 Relationships between the categories of description

The seven qualitatively different ways of promoting critical thinking can be explained by the differences between the two interrelated variations (dimensions), which help to reveal the relationships between the categories: creating conditions for critical thinking to manifest itself, and developing critical thinking. The main features of the above relationships are summarised in Table 24. This reveals a broadening of the research participants' experience in different dimensions of variations across all categories.

Tab. 24: *Relationships between the categories*

Category / Dimension	**Fostering open-mindedness**	**Using organisational measures**	**Using motivational measures**	**Promoting independence**	**Asking questions**	**Showing personal example or someone else's**	**Challenging**
Creating conditions for critical thinking to manifest itself	Building relationships based on trust; respect for every opinion	Encouraging employees to raise and solve emerging problems in the team by organising meetings	The value and importance of critical thinking to the organisation is acknowledged through moral and material incentive	Encouragement to think and look into a problem, situation, empowerment to act through trust	Encouragement to substantiate, prove and explain by asking thought-provoking questions	The value and importance of critical thinking in the organisation is acknowledged by demonstrating achievements	Challenging tasks enable employees to act and not be afraid of making mistakes
Developing critical thinking	Open and constructive feedback	Methods that promote active involvement in the thinking process are used	Motivated to learn and taught in practical activities	Delegation of work tasks that develop self-control abilities	The questions presented focus on the development of analytical and generalisation abilities	Demonstrate how to reflect or think with concrete examples	Provocation to reflect on one's activities, results

Dimension I: Critical thinking is promoted by creating conditions for its manifestation. This dimension reveals the promotion of critical thinking that describes the topic as the creation of certain conditions for critical thinking to manifest itself. In the first category, the promotion of critical thinking manifests itself as an openness inspired and fostered by the employer in the organisation at the personal and organisational level. This is an organisational environment where people trust one another, where every employee is encouraged to speak and is heard, and where there is respect for every opinion expressed:

> *They shouldn't be afraid of you; they should trust you. As far as I've come across, there are managers who want to earn that authority through fear ... well, they'll be scared, so they'll listen and do everything you say. ... There should also be trust-based relationships when the educator trusts the manager, exactly the same way as children trust the educator, so they're not afraid of expressing their opinion, that's through that trust.* (A22)
> *So those of us who are more senior or are managers, we have to be able to open up adults, so that they think, so that they make suggestions, don't hesitate to speak up.* (A4)
> *... we apply a positive approach to any discussions that arise. We don't say 'yes' or 'no', we say 'let's think, maybe that'll be good, or maybe like that'.* (A14)

In the second category, the creation of conditions for critical thinking is manifested through the use of external means: the organisation of meetings and discussions, the initiation of working groups. According to the employers, the use of these organisational measures creates conditions for employees to interact and evaluate a situation, look for alternative solutions to a problem, or share ideas with others:

> *We do meetings every Monday, we discuss everything, analyse and prepare for each week. Our activities are focused and prepared. To quickly evaluate the situation on the spot and find a solution to the problem – I think that's also critical thinking, also a part of it, because you don't know the person's true situation, he came in with this problem or he came in with a very negative emotion, and you have to nicely prove it to him and quickly find a solution on the spot, because people are now usually in a rush and don't have time, and maybe you'll even have to be a psychologist, caressing, supporting, explaining and resolving the situation. We have to be prepared for this and we know that and we get around those various situations.* (A14)

Thus, employers, as managers with the main role and responsibility for decision-making, ensure that the organisation's employees who report to them have the opportunity to make collegial decisions or evaluations of situations by organising meetings and consultations:

> *A lot of times when we're faced with difficult situations, we do this case analysis method where specialists from all areas get together and we talk about that case study. Everyone presents their arguments, their vision, the arguments for their decision. Everyone has to somehow come to an agreement. It's this sort of team critical thinking.* (A21)

The conditions for critical thinking to manifest itself in this category are revealed as the realisation of opportunities to collaborate, express one's own opinion and hear the opinions of others, and put forth and evaluate proposals through initiated meetings, consultations or group work. It should be noted that in the opinion of the employers, group thinking is always superior to that of one person:

> *There are geniuses, but unfortunately, I can see that it can be reached both easier and faster in a team.* (A15)

So by creating conditions to cooperate on professional matters, the employers expect optimal decision-making and progress:

> *On the other hand, by interacting through that activity, analysis, everyone sees how strong the other is, how much he's able to prove his idea. If he put it into words, he has to justify it – that's the principle we follow. In the team, we analyse and immediately evaluate how much we can apply that proposal of his in this area. Everything goes in a targeted manner, to one point, to innovations, the latest technologies, to the possibility of delivering it all. Sometimes the proposal seems crazy, but later we see the situation, that it wasn't completely crazy.* (A14)

The third category stresses the factor of applying motivational measures as a condition for critical thinking to manifest itself. The employers try to motivate employees by praising them or otherwise, not by providing material incentives for the work done, the proposal made, or the problem solved. According to the employers, demonstrating that critical thinking is recognised and valued creates an environment conducive to its manifestation:

> *Praise, encouragement and incentive for ideas, for thinking at work, for not applying the same job to all seniors, for adapting to them, for the home environment created. We give certificates of appreciation ...* (A13)

In this category too, the creation of conditions for critical thinking manifests itself as a material incentive to achieve the set goals by providing the highest level of services. Thus, in an organisation, a financial incentive, in a sense, creates the conditions to achieve the goals of the organisation by analysing the situation, choosing appropriate measures, and providing paths for solutions and their implementation. In other words, existing financial incentives create conditions to encourage employees to think critically:

> *The only incentive is financial; they have financial goals set. That's actually the only measure of success that I'd say works. We have a really competitive environment, everything is based solely on the financial plan. There's no ceiling on how much you can earn, everything is in the sense of commission – there's no salary, just commissions. The market is very competitive and small, plus people compete internally, everyone works with all of the customers, so that especially raises competition.* (A16)

The fourth category stresses employee independence, which is manifested in taking responsibility or delegating it through empowerment at the personal level:

Specifically as the manager, I delegate that you are now in charge. I just grant those rights and then, since I'm granting them, I can't somehow demand it from him. I mean, we can discuss, but … (A1)

I say: 'But wait, you're in charge of that bar, you can do that, you have enough experience and you know best and after all you're delegated by the state at the moment and you can do that'. (A9)

This category deals with employee independence, which is manifested in taking responsibility or delegating it through empowerment at the organisational level as well:

A working group is then asked to meet separately to prepare arguments and prepare proposals that they would come back with, like in the Seimas. Then we try again to hear the arguments and express our observations, so that a general decision can nonetheless be made. (A17)

The employers create conditions for employees to make independent decisions by demonstrating their confidence in them as professionals:

… I would think that if a person has already come in, then the social worker must – after assessing the information, the situation, the context of the day – come up with what to do. Or even draw up an individual plan for the disabled person. But I would completely be inclined not to butt in, because I think the social worker knows the person best in everyday life and that trust in him would be very important as a professional because he should demonstrate critical thinking with his work. (A21)

In the fifth category, the creation of conditions for critical thinking is expressed through constantly asking the question of 'why?' By asking the question of 'why?' – why the employee made such a decision, why the employee performed the task in that way, why the employee behaved one way or another in a specific situation – the employers create conditions for the employees to analyse their professional activities, such as a certain situation or decisions made, and compare and evaluate alternative solutions and risks. That is, through questions that require giving an opinion, arguing a decision, or substantiating or explaining a situation, an environment is created that encourages employees to think:

Try to extract from them why they need to think critically, why they acted that way in that situation, maybe they should have acted differently, let's think about it together what to do now (A13).

… I ask: 'OK, so what's your opinion, what are the alternatives, what are the pros of choosing one solution and what are the cons, and what are the pros and cons of choosing the second solution?' (A25)

Much like in the third category, the creation of conditions for critical thinking manifests itself in the sixth category through acknowledgement of the value and benefits of critical thinking in the organisation. Only in this category, acknowledgement of the value and benefits of critical thinking is stressed through personal example, that is, through the individual level:

> *So I personally share my experience, as a manager, in critical situations, I share it with the employees themselves as my personal example.* (A1)
> *Just by talking, I try to show by examples that it's useful, if that comes out of the conversation.* (A20)

The creation of conditions for critical thinking to manifest itself is stressed in the seventh category as the employer giving challenges or creating situations/tasks that pose a challenge. When creating or making such situations, the employers seek to enable employees to take responsibility and act:

> *So I say, do what seems right, and then if it was/will be bad, be prepared to get blasted, but it'll still be better than if you hadn't done anything. ... With me, that's how things are taught – do it the way you can, and then get blasted for it, but it'll be a lot less shameful than doing nothing at all. At least you'll still do it somehow. And then this critical thinking will grow so that next time I'll be able to do more and more.* (A1)

This dimension also emphasises the possibility of errors 'occurring' in professional activities as a challenge that the employee is able to cope with. Recognition of the element of error culture in professional activities creates a space in an organisation where the employee is free to act independently, but also to take responsibility for his or her decisions and change them:

> *If you have some established model of your own, don't be afraid to change it, be free and bold in critical thinking, don't be afraid to make mistakes. This is where we differentiate, we see that age is hard to beat, and it can. We'll show you – you just want, want to know, we'll open the way for you, we'll show you.* (A14)

Dimension II: Critical thinking is promoted by developing critical thinking skills. This dimension reveals the promotion of critical thinking that describes the topic as the application of different strategies in order to develop critical thinking.

In the first category, the development of critical thinking is manifested through the fostering of open-mindedness through constructive feedback, which creates a situation enabling reflection of one's activity or decision. The employers stress that by openly considering and discussing successful situations, they develop responsibility and self-awareness:

> *... publicising successful examples of how we managed to solve a problem. You have to talk to people and tell, present, develop self-awareness and at the same time critical thinking as well. Because after all, if a person works for a company and wants to work, then he more or less consciously, or maybe unconsciously, tries to ensure that the company is in good standing, that its position is good, and then through the company's openness, transparency this is possible.* (A19)

The aspect of critical thinking development in the second category is revealed through the methods used by employers to conduct meetings, discussions or training, when the aim is to develop specific critical thinking skills. According to the employers, they try to make sure that the meetings do not become routine and that the employees *are engaged and participate, not that one presents and the others listen* (A22). To encourage employees to actively express their position and make suggestions, the employers use a variety of proactive methods:

> *... so that work in small groups, like during those consultations and stuff like that, so that everyone can act proactively and not be passive, but active, and that experience of theirs that they gained here, so that they can apply that experience in their work.* (A22)

Mentioned in this dimension is another educational aspect manifested in this category: the training process in professional activities organised by the employers themselves. As the employers point out, they train their employees. Some directly motivate them to learn and organise training themselves:

> *So my suggestions are always go and learn. ... Next, I really encourage learning ... there's in-house training, I do it myself.* (A23)

Others take on the role of teacher, but not by organising training, but by organising the learning process in practice:

> *Another thing is I encourage people to learn. For example, a student comes in knowing everything, knowing how to do everything, and you say: 'Here's a cable for you, here's the pliers, here's the tip for you, please put it on.' The person takes maybe five times to get it on, and you ask: 'Did you put it on right?' He says: 'Right.' The person doesn't have experience. When you explain to him what the standard is, how it should be done, then he gets upset, but you say: 'Watch this film, there's this teaching material.' Six months later, when you see how he puts it on, you understand that the person has learned by himself, he knows the criteria, and when a colleague came who also put one on and asked: 'Did I put it on right?', he says: 'Wrong' – and what's wrong? And he already knows how to argue and explain.* (A15)

The development of critical thinking in the third category manifests itself as a result of qualification development. The employers organise outings and trips during which the employees improve their abilities and have the opportunity to learn good practice:

> *... we motivate through qualification development trips – these are the traditional means of motivation that we have. For employees who think critically.* (A13)
> *... plus I encourage it by organising outings where we can gain some professional experience and re-evaluate, maybe we can do it that way too.* (A14)

Mentioned as one of the organisational measures that creates preconditions for the promotion of critical thinking in employees is holding specific meetings for employee development. At this type of meeting, employees are encouraged to critically analyse professional literature, select key conclusions, and present them:

> *For example, there's a journal club. ... we sit down for an hour once a week every two months and discuss literature. You pick an interesting new article and present it in 15–20 minutes. You have to think critically about what's most important. All of us won't have*

> *time to read it. You have to take out the gems and show what they saw, that they did it like this and that, and that and that is what came out of it. You have to review at least 20–30 articles and decide that this one is the most valuable. Then you present it – they did this and let's try it too, they did this and got that.* (A12)

In the fourth category, the development of critical thinking is revealed through the presentation of tasks that promote independence and develop self-control at the individual level:

> *A person has to constantly check himself on the qualitative and quantitative indicators of his work. He has to collect the data himself, analyse them, process them himself, sort, group, and check within those broad tasks what goals he has to set for himself; he has to make a work plan for himself and regularly checked for quality and quantity.* (A28)

In the fifth category, the aspect of developing critical thinking is stressed as the development of analytical skills through questions asked by the employer both at the individual level and when working in a team. Constantly asking employees questions about the work they have done and the decisions they have made, on the one hand, encourages employees to evaluate the reliability and validity of the decisions and arguments here and now, and on the other hand, develops their ability to analyse and generalise information:

> *A person drives off and something needs to be installed. So then he immediately evaluates that situation and not that he does it according to that task, but he evaluates it. It's usually an ongoing discussion of how he did it, why he did it, and why he changed it here now. It's this ongoing interaction. Maybe that's what leads to an educational situation, that each time we decide.* (A7)
> *I have a good example: after a meeting, I often ask, so what did we decide? And it was like it was clear to everyone before I asked this question. And then critical thinking is when a person understands what we decided. Sometimes I even ask them to write it down, to repeat what we decided in order to name it. But this is a skill of sorts ...* (A15)

The aspect of critical thinking development in the sixth category manifests itself through a personal demonstration of the thinking process as an example that outlines the way of thinking:

> *It's important not to criticise, but to argue, if, say, we're going to talk about monitoring open activities, because educators are very sensitive to this, so for it not to sound like criticism or a discussion of open activities, but as advice based on certain theoretical knowledge. For example, if I say that a certain method should be used in such a way, then I have to explain why, because that and that scientist says so. Then the educators understand that this wasn't some kind of criticism on my part, but that it's scientifically based facts, evidence. So I'd say that I show them this example of mine of how this can be practiced.* (A22)

The dimension of critical thinking development that emerges in the seventh category is related to certain provocations and challenges that the employers present:

Sometimes there are these miracles where there's too good of a result. I say – abnormally not good. People get confused, and I say: 'I'd like to know why you got too good of a result, because in my imagination, it shouldn't have been that good.' At first, they get sad when I ask that, but maybe, I say, it's some kind of business niche, a new business might be born. But with me, people understand – it doesn't matter if it's really bad or really good, you have to know the arguments why it happened like that. Here, I think, the ability to explain the result is also very important. (A15)

5.1.4 Outcome space

Analysis of the outcome space reveals that the employers encourage critical thinking by creating favourable conditions for it, both for each employee individually, and collectively in the team, so that they make a personal contribution to the development of the organisation (Table 25).

Tab. 25: *Outcome space. Referential and structural components: How employers encourage critical thinking*

Referential component (what the experience is, how it is manifested)	**Structural component (what that experience is for)**
Fostering open-mindedness	Personal Organisational
Using organisational measures	Personal Organisational
Using motivational measures	Personal Organisational
Promoting independence	Personal Organisational
Asking questions	Personal Organisational
Showing personal example	Personal Organisational
Challenging	Personal Organisational Social

The most pronounced are the personal and organisational aspects, which are found in all categories. The least pronounced is the social aspect, which is only tangible in one category – critical thinking as a challenge.

The hierarchical relationships between the structural components and the categories are presented in Figure 13.

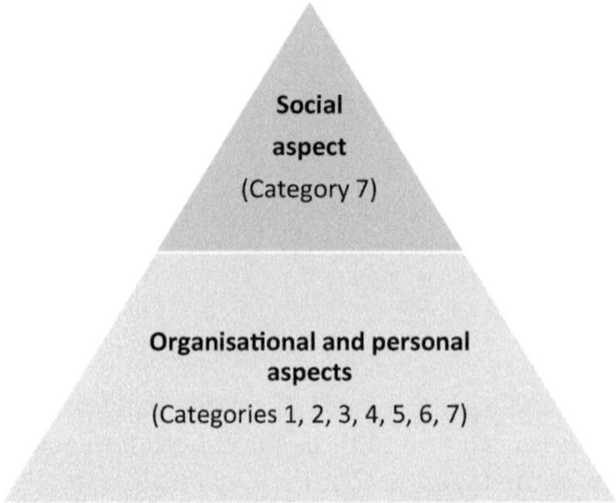

Fig. 13: *Hierarchical relationships between the structural components and the categories*

Through analysis of the hierarchical relationships between the categories, personal and organisational aspects of equal value were established. Critical thinking is promoted in employees in interaction between the employee and the employer and between the employee and other employees. Critical thinking is encouraged by the employers for the professional growth of each employee: by ensuring autonomy at work, providing feedback, and using various organisational and/or motivating measures. All of these aspects increase employee engagement, which can potentially help ensure the effective operation of the organisation.

5.2. How employees experience critical thinking

In order to reveal how the employees experience critical thinking in their professional activities, four categories are singled out, of which three are dominant. Employees experience critical thinking as: (1) constant questioning; (2) contemplation of a situation, phenomenon, problem personal position from various perspectives; (3) a response to a challenge. There is one non-dominant category (4) that reveals the experience of critical thinking as a manifestation of personal position/opinion in a controversial context.

5.2.1 Dominant categories

Category 1: The experience of critical thinking as constant questioning. This category reveals the employees' experience of critical thinking as asking yourself and the environment questions in daily work activities about activities, emerging or proposed ideas, information received, and assignments. In this category, it comes to light that asking questions is perceived as something like constantly *poking little needles in all the places* (B4), and this helps think over why the proposed idea works or could work, or why the information or decision should be accepted or abandoned. Continuous questioning helps in situations when each decision has to be selected by arguing and/or presenting an alternative. This encourages thinking over the things experienced in professional activities (information received, tasks, assignments) from different perspectives, thus penetrating the true meaning of things. From this follows the experience of critical thinking as asking the question of 'why?' continually. The philosophical question of 'why?' *must constantly provoke* critical thinking (B9). It is like a habit that encourages depth of analysis, when, in checking sources and information and deciding on their reliability, not only is there questioning, but alternative answers and solutions are sought as well:

> *The fact that someone told you one way or another, that's not necessarily the case. You have to try to go through your filters yourself and see if that's really the case. But then you're obliged not only to question things, but to go into the heart of the matter as well. Then you're forced to go deeper. If some politician talks about one thing or another, how he would do this and that, promises this and that, you have to look – aha, that's what he's saying now, but what did he say before, what was his position? Why did it suddenly change? Is it because it really has changed, or is it because it's pleasant to the voters' ears? Are those sources checked, was it looked at from other angles, and what would the same image look like from those other angles? Comparing other sources, and a third and a fourth, looking from their point of view and thinking, so what's their goal, why do they want to present this and that idea and so on. You have to husk it and see – not everything is true there either.* (B9)

Another aspect that is revealed in this category has to do with the search for truth, authenticity. The employees stress that the questions they raise in their daily professional activities are necessary when faced with situations where they have to choose which information to call correct and not fall victim to fake news. It is precisely constant questioning that helps not only to question the information being worked on, but also to resist manipulation. And it helps to see what lies behind the kept quiet, when looking for the time, place and addressee of the subtext of the authenticity of the information in terms of cause-effect aspects:

> *As well as all the information that other people have prepared for you, be it the media or the public institutions that broadcast it – you also understand that everything you see is important, but sometimes what lies behind it may be more important. You have to ask about what you see. From what you see, you go to the things that you don't see. Then you go from all angles: and where is that from, and who is that for, and why is that, what, why, with whom – you have to cover the whole range of questions. ... Evaluate the subtext of that information, what's trying to be achieved by it, why, for example, that information came out now and not sooner or later.* (B3)

On the one hand, the experience of critical thinking as constant questioning manifests itself in contemplating the appropriateness of a solution or the reliability of information or sources, prioritising activities, and evaluating and arguing the appropriateness of their choice. On the other hand, it unfolds through searches for truth, authenticity, by constantly questioning what is being said or done; looking for the meaning of what has been said or done; and trying to perceive what lies behind the presented fact, task or information – as if trying to read between the lines.

Category 2: The experience of critical thinking as contemplation of a situation/phenomenon/problem/personal position from various perspectives. This category reveals the employees' experience of critical thinking as the contemplation of a situation/phenomenon/problem experienced in professional activities from various perspectives. In this category, it comes to light that constantly contemplating things from different perspectives is perceived as something akin to *arranging elements into a mosaic* (B9), when, in performing a specific professional task, you have to evaluate the received data, *you have to dig, take a lot of information, read a lot, compare a lot* (B9), rely on various sources, and not follow the opinion already formed, the conclusions already reached, and not accept the phenomenon as black and white, but look into it, become acquainted with it and rethink it, and only then provide substantiated, reasoned conclusions:

> *Not becoming attached to formed opinions, but searching, not conforming. The monk Pilypas said that people are very quick to form an opinion. So it is, and I notice it in myself, that someone said something, a few words, some behaviour, a reaction – and you have a conclusion about the person. But in order to discover a person, to see him in every way, you might have to also go to the mountains or swim across the sea. Then he shows his true colours. You can't say black and white.* (B9)

Another aspect revealed in the analysed category is when contemplation from various perspectives is related not to the decisions you make yourself, but to helping someone else by evaluating a certain problem and looking for the most optimal solution alternatives. This is like contemplating a possible solution in perspective, evaluating the situation that the person is in as well as the path to the situation that the person would like to be in:

> *... say he has two employees, but would like for ten employees to work at his company. And you lay out that path, what'll have to be sacrificed, what'll have to be done for him to get to that situation. ... Really, what step and what bad or good can come of it.* (B4)

Such professional behaviour is not seen as an end in itself, but is associated with the search for the fairest, most optimal solutions in a particular situation and the reduction of possible errors or risks when solutions are thought over in advance, modelling what may happen after adopting one or another alternative, and what challenges may accompany one or another decision:

> *... you want to put that airbag in front instead of later saying – we got burned.* (B4)

Another aspect is the contrast between objectivity and subjectivity, when opposite points of view are evaluated, between which there are certain differences and discrepancies. It is like a constant, impartial evaluation of the facts, going from the global whole, a generalised position, material to specific, clearly discernible details, facts in search of objective evidence that refutes a subjective, preconceived notion, position, and version:

> *This turns into this puzzle, when you have objective data in one hand – a puzzle that's one shape, and you take another piece of the puzzle that's given to you of subjective data and you try to match them up. If the subjective data don't match, you ask for another puzzle or your raise another version so that those two pieces of objective and subjective factors match. There are objective and subjective data. Subjective data, which are usually provided to us by police officers: these are certain locations where the remains were found, even the causes of death for those individuals are given sometimes, sometimes they enter that he was found after hanging himself in a noose, they even give the entire mechanism, even though it's not actually clear whether he hanged himself or was hung. Or drowned – maybe he was thrown in the water already dead. You look for facts, objective evidence, based on which you can confirm to the investigator according to the task that this is the case or present other facts so that he can investigate those facts and change that subjective initial opinion of his in the course of the pre-trial investigation. ... You go from the global whole to the micro signs, rejecting them one by one, like you pull out the dandelion fluff that blocks the overall image of the dandelion. And then you see, after removing most of the signs, that there's one left.* (B5)

The data reveal that employees experience critical thinking when contemplating not only a situation, problem or phenomenon, but also a personal opinion/position – how much it responds to or reflects their personal situation, how substantiated it is:

> *... what am I doing, what have I done, am I really worth that bigger money, am I capable of taking on greater responsibility? If you feel like you are, you write, you go to talk and you can try to prove it.* (B9)

Contemplation of a personal position and self-reflection are extremely important in order to weigh it: *you check twice as hard that it really is so* (B4). When contemplating a personal position or opinion, the importance of the ability to look from someone else's (the manager's, the customer's, the student's) perspective is revealed. One considers how I would act in such a situation if I was the manager, a student, a customer. All of this is important in order to believe in what you say and have peace of mind *that you did the best you could* (B16).

The need to contemplate a situation/phenomenon/problem experienced from various perspectives is associated with an employee's erudition and desire to go into the heart of the matter. The employees note that it would be possible to substantiate and argue not only how you think and what assumptions you make, but also what facts and evidence support it, but this requires knowledge, a wide field of vision of the problem, and a desire to look into the situation. This requires a lot of effort ... *because the larger your field of vision, the more angles you see* (B7). The employees emphasise the importance of context in order to not just perform a task primitively, as if it were a simple *game of chess* (B13), but also to give it context and evaluate which solution is more appropriate for the particular environment, and how others will react to one solution or another. It is important for employees to understand the task in the broader context of interest groups, time periods and cultures and thus avoid miscommunication. It is, therefore, extremely important to know the person you are talking to, his or her character traits and culture, and to be able to understand and decode the information provided by the speaker, which may have completely different meanings:

> *... you have to grasp that when one thing or another is said, it doesn't necessarily mean the same thing as it does in my understanding, because this is a person from another country, one who reacts differently and expresses emotion differently. By understanding that, you avoid misunderstandings, you then realise that these are not some ultimatums, it's not something, it's just that an Italian's character is one thing, mine is another, and northerners are again something else, and that silence, taciturnity or reaction and wording of remarks doesn't mean malice.* (B9)

The experience of critical thinking in this category is revealed as an integral part of daily professional activities. Contemplation of a situation, phenomenon or problem from various perspectives is very clearly linked to the question of meaning – what it is being done for, why it is necessary.

Category 3: The experience of critical thinking as a response to a challenge. This category reveals the employees' experience of critical thinking as a response to a challenge in professional activities, which is understood as stress and difficulty, and is associated with verification of the employee's abilities. Challenges are experienced in professional situations which call for the need to think, act, do something differently than usual, and create a new experience. Challenging situations invite employees to leave their comfort zone.

Employees experience critical thinking in their professional activities when faced with a challenge like an unexpected provocation, or even a slap in the face. Then there is an inadequately emotional, aggressive reaction, and awkward, unexpected questions – *you stand there caught off guard, you don't know what they'll ask you, and they attack you* (B7). Such situations inspire a feeling of being caught, attacked from all sides, that you must not give in to – you must remain calm, and recognise and understand what the aim of the awkward question is, what the expectation is, and solve the problem *with a cool head ... so that you don't start to panic or console yourself* (B10). Such situations always require weighty, well-thought-out arguments, answers or solutions so that the position represented or the insight or conclusion presented is not belittled.

Employees also experience critical thinking as a response to the challenge of the unknown, when they encounter non-standard situations in their professional activities, *where I'm not that versed* (B10), *where it's like there's no way out, it's unclear what to do* (B7). These are often situations where the action is not clearly described or regulated, or has more than one possible solution. Both situations require new, atypical, authentic behaviour, and it is as if the employees experience an external stimulus to act, to think differently:

... some situations are not described and then, after you turn on your critical thinking, you have to apply some template from the material resources, the ability resources that you have ... (B16)

Another aspect of the challenge is the challenge of responsibility. This is experienced as a delegated and assumed responsibility 'for what'. Managers entrust the employee with larger, more responsible projects. In such situations, performing the task itself requires looking at the task at hand and your relationship to it from a radically different perspective:

Not to do some simple task, but broader and more responsibilities. ... more tasks that are more interesting and newer, not making the same old poster, but some different kind of stand that's going to stand there in the middle of the room. From new tasks like that, critical vision emerges in new challenges. (B11)

When acting in such situations, employees take responsibility for certain decisions in order to achieve the best possible operating result.

In sharing their critical thinking experience, the employees also single out the challenge of quick decision-making. This challenge is experienced in professional situations where a quality result must be delivered in a very short time – when *you can't drift between fantastic ideas, but need a concrete and quick answer* (B11). In these situations, the employee must recognise what is going on, understand what to do, and evaluate what will happen and what measures to take if the situation worsens. This requires a lightning-fast reaction – *I can see that the situation is critical, so my job is to deal with it in fifteen minutes so that I don't suffer myself and there is no harm done to the person* (B6). Such a challenge is often accompanied by constant, often even unconscious, tension and maintaining vigilance.

The employees experience critical thinking as a response to a challenge – provocation, the unknown, responsibility, and a quick decision. In the context of the research data, employees attach a positive meaning to these challenges and see them not as hindering, but as encouraging them to move forward, look for original solutions, and change their thinking.

5.2.2 Non-dominant category

Category 4: The experience of critical thinking as a manifestation of personal position/opinion in a controversial context. This category reveals the employees' experience of critical thinking as a manifestation of personal position/opinion in a controversial context. Employees experience the manifestation of their personal position in a controversial context in professional situations where the personal opinion they are positioning is not accepted or differs from the position declared by the manager. The employees emphasise that situations like this require *having a spine* (B2) and thinking with your head, regardless of what the manager says and what position the manager represents:

> *... I have some different opinion of my own, then I understand that I'm thinking a little. That opinion is usually a little different from what's presented to me as the single, undisputed opinion. ... You have to be guided by your critical thinking ... you have to not trust just the manager a little, because he's shaping a certain policy.* (B13)

This aspect of experiencing critical thinking is particularly stressed in the context of the relationship with the employer, when it is important to express your position in a certain situation or problem not only by criticising it or rejecting certain ideas, but by making clear, specific suggestions to the employer about other possible behaviours or solutions:

> *For my part, I also have a very clear methodology for myself, with one manager, that if you come to criticise or express dissatisfaction in a certain situation, bring three solutions. Like for example, if I come to see Aloyzas Antanaitis, I hope I didn't guess anyone's name and surname, I say: 'I don't like that the warehouse is dirty' and I suggest giving everyone cleaner shoes or I suggest everyone taking turns sweeping the warehouse, or let's chip in two euros each and hire a better cleaner. And the manager either adopts one of my decisions, or something else, but so it's not just what we call 'hanging monkeys': 'let's solve this – our warehouse is dirty' and we leave.* (B4)

In such situations, the manifestation of a personal position is primarily associated with the courage to make it public, to communicate it publicly, as well as with resisting destructive criticism of the environment and focusing on constructive observations that promote a person's proactivity:

> *... how much courage it takes to spread the message, to communicate it publicly. An artist who has critical thinking always has to arm himself with a certain patience and even a certain kind of armour, protection, because all those critical comments can be useful for future activities if they're constructive, but more often than not they're so destructive that they don't give pretext to continue working, but just encourage you to continue hiding. I just distance myself from comments like that and pay attention to the constructive comments.* (B15).

Thus, the employees' experience of critical thinking as a manifestation of personal opinion/position is experienced in certain controversial professional situations where the personal position may be unacceptable or radically different from that of others. Employees then need the courage to express their personal opinion in the controversial professional context.

A qualitative difference was found between the categories. The experience described in the first and second categories is associated with active consideration of what the action is being done for, for what purpose, and whom it is important to and why. The experience described in the third and fourth categories stresses the challenges faced, and the need for a strong personal position in the context of stressful and sometimes controversial professional activities.

5.2.3 Relationships between the categories of description

The four qualitatively different ways of experiencing critical thinking can be explained by the differences between the two interrelated variations (dimensions), which help to reveal the relationships between the categories: evidence-based professional practice, and action in uncertain/non-standard professional situations (Table 26). This shows a broadening of the participants' experience in both different dimensions of variations in all four main categories.

Tab. 26: *Relationships between the categories (how employees experience critical thinking)*

Category / Dimension	As constant questioning	As contemplation of a situation, problem, phenomenon from various perspectives	As a response to a challenge	As a manifestation of personal position, opinion in a controversial context
Through evidence-based professional practice	The search for truth, authenticity by evaluating the reliability and validity of information, solutions and arguments	Contemplation of professional content from different perspectives by generating different solution alternatives and analysing sources in search of objectivity	The search for atypical, alternative arguments and solutions and taking responsibility in acting	Standing up for a personal position and supporting the statement by making clear and specific suggestions
Action in uncertain, non-standard professional situations	Constant doubt, reflection on what is said and done; what lies behind the decision or information.	Not conforming to an already formed opinion, not following a decision that has been made.	Acting in stressful, uncertain, new situations that push you out of your comfort zone.	Positioning an opinion when it is unacceptable to others; resisting destructive criticism of the environment; having a spine

Dimension I: Evidence-based decision-making. This dimension reveals an experience of critical thinking that describes the topic as evidence-based decision-making in professional activities. In the first category, the employees' experience of critical thinking manifests itself as the search for truth and authenticity in professional activities by evaluating the reliability and validity of information, solutions and arguments both at the individual level and when working in a team. Evidence-based professional practice is constructed on the basis of factual information (quantitative and qualitative data), scientific and expert research and their analysis, when it is necessary to substantiate the decisions made:

> *... you always have to ask, ask a lot of questions, why that's said, why that is ... comparing other sources, and a third and a fourth, looking from their point of view and thinking, so what's their goal, why do they want to present this and that idea and so on. You have to husk it and see – not everything is true there either.* (B9)

The second category stresses the procedural elements of the critical thinking experience that are manifested in the performance of specific professional tasks which are very clearly given meaning to, what is it being done for. The importance is noted of contemplating professional content from different perspectives in generating different solution alternatives, analysing sources, searching for objective information, and searching for facts and evidence that refute subjective information. This is associated with operational performance quality, professional action:

> *For example, you get a complaint and you have to assess what the building is, if that case warrants a complaint or not, if we examine cases like that, if the building need a permit or not, if you have to go and inspect the site or if you can make a decision on the spot, if you need additional documents. You have to evaluate a lot of things right away so you can decide how to proceed and how much time it'll take you (B12).*
> *Those initial options that are raised often trip you up, and during the investigation you think that that's how it must have been done, but you have to push that subjective data aside and see the totality of objective data, and only then go to the subjective data and see if they coincide or not. Let's say, they send pictures of a few people, and it's unknown if they fit that skull that was found or not. And you compare those marks on the skull with the marks of the portrait and gradually filter out that these marks in that portrait don't fit that skull. You put aside what was presented to you in the first option as a suitable option because you don't know which of those three portraits corresponds to that skull. The same goes for the destructive tools – you gradually filter them out, thinning out that filter: you sift some marks through a larger sieve, then turn off the next level of critical thinking and go to the group marks, that you already have to take a finer sieve and filter out the ones that don't fit, and then take a paper filter that only that one mark seeps though. You critically reject those other destructive tools or individuals and present a concrete conclusion.* (B5)

The third category highlights the experience of critical thinking in professional situations where employees experience stress and encounter atypical difficulties that are not characteristic of daily activities. Such situations are experienced when acting individually and with others. They seemingly push employees out of their comfort zone and impel them to look for atypical arguments, solutions and alternatives.

... you get some bugged page, some error, where you sit there for a few hours and then you finally start doing everything all over again, you start changing your thinking. ... there's a new problem and not all problems have a one-size-fits-all solution. (B10)
Or even when we get a difficult situation, and it seems like there's no way out, it's unclear what to do. So we sit down together and everyone, using their critical thinking, speaks out loud and then we can make some kind of joint decision. In my opinion, this has to do with talking to each other. Of course, if you're alone, then you reach something based on your critical thinking, but we usually use it when we're deciding among ourselves, when we're looking for a solution or developing something, or we're solving a problem. (B7)

Like the third category, the fourth category stresses the experience of critical thinking as a certain response to atypical, controversial situations, but very clearly emphasises the personal aspect – the manifestation/manifestation/representation of a personal position in activities, solutions and processes. In every situation, the employee's posture when expressing his or her arguments is important:

You're always thinking about whether that's right or whether what you're being told to do is wrong. ... because you see that the remarks of the symphony conductor are almost cardinally different from the remarks that the director made before that. Then you think you were right in asking these questions of whether it really is right, what's being required of you. (B13)

Dimension II: Action in uncertain/non-standard professional situations. This dimension reveals an experience of critical thinking that describes the topic when acting in situations that are uncertain, non-standard or atypical for the employee. In the first category, the experience of critical thinking manifests itself at the personal level, when it is as if the uncertainty of a situation is created by the employees themselves through constant doubts and reflection on what is being said, what lies behind the decision or information. On the one hand, this seems to create a background of mistrust of the environment and oneself, but on the other hand, it is associated with the disposition of operational efficiency in order to achieve the best operating results:

... after receiving that information, it's important to know what your partner wants to say, what his aim is. He says such and such, this and that – then you have to go a lot deeper: aha, really, if not quite that, then why is he carrying that message? What's the point of him carrying that message? Why is he doing that? What are his motives? Maybe there are some connections to other elements and then to look for points. You can't be paranoid at all, but you have to constantly look and ask, so what's behind that, why do they want this, why do they want that. (B9)

In the second category, acting in uncertain, atypical professional situations very clear manifests itself through not conforming to an already formed opinion, not following a single decision that has been made, and through the search for objectivity:

Those same symptoms can be caused by a lot of diseases: the flu, catarrh, tracheitis. It's a long list. You have to diagnose one. You look to see where the nidus is, whether there's a nidus in the bronchi or the lungs that those symptoms are coming from. There are clinical signs that you see yourself when the patient comes in, and there are subjective ones – all those complaints. Then you objectively look at what it is, you put the objective signs together with the subjective ones, and you have a diagnsosis. If you can't confirm it, you refer [the patient] to another specialist for tests, say, to do an X-ray. If you can't feel it, you can't see it – you do an ultrasound. You put the clinical symptomatology together with the instrumental analysis and you think critically – could it be this disease, or this one? (B5)

In the third category, acting in uncertain/atypical professional situations is particularly stressed as the challenge created by the situation for the employee – tension, vagueness, newness:

... there are situations that seem simple, and then unroll into terrible things, to inpatient treatment, to surgery. You have to plan not to interfere, all those delayed-action abscesses, that if you don't touch the person will walk, and you'll go to the right help, but not today. If you start doing what you can without the tools, knowledge and capabilities, it won't be help, but a sudden exacerbation of the problem. (B16)

The fourth category stresses expressing a personal position when it is not accepted by others, and resisting destructive criticism of the environment. In such situations, the importance of expressing a personal position is compared to having a spine.

... I don't accept remarks that are made to me blindly; after critically evaluating them, I accept them and apply them to myself. It's usually a piece of music, it has to be performed, fulfilled, and there are certain instructions on how that piece should be fulfilled – the tempo, the mood, and a lot of times, the director's remarks don't really correspond to those instructions. You have to be guided by your critical thinking. (B13)

5.2.4 Outcome space

The outcome space, which summarises the referential and structural components of the outcome and their relationships, is given in Table 27. The referential component describes what the experience is, how it is manifested in professional practice. It corresponds to the categories described above. The structural component describes what that experience is for.

Analysis of the outcome space reveals that critical thinking is experienced not only as a direct function performed professionally, but also as an employee's personal contribution to the development of the organisation and society. The most pronounced is the personal aspect, which is found in all categories (Figure 14).

Critical thinking is first and foremost experienced through the creation of added value for oneself as an employee in order to perform tasks as well as possible and to act effectively in uncertain situations. This manifests itself as proof of

Tab. 27: *Referential and structural components: How employees experience critical thinking*

Reference component (what the experience is, how it is manifested)	**Structural component (what that experience is for)**
As constant questioning	Personal
As contemplation of a situation, problem, phenomenon, personal position from various perspectives	Personal Organisational Social
As a response to a challenge	Personal Organisational
As a manifestation of personal position/opinion in a controversial context	Personal Social

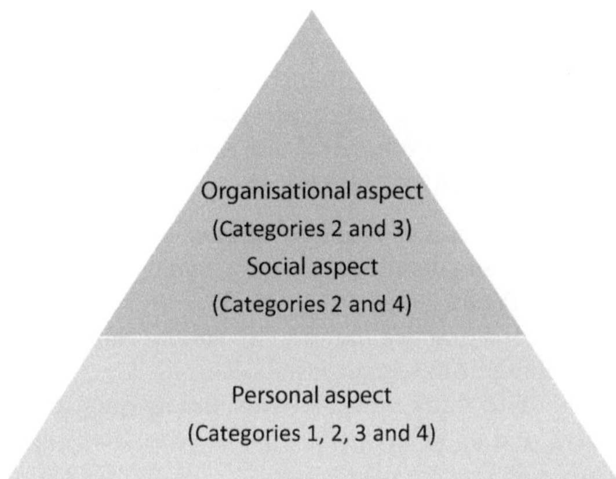

Fig. 14: *Hierarchical relationships between the structural components and the categories*

the employee's professionalism, mastery and erudition. The organisational aspect is most pronounced in the second and third categories when acting with others, in a team at the organisational level, when it is very clearly perceived that one or another behaviour is related to someone else's (a customer's, the team's, the very organisation's) well-being. This is taking responsibility not only for yourself and your decisions but for the organisation as well. It is as though this is important not only for my own well-being as a professional but also for the well-being of the organisation. The social aspect manifests itself in the second and fourth categories as the experience of critical thinking in a broader context that goes beyond the specific position, professional field or organisation, when professional activities contribute to the creation of value for society.

Conclusions

The study revealed the subjective conceptions and experiences of critical thinking among higher education teachers and students, as well as employers and employees. Analysis of the research data revealed the differences and similarities in the conceptions and experiences of each of the groups of research participants. We present summarised conclusions from the analysis of data from two large groups – the academic community (teachers and students) and the professional community (employers and employees).

Conceptions of critical thinking and experience of the phenomenon of critical thinking among teachers and students. The treatment of critical thinking by the representatives of both groups is related both to action in the academic space, and to the general experience of the phenomenon in the personal and professional space. Both groups stressed that they did not have a previously formed conception of critical thinking. The teachers stressed that they do not have a special aim to teach critical thinking. Their teaching is an integral part of academic activities, in pursuit of a deeper understanding of the subject being studied, preparation for the profession, and the development of thinking and broadening one's outlook in general. We can, therefore, say that in their conception, critical thinking is associated with the development of both professional and generic competences.

Both groups understand critical thinking as:

- the development of a person's cognitive abilities by working with the specific content of the subject being studied – to select, compare, convey, interpret, evaluate, and draw conclusions;
- a tool or instrument of a practical nature – to solve a problem or find and apply a solution by modelling professional situations;
- a person's disposition to think independently, boldly question the opinions and decisions of others, and build an open, empathetic relationship with others.

The following differences between the teachers and the students in the understanding of critical thinking were identified:

- The teachers understand critical thinking as a holistic overall competence that provides the basis for the development of their own thinking as well as for the creation of a multifaceted, open relationship with the environment;
- The students perceive critical thinking in relation to the environment more narrowly – as the ability to reflect on phenomena in the light of various perspectives;
- The teachers perceive critical thinking as a learning process – to become acquainted, understand, choose, evaluate;
- The students associate critical thinking more with the process of solving topical problems;
- The teachers associate critical thinking with other phenomena, such as creativity or civil and democratic society;
- The students do not stress the connections between critical thinking and other phenomena.

The conception of critical thinking is revealed at the personal, interpersonal and social levels. Both the teachers and the students see the value of critical thinking for personal growth and professional development. In relation to other people, critical thinking is seen as an opportunity to improve one's thinking by studying and working together, as well as by solving relevant professional problems. In relation to society, critical thinking is seen as openness to change, progress, creative solutions and innovation. However, the latter aspect is only highlighted in the teachers' experiences.

Both the teaching and learning of critical thinking are exclusively related to delving into the subject being studied, better knowledge acquisition, and the development of analytical skills. Comparison of the teachers' teaching experiences and the students' learning experiences reveals several key aspects common to both groups:

- Critical thinking teaching and learning takes place in two ways: by organising joint activities, and by assigning independent tasks;
- The teacher takes an active role in teaching, explaining, demonstrating, modelling; the students engage in the activities offered by the teacher;
- Passive teaching occurs when the teacher delegates learning responsibilities to students, monitoring and coordinating the learning process; the students engage in learning feeling the freedom to choose, decide, create;
- The teachers use and the students recognise a wide range of methods for developing critical thinking: case and problem analysis, text analysis and evaluation, questioning, situation simulation, experimentation, discussions.

Several differences in the teaching and learning experiences also became evident:

- The teachers value teaching through independent tasks in terms of personal empowerment, better immersion into the content being studied, and professional effectiveness;
- The students tend to associate independent learning more with personal maturity and their recognition and evaluation as a person than with the development of abilities applicable in studies and professional life;
- The teachers claim to teach by personal example – sharing experience and scientific achievements – and clearly declare the values of openness to the truth, the pursuit of rightness, and the search for unique solutions and creativity;
- In their experiences, the students do not recognise the method of learning from the teacher's example.

The teachers also claim that no one taught them how to teach critical thinking. They develop their critical thinking competencies individually, through self-education – by reading, observing and analysing the environment – and collectively, during organised qualification development training events – by listening to speeches and colleagues and discussing amongst themselves. The students also could not recall the teachers mentioning that they are specially teaching them critical thinking. The students' experiences reflected the learning of critical thinking in the usual lectures and practical classes organised by teachers. The students, like the teachers, associate the learning of critical thinking with a better understanding of the subject being studied, knowledge of the profession, deeper thinking, and the broadening of one's outlook.

Conceptions of critical thinking and experience of the phenomenon of critical thinking among employees and employers. The treatment of critical thinking by the representatives of both groups is inextricably linked to their daily professional activities. The conception of critical thinking is formed by contemplating an experience of the phenomenon and, conversely, the experience/ordeal of critical thinking in the course of daily professional activities forms subjective conceptions of critical thinking.

The common components of the employers' and employees' understanding of critical thinking are revealed as individual abilities focused on the search for truth, and as a person's specific qualities that reflect the manifestation of courage in professional activities. It should be noted that both the employers and the employees understand critical thinking not only as cognitive abilities, but also as their manifestation in the course of daily professional activities. The practical applicability of this competence and the tangibleness of concrete results are highlighted in both groups' understanding of subjective critical thinking. Both groups understand critical thinking as:

- free thinking without preconceptions, when a person is not guided solely by his or her personal experience or attitude and does not succumb to environmental pressures;
- the ability to see and analyse a situation from different perspectives, anticipating and evaluating all possible risks;
- reasoned decision-making and communication of those arguments based on reasoning;
- questioning the absolute, indisputable truth, scepticism, the desire not to become attached to subjective opinions, doubt as to the existence of any reliable criterion of truth;
- self-confidence in expressing opinions and taking on challenges;
- the ability to act independently and take responsibility without fear of making mistakes.

The identified variations in the employers' and employees' understanding of critical thinking are linked to certain features:

- in the employers' understanding of critical thinking, the manifestation of personal qualities – independence and self-confidence – is more pronounced; these aspects of the employers' conception of critical thinking are revealed through the context of creating added value for the organisation.
- The employees' conception of critical thinking highlights the importance of empathy, which is revealed at the interpersonal and social levels as an emotional response to other people's experiences, encouraging them to help or change their situation.

In summarising the experience of critical thinking among employees and employers in daily professional activities, commonalities were established between how employers encourage critical thinking and how employees experience critical thinking. These are:

- Asking themselves and others questions. For employers, this is one of the forms of promoting critical thinking in employees, and for employees, it is a process that creates personal added value in professional activities.
- Challenging experiences. For employers, this is a provocation that stimulates critical thinking in employees, and for employees, it is a departure from their comfort zone. Challenges are given the meaning of a growing experience: they encourage you to move forward, look for original solutions, change your thinking, and create new experiences.
- Delegating and taking on responsibility. For employers, this means encouraging employees to take on responsibility through increasing confidence in the employees and developing their responsibilities, and for employees, this means not being afraid to make mistakes and being able to learn from their mistakes.
- Expressing a personal position/opinion. For both employers and employees, the emphasis is on a supportive environment that includes organisational and motivational measures.
- Creating added value. Both the employers and the employees stress not only the creation of added value for the individual, but also the contribution to the development of the organisation and the well-being of society.

The main difference that distinguishes the employers' and employees' experience of critical thinking is that the employers stress the importance of promoting critical thinking in employees, and the employees do not underscore the role of the employer in promoting their critical thinking. The employees associate the experience of critical thinking in professional activities more with their own dispositions and behaviour at work.

References

Akerlind, G. S. & Akerlind, G. S. (2005). Variation and commonality in phenomenographic research methods. *Higher Education Research and Development, 24*(4), 321–334. doi:10.1080/07294360500284672.

Barnard, A. McCosker, H. & Gerber, R. (1999). Phenomenography: A qualitative research approach for exploring understanding in health Care. *Qualitative Heath Research, 9*(2), 212–226. doi:10.1177/104973299129121794.

Baysen, E. & Baysen, F. (2020). Waste and Waste Management Awareness Among Teachers: A Phenomenographic Approach. In D. Flaut, Š. Hošková-Mayerová, C. Ispas, F. Maturo & C. Flaut (Eds.), *Decision Making in Social Sciences: Between Traditions and Innovations.* Cham, Switzerland: Springer.

Blimling, G. S. (2013). Challenges of assessment in student affairs. In J. H. Schuh (Ed.), *New Directions for Student Services, 142*, 5–14. Selected contemporary assessment issues. San Francisco, CA: Jossey-Bass.

Bortkevičienė, V. (2015). *Verslumo kompetencijos virsmas veikloje: teorinės žinios ar praktinis žinojimas? [Transformations of entrepreneurial competence in activities: Theoretical knowledge or practical knowledge?]* (Dissertation project, Vytauto Didžiojo University, Kaunas, Lithuania). Retrieved from http://sbk.vdu.lt/wp-content/uploads/2014/05/VERSLUMO-KOMPETENCIJOS-VIRSMAS-VEIKLOJE-TEORIN%C4%96S-%C5%BDINIOS-A.pdf.

Bresciani, M. J. (2013). Afterword: Considerations for Future Practice of Assessment and Accountability. *New Directions for Student Services, 2013*(142), 99–105. doi:10.1002/ss.20053.

Bresciani, M. J. (2015). The neuroscience of learning and development and its implications for inquiry. *Journal of Student Affairs Inquiry, 1*, 1–11. Retrieved from https://vcsa.ucsd.edu/assessment/coalition/april-6_bresciani_the_neurosciene_of_learning_implications_for_inquiry.pdf.

Cope, C. J. (2004). Ensuring validity and reliability in phenomenographic research using the analytical framework of a structure of awareness. *Qualitative Research Journal, 4*(2), 5–18.

Dahlgren, L. & Marton, F. (1978). Students' conceptions of subject matter: An aspect of learning and teaching in higher education. *Studies in Higher Education, 3*(1), 25–35. doi:10.1080/03075077812331376316.

Dall'Alba, G. (2000). Reflections on some faces of phenomenography. In J. Bowden & E. Walsh (Eds.), *Phenomenography* (pp. 83–101). Melbourne, Australia: RMIT University Press.

Entwistle, N. (1997). Introduction: Phenomenography in higher education. *Higher Education Research and Development, 16*(2), 127–134. doi:10.1080/0729436970160202.

Francis, H. (1993). Advancing phenomenography: Questions of method. *Nordisk Pedagogik, 13*(2), 68–75.

Gibbings, P., Lidstone, J. & Bruce, C. (2015). Engineering Phenomenography. *In Theory and Method in Higher Education Research* (pp. 295–309). Bingley, England: Group Publishing Limited.

Han, F. & Ellis, R. A. (2019). Using phenomenography to tackle key challenges in science education. *Frontiers in Psychology, 10*(1414) doi:10.3389/fpsyg.2019.01414.

Hsieh W. & Tsai C. C. (2017). Taiwanese high school teachers' conceptions of mobile learning. Computers & Education *115*, 82–95. doi:10.1016/j.compedu.2017.07.013.

Karnieli-Miller, O., Vu, T. R., Holtman, M. C., Clyman, S. G. & Inui, T. S. (2010). Medical students' professionalism narratives: A window on the informal and hidden curriculum. *Academic Medicine: Journal of the Association of American Medical Colleges, 85*(1), 124–133. https://doi.org/10.1097/ACM.0b013e3181c42896.

Khan, M. S. H. & Markauskaitė, L. (2017). Technical and vocational teachers' conceptions of ICT in the workplace: Bridging the gap between teaching and professional practice. *Journal of Educational Computing Research, 56*(7), 1099–1128. doi:10.1177/0735633117740396.

Kvale, S. (1994). *Validation as communication and action: On the social construction of validity.* New Orleans, LA: ERIC.

Larsson, J. & Holmstrom, I. (2007). Phenomenographic or phenomenological analysis: Does it matter? Examples from a study on anaesthesiologists' work. *International Journal of Qualitative Studies on Health and Well-being, 2*(1), 55–64. doi:10.1080/17482620601068105.

Laurillard, D. (1993). *Rethinking university teaching: A framework for the effective use of educational technology.* London, England: Routledge.

Lepp, M. & Ringsberg, K. C. (2011). Phenomenography – a qualitative research approach. In *Qualitative Methods in Public Health Research – Theoretical Foundations and Practical Examples* (pp. 105–135). Lund, Sweden: Studentlitteratur.

Limberg, L. (2008). Phenomenography. In L. Given (Ed.), *The SAGE encyclopedia of qualitative research methods* (pp. 612–615). Thousand Oaks, CA: Sage.

Mann, L., Dall'Alba, G. & Radcliffe, D. (2007). *Using phenomenography to investigate different ways of experiencing sustainable design.* Honolulu, HI: American Society for Engineering Education.

Marton, F. (1981). Phenomenography—Describing conceptions of the world around us. *Instructional Science, 10*(2), 177–200. doi:10.1007/BF00132516.

Marton, F. (1994). Phenomenography. In T. Husen & T. N. Postlethwaite (Eds.), *International encyclopedia of education* (pp. 4424–4429). Oxford, England: Pergamon.

Marton, F. & Booth, S. (1997). *Learning and awareness.* Mahwah, NJ: Lawrence Earlbaum Assoc.

Marton, F. & Pong, W. Y. (2005). On the unit of description in phenomenography. *Higher Education Research & Development, 24*(4), 335–348. doi:10.1080/07294360500284706.

Marton, F. & Saljo, R. (1976). On qualitative differences in learning: I. Outcome and process. *British Journal of Educational Psychology, 46*(1), 4–11. doi:10.1111/j.2044-8279.1976.tb02980.x.

Merriam, S. B. (2002). Assessing and evaluating qualitative research. In S. B. Merriam (Ed.), *Assessing and evaluating qualitative research in practice* (pp. 18–33). San Francisco, CA: Jossy-Bass.

Penkauskienė, D. (2017). Reflexivity and scientific rigorousness: Testimony from reflective lifeworld studies. *Social work, 17*(2), 152–162. doi:10.13165/SD-19-17-2-02.

Rands, M. & Gansemer-Topf, A. M. (2016). Phenomenography: A methodological approach for assessment in student affairs. *Journal of Student Affairs Inquiry, 1*(2), 1–22. Retrieved from: https://lib.dr.iastate.edu/cgi/viewcontent.cgi?article=1044&context=edu_pubs.

Ruškė, J. (2014). *Asmenų su negalia orumo konstravimas sąmoningumo ugdymo strategijomis [Constructing the dignity of the disabled with awareness raising strategies]* (Doctoral dissertation, Šiauliai University, Šiauliai, Lithuania).

Sabaliauskas, S., Poteliūnienė, S., Česnavičienė, J. & Juškevičienė A. (2018). *Dalykinių kompetencijų tobulinimo poreikio ir turinio analizė. [Analysis of the need for and content of subject competences development.]*.Vilnius: Ugdymo plėtotės centras. Retrieved from https://www.upc.smm.lt/projektai/bendal/failai/Tyrimo-ataskaita-Dalykines-kompetencijos.pdf.

Sin, S. (2010). Considerations of quality in phenomenographic research. *International Journal of Qualitative Methods, 9*(4), 305–319. doi:10.1177/160940691000900401.

Stamouli, I. & Huggard, M. (2007). *Phenomenography as a tool of understanding our students.* Ireland, Dublin: Dublin City University.

Teeter, P. & Sandberg, J. (2016). Constraining or enabling green capability development? How policy uncertainty affects organizational responses to flexible environmental regulations. *British Journal Management, 28,* 649–665. https://doi.org/10.1111/1467-8551.12188.

Tight, M. (2016). Phenomenography: The development and application of an innovative research design in higher education research. *International Journal of Social Research Methodology, 19*(3), 319-338. doi:10.1080/13645579.2015.1010284.

Trigwell, K. (2000). A phenomenographic interview on phenomenography. In J. Bowden & E. Walsh (Eds.) *Phenomenography* (pp. 63–82). Melbourne, Australia: RMIT University Press.

Vermunt J. D. & Donche, V. (2017). A learning patterns perspective on student learning in higher education: state of the art and moving forward. *Educational Psychology Review, 29,* 269–299. doi:10.1007/s10648-017-9414-6.

Yates, C., Partridge, H. & Bruce, C. (2012). Exploring information experiences through phenomenography. *Library and Information Research, 36*(112), 96–119. doi:10.29173/lirg496.

Zou, T. X., Chu, B. C., Law, L. Y., Lin, V., Ko, T., Yu, M. & Mok P. Y. (2019). University teachers' conceptions of internationalisation of the curriculum: A phenomenographic study. *Higher Education, 80*(4), 1–20. doi:10.1007/s10734-019-00461-w.

Critical Thinking Competence in Study Process and Labour Market: A Quantitative Study

Abstract: Critical thinking is considered to be one of the most important competences that determine well-being of the individual and society. In the rapidly changing world of information flow, critical thinking is often identified as the goal of higher education. In the modern labour market, employers are increasingly emphasising the importance of critical thinking skills when making decisions in challenging conditions.

The purpose of this chapter is to reveal how teachers, students, employers and employees define critical thinking, and what their attitude is towards the development of critical thinking skills and dispositions and their importance in the modern labour market. This chapter consists of four sections. The first section discusses the quantitative research methodology. The construction and validation of the research instrument, the methods of data analysis, the sampling and characteristics of the respondents, the research ethics, and limitations are presented in detail. The second section presents the attitude of the teachers and students towards the manifestation and development of critical thinking skills and dispositions. The evaluation of higher education participants – teachers and students – of the importance of critical thinking skills and dispositions in the modern labour market is presented. The teachers' need to improve critical thinking skills is revealed. The third section introduces the attitude of employers and employees towards the manifestation and development of critical thinking skills and dispositions. The evaluation of labour market participants – employers and employees – of the importance of critical thinking skills and dispositions in the modern labour market is presented. The manifestation of critical thinking in employees' professional activities is presented, and the need to improve critical thinking skills in labour market participants is revealed. The fourth section presents a comparison of the manifestation of critical thinking in higher education and in labour market, from the point of view of higher education and labour market participants.

Keywords: critical thinking skills and dispositions, attitudes of teachers, students, employers, employees, quantitative research.

1. Research Methodology

In order to reveal the links between critical thinking in higher education and in the labour market, a quantitative research methodology which is based on a positivist paradigm (Phillips and Burbules, 2000; Creswell and Guetterman, 2019) was purposefully chosen. It emphasises the importance of empirical methods for scientific knowledge. Quantitative research is chosen when the problem under study is insufficiently researched and written up; when it is impossible to become acquainted with and examine the subject under study or its individual characteristics through observation; when the subject under study consists of elements of social or individual consciousness (opinions, needs, interests, beliefs, etc.) (Creswell and Creswell, 2021); or when empirically based findings from large sample sizes are needed for generalisable inferences, replication of findings (Park, Konge and Artino, 2020). Such a study makes it possible to investigate the causes that lead to specific results or consequences, and to answer the research questions raised.

The research responds to all of the following arguments for the choice of quantitative methodology: not a single representative quantitative study has been performed in Lithuania about critical thinking in higher education and in the labour market; the opinions of different groups about critical thinking are best explored by survey rather than by other methods; the representative data collected in the four groups of respondents (teachers, students, employers and employees) make it possible to generalise the conclusions for the country's higher education and labour market. Particular attention to the accuracy of the research procedures and the use of statistical methods allowed for a reasoned disclosure of the links between higher education and the labour market.

This quantitative research is a consistent continuation of the antecedent systematic literature review, quantitative and qualitative content analysis of study programmes at Lithuanian higher education institutions, and phenomenographic research. It completes the process to identify the links between higher education and the labour market and thus integrally complements triangulation.

This study addresses the following research questions:

- What are the opinions of teachers and students about critical thinking and critical thinking skills and dispositions?
- What are the opinions of employers and employees about critical thinking and critical thinking skills and dispositions?
- What are the similarities and differences between the manifestation of critical thinking in higher education and in the labour market?

1.1 Data collection method and instrument

A survey was chosen for data collection. This is one of the most popular methods of quantitative research, as it creates possibilities to gather data in a short time at low time and financial cost (Tracy, 2019; Creswell and Creswell, 2021). This method uses a standardised data collection procedure which ensures that each respondent has the opportunity to answer the questions under the same conditions, and minimises biased intervention on the part of the researcher that could affect the research results. In the survey, data is collected through a questionnaire, which is a set of questions with a certain structure and coherence, designed to gather information from respondents. The questionnaire is a formalised set of quantitative data (Bitinas, 2006) that helps to verify statements. The written survey method is used when a large group of respondents needs to be reached. In addition, data collected through a questionnaire can be compared, their statistical reliability can be checked (Tracy, 2019), and by following the statistical requirements of the study sample size, the results can be generalised to the entire population. When using the survey method, the respondents complete the questionnaire independently; they are given the opportunity to complete the questionnaire at a convenient time, ensuring their anonymity (Tijūnėlienė and Virbalienė, 2006; Bourke, Kirby and Doran, 2016).

Original questionnaires were constructed for the study. Before preparing the questionnaires, the researchers analysed scientific publications related to the research topic. The synchronic approach to scientific analysis made it possible to analyse the conception of critical thinking as one of a specific field (domain-specific) or as being independent of a specific field or discipline (domain-general) (Hathcoat, Penn, Barnes and Comer, 2016; Dwyer, 2017). Researchers of the conception of critical thinking as domain-general (Davies, 2013; Ennis, 1989; Halpern, 199; Kuhn, 1999) argue that there exists a certain set of critical thinking skills that are common and applicable in various fields. On the other hand, researchers who define critical thinking as being domain-specific (McPeck, 1999; Moore, 2011) emphasise the dependence of critical thinking on the knowledge of a particular field. The development of critical thinking is, therefore, only implemented in the context of the specific field. The analysis of scientific sources that was performed showed that critical thinking is understood both as the transfer of an aggregate competence, and as a set of certain skills that emerge in a particular study area. This became the main conclusion, and was used as the basis for construction the research instrument.

The chosen data collection method makes it possible to compare the opinions of the teachers and students, employers and employees, and this helps to reveal similarities and differences between the study groups. The questionnaire consisted of 19 questions. All four groups were presented with three identical blocks of questions: the understanding of critical thinking (two questions); the importance of critical thinking skills in the labour market (one question); and the importance of critical thinking dispositions for the labour market (one question). The higher education representatives (teachers and students) were given eight identical blocks of questions with additional questions for the teachers, and the labour market representatives (employers and employees) were given eight identical blocks of questions. In addition, a separate block of socio-demographic questions was constructed for each study group. The presentation of identical blocks of questions to the four study groups can be considered a reference of the principle of triangulation (Bitinas, 2006, p. 252).

The following recommendations were followed in preparing the questionnaires (Bitinas, Rupšienė and Židžiūnaitė, 2008; De Vaus, 2013; Kardelis, 2016) the questions must be clear, unambiguous, reliable, attractive, and in line with the respondents' experience and competence. Clear instructions are provided at the beginning of each questionnaire. The questionnaire begins with relatively easy, motivating questions that introduce the context of the problem under study and pique the respondent's interest. From there, the questions become increasingly complex, gradually engaging the respondent into completion of the questionnaire.

The questionnaires used different types of closed-ended questions. Open-ended questions were used for socio-demographic information (age, years of teaching experience, management experience); single best answer questions were used to address the conception of critical thinking. An ordinal scale was used to determine the level of education and size of the organisation. The majority of the questions were constructed using a Likert scale, where respondents were asked to evaluate statements using a 7-point scale (*where 1 is 'not important at all' and 7 is 'very important'*) or a 5-point scale (*'strongly disagree', 'disagree', 'neither agree nor disagree', 'agree', 'strongly agree'*). The use of a Likert scale in the research instrument was based on the assumption that the more positive the respondent's evaluation is of the relevant disposition, the more pronounced the manifestation of that disposition is in the respondent's behaviour (Bitinas, 2006). Such an assumption is particularly substantiated in order to reveal the attitudes of the teachers, students, employers and employees towards the manifestation of critical thinking. Each questionnaire ended with demographic questions.

1.2 Construction of the research instrument

The questionnaires consisted of three identical blocks of questions. The first block of questions was designed to examine the respondents' understanding of critical thinking. When asked which description of critical thinking is closest, the respondents had to choose the definition that was most appropriate.

- Critical thinking is the improvement of a person's thinking by changing habitual thinking patterns.
- Critical thinking is the ability to argumentatively question unreasoned assumptions and reasoning in pursuit of truth and rightness.
- Critical thinking is the ability to be guided by reasoned arguments in various contexts in pursuit of reasoned and rational decisions.
- Critical thinking is the ability to reason, reflect and act critically for the good of oneself, others and society.
- Critical thinking is the totality of a person's cognitive skills and dispositions. Skills: to interpret and analyse, to explain and evaluate, and to draw conclusions and make the corrections stemming from them. Personal dispositions: open-mindedness and inquisitiveness, analyticity and systematicity, trust in soundness and the pursuit of truth.
- Critical thinking is a strong human development thinking based on firm knowledge, cognitive abilities and honest, moral behaviour in all life situations.
- Critical thinking is reflexive thinking when making a reasoned decision about what and what not to believe.

The respondents were asked to evaluate statements about the manifestation and development of critical thinking on a 5-point scale (*'strongly disagree', 'disagree', 'neither agree nor disagree', 'agree', 'strongly agree'*).

- Critical thinking can be developed.
- A person can think critically if he or she wants and tries to.
- A person's ability to think critically is unchanging.
- Critical thinking only occurs when criticising.
- There are various ways to demonstrate critical thinking.
- Critical thinking is possible in every situation.

The second block of questions was designed to determine what critical thinking skills are important in the modern labour market. This block consisted of eight skill groups: decision-making, inference, explanation, analysis, self-regulation, argumentation, interpretation, evaluation. Each group of critical thinking skills was made up of particular constituents that had to be evaluated on a 7-point scale (*where 1 is 'not important at all' and 7 is 'very important'*):

Decision-making

- Make decisions independently
- Make decisions collegially
- Justify a decision made to others
- Make decisions according to the procedures established in the organisation

Inference

- Summarise information
- Formulate evidence-based conclusions
- Formulate conclusions with regard to the context
- Formulate conclusions in anticipation of possible consequences

Explanation

- Formulate questions for others
- Answer others' questions
- Explain an analysis carried out and the results obtained
- Explain the decision-making path
- Explain complex concepts
- Reveal the essence of a phenomenon

Analysis

- Reveal connections between statements, facts, concepts
- Examine a situation from different points of view
- Find connections between the whole and its parts
- Collect data/information and link it to other data/sources

Self-regulation

- Know oneself
- Reflect (on one's thoughts, feelings, actions)
- Change according to the situation

Argumentation

- Think based on facts/evidence
- Justify one's choices
- Base actions on reflection

Interpretation

- Classify data/information
- Understand the content of data/information
- Convey data/information in one's own words
- Discern essential information from supplementary information

Evaluation

- Evaluate data/information with regard to different opinions
- Evaluate data/information without prejudice
- Evaluate a situation on the basis of data/information
- Evaluate/self-evaluate the decisions/conclusions made

The third block of questions was designed to determine what critical thinking dispositions are important in the modern labour market. This block consisted of 14 critical thinking dispositions. The respondents had to evaluate the critical thinking constituents presented on a 7-point scale (*where 1 is 'not important at all' and 7 is 'very important'*):

- Impartiality
- Accuracy
- Fairness
- Caring for other people
- Inquisitiveness
- Self-confidence
- Flexibility
- Attentiveness
- Endurance
- Courage
- Perseverance
- Scepticism
- Open-mindedness
- Rightness

The higher education representatives (teachers and students) were additionally given questions about the development of critical thinking skills and dispositions. The teachers and students were asked what critical thinking skills are given the most attention in the study process. This block consisted of eight skill groups: decision-making, inference, explanation, analysis, self-regulation, argumentation, interpretation, evaluation. Each group of critical thinking skills was made up of particular constituents that had to be evaluated on a 7-point scale (*where 1 is 'no attention at all' and 7 is 'particular attention'*):

Decision-making

- Make decisions independently
- Make decisions collegially
- Justify a decision made to others
- Make decisions according to the procedures established in the organisation

Inference

- Summarise information
- Formulate evidence-based conclusions
- Formulate conclusions with regard to the context
- Formulate conclusions in anticipation of possible consequences

Explanation

- Formulate questions for others
- Answer others' questions
- Explain an analysis carried out and the results obtained
- Explain the decision-making path
- Explain complex concepts
- Reveal the essence of a phenomenon

Analysis

- Reveal connections between statements, facts, concepts
- Examine a situation from different points of view
- Find connections between the whole and its parts
- Collect data/information and link it to other data/sources

Self-regulation

- Know oneself
- Reflect (on one's thoughts, feelings, actions)
- Change according to the situation

Argumentation

- Think based on facts/evidence
- Justify one's choices
- Base actions on reflection

Interpretation

- Classify data/information
- Understand the content of data/information
- Convey data/information in one's own words
- Discern essential information from supplementary information

Evaluation

- Evaluate data/information with regard to different opinions
- Evaluate data/information without prejudice
- Evaluate a situation on the basis of data/information
- Evaluate/self-evaluate the decisions/conclusions made

The teachers and students were asked what critical thinking dispositions are given the most attention in study programmes. The teachers were asked how much attention they give to developing these dispositions, and the students were asked how often teachers develop these critical thinking dispositions. This block consisted of 14 critical thinking dispositions that had to be evaluated on a 7-point scale (*where 1 is 'no attention at all' and 7 is 'particular attention'*):

- Impartiality
- Accuracy
- Fairness
- Caring for other people
- Inquisitiveness
- Self-confidence
- Flexibility
- Attentiveness
- Endurance
- Courage
- Perseverance
- Scepticism
- Open-mindedness
- Rightness

The teachers and students were asked about the ways in which critical thinking is developed at institutions of higher education. The teachers and students were asked to evaluate the following ways on a 5-point scale (*'very often', 'often', 'neither often nor rarely', 'rarely', 'very rarely'*):

- Teaching to analyse information, data, phenomena
- Teaching to ask questions
- Teaching to find the interrelations between phenomena
- Teaching to justify a choice/decision
- Teaching to link practice and theory
- Organising discussions
- Purposefully provoking
- Examining cases, situations
- Solving complex tasks, problems
- Demonstrating personal example
- Teaching to link causes and consequences
- Using role-playing games

- Teaching to doubt, not trust a single truth
- Giving non-standard tasks
- Teaching to know oneself
- Teaching to evaluate data reliability
- Giving creative tasks
- Teaching to explore the environment
- Teaching to take responsibility for one's actions
- Creating opportunities to learn from one another
- Teaching to evaluate alternatives
- Teaching to look at phenomena from different perspectives
- Teaching to accept the opinions of others
- Providing feedback
- Teaching to recognise mistakes
- Providing opportunities to learn from mistakes
- Providing opportunities to select tasks and the way they are performed

The teachers and students were asked what techniques they use to improve their critical thinking skills. They had to evaluate the following statements on a 5-point scale (*'very often', 'often', 'neither often nor rarely', 'rarely', 'very rarely'*):

- You read books
- You analyse the environment, events, phenomena
- You analyse the attitudes of others
- You engage in self-reflection
- You participate in seminars, conferences
- You discuss with others
- You take an interest in current social issues

The teachers and students were asked who should be responsible for developing critical thinking (the higher education institution, the organisation where the individual works, or the individual him or herself) and how higher education institutions prepare professionals for the modern labour market *('very well', 'well', 'neither well nor poorly', 'poorly', 'very poorly').*

The teachers were additionally asked about the need to improve critical thinking skills. The teachers were asked if they see a need to improve critical thinking skills. This block consisted of eight skill groups: decision-making, inference, explanation, analysis, self-regulation, argumentation, interpretation, evaluation. Each group of critical thinking skills was made up of particular constituents that had to be evaluated on a 7-point scale (*where 1 is 'no need at all' and 7 is 'a very strong need'*):
Decision-making

- Make decisions independently
- Make decisions collegially
- Justify a decision made to others
- Make decisions according to the procedures established in the organisation

Inference

- Summarise information
- Formulate evidence-based conclusions
- Formulate conclusions with regard to the context
- Formulate conclusions in anticipation of possible consequences

Explanation

- Formulate questions for others
- Answer others' questions
- Explain an analysis carried out and the results obtained
- Explain the decision-making path
- Explain complex concepts
- Reveal the essence of a phenomenon

Analysis

- Reveal connections between statements, facts, concepts
- Examine a situation from different points of view
- Find connections between the whole and its parts
- Collect data/information and link it to other data/sources

Self-regulation

- Know oneself
- Reflect (on one's thoughts, feelings, actions)
- Change according to the situation

Argumentation

- Think based on facts/evidence
- Justify one's choices
- Base actions on reflection

Interpretation

- Classify data/information
- Understand the content of data/information
- Convey data/information in one's own words
- Discern essential information from supplementary information

Evaluation

- Evaluate data/information with regard to different opinions
- Evaluate data/information without prejudice
- Evaluate a situation on the basis of data/information
- Evaluate/self-evaluate the decisions/conclusions made

The teachers were additionally asked about the need to improve personal qualities. The teachers were asked if they see a need to improve personal qualities. This block consisted of 14 qualities that had to be evaluated on a 7-point scale (*where 1 is 'no need at all' and 7 is 'a very strong need'*):

- Impartiality
- Accuracy
- Fairness
- Caring for other people
- Inquisitiveness
- Self-confidence
- Flexibility
- Attentiveness
- Endurance
- Courage
- Perseverance
- Scepticism
- Open-mindedness
- Rightness

In the questionnaires, there was a separate block of socio-demographic questions. Some of the questions reflecting the characteristics of the teachers and students were the same (gender, age, type of higher education institution), and some of the questions differed according to the specifics of the group. The teachers were asked to indicate the following: years of teaching experience in higher education, programme and cycle of study that they teach in, participation in qualification development events. The students were asked to specify the following: study area, cycle of study that they are studying in, study year, employment (i.e. just study or study and work).

The employers and employees were asked about the manifestation of critical thinking in professional activities. The employers were asked how critical thinking is manifested in the activities of their direct subordinates, and the employees were asked how critical thinking is manifested in their professional activities. This block consisted of 13 statements that had to be evaluated on a 5-point scale (*'strongly disagree', 'disagree', 'neither agree nor disagree', 'agree', 'strongly agree'*):

- Independent problem-solving
- Expeditious problem-solving
- Collegial decision-making in crisis situations
- Justified and motivated decisions
- Verifying the reliability of information
- Comprehensive problem analysis
- Raising hypotheses and searching for alternative solutions
- Constant analysis of one's actions
- Targeted knowledge application in practice
- Innovative solutions

- The ability to spot errors and imperfections in existing systems in order to improve them
- Personal assumption of responsibility in acting
- The ability to act in non-standard situations

The employers and employees were asked about the need to improve critical thinking skills. The employers were asked what critical thinking skills their direct subordinates should improve, and the employees were asked if they see a need to improve the respective critical thinking skills. This block consisted of eight skill groups: decision-making, inference, explanation, analysis, self-regulation, argumentation, interpretation, evaluation. Each group of critical thinking skills was made up of particular constituents that had to be evaluated on a 7-point scale (*where 1 is 'no need' and 7 is 'a very strong need'*):

Decision-making

- Make decisions independently
- Make decisions collegially
- Justify a decision made to others
- Make decisions according to the procedures established in the organisation

Inference

- Summarise information
- Formulate evidence-based conclusions
- Formulate conclusions with regard to the context
- Formulate conclusions in anticipation of possible consequences

Explanation

- Formulate questions for others
- Answer others' questions
- Explain an analysis carried out and the results obtained
- Explain the decision-making path
- Explain complex concepts
- Reveal the essence of a phenomenon

Analysis

- Reveal connections between statements, facts, concepts
- Examine a situation from different points of view
- Find connections between the whole and its parts
- Collect data/information and link it to other data/sources

Self-regulation

- Know oneself
- Reflect (on one's thoughts, feelings, actions)
- Change according to the situation

Argumentation

- Think based on facts/evidence
- Justify one's choices
- Base actions on reflection

Interpretation

- Classify data/information
- Understand the content of data/information
- Convey data/information in one's own words
- Discern essential information from supplementary information

Evaluation

- Evaluate data/information with regard to different opinions
- Evaluate data/information without prejudice
- Evaluate a situation on the basis of data/information
- Evaluate/self-evaluate the decisions/conclusions made

The employers and employees were asked about the need to improve critical thinking dispositions. The employers were asked what qualities their direct subordinates should improve, and the employees were asked if they see a need to improve the respective qualities. This block consisted of 14 personal qualities that had to be evaluated on a 7-point scale (*where 1 is 'no need' and 7 is 'a very strong need'*):

- Impartiality
- Accuracy
- Fairness
- Caring for other people
- Inquisitiveness
- Self-confidence
- Flexibility
- Attentiveness
- Endurance
- Courage
- Perseverance
- Scepticism
- Open-mindedness
- Rightness

The employers and employees were asked a question to determine who should be responsible for developing critical thinking (the higher education institution, the organisation where the individual works, or the individual him or herself) and how higher education institutions prepare professionals for the modern labour market (*'very well', 'well', 'neither well nor poorly', 'poorly', 'very poorly')*.

In the questionnaires, there was a separate block of socio-demographic questions. Some of the questions reflecting the characteristics of the employers and employees were the same (gender, age, education, type of organisation, size of organisation, sector of economic activity) and some of the questions differed according to the specifics of the group (for employers: management experience; for employees: length of employment, position at work).

1.3 Validation of the research instrument

Approbation of the prepared questionnaire is expedient; 80 respondents were selected for this purpose, that is, 20 respondents from each target group: teachers and students, employers and employees. Through direct contact between the researcher and the respondent, that is, through individual interview, where the respondent answered and the researcher marked the corresponding answers, all inaccuracies and ambiguities in the statements were noted. Analysis of the answers received made it possible to eliminate twofold, tendentious, ambiguous and repetitive statements and edit the language.

Cronbach's alpha (α) measure of internal consistency was used to validate the instrument. This measure helps determine if each individual variable making up the scale serves the overall purpose of the scale. In other words, Cronbach's alpha coefficient is based on the correlation of different questions and evaluates whether all of the questions on the scale are closely related (Aiken, 2002; Drost, 2011). The closer coefficient alpha gets to one, the higher the internal consistency of the question group, the stronger the correlations between the scale variables, the more consistent they are, and the more reliable the scale is (Rupšienė and Rutkienė, 2016). Cronbach's alpha coefficient should be at least 0.7 (Vaitkevičius and Saudargienė, 2006; Vaitkevičius and Saudargienė, 2010).

The Cronbach's alpha coefficient values varied considerably. When evaluating the statements on the teacher's questionnaire about the manifestation and development of critical thinking, coefficient alpha was positive (α=0.088). As the opinions of all four study groups are being evaluated and compared, the statements about the manifestation and development of critical thinking on the questionnaires for the other target groups were evaluated in parallel. Cronbach's alpha coefficient was found to range from 0.692 for students to 0.456 for employers, so it was decided to keep the statements about the manifestation and development of critical thinking. The majority of the scales constructed in the study had good internal consistency (i.e. well suited for statistical analysis). The following results were obtained when evaluating the internal consistency (reliability) of the scales (Table 28):

- Cronbach's alpha coefficients for the teacher questionnaires (0.961–0.088)
- Cronbach's alpha coefficients for the student questionnaires (0.974–0.692)
- Cronbach's alpha coefficients for the employer questionnaires (0.966–0.456)
- Cronbach's alpha coefficients for the employee questionnaires (0.967–0.690)

The Cronbach's alpha coefficient values for the teacher and student questionnaires are presented in Table 28.

Tab. 28: *Cronbach's alpha coefficient values*

Questionnaire blocks	Teacher questionnaire	Student questionnaire	Employer questionnaire	Employee questionnaire
	Cronbach's alpha (α) values			
Manifestation and development of critical thinking	0.088	0.692	0.456	0.690
The importance of critical thinking skills in the labour market Ability blocks				
Decision-making	0.880	0.890	0.745	0.891
Inference	0.932	0.934	0.869	0.938
Explanation	0.926	0.944	0.891	0.945
Analysis	0.926	0.929	0.879	0.944
Self-regulation	0.842	0.875	0.810	0.879
Argumentation	0.903	0.895	0.834	0.914
Interpretation	0.928	0.911	0.869	0.941
Evaluation	0.920	0.872	0.872	0.938
The importance of critical thinking dispositions in the labour market	0.946	0.949	0.916	0.933
Development of critical thinking skills Ability blocks				
Decision-making	0.667	0.920		
Inference	0.813	0.944		
Explanation	0.809	0.951		
Analysis	0.842	0.941		
Self-regulation	0.873	0.929		
Argumentation	0.823	0.929		
Interpretation	0.825	0.941		
Evaluation	0.862	0.939		
Development of critical thinking constituents	0.906	0.960		
Ways to develop critical thinking skills	0.961	0.974		

Tab. 28: *Continued*

Questionnaire blocks	Teacher questionnaire	Student questionnaire	Employer questionnaire	Employee questionnaire
	Cronbach's alpha (α) values			
The need to improve critical thinking skills Ability blocks			The need to improve critical thinking skills Ability blocks	
Decision-making	0.942		0.901	0.920
Inference	0.976		0.944	0.954
Explanation	0.979		0.949	0.960
Analysis	0.974		0.939	0.952
Self-regulation	0.939		0.902	0.934
Argumentation	0.970		0.925	0.952
Interpretation	0.980		0.943	0.954
Evaluation	0.980		0.939	0.952
The need to improve critical thinking dispositions	0.979		0.966	0.967
Ways to improve critical thinking skills	0.682	0.860		
Manifestation of critical thinking in professional activities			0.918	0.932

Cronbach's alpha shows that the critical thinking skills scales can be used in statistical analysis (Vaitkevičius and Saudargienė, 2006) and that these scales are reliable (Rupšienė and Rutkienė, 2016).

1.4 Methods for statistical analysis of the research data

Quantitative data analysis was performed using IBM® SPSS® 23.0 statistical software, and Microsoft Excel 2007 was selected for graphic illustration of the data. Descriptive and inferential statistical methods were used.

The following main methods of descriptive statistics were used:

- Measures of frequency to determine the distribution of features.
- Measures of central tendency (mean, mode). Mean (M) – a quantitative indicator that summarises and expresses the typical level of a certain variable feature of homogeneous phenomena; Mode (M_o) – the most commonly recurring value (Vaitkevičius and Saudargienė, 2006).
- Measure of variability (standard deviation).

Measures of skewness and kurtosis as well as the Kolmogorov-Smirnov Z test were used to identify the normality of the distribution. Since it was assessed that the data are not normally distributed, the following non-parametric methods of statistical inference were used:

- Analysis of variance methods to evaluate the statistical significance of Mann-Whitney U and Kruskal-Wallis H. The Mann-Whitney U test is used to compare differences between two independent groups when the dependent variable is ordinal or continuous. It is non-parametric alternative to a two-sample t-test. The Kruskal-Wallis H test is a non-parametric alternative to the One Way ANOVA to compare three or more independent groups. Post-hoc Dunn's tests were performed after the Kruskal-Wallis H test recorded statistically significant differences between the groups. Since multiple tests were performed, the Bonferroni adjustment was applied. The purpose of the Bonferroni adjustment is to reduce the probability of identifying significant results that do not exist in reality (Salkind, 2010).
- The non-parametric Chi-square ($\chi 2$) test of independence, in order to establish statistically significant relationships between the four study groups (teachers and students, employers and employees).
- Correlation analysis by calculating the Spearman's rank correlation coefficient (r_s) in order to determine the interrelationships of the variables. Spearman's (r_s) was chosen because it is suitable for variables whose distributions are far from the normal distribution (Bilevičiūtė and Jonušauskas, 2011). The interpretation of correlation associations was based on the distribution of correlation association strength put forward by Bitinas (2006), where a correlation coefficient: from 0 to 0.20 indicates that the association between the variables is essentially non-existent or very weak; from 0.20 to 0.40 – that the association is weak; from 0.40 to 0.60 – that the association is moderate; from 0.60 to 0.80 – that the association is strong; from 0.80 to 1– that the association is very strong.

1.5 Selection, sampling and characteristics of the respondents

In order to ensure that the sample was representative of the entire statistical population, a multistage probability sampling method was used. Four samples were drawn for the survey of each group: teachers, students, employers and employees from all regions of Lithuania. Representative samples were generated on the basis of 2020 data from the Official Statistics Portal[6] and the State Social Insurance Fund SODRA.[7]

6 Official Statistics Portal. (n.d.a). Statistics by themes. Retrieved from https://osp.stat.gov.lt/temines-lenteles7 (A).

7 Sodra. (n.d.). Retrieved from https://www.sodra.lt/.

Sampling of Lithuanian higher education teachers (N=152). The general population of university and college teachers in the country at the time of planning the study was 11,266. If the planned sample size is 152 respondents, then the margin of error at 95 % confidence and 50 % population proportion is 9.5 %.

Tab. 29: *Control figures for the teacher sampling plan according to socio-demographic parameters, when* $N_{teachers}=152$

Controlled parameter of the internal structure of the sample	Sampling plan: recommended absolute and relative sizes					
Gender	N_{men}	Men %	N_{women}	Women %		
Planned sample	≈67	≈44	≈85	≈56		
Age	$N \geq_{50\ years}$	≥ 50 years %	$N_{\leq 49\ years}$	≤ 49 years %		
Planned sample	≈60	≈40	≈92	≈60		
University and college	$N_{uni\ teach}$	Uni. teachers %	$N_{coll\ teach}$	Coll. teachers %		
Planned sample	≈107	≈71	≈45	≈29		
Parameter of the internal structure of the sample	**Sampling plan: recommended absolute and relative sizes**					
Study field	Biomedical and Physical Sciences		Social Sciences, Humanities, Arts		Technology	
Planned sample	$N_{teachers}$	Teachers %	$N_{teachers}$	Teachers %	N	Teachers %
	≈38	≈25	≈82	≈54	≈3	≈21

The quantitative parameters and relative sizes of the internal structure of the sample according to the main socio-demographic criteria are presented in Table 29.

Sampling of Lithuanian higher education students (N=1,512). The general population of university and college students in the country at the time of planning the study was 111,000. If the planned sample size is 1,512 observations, then the margin of error at 95 % confidence and 50 % population proportion is 2.8 %.

The quantitative parameters and relative sizes of the internal structure of the sample according to the main socio-demographic criteria are presented in Table 30.

Tab. 30: *Control figures for the student sampling plan according to socio-demographic parameters, when $N_{students}$=1,512*

Controlled parameter of the internal structure of the sample	Sampling plan: recommended absolute and relative sizes			
Gender	N_{men}	Men %	N_{women}	Women %
Planned sample	≈604	≈40	≈908	≈60
University and college	N_{uni}	Uni %	N_{coll}	Coll. %
Planned sample	≈1,058	≈70	≈453	≈30
Private/public	N_{public}	Public %	$N_{private}$	Private %
Planned sample	≈1,383	≈91.5	≈128	≈8.5

Parameter of the internal structure of the sample	Sampling plan: recommended absolute and relative sizes											
Study field	Biomed.		Physical		Humanities		Arts		Social		Technology	
Planned sample	N	%	N	%	N	%	N	%	N	%	N	%
	287	19	91	6	76	5	76	5	665	44	317	21

The sampling of Lithuanian business and public sector employees (N=2,012). The general population of the business and public sector employees in the country covered by compulsory insurance was 1,356,000 at the time of planning the study. If the planned sample size of business and public sector employees is 2,012 respondents, then the margin of error at 95 % confidence and 50 % population proportion is 2.5 %. It should be noted that regardless of whether it is calculated from all (1.36 million) insured employees or from a much smaller sample (1 million), the margin of error remains stable at 2.5 %.

The quantitative parameters and relative sizes of the internal structure of the sample according to the main socio-demographic criteria are presented in Table 31.

Tab. 31: *Control figures for the employee sampling plan according to socio-demographic parameters, when $N_{employees}$=2,012*

Controlled parameter of the internal structure of the sample	**Sampling plan: recommended absolute and relative sizes**			
Gender	N_{men}	Men %	N_{women}	Women %
Planned sample	≈905	≈45	≈1,107	≈55
Business/public sector	$N_{business}$	Business %	N_{public}	Public %
Planned sample	≈1,006	≈50	≈1,006	≈50
Age of employees	$N_{\leq 40\ years}$	≤ 40 years, %	$N_{> 40\ years}$	> 40 years, %
Planned sample	≈925	≈46	≈1,087	≈54

Parameter of the internal structure of the sample	**Sampling plan: recommended absolute and relative sizes**			
Level of education of employees	University and non-university higher, post-secondary		All other lower education categories	
Planned sample	N	%	N	%
	≈1,167	≈58	≈845	≈42

Parameter of the internal structure of the sample	**Sampling plan: recommended absolute and relative sizes**							
Number of employees	Very small ≤ 10 employees		Small 11–50 employees		Average 51–250 employees		Large > 250 employees	
Planned sample	N	%	N	%	N	%	N	%
	603	30	704	35	503	25	202	10

Parameter of the internal structure of the sample	**Sampling plan: recommended absolute and relative sizes**											
County	Vilnius County		Kaunas County		Klaipėda County		Šiauliai County		Panevėžys County		Remaining small counties	
Planned sample	N	%	N	%	N	%	N	%	N	%	N	%
	603	30	402	20	221	11	201	10	160	8	425	21

Sampling of Lithuanian business and public sector employers (N=528). The general population of business and public sector employers in the country at the time of planning the study was 47,000 persons. If the planned sample size of the employer survey is 528 observations, then the margin of error at 95 % confidence and 50 % population proportion is 5 %.

The quantitative parameters and relative sizes of the internal structure of the sample according to the main socio-demographic criteria are presented in Table 32.

Tab. 32: *Control figures for the employer sampling plan according to socio-demographic parameters, when $N_{employers}$=528*

Controlled parameter of the internal structure of the sample	**Sampling plan: recommended absolute and relative sizes**			
Gender	N_{men}	Men %	N_{women}	Women %
Planned sample	≈264	≈50	≈264	≈50
Business/public sector	$N_{business}$	Business %	N_{public}	Public %
Planned sample	≈264	≈50	≈264	≈50
Age of employers	$N_{\leq 40\ years}$	≤ 40 years, %	$N_{> 40\ years}$	> 40 years, %
Planned sample	≈242	≈46	≈286	≈54

Parameter of the internal structure of the sample	**Sampling plan: recommended absolute and relative sizes**			
Level of education of employers	University and non-university higher, post-secondary		All other lower education categories	
Planned sample	N	%	N	%
	≈449	≈85	≈79	≈15

Parameter of the internal structure of the sample	**Sampling plan: recommended absolute and relative sizes**											
County	Vilnius County		Kaunas County		Klaipėda County		Šiauliai County		Panevėžys County		Remaining small counties	
Planned sample	N	%	N	%	N	%	N	%	N	%	N	%
	158	30	106	20	58	11	52	10	42	8	112	21

In summary, the calculated sample sizes are 152 teachers, 1,512 students, 528 employers and 2,012 employees. Absolute and relative sample sizes were periodically checked during sampling to ensure that there were no significant deviations from the control figure set. The sample sizes of all four groups surveyed were larger than planned.

Characteristics of the respondents. Teachers and students. A total of 152 teachers and 1,512 students participated in the study. The socio-demographic data for the teacher and student groups are summarised in Table 33.

Tab. 33: *Socio-demographic data for the teacher and student groups (%)*

	Teachers	Students
Gender		
Women	64.0	60.3
Men	36.0	39.7
Type of higher education institution		
College	56.6	28.2
University	63.2	71.8
Cycle of study		
Bachelor's	84.9	80.8
Master's	45.4	17.3
Doctoral	11.2	0.9
Group of study fields		
Physical Sciences	5.3	1.8
Life Sciences	2.6	2.2
Humanities	13.8	8.1
Informatics	7.2	11.6
Engineering	17.8	14.6
Mathematics	6.6	5.8
Arts	6.6	5.6
Social Sciences	43.4	15.7
Sport	4.6	1.3
Health Sciences	10.5	8.2
Technological Sciences	15.1	11.0
Law	4.6	12.2
Education Sciences	7.9	6.0
Business and Public Administration	13.2	13.0

Tab. 33: *Continued*

	Teachers	Students
Veterinary Sciences	2.0	2.3
Agriculture	3.3	2.2
County		
Alytus County	5.0	1.5
Kaunas County	24.0	19.5
Klaipėda County	24.0	11.2
Marijampolė County	1.0	2.4
Panevėžys County	4.0	1.7
Šiauliai County	14.0	22.7
Tauragė County	-	-
Telšiai County	3.0	0.5
Utena County	1.0	1.5
Vilnius County	24.0	39.0

The teacher and student respondent groups represent the Lithuanian teacher and student populations according to the parameters of gender, study cycle, study field group and higher education institution location, which is reflected in the description of the research data below when comparing them with Lithuanian statistics.

In 2019, Lithuania had a population of 2,794,184, of which 1,498,593 were women and 1,295,591 were men,[8] which accounts for 54.0 % and 46.0 % of the population respectively.[9] Of the 1,512 students who participated in the study, 601 (60.3 %) were women and 911 (39.7 %) were men; of the 152 teachers, 97 (63.8 %) were women and 55 (36.2 %) were men.

The mean age of the teachers was 48.9 years, the youngest respondent was 28 years old, and the oldest was 75. 53.0 % of the teachers who participated in the study were 49 or younger, and 47.0 % were 50 or over. The mean age of the students was 23.8 years, the youngest respondent was 18 years old, and the oldest was 59. 26.5 % of the students who participated in the study were 20 or younger, 56.7 % were between 21 and 25 years old, and 16.7 % were 26 or older.

8 Official Statistics Portal. (n.d.b.). Resident population by sex and age at the beginning of the year. Retrieved from https://osp.stat.gov.lt/temines-lenteles7.

9 Official Statistics Portal. (2019). Statistical yearbook of Lithuania. Resident population. Retrieved from https://osp.stat.gov.lt/lietuvos-statistikos-metrastis/lsm-2019/gyventojai-ir-socialine-statistika/nuolatiniai-gyventojai.

Since 2000, there have been two types of higher education institutions in Lithuania: universities and colleges. Universities are more focused on theoretical and academic training; they offer university studies, and carry out fundamental and applied scientific research, experimental development, and/or high-level professional art. Colleges are more focused on professional preparation; they offer higher education college studies and carry out applied scientific research and/or professional art.[10] According to Statistics Lithuania,[11] there were 22 colleges and 19 universities in Lithuania in 2019–2020. The colleges had 32,931 students and 2,444 teachers, and the universities had 73,011 students and 7,536 teachers. Of the respondents, 71.5 % of the students and 63.2 % of the teachers were from universities, and 28.5 % of the students and 36.8 % of the teachers were from colleges, which represents the general distribution of students and teachers in universities and colleges in Lithuania.

The system of degree-granting studies, which is based on a structure of three study cycles – bachelor-master-doctor of science – was put in place in Lithuania in 1993–1994. There is a coherent transition between the cycles, so the learning outcomes achieved in one cycle are used and deepened/expanded accordingly in the next cycle. Higher education college studies are only conducted in the first cycle, but universities offer all three cycles of study. Upon completion of the first cycle, a bachelor's or professional bachelor's (for college graduates) degree is awarded. Upon completion of the second study cycle, a master's degree or a master's degree and a professional qualification are awarded. It should be noted here that a master's degree can also be obtained by completing integrated studies covering the first and second study cycles. Universities and colleges can also offer professional studies (residency and pedagogy studies). These are designed for students to acquire a qualification or prepare for independent practical activities.[12]

The questionnaire was formulated according to the three-cycle structure of higher education, but there was also the choice of 'other' for professional or residency studies. Of the respondents, 80.8 % of the students and 84.9 % of the teachers were studying/teaching in bachelor's studies, 17.3 % of the students and 45.4 % of the teachers were studying/teaching in master's/integrated studies, and 0.9 % of the students and 11.2 % of the teachers were studying/teaching in doctoral studies. The number of teachers exceeds the number of respondents because some teachers teach in both colleges and universities.

---

10 Centre for quality assessment in higher education. (n.d.). Aukštasis mokslas. [Higher education]. Retrieved from https://www.skvc.lt/default/lt/lietuvos-svietimo-sistema/aukstasis-mokslas

11 Official Statistics Portal. (n.d.c.). Number of educational institutions, pupils, students and pedagogues. Retrieved from https://osp.stat.gov.lt/statistiniu-rodikliu-analize?hash=b331cbcd-c8ae-4560-b695-f7380924efcc#/.

12 Centre for quality assessment in higher education. (n.d.). Aukštasis mokslas. [Higher education]. Retrieved from https://www.skvc.lt/default/lt/lietuvos-svietimo-sistema/aukstasis-mokslas

Teachers and students from various study field programmes participated in the study. The highest proportion of teachers – 43.4 % – stated that they teach in Social Sciences programmes. Slightly fewer teachers were from the following study fields: Engineering (17.8 %), Technological Sciences (15.1 %), Humanities (13.8 %), Business and Public Administration (13.2 %) and Health Sciences (10.5 %). The following study fields were least represented: Education Sciences (7.9 %), Informatics Science (7.2 %), Arts (6.6 %), Mathematics (6.6 %), Physical Sciences (5.3 %), Sport (4.6 %), Law (4.6 %), Agriculture (3.3 %), Life Sciences (2.6 %) and Veterinary Sciences (2.0 %). The students' responses were similarly distributed: 15.7 % study Social Sciences, 14.6 % – Engineering Sciences, 13.0 % – Business and Public Administration, 12.2 % – Law, 11.6 % – Informatics, 11.0 % – Technological Sciences, 8.2 % – Health Sciences, 8.1 % – Humanities, 6.0 % – Education Sciences, 5.8 % – Mathematics, 5.6 % – Arts, 2.3 % – Veterinary Sciences, 2.2 % – Agricultural Sciences, 2.2 % – Life Sciences, 1.8 % – Physical Sciences, and 1.3 % – Sport.

The largest number of higher education institutions are located in Lithuania's three major cities: Vilnius, Kaunas and Klaipėda. Therefore, the study primarily included teachers teaching at institutions of higher education in these cities (23.7 % each). The distribution of students was not as even, but these cities still accounted for the largest percentage (39.0 %, 19.5 % and 11.2 %, respectively). In the student group, a significant share of the respondents (22.7 %) study in Šiauliai, the fourth largest city in Lithuania.

The teachers were additionally asked about their years of teaching experience at institutions of higher education, and the students were asked if they were only studying or both studying and working.

Analysis of the distribution of teachers by their years of teaching experience at institutions of higher education shows that experienced teachers participated in the study. Slightly more than a third (35.5 %) of the teachers indicated that they have been working at institutions of higher education for 11–20 years, while a third (31.6 %) have been working for 10 years or less, a fifth (22.4 %) have been working for 21–30 years, and a tenth (9.2 %) have been working for 31–40 years; 1.3 % of the teachers have more than 40 years of teaching experience at institutions of higher education. It was established that the average length of teaching experience at institutions of higher education was 17 years. It should be noted that 53.0 % of the students only study, and 47.0 % both study and work.

Employers and employees. A total of 528 employers and 2,012 employees participated in the study. The socio-demographic data for the employer and employee groups are summarised in Table 34.

Tab. 34: *Socio-demographic data for the employer and employee groups (%)*

	Employers	**Employees**
Gender		
Women	59.1	59.8
Men	40.9	40.2
Age		
≤ 40 years	33.1	52.0
≥ 41 years	66.9	48.0
Education		
Higher university	70.3	44.2
Higher non-university	11.4	21.0
Post-secondary	7.0	14.8
Other	11.4	20.0
Management/work experience		
≤ 10 years	49.4	37.3
11–20 years	30.9	25.5
21–30 years	13.3	20.8
31–40 years	5.5	14.2
41–50 years	0.9	2.1
≥ 51 years	-	0.0
Type of organisation		
Public	50.9	41.3
Private	45.1	55.5
Non-governmental	4.0	2.6
Other or not specified	-	0.6
Sector of professional activity*		
Agriculture, forestry and fishing	4.1	2.3
Manufacturing	6.7	0.9
Electricity, gas, steam and air conditioning supply	1.0	7.7
Water supply, sewerage, waste management and remediation	1.4	1.7
Construction	6.7	2.3
Wholesale and retail trade	8.6	10.7
Repair of motor vehicles and motorcycles	2.0	7.9

Tab. 34: *Continued*

	Employers	**Employees**
Transportation and storage	2.3	3.0
Accommodation and food service activities	4.1	2.4
Information and communication	2.9	5.4
Financial and insurance activities	2.9	5.0
Real estate activities	0.4	2.9
Other professional, scientific and technical activities	1.4	1.3
Administrative and support service activities	21.9	1.8
Education	18.4	21.1
Human health services and social work activities	9.4	12.2
Arts, entertainment and recreation	5.9	8.4
Other	3.2	3.9
Organisation size		
Microenterprise (≤ 10 employees)	4.7	22.8
Small enterprise (11–50 employees)	50.4	31.8
Medium-sized enterprise (51–250 employees)	38.1	37.8
Large enterprise (> 250 employees)	6.8	7.7
County		
Alytus County	3.8	3.5
Kaunas County	15.2	15.2
Klaipėda County	7.2	8.3
Marijampolė County	3.8	2.6
Panevėžys County	17.0	14.2
Šiauliai County	15.0	16.8
Tauragė County	4.0	3.2
Telšiai County	4.0	5.3
Utena County	9.7	8.1
Vilnius County	20.5	22.8

**percentage of the respondents who answered*

The employer and employee respondent groups reflect the Lithuanian labour market according to the parameters of management/work experience, type of organisation, sector of professional activity, and organisation size and location, which is revealed in the description of the research data below when comparing them with Lithuanian statistics.

As already mentioned, in 2019, Lithuania had a population of 2,794,184, of which 1,498,593 were women and 1,295,591 were men,[13] which accounts for 54.0 % and 46.0 % of the population respectively.[14] Of the 528 employers who participated in the study, 312 (59.1 %) were women and 216 (40.9 %) were men; of the 2,012 employees, 1,203 (59.8 %) were women and 809 (40.2 %) were men.

The mean age of the employers was 46.3 years – the youngest respondent was 24 years old, and the oldest was 71. 33.1 % of the employers who participated in the study were 40 or younger, and 66.9 % were over 40. The mean age of the employees was 41.9 years – the youngest respondent was 18 years old, and the oldest was 71. 52.0 % of the employees who participated in the study were 40 or younger, and 48.0 % were over 40. The employer group is older than the employee group.

Both groups are dominated by persons with higher university education, accounting for 70.3 % of all respondents in the employer group and 44.2 % in the employee group. 11.4 % of the employers have higher non-university education, and 7.0 % have post-secondary education. Meanwhile, 21.0 % of the employees have higher non-university education, and 14.8 % have post-secondary education. 11.4 % of the employers and 20.0 % of the employees chose the answer 'other'. The employers mentioned the following options: professional (5.5 %), secondary (3.2 %), basic (2.3 %), incomplete higher education (0.2 %), incomplete university (0.2 %); this shows that just over a tenth of the employers surveyed have less than post-secondary education. In the employee group, this makes up a fifth of the respondents, who listed their education as professional (11.4 %), secondary (5.4 %), basic (2.0 %), vocational secondary (0. 1 %). One respondent each answered: incomplete higher, incomplete post-secondary, incomplete secondary, secondary or courses, vocational secondary. 0.8 % of the employees did not specify their education.

In both groups, the highest proportion of respondents have 10 years or less of managing or work experience, accounting for 49.4 % in the employer group and 37.3 % in the employee group. As the years of experience increase, the number of respondents in both groups decreases. 0.9 % of the employers have management experience of 41–50 years, and 2.1 % of the employees have that much work experience. Only one respondent had 51 year or more of work experience. The average

13 Official Statistics Portal. (n.d.b.). Resident population by sex and age at the beginning of the year. Retrieved from https://osp.stat.gov.lt/temines-lenteles7.

14 Official Statistics Portal. (n.d.b.). Resident population by sex and age at the beginning of the year. Retrieved from https://osp.stat.gov.lt/lietuvos-regionai/lietuvos-regionai-2019/zmones/moterys-ir-vyrai.

length of managing experience is 13.49 years, and the average length of employment in the employee group is 17.21 years. It should be noted that 6.4 % of the employers and 16.3 % of the employees have accumulated the minimum length of employment, which was 31 years in Lithuania in 2019.[15]

The respondents in the employee group were asked about the nature of their employment relationship. 1.5 % of the respondents did not answer this question. Of the respondents who answered, 88.2 % are hired employees, 4.2 % are hired employees who run their own business, 4.2 % work according to a business certificate/self-employment certificate, and 3.3 % are hired employees who also work according to a business certificate/self-employment certificate. The following options were mentioned as 'other': in employment training, work on a social basis, doctoral student, politician, and so on.

The socio-demographic research data reflect the country's economic structure which is analysed by the form of ownership of the economic operator, the size of the economic operator, the territorial principle, and the sector.

Half (50.9 %) of the employers who participated in the study manage public institutions, and slightly more than half (55.5 %) of the employees work in private organisations. Non-governmental organisations account for the smallest share of respondents: 4.0 % of the employers and 2.6 % of the employees. In the employee group, 0.6 % of the respondents selected 'other' and mentioned these options: AB (public limited liability company), budgetary institution.

There were 84,900 companies operating in Lithuania in 2019. More than 80 % of the operating companies had nine employees or less.[16] The respondents are managers/employees at establishments of various sizes. Half (50.4 %) of the employers are managers at small enterprises with 11–50 employees. 38.1 % of the respondents are managers at medium-sized enterprises (51–250 employees), while 6.8 % are managers at larenterprises (> 250 employees) and 4.7 % – at microenterprises (≤ 10 employees). The respondents in the employee group were more evenly distributed: 37.8 % work at a medium-sized enterprise (51–250 employees), 31.8 % – at a small enterprise (11–50 employees), 22.8 % – at a microenterprise (≤ 10 employees), and 7.7 % – at a large enterprise (> 250 employees).

Most of the respondents are from Vilnius County (20.5 % of the employers and 22.8 % of the employees), followed by three large, fairly equal combined groups of respondents from Šiauliai (15.0 % and 16.8 %), Panevėžys (17.0 % and 14.2 %) and Kaunas (15.2 % and 15.2 %).

---

15 Ministry of Social Security and Labour. (n.d.). Būtinasis stažas senatvės pensijai [Required seniority for old-age pension]. Retrieved from https://socmin.lrv.lt/lt/veiklos-sritys/socialinis-draudimas/socialinio-draudimo-ismokos/butinasis-stazas-senatves-pensijai.

16 Versli Lietuva. (2019). Verslumo tendencijos Lietuvoje 2019 m. pradžioje [Entrepreneurship trends in Lithuania in early 2019]. Retrieved from https://www.verslilietuva.lt/wp-content/uploads/2019/10/2019.09.30_verslumo_apzvalga.pdf

The second revision of the Statistical Classification of Economic Activities (NACE Rev. 2) was in force in Lithuania at the time of the study.[17] The research data show that the employer group is the most represented in administrative and support service activities (21.9 %), and the employee group – in education (21.9 %). The latter activity is in second place (18.4 %) in the employer group. In the employee group, human health services and social work activities are in second place (12.2 %). The employers who selected 'other' listed the following activities: library and archives; accounting and finance; electronics; energy; passenger transport activities; consulting activities; culture; culture and information; repair of industrial machinery; process automation; design, scientific and consultancy activities; design services; religion; law; business consulting; public administration. The employees listed the following activities as 'other': administration; environmental protection; audit; kindergarten teacher; accounting, legal services; finance and control; production, trade and services; beauty services; investments; equipment design; external audit; culture; cultural activities; metal industry; science, innovation and technology; services; recruitment; politics; design and production; psychological assistance; social field; social work; social services; organising and conducting sporting events, competitions; legal services and consultancy; rights representation, advocacy; tourism; cleaners; civil servant; public administration; public audit; business services; internal audit; public administration; public procurement; public population services; social activities; human resources.

1.6 Research ethics

The quantitative research was conducted according to the basic ethical rules of anonymity, voluntary participation, and no harm to the participants (Panter and Sterba, 2011; Jones, 2015; Creswell and Creswell, 2021).

At the beginning of the study, before filling in the questionnaire, the respondents were introduced to the research aim and were given a brief description of it, emphasising that they could terminate their participation at any stage of completing the questionnaire. The respondents were assured that the data submitted would remain anonymous and only be made public in an aggregated form, and were given the names of the research and data collection organisations. It is considered that by continuing to complete the questionnaire with this information, the respondents give their informed consent.

17 Classificator of types of economic activity. (2007). Retrieved from https://e-seimas.lrs.lt/portal/legalAct/lt/TAD/TAIS.309099.

When conducting the survey remotely, additional measures were taken to ensure the anonymity of the respondents. The organisation that collected the data ensured that the IP network identifiers (IP addresses) of the digital devices used to complete the questionnaires would not be captured and stored.

The collected data is kept in the university's data repositories, which cannot be accessed by third parties without the consent of the university and the researchers.

1.7 Study limitations

The main limitation of the study is that conducting a survey remotely may result in breaches of the internal structure of the sample, that is, representativeness. To avoid this error, the internal structure of the sample was continuously monitored during the survey according to the selected parameters, that is, observation of the absolute and relative numbers of respondents to ensure that they correspond to the internal structure of the planned sample. For example, if it is observed at the data collection stage that according to the 'type of higher education institution' variable, the sample of respondents from universities is completely filled, then further data collection is done only at colleges. All independent variables were monitored and controlled in this way.

2. Attitude of Teachers and Students Towards Critical Thinking

2.1 Definition of critical thinking

The study was designed to determine how teachers and students describe critical thinking. The teachers and students were given seven descriptions of critical thinking and asked to choose the one description that is most acceptable to them.

It was found (Figure 15) that both the teachers and the students most agree with the description that critical thinking is the totality of a person's cognitive skills (to interpret and analyse, to explain and evaluate, and to draw conclusions and make the corrections stemming from them) and dispositions (open-mindedness and inquisitiveness, analyticity and systematicity, trust in soundness and the pursuit of truth). Just over a third (36.2 %) of the teachers and a quarter (24.1 %) of the students agree with this description.

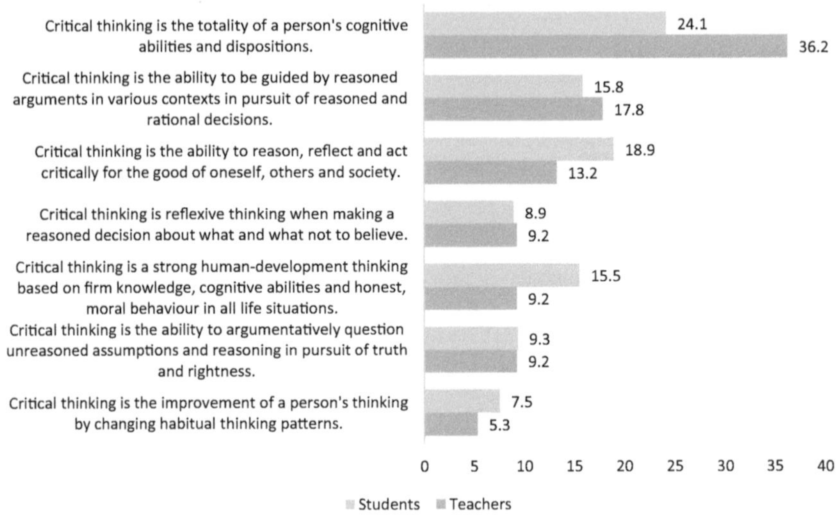

Fig. 15: *Definition of critical thinking, comparison of teachers' and students' opinions, %*

The positions of the teachers and the students differ slightly concerning the other definitions of critical thinking provided. A difference in opinion was established in the description that critical thinking is the ability to reason, reflect and act critically for the good of oneself, others and society – more than a tenth (13.2 %) of the teachers and almost a fifth (18.9 %) of the students agree with this statement. A more pronounced difference of opinion came to light in the description that critical thinking is reflexive thinking when making a reasoned decision about what and what not to believe – 9.2 % of the teachers and 15.5 % of the students agree with this definition of critical thinking. The evaluations of the other descriptions are similar. For example, 17.8 % of the teachers and 15.8 % of the students agree that critical thinking is the ability to be guided by reasoned arguments in various contexts in pursuit of reasoned and rational decisions. An equal percentage of the teachers (9.2 %) and the students (9.3 %) are convinced that critical thinking is the ability to argumentatively question unreasoned assumptions and reasoning in pursuit of truth and rightness. Only a small proportion of the students (7.5 %) and even fewer teachers (5.3 %) believe that critical thinking is the improvement of a person's thinking by changing habitual thinking patterns.

Looking at all of the descriptions of critical thinking presented, one statistically significant difference was found: the teachers agree more than the students that critical thinking is the totality of a person's cognitive skills and dispositions ($\chi2=15.560$; $df=6$; $p<0.05$). Thus, the conception of critical thinking of higher education teachers and students is related to a person's skills and dispositions, which enable the person to be self-confident when making decisions in both daily and professional activities. This suggests that the teachers' and students' understanding of critical thinking is close to the conceptions of critical thinking defined by Facione (1990). Although the teachers and students associate the conception of critical thinking least with the process of improving thinking, they do highlight the importance of critical thinking as a certain process that results in the right decision.

2.2 Manifestation and development of critical thinking

This study also aimed to evaluate the attitudes of teachers and students towards the manifestation and development of critical thinking (Figure 16 and 17). Using a 5-point Likert scale *('strongly disagree', 'disagree', 'neither agree nor disagree', 'agree', 'strongly agree')*, the respondents were asked to evaluate the extent to which they agree or disagree with the six statements presented.

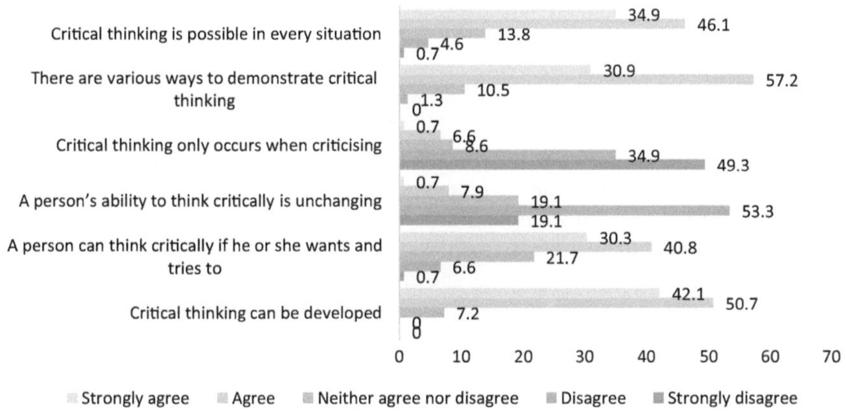

Fig. 16: *Manifestation and development of critical thinking, teacher evaluation, %*

Evaluation of **the attitude of the teachers** towards the manifestation and development of critical thinking (Figure 16) revealed that the majority of the teachers (92.8 %) tend to agree with the statement that critical thinking can be developed. Only 7.2 % of the teachers neither agreed nor disagreed with this statement. There was not a single teacher who disagreed with the statement that critical thinking can be developed.

Almost two-thirds (72.4 %) of the teachers who participated in the study did not agree with the statement that a person's ability to think critically is unchanging. Approximately one-fifth (19.1 %) of the teachers said that they neither agreed nor disagreed with this statement, and 8.6 % said that they did agree with this statement.

The opinions of the teachers differed more regarding the statement that a person can think critically if he or she wants and tries to, which 71.1 % of the teachers who participated in the study agreed with. However, slightly more than a fifth (21.7 %) of the survey participants neither agreed nor disagreed with this statement, and 7.3 % did not agree with the statement.

The teachers also almost unanimously (88.1 %) agreed with the statement that there are various ways to demonstrate critical thinking. Roughly a tenth (10.5 %) of the teachers neither agreed nor disagreed with this statement. 1.3 % of the respondents disagreed with this statement, but there was not a single respondent who strongly disagreed.

The majority of the teachers (84.2 %) were inclined to disagree with the statement that critical thinking only occurs when criticising. Less than a tenth (8.6 %) of the teachers who participated in the study neither agreed nor disagreed with this statement. 7.3 % agreed with the statement that critical thinking only occurs when criticising.

The statement that critical thinking is possible in every situation was something that 81 % of the teachers who participated in the study agreed with. More than a tenth (13.8 %) of the teachers who participated in the survey neither agreed nor disagreed with this statement, while 5.3 % of the respondents did not agree with the said statement.

No statistically significant differences were found between attitudes of the teachers and demographic and social factors (gender, age, years of teaching experience, type of higher education institution).

It can be argued that the teachers view critical thinking as a dynamic process – one that is developing and changing, and is necessary for every person in different situations. From the point of view of the teachers, critical thinking does not only occur when criticising.

Evaluation **of the attitude of the students** towards the manifestation and development of critical thinking (Figure 17) revealed that more than three-quarters (76 %) of the students who participated in the study tend to agree with the statement that critical thinking can be developed. More than two-thirds of the respondents tend to agree with the statements that *t*here are various ways to demonstrate critical thinking (70.8 %), that critical thinking is possible in every situation (69.1 %) and that a person can think critically if he or she wants and tries to (68 %).

Fig. 17: *Manifestation and development of critical thinking, student evaluation, %*

More than a third of the students who participated in the study tend to agree that critical thinking only occurs when criticising (38.8 %), and that a person's ability to think critically is unchanging (38.3 %). It should be noted, however, that approximately a third (35.8 %) of the students who participated in the study disagreed with the statement that a person's ability to think critically is unchanging. 37.7 % of the students who participated in the survey disagreed with the statement that critical thinking only occurs when criticising. Nearly a quarter of the students (23.5 %) neither agreed nor disagreed with this statement.

It was found that the students aged 26 and over tend to disagree more frequently than the others that a person's ability to think critically is unchanging, while students aged 21–25 are most likely to agree with this statement ($\chi2=140.016$; df=8; $p<0.0001$). It was noted that the students aged 26 and over tend to disagree more frequently than the others that critical thinking only occurs when criticising, while students aged 21–25 agree with this statement the most ($\chi2=201.866$; df=8; $p<0.0001$).

University students are more likely than college students to agree with the following statements: a person's ability to think critically is unchanging ($\chi2=40.302$; df=4; $p<0.0001$); critical thinking only occurs when criticising ($\chi2=42.001$; df=4; $p<0.0001$).

Thus, the students are of the opinion that critical thinking can be developed and demonstrated in each situation and in a variety of ways if personal effort is put into it. It is worth noting that while most students view critical thinking as a changing process and do not think that critical thinking only occurs when criticising, there are still a considerable number of students who think the opposite.

The study aimed to compare the attitudes of teachers and students towards the manifestation and development of critical thinking. Based on the Mann-Whitney[18] non-parametric test for comparing independent samples, it was found that the teachers, compared to the students, agree more that:

- there are various ways to demonstrate critical thinking, $p<0.001$ (mean rank, teacher responses – 1212.09; mean rank, student responses – 794.34);
- critical thinking is possible in every situation, $p<0.001$ (mean rank, teacher responses – 1136.34; mean rank, student responses – 801.96);
- a person's ability to think critically is unchanging, $p<0.001$ (mean rank, teacher responses – 997.2; mean rank, student responses – 815.94);
- critical thinking only occurs when criticising, $p<0.001$ (mean rank, teacher responses – 980.96; mean rank, student responses – 817.58);
- critical thinking can be developed, $p<0.001$ (mean rank, teacher responses – 957.55; mean rank, student responses – 819.93).

In summary, it can be argued that the teachers and students view the manifestation of critical thinking as a changing process that helps a person demonstrate critical thinking skills in different ways, depending on the situation. In evaluating the manifestation of critical thinking, both groups associate it with the efforts of each person. The majority do not believe that critical thinking only occurs when criticising, but a considerable proportion of both the teachers and the students say the opposite.

2.3 Development of critical thinking skills

The study sought to determine how much attention the **teachers** give to the development of students' critical thinking skills in the study process. To this end, eight groups of critical thinking skills were singled out: explanation, analysis, decision-making, inference, self-regulation, interpretation, evaluation, and argumentation. In each group, three to six constituents – specific abilities – of that group were presented. Using a 7-point Likert scale *(where 1 is 'no attention at all' and 7 is 'particular attention')*, the teachers were asked to evaluate how much attention they give in the study process to developing the abilities of each group.

The study revealed that in developing students' critical thinking skills, the teachers give attention to the development of all critical thinking skills. The teachers allocate particular attention to developing the constituents of the inference (M=5.95), interpretation (M=5.93) and argumentation (M=5.92) skill groups.

The teachers give a bit less attention to developing the abilities in the other groups – analysis (M=5.85), evaluation (M=5.77) and explanation (M=5.76). The least attention is given to developing decision-making (M=5.52) and self-regulation (M=5.26) abilities.

---

18 *The Mann-Whitney test applied because in the one sample Kolmogorov-Smirnov test $p < 0.05$, and null hypothesis of normal population distribution was rejected, therefore, parametric analysis was not possible.*

In developing students' ability to formulate conclusions, the teachers allocate the most attention to developing their ability to formulate evidence-based conclusions (M=6.09) and to summarise information (M=6.03), placing slightly less emphasis on the ability to formulate conclusions with regard to the context (M=5.89) and in anticipation of possible consequences (M=5.8). These research data call attention to the depth of the teachers' understanding of critical thinking: evaluating the context and anticipating possible consequences are considered to be less significant constituents of critical thinking development.

The teachers are of the opinion that the ability to interpret is also an important mark of critical thinking. Here, the most attention is given to developing the ability to understand the content of data/information (M=6) and to convey data/information in one's own words (M=6). A bit less attention is given to developing the ability to discern essential information from supplementary information (M=5.95) and to classify data/information (M=5.85). It can be assumed that in the opinion of the teachers, the ability to interpret is more related to simply conveying the content of information than it is to 'arranging' the content being conveyed.

When developing argumentation skills, the teachers first develop students' ability to reason their choices (M=6.04), then to think based on facts/evidence (M=5.96), and finally to base actions on reflection (M=5.77).

In the group of analysis skills, the teachers allocate the most attention to developing the ability to collect data/information and link it to other data/sources (M=5.98), followed by the ability to find the connections between the whole and its parts (M=5.85) and to reveal connections between statements, facts, concepts (M=5.82), and finally the ability to examine a situation from different points of view (M=5.76). These data show that in the teachers' understanding, the development of analysis skills is most related to the collection and summarisation of information. However, less attention is given to the evaluation of that information using different sources and standpoints and discussing them.

In the group of evaluation skills, the teachers allocate the most attention to developing the ability to evaluate a situation on the basis of data/information (M=5.88) and to evaluate/self-evaluate the decisions/conclusions made (M=5.8). According to the teachers, a bit less attention is given in the study process to developing the ability to evaluate data/information without prejudice (M=5.76) and to evaluate data/information with regard to different opinions (M=5.67). These research data show that evaluation skills are more focused on practical activities than on personal dispositions to perform those activities.

In developing explanation skills, attention is first given to developing the ability to explain an analysis carried out and the results obtained (M=6), to reveal the essence of a phenomenon (M=5.89) and to answer others' questions (M=5.81). Less attention is given to developing the ability to explain complex concepts (M=5.72) and to explain the decision-making path (M=5.7), and even less is given to developing the ability to formulate questions for others (M=5.4). So again, a reasoned question arises as to why teachers, in developing students' explanation skills, prioritise the ability to explain and reveal the essence of a phenomenon, and pay less attention to giving meaning to explanation through the formulation of questions to others and through reasoning the decision-making path.

The study revealed that in developing students' decision-making skills, the teachers single out the ability to formulate conclusions (M=5.76) and to justify a decision made to others (M=5.7). A bit less attention is given to developing the ability to make decisions collegially (M=5.49) and according to the procedures established in the organisation (M=5.17). This suggests that in developing critical thinking, the teachers consider students' independence and the influence of interpersonal relationships on those decisions to be important. Of distinction is the emphasis on the importance of value orientations or interiorisation of the procedure established in the organisation.

The teachers give the least attention to developing self-regulation skills. It can be argued that the abilities to reflect (on one's thoughts, feelings, actions) (M=5.4), to change according to the situation (M=5.23) and to know oneself (M=5.18) are valued by the teachers less than all the others.

No statistically significant differences were found between development of critical thinking skills and demographic and social factors (gender, age, years of teaching experience, type of higher education institution).

Thus, the teachers develop all critical thinking skills in the study process, giving a bit more attention to the development of argumentation, interpretation and inference skills. However, the research data show that in the study process, the teachers give less attention to abilities that are related to evaluating context, different attitudes and perspectives or presenting them to others. There are, therefore, reasoned doubts about how 'deeply' the teachers understand the essence/phenomenon of critical thinking.

The study sought to determine the **students'** evaluation of how much attention is given to the development of critical thinking skills in the study programmes that they are in.[19] The students were asked to evaluate the development of all eight skill groups mentioned above on a 7-point Likert scale.

According to the students, the most attention is given in the study programme to developing argumentation (M=5.33), inference (M=5.25) and decision-making (M=5.22) skills. A bit less attention is given to self-regulation (M=5.19) and explanation (M=5.17) skills, and the least attention is given to interpretation (M=5.1), analysis (M=5.06) and evaluation (M=5.05) skills. It was found that in the study programmes, special attention is given to the abilities in the argumentation group of justifying one's choices (M=5.37), thinking based on facts/evidence (M=5.36) and basing actions on reflection (M=5.28).

In developing inference skills, the most attention is given to developing the ability to formulate evidence-based conclusions (M=5.31) and summarise information (M=5.29), and a bit less to the ability to formulate conclusions with regard to

19 *The arithmetic mean (M) is calculated. The frequency of each statement was evaluated on a 7-point scale, where 1 is 'no attention at all' and 7 is 'significant attention'.*

the context (M=5.23) and in anticipation of possible consequences (M=5.2). This suggests that according to the students, the ability to make inferences is more closely related to the ability to make evidence-based conclusions and summarise the information available. The context and anticipation of possible consequences are less significant here.

In developing decision-making skills in the study programmes, it is the evaluation of the students that the most attention is given to developing the ability to make decisions according to the procedures established in the organisation (M=5.27), independently (M=5.24) and collegiately (M=5.22), and a bit less to the ability to justify a decision made to others (M=5.15).

According to the students, the most attention is given in their studies to the self-regulation skill of knowing oneself (M=5.25). A bit less attention is given to the ability to change according to the situation (M=5.19) and to reflect (on one's thoughts, feelings, actions) (M=5.16).

The development of explanation skills is mainly related to the ability to explain an analysis carried out and the results obtained (M=5.26) and to reveal the essence of a phenomenon (M=5.23). It is the evaluation of the students that teachers give less attention to developing the ability to explain the decision-making path (M=5.18), to answer others' questions (M=5.16) and to explain complex concepts (M=5.14). The least attention is given to developing the ability to formulate questions for others (M=5.09).

Very equal attention is given in study programmes to developing the interpretation skill to understand the content of data/information (M=5.14), to discern essential information from supplementary information (M=5.13), to convey data/information in one's own words (M=5.1) and to classify data/information (M=5.06).

In the group of analysis skills, the students claim that the most attention is given to developing the ability to collect data/information and link it to other data/sources (M=5.17), and a bit less to the ability to examine a situation from different points of view (M=5.05) and to find connections between the whole and its parts (M=5.03). Meanwhile, the least attention is given to developing the ability to reveal connections between statements, facts, concepts (M=4.99).

In the group of evaluation skills, the students believe that the most attention is given in study programmes to the ability to evaluate a situation on the basis of data/information (M=5.13) and to evaluate/self-evaluate the decisions/conclusions made (M=5.13). A bit less attention is given in the study process to developing the ability to evaluate data/information without prejudice (M=5.03) and with regard to different opinions (M=4.95).

It was found that the students who were over 20 years old noted more frequently than the students who were 20 years old or younger that the teachers in their study programmes give the most attention to abilities such as formulating questions for others ($\chi2=56.281$; df=12; $p<0.001$). The students in the 21–25 age group note more frequently than the others that their teachers give the most attention to the ability to know oneself ($\chi2=58.653$; df=12; $p<0.001$), to reflect (on one's thoughts, feelings, actions) (χ2=54.323; df=12; p<0.001) and to change according to the situation (χ2=55.782; df=12; p<0.001).

The students who were only studying note more frequently than the students who were both studying and working that the teachers in their study programmes give more attention to the ability to formulate conclusions (χ2=38.193; df=6; p<0.001), make decisions collegially (χ2=34.73; df=6; p<0.001), make decisions according to the procedures established in the organisation (χ2=29.807; df=6; p<0.001), formulate conclusions with regard to the context (χ2=25.175; df=6; p<0.001), formulate conclusions in anticipation of possible consequences (χ2=37.624; df=6; p<0.001), formulate questions for others (χ2=19.638; df=6; p<0.001), reveal connections between statements, facts, concepts (χ2=26.570; df=6; p<0.001), know oneself (χ2=33.337; df=6; p<0.001), reflect (on one's thoughts, feelings, actions) (χ2=20.863; df=6; p<0.01), change according to the situation (χ2=26.118, df=6; p<0.001), base actions on reflection (χ2=27.184; df=6; p<0.001), classify data (χ2=35.324; df=6; p<0.001) and discern essential information from supplementary information (χ2=18.324; df=6; p<0.05).

The students who were both studying and working note more frequently than the students who were only studying that the teachers in their study programmes give more attention to the ability to summarise information (χ2=36.615; df=6; p<0.001) and to evaluate data/information with regard to different opinions (χ2=31.209; df=6; p<0.001).

Compared to the students who were only studying, the students who were both studying and working were more likely to disagree that the teachers in their study programmes give attention to developing the ability to justify a decision made to others (χ2=26.170; df=6; p<0.001), answer others' questions (χ2=25.819; df=6; p<0.001), explain an analysis carried out and the results obtained (χ2=16.776; df=6; p<0.05), explain the decision-making path (χ2=26.170; df=6; p<0.001), (χ2=22.541; df=6; p<0.001), explain complex concepts (χ2=21.966; df=6; p<0.001), reveal the essence of a phenomenon (χ2=22.541; df=6; p<0.001), collect data/information and link it to other data/sources (χ2=18.569; df=6; p<0.05) and evaluate/self-evaluate the decisions/conclusions made (χ2=16.673; df=6; p<0.05).

It came to light that university students note more frequently than college students that the teachers in their study programmes give the most attention to developing the ability to know oneself (χ2=16.019; df=6; p<0.01).

Data distribution by gender showed that women more often than men stated that in their study programme, more attention was given to the ability to formulate conclusions (χ2=23.688; df=6; p<0.01), formulate conclusions with regard to the context (χ2=22.297; df=6; p<0.01), formulate questions for others (χ2=14.469; df=6; p<0.05), think based on facts/evidence (χ2=18.786; df=6; p<0.01), base actions on reflection (χ2=17.912; df=6; p<0.05), classify data/information (χ2=17.616; df=6; p<0.05), understand the content of data/information (χ2=15.991; df=6; p<0.05), evaluate data/information with regard to different opinions (χ2=23.129; df=6; p<0.01), evaluate data/information without prejudice (χ2=25.012; df=6; p<0.001), evaluate a situation on the basis of data/information (χ2=17.415; df=6; p<0.01), evaluate the decisions/conclusions made ($\chi2=13.189$; df=6; $p<0.05$). Meanwhile, men were more likely than women to disagree that their ability to answer others' questions was developed in the study process ($\chi2=20.416$; df=6; $p<0.05$).

The student evaluations showed that attention is given in study programmes to the development of all critical thinking skills, but a bit more attention is given to developing argumentation, inference and decision-making skills. It should be noted that the students believe that teachers give the least attention to developing analysis, interpretation and evaluation skills.

Students over the age of 25 and students who also worked during their studies noted more frequently that during lectures, teachers give the most attention to their self-knowledge and self-improvement, that is, to developing self-regulation skills at the personal and interpersonal level. It is worth noting that students who both studied and worked during their studies were more likely to believe that teachers do not give enough attention to developing argumentation and evaluation skills. Meanwhile, women noted more frequently than men that during lectures, more attention is given to developing analysis and interpretation skills.

The study **sought to compare how much attention teachers give to the development of critical thinking skills when working with students, and how students evaluate the intensity of the time that is given**, that is, in the opinion of the students, how much attention is given to the development of critical thinking skills in the study programme.

Based on the Mann-Whitney[20] non-parametric test for comparing independent samples, it was found that the teachers note more than the students that attention is given in the study process to the following critical thinking skills:

- interpretation $p<0.001$ (mean rank, teacher responses – 1110.44; mean rank, student responses – 804.56);
- analysis $p<0.001$ (mean rank, teacher responses – 1108.32; mean rank, student responses – 804.77);
- evaluation $p<0.001$ (mean rank, teacher responses – 1087.65; mean rank, student responses – 808.86);
- inference $p<0.001$ (mean rank, teacher responses – 1059.23; mean rank, student responses – 809.71);
- argumentation $p<0.001$ (mean rank, teacher responses – 1030.34; mean rank, student responses – 812.61);
- explanation $p<0.001$ (mean rank, teacher responses – 1029.92; mean rank, student responses – 812.65);

20 *The Mann-Whitney criterion is calculated because the Kolmogorov-Smirnov statistics for the teacher sample showed that $p<0.05$, which means that the difference in the distribution from the normal is statistically significant, that is, the distribution is not normal and parametric analysis is not possible.*

- decision-making $p<0.05$ (mean rank, teacher responses – 956.83; mean rank, student responses – 823.02).

Meanwhile, the opinions of the teachers and the students are similar concerning the attention given to developing self-regulation skills. There was no statistically significant difference between the evaluation of the teachers and the students.

The study sought not only to compare the critical thinking skill groups, but also to evaluate the constituents of the relevant skill groups. Based on the Mann-Whitney[21] non-parametric test for comparing independent samples, it was found that the teachers, far more than the students, agree that attention is given in the study process to certain abilities from the analysis, interpretation, inference, explanation, evaluation and decision-making skill groups. The evaluations of the specific constituents of the critical thinking skills groups are given below.

Analysis skills:

- reveal connections between statements, facts, concepts $p<0.001$ (mean rank, teacher responses – 1095.66; mean rank, student responses – 806.04);
- find connections between the whole and its parts $p<0.001$ (mean rank, teacher responses – 1095.63; mean rank, student responses – 806.05);
- collect data/information and link it to other data/sources $p<0.001$ (mean rank, teacher responses – 1081.13; mean rank, student responses – 807.51).

Interpretation skills:

- understand the content of data/information $p<0.001$ (mean rank, teacher responses – 1092.93; mean rank, student responses – 806.32);
- discern essential information from supplementary information $p<0.001$ (mean rank, teacher responses – 1090.19; mean rank, student responses – 806.59);
- convey data/information in one's own words $p<0.001$ (mean rank, teacher responses – 1080.32; mean rank, student responses – 807.59);
- classify data/information $p<0.001$ (mean rank, teacher responses – 1079.92; mean rank, student responses – 807.63).

Inference skills:

- formulate evidence-based conclusions $p<0.001$ (mean rank, teacher responses – 1073.11; mean rank, student responses – 808.31);
- summarise information $p<0.001$ (mean rank, teacher responses – 1068.86; mean rank, student responses – 808.74);
- formulate conclusions with regard to the context $p<0.001$ (mean rank, teacher responses – 1036.14; mean rank, student responses – 812.03);

---

21 *The Mann-Whitney criterion is calculated because the Kolmogorov-Smirnov statistics for the teacher sample showed that $p<0.05$, which means that the difference in the distribution from the normal is statistically significant, that is, the distribution is not normal and parametric analysis is not possible.*

- formulate conclusions in anticipation of possible consequences p<0.001 (mean rank, teacher responses – 1002.84; mean rank, student responses – 815.38).

Explanation skills:

- explain an analysis carried out and the results obtained p<0.001 (mean rank, teacher responses – 1070.07; mean rank, student responses – 808.62);
- reveal the essence of a phenomenon p<0.001 (mean rank, teacher responses – 1040.34; mean rank, student responses – 811.61);
- answer others' questions p<0.001 (mean rank, teacher responses – 1035.47; mean rank, student responses – 812.1);
- explain complex concepts p<0.001 (mean rank, teacher responses – 1010.55; mean rank, student responses – 814.6);
- explain the decision-making path p<0.001 (mean rank, teacher responses – 1004.08; mean rank, student responses – 815.25);
- formulate questions for others p<0.01 (mean rank, teacher responses – 941.33; mean rank, student responses – 821.56).

Evaluation skills:

- evaluate data/information with regard to different opinions p<0.001 (mean rank, teacher responses – 1055.22; mean rank, student responses – 810.11);
- examine a situation from different points of view p<0.001 (mean rank, teacher responses – 1054.45; mean rank, student responses – 810.19);
- evaluate data/information without prejudice p<0.001 (mean rank, teacher responses – 1052.74; mean rank, student responses – 810.36);
- evaluate a situation on the basis of data/information p<0.001 (mean rank, teacher responses – 1052.43; mean rank, student responses – 810.39);
- evaluate/self-evaluate the decisions/conclusions made p<0.001 (mean rank, teacher responses – 1029.24; mean rank, student responses – 812.72).

Argumentation skills:

- justify one's choices p<0.001 (mean rank, teacher responses – 1048.7; mean rank, student responses – 810.77);
- think based on facts/evidence p<0.001 (mean rank, teacher responses – 1018.49; mean rank, student responses – 813.8);
- base actions on reflection p<0.001 (mean rank, teacher responses – 987.13; mean rank, student responses – 816.95);
- Decision-making skills:
- formulate conclusions p<0.001 (mean rank, teacher responses – 991.15; mean rank, student responses – 816.55);
- make decisions collegially p<0.05 (mean rank, teacher responses – 910.9; mean rank, student responses – 824.62).

Analysis of the data showed that in the opinion of the teachers, they give much more attention to the development of critical thinking skills when teaching study subjects than in the opinion of the students. More so than the students, the teachers believe that when teaching study subjects, they give the most attention to developing analysis and interpretation skills, and a bit less to inference, explanation and argumentation skills. The smallest difference of opinion was found in the evaluation of decision-making skills.

Analysis of the constituents of the critical thinking skill groups shows that in the group of decision-making skills, the teachers note that they give more attention to developing independent decision-making skills. Meanwhile, the students believe that more attention is given to developing the ability to make decisions according to the procedures established in the organisation. The teachers and the students have equal evaluations of the attention that is given to developing inference, argumentation and self-regulation skills. However, from the point of view of both the teachers and the students, the least attention is given in the study process to developing self-regulation skills.

The study sought to determine **which groups of critical thinking skills the teachers give the most attention to when teaching their subject**[22] (Table 35).

Tab. 35: *Spearman's rank correlation coefficient (r_s)*

Skill group	**Decision-making**	**Inference**	**Explanation**	**Analysis**	**Self-regulation**	**Argumentation**	**Interpretation**	**Evaluation**
Decision-making		0.614**	0.610**	0.571**	0.435**	0.620**	0.463**	0.562**
Inference			0.723**	0.743**	0.350**	0.722**	0.680**	0.657**
Explanation				0.747**	0.448**	0.741**	0.641**	0.655**
Analysis					0.406**	0.774**	0.724**	0.678**
Self-regulation						0.545**	0.358**	0.434**
Argumentation							0.671**	0.708**
Interpretation								0.668**
Evaluation								

* *p<0.05; **p<0.01; ***p<0.001*

22 *To this end, the Spearman's rank correlation coefficient (rs) is calculated. Only statistically significant (p<0.05) values of the correlation coefficient are presented for the analysis; the closer the obtained correlation coefficient is to the interval [-1; 1] endpoint, the stronger the relationship (Čekanavičius, V. & Murauskas, G. Statistika ir jos taikymai. Vilnius: TEV, 2003).*

Spearman's rank correlation coefficient was used to evaluate the groups of critical thinking skills. It was found (Table 35) that the more attention teachers give to developing decision-making skills, the more attention they give to developing inference (r_s=0.614; p<0.01), explanation (r_s=0.610; p<0.01) and argumentation (r_s=0.620; p<0.01) skills. It was also found that the more attention teachers give to developing inference skills, the more attention they give to developing explanation (r_s=0.723; p<0.01), analysis (r_s=0.743; p<0.01) and argumentation (r_s=0.722; p<0.01) skills. Furthermore, the more attention teachers give to developing explanation skills, the more attention they give to developing inference (r_s=0.723; p<0.01), analysis (r_s=0.747; p<0.01) and argumentation (r_s=0.741; p<0.01) skills. The more attention teachers give to developing analysis skills, the more attention they give to developing inference (r_s=0.743; p<0.01), explanation (r_s=0.747; p<0.01), argumentation (r_s=0.774; p<0.01) and interpretation (r_s=0.724; p<0.01) skills. The more attention teachers give to developing argumentation skills, the more attention they give to developing inference (r_s=0.722; p<0.01), explanation (r_s=0.741; p<0.01), analysis (r_s=0.774; p<0.01) and evaluation (r_s=0.708; p<0.01) skills. Analysis of the data shows that the more attention that is given to developing interpretation skills, the more attention is also given to developing analysis skills (r_s=0.724; p<0.01), and the more attention that is given to developing evaluation skills, the more attention is also given to developing argumentation skills (r_s=0.708; p<0.01). This is illustrated by the strong correlation found between the skill groups analysed (Table 35). A slightly weaker correlation was found when evaluating the abilities in the self-regulation skill group. A moderate strength of correlation was found in the argumentation skill group, which means that by giving more attention to developing self-regulation skills, more attention is given to developing argumentation skills (r_s=0.545; p<0.01).

Analysis of the data showed that the teachers give more attention to the explanation, analysis and argumentation skill groups. It was found that by giving more attention to the development of these skills, the attention given to the development of other skills increases as well.

In summary, it can be argued that teachers do give attention in the study process to the development of critical thinking skills, which is also recognised by the students. However, the teachers believe that the attention given to the development of critical thinking skills is also more intense than the students note. Analysis of the constituents of the critical thinking skill groups revealed that the teachers give less attention in the study process to developing the ability to see, understand and explain the wider context, the processes taking place in it, and their links.

2.4 Development of critical thinking dispositions

The study sought to determine how much attention the teachers give to the development of students' critical thinking dispositions (impartiality, accuracy, fairness, caring for other people, inquisitiveness, self-confidence, flexibility, attentiveness, endurance, courage, perseverance, scepticism, open-mindedness, rightness) in the study process.

To this end, the **teachers** were asked to evaluate, using a 7-point Likert scale *(where 1 is 'no attention at all' and 7 is 'particular attention')*, how much attention they give to developing these critical thinking dispositions when working with students.

Analysis of the research data revealed that the teachers, when working with students, give attention to developing all critical thinking dispositions.[23] When working with students, the teachers give considerable attention to developing the dispositions of fairness (M=6.2), rightness (M=6.02) and accuracy (M=5.9). These dispositions are united by faithfulness to the truth/the search for truth. In the study process, the teachers also give attention to developing the dispositions of self-confidence (M=5.82), attentiveness (M=5.7), inquisitiveness (M=5.63), flexibility (M=5.62), impartiality (M=5.57) and open-mindedness (M=5.52). When working with students, the teachers also develop the dispositions of perseverance (M=5.47), caring for other people (M=5.45), courage (M=5.22) and endurance (M=5.11). The teachers give the least attention to developing scepticism (M=4.21).

No statistically significant differences were found between development of critical thinking disposition and demographic and social factors (gender, age, years of teaching experience, type of higher education institution).

The students were also asked to evaluate, using a 7-point Likert scale (*where 1 is 'no attention at all' and 7 is 'particular attention'*), how much attention is given in their study programmes to the development of critical thinking dispositions.

Analysis of the research data revealed that **in the opinion of the students**,[24] special attention is given to the development of inquisitiveness (M=5.9) in their study programmes. Considerable attention is given in studies to developing the dispositions of rightness (M=5.48), accuracy (M=5.48), fairness (M=5.47) and attentiveness (M=5.45). The dispositions of self-confidence (M=5.37), flexibility (M=5.35), perseverance (M=5.28), caring for other people (M=5.27) and endurance (M=5.22) are also developed in the study process. According to the students, dispositions such as scepticism (M=4.5), impartiality (M=5.08), open-mindedness (M=5.1) and courage (M=5.16) are developed the least in their study programmes.

It was found that the students in the 21–25 age group note more frequently than the others that the teacher in their study programme gives greater attention to developing courage ($\chi 2=47.712$; df=12; $p<0.001$). Meanwhile, the students aged 26 and over tend to disagree more frequently than the others that the teacher has given more attention to developing the dispositions of perseverance ($\chi 2=51.254$; df=12; $p<0.001$), scepticism ($\chi 2=37.661$; df=12; $p<0.001$) and open-mindedness ($\chi 2=38.791$; df=12; $p<0.001$).

The students who were both studying and working note more frequently than the students who were only studying that the teacher has given more attention

---

23 *The arithmetic mean (M) is calculated. The frequency of each statement was evaluated on a 7-point scale, where 1 is 'no attention at all' and 7 is 'significant attention'.*

24 *The arithmetic mean (M) is calculated. The frequency of each statement was evaluated on a 7-point scale, where 1 is 'no attention at all' and 7 is 'significant attention'.*

to developing the dispositions of impartiality ($\chi2=36.494$; df=6; $p<0.001$), accuracy ($\chi2=22.290$; df=6; $p<0.001$), self-confidence ($\chi2=15.940$; df=6; $p<0.05$), attentiveness ($\chi2=28.867$; df=6; $p<0.001$) and endurance ($\chi2=32.258$; df=62; $p<0.001$). The students who were only studying were more likely to agree that the teacher has given more attention to developing the dispositions of courage ($\chi2=29.855$; df=6; $p<0.001$), perseverance ($\chi2=18.818$; df=6; $p<0.05$) and rightness ($\chi2=49.986$; df=6; $p<0.001$). Representatives of this group also note more frequently than others that the teacher has given less attention to the development of scepticism ($\chi2=29.934$; df=6; $p<0.001$).

Compared with the university students, the college students were more likely to note that the teacher has given more attention to developing impartiality ($\chi2=29.934$; df=6; $p<0.001$), and given less attention to developing inquisitiveness ($\chi2=18.627$; df=6; $p<0.01$), endurance ($\chi2=16.746$; df=6; $p<0.05$), open-mindedness ($\chi2=18.043$; df=6; $p<0.05$), rightness ($\chi2=14.371$; df=6; $p<0.05$) and accuracy ($\chi2=21.846$; df=6; $p<0.05$).

When evaluating the responses by gender, it was found that women note more frequently than men that during lectures, the teacher has given more attention to developing endurance ($\chi2=14.329$; df=6; $p<0.05$) and courage ($\chi2=14.509$; df=6; $p<0.05$). Meanwhile, the men were more likely than the women to disagree that the teacher has given more attention to developing open-mindedness ($\chi2=16.550$; df=6; $p<0.05$) and rightness ($\chi2=14.88$; df=6; $p<0.05$).

In summary, it can be argued that the students aged 26 and over note more frequently than the younger students that in the study process, teachers give less attention to developing dispositions such as open-mindedness and scepticism. On the other hand, the students in this age group believe that teachers give the most time in their lectures to developing courage. In evaluating attention to the development of critical thinking dispositions, it was revealed that compared to the students who were both studying and working, the students who were only studying were more likely to note the teachers' attention to the development of self-confidence and endurance. The college students were more likely to believe that they were being taught impartiality, open-mindedness and rightness.

The study sought to compare how much attention teachers give to the development of critical thinking dispositions in the study process, and how students evaluate the intensity of the time that is given, that is, in the opinion of the students, how much attention is given to the development of critical thinking dispositions in the study process.

Based on the Mann-Whitney[25] non-parametric test for comparing independent samples, it was found that compared to the students, the teachers believe that they give much more attention to developing the dispositions of:

25 *The Mann-Whitney criterion is calculated because the Kolmogorov-Smirnov statistics for the teacher sample showed that $p<0.05$, which means that the difference in the distribution from the normal is statistically significant, that is, the distribution is not normal and parametric analysis is not possible.*

- impartiality $p<0.001$ (mean rank, teacher responses – 992.28; mean rank, student responses – 816.44);
- accuracy $p<0.001$ (mean rank, teacher responses – 969.95; mean rank, student responses – 818.68);
- fairness $p<0.001$ (mean rank, teacher responses – 1086.98; mean rank, student responses – 806.92);
- inquisitiveness $p<0.001$ (mean rank, teacher responses – 961.53; mean rank, student responses – 819.53);
- self-confidence $p<0.01$ (mean rank, teacher responses – 948.32; mean rank, student responses – 820.86);
- open-mindedness $p<0.01$ (mean rank, teacher responses – 956.07; mean rank, student responses – 820.08);
- rightness $p<0.001$ (mean rank, teacher responses – 1003.16; mean rank, student responses – 815.34).

Analysis of the data showed that in the opinion of the teachers, they give much more attention to the development of individual dispositions related to critical thinking when teaching their subjects than in the opinion of the students. Analysis of the results revealed a major difference of opinion in evaluating the development of dispositions such as impartiality, accuracy, fairness, inquisitiveness, self-confidence, open-mindedness and rightness.

However, both the teachers and the students stress that the most attention in the study process is given to developing the disposition of fairness. Efforts are made for the students' beliefs and attitudes to be presented honestly and to direct them to the search for truth. Both the teachers and the students noted that the development of scepticism is given the least attention. It can be assumed that this evaluation may have been due to the ambiguous meaning of the term 'scepticism'.

2.5 The importance of critical thinking skills in the modern labour market

The study sought to determine how teachers evaluate the importance of critical thinking skills in the modern labour market.[26] Using a 7-point Likert scale (*where 1 is 'not important at all' and 7 is 'very important'*), the teachers were asked to evaluate the importance in the modern labour market of the constituents of each critical thinking skill group.

The study identified which critical thinking skills the teachers consider essential in the modern labour market. The teachers identified the following as being the most important critical thinking skills in the modern labour market: inference (M=5.89), argumentation (M=5.87), interpretation (M=5.82). The teachers put

26 *The arithmetic mean (M) is calculated. The frequency of each statement was evaluated on a 7-point scale, where 1 is 'not important at all' and 7 is 'very important'.*

slightly less emphasis on the importance of decision-making (M=5.8), evaluation (M=5.79), and analysis (M=5.77) skills in the modern labour market, and the least on the importance of explanation (M=5.71) and self-regulation (M=5.63) skills.

In the group of inference skills, the teachers believe that the ability to make inferences in anticipation of possible consequences (M=5.99) is of particular importance in the labour market. The ability to formulate evidence-based conclusions (M=5.9) and to summarise information (M=5.84) were given as being slightly less important. The ability to formulate conclusions with regard to the context has the lowest average (M=5.78).

As the most important argumentation skills in the modern labour market, the teachers identified the ability to think based on facts/evidence (M=5.99) and to justify one's choices (M=5.95); the ability to base actions on reflection (M=5.7) was identified as less important.

The teachers consider interpretation and evaluation skills to be slightly less important. Of these skill groups, the key interpretation skills that were distinguished were the ability to discern essential information from supplementary information (M=5.93) and to understand the content of data/information (M=5.93).

In the group of evaluation skills, the most important are considered to be the ability to evaluate a situation on the basis of data/information (M=5.93) and to evaluate/self-evaluate the decisions/conclusions made (M=5.91). The teachers attach less importance to the interpretive ability to classify data/information (M=5.74) and to convey data/information in one's own words (M=5.7). Less importance was also given to the ability in the group of evaluation skills to evaluate data/information without prejudice (M=5.7) and to evaluate data/information with regard to different opinions (M=5.65). The abilities of the other two groups – decision-making and explanation – were similarly evaluated by the teachers.

The teachers believe that in the modern labour market, the most important ability when making decisions is to make decisions collegially (M=5.91); slightly less importance was given to the ability to justify a decision made to others (M=5.88) and to formulate conclusions (M=5.84), and the least importance was given to the ability to make decisions according to the procedures established in the organisation (M=5.61).

When evaluating the importance of individual explanation skills in the modern labour market, the teachers identified the ability to explain an analysis carried out and the results obtained (M=5.97) and to answer others' questions (M=5.91) as being the most important. The ability to reveal the essence of a phenomenon (M=5.82) and to explain the decision-making path (M=5.7) were given slightly less importance. The ability to formulate questions for others (M=5.53) and to explain complex concepts (M=5.44) have the lowest average among teachers.

According to the teachers, the most important analysis skill in the modern labour market is to collect data/information and link it to other data/sources (M=5.87). Also noted as important skills in the modern labour market were the ability to examine a situation from different points of view (M=5.79) and to find connections between the whole and its parts (M=5.78), while the least important was considered to be the ability to reveal connections between statements, facts, concepts (M=5.66).

When evaluating the importance of self-regulation skills in the modern labour market, the teachers identified the ability to change according to the situation (M=5.9) as being the most important, and the ability to know oneself (M=5.57) and to reflect (on one's thoughts, feelings, actions) (M=5.43) as being much less important.

The research data show that the older teachers are more likely to note that a person's ability to work with data and information is valued in the modern labour market. It was found that teachers aged 50 and over are more likely than the younger teachers to state that it is very important for the modern labour market to collect data/information and link it to other data/sources ($\chi2=13.680$; df=6; $p<0.05$) and to discern essential information from supplementary information ($\chi2=14.417$; df=6; $p<0.05$).

When evaluating the teachers' responses by gender, it was found that women were more likely than men to say that the ability to evaluate a situation on the basis of data/information ($\chi2=21.571$; df=6; $p<0.01$) is very important for the modern labour market.

It can be assumed that the teachers consider self-regulation and explanation skills not so important in the modern labour market as other skills, and the most important are inference, argumentation and interpretation skills.

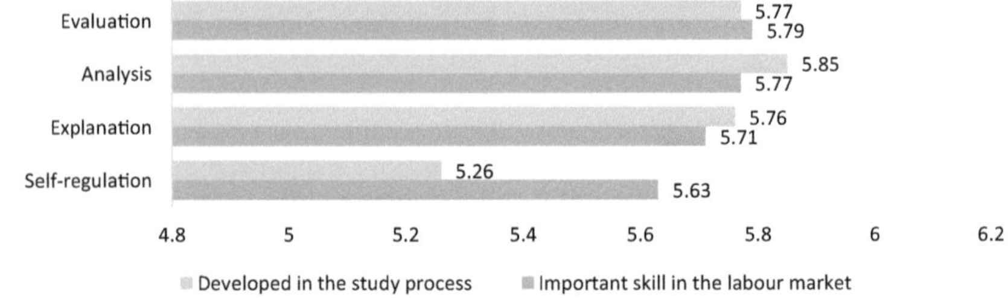

Fig. 18: *Relationship between the teachers' attitudes to the importance of critical thinking skills in the modern labour market and their development.*

Relationship between the teachers' attitude to the importance of critical thinking skills in the modern labour market and their development.[27] It was found (Figure 18) that when identifying the most important abilities in the modern labour market, the teachers specified inference (M=5.89), argumentation (M=5.87) and interpretation (M=5.82) skills, and claimed to give attention to their development: inference (M=5.95), interpretation (M=5.93), argumentation (M=5.92).

Statistically significant differences were found in the relationship between the teachers' attitude to the importance of critical thinking skills in the modern labour market and their development. Analysis of the research results revealed that the more the teachers believe that inference is important in the labour market, the more attention they give to the development of this ability (r_s=0.513; $p<0.001$). A similar trend was found with argumentation (r_s=0.439; $p<0.001$) and interpretation (r_s=0.544; $p<0.001$) skills.

The study also sought to determine how students[28] evaluate the importance of critical thinking skills in the modern labour market. Using a 7-point Likert scale (*where 1 is 'not important at all' and 7 is 'very important'*), the students were asked to evaluate the importance in the modern labour market of the constituents of each critical thinking skill group.

It was found that the students consider the most important critical thinking skills in the modern labour market to be self-regulation (M=5.59), argumentation (M=5.54) and inference (M=5.5) skills. They rated decision-making (M=5.49) and explanation (M=5.43) skills as being slightly less important in the labour market. And in the opinion of the students, the least significant skills in the modern labour market are analysis (M=5.31), evaluation (M=5.31) and interpretation (M=5.3) skills.

Analysis of the research data revealed that the students consider the most important self-regulation skills in the modern labour market to be the ability to know oneself (M=5.68), reflect (on one's thoughts, feelings, actions) (M=5.55) and change according to the situation (M=5.55). In this skill group, the ability to change according to the situation (M=5.55) and the ability to reflect (on one's thoughts, feelings, actions) (M=5.55) were identified as being slightly less important.

In the group of argumentation skills, the students consider the ability to think based on facts/evidence (M=5.6) and justify one's choices (M=5.58) to be important in the modern labour market; the ability to base actions on reflection (M=5.46) was identified as being less important.

It was found that in the group of inference skills, the students attached the greatest importance to the ability to formulate conclusions in anticipation of possible consequences (M=5.56) and to formulate evidence-based conclusions

27 *The arithmetic mean (M) is calculated. The frequency of each statement was evaluated on a 7-point scale, where 1 is 'not important at all' and 7 is 'very important'.*

28 *The arithmetic mean (M) is calculated. The frequency of each statement was evaluated on a 7-point scale, where 1 is 'not important at all' and 7 is 'very important'.*

(M=5.51), and a bit less to the ability to summarise information (M=5.47). Even less importance is given to the ability to evaluate data/information without prejudice (M=5.36) and with regard to different opinions (M=5.15).

According to the students, the most important ability when making decisions in the modern labour market is to make decisions according to the procedures established in the organisation (M=5.53) and make decisions collegially (M=5.5); slightly less importance was given to the ability to justify a decision made to others (M=5.48) and to formulate conclusions (M=5.48).

When evaluating the importance of the constituents of the group of explanation skills in the modern labour market, the students gave the ability to explain an analysis carried out and the results obtained (M=5.48) and the ability to reveal the essence of a phenomenon (M=5.48) as being the most important. From the students' point of view, the ability to formulate questions for others (M=5.4), explain the decision-making path (M=5.39) and explain complex concepts (M=5.36) are considered slightly less important in the modern labour market. Meanwhile, the ability to answer others' questions has the lowest average (M=4.49).

According to the students, the most important analysis skill in the modern labour market is to collect data/information and link it to other data/sources (M=5.4). The ability to examine a situation from different points of view (M=5.34) and find connections between the whole and its parts (M=5.29) are also evaluated as being important. From the point of view of the students, ability in the modern labour market to reveal connections between statements, facts, concepts (M=5.22) is not so important.

Among the interpretation skills, the students attached importance to the ability to understand the content of data/information (M=5.39) and to discern essential information from supplementary information (M=5.37). Less importance was given to the ability to convey data/information in one's own words (M=5.26) and to classify data/information (M=5.19).

The students identified the most important evaluation skills in the modern labour market as being the ability to evaluate/self-evaluate the decisions/conclusions made (M=5.39) and to evaluate a situation on the basis of data/information (M=5.38).

It was found that the students who were only studying noted more frequently than the students who were both studying and working that the ability to know oneself ($\chi2=13.978$; df=6; $p<0.05$) is important for the modern labour market. The male respondents were more likely than the female respondents to disagree that the ability to know oneself ($\chi2=22.493$; df=6; $p<0.01$) is important for the modern labour market.

Similar results were obtained by comparing the ability to classify data/information by the respondents' gender and employment status. The students who were both studying and working noted more frequently than the students who were only studying that the ability to classify data/information ($\chi2=27{,}501$; df=6; $p<0.001$) is needed more by the labour market. The same evaluation is more common among women than among men ($\chi2=19.564$; df=6; $p<0.05$).

Thus, the students consider self-regulation, argumentation and inference skills to be the most important skills for the modern labour market. Although the difference in evaluation is not significant, there is a clear tendency for these abilities to be evaluated rather narrowly. That is, abilities that are contextualised/put in context, in terms of evaluation without prejudice or evaluation with regard to the opinions of others, and reasoning of actions with reflection, are considered less important by students.

Relationship between the students' attitude to the importance of critical thinking skills in the modern labour market and their development in the study process.[29] It was found (Figure 19) that the students, in identifying the most important skills in the modern labour market as inference (M=5.5) and decision-making (M=5.49), noted that teachers give more attention to the development of these skills in the study process as well: inference (M=5.25), decision-making (M=5.22). It should be noted that the students believe that self-regulatory skills are important for the labour market (M=5.49), but they admit that teachers do not give enough attention to the development of these skills (M=5.19).

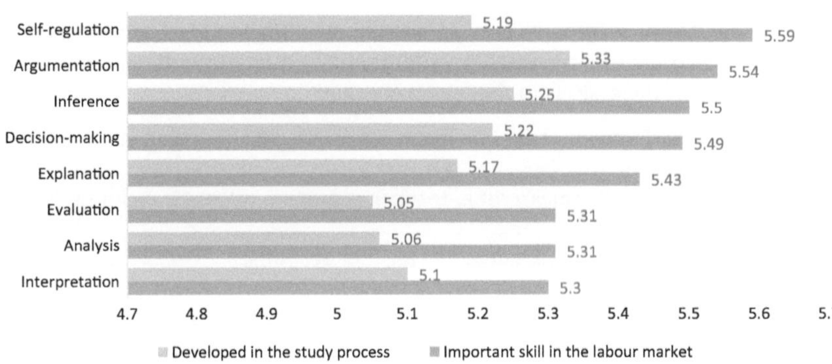

Fig. 19: *Relationship between the students' attitude to the importance of critical thinking skills for the modern labour market and their development in the study process*

Statistically significant differences were found in the relationship between the students' attitude to the importance of critical thinking skills for the modern labour market and the development of these skills in the study process. Analysis of the research results revealed that the more the students believe that decision-making is an important skill in the labour market, the more they note that teachers

29 *The arithmetic mean (M) is calculated.* The frequency of each statement was evaluated on a 7-point scale, where 1 is 'not important at all' and 7 is 'very important'.

give more attention to this skill (r_s=0.554; p<0.001) in the study process. A similar trend was found with inference (r_s=0.577; p<0.001) and self-regulation (r_s=0.486; p<0.001) skills.

The study sought to compare how the groups of higher education representatives (teachers and students) evaluate the importance of critical thinking skills in the labour market. It turned out that the opinions of the teachers and students differ, and a statistically significant difference was found in the evaluation of almost all critical thinking skills.

Based on the Mann-Whitney[30] non-parametric test for comparing independent samples, it was found that the teachers, much more than the students, emphasise the importance of these skills in the modern labour market:

- interpretation p<0.001 (mean rank, teacher responses – 1032.03; mean rank, student responses – 812.44);
- evaluation p<0.001 (mean rank, teacher responses – 1018.57; mean rank, student responses – 813.79);
- analysis p<0.01 (mean rank, teacher responses – 1006.13; mean rank, student responses – 815.05).

Based on the Mann-Whitney[31] non-parametric test for comparing independent samples, it was found that the teachers, slightly more than the students, emphasise the importance of these skills in the labour market:

- inference p<0.001 (mean rank, teacher responses – 983.08; mean rank, student responses – 817.36);
- argumentation p<0.001 (mean rank, teacher responses – 969.45; mean rank, student responses – 818.73);
- decision-making p<0.001 (mean rank, teacher responses – 962.24; mean rank, student responses – 819.46);
- explanation p<0.01 (mean rank, teacher responses – 936.99; mean rank, student responses – 822).

It should be noted that the opinions of the teachers and students are similar (no statistically significant difference was found) in evaluating the importance of self-regulation skills in the modern labour market p<0.001 (mean rank, teacher responses – 854.57; mean rank, student responses – 830.28).

30 *The Mann-Whitney criterion is calculated because the Kolmogorov-Smirnov statistics for the teacher sample showed that p<0.05, which means that the difference in the distribution from the normal is statistically significant, that is, the distribution is not normal and parametric analysis is not possible.*

31 *The Mann-Whitney criterion is calculated because the Kolmogorov-Smirnov statistics for the teacher sample showed that p<0.05, which means that the difference in the distribution from the normal is statistically significant, that is, the distribution is not normal and parametric analysis is not possible.*

The study sought to compare how the teachers and students evaluate the importance of constituents of critical thinking skills in the labour market. Based on the Mann-Whitney[32] non-parametric test for comparing independent samples, it was found that the teachers stress much more strongly than the students the importance of the following constituents of critical thinking skills in the modern labour market:

Interpretation skills:

- discern essential information from supplementary information $p<0.001$ (mean rank, teacher responses – 1031.39; mean rank, student responses – 812.51);
- understand the content of data/information $p<0.001$ (mean rank, teacher responses – 1012.64; mean rank, student responses – 814.39);
- classify data/information $p<0.001$ (mean rank, teacher responses – 1006.54; mean rank, student responses – 8015.00).

Evaluation skills:

- evaluate a situation on the basis of data/information $p<0.001$ (mean rank, teacher responses – 1019.30; mean rank, student responses – 813.72);
- evaluate/self-evaluate the decisions/conclusions made $p<0.001$ (mean rank, teacher responses – 1013.96; mean rank, student responses – 814.26).

Explanation skills:

- explain an analysis carried out and the results obtained $p<0.001$ (mean rank, teacher responses – 1003.82; mean rank, student responses – 815.28).

Based on Mann-Whitney[33] test, the teachers stress more strongly than the students the importance of the following critical thinking skills for the labour market:

Analysis skills:

- collect data/information and link it to other data/sources $p<0.001$ (mean rank, teacher responses – 993.43; mean rank, student responses – 816.32);
- examine a situation from different points of view $p<0.001$ (mean rank, teacher responses – 992.38; mean rank, student responses – 816.43);
- find connections between the whole and its parts $p<0.001$ (mean rank, teacher responses – 991.28; mean rank, student responses – 816.54).

---

32 *The Mann-Whitney criterion is calculated because the Kolmogorov-Smirnov statistics for the teacher sample showed that p<0.05, which means that the difference in the distribution from the normal is statistically significant, that is, the distribution is not normal and parametric analysis is not possible.*

33 *The Mann-Whitney criterion is calculated because the Kolmogorov-Smirnov statistics for the teacher sample showed that p<0.05, which means that the difference in the distribution from the normal is statistically significant, that is, the distribution is not normal and parametric analysis is not possible.*

Evaluation skills:

- evaluate data/information with regard to different opinions $p<0.001$ (mean rank, teacher responses – 987.94; mean rank, student responses – 816.87).

Inference skills:

- formulate conclusions in anticipation of possible consequences $p<0.001$ (mean rank, teacher responses – 979.58; mean rank, student responses – 817.71);
- formulate evidence-based conclusions $p<0.001$ (mean rank, teacher responses – 944.41; mean rank, student responses – 819.04);
- formulate conclusions with regard to the context $p<0.01$ (mean rank, teacher responses – 934.50; mean rank, student responses – 822.25).

Decision-making skills:

- justify a decision made to others $p<0.001$ (mean rank, teacher responses – 978.50; mean rank, student responses – 818.07);
- make decisions collegially $p<0.001$ (mean rank, teacher responses – 976.07; mean rank, student responses – 819.04).

Argumentation skills:

- justify one's choices $p<0.001$ (mean rank, teacher responses – 974.01; mean rank, student responses – 818.27);
- think based on facts/evidence (mean rank, teacher responses – 973.95; mean rank, student responses – 818.28).

Based on Mann-Whitney[34] test, the teachers stress a bit more strongly than the students the importance of the following critical thinking skills for the labour market:

Inference skills:

- summarise information $p<0.001$ (mean rank, teacher responses – 981.27; mean rank, student responses – 817.54).

Analysis skills:

34 *The Mann-Whitney criterion is calculated because the Kolmogorov-Smirnov statistics for the teacher sample showed that $p<0.05$, which means that the difference in the distribution from the normal is statistically significant, that is, the distribution is not normal and parametric analysis is not possible.*

- reveal connections between statements, facts, concepts $p<0.001$ (mean rank, teacher responses – 973.23; mean rank, student responses – 818.35).

Interpretation skills:

- convey data/information in one's own words $p<0.001$ (mean rank, teacher responses – 968.77; mean rank, student responses – 818.80).

Decision-making skills:

- formulate conclusions $p<0.001$ (mean rank, teacher responses – 958.74; mean rank, student responses – 819.81).

Explanation skills:

- answer others' questions $p<0.01$ (mean rank, teacher responses – 949.86; mean rank, student responses – 820.70);
- explain the decision-making path $p<0.01$ (mean rank, teacher responses – 937.32; mean rank, student responses – 821.96);
- explain complex concepts $p<0.001$ (mean rank, teacher responses – 862.72; mean rank, student responses – 829.36).

Evaluation skills:

- evaluate data/information without prejudice $p<0.01$ (mean rank, teacher responses – 946.99; mean rank, student responses – 820.99).

Argumentation skills:

- base actions on reflection $p<0.05$ (mean rank, teacher responses – 911.76; mean rank, student responses – 824.53).

In summary, it can be stated that the teachers place more emphasis than the students on the importance of interpretation, evaluation and explanation skills for the modern labour market. Both the teacher and the students consider argumentation and inference skills to be the most important skills in the modern labour market. From the point of view of both the teachers and the students, the ability to base actions on reflection is not so important in the argumentation skill group. The students believe that self-regulation skills are also one of the most important, while the teachers consider these skills to be not so important in the modern labour market. The teachers consider interpretation skills to be the most important in the modern labour market, while the students evaluate these skills as being the least important.

It has been observed that the more teachers recognise the importance of specific critical thinking skills in the modern labour market, the more attention they give to their development in the study process. The more importance students attach to specific critical thinking skills, the higher they evaluate the attention the teachers give to their development.

2.6 The importance of critical thinking dispositions in the modern labour market

The study revealed how teachers evaluate the importance of individual critical thinking dispositions in the modern labour market.[35] Using a 7-point Likert scale (*where 1 is 'not important at all' and 7 is 'very important'*), the teachers were asked to evaluate the importance in the modern labour market of each critical thinking disposition presented.

Analysis of the research data suggests that, in the evaluation of the teachers, the most important critical thinking dispositions in the modern labour market are fairness (M=5.98), flexibility (M=5.95) self-confidence (M=5.95) and accuracy (M=5.94). Important dispositions are perseverance (M=5.83), rightness (M=5.76), endurance (M=5.72), attentiveness (M=5.68) and courage (M=5.6). The teachers identified scepticism (M=4.22), open-mindedness (M=5.07), caring for other people (M=5.34), impartiality (M=5.48) and inquisitiveness (M=5.49) as being not so important critical thinking dispositions in the modern labour market.

Distributing the answers to this question according to the age of the respondents shows that the younger teachers (≤ 49 years old) were more likely than the older teachers to not have an opinion in evaluating inquisitiveness ($\chi2=15.944$; df=6; $p<0.05$) as a critical thinking disposition that is important in the modern labour market. Meanwhile, the older teachers (≥ 50 years old) were more likely than the younger teachers to note the importance of inquisitiveness ($\chi2=15.422$; df=6; $p<0.05$) and perseverance ($\chi2=14.099$; df=6; $p<0.05$) in the modern labour market. Analysis by gender showed that women tend more than men to emphasise the importance of impartiality ($\chi2=15.907$; df=6; $p<0.05$) and endurance ($\chi2=13.096$; df=6; $p<0.05$) in the modern labour market. Meanwhile, men note the importance of fairness ($\chi2=15.125$; df=6; $p<0.05$) and caring for other people ($\chi2=13.619$; df=6; $p<0.05$) more than women do. In addition, men were more likely than women to not have an opinion in evaluating the importance of inquisitiveness ($\chi2=22.203$; df=6; $p<0.01$) and rightness ($\chi2=14.657$; df=6; $p<0.05$) in the modern labour market. Men were also more likely than women to believe that perseverance is not an important critical thinking disposition in the modern labour market ($\chi2=20.506$; df=6; $p<0.05$).

In summary, it can be stated that inquisitiveness is more appreciated by older teachers as a critical thinking disposition that is important in the modern labour market. The research data suggest that the female respondents single out the importance of impartiality and endurance in the modern labour market, while the male respondents single out fairness and caring for other people.

---

35 *The arithmetic mean (M) is calculated. The frequency of each statement was evaluated on a 7-point scale, where 1 is 'not important at all' and 7 is 'very important'.*

Relationship between the teachers' attitude to the importance of critical thinking dispositions in the modern labour market and their development.[36] It was found (Figure 20) that when identifying the most important critical thinking dispositions in the modern labour market, the teachers specified fairness (M=5.98) and accuracy (M=5.94) skills, and claimed to give greater attention to their development in the study process: fairness (M=6.2), accuracy (M=5.9). However, an obvious discrepancy is visible: from the teachers' point of view, an important critical thinking disposition in the modern labour market is rightness (M=6.02), but this disposition is not given the most attention in the teaching process (M=5.76).

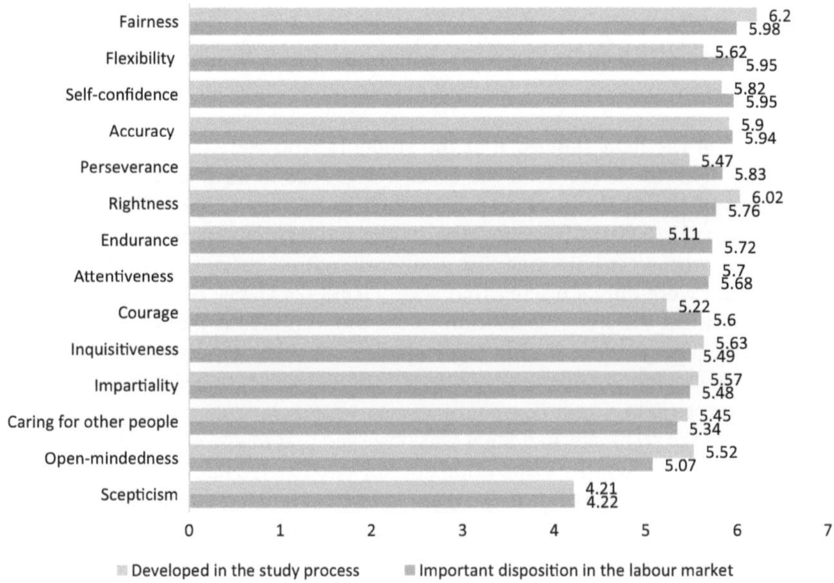

Fig. 20: *Relationship between the teachers' attitude to the importance of critical thinking dispositions in the modern labour market and their development*

Statistically significant differences were found in the relationship between the teachers' attitude to the importance of critical thinking dispositions in the modern labour market and their development. Analysis of the research results revealed that the more the teachers believe that fairness is important in the modern labour

36 *The arithmetic mean (M) is calculated. The frequency of each statement was evaluated on a 7-point scale, where 1 is 'not important at all' and 7 is 'very important'.*

market, the more attention they give to the development of this critical thinking disposition (r_s=0.459; $p<0.001$). A similar trend was observed with regard to accuracy (r_s=0.414; $p<0.001$).

The study revealed **how students evaluate the importance of individual critical thinking dispositions in the modern labour market**.[37] Using a 7-point Likert scale (*where 1 is 'not important at all' and 7 is 'very important'*), the students were asked to evaluate the importance in the modern labour market of each critical thinking disposition presented.

According to the students, the most important critical thinking dispositions in the modern labour market are self-confidence (M=5.8), fairness (M=5.69), attentiveness (M=5.65), accuracy (M=5.64) and flexibility (M=5.61). Important dispositions are perseverance (M=5.57), rightness (M=5.56), courage (M=5.4) and caring for other people (M=5.37). The students identified the dispositions of scepticism (M=4.72), open-mindedness (M=5.09), endurance (M=5.2), impartiality (M=5.25) and inquisitiveness (M=5.29) as being of average importance in the modern labour market.

Analysis of the data showed that the students who were 20 or younger were more likely than the students in the other age groups to be able to decide on the importance of the qualities of scepticism ($\chi2$=36.752; df=12; $p<0.001$) and open-mindedness ($\chi2$=33.901; df=12; $p<0.01$) in the modern labour market. However, the students who were both studying and working note more frequently than the students who were only studying that scepticism ($\chi2$=41.134; df=6; $p<0.001$) is an important critical thinking disposition in the modern labour market. In addition, the students who worked during their studies consider impartiality ($\chi2$=64.505; df=6; $p<0.001$) and inquisitiveness ($\chi2$=18.678; df=6; $p<0.01$) to be important critical thinking dispositions.

Looking at the results by gender, it was observed that men were more likely than women to disagree that the dispositions of impartiality ($\chi2$=39.991; df=6; $p<0.001$) and rightness ($\chi2$=16.069; df=6; $p<0.05$) are important in the modern labour market. Meanwhile, women agree more on the importance of the dispositions of caring for other people ($\chi2$=19.457; df=6; $p<0.05$) and inquisitiveness ($\chi2$=26.793; df=6; $p<0.001$) in the modern labour market.

Relationship between the students' attitude to the importance of critical thinking skills for the modern labour market and their development in the study process.[38] It was found that the students, in identifying the most important critical thinking disposition in today's labour market as self-confidence (M=5.8), noted that teachers also give attention to its development (M=5.48).

---

37 *The arithmetic mean (M) is calculated. The frequency of each statement was evaluated on a 7-point scale, where 1 is 'not important at all' and 7 is 'very important'.*

38 *The arithmetic mean (M) is calculated. The frequency of each statement was evaluated on a 7-point scale, where 1 is 'not important at all' and 7 is 'very important'.*

However, an obvious discrepancy is visible in the evaluation of other critical thinking dispositions except of courage (Figure 21).

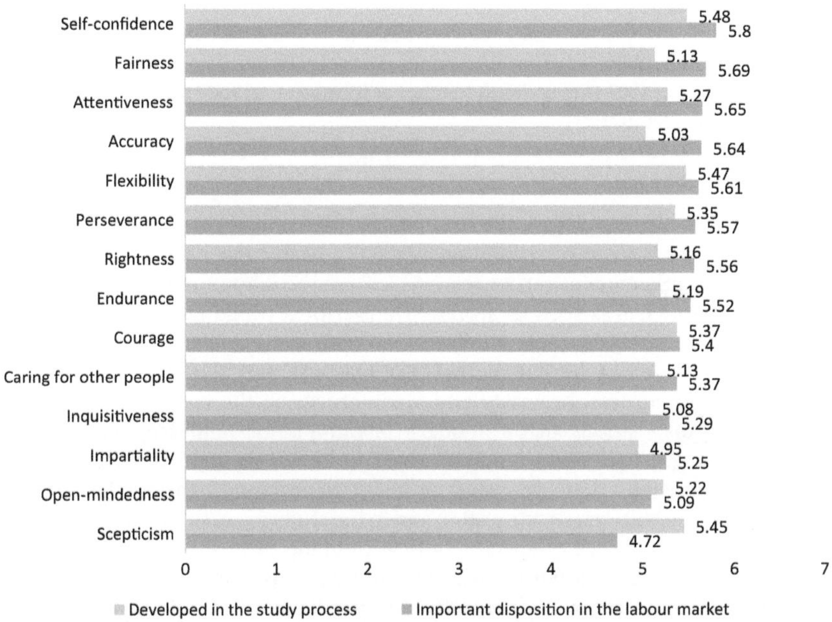

Fig. 21: *Relationship between the students' attitude to the importance of critical thinking dispositions for the modern labour market and their development in the study process*

Analysis of the research results revealed that the more the students believe that self-confidence is important in the modern labour market, the more attention they believe the teachers give to the development of this critical thinking disposition ($r_s=0.484$; $p<0.001$).

The study sought to compare the opinion of the teachers and the students on the importance of critical thinking dispositions in the modern labour market. Based on the Mann-Whitney[39] non-parametric test for comparing independent samples, it was found that the teachers stress much more strongly than the students the importance of the following critical thinking dispositions in the modern labour market:

39 *The Mann-Whitney criterion is calculated because the Kolmogorov-Smirnov statistics for the teacher sample showed that $p<0.05$, which means that the difference in the distribution from the normal is statistically significant, that is, the distribution is not normal and parametric analysis is not possible.*

- flexibility $p<0.01$ (mean rank, teacher responses – 952.47; mean rank, student responses – 820.44);
- accuracy $p<0.01$ (mean rank, teacher responses – 949,00; mean rank, student responses – 820.79);
- fairness $p<0.001$ (mean rank, teacher responses – 943.87; mean rank, student responses – 821.30);
- perseverance $p<0.01$ (mean rank, teacher responses – 930.31; mean rank, student responses – 8222.67);
- impartiality $p<0.05$ (mean rank, teacher responses – 908.78; mean rank, student responses – 824.83).

Based on Mann-Whitney[40] test, the students stressed much more strongly than the teachers the importance of scepticism $p<0.001$ (mean rank, teacher responses – 684.52; mean rank, student responses – 847.38) in the labour market. It should be noted that scepticism is seen as an important critical thinking disposition in the modern labour market by those students who both study and work.

In summary, it can be stated that the teachers and the students consider self-confidence, fairness, accuracy and flexibility to be the most important critical thinking dispositions in the modern labour market, and scepticism, open-mindedness, impartiality and inquisitiveness to be not so important. The critical thinking dispositions that are noted as being important in the modern labour market by teachers are given more attention in the study process. The more teachers recognise the importance of specific critical thinking dispositions in the modern labour market, the more attention they give to their development in the study process. The more importance students attach to specific critical thinking dispositions, the higher they evaluate the attention the teachers give to their development.

2.7 Opportunities for developing critical thinking

Analysis of the research data revealed **how often, when developing critical thinking in students, teachers apply various methods for the development of critical thinking**. Using a 5-point Likert scale (*'very often', 'often', 'neither often nor rarely', 'rarely', 'very rarely'*), the teachers were asked to evaluate how often, when developing critical thinking in students, they apply various methods for the development of critical thinking. In order to show the difference in opinion among respondents, the responses *'very often' and 'often'* were combined into one level – *'often'*, and the responses *'very rarely' and 'rarely'* were combined into one level – *'rarely'* (Figure 22).

40 *The Mann-Whitney criterion is calculated because the Kolmogorov-Smirnov statistics for the teacher sample showed that p<0.05, which means that the difference in the distribution from the normal is statistically significant, that is, the distribution is not normal and parametric analysis is not possible.*

The majority of the teachers who participated in the study claim that they often or very often develop critical thinking in students by teaching to link practice and theory (83.6 %), teaching to analyse information, data, phenomena (82.9 %), examining cases, situations (82.9 %), providing feedback (82.2 %) or teaching to justify a choice/decision (80.3 %).

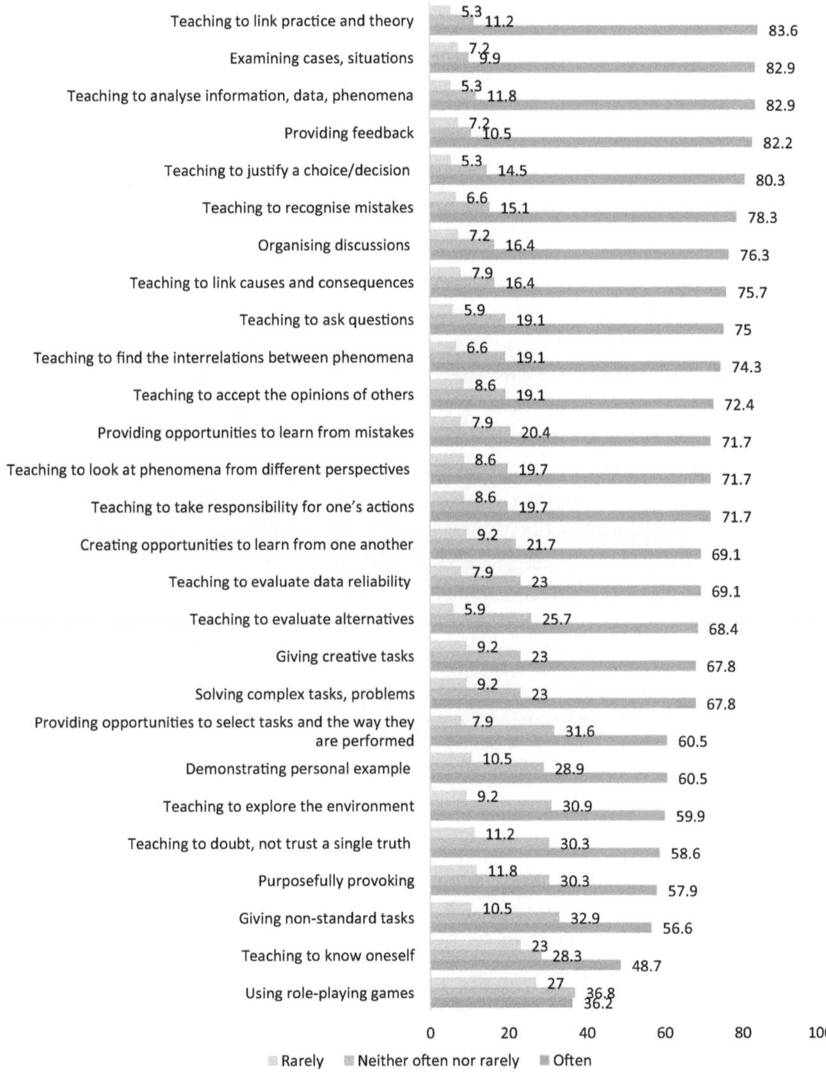

Fig. 22: *Opportunities for developing critical thinking, teacher evaluation, %*

Most of the **teachers** note that they often or very often develop critical thinking in students by teaching to recognise mistakes (78.3 %), organising discussions (76.3 %), teaching to link causes and consequences (75.6 %), teaching to ask questions (75 %), teaching to find the interrelations between phenomena (74.3 %) and teaching to accept the opinions of others (72.6). The teachers also provide opportunities to learn from mistakes (71.7 %) and teach to take responsibility for one's actions (71.7 %).

Analysis of the research data revealed that when developing critical thinking in **students**, teachers are the least likely to use role-playing games (26.9 %) and teach to know oneself (23 %).

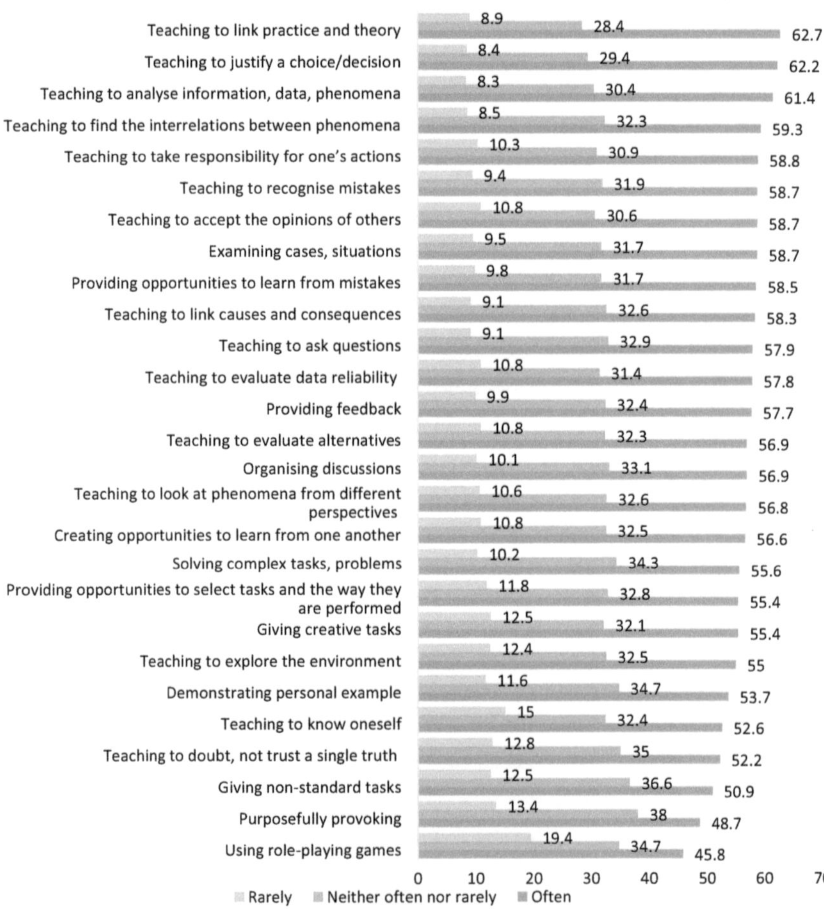

Fig. 23: *Opportunities for developing critical thinking, student evaluation, %*

The students were also asked to use a 5-point scale (*'very often', 'often', 'neither often nor rarely', 'rarely', 'very rarely'*) to evaluate how often teachers use the said methods to develop their critical thinking. In order to show the difference in opinion among respondents, the responses *'very often' and 'often'* were combined into one level – *'often'*, and the responses *'very rarely' and 'rarely'* were combined into one level – *'rarely'* (Figure 23).

Analysis of the research data revealed the **students'** opinion of how often teachers apply various methods for the development of critical thinking in students. The majority of the students who participated in the study said that teachers often or very often teach to link practice and theory (62.7 %), teach to reason the chosen solution (62.2 %), and teach to analyse information, data, phenomena (61.4 %).

Teachers teach the students, from the point of view of students, to find the interrelations between phenomena (59.3 %), to take responsibility for their actions (58.8 %), to accept the opinions of others (58.7 %); they provide opportunities to learn from mistakes (58.6 %), teach to recognise mistakes (58.6 %), teach to link causes and consequences (58.3 %), teach to ask questions (58 %), teach to evaluate data reliability (57.8 %), provide feedback (57.7 %), teach to evaluate alternatives (57 %), organise discussions (56.9 %), teach to look at phenomena from different perspectives (56.8 %), create opportunities to learn from one another (56.6 %), and solve complex tasks, problems (55.6 %).

According to the students, teachers are the least likely to use role-playing games (19.5 %), to teach to know oneself (15 %), to give non-standard tasks (12.5 %), to purposefully provoke (13.3 %), to demonstrate personal example (11.7 %), to give creative tasks (12.5 %), to teach to explore the environment (12.4 %), and to provide opportunities to select tasks and the way they are performed (11.7 %).

Comparing the research data according to different groups of respondents, it was found that the students aged 21–25 note more frequently than the other students that the teachers in their study programme develop critical thinking by teaching to analyse information, data, phenomena ($\chi2$=58560; df=8; $p<0.001$), purposefully provoking (χ=39.223; df=8; $p<0.001$), using role-playing games ($\chi2$=71.174; df=8; $p<0.001$) and teaching to doubt, not trust a single truth ($\chi2$=91.214; df=8; $p<0.001$). Meanwhile, younger students ($\leq$ 20 years old) note more frequently than others that teachers develop critical thinking by teaching to link practice and theory ($\chi2$=42.995; df=8; $p<0.001$) and by organising discussions ($\chi2$=46.646; df=8 $p<0.001$).

The students aged 26 years and over note more frequently than others that teachers very rarely/never teach critical thinking by: suggesting that they solve complex tasks, problems ($\chi2$=48.437; df=8; $p<0.001$), demonstrating personal example ($\chi2$=35.210; df=8; $p<0.001$), teaching to link causes and consequences ($\chi2$=46.276; df=8; $p<0.001$), giving non-standard tasks ($\chi2$=59.713; df=8; $p<0.001$), teaching to know oneself ($\chi2$=71.370; df=8; $p<0.001$), teaching to evaluate data reliability ($\chi2$=64.531; df=8; $p<0.001$), giving creative tasks ($\chi2$=77.596; df=8; $p<0.001$), teaching to explore the environment ($\chi2$=80.453; df=8; $p<0.001$), teaching to take responsibility for one's actions ($\chi2$=59.131; df=8; $p<0.001$), creating opportunities to learn from one another ($\chi2$=51.375; df=8; $p<0.001$), teaching to evaluate alternatives ($\chi 2=66.239$; df=8; $p<0.001$), teaching to look at the phenomenon from different perspectives ($\chi 2=81.458$; df=8; $p<0.001$), teaching to accept the opinions of others ($\chi 2=76.263$; df=8; $p<0.001$), teaching to recognise mistakes ($\chi 2=62.472$; df=8; $p<0.001$), creating opportunities to learn from mistakes ($\chi 2=85.186$; df=8; $p<0.001$) or providing opportunities to select tasks and the way they are performed ($\chi 2=67.926$; df=8; $p<0.001$).

Analysing the distribution of research data by the employment status of the students, it was found that the students who were only studying noted more frequently than the students who were both studying and working that during lectures and seminars, teachers often developed critical thinking by teaching to ask questions ($\chi 2=17.059$; df=4; $p<0.01$), organising discussions ($\chi 2=13.755$; df=4; $p<0.05$), teaching to link causes and consequences ($\chi 2=10.057$; df=4; $p<0.05$), teaching to know oneself ($\chi 2=30.789$; df=4; $p<0.001$) and providing opportunities to learn from mistakes ($\chi 2=23.263$; df=4; $p<0.001$).

The students who were both studying and working noted more frequently than the students who were only studying that during lectures and seminars, teachers rarely developed critical thinking by teaching to justify a choice/decision ($\chi 2=14.385$; df=4; $p<0.01$), using role-playing games ($\chi 2=19.279$; df=4; $p<0.01$) or teaching to take responsibility for one's actions ($\chi 2=16.820$; df=4; $p<0.01$).

Differences in the distribution of responses emerged when comparing the research data by type of higher education institution. The college students note more frequently than the university students that teachers often develop critical thinking by examining cases, situations ($\chi 2=15.527$; df=4; $p<0.01$) and solving complex tasks, problems ($\chi 2=17.981$; df=4; $p<0.01$). However, the college students note more frequently than the university students that teachers very rarely develop critical thinking by: teaching to link causes and consequences ($\chi 2=15.239$; df=4; $p<0.05$), teaching to evaluate data reliability ($\chi 2=16.117$; df=4; $p<0.05$), teaching to evaluate alternatives ($\chi 2=11.547$; df=4; $p<0.05$); teaching to accept the opinions of others ($\chi 2=16.80$; df=4; $p<0.05$) teaching to recognise mistakes ($\chi 2=22.666$; df=4; $p<0.001$) and providing opportunities to learn from mistakes ($\chi 2=11.699$; df=4; $p<0.05$). The university students note more frequently than the college students that teachers very often develop critical thinking by teaching to doubt, not trust, a single truth ($\chi 2=17.571$; df=4; $p<0.05$).

Evaluating the distribution of responses by gender, it was found that women note more frequently than men that teachers develop critical thinking by teaching to analyse information, data, phenomena ($\chi 2=19.611$; df=4; $p<0.01$), teaching to justify a choice/decision ($\chi 2=16.275$; df=4; $p<0.05$), teaching to link practice and theory ($\chi 2=17.112$; df=4; $p<0.05$), examining cases, situations ($\chi 2=20.654$; df=4; $p<0.001$), demonstrating personal example ($\chi 2=17.166$; df=4; $p<0.05$), teaching to link causes and consequences ($\chi 2=11.839$; df=4; $p<0.05$); giving creative tasks ($\chi 2=13.180$; df=4; $p<0.05$), creating opportunities to learn from one another ($\chi 2=13.748$; df=4; $p<0.05$), providing opportunities to learn from mistakes ($\chi 2=13.686$; df=4; $p<0.05$) and providing opportunities to select tasks and the way they are performed ($\chi 2=14.645$; df=4; $p<0.05$).

Students over the age of 26 and working students are more likely to believe that during lectures, teachers rarely teach to justify a choice/decision and take responsibility for one's actions.

The study sought to compare the ways in which critical thinking is most commonly developed. The teachers were, therefore, asked how often they use certain methods when working with students, and the students were asked how often teachers use the corresponding methods in developing critical thinking.

Based on the Mann-Whitney[41] non-parametric test for comparing independent samples, it was found that the students claimed much more strongly than the teachers that teachers develop critical thinking by:

- teaching to analyse information, data, phenomena, $p<0.001$ (mean rank, teacher responses – 596.68; mean rank, student responses – 856.21);
- examining cases, situations $p<0.001$ (mean rank, teacher responses – 614.2; mean rank, student responses – 854.45);
- providing feedback $p<0.001$ (mean rank, teacher responses – 615.75; mean rank, student responses – 854.29);
- organising discussions $p<0.001$ (mean rank, teacher responses – 627.33; mean rank, student responses – 853.13);
- teaching to link practice and theory $p<0.001$ (mean rank, teacher responses – 660.15; mean rank, student responses – 849.83);
- teaching to find the interrelations between phenomena $p<0.001$ (mean rank, teacher responses – 685.36; mean rank, student responses – 847.29);
- teaching to link causes and consequences $p<0.001$ (mean rank, teacher responses – 686.07; mean rank, student responses – 847.22);
- teaching to justify a choice/decision $p<0.001$ (mean rank, teacher responses – 686.73; mean rank, student responses – 847.15);
- teaching to ask questions $p<0.001$ (mean rank, teacher responses – 692.14; mean rank, student responses – 846.61);
- teaching to recognise mistakes $p<0.001$ (mean rank, teacher responses – 699.39; mean rank, student responses – 845.88);
- giving creative tasks $p<0.001$ (mean rank, teacher responses – 725.77; mean rank, student responses – 843.23);
- teaching to take responsibility for one's actions $p<0.01$ (mean rank, teacher responses – 731.33; mean rank, student responses – 842.67);
- solving complex tasks, problems $p<0.01$ (mean rank, teacher responses – 737.02; mean rank, student responses – 842.1);

41 *The Mann-Whitney criterion is calculated because the Kolmogorov-Smirnov statistics for the teacher sample showed that $p<0.05$, which means that the difference in the distribution from the normal is statistically significant, that is, the distribution is not normal and parametric analysis is not possible.*

- providing opportunities to learn from mistakes $p<0.01$ (mean rank, teacher responses – 742.91; mean rank, student responses – 841.51);
- creating opportunities to learn from one another $p<0.05$ (mean rank, teacher responses – 743.81; mean rank, student responses – 841.42);
- teaching to evaluate data reliability $p<0.05$ (mean rank, teacher responses – 750.5; mean rank, student responses – 840.74);
- purposefully provoking $p<0.05$ (mean rank, teacher responses – 758.57; mean rank, student responses – 839.93);
- teaching to accept the opinions of others $p<0.001$ (mean rank, teacher responses – 692.14; mean rank, student responses – 846.61);
- teaching to evaluate alternatives $p<0.05$ (mean rank, teacher responses – 755.87; mean rank, student responses – 840.23);
- teaches to look at phenomena from different perspectives $p<0.05$ (mean rank, teacher responses – 757.87; mean rank, student responses – 840.00);
- teachers claimed much more strongly than the students that they develop critical thinking by using role-playing games $p<0.05$ (mean rank, teacher responses – 914.15; mean rank, student responses – 824.29).

Analysis of the results revealed a significant difference of opinion in evaluating the following educational methods: teaching to analyse information, data, phenomena; examining cases, situations; organising discussions; teaching to link practice and theory; teaching to find the interrelations between phenomena.

It is important to note that the teachers believe that they use role-playing games more often during their lectures than the students do. When evaluating the other methods, the students note their use in the study process much more frequently than the teachers.

In summary, it can be stated that teachers develop critical thinking in the study process by teaching to link practice and theory, teaching to justify the chosen solution, and teaching to analyse information, data, phenomena. Role-playing games and teaching to know oneself are not popular ways of developing critical thinking in the study process.

2.8 The need to improve critical thinking skills

The study revealed how the teachers evaluate the need to improve their own critical thinking skills.[42] Using a 7-point Likert scale (*where 1 is 'no need at all' and 7 is 'a very strong need'*), the teachers were asked to evaluate the need for them, as teachers, to improve the abilities presented. Each statement had to be evaluated.

Analysis of the data obtained revealed that there is a very strong need among the teachers to improve their inference ability to formulate evidence-based conclusions (M_0=7), decision-making ability to make decisions collegially (M_0=6)

42 *The mode (Mo) is calculated – the most commonly recurring data set value.*

and justify a decision made to others (M_0=6), explanation ability to formulate questions for others (M_0=6) and answer others' questions (M_0=6), and analytical ability to examine a situation from different points of view (M_0=6) and collect data/information and link it to other data/sources (M_0=6).

The greatest need expressed by the teachers concerning development of inference skills was the ability to formulate evidence-based conclusions (M_0=7). They expressed slightly less of a need to improve their ability to formulate conclusions in anticipation of possible consequences (M_0=5), and the least need to improve their ability to summarise information (M_0=4) and formulate conclusions with regard to the context (M_0=4).

Among the constituents in the group of decision-making skills, the teachers expressed the greatest need to develop their ability to make decisions collegially (M_0=6) and justify a decision made to others (M_0=6). The teachers have a slightly lower need to improve their ability to formulate conclusions (M_0=4) and make decisions according to the procedures established in the organisation (M_0=4).

Among the explanation skills, it is most important for teachers to improve their ability to formulate questions for others (M_0=6), answer others' questions (M_0=6) and explain the decision-making path (M_0=5). The least relevant for teachers is to improve their ability to explain an analysis carried out and the results obtained (M_0=4), explain complex concepts (M_0=4) and reveal the essence of a phenomenon (M_0=4).

Regarding the analysis skills, it is most important for teachers to improve their ability to examine a situation from different points of view (M_0=6) and collect data/information and link it to other data/sources (M_0=6). It is somewhat less relevant for them to improve their ability to reveal connections between statements, facts, concepts (M_0=5) and find connections between the whole and its parts (M_0=4).

There is an equal need to improve all self-regulation skills, that is, the ability to know oneself (M_0=5), reflect (on one's thoughts, feelings, actions) (M_0=5) and change according to the situation (M_0=5).

The need for teachers to develop argumentation skills is also very even, that is, the ability to think based on facts/evidence (M_0=5), justify one's choices (M_0=5) and base actions on reflection (M_0=5).

In the group of interpretation skills, it is most important for teachers to improve their ability to classify data/information (M_0=5), convey data/information in one's own words (M_0=5) and discern essential information from supplementary information (M_0=5). Least relevant, in the evaluation of the teachers, is to improve their ability to understand the content of data/information (M_0=4).

As for the group of evaluation skills, it is most important for teachers to improve their ability to evaluate data/information with regard to different opinions (M_0=5) and evaluate a situation on the basis of data/information (M_0=5). Of slightly less relevance is improving their ability to evaluate/self-evaluate the decisions/conclusions made (M_0=4), and improving their ability to evaluate data/information without prejudice (M_0=3) is of the least relevance.

It was found that the older teachers (aged 50 and over) are more likely than the younger teachers to see a greater need to improve the ability in the group of interpretation skills to discern essential information from supplementary information. This is illustrated by the statistically significant difference found ($\chi2=14.417$; df=6; $p<0.05$).

The study also sought to determine how the teachers evaluate the need to improve their own critical thinking dispositions.[43] Using a 7-point Likert scale (*where 1 is 'no need at all' and 7 is 'a very strong need'*), the teachers were asked to evaluate the need for them, as teachers, to improve the critical thinking dispositions presented. Each statement had to be evaluated.

Analysis of the data obtained revealed that the teachers feel a strong need to improve their dispositions of courage ($M_0=6$) and perseverance ($M_0=6$). A bit less emphasis was placed on impartiality ($M_0=5$) and accuracy ($M_0=5$). It was least relevant for teachers to develop the dispositions of caring for other people ($M_0=4$), inquisitiveness ($M_0=4$), flexibility ($M_0=4$), attentiveness ($M_0=4$), scepticism ($M_0=4$), rightness ($M_0=4$), self-confidence ($M_0=3$) and open-mindedness ($M_0=3$). It should be noted that in the evaluation of the teachers, it is least relevant for them to develop a critical thinking disposition such as fairness ($M_0=1$).

It was found that the older teachers (aged 50 and over) are more likely than the younger teachers to see a greater need to improve the dispositions of impartiality ($\chi2=15.944$; df=6; $p<0.05$) and perseverance ($\chi2=14.099$; df=6; $p<0.05$).

The study sought to determine **the ways in which teachers improve their critical thinking skills**.[44] The teachers were asked to evaluate how often they use the different methods of developing critical thinking by ranking them on a 5-point scale (*'very rarely', 'rarely', 'neither rarely nor often', 'often', 'very often'*).

Analysis of the data obtained revealed that the teachers improve their critical thinking skills in different ways. Most often, the teachers read books (M=4.18). Less often, they engage in self-reflection (M=2.42) and participate in seminars, conferences (M=2.36), and least often they analyse the attitudes of others (M=1.96), analyse the environment, events, phenomena (M=1.78) and take an interest in current social issues (M=1.78). Thus, it can be argued that the main way of improving critical thinking skills is self-education.

The study also sought to determine the ways in which students improve their critical thinking skills. Analysis of the data obtained revealed that the students are fairly sluggish in improving their critical thinking skills.[45] Most often, the students participate in seminars, conferences (M=2.66), engage in self-reflection (M=2.59),

---

43 *The mode (Mo) is calculated – the most commonly recurring data set value.*

44 *The arithmetic mean (M) is calculated. The frequency of each statement was evaluated on a 5-point scale ('very rarely', 'rarely', 'neither rarely nor often', 'often', 'very often').*

45 *The arithmetic mean (M) is calculated. The frequency of each statement was evaluated on a 5-point scale ('very rarely', 'rarely', 'neither rarely nor often', 'often', 'very often').*

read books (M=2.54) and analyse the attitudes of others (M=2.5). Less often, they analyse the environment, events, phenomena (M=2.41) and take an interest in current social issues (M=2.41), and least often, they discuss with others (M=2.35).

The teachers' need to improve their critical thinking skills focuses on the level of interpersonal relationships – they try to improve their ability to make reasoned decisions collegially by arguing and presenting, and by arguing their choices. The greatest need to improve critical thinking dispositions is associated with the dispositions of courage and perseverance. The teachers expressed the least need for improvement in terms of the disposition of fairness.

Both the teachers and students develop their critical thinking skills by reading books, engaging in self-reflection and participating in training.

2.9 Attitude regarding who is responsible for developing critical thinking

The teachers and students were asked who they thought should be responsible for developing a person's critical thinking. The respondents had to evaluate the statements presented on a 7-point Likert scale (*'strongly disagree', 'disagree', 'somewhat disagree', 'neither agree nor disagree', 'somewhat agree', 'agree', 'strongly agree'*).

The higher education representatives (teachers and students) were found to agree that the person is responsible for developing his or her own critical thinking (teachers – M=6.32; students – M=6.1), and to a lesser extent that the organisation where the person works is responsible (teachers – M=4.79; students – M=4.7).[46] It should be noted that the attitude of the teachers and the students differs when evaluating the position of the higher education institution (teachers – M=5.12; students – M=4.85). The teachers note the role of the higher education institution more than the students do. Based on the Mann-Whitney[47] non-parametric test for comparing independent samples, it was found that the teachers agree much more strongly than the students that the higher education institution should be responsible for developing a person's critical thinking, $p<0.01$ (mean rank, teacher responses – 925.63; mean rank, student responses – 823.14).

It was important to clarify how the teachers and students think that the higher education institution where they work/study prepares professionals for the modern labour market. It turned out that the majority of the teachers (71.7 %) and students (74.4 %) have a positive view of the role of the higher education

46 *The arithmetic mean (M) is calculated. The frequency of each statement was evaluated* on a 7-point scale *('strongly disagree', 'disagree', 'somewhat disagree', 'neither agree nor disagree', 'somewhat agree', 'agree', 'strongly agree').*

47 *The Mann-Whitney criterion is calculated because the Kolmogorov-Smirnov statistics for the teacher sample showed that p<0.05, which means that the difference in the distribution from the normal is statistically significant, that is, the distribution is not normal and parametric analysis is not possible.*

institution in preparing professionals for the modern labour market. More than a quarter (27.6 %) of the teachers and a fifth (21.9 %) of the students do not have an opinion about how the higher education institution where they work/study prepares professionals for the modern labour market. Meanwhile, 0.7 % of the teachers and 3.7 % of the students have a negative view of preparation at the higher education institution.

The higher education representatives agree that the person is responsible for developing his or her own critical thinking, and to a lesser extent – that the organisation where the person works is responsible. The responsibility of the higher education institution is emphasised more by teachers than by students. This group has a positive view of the role of the higher education institution in preparing future professionals.

3. Attitude of Employers and Employees Towards Critical Thinking

3.1 Definition of critical thinking

The study sought to determine which of the definitions of critical thinking presented was the closest to the employers and employees who participated in the study. The employers and employees were given seven descriptions of critical thinking and asked to choose the one description that is most acceptable to them (Figure 24).

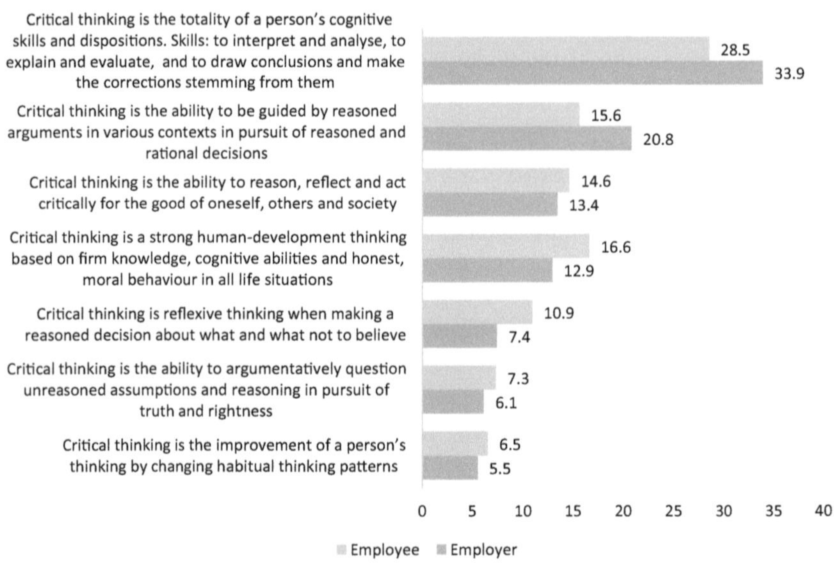

Fig. 24: *Definition of critical thinking, attitude of employers and employees, %*

It was found that both groups of respondents are most likely to describe critical thinking as the totality of a person's cognitive skills and dispositions (skills: to interpret and analyse, to explain and evaluate, and to draw conclusions and make the corrections stemming from them; personal dispositions: open-mindedness and inquisitiveness, analyticity and systematicity, trust in soundness and the pursuit of truth). Approximately, a third of the representatives of each study group (employers – 33.9 %; employees – 28.5 %) agree with this description.

However, the positions of the employers and the employees differ slightly concerning the other definitions of critical thinking. The most pronounced difference of opinion was found concerning the definition that critical thinking is the ability to be guided by reasoned arguments in various contexts in pursuit of reasoned and rational decisions, which a fifth (20.8 %) of the employers and a sixth (15.6 %) of the employees agree with. Meanwhile, 12.9 % of the employers and a 16.6 % of the employees agree with the statement that critical thinking is a strong human development thinking based on firm knowledge, cognitive abilities and honest, moral behaviour in all life situations. The third most popular in the evaluations of the employers (13.4 %) is the description of critical thinking as the ability to reason, reflect and act critically for the good of oneself, others and society; this description was fourth in the evaluations of the employees (14.6 %).

The evaluations of the other descriptions are similar. A tenth of the employees (10.9 %) and a slightly smaller percentage of the employers (7.4 %) agree with the statement that critical thinking is reflexive thinking when making a reasoned decision about what to and what not to believe. A similar portion of the employers (6.1 %) and the employees (7.3 %) tend to agree with the statement that critical thinking is the ability to argumentatively question unreasoned assumptions and reasoning in pursuit of truth and rightness. Only a small percentage of the employers (5.5 %) and employees (6.5 %) claim that critical thinking is the improvement of a person's thinking by changing habitual thinking patterns.

When analysing the opinions of the employers and employees on the conception of critical thinking, statistically significant differences were found. The employers agree more than the employees that critical thinking is the totality of a person's cognitive skills and dispositions, and that critical thinking is the ability to be guided by reasoned arguments in various contexts in pursuit of reasoned and rational decisions ($\chi 2=21.826$; $df=6$; $p<0.001$).

It can be argued that for the employers and employees, the conception of critical thinking is associated with certain personal skills and dispositions. However, the definition of critical thinking which focuses on the abilities necessary for the effectiveness of an organisation is more acceptable to the employers than to the employees. The least acceptable definition of critical thinking for both the employers and the employees is the understanding that critical thinking is the improvement of a person's thinking by changing habitual thinking patterns.

3.2 Manifestation and development of critical thinking

The study aimed to evaluate the attitude of employers towards the manifestation and development of critical thinking (Figure 25). Using a 7-point Likert scale (*where 1 is 'no attention at all' and 7 is 'particular attention'*), the employees were asked to evaluate the extent to which they agree or disagree with the statements presented about the manifestation and development of critical thinking.

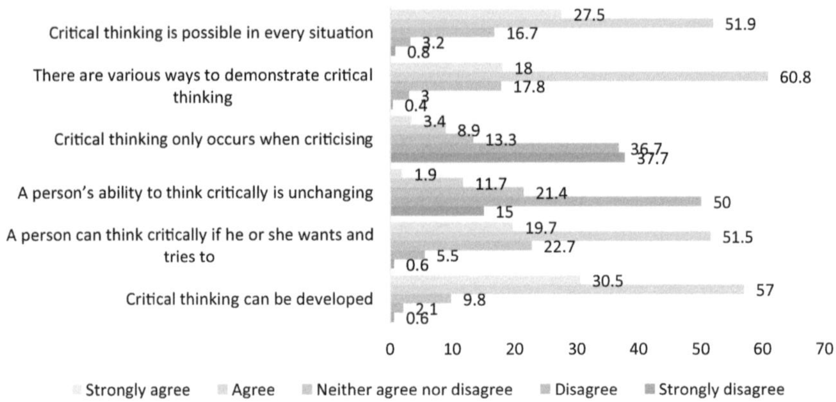

Fig. 25: *Manifestation of critical thinking, employer evaluation, %*

Evaluation of the attitude of the **employers** towards the manifestation and development of critical thinking (Figure 25) revealed that the majority of the employers (87.5 %) agree with the statement that critical thinking can be developed (30.5 % strongly agree; 57 % agree). Almost a tenth (9.8 %) of the employers who participated in the study said that they neither agreed nor disagreed with this statement, and 2.7 % of the subjects said that they did not agree.

The majority (79.4 %) of the employers who participated in the study agreed with the statement that critical thinking is possible in every situation (27.5 % strongly agreed; 51.9 % agreed). 16.7 % of the employers neither agreed nor disagreed with this statement, and 4 % did not agree (3.2 % disagreed; 0.8 % strongly disagreed).

Slightly more than three-quarters of the employers (78 %) agree with the statement that there are various ways to demonstrate critical thinking (18 % strongly agree; 60 % agree). Slightly less than a fifth (17.8 %) of the respondents neither agreed nor disagreed with this statement, and only 3.4 % did not agree with this statement (0.4 % strongly disagreed; 3 % disagreed).

Almost two-thirds (65 %) of the employers who participated in the study did not agree with the statement that a person's ability to think critically is unchanging (15 % strongly disagreed; 50 % disagreed). Meanwhile, a fifth (21.4 %) of the employers who participated in the study said they neither agree nor disagree with this statement, and 13.6 % agreed with it (1.9 % strongly agreed; 11.7 % agreed).

The opinions of the employers differed more regarding the statement that a person can think critically if he or she wants and tries to, which 71.2 % of the employers who participated in the study agreed with (19.7 % strongly agreed; 51.5 % agreed). However, more than a fifth (22.7 %) said they neither agreed nor disagreed with this statement, and 6.1 % did not agree with this statement (0.6 % strongly disagreed; 5.5 % disagreed).

Three-quarters of the employers (74.4 %) disagreed with the statement that critical thinking only occurs when criticising (37.7 % strongly disagreed; 36.7 % disagreed). The statement that critical thinking only occurs when criticising was something that slightly over a tenth of the employers agreed with (12.3 %: 3.4 % strongly agreed; 8.9 % agreed), while 13.3 % neither agreed nor disagreed with this statement.

Analysis of the data showed that compared to the older employers, the employers aged 40 or less more frequently do not have a clear opinion in evaluating the statement that critical thinking only occurs when criticising ($\chi2=15.506$; df=4; $p<0.05$). However, comparing the distribution by gender revealed that men are more likely to agree than women with the statement that critical thinking only occurs when criticising ($\chi2=18.822$; df=4; $p<0.01$).

The research data obtained suggest that the employers tend to view critical thinking as a dynamic ability, that is, one that is developing and changing. However, every tenth employer notes that critical thinking only occurs when criticising, and this is more typical of male respondents.

The study aimed to evaluate **the attitude of employees towards the manifestation and development of critical thinking** (Figure 26). Using a 5-point Likert scale (*'strongly disagree', 'disagree', 'neither agree nor disagree', 'agree', 'strongly agree'*), the employees were asked to evaluate the extent to which they agree or disagree with the statements presented about the manifestation and development of critical thinking (Figure 26).

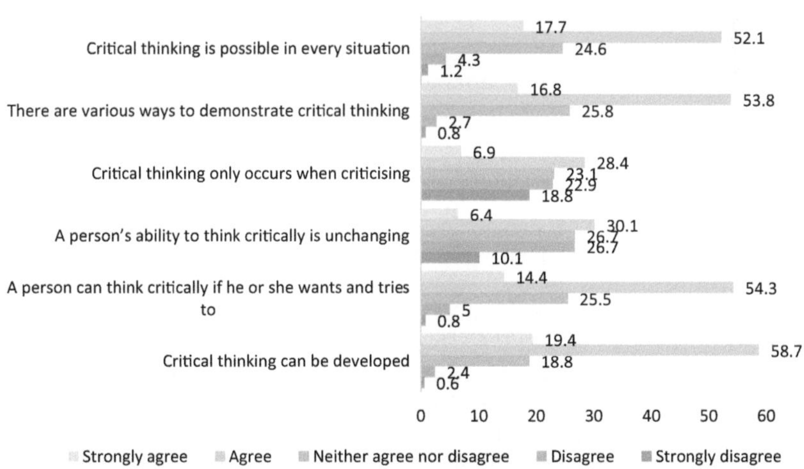

Fig. 26: *Manifestation of critical thinking, employee evaluation, %*

Evaluation of the attitude of the employees towards the manifestation and development of critical thinking (Figure 27) revealed that the majority of the employees (78.1 %) agree with the statement that critical thinking can be developed (19.4 % strongly agree; 58.7 % agree). Almost a fifth (18.8 %) of the employers who participated in the study said that they neither agreed nor disagreed with this statement, and 3 % of the subjects said that they did not agree (0.6 % strongly disagreed; 2.4 % disagreed).

Slightly less than three-quarters (70.6 %) of the employees agreed with the statement that there are various ways to demonstrate critical thinking (16.8 % strongly agreed; 53.8 % agreed). Roughly a quarter (25.8 %) of the respondents neither agreed nor disagreed with this statement, and only 3.5 % did not agree with the statement (0.8 % strongly disagreed; 2.7 % disagreed).

The statement that critical thinking is possible in every situation was something that 69.8 % of the employers who participated in the survey agreed with (17.7 % strongly agreed; 52.1 % agreed). 24.6 % of the respondents neither agreed nor disagreed with this statement, and 5.5 % did not agree (1.2 % strongly disagreed; 4.3 % disagreed).

Almost 68.7 % of the employees who participated in the study agreed with the statement that a person can think critically if he or she wants and tries to (14.4 % strongly agree; 54.3 % agree). However, more than a fifth (25.5 %) said they neither agreed nor disagreed with this statement, and 5.8 % did not agree with this statement (0.8 % strongly disagreed; 5 % disagreed).

The employees more or less evenly evaluate the statement that a person's ability to think critically is unchanging. Almost 36.8 % of the respondents did not agree with this statement (10.1 % strongly disagreed; 26.7 % disagreed), while 36.5 % did agree with this statement (6.4 % strongly agreed; 30.1 % agreed), and more than a quarter (26.7 %) of respondents said that they neither agreed nor disagreed with this statement.

More than a third (35.3 %) of the employees agreed with the statement that critical thinking only occurs when criticising (6.9 % strongly agreed; 28.4 % agreed). Just less than half (41.7 %) of the respondent did not agree with this statement (18.8 % strongly disagreed; 22.9 % disagreed). Approximately, a fifth (22.9 %) of the respondents disagree with the statement, and almost a quarter (23.1 %) neither agree nor disagree.

Comparing the distribution by gender revealed that men are more likely to agree than women with the statements that critical thinking can be developed ($\chi 2=44.283$; df=4; $p<0.001$) and that a person can think critically if he or she wants and tries to ($\chi 2=10.607$; df=4; $p<0.05$). Men are also more likely not to have an opinion when evaluating the statements that there are various ways to demonstrate critical thinking ($\chi 2=14.192$; df=4; $p<0.05$) and that critical thinking is possible in every situation ($\chi 2=12.178$; df=4; $p<0.05$). Meanwhile, women are more likely than men to strongly disagree with the statement that critical thinking only occurs when criticising ($\chi 2=132.956$; df=4; $p<0.001$).

The employees who had a post-secondary education were more likely than the other employees to agree that a person's ability to think critically is unchanging

($\chi 2=117.900$; df=8; $p<0.001$). Those with higher university education were more likely than the other employees to agree that critical thinking only occurs when criticising ($\chi 2=165.606$; df=8; $p<0.001$).

Comparing the responses by age revealed that the employers aged 40 or less were more likely than the employees over 40 years old to neither agree nor disagree that critical thinking can be developed ($\chi 2=45.156$; df=4; $p<0.001$), a person can think critically if he or she wants and tries to ($\chi 2=13.996$; df=4; $p<0.01$), critical thinking only occurs when criticising ($\chi 2=131.608$; df=4; $p<0.001$) and there are various ways to demonstrate critical thinking ($\chi 2=37.115$; df=4; $p<0.01$).

It turned out that the employers aged 40 or less were more likely than the older employees to agree that a person's ability to think critically is unchanging ($\chi 2=74.468$; df=4; $p<0.01$). Meanwhile, the older employers (≥ 41 years) were more likely than the younger employees to strongly agree that critical thinking is possible in every situation ($\chi 2=58.263$; df=4; $p<0.01$).

It was found that the employees who work in a medium-sized enterprise (51–250 employees) were more likely than the other employees to disagree that a person's ability to think critically is unchanging ($\chi 2=162.505$; df=12; $p<0.001$). Meanwhile, the employees who work in small enterprises (11–50 employees) are more likely than the others to agree that a person's ability to think critically is unchanging ($\chi 2=162.505$; df=12; $p<0.001$) and to strongly agree with the statement that critical thinking only occurs when criticising ($\chi 2=223.145$; df=12; $p<0.001$).

It can thus be argued that employees tend to think that critical thinking can manifest itself in different ways and in different situations, and depends on a person's desire and efforts. It is worth noting that while the employees agree with the statement that critical thinking can be developed, more than a third indicate that the ability to think critically is unchanging. The same percentage of respondents believe that critical thinking only occurs when criticising. Furthermore, this statement illustrating the manifestation of critical thinking is more often supported by men and employees with a university education. The study found that younger employees are more likely not to have an opinion when evaluating the manifestation of critical thinking and opportunities for developing it. Male respondents are more likely to agree that critical thinking depends on the person and can be developed.

Comparing the employer and employee evaluations of the manifestation and development of critical thinking, a statistically significant difference was found between the opinions of the employers and the employees. Based on the Mann-Whitney[48] non-parametric test for comparing independent samples, it was found that the employers, compared to the employees, agree more that:

---

48 *The Mann-Whitney criterion is calculated because the Kolmogorov-Smirnov statistics for the employer sample showed that $p<0.05$, which means that the difference in the distribution from the normal is statistically significant, that is, the distribution is not normal and parametric analysis is not possible.*

- critical thinking only occurs when criticising, $p<0.001$ (mean rank, employer responses – 1632.48; mean rank, employee responses – 1175.51);
- a person's ability to think critically is unchanging, $p<0.001$ (mean rank, employer responses – 1586.56; mean rank, employee responses – 1187.56);
- critical thinking can be developed, $p<0.001$ (mean rank, employer responses – 1431.77; mean rank, employee responses – 1228.18);
- there are various ways to demonstrate critical thinking, $p<0.01$ (mean rank, employer responses – 1344.9; mean rank, employee responses – 1250.97);
- critical thinking is possible in every situation, $p<0.001$ (mean rank, employer responses – 1416.81; mean rank, employee responses – 1323.1);
- a person can think critically if he or she wants and tries to $p<0.05$ (mean rank, employer responses – 1327.54; mean rank, employee responses – 1255.53).

Evaluation of the data presented revealed a highly significant difference of opinion regarding two statements that the employers agree with more than the employees – that critical thinking only occurs when criticising and that a person's ability to think critically is unchanging. A small but significant difference of opinion was found regarding one statement that the employers tended to agree with more than the employees – that critical thinking can be developed. Very small but still significant differences of opinion were found regarding three other statements that the employers tended to agree with more than the employees – that there are various ways to demonstrate critical thinking, that critical thinking is possible in every situation, and that a person can think critically if he or she wants and tries to.

In summarising the opinions of the employees and employers about the manifestation and development of critical thinking, it can be stated that both groups of respondents see critical thinking as a person's abilities that can manifest themselves in various situations. It is important to note that the prevailing opinion in both groups is that critical thinking is developed and depends on each person's desire and efforts.

3.3 The importance of critical thinking skills in the modern labour market

The study sought to determine how employers evaluate the importance of critical thinking skills in the modern labour market.[49] Using a 7-point Likert scale (*where 1 is 'not important at all' and 7 is 'very important'*), the employers were asked to evaluate the importance in the modern labour market of each ability presented.

The employers identified the following as being the most important critical thinking skills in the modern labour market: inference (M=6.02), argumentation (M=5.95), interpretation (M=5.92), evaluation (M=5.91) and self-regulation

49 *The arithmetic mean (M) is calculated. The frequency of each statement was evaluated on a 7-point scale, where 1 is 'not important at all' and 7 is 'very important'.*

(M=5.91). They put slightly less emphasis on the importance of explanation (M=5.86) and decision-making (M=5.84) skills. According to the employers, analysis skills (M=5.79) are not so important in the modern labour market.

In the group of inference skills, the employers believe that the ability to formulate conclusions in anticipation of possible consequences (M=6.13), the ability to formulate evidence-based conclusions (M=6.09) and the ability to summarise information (M=6.06) are of particular importance in the labour market. The employers consider the ability to formulate conclusions with regard to the context (M=5.83) to be of less significance here.

As the most important argumentation skills in the modern labour market, the employers identified the ability to think based on facts/evidence (M=6.04) and to justify one's choices (M=6.04); the ability to base actions on reflection (M=5.79) was identified as less important.

Among the interpretation skills, the employers believe that the ability to understand the content of data/information (M=6.06) and the ability to discern essential information from supplementary information (M=6.06) are particularly important in the modern labour market. The employers consider the ability to classify data/information (M=5.8) and the ability to convey data/information in one's own words (M=5.79) to be of less importance.

The employers identified the most important evaluation skills in the modern labour market as being the ability to evaluate a situation on the basis of data/information (M=6.03) and to evaluate/self-evaluate the decisions/conclusions made (M=6.02). They attach the less importance to the ability to evaluate data/information without prejudice (M=5.95) and to evaluate data/information with regard to different opinions (M=5.67).

When evaluating the importance of self-regulation skills in the modern labour market, the employers identified the ability to change according to the situation (M=6.02) and to know oneself (M=5.96) as being the most important. Less importance is given to the ability to reflect (on one's thoughts, feelings, actions) (M=5.75).

When evaluating the importance of explanation skills in the modern labour market, the employers identified the ability to explain an analysis carried out and the results obtained (M=6.07) as being the most important; a bit less importance was given to the ability to reveal the essence of a phenomenon (M=5.96), to answer others' questions (M=5.95) and to formulate questions for others (M=5.91). Less important in the modern labour market, according to the employers, are the ability to explain the decision-making path (M=5.69) and the ability to explain complex concepts (M=5.63).

According to the employers, the most important ability when making decisions in the modern labour market is to justify the decision made to others (M=5.93); slightly less importance is given to the ability to formulate conclusions (M=5.85), to make decisions collegially (M=5.84) and to make decisions according to the procedures established in the organisation (M=5.79).

In the group of analysis skills, the employers single out the ability to examine a situation from different points of view (M=5.88) and to collect data/information and link it to other data/sources (M=5.85). They consider the ability to find connections between the whole and its parts (M=5.77) to be important, and the ability to reveal connections between statements, facts, concepts (M=5.68) to be not so important. No statistically significant differences were found between the critical thinking skills and demographic and social factors (gender, age, type of organisation, education, size of organisation, management experience).

The study also sought to determine **the employees' opinion regarding the most important abilities in the modern labour market**. Using a 7-point Likert scale *(where 1 is 'not important at all' and 7 is 'very important')*, the employees were asked to evaluate the importance in the modern labour market of each ability presented.[50]

The employees identified the following as being the most important critical thinking skills in the modern labour market: self-regulation (M=5.7), argumentation (M=5.62), decision-making (M=5.51) and inference (M=5.5). The employees put slightly less emphasis on the importance of explanation (M=5.46) and interpretation (M=5.3) skills in the modern labour market, and the least on analysis (M=5.23) and evaluation (M=5.23) skills.

When evaluating the importance of self-regulation skills in the modern labour market, the employees identified the ability to know oneself (M=5.8) and the ability to change according to the situation (M=5.7) as being the most important. Less importance was given to the ability to reflect (on one's thoughts, feelings, actions) (M=5.61).

As the most important argumentation skills in the modern labour market, the employees identified the ability to justify one's choices (M=5.69) and to think based on facts/evidence (M=5.66). The ability to base actions on reflection (M=5.51) was noted as less important.

According to the employees, the most important ability when making decisions in the modern labour market is to make decisions according to the procedures established in the organisation (M=5.56); slightly less importance is given to the ability to justify a decision made to others (M=5.53) and to make decisions collegially (M=5.51). Even less importance is attached to the ability to formulate conclusions (M=5.45).

In the group of inference skills, the employees believe that the ability to formulate conclusions in anticipation of possible consequences (M=5.86) and the ability to formulate evidence-based conclusions (M=5.54) are of particular importance in the labour market; of less importance are the ability to summarise information (M=5.49) and the ability to formulate conclusions with regard to the context (M=5.41).

---

50 *The arithmetic mean (M) is calculated. The frequency of each statement was evaluated on a 7-point scale, where 1 is 'not important at all' and 7 is 'very important'.*

When evaluating the importance of individual explanation skills in the modern labour market, the employees identified the ability to explain an analysis carried out and the results obtained (M=5.56), to reveal the essence of a phenomenon (M=5.55) and to answer others' questions (M=5.5) as being the most important. The ability to explain the decision-making path (M=5.41), to formulate questions for others (M=5.39) and to explain complex concepts (M=5.38) were identified as being slightly less important.

Among the interpretation skills, the employees believe that the ability to understand the content of data/information (M=5.39) and the ability to discern essential information from supplementary information (M=5.38) are particularly important in the modern labour market. Less importance was given to the ability to convey data/information in one's own words (M=5.24) and to classify data/information (M=5.18).

According to the employees, the most important analysis skills in the modern labour market are the ability to collect data/information and link it to other data/sources (M=5.31) and to examine a situation from different points of view (M=5.28). The ability to find connections between the whole and its parts (M=5.23) is noted as an important skill in the modern labour market, and the ability to reveal connections between statements, facts, concepts (M=5.14) is considered to be not so important skill in this group.

The employees identified the most important evaluation skills in the modern labour market as being the ability to evaluate/self-evaluate the decisions/conclusions made (M=5.36) and to evaluate a situation on the basis of data/information (M=5.29); of less importance were the ability to evaluate data/information without prejudice (M=5.24) and to evaluate data/information with regard to different opinions (M=5.02).

Comparing the distribution by gender revealed that female employees are more likely than male employees to recognise the importance in the modern labour market of the ability to answer others' questions ($\chi2=130.977$; df=6; $p<0.001$) and to evaluate data/information with regard to different opinions ($\chi2=78.816$; df=6; $p<0.001$).

The employees aged 41 years and over noted more frequently than the employees in the other age groups that it is very important in the modern labour market to be able to reason a decision made to others ($\chi2=121.465$; df=6; $p<0.001$), formulate questions for others ($\chi2=119.414$; df=6; $p<0.001$), answer others' questions ($\chi2=135.692$; df=6; $p<0.001$), reveal the essence of a phenomenon ($\chi2=166.143$; df=6; $p<0.001$), know oneself ($\chi2=166.135$; df=6; $p<0.001$), reflect ($\chi2=135.221$; df=6; $p<0.001$), evaluate data/information with regard to different opinions ($\chi2=98.777$; df=6; $p<0.001$), evaluate data/information without prejudice ($\chi2=102.674$; df=6; $p<0.001$).

The study sought to compare how the group of labour market representatives (employers and employees) evaluates the importance of critical thinking skills in the modern labour market. Based on the Mann-Whitney[51] non-parametric test for comparing independent samples, it was found that the employers, more than the employees, emphasise the importance of these skills in the modern labour market:

- evaluation p<0.001 (mean rank, employer responses – 1567.67; mean rank, employee responses – 1192.51);
- interpretation p<0.001 (mean rank, employer responses – 1547.61; mean rank, employee responses – 1197.78);
- argumentation p<0.001 (mean rank, employer responses – 1433.44; mean rank, employee responses – 1221.63);
- analysis p<0.001 (mean rank, employer responses – 1511.49; mean rank, employee responses – 1207.28);
- inference p<0.001 (mean rank, employer responses – 1508.15; mean rank, employee responses – 1208.13);
- explanation p<0.001 (mean rank, employer responses – 1221.63; mean rank, employee responses – 1456.73);
- decision-making p<0.001 (mean rank, employer responses – 1433.07; mean rank, employee responses – 1227.84).

It should be noted that the opinions of the employers and employees were similar (no statistically significant difference was found) in evaluating the importance of self-regulation skills in the modern labour market p<0.001 (mean rank, employer responses – 1376.05; mean rank, employee responses – 1242.8).

However, a pronounced difference of opinion was found in the evaluation of the importance of interpretation, evaluation, analysis and inference skills. The employers emphasise the importance of these skills in the modern labour market more than the employees do. A slightly smaller difference of opinion was found in the evaluation of the importance of argumentation, decision-making and explanation skills in the modern labour market.

The study asked the employers and employees to evaluate the importance in the modern labour market of the constituents of each critical thinking skill group. Based on the Mann-Whitney[52] non-parametric test for comparing independent samples, it was found that the employers stress more strongly than the employees the importance of the following constituents of critical thinking skills in the labour market:

---

51 *The Mann-Whitney criterion is calculated because the Kolmogorov-Smirnov statistics for the employer sample showed that p<0.05, which means that the difference in the distribution from the normal is statistically significant, that is, the distribution is not normal and parametric analysis is not possible.*

52 *The Mann-Whitney criterion is calculated because the Kolmogorov-Smirnov statistics for the employer sample showed that p<0.05, which means that the difference in the distribution from the normal is statistically significant, that is, the distribution is not normal and parametric analysis is not possible.*

Evaluation skills:

- evaluate a situation on the basis of data/information p<0.001 (mean rank, employer responses – 1557.84; mean rank, employee responses – 1195.09);
- evaluate data/information without prejudice p<0.001 (mean rank, employer responses – 1540.43; mean rank, employee responses – 1199.66);
- evaluate/self-evaluate the decisions/conclusions made p<0.001 (mean rank, employer responses – 1537.1; mean rank, employee responses – 1200.54);
- evaluate data/information with regard to different opinions p<0.001 (mean rank, employer responses – 1526.41; mean rank, employee responses – 1203.34).

Interpretation skills:

- discern essential information from supplementary information p<0.001 (mean rank, employer responses – 1549.48; mean rank, employee responses – 1197.29);
- understand the content of data/information p<0.001 (mean rank, employer responses – 1536.88; mean rank, employee responses – 1200.6);
- classify data/information p<0.001 (mean rank, employer responses – 1525.88; mean rank, employee responses – 1203.48);
- convey data/information in one's own words p<0.001 (mean rank, employer responses – 1486.9; mean rank, employee responses – 1213.71).

Inference skills:

- summarise information p<0.001 (mean rank, employer responses – 1511.19; mean rank, employee responses – 1207.34);
- formulate conclusions in anticipation of possible consequences p<0.001 (mean rank, employer responses – 1498.91; mean rank, employee responses – 1210.56);
- formulate evidence-based conclusions p<0.001 (mean rank, employer responses – 1469.4; mean rank, employee responses – 1211.22);
- formulate conclusions with regard to the context p<0.001 (mean rank, employer responses – 1447.34; mean rank, employee responses – 1224.09).

Analysis skills:

- examine a situation from different points of view p<0.001 (mean rank, employer responses – 1506.36; mean rank, employee responses – 1208.6);
- reveal connections between statements, facts, concepts p<0.001 (mean rank, employer responses – 1497.05; mean rank, employee responses – 1211.05);
- find connections between the whole and its parts p<0.001 (mean rank, employer responses – 1492.57; mean rank, employee responses – 1212.22);
- collect data/information and link it to other data/sources p<0.001 (mean rank, employer responses – 1486.52; mean rank, employee responses – 1213.81).

Explanation skills:

- explain an analysis carried out and the results obtained p<0.001 (mean rank, employer responses – 1501.19; mean rank, employee responses – 1209.96);

- formulate questions for others $p<0.001$ (mean rank, employer responses – 1493.23; mean rank, employee responses – 1212.05);
- answer others' questions $p<0.001$ (mean rank, employer responses – 1458.94; mean rank, employee responses – 1221.05);
- explain the decision-making path $p<0.001$ (mean rank, employer responses – 1391.21; mean rank, employee responses – 1238.82);
- explain complex concepts $p<0.001$ (mean rank, employer responses – 1374.41; mean rank, employee responses – 1243.23);
- reveal the essence of a phenomenon $p<0.001$ (mean rank, employer responses – 1445.45; mean rank, employee responses – 1224.59).

Decision-making skills:

- make decisions collegially $p<0.001$ (mean rank, employer responses – 1423.06; mean rank, employee responses – 1230.46);
- make decisions according to the procedures established in the organisation $p<0.001$ (mean rank, employer responses – 1371.48; mean rank, employee responses – 1244);
- formulate conclusions $p<0.001$ (mean rank, employer responses – 1451.71; mean rank, employee responses – 1222.94);
- justify a decision made to others $p<0.001$ (mean rank, employer responses – 1463.68; mean rank, employee responses – 1219.8).

Argumentation skills:

- base actions on reflection $p<0.001$ (mean rank, employer responses – 1397.61; mean rank, employee responses – 1237.14);
- think based on facts/evidence $p<0.001$ (mean rank, employer responses – 1453.42; mean rank, employee responses – 1222.5);
- justify one's choices $p<0.001$ (mean rank, employer responses – 1430.47; mean rank, employee responses – 1228.52).

Self-regulation skills:

- reflect (on one's thoughts, feelings, actions) $p<0.05$ (mean rank, employer responses – 1340.79; mean rank, employee responses – 1252.05);
- know oneself $p<0.01$ (mean rank, employer responses – 1346.51; mean rank, employee responses – 1250.55);
- change according to the situation $p<0.001$ (mean rank, employer responses – 1418.68; mean rank, employee responses – 1231.61).

The employers put considerably more emphasis than the employees on evaluation skills (evaluate a situation on the basis of data/information; evaluate data/information without prejudice; evaluate/self-evaluate the decisions/conclusions made; evaluate data/information with regard to different opinions) and on interpretation skills (discern essential information from supplementary information; understand the content of data/information; classify data/information).

Analysis of the data revealed a significant difference of opinion between the employers and the employees. The employers put stronger emphasis than the employees on inference skills (summarise information; formulate conclusions in anticipation of possible consequences; formulate evidence-based conclusions), analysis skills (examine a situation from different points of view; reveal connections between statements, facts, concepts; find connections between the whole and its parts; collect data/information and link it to other data/sources), and explanation skills (explain an analysis carried out and the results obtained; formulate questions for others).

A small but significant difference of opinion between the employers and the employees was found in their evaluation of decision-making skills (make decisions collegially; make decisions according to the procedures established in the organisation) and argumentation skills (base actions on reflection). A very small but still significant difference of opinion between the employers and the employees was found in their evaluation of the importance in the modern labour market of the self-regulation skills of reflecting (on one's thoughts, feelings, actions) and knowing oneself.

In summary, it can be stated that the employers consider the abilities in the groups of evaluation and interpretation skills to be more important than the employees do. It should be noted that the employers value the importance of self-regulation skills slightly more than the employees do. However, in the opinion of the employees, the ability to know oneself and the ability to reflect (on one's thoughts, feelings, actions) are the most important skills in the labour market.

Both the employers and the employees consider the abilities attributed to the group of inference skills as being the most important critical thinking skills in the modern labour market. The employers also consider explanation and interpretation skills to be important. Meanwhile, the employees consider the abilities in the group of self-regulation skills as well as the abilities in the groups of argumentation and decision-making skills to be the most important. Both the employees and the employers consider abilities related to anticipating, explaining and evaluating a particular process or decision path in the broader context as being the less important.

3.4 The importance of critical thinking dispositions in the modern labour market

The study sought to determine how employers evaluate the importance of critical thinking dispositions in the modern labour market.[53] Using a 7-point Likert scale (*where 1 is 'not important at all' and 7 is 'very important'*), the employers were

53 *The arithmetic mean (M) is calculated. The frequency of each statement was evaluated on a 7-point scale, where 1 is 'not important at all' and 7 is 'very important'.*

asked to evaluate the importance in the modern labour market of each critical thinking disposition presented.

According to the employers, the most important critical thinking dispositions in the modern labour market are fairness (M=6.27), rightness (M=6.23), accuracy (M=6.09), flexibility (M=6.02) and self-confidence (M=6.02). Important dispositions are attentiveness (M=5.97), impartiality (M=5.95), caring for other people (M=5.9), perseverance (M=5.89) and endurance (M=5.79).

The employers identified scepticism (M=4.45), open-mindedness (M=5.32), inquisitiveness (M=5.4) and courage (M=5.71) as being the less important critical thinking dispositions in the modern labour market.

No statistically significant differences were found between dispositions and demographic and social factors (gender, age, type of organisation, education, size of organisation, management experience).

Using a 7-point Likert scale (*where 1 is 'not important at all' and 7 is 'very important'*), the **employees** were asked to evaluate the importance in the modern labour market of each critical thinking disposition presented.[54]

According to the employees, the most important critical thinking dispositions in the modern labour market are rightness (M=5.9), self-confidence (M=5.87), fairness (M=5.83), attentiveness (M=5.78) and flexibility (M=5.73). Important dispositions are accuracy (M=5.71), perseverance (M=5.65), endurance (M=5.62), courage (M=5.55) and caring for other people (M=5.53).

The employees identified scepticism (M=4.47), open-mindedness (M=5.13), inquisitiveness (M=5.22) and impartiality (M=5.3) as being the less important critical thinking dispositions in the modern labour market.

Comparing the distribution by gender revealed that female employees are more likely than male employees to recognise the importance of the following critical thinking dispositions in the modern labour market: impartiality ($\chi2=176.536$; df=6; $p<0.001$); fairness ($\chi2=148.816$; df=6; $p<0.001$), caring for other people ($\chi2=104.872$; df=6; $p<0.001$), flexibility ($\chi2=122.249$; df=6; $p<0.001$), endurance ($\chi2=68.142$; df=6; $p<0.001$), courage ($\chi2=35.580$; df=6; $p<0.001$), perseverance ($\chi2=61.132$ df=6; $p<0.001$), rightness ($\chi2=85.172$; df=6; $p<0.001$). Meanwhile, men noted more frequently than women that inquisitiveness is not important at all for the modern labour market ($\chi2=29.728$; df=6; $p<0.001$).

The employees who had a post-secondary education were more likely than the other employees to note that open-mindedness is very important for the modern labour market ($\chi2=22.180$; df=12; $p<0.05$).

The employers who were over 40 years old were more likely than the younger employees to note that the following dispositions are very important for the modern labour market: impartiality ($\chi2=122.122$; df=6; $p<0.001$), fairness ($\chi2=137.912$; df=6; $p<0.001$), caring for other people ($\chi2=102.260$; df=6; $p<0.001$),

54 *Importance in the labour market on a 7-point scale, where 1 is 'not important at all' and 7 is 'very important'.*

inquisitiveness ($\chi 2=26.516$; df=6; $p<0.001$), flexibility ($\chi 2=78.915$; df=6; $p<0.001$), attentiveness ($\chi 2=103.942$; df=6; $p<0.001$), endurance ($\chi 2=72.038$; df=6; $p<0.001$), courage ($\chi 2=76.504$; df=6; $p<0.001$), perseverance ($\chi 2=93.992$; df=6; $p<0.001$), open-mindedness ($\chi 2=49.4963$; df=6; $p<0.001$), rightness ($\chi 2=167.425$; df=6; $p<0.001$). Meanwhile, the younger employers (≤ 40 years) were more likely than the others to note that scepticism is not important at all for the modern labour market ($\chi 2=65.526$; df=6; $p<0.001$).

Furthermore, the employees who work in a microenterprise (≤ 10 employees) note more frequently than the others that scepticism is not important at all in the modern labour market ($\chi 2=147.136$; df=18; $p<0.001$).

Analysis of the research data was aimed at comparing how employers and employees evaluate the importance of individual dispositions in the labour market. Based on the Mann-Whitney[55] non-parametric test for comparing independent samples, it was found that the employers stress much more strongly than the employees the importance of the following critical thinking dispositions in the modern labour market:

- impartiality $p<0.001$ (mean rank, employer responses – 1535.92; mean rank, employee responses – 1200.85);
- fairness $p<0.001$ (mean rank, employer responses – 1489.66; mean rank, employee responses – 1212.99);
- accuracy $p<0.001$ (mean rank, employer responses – 1452.44; mean rank, employee responses – 1222.75);
- caring for other people $p<0.001$ (mean rank, employer responses – 1429.1; mean rank, employee responses – 1228.88);
- rightness $p<0.001$ (mean rank, employer responses – 1414.09; mean rank, employee responses – 1232.82);
- flexibility $p<0.001$ (mean rank, employer responses – 1399.37; mean rank, employee responses – 1236.68);
- perseverance $p<0.001$ (mean rank, employer responses – 1374.77; mean rank, employee responses – 1243.14);
- attentiveness $p<0.01$ (mean rank, employer responses – 1357.78; mean rank, employee responses – 1247.6);
- endurance $p<0.05$ (mean rank, employer responses – 1335.63; mean rank, employee responses – 1253.41);
- inquisitiveness $p<0.05$ (mean rank, employer responses – 1334.23; mean rank, employee responses – 1253.78);

55 *The Mann-Whitney criterion is calculated because the Kolmogorov-Smirnov statistics for the employer sample showed that $p<0.05$, which means that the difference in the distribution from the normal is statistically significant, that is, the distribution is not normal and parametric analysis is not possible.*

- self-confidence $p<0.05$ (mean rank, employer responses – 1334.82; mean rank, employee responses – 1253.62);
- courage $p<0.05$ (mean rank, employer responses – 1325.29; mean rank, employee responses – 1256.12).

It should be noted that when evaluating critical thinking dispositions such as open-mindedness and scepticism, no difference of opinion was found ($p> 0.05$).

Thus, a highly significant difference of opinion was found in that the employers stress much more strongly than the employees the importance of the qualities of impartiality, fairness and accuracy for the labour market. A small but significant difference of opinion was found in that the employers put stronger emphasis than the employees on the importance of caring for other people, rightness and flexibility for the labour market. A very small but still significant difference of opinion was recorded between how the employers and the employees evaluated the importance of courage, inquisitiveness and self-confidence in the labour market.

The opinions of both the employers and the employees on the critical thinking dispositions that are important for the modern labour market were basically the same. Fairness, rightness, flexibility and self-confidence are valued. Meanwhile, scepticism, open-mindedness and inquisitiveness are valued the least. Impartiality, caring for other people, endurance, courage and perseverance are the qualities that women and older employees consider the most important. Scepticism is the least important critical thinking disposition for those working in small enterprises and for younger employees.

3.5 Manifestation of critical thinking in the professional activities of employees

Analysis of the research data revealed the attitude of employers towards how their employees' critical thinking is manifested in professional activities (Figure 27). Using a 5-point Likert scale (*'strongly disagree', 'disagree', 'neither agree nor disagree', 'agree', 'strongly agree'*), the employers were asked to evaluate how the critical thinking of their direct subordinates is manifested (in order to show the differences, the responses *'strongly disagree'* and *'disagree'* were combined into one level – *'disagree'*, and the responses *'agree'* and *'strongly agree'* were combined into one level – *'agree'*).

According to the **employers** (Figure 27), the critical thinking of their direct subordinates is manifested the most in crisis situations, when problems have to be solved. The majority of the employers who participated in the survey agreed (i.e. agreed or strongly agreed) that in professional activities, employees' critical thinking is manifested in justified and motivated decisions (82 %), targeted knowledge application in practice (79.7 %), the ability to act in non-standard situations (76.9 %) and collegial decision-making in crisis situations (76.3 %). Also noted were the ability to make decisions expeditiously (75.4 %), formulate conclusions (74.4 %) and verify the reliability of information (73.7 %). It was found that the employers associate the manifestation of critical thinking with the ability to spot errors and imperfections at work (73.3 %), the personal assumption of responsibility in acting (73.1 %) and the ability to perform comprehensive problem analysis (72.8 %).

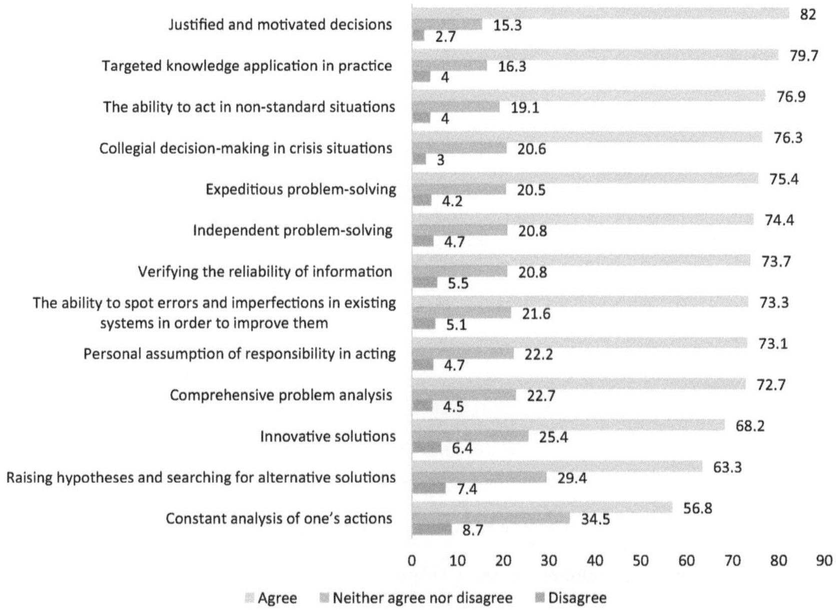

Fig. 27: *Manifestation of critical thinking in employees' professional activities, attitude of employers, %*

Analysis of the data showed that the employers aged 40 or less were more likely than the older employers to disagree that the critical thinking of their direct subordinates is manifested in justified and motivated decisions ($\chi 2=18.092$; df=3; $p<0.001$).

When evaluating the responses by gender, it was found that the male employers were more likely than the female employers to neither agree nor disagree that the critical thinking of their direct subordinates is manifested in collegial decision-making in crisis situations ($\chi 2=16.098$; df=3; $p<0.01$).

Thus, the manifestation of critical thinking in professional activities is most associated by the employers with the employees' ability to react expeditiously to the situation at hand and responsibly make a reasoned decision, either independently or in interpersonal interaction. From the point of view of the employers, employees' critical thinking is also reflected in the ability to delve fully into a problem, using existing knowledge and looking for new knowledge.

The employees were also asked how critical thinking manifests itself in their professional activities. Using a 5-point Likert scale (*'strongly disagree', 'disagree', 'neither agree nor disagree', 'agree', 'strongly agree'*), the employees were asked to evaluate how critical thinking manifests itself in their professional activities (in order to show the differences, the responses *'strongly disagree'* and *'disagree'* were combined into one level – *'disagree'*, and the responses *'agree'* and *'strongly agree'* were combined into one level – *'agree'*).

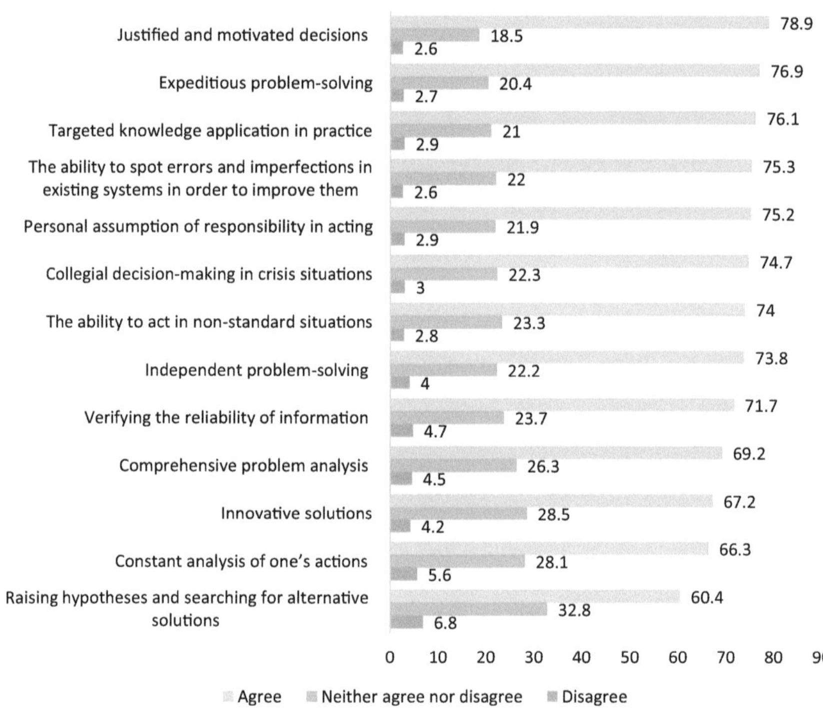

Fig. 28: *Manifestation of critical thinking in employees' professional activities, attitude of employees, %*

The majority of the employees agreed (Figure 28) that in their professional activities, critical thinking is manifested in justified and motivated decisions (78.9 %), expeditious problem-solving (76.9 %), targeted knowledge application in practice (76.1 %), the ability to spot errors and imperfections at work (75.3 %) and personal assumption of responsibility in acting (75.2 %). The employees associate the manifestation of critical thinking with the level of independent problem-solving. The employees broadly agreed with the statements that critical thinking is manifested in collegial decision-making in crisis situations (74.7 %), the ability to act in non-standard situations (74 %) and independent problem-solving (73.8 %).

The vast majority of the respondents agreed with the statements that critical thinking is manifested in verifying the reliability of information (71.7 %) and comprehensive problem analysis (69.2 %).

Data distribution by gender shows that female employees are more likely than male employees to strongly agree that in their professional activities, critical thinking manifests itself as collegial decision-making in crisis situations ($\chi2=54.178$; $df=4$; $p<0.001$), verifying the reliability of information ($\chi2=65.347$; $df=4$; $p<0.001$) and comprehensive problem analysis ($\chi2=55.611$; $df=4$; $p<0.001$). Meanwhile, the male employers were more likely than the female employers to not have an opinion (neither agree nor disagree) that in their professional activities, critical thinking manifests itself as raising hypotheses and searching for alternative solutions ($\chi2=17.158$; $df=4$; $p<0.01$) or constant analysis of one's actions ($\chi2=23.631$; $df=4$; $p<0.001$).

The older employers (≥ 41 years) were more likely than the others to agree that in their professional activities, critical thinking is manifested through justified and motivated decisions ($\chi2=79.858$; $df=4$; $p<0.001$), comprehensive problem analysis ($\chi2=98.474$; $df=4$; $p<0.001$), raising hypotheses and searching for alternative solutions ($\chi2=32.908$; $df=4$; $p<0.001$), constant analysis of one's actions ($\chi2=77.624$; $df=4$; $p<0.001$) and innovative solutions ($\chi2=88.820$; $df=4$; $p<0.001$).

Hence, the manifestation of critical thinking in professional activities is most associated by the employees with decision-making abilities at the personal and interpersonal level. According to the employees, critical thinking is also strongly expressed in the context of information and knowledge management. The research data show that the female employees and the older male employees are more inclined to agree that critical thinking is manifested in professional activities through the ability to analyse and verify information.

Analysis of the data was aimed at comparing the attitudes of the employers and the employees towards how critical thinking is manifested in the professional activities of employees. Based on the Mann-Whitney[56] non-parametric test for comparing independent samples, it was found that the employers are more likely than the employees to believe that critical thinking is manifested in the professional activities of employees through collegial decision-making in crisis situations $p<0.05$ (mean rank, employer responses – 1336.17; mean rank, employee responses – 1253.27) and justified and motivated decisions $p<0.05$ (mean rank, employer responses – 1324.7; mean rank, employee responses – 1256.28).

56 *The Mann-Whitney criterion is calculated because the Kolmogorov-Smirnov statistics for the employer sample showed that p<0.05, which means that the difference in the distribution from the normal is statistically significant, that is, the distribution is not normal and parametric analysis is not possible.*

Meanwhile, the employees are more likely than the employers to believe that critical thinking is manifested in the professional activities of employees through constant analysis of one's actions p<0.001 (mean rank, employer responses – 1170.53; mean rank, employee responses – 1296.73).

Evaluation of the data presented revealed a significant difference of opinion in that the employers stress much more strongly than the employees that critical thinking is manifested in collegial decision-making in crisis situations and justified and motivated decisions. Meanwhile, the employees, differently from the employers, put more emphasis on critical thinking as the constant analysis of one's actions.

3.6. The need to improve critical thinking skills

The employers were asked to evaluate the need for their direct subordinates to improve their critical thinking skills.[57] Using a 7-point Likert scale (*where 1 is 'no need at all' and 7 is 'a very strong need'*), the employers were asked to evaluate the need for their direct subordinates to improve the abilities presented. The respondents had to evaluate each statement presented.

It was found that in the opinion of the employers, the greatest need for their direct subordinates is to improve their inference (M=4.99), decision-making (M=4.92), argumentation (M=4.87) and self-regulation (M=4.85) skills. The need to improve their evaluation (M=4.79), explanation (M=4.78), analysis (M=4.72) and interpretation (M=4.72) skills was moderate.

Analysis of the research data according to the constituents of the critical thinking skills revealed that in the group of inference skills, the employers believe that employees first and foremost need to improve their ability to formulate conclusions in anticipation of possible consequences (M=5.13) and their ability to formulate evidence-based conclusions (M=4.98). The employers evaluated the ability to summarise information (M=4.95) and to formulate conclusions with regard to the context (M=4.92) as being slightly less important.

In evaluating the need for their direct subordinates to improve their decision-making skills, the employers primarily stressed the need to improve their ability to formulate conclusions (M=4.99), to justify a decision made to others (M=4.96) and to make decisions collegially (M=4.93). Less emphasis was placed on the need to improve the ability to make decisions according to the procedures established in the organisation (M=4.81).

In the argumentation skill group, the employers rated the ability to think based on facts/evidence (M=4.92) and to justify one's choices (M=4.88) as the most important abilities that their employees need to improve. The need for employees

57 *The arithmetic mean (M) is calculated. The frequency of each statement was evaluated on a 7-point scale, where 1 is 'no need at all' and 7 is 'a very strong need'.*

to improve their ability to base actions on reflection (M=4.82) was evaluated as being slightly less important.

In the self-regulation group, the employers especially emphasised the need for their direct subordinates to improve their ability to change according to the situation (M=5.12), but improving their ability to know themselves (M=4.71) and to reflect (on their thoughts, feelings, actions) (M=4.72) was considered much less important.

In evaluating the need for their direct subordinates to improve their evaluation skills, the employers first identified the need to improve their ability to evaluate data/information without prejudice (M=4.86) and to evaluate/self-evaluate the decisions/conclusions made (M=4.83). The need for employees to improve their ability to evaluate a situation on the basis of data/information (M=4.77) and to evaluate data/information with regard to different opinions (M=4.72) was less expressed.

In terms of the constituents of the group of explanation skills, the employers believe that employees should concentrate on improving their ability to explain an analysis carried out and the results obtained (M=4.87) and to reveal the essence of a phenomenon (M=4.86). The ability to formulate questions for others (M=4.83) and to answer others' questions (M=4.83) were seen as being in slightly less need of improvement. The employers are of the opinion that it is of average importance for employees to improve their ability to explain the decision-making path (M=4.76) and to explain complex concepts (M=4.75).

In evaluating the need for their direct subordinates to improve their analysis skills, the employers noted that the most important thing for employees would be to improve their ability to examine a situation from different points of view (M=4.82) and to find connections between the whole and its parts (M=4.78). Less in need of improvement are the ability to collect data/information and link it to other data/sources (M=4.83) and the ability to reveal connections between statements, facts, concepts (M=4.7).

In the group of interpretation skills, the employers believe that their employees should improve their ability to discern essential information from supplementary information (M=4.83) more than their ability to understand the content of data/information (M=4.7), to classify data/information (M=4.67) or to convey data/information in their own words (M=4.67).

No statistically significant differences were found between critical thinking skills and demographic and social factors (gender, age, type of organisation, education, size of organisation, management experience).

In summary, it should be noted that the employers single out the ability to formulate conclusions in anticipation of possible consequences and to change according to the situation as the most important abilities that their employees need to improve. However, the employers point to inference and decision-making skills as the greatest need in terms of employee development. The employers see the least need for employee improvement in the interpretation and analysis skill groups.

Relationship between the employers' attitudes to the importance of critical thinking skills in the modern labour market and the need for their improvement among subordinates (Figure 29).[58] It was found that employers, in identifying the most important ability in the modern labour market as being the ability to formulate conclusions (M=6.02), specify a need to improve this ability in terms of their subordinates (M=4.99). Analysis of the research data revealed that the more the employers note that inference is important in the modern labour market, the more they believe that their subordinates need to improve this ability (r_s=0.218; p<0.001).

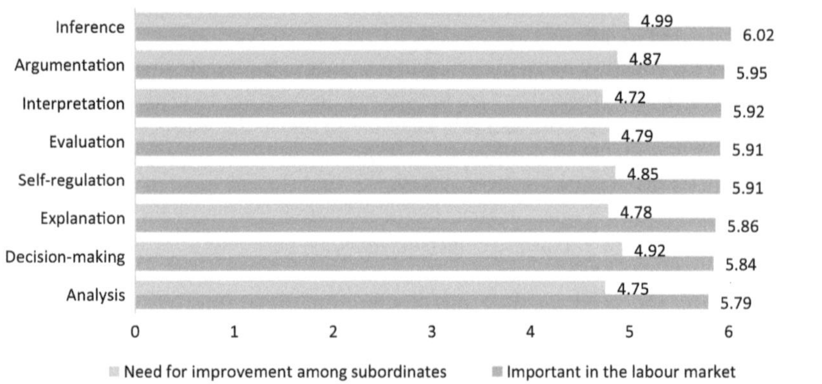

Fig. 29: *Relationship between the employers' attitudes to the importance of critical thinking skills in the modern labour market and the need for their improvement among subordinates.*

The **employees** were asked to evaluate how much they need to improve their critical thinking skills.[59] To this end, they were asked to use a 7-point Likert scale (*where 1 is 'no need at all' and 7 is 'a very strong need'*) to evaluate their need, as employees, to improve their critical thinking skills. The respondents had to evaluate each statement presented.

It was found that the employees expressed the greatest need to improve their decision-making (M=5.12), argumentation (M=5.06), self-regulation (M=5.1) and inference (M=5) skills. The need for employees to improve their explanation

58 *The arithmetic mean (M) is calculated. The frequency of each need was evaluated on a 7-point scale, where 1 is 'no need at all' and 7 is 'a very strong need'. Importance in the labour market on a 7-point scale, where 1 is 'not important at all' and 7 is 'very important'.*

59 *The arithmetic mean (M) is calculated. The frequency of each need was evaluated on a 7-point scale, where 1 is 'no need at all' and 7 is 'a very strong need'.*

(M=4.97), analysis (M=4.72), interpretation (M=4.69) and evaluation (M=4.64) skills was considered to be of average importance.

Analysis of the research data according to the constituents of the critical thinking skills revealed that in the group of decision-making skills, the employees put the most emphasis on the need to improve their ability to make decisions collegially (M=5.16) and to make decisions according to the procedures established in the organisation (M=5.14). The need to improve the ability to reason a decision made to others (M=5.12) and to formulate conclusions (M=5.09) was considered to be slightly less important.

In evaluating the need to improve their argumentation skills, the employees first and foremost identified the ability to reason their choices (M=5.11) and to think based on facts/evidence (M=5.08). The employees expressed less of a need to improve their ability to base actions on reflection (M=5.01).

The employees particularly expressed a need to improve their self-regulation skills of knowing themselves (M=5.27), changing according to the situation (M=5.24) and reflecting (on their thoughts, feelings, actions) (M=5.12).

Of the inference skills presented, the employees felt that they should concentrate on improving their ability to formulate conclusions in anticipation of possible consequences (M=5.09) and to formulate evidence-based conclusions (M=5.03). However, the employees consider the other inference skills presented to be equally important, namely, the ability to formulate conclusions with regard to the context (M=4.96) and to summarise information (M=4.95).

In the group of explanation skills, the employees felt that they most needed to improve their ability to reveal the essence of a phenomenon (M=5.03) and to answer others' questions (M=5). The ability to explain complex concepts (M=4.98), to explain an analysis carried out and the results obtained (M=4.98) and to explain the decision-making path (M=4.96) require slightly less improvement. According to the employees, the need to improve their ability to formulate questions for others (M=4.92) was less pronounced.

In the group of analysis skills, the employees felt that they most needed to improve their ability to examine a situation from different points of view (M=4.75) and to collect data/information and link it to other data/sources (M=4.75). The employees note the ability to find connections between the whole and its parts (M=4.74) and to reveal connections between statements, facts, concepts (M=4.66) as being in need of improvement.

In the group of interpretation skills, the employees believe that they should improve their ability to discern essential information from supplementary information (M=4.75) and to understand the content of data/information (M=4.73). The employees expressed slightly less of a need to improve their ability to convey data/information in their own words (M=4.68) and to classify data/information (M=4.62).

Compared to the other skill groups, the employees expressed less of a need to improve their evaluation skills. In this skill group, the greatest need is to improve their ability to evaluate/self-evaluate the decisions/conclusions made (M=4.76) and to evaluate a situation on the basis of data/information (M=4.67). The employees are of the opinion that there is slightly less of a need to improve their ability to evaluate data/information without prejudice (M=4.64) and to evaluate data/information with regard to different opinions (M=4.52).

Data distribution by gender shows that female employees are more likely than male employees to note that there is a strong need to improve their ability to formulate conclusions (χ2=37.749; df=6; p<0.001), summarise information (χ2=28.963; df=6; p<0.001), formulate evidence-based conclusions (χ2=22.870; df=6; p<0.001), formulate conclusions with regard to the context (χ2=14.145; df=6; p<0.001), formulate conclusions in anticipation of possible consequences (χ2=19.360; df=6; p<0.001), formulate questions for others (χ2=34.629; df=6; p<0.001), answer others' questions (χ2=30.379; df=6; p<0.001), explain an analysis carried out and the results obtained (χ2=32.146; df=6; p<0.001), explain the decision-making path (χ2=30.061; df=6; p<0.001), explain complex concepts (χ2=25.221; df=6; p<0.001), examine a situation from different points of view (χ2=19.910; df=6; p<0.001), classify data/information (χ2=34.279; df=6; p<0.001), understand the content of data/information (χ2=19.954; df=6; p<0.001), convey data/information in one's own words (χ2=24.582; df=6; p<0.001), evaluate data/information without prejudice (χ2=25.882; df=6; p<0.001).

Meanwhile, men are more likely than women to note that there is a sufficiently strong need to improve their ability to make decisions collegially (χ2=26.843; df=6; p<0.001) and to know themselves (χ2=35.089; df=6; p<0.001).

Male employees are also more likely than female employees not to have an opinion (to neither agree nor disagree) when evaluating the ability to justify a decision made to others (χ2=40.824; df=6; p<0.001) and to make decisions according to the procedures established in the organisation (χ2=55.489; df=6; p<0.001).

Those with a non-university higher education specify more frequently than the others that there is a serious/very strong need to improve their ability to explain an analysis carried out and the results obtained (χ2=22.205; df=12; p<0.01), explain the decision-making path (χ2=27.024; df=12; p<0.01), reflect (χ2=39.419; df=12; p<0.001). These employees are also more likely than the others to not have an opinion regarding the ability to classify data/information (χ2=42.125; df=12; p<0.001) and to understand the content of data/information (χ2=39.199; df=12; p<0.001).

The older employers (≥ 41 years) were more likely than the others to note that there is a very strong need to improve their ability to make decisions collegially (χ2=82.451; df=6; p<0.001), justify a decision made to others (χ2=91.148; df=6; p<0.001), make decisions according to the procedures established in the organisation (χ2=110.990; df=6; p<0.001), summarise information (χ2=76.140; df=6; p<0.001), formulate evidence-based conclusions (χ2=80.658; df=6; p<0.001), formulate conclusions with regard to the context (χ2=65.088; df=6; p<0.001), formulate conclusions in anticipation of possible consequences (χ2=84.296; df=6; p<0.001), formulate questions for others (χ2=77.547; df=6; p<0.001), answer others' questions (χ2=111.946; df=6; p<0.001), explain an analysis carried out and the results obtained ($\chi2=81.709$; df=6; $p<0.001$), explain the decision-making path ($\chi2=89.412$; df=6; $p<0.001$), explain complex concepts ($\chi2=76.421$; df=6; $p<0.001$), reveal the essence of a phenomenon ($\chi2=113.677$; df=6; $p<0.001$), reveal connections between statements, facts, concepts ($\chi2=34.140$; df=6; $p<0.001$), examine a situation from different points of view ($\chi2=56.477$; df=6; $p<0.001$), find connections between the whole and its parts ($\chi2=37.411$; df=6; $p<0.001$), collect data/information and link it to other data/sources ($\chi2=61.571$; df=6; $p<0.001$), know oneself ($\chi2=82.451$; df=6; $p<0.001$), reflect ($\chi2=76.751$; df=6; $p<0.001$), change according to the situation ($\chi2=109.379$; df=6; $p<0.001$), think based on facts/evidence ($\chi2=64.443$; df=6; $p<0.001$), justify one's choices ($\chi2=72.873$; df=6; $p<0.001$), base actions on reflection ($\chi2=54.153$; df=6; $p<0.001$), classify data/information ($\chi2=49.481$; df=6; $p<0.001$), understand the content of data/information ($\chi2=76.563$; df=6; $p<0.001$), convey data/information in one's own words ($\chi2=69.806$; df=6; $p<0.001$), discern essential information from supplementary information ($\chi2=70.332$; df=6; $p<0.001$), evaluate data/information with regard to different opinions ($\chi2=40.706$; df=6; $p<0.001$), evaluate data/information without prejudice ($\chi2=45.087$; df=6; $p<0.001$), evaluate a situation on the basis of data/information ($\chi2=69.495$; df=6; $p<0.001$), evaluate the decisions/conclusions made ($\chi2=65.382$; df=6; $p<0.001$).

In summarising the need expressed by the employees for improving skills, it should be noted that the representatives of this group consider the most important skills that need improvement to be abilities attributed to the decision-making and argumentation skill groups, expressed at both the personal and interpersonal level. It is also very important for the employees to improve their self-regulation skills. It can be argued that the need for employees to improve their ability to know themselves, to reflect on their thoughts and actions, and to change is focused on each employee's personal development, that is, it is attributable to the personal level. The employees expressed the least need to improve abilities related to information or data processing.

It should be noted that the male employees feel a greater need than the female employees to improve skills related to self-knowledge and the ability to solve problems in cooperation with colleagues. The employees with a higher non-university education feel a greater need to improve abilities related to explaining to others. In addition, the employees aged 41 and over feel a greater need to develop all of their critical thinking skills.

Relationship between the employees' attitudes to the importance of critical thinking skills in the modern labour market and the need for their improvement (Figure 30).[60]

60 *The arithmetic mean (M) is calculated. The frequency of each need was evaluated on a 7-point scale, where 1 is 'no need at all' and 7 is 'a very strong need'. Importance in the labour market on a 7-point scale, where 1 is 'not important at all' and 7 is 'very important'.*

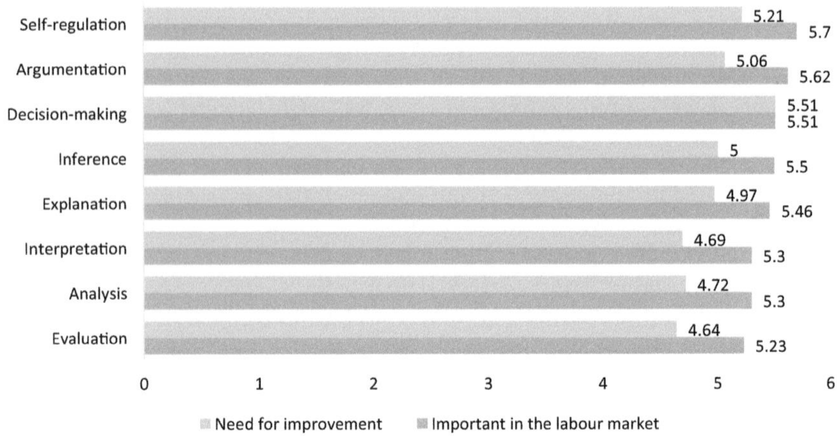

Fig. 30: *Relationship between the employees' attitudes to the importance of critical thinking skills in the modern labour market and the need for their improvement*

It was found that employees, in identifying self-regulation (M=5.7) as the most important critical thinking skill in today's labour market, specify a need to improve this ability (M=5.21). Analysis of the research data revealed that the more the employees believe that self-regulation is important in the modern labour market, the more they note that they need to improve this ability (r_s=0.452; p<0.001). The study compares the attitudes of the employers and the employees regarding the extent to which employees need to develop specific critical thinking skills. Based on the Mann-Whitney[61] non-parametric test for comparing independent samples, it was found that the employees note more frequently than the employers that they need to improve the following skills:

- decision-making p<0.01 (mean rank, employer responses – 1175.07; mean rank, employee responses – 1295.54);
- explanation p<0.01 (mean rank, employer responses – 1178.19; mean rank, employee responses – 1294.73);
- self-regulation p<0.001 (mean rank, employer responses – 1096.81; mean rank, employee responses – 1316.08);

61 *The Mann-Whitney criterion is calculated because the Kolmogorov-Smirnov statistics for the employer sample showed that p<0.05, which means that the difference in the distribution from the normal is statistically significant, that is, the distribution is not normal and parametric analysis is not possible.*

- argumentation $p<0.01$ (mean rank, employer responses – 1180.88; mean rank, employee responses – 1294.02).

Based on Mann-Whitney test,[62] it was found that the employees note more frequently than the employers that they need to improve the following constituents of critical thinking skills:

Self-regulation skills:

- know oneself $p<0.001$ (mean rank, employer responses – 1043.19; mean rank, employee responses – 1330.15);
- reflect (on one's thoughts, feelings, actions) $p<0.001$ (mean rank, employer responses – 1108.29; mean rank, employee responses – 1313.07).

Decision-making skills:

- make decisions according to the procedures established in the organisation $p<0.001$ (mean rank, employer responses – 1152.51; mean rank, employee responses – 1301.46);
- make decisions collegially $p<0.01$ (mean rank, employer responses – 1180.21; mean rank, employee responses – 1294.19);
- change according to the situation $p<0.05$ (mean rank, employer responses – 1205; mean rank, employee responses – 1287.69).

Explanation skills:

- answer others' questions $p<0.001$ (mean rank, employer responses – 1162.44; mean rank, employee responses – 1298.86);
- formulate questions for others $p<0.01$ (mean rank, employer responses – 1184.3; mean rank, employee responses – 1293.12);
- explain complex concepts $p<0.01$ (mean rank, employer responses – 1184.71; mean rank, employee responses – 1293.01);
- explain the decision-making path $p<0.01$ (mean rank, employer responses – 1193.02; mean rank, employee responses – 1290.83);
- reveal the essence of a phenomenon $p<0.05$ (mean rank, employer responses – 1199.58; mean rank, employee responses – 1289.11).

Argumentation skills:

- justify one's choices $p<0.01$ (mean rank, employer responses – 1180.93; mean rank, employee responses – 1294.01);
- base actions on reflection $p<0.05$ (mean rank, employer responses – 1187.58; mean rank, employee responses – 1292.26);

62 *The Mann-Whitney criterion is calculated because the Kolmogorov-Smirnov statistics for the employer sample showed that $p<0.05$, which means that the difference in the distribution from the normal is statistically significant, that is, the distribution is not normal and parametric analysis is not possible.*

- think based on facts/evidence $p<0.05$ (mean rank, employer responses – 1203.03; mean rank, employee responses – 1288.21).

Meanwhile, the employers note more frequently than the employees that employees need to improve the following evaluation skill constituents:

- evaluate data/information without prejudice $p<0.01$ (mean rank, employer responses – 1343.28; mean rank, employee responses – 1251.4);
- evaluate data/information with regard to different opinions $p<0.05$ (mean rank, employer responses – 1339.9; mean rank, employee responses – 1252.29).

Thus, a statistically significant difference between the employers and the employees was found in their evaluation of the need for employees to improve their decision-making skills (make decisions according to the procedures established in the organisation; make decisions collegially) and their explanation skills (formulate questions for others; explain complex concepts).

Analysis of the research data revealed that the employees stress much more strongly than the employers that they need to improve their self-regulation skills (know oneself; reflect [on one's thoughts, feelings, actions]). So, unlike the employers who evaluated the need of the employees working in their company to improve individual abilities, the employees placed particular emphasis on the need to improve their self-regulation skills.

3.7 The need to improve critical thinking dispositions

In the questionnaire, the employers were asked to evaluate how much their direct subordinates need to improve the critical thinking dispositions given.[63] Using a 7-point Likert scale (*where 1 is 'no need at all' and 7 is 'a very strong need'*), the employers were asked to evaluate the need for their direct subordinates to improve the critical thinking dispositions given. The respondents had to evaluate each statement.

According to the employers, their direct subordinates most need to improve the dispositions of flexibility (M=4.81), self-confidence (M=4.77) and accuracy (M=4.7); the need to improve the dispositions of attentiveness (M=4.64), impartiality (M=4.64), rightness (M=4.59), perseverance (M=4.57), courage (M=4.47), endurance (M=4.41), caring for other people (M=4.4) and open-mindedness (M=4.39) was considered to be slightly less important. The employers believe that their direct subordinates moderately need to improve the critical thinking dispositions of scepticism (M=3.67), inquisitiveness (M=4.29) and fairness (M=4.3).

Analysis of the data showed that the employers aged 40 or less were more likely than the older employers to be undecided as to whether their direct subordinates

63 *The arithmetic mean (M) is calculated. The frequency of each statement was evaluated on a 7-point scale, where 1 is 'no need at all' and 7 is 'a very strong need'.*

need to improve the following critical thinking dispositions: impartiality ($\chi2=14.388$; df=6; $p<0.05$), accuracy ($\chi2=33.734$; df=6; $p<0.001$); self-confidence ($\chi2=28.998$; df=6; $p<0.001$); rightness ($\chi2=25.316$; df=6; $p<0.001$). These employers were also more inclined to agree that their direct subordinates do not need to improve the following critical thinking dispositions: fairness ($\chi2=28.678$; df=6; $p<0.001$); inquisitiveness ($\chi2=20.144$; df=6; $p<0.01$); attentiveness ($\chi2=22.577$; df=6; $p<0.01$); endurance ($\chi2=17.757$; df=6; $p<0.01$); perseverance ($\chi2=14.210$; df=6; $p<0.05$); open-mindedness ($\chi2=22.214$; df=6; $p<0.01$). The employers aged 40 and under especially note that there is absolutely no need to develop scepticism ($\chi2=12.754$; df=6; $p<0.05$) as a critical thinking disposition.

During the study, **the employees were also asked to evaluate their need, as employees, to improve their critical thinking dispositions.**[64] To this end, they were asked to use a 7-point Likert scale (*where 1 is 'no need at all' and 7 is 'a very strong need'*) to evaluate their need to improve the given critical thinking dispositions. The respondents had to evaluate each statement.

It was found that the employees believe that they most need to improve their dispositions of self-confidence (M=5.21), rightness (M=4.96), perseverance (M=4.96), courage (M=4.96), attentiveness (M=4.92) and flexibility (M=4.92). The employees expressed the least need to improve their dispositions of scepticism (M=4.15), impartiality (M=4.47), open-mindedness (M=4.56) and inquisitiveness (M=4.59).

Data distribution by gender shows that female employees are more likely than male employees to note that there is a very strong need to improve the following critical thinking dispositions: impartiality ($\chi2=37.766$; df=6; $p<0.001$), accuracy ($\chi2=42.176$; df=6; $p<0.001$), caring for other people ($\chi2=69.360$; df=6; $p<0.001$), self-confidence ($\chi2=39.701$; df=6; $p<0.001$), flexibility ($\chi2=44.212$; df=6; $p<0.001$).

The employees who had a post-secondary education were more likely than the others to note that there is a very strong need to improve the following critical thinking dispositions: accuracy ($\chi2=44.041$; df=12; $p<0.001$), fairness ($\chi2=82.402$; df=12; $p<0.001$), caring for other people ($\chi2=62.306$; df=12; $p<0.001$), inquisitiveness ($\chi2=55.501$; df=12; $p<0.001$), attentiveness ($\chi2=51.337$; df=12; $p<0.001$), endurance ($\chi2=42.127$; df=12; $p<0.001$), perseverance ($\chi2=39.469$; df=12; $p<0.001$), open-mindedness ($\chi2=44898$; df=12; $p<0.001$).

It was found that the employees who work according to a business certificate/self-employment certificate were more likely than the others to note that there is a very strong need to improve the critical thinking disposition of fairness ($\chi2=30.996$; df=18; $p<0.001$). On the other hand, the same group of respondents claimed more often than any other that there is no need to improve open-mindedness ($\chi2=29.635$; df=12; $p<0.001$).

64 *The arithmetic mean (M) is calculated. The frequency of each statement was evaluated on a 7-point scale, where 1 is 'no need at all' and 7 is 'a very strong need'.*

Analysis of the data showed that the employees who work in small enterprises (11–50 employees) were more likely than the other employees to note that there is a very strong need to improve the following critical thinking dispositions: impartiality ($\chi2=170.670$; df=18; $p<0.001$), accuracy ($\chi2=122.770$; df=18; $p<0.001$), fairness ($\chi2=169.350$; df=18; $p<0.001$), caring for other people ($\chi2=117.209$; df=18; $p<0.001$), inquisitiveness ($\chi2=91.668$; df=18; $p<0.001$), flexibility ($\chi2=130.592$; df=18; $p<0.001$), attentiveness ($\chi2=130.969$; df=18; $p<0.001$), endurance ($\chi2=114.935$; df=18; $p<0.001$), courage ($\chi2=115.140$; df=18; $p<0.001$), perseverance ($\chi2=148.558$; df=18; $p<0.001$), open-mindedness ($\chi2=128.663$; df=18; $p<0.001$), rightness ($\chi2=239.793$; df=18; $p<0.001$).

The employees aged 41 or more were more likely than the others to note that there is a very strong need to improve the following critical thinking dispositions: fairness ($\chi2=85.905$; df=6; $p<0.001$), caring for other people ($\chi2=52.751$; df=6; $p<0.001$), inquisitiveness ($\chi2=21.992$; df=6; $p<0.001$), self-confidence ($\chi2=51.518$; df=6; $p<0.001$), flexibility ($\chi2=53.701$; df=6; $p<0.001$), attentiveness ($\chi2=71.836$; df=6; $p<0.001$), endurance ($\chi2=50.813$; df=6; $p<0.001$), courage ($\chi2=45.184$; df=6; $p<0.001$), open-mindedness ($\chi2=50.770$; df=6; $p<0.001$), rightness ($\chi2=139.782$; df=6; $p<0.001$).

In summary, it can be stated that the need to improve the disposition of impartiality was expressed more by women and employees in small enterprises. The need to improve the disposition of caring for other people was also expressed more by women and employees in small enterprises with post-secondary education. Women, employees in small enterprises and employees aged 41 and over are inclined to want to improve flexibility. The need to improve the quality of fairness is most expressed in employees who work according to a business certificate or a self-employment certificate. The employees with a higher education who are self-employed or work in small enterprises as well as the older employees would also like to improve this disposition.

Relationship between the employers' attitudes to the importance of critical thinking dispositions in the modern labour market and the need for their improvement in terms of their subordinates (Figure 31).[65] It was found that the employers consider fairness (M=6.27), rightness (M=6.23) and accuracy (M=6.09) to be the most important critical thinking dispositions in the modern labour market. Meanwhile, in evaluating the need to improve critical thinking dispositions in terms of their subordinates, the employers note that their employees need to improve their dispositions of flexibility (M=4.81) and self-confidence (M=4.77).

---

65 *The arithmetic mean (M) is calculated. The frequency of each need was evaluated on a 7-point scale, where 1 is 'no need at all' and 7 is 'a very strong need'. Importance in the labour market on a 7-point scale, where 1 is 'not important at all' and 7 is 'very important'.*

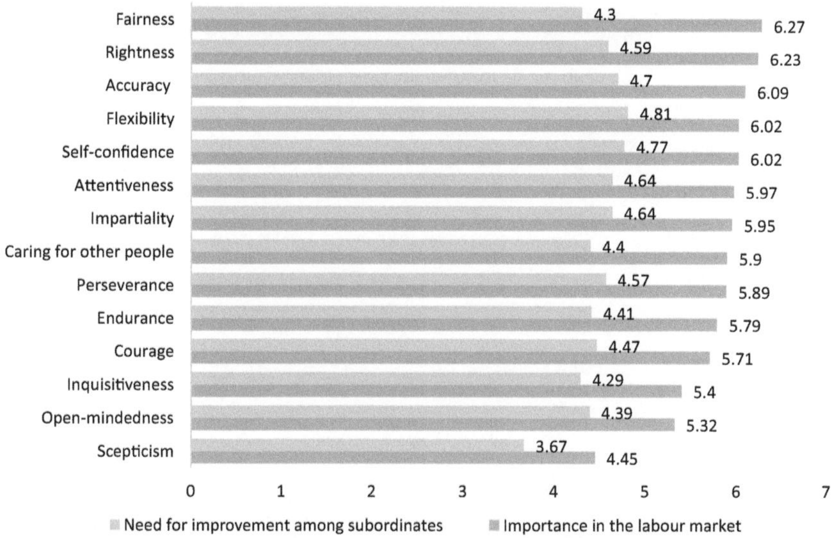

Fig. 31: *Relationship between the employers' attitudes to the importance of critical thinking dispositions in the modern labour market and the need for their improvement in terms of their subordinates*

Relationship between the employees' attitudes to the importance of critical thinking dispositions in the modern labour market and the need for their improvement (Figure 32).[66] It was found that the employees consider self-confidence (M=5.87) and rightness (M=5.9) to be the most important critical thinking dispositions in the modern labour market. It should be noted that these are also the critical thinking dispositions that they express a need to improve (M=5.21 and M=4.96 respectively). Statistically significant differences were found in the relationship between the employees' attitudes to the importance of critical thinking dispositions in the modern labour market and the need for their improvement. Analysis of the research results revealed that the more the employees believe that self-confidence is important in the modern labour market, the more they note that they need to improve this disposition ($r_s=0.305$; $p<0.001$). A similar trend was found in evaluating the disposition of rightness ($r_s=0.307$; $p<0.001$).

66 *The arithmetic mean (M) is calculated. The frequency of each need was evaluated on a 7-point scale, where 1 is 'no need at all' and 7 is 'a very strong need'. Importance in the labour market on a 7-point scale, where 1 is 'not important at all' and 7 is 'very important'.*

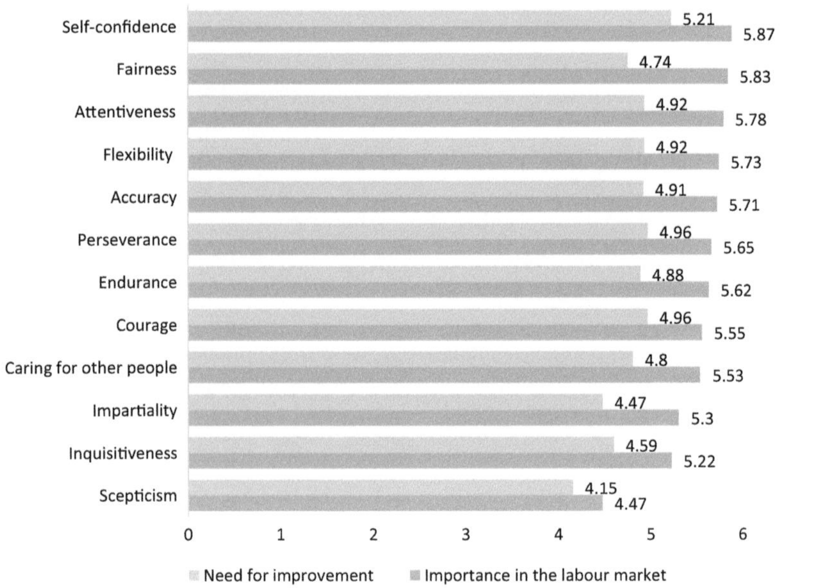

Fig. 32: *Relationship between the employees' attitudes to the importance of critical thinking dispositions in the modern labour market and the need for their improvement*

The following is a comparison of the evaluations of **the employers and the employees** regarding the extent to which employees need to improve individual critical thinking dispositions.

Based on the Mann-Whitney[67] non-parametric test for comparing independent samples, it was found that the employees note more frequently than the employers that they need to improve the following critical thinking dispositions:

- courage $p<0.001$ (mean rank, employer responses – 1092.65; mean rank, employee responses – 1317.17);
- endurance $p<0.001$ (mean rank, employer responses – 1100.13; mean rank, employee responses – 1315.21);

67 *The Mann-Whitney criterion is calculated because the Kolmogorov-Smirnov statistics for the employer sample showed that $p<0.05$, which means that the difference in the distribution from the normal is statistically significant, that is, the distribution is not normal and parametric analysis is not possible.*

- scepticism $p<0.001$ (mean rank, employer responses – 1108.68; mean rank, employee responses – 1312.97);
- self-confidence $p<0.001$ (mean rank, employer responses – 1109.77; mean rank, employee responses – 1312.68);
- perseverance $p<0.001$ (mean rank, employer responses – 1121.84; mean rank, employee responses – 1309.51);
- fairness $p<0.001$ (mean rank, employer responses – 1122.96; mean rank, employee responses – 1309.22);
- caring for other people $p<0.001$ (mean rank, employer responses – 1124.31; mean rank, employee responses – 1308.86);
- rightness $p<0.001$ (mean rank, employer responses – 1145.55; mean rank, employee responses – 1303.29);
- inquisitiveness $p<0.001$ (mean rank, employer responses – 1161.27; mean rank, employee responses – 1299.16);
- attentiveness $p<0.001$ (mean rank, employer responses – 1169.6; mean rank, employee responses – 1297.09);
- accuracy $p<0.01$ (mean rank, employer responses – 1190.91; mean rank, employee responses – 1291.39);
- open-mindedness $p<0.01$ (mean rank, employer responses – 1199.36; mean rank, employee responses – 1289.17).

Meanwhile, the opinions of the employers and the employees are similar in terms of flexibility and impartiality (no statistically significant difference was found).

Thus, there were significant differences of opinion between the employers and the employees in two cases. Compared to how the employers evaluated what dispositions their direct subordinates should improve, the employees were more likely to agree with statements that they need to develop courage, perseverance, scepticism and self-confidence. The employees also agree more than the employers with statements that they need to develop perseverance, fairness, caring for other people and rightness.

Small but significant differences of opinion were found regarding the need to improve the dispositions of flexibility, open-mindedness, accuracy and attentiveness. Compared to how the employers evaluated what qualities their direct subordinates should improve, the employees were more likely to agree that they should develop these dispositions; however, the differences are not significant.

3.8 Attitude regarding who is responsible for developing critical thinking

The employers and employees were asked who they thought should be responsible for developing a person's critical thinking. The items presented had to be evaluated on a 7-point Likert scale (*'strongly disagree', 'disagree', 'somewhat disagree', 'neither agree nor disagree', 'somewhat agree', 'agree', 'strongly agree'*). The respondents had to evaluate all of the items presented.

It was found that the labour market representatives (employers and employees) agree that the person is responsible for developing his or her own critical thinking (employers – M=6.18; employees – M=6.05), and somewhat agree that the organisation where the person works (employers – M=5.02; employees – M=4.76) and the higher education institution (employers – M=5.09; employees – M=4.78) are responsible.[68] Based on the Mann-Whitney[69] non-parametric test for comparing independent samples, it was found that the employers agree more strongly than the employees that the higher education institution, $p<0.01$ (mean rank, employer responses –1411.28; mean rank, employee responses – 1233.56) and the organisation where the person works, $p<0.01$ (mean rank, employer responses –1393.19; mean rank, employee responses – 1238.30) should be responsible for developing a person's critical thinking.

It was also important to determine what the employers and employees think about how higher education institutions prepare professionals for the modern labour market. It was revealed that slightly more than half (62.4 %) of the employees and slightly less than half (44.5 %) of the employers have a positive view of the role of the higher education institution in preparing professionals for the modern labour market. Meanwhile, almost half of the employers (46.8 %) and a third of the employees (32.5 %) have no opinion, and 8.7 % of the employers and 5.1 % of the employees have a negative view of the preparation of professionals at higher education institutions.

Hence, the labour market representatives agree that the person is responsible for developing his or her own critical thinking, and somewhat agree that the organisation where the person works and the higher education institution are responsible. This group has a positive view of the role of the higher education institution in preparing professionals.

68 *The arithmetic mean (M) is calculated. The statements were evaluated on a 7-point scale ('strongly disagree', 'disagree', 'somewhat disagree', 'neither agree nor disagree', 'somewhat agree', 'agree', 'strongly agree').*

69 *The Mann-Whitney criterion is calculated because the Kolmogorov-Smirnov statistics for the employer sample showed that $p<0.05$, which means that the difference in the distribution from the normal is statistically significant, that is, the distribution is not normal and parametric analysis is not possible.*

4. Comparison of the Manifestation of Critical Thinking in Higher Education and in the Labour Market

4.1 Attitude to the conception of critical thinking

In order to reveal the respondents' attitude on what they consider to be critical thinking, the research instrument provided them with seven definitions of critical thinking that respond to different theoretical concepts of critical thinking:

- Critical thinking is the improvement of a person's thinking by changing habitual thinking patterns.
- Critical thinking is the ability to argumentatively question unreasoned assumptions and reasoning in pursuit of truth and rightness.
- Critical thinking is the ability to be guided by reasoned arguments in various contexts in pursuit of reasoned and rational decisions.
- Critical thinking is the ability to reason, reflect and act critically for the good of oneself, others and society.
- Critical thinking is the totality of a person's cognitive skills and dispositions. Skills: to interpret and analyse, to explain and evaluate, and to draw conclusions and make the corrections stemming from them. Personal dispositions: open-mindedness and inquisitiveness, analyticity and systematicity, trust in soundness and the pursuit of truth.
- Critical thinking is a strong human development thinking based on firm knowledge, cognitive abilities and honest, moral behaviour in all life situations.
- Critical thinking is reflexive thinking when making a reasoned decision about what and what not to believe.

In analysing the answers of the respondents by group, it was found that in all four groups (teachers – 36.2 %; employers – 33.9 %; employees – 28.5 % and students – 21.1 %), the dominant concept of critical thinking is that *'Critical thinking is the totality of a person's cognitive skills and dispositions. Skills: to interpret and analyse, to explain and evaluate, and to draw conclusions and make the corrections stemming from them. Personal dispositions: open-mindedness and inquisitiveness, analyticity and systematicity, trust in soundness and the pursuit of truth'*. No statistically significant differences were found between the surveyed groups.

In evaluating the conception of critical thinking as a certain phenomenon, two aspects of the similarity of understanding between the higher education representatives (teachers and students) and the labour market representatives (employees and employers) emerged. First of all, the representatives of both higher education and the labour market understand critical thinking as a set of skills and dispositions through which a person makes decisions in daily and professional activities. That is, the higher education system prepares future labour market participants who are able and have the appropriate dispositions to make reasoned decisions independently and collegially in order to achieve organisational efficiency. Accordingly, priority is given in the modern labour market to individuals who have the abilities necessary to ensure the development of the organisation.

Another similarity of the conception of critical thinking between the higher education and labour market representatives is related to the improvement of critical thinking as the thought process itself. The description of critical thinking as the improvement of a person's thinking by changing habitual thinking patterns was selected by the smallest share of the representatives of both higher education and the labour market. This understanding is based on the assumption that critical thinking cannot be developed.

4.2 Attitude towards critical thinking and the development of critical thinking

In analysing the opinion of the different groups of respondents about critical thinking, it was found that the majority of respondents in each group agree with the statements that:

- critical thinking can be developed (teachers M=4.35; students M=4.01; employers M=4.15; employees M=3.94);
- there are various ways to demonstrate critical thinking (teachers M=4.18; students M=3.88; employers M=3.93; employees M=3.83);
- critical thinking is possible in every situation (teachers M=4.1; students M=3.85; employers M=4.02; employees M=3.81).

Based on the Kruskal-Wallis test for comparing independent samples, it was found that the teachers were more likely than the employers, students and employees to agree with the statements that:

- critical thinking can be developed, $p<0.001$ (mean rank, teacher responses – 2603.66; employer responses – 2319.60; employee responses – 1992.01; student responses – 2123.33);
- critical thinking is possible in every situation, $p<0.001$ (mean rank, teacher responses – 2452.00; employer responses – 2324.50; employee responses – 2024.00; student responses – 2094.30);
- a person can think critically if he or she wants and tries to, $p<0.001$ (mean rank, teacher responses – 2287.16; employer responses – 2144.40; employee responses – 2027.45; student responses – 2169.17);
- there are various ways to demonstrate critical thinking, $p<0.001$ (mean rank, teacher responses – 2545.99; employer responses – 2186.18; employee responses – 2035.41; student responses – 2117.97).

Meanwhile, the students were more likely than the teachers, employees and employers to agree with the statements that:

- a person's ability to think critically is unchanging, $p<0.001$ (mean rank, teacher responses – 1368.00; employer responses – 1553.29; employee responses – 2200.06; student responses – 2238.31);
- critical thinking only occurs when criticising, $p<0.001$ (mean rank, teacher responses – 1191.23; employer responses – 1463.00; employee responses – 2197.97; student responses – 2290.38).

In terms of the manifestation and development of critical thinking, the higher education and labour market representatives were in agreement that critical thinking is something that can be developed. Although none of the respondents associate critical thinking much with improvement of the thought process by changing habitual thinking patterns, they do acknowledge that critical thinking can be developed. In general, the research participants all agree that critical thinking is changing, can be expressed in different ways in all situations, and depends on each person's desire and efforts. This suggests that in higher education and the labour market, the manifestation of critical thinking is considered valuable and desirable.

It should be noted that among the representatives of both higher education and the labour market, the attitude is nevertheless revealed that critical thinking only occurs when criticising. This attitude is more typical of the employees and students than of the employers and teachers.

4.3 Attitude towards the importance of critical thinking skills in the modern labour market

In evaluating the distribution of the respondents' opinions on the importance of critical thinking skills in the labour market by study group, it was found that their opinions on this issue differed somewhat. The teachers ($M=5.89$) and the employers ($M=6.02$) consider the most important skill in the modern labour market to be the ability to formulate conclusions, while the students ($M=5.59$) and the employees ($M=5.7$) consider it to be self-regulation. It should be noted that all groups of respondents consider argumentation to be equally important in the modern labour market (teachers $M=5.87$; students $M=5.54$; employers $M=5.95$; employees $M=5.62$).

Based on the Kruskal-Wallis test for comparing independent samples, it was found that the employers were more likely than the teachers, students and employees to consider the most important skills in the modern labour market to be:

- decision-making, $p<0.001$ (mean rank, teacher responses – 2397.11; employer responses – 2398.24; employee responses – 2058.55; student responses – 2028,09);
- inference, $p<0.001$ (mean rank, teacher responses – 2425.91; employer responses – 2537.66; employee responses – 2058.55; student responses – 2004.32);
- explanation, $p<0.001$ (mean rank, teacher responses – 2300.12; employer responses – 2456.34; employee responses – 2063.12; student responses – 2011.47);
- self-regulation, $p<0.001$ (mean rank, teacher responses – 2062.20; employer responses – 2341.50; employee responses – 2121.81; student responses – 1997.39);

- argumentation, $p<0.001$ (mean rank, teacher responses – 2369.03; employer responses – 2428.49; employee responses – 2086.03; student responses – 1983.78);
- interpretation, $p<0.001$ (mean rank, teacher responses – 2539.18; employer responses – 2613.67; employee responses – 2025.00; student responses – 1983.22);
- evaluation, $p<0.001$ (mean rank, teacher responses – 2540.34; employer responses – 2621.85; employee responses – 1990.68; student responses – 2025.92).

Meanwhile, the teachers are more likely to identify analysis skills as being important in the modern labour market, $p<0.001$ (mean rank, teacher responses – 2528.44; employer responses – 2515.45; employee responses – 2004.22; student responses – 2046.25).

In evaluating the importance of critical thinking skills in the modern labour market, similarities between the higher education and labour market representatives emerged. Both groups specify inference skills as being key in the modern labour market, with the most important being the ability to formulate evidence-based conclusions and to formulate conclusions in anticipation of possible consequences. Meanwhile, the ability to formulate conclusions with regard to the context is considered to be of average importance.

Another similarity between the labour market and higher education representatives is related to their evaluation of self-regulation skills. The students and the employees rank self-regulation as the most important skills in the modern labour market. Meanwhile, the employers and the teachers rank them as being skills of average importance in the modern labour market.

Another overlap in the evaluations emerged in the group of explanation skills. According to the representatives of both groups, the most important explanation skills are the ability to explain an analysis carried out and the results obtained, to reveal the essence of a phenomenon, and to answer others' questions. All of the groups consider the ability to explain the decision-making path and to formulate questions for others to be less important. A similar trend, that the ability to take the broader context into account when evaluating, argumenting and interpreting is less important, also emerged in the other critical thinking skill groups. It can be assumed that in higher education and the labour market, critical thinking skills which enable a person to consider key issues, make decisions responsibly and act independently are important, while the ability to 'exit' one's professional/study field into a broader context is less important. In other words, the importance of critical thinking skills in the modern labour market is viewed more from the personal and interpersonal aspect, while the social aspect is seemingly ignored.

In this part of the evaluation of the phenomenon of critical thinking, links also emerged within the group of higher education representatives. It was found that the more importance the teachers and students attach to specific critical thinking skills in the modern labour market, the more attention they give to their development in the study process.

Links were also revealed within the group of labour market representatives. It was found that the more importance the employers attach to the ability to formulate conclusions in the modern labour market, the more they believe that their subordinates need to improve this ability. The more importance the employees attach to self-regulation skills in the modern labour market, the more they express a need to improve them.

4.4 Attitude to the importance of improving the constituents of critical thinking skills in the modern labour market

In evaluating the distribution of the respondents' opinions on the importance of improving the constituents of critical thinking skills in the labour market by study group, it was found by applying the Kruskal-Wallis test that their opinions on this issue differed somewhat.

Decision-making:

- formulate conclusions $p<0.001$ (mean rank, employer responses – 2411.49; teacher responses – 2409.58; employee responses – 2034.15; student responses – 2054.68);
- make decisions collegially $p<0.001$ (mean rank, teacher responses – 2433.77; employer responses – 2376.36; employee responses – 2057.38; student responses – 2033.61);
- justify a decision made to others $p<0.001$ (mean rank, employer responses – 2456.40; teacher responses – 2421.79; employee responses – 2057.45; student responses – 2006.76);
- make decisions according to the procedures established in the organisation $p<0.001$ (mean rank, employer responses – 2307.55; teacher responses – 2104.38; employee responses – 2094.74; student responses – 2041.03).

Inference:

- summarise information $p<0.001$ (mean rank, employer responses – 2549.21; teacher responses – 2405.11; employee responses – 2042.75; student responses – 1995.59);
- formulate evidence-based conclusions $p<0.001$ (mean rank, employer responses – 2522.46; teacher responses – 2375.61; employee responses – 2048.55; student responses – 2000.18);
- formulate conclusions with regard to the context $p<0.001$ (mean rank, employer responses – 2407.04; teacher responses – 2340.50; employee responses – 2037.92; student responses – 2058.16);
- formulate conclusions in anticipation of possible consequences $p<0.001$ (mean rank, employer responses – 2527.83; teacher responses – 2403.93; employee responses – 2047.77; student responses – 1996.50).

Explanation:

- formulate questions for others $p<0.001$ (mean rank, employer responses – 2515.90; teacher responses – 2106.98; employee responses – 2047.96; student responses – 2030.26);
- answer others' questions $p<0.001$ (mean rank, employer responses – 2449.43; teacher responses – 2343.78; employee responses – 2055.59; student responses – 2019.52);
- explain an analysis carried out and the results obtained $p<0.001$ (mean rank, employer responses – 2535.70; teacher responses – 2464.78; employee responses – 2057.21; student responses – 1975.08);
- explain the decision-making path $p<0.001$ (mean rank, employer responses – 2330.50; teacher responses – 2320.78; employee responses – 2078.07; student responses – 2033.44);
- explain complex concepts $p<0.001$ (mean rank, employer responses – 2304.06; teacher responses – 2134.81; employee responses – 2085.36; student responses – 2051.68);
- reveal the essence of a phenomenon $p<0.001$ (mean rank, employer responses – 2439.98; teacher responses – 2367.83; employee responses – 2072.98; student responses – 1997.26).

Analysis:

- reveal connections between statements, facts, concepts $p<0.001$ (mean rank, employer responses – 2484.52; teacher responses – 2448.25; employee responses – 2008.59; student responses – 2059.30);
- examine a situation from different points of view $p<0.001$ (mean rank, employer responses – 2508.54; teacher responses – 2488.54; employee responses – 2013.69; student responses – 2040.08);
- find connections between the whole and its parts $p<0.001$ (mean rank, teacher responses – 2490.28; employer responses – 2479.67; employee responses – 2013.47; student responses – 2050.28);
- collect data/information and link it to other data/sources $p<0.001$ (mean rank, teacher responses – 2494.11; employer responses – 2471.35; employee responses – 2012.20; student responses – 2054.48).

Self-regulation:

- know oneself $p<0.001$ (mean rank, employer responses – 2288.93; teacher responses – 1939.19; employee responses – 2131.31; student responses – 2015.47);
- reflect (on one's thoughts, feelings, actions) $p<0.05$ (mean rank, employer responses – 2256.79; teacher responses – 1990.74; employee responses – 2111.33; student responses – 2048.11);

- change according to the situation $p<0.001$ (mean rank, employer responses – 2414.66; teacher responses – 2304.99; employee responses – 2108.84; student responses – 1964.70).

Argumentation:

- think based on facts/evidence $p<0.001$ (mean rank, employer responses – 2452.14; teacher responses – 2386.78; employee responses – 2072.14; student responses – 1992.22);
- justify one's choices $p<0.001$ (mean rank, employer responses – 2426.30; teacher responses – 2373.70; employee responses – 2091.86; student responses – 1976.32);
- base actions on reflection $p<0.001$ (mean rank, employer responses – 2350.25; teacher responses – 2245.62; employee responses – 2084.16; student responses – 2026.00).

Interpretation:

- classify data/information $p<0.001$ (mean rank, employer responses – 2554.40; teacher responses – 2499.25; employee responses – 2019.38; student responses – 2015.42);
- understand the content of data/information $p<0.001$ (mean rank, employer responses – 2592.61; teacher responses – 2490.00; employee responses – 2028.74; student responses – 1990.54);
- convey data/information in one's own words $p<0.001$ (mean rank, employer responses – 2493.13; teacher responses – 2397.66; employee responses – 2036.89; student responses – 2023.72);
- discern essential information from supplementary information $p<0.001$ (mean rank, employer responses – 2617.17; teacher responses – 2533.85; employee responses – 2027.06; student responses – 1979.79).

Evaluation:

- evaluate data/information with regard to different opinions $p<0.001$ (mean rank, employer responses – 2527.51; teacher responses – 2533.85; employee responses – 1987.50; student responses – 2067.79);
- evaluate data/information without prejudice $p<0.001$ (mean rank, employer responses – 2566.54; teacher responses – 2369.15; employee responses – 1994.55; student responses – 2057.29);
- evaluate a situation on the basis of data/information $p<0.001$ (mean rank, employer responses – 2602.13; teacher responses – 2542.66; employee responses – 1994.04; student responses – 2028.10);
- evaluate/self-evaluate the decisions/conclusions made $p<0.001$ (mean rank, employer responses – 2581.21; teacher responses – 2509.46; employee responses – 2019.68; student responses – 2004.62).

The results of the Kruskal-Wallis test showed that the employers and the teachers have a similar evaluation of the importance of the constituents of critical thinking skills in the labour market. Next, we will present in detail how these groups of respondents (employers, teachers, employees, students) evaluate the importance of each critical thinking ability in the labour market. The respondents were asked in the questionnaire to evaluate the importance of the given abilities for the labour market.

For each skill, a Kruskal-Wallis test provided a significant difference ($p<0.001$) between the mean ranks of at least one pair of groups. Post-hoc Dunn's tests were carried out for the six pairs of groups (employees-employers, employees-teachers, employees-students, employers-students, teachers-students, employers-teachers) with the Bonferroni adjustment (Figures 33–40).

For the ability to *make decisions independently*, a Kruskal-Wallis test showed that there was a significant difference between means ($H=56.063$; $df=3$; $p<0.001$). Post-hoc tests of pairwise comparisons showed that the importance in the labour market of the ability to *make decisions independently* is evaluated similarly by the employees and the students, but compared to the teachers ($p<0.01$) and the employers ($p<0.001$), the employees rate this ability as being **less important**. Compared with the attitude of the teachers ($p<0.01$) and the employers ($p<0.001$), the students rate the ability to *make decisions independently* as being **less important**. But between the teachers and the employers there is no statistically significant difference (Figure 33, a).

For the ability to *make decisions collegially*, a Kruskal-Wallis test showed that there was a significant difference between means ($H=49.054$; $df=3$; $p<0.001$). Post-hoc tests of pairwise comparisons showed that the importance in the labour market of the ability to *make decisions collegially* is evaluated similarly by the employees and the students, but compared to the teachers ($p<0.01$) and the employers ($p<0.001$), the employees rate this ability as being **less important**. Compared with the attitude of the teachers ($p<0.001$) and the employers ($p<0.001$), the students rate the ability to *make decisions collegially* as being **less important**. But between the teachers and the employers there is no statistically significant difference (Figure 33, b).

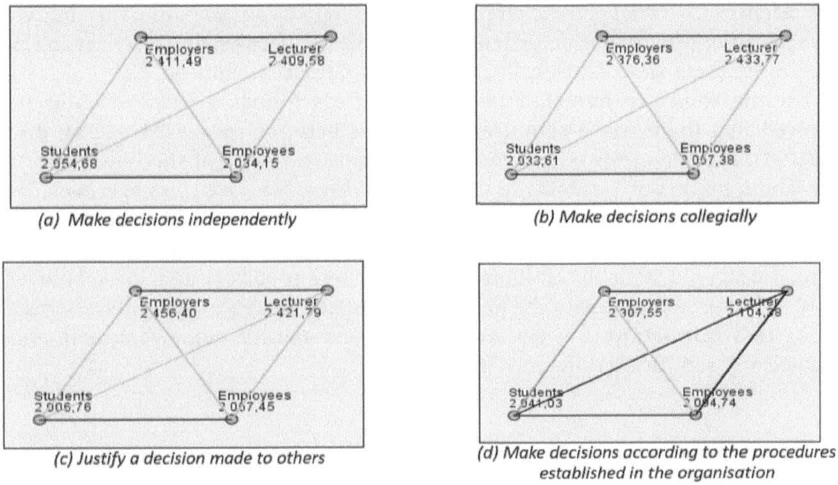

Fig. 33: *Decision-making block*

For the ability to *justify a decision made to others*, a Kruskal-Wallis test showed that there was a significant difference between means (H=72.071; df=3; p<0.001). Post-hoc tests of pairwise comparisons showed that the importance in the labour market of the ability to *justify a decision made to others* is evaluated similarly by the employees and the students, but compared to the teachers (p<0.01) and the employers (p<0.001), the employees rate this ability as being **less important**. Compared with the attitude of the teachers (p<0.001) and the employers (p<0.001), the students rate the ability to *justify a decision made to others* as being **less important**. But between the teachers and the employers there is no statistically significant difference (Figure 33, c).

For the ability to make decisions according to the procedures established in the organisation, a Kruskal-Wallis test showed that there was a significant difference between means (H=20.346; df=3; p<0.001). Post-hoc tests of pairwise comparisons showed that the employers consider the ability to make decisions according to the procedures established in the organisation to be more important in the labour market than the students (p<0.001) and employees (p<0.001) do. No statistically significant differences were found in the other pairs (Figure 33, d).

For the ability to *summarise information*, a Kruskal-Wallis test showed that there was a significant difference between means (H=104.068; df=3; p<0.001). Post-hoc tests of pairwise comparisons showed that the importance in the labour market of the ability to *summarise information* is evaluated similarly by the employees and the students, but compared to the teachers (p<0.01) and the employers (p<0.001), the employees rate this ability as being **less important**. Compared with the attitude of the teachers (p<0.001) and the employers (p<0.001), the students rate the ability to *summarise information* as being **less important**. But between the teachers and the employers there is no statistically significant difference (Figure 34, a).

For the ability to *formulate evidence-based conclusions*, a Kruskal-Wallis test showed that there was a significant difference between means (H=91.584; df=3; p<0.001). Post-hoc tests of pairwise comparisons showed that the importance in the labour market of the ability to *formulate evidence-based conclusions* is evaluated similarly by the employees and the students, but compared to the teachers (p<0.01) and the employers (p<0.001), the employees rate this ability as being **less important**. Compared with the attitude of the teachers (p<0.001) and the employers (p<0.001), the students rate the ability to *formulate evidence-based conclusions* as being **less important**. But between the teachers and the employers there is no statistically significant difference (Figure 34, b).

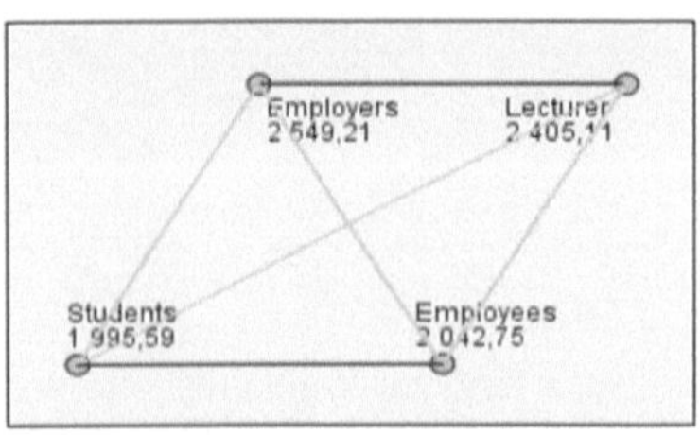

(a) Summarise information

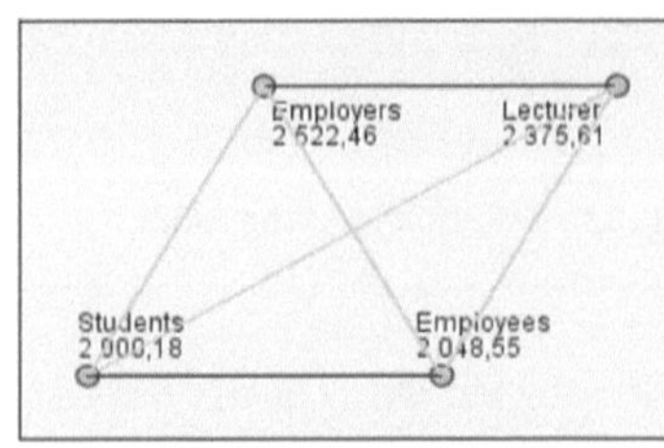

(b) Formulate evidence-based conclusions

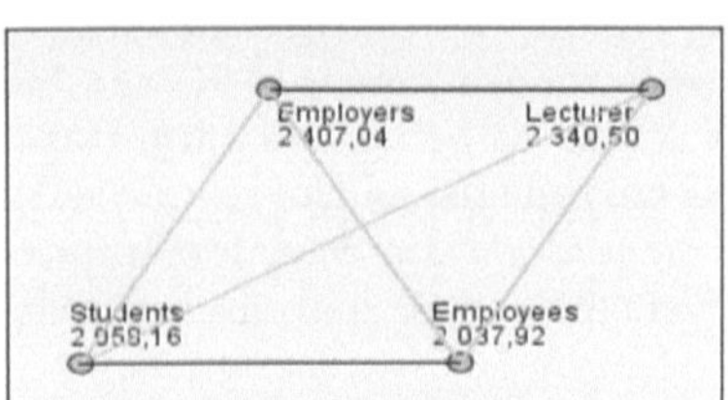

(c) Formulate conclusions with regard to the context

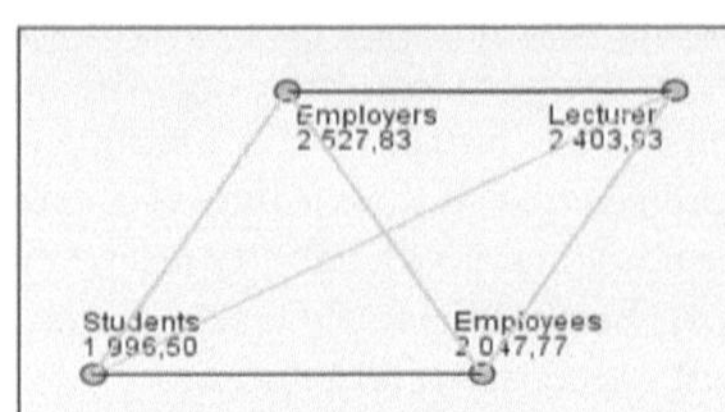

(d) Formulate conclusions in anticipation of possible consequences

Fig. 34: *Inference block*

For the ability to *formulate conclusions with regard to the context*, a Kruskal-Wallis test showed that there was a significant difference between means (H=49.978; df=3; p<0.001). Post-hoc tests of pairwise comparisons showed that the importance in the labour market of the ability to *formulate conclusions with regard to the context* is evaluated similarly by the employees and the students, but compared to the teachers (p<0.01) and the employers (p<0.001), the employees rate this ability as being **less important**. Compared with the attitude of the teachers (p<0.001) and the employers (p<0.001), the students rate the ability to *formulate conclusions with regard to the context* as being **less important**. But between the teachers and the employers there is no statistically significant difference (Figure 34, c).

For the ability to *formulate conclusions in anticipation of possible consequences*, a Kruskal-Wallis test showed that there was a significant difference between means (H=96.335; df=3; p<0.001). Post-hoc tests of pairwise comparisons showed that the importance in the labour market of the ability to *formulate conclusions in anticipation of possible consequences* is evaluated similarly by the employees and the students, but compared to the teachers (p<0.01) and the employers (p<0.001), the employees rate this ability as being **less important**. Compared with the attitude of the teachers (p<0.001) and the employers (p<0.001), the students rate the ability to *formulate conclusions in anticipation of possible consequences* as being **less important**. But between the teachers and the employers there is no statistically significant difference (Figure 34, d).

For the ability to *formulate questions for others*, a Kruskal-Wallis test showed that there was a significant difference between means (H=75.187; df=3; p<0.001). Post-hoc tests of pairwise comparisons showed that the employers consider the ability to *formulate questions for others* to be **more important** in the labour market than the teachers (p<0.001), students (p<0.001) and employees (p<0.001) do. No statistically significant differences were found in the other pairs (Figure 35, a).

For the ability to *answer others' questions*, a Kruskal-Wallis test showed that there was a significant difference between means (H=63.270; df=3; p<0.001). Post-hoc tests of pairwise comparisons showed that the importance in the labour market of the ability to *answer others' questions* is evaluated similarly by the employees and the students, but compared to the teachers (p<0.01) and the employers (p<0.001), the employees rate this ability as being **less important**. Compared with the attitude of the teachers (p<0.001) and the employers (p<0.001), the students rate the ability to *answer others' questions* as being **less important**. But between the teachers and the employers there is no statistically significant difference (Figure 35, b).

For the ability to *explain an analysis carried out and the results obtained*, a Kruskal-Wallis test showed that there was a significant difference between means (H=107.356; df=3; p<0.001). Post-hoc tests of pairwise comparisons showed that the importance in the labour market of the ability to *explain an analysis carried out and the results obtained* is evaluated similarly by the employees and the students, but compared to the teachers (p<0.001) and the employers (p<0.001), the employees rate this ability as being **less important**. Compared with the attitude of the teachers (p<0.001) and the employers (p<0.001), the students rate the ability to *explain an analysis carried out and the results obtained* as being **less important**. But between the teachers and the employers there is no statistically significant difference (Figure 35, c).

For the ability to *explain the decision-making path*, a Kruskal-Wallis test showed that there was a significant difference between means (H=31.023; df=3; p<0.001). Post-hoc tests of pairwise comparisons showed that the importance in the labour market of the ability to *explain the decision-making path* is evaluated similarly by the employees and the students, but compared to the employers ($p<0.001$), the employees rate this ability as being **less important**. Compared with the attitude of the teachers ($p<0.001$) and the employers ($p<0.001$), the students rate the ability to *explain the decision-making path* as being **less important**. But between the teachers and the employers there is no statistically significant difference (Figure 35, d).

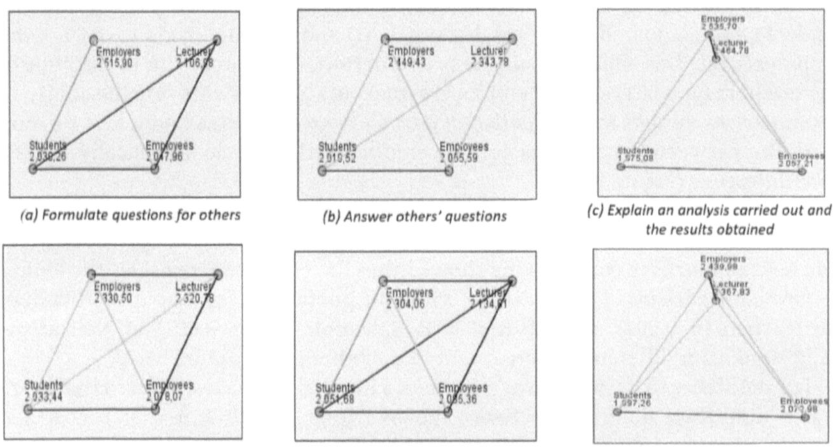

(a) Formulate questions for others
(b) Answer others' questions
(c) Explain an analysis carried out and the results obtained
(d) Explain the decision-making path
(e) Explain complex concepts
(f) Reveal the essence of a phenomenon

Fig. 35: *Explanation skills block*

For the ability to *explain complex concepts*, a Kruskal-Wallis test showed that there was a significant difference between means ($H=18.772$; $df=3$; $p<0.001$). Post-hoc tests of pairwise comparisons showed that the employers consider the ability to *explain complex concepts* to be **more important** in the labour market than the students ($p<0.001$) and employees ($p<0.001$) do. No statistically significant differences were found in the other pairs (Figure 35, e).

For the ability to *reveal the essence of a phenomenon*, a Kruskal-Wallis test showed that there was a significant difference between means ($H=64.702$; $df=3$; $p<0.001$). Post-hoc tests of pairwise comparisons showed that the importance in the labour market of the ability to *reveal the essence of a phenomenon* is evaluated similarly by the employees and the students, but compared to the teachers ($p<0.01$) and the employers ($p<0.001$), the employees rate this ability as being **less important**. Compared with the attitude of the teachers ($p<0.01$) and the employers ($p<0.001$), the students rate the ability to *reveal the essence of a phenomenon* as being **less important**. But between the teachers and the employers there is no statistically significant difference (Figure 35, f).

For the ability to *reveal connections between statements, facts, concepts*, a Kruskal-Wallis test showed that there was a significant difference between means (H=83.030; df=3; p<0.001). Post-hoc tests of pairwise comparisons showed that the importance in the labour market of the ability to *reveal connections between statements, facts, concepts* is evaluated similarly by the employees and the students, but compared to the teachers (p<0.001) and the employers (p<0.001), the employees rate this ability as being **less important**. Compared with the attitude of the teachers (p<0.01) and the employers (p<0.001), the students rate the ability to *reveal connections between statements, facts, concepts* as being **less important**. But between the teachers and the employers there is no statistically significant difference (Figure 36, a).

For the ability to *examine a situation from different points of view*, a Kruskal-Wallis test showed that there was a significant difference between means (H=94.474; df=3; p<0.001). Post-hoc tests of pairwise comparisons showed that the importance in the labour market of the ability to *examine a situation from different points of view* is evaluated similarly by the employees and the students, but compared to the teachers (p<0.001) and the employers (p<0.001), the employees rate this ability as being **less important**. Compared with the attitude of the teachers (p<0.001) and the employers (p<0.001), the students rate the ability to *examine a situation from different points of view* as being **less important**. But between the teachers and the employers there is no statistically significant difference (Figure 36, b).

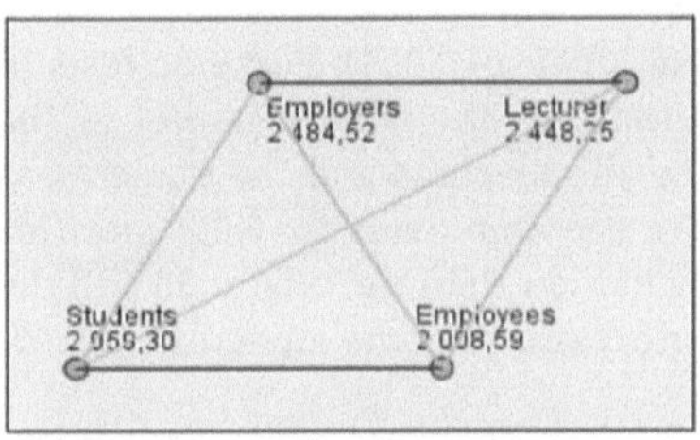

(a) Reveal connections between statements, facts, concepts

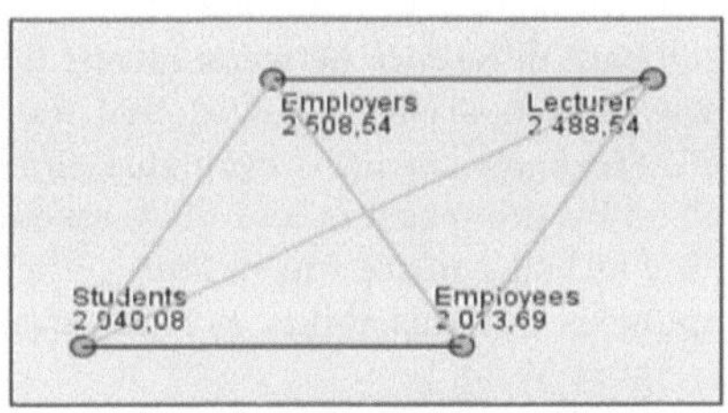

(b) Examine a situation from different points of view

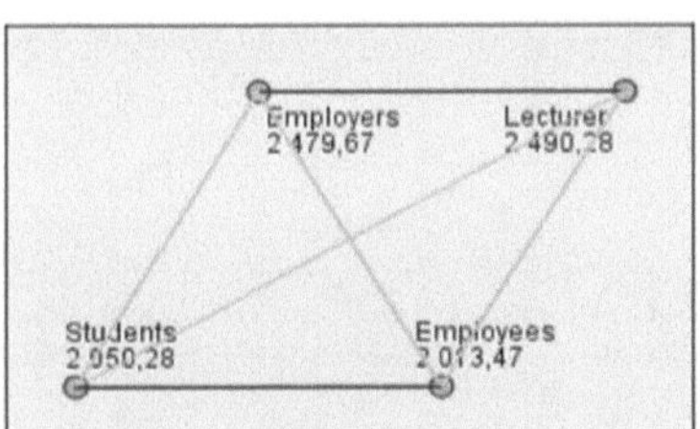

(c) Find connections between the whole and its parts

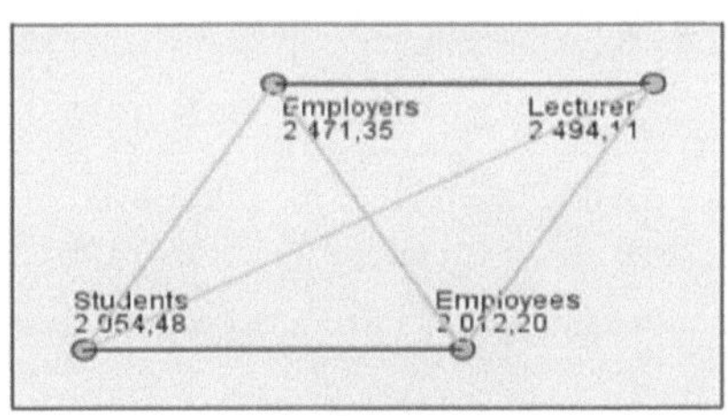

(d) Collect data/information and link it to other data/sources

Fig. 36: *Analysis skills block*

For the ability to *find connections between the whole and its parts,* a Kruskal-Wallis test showed that there was a significant difference between means (H=84.930; df=3; p<0.001). Post-hoc tests of pairwise comparisons showed that the importance in the labour market of the ability to *find connections between the whole and its parts* is evaluated similarly by the employees and the students, but compared to the teachers (p<0.001) and the employers (p<0.001), the employees rate this ability as being **less important**. Compared with the attitude of the teachers (p<0.001) and the employers (p<0.001), the students rate the ability to *find connections between the whole and its parts* as being **less important**. But between the teachers and the employers there is no statistically significant difference (Figure 36, c).

For the ability to *collect data/information and link it to other data/sources,* a Kruskal-Wallis test showed that there was a significant difference between means (H=82.767; df=3; p<0.001). Post-hoc tests of pairwise comparisons showed that the importance in the labour market of the ability to *collect data/information and link it to other data/sources* is evaluated similarly by the employees and the students, but compared to the teachers (p<0.001) and the employers (p<0.001), the employees rate this ability as being **less important**. Compared with the attitude of the teachers (p<0.001) and the employers (p<0.001), the students rate the ability to *collect data/information and link it to other data/sources* as being **less important**. But between the teachers and the employers there is no statistically significant difference (Figure 36, d).

For the ability to *know oneself,* a Kruskal-Wallis test showed that there was a significant difference between means (H=26.140; df=3; p<0.001). Post-hoc tests of pairwise comparisons showed that the importance in the labour market of the ability to *know oneself* is evaluated similarly by the teachers and the students as well as by the teachers and the employees. But the employers (p<0.05) rate this ability as being **more important** in the labour market than the others do and the employees rate this ability as being **more important** than the students (p<0.05) do (Figure 37, a).

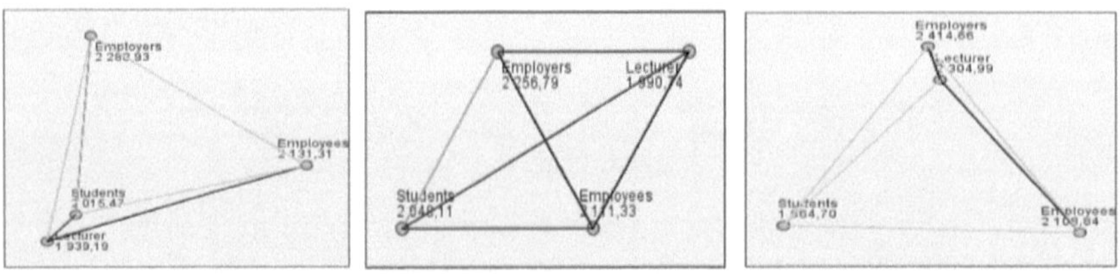

(a) Know oneself *(b) Reflect (on one's thoughts, feelings, actions)* *(c) Change according to the situation*

Fig. 37: *Self-regulation skills block*

For the ability to *reflect (on one's thoughts, feelings, actions)*, a Kruskal-Wallis test showed that there was a significant difference between means (H=13.929; df=3; p<0.001). Post hoc tests of pairwise comparisons showed that the employers rate the ability to *reflect* (*on one's thoughts, feelings, actions*) as being **more important** in the labour market than the students (p<0.001) do. No statistically significant differences were found in the other pairs (Figure 37, b).

For the ability to *change according to the situation*, a Kruskal-Wallis test showed that there was a significant difference between means (H=63.191; df=3; p<0.001). Post-hoc tests of pairwise comparisons showed that the importance in the labour market of the ability to *change according to the situation* is evaluated similarly by the employees and the teachers, but compared to the employers (p<0.001), the employees rate this ability as being **less important**. Compared with the attitude of the teachers (p<0.01), the employers (p<0.01) and the employees (p<0.05), the students rate the ability to *change according to the situation* as being **less important**. But between the teachers and the employers there is no statistically significant difference (Figure 37, c).

For the ability to *think based on facts/evidence*, a Kruskal-Wallis test showed that there was a significant difference between means (H=71.109; df=3; p<0.001). Post-hoc tests of pairwise comparisons showed that the importance in the labour market of the ability to *think based on facts/evidence* is evaluated similarly by the employees and the students, but compared to the employers (p<0.001) and the teachers (p<0.01), the employees rate this ability as being **less important**. Compared with the attitude of the teachers (p<0.01) and the employers (p<0.01), the students rate the ability to *think based on facts/evidence* as being **less important**. But between the teachers and the employers there is no statistically significant difference (Figure 38, a).

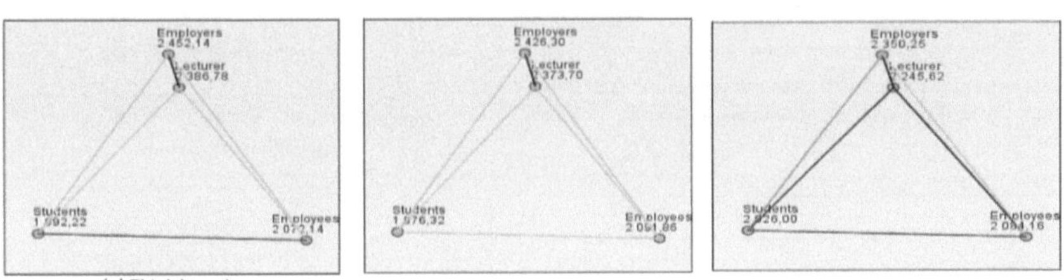

(a) Think based on facts/evidence (b) Justify one's choices (c) Base actions on reflection

Fig. 38: *Argumentation skills block*

For the ability to *justify one's choices*, a Kruskal-Wallis test showed that there was a significant difference between means (H=66.681; df=3; p<0.001). Post-hoc tests of pairwise comparisons showed that the importance in the labour market of the ability to *justify one's choices* is evaluated similarly by the employers and the teachers, but compared to the employers ($p<0.001$) and the teachers ($p<0.01$), the employees rate this ability as being **less important**. Compared with the attitude of the teachers ($p<0.01$), the employers ($p<0.01$) and employees ($p<0.05$), the students rate the ability to *justify one's choices* as being **less important** (Figure 38, b).

For the ability to *base actions on reflection*, a Kruskal-Wallis test showed that there was a significant difference between means ($H=32.750$; $df=3$; $p<0.001$). Post hoc tests of pairwise comparisons showed that the employers rate the ability to *base actions on reflection* as being **more important** in the labour market than the students ($p<0.001$) and employees ($p<0.001$) do. No statistically significant differences were found in the other pairs (Figure 38, c).

For the ability to *classify data/information*, a Kruskal-Wallis test showed that there was a significant difference between means ($H=112.527$; $df=3$; $p<0.001$). Post-hoc tests of pairwise comparisons showed that the importance in the labour market of the ability to *classify data/information* is evaluated similarly by the employees and the students, but compared to the teachers ($p<0.001$) and the employers ($p<0.001$), the employees rate this ability as being **less important**. Compared with the attitude of the teachers ($p<0.001$) and the employers ($p<0.001$), the students rate the ability to *classify data/information* as being **less important**. But between the teachers and the employers there is no statistically significant difference (Figure 39, a).

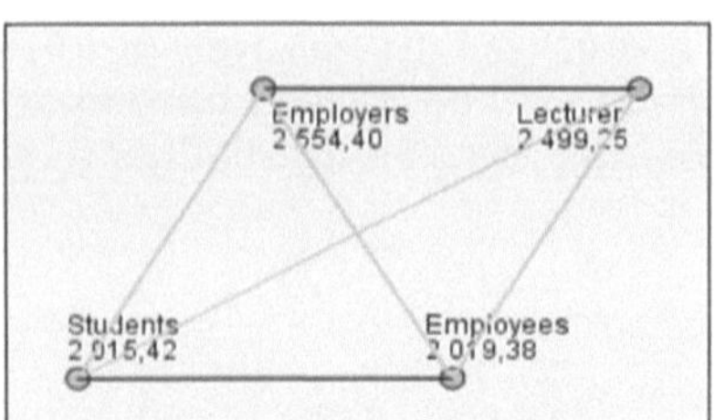

(a) Classify data/information

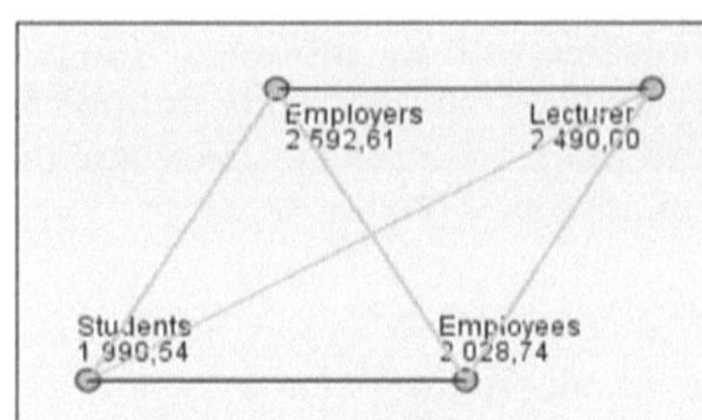

(b) Understand the content of data/information

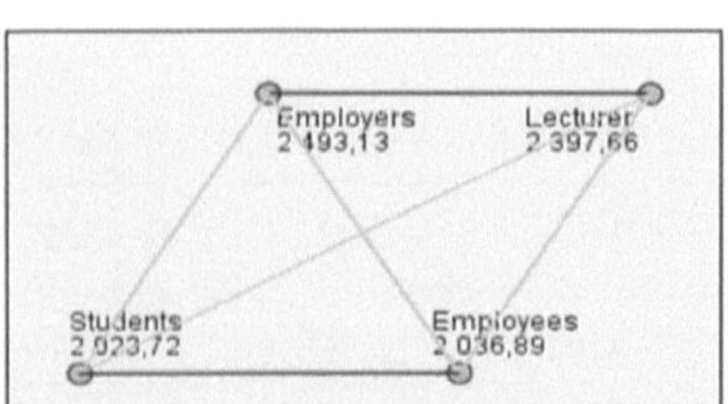

(c) Convey data/information in one's own words

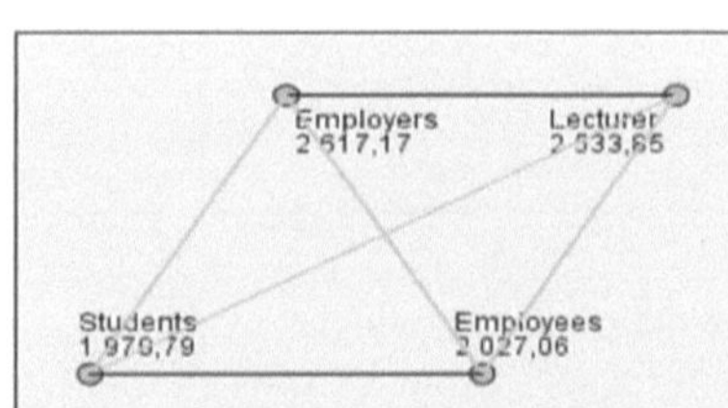

(d) Discern essential information from supplementary information

Fig. 39: *Interpretation skills block*

For the ability to *understand the content of data/information*, a Kruskal-Wallis test showed that there was a significant difference between means (H=129.312; df=3; p<0.001). Post-hoc tests of pairwise comparisons showed that the importance in the labour market of the ability to *understand the content of data/information* is evaluated similarly by the employees and the students, but compared to the teachers (p<0.001) and the employers (p<0.001), the employees rate this ability as being **less important**. Compared with the attitude of the teachers (p<0.001) and the employers (p<0.001), the students rate the ability to *understand the content of data/information* as being **less important**. But between the teachers and the employers there is no statistically significant difference (Figure 39, b).

For the ability to *convey data/information in one's own words*, a Kruskal-Wallis test showed that there was a significant difference between means (H=80.238; df=3; p<0.001). Post-hoc tests of pairwise comparisons showed that the importance in the labour market of the ability to *convey data/information in one's own words* is evaluated similarly by the employees and the students, but compared to the teachers (p<0.01) and the employers (p<0.001), the employees rate this ability as being **less important**. Compared with the attitude of the teachers (p<0.001) and the employers (p<0.001), the students rate the ability to *convey data/information in one's own words* as being **less important**. But between the teachers and the employers there is no statistically significant difference (Figure 39, c).

For the ability to *discern essential information from supplementary information*, a Kruskal-Wallis test showed that there was a significant difference between means (H=145.759; df=3; p<0.001). Post-hoc tests of pairwise comparisons showed that the importance in the labour market of the ability to *discern essential information from supplementary information* is evaluated similarly by the employees and the students, but compared to the teachers (p<0.001) and the employers (p<0.001), the employees rate this ability as being **less important**. Compared with the attitude of the teachers (p<0.001) and the employers (p<0.001), the students rate the ability to *discern essential information from supplementary information* as being **less important**. But between the teachers and the employers there is no statistically significant difference (Figure 39, d).

For the ability to *evaluate data/information with regard to different opinions*, a Kruskal-Wallis test showed that there was a significant difference between means (H=105.071; df=3; p<0.001). Post-hoc tests of pairwise comparisons showed that the importance in the labour market of the ability to *evaluate data/information with regard to different opinions* is evaluated similarly by the employees and the students, but compared to the teachers (p<0.001) and the employers (p<0.001), the employees rate this ability as being **less important**. Compared with the attitude of the teachers (p<0.001) and the employers (p<0.001), the students rate the ability to *evaluate data/information with regard to different opinions* as being **less important**. But between the teachers and the employers there is no statistically significant difference (Figure 40, a).

For the ability to *evaluate data/information without prejudice*, a Kruskal-Wallis test showed that there was a significant difference between means (H=108.113;

df=3; p<0.001). Post-hoc tests of pairwise comparisons showed that the importance in the labour market of the ability to *evaluate data/information without prejudice* is evaluated similarly by the employees and the students, but compared to the teachers (p<0.01) and the employers (p<0.001), the employees rate this ability as being **less important**. Compared with the attitude of the teachers (p<0.01) and the employers (p<0.001), the students rate the ability to *evaluate data/information without prejudice* as being **less important**. But between the teachers and the employers there is no statistically significant difference (Figure 40, b).

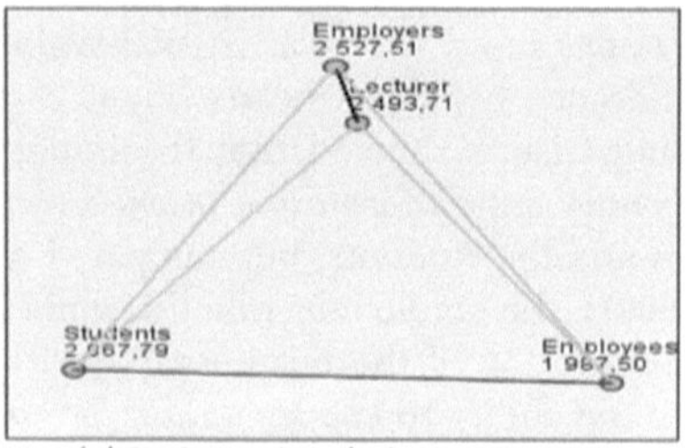

(a) Evaluate data/information with regard to different opinions

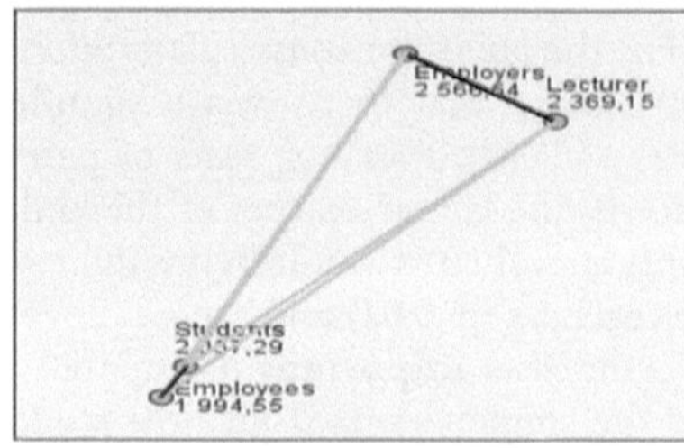

(b) Evaluate data/information without prejudice

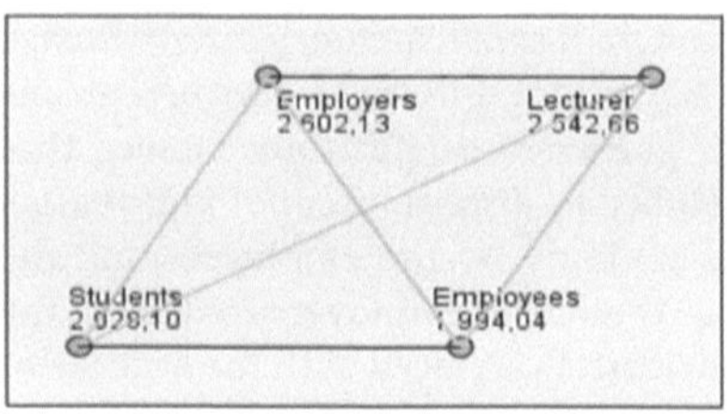

(c) Evaluate a situation on the basis of data/information

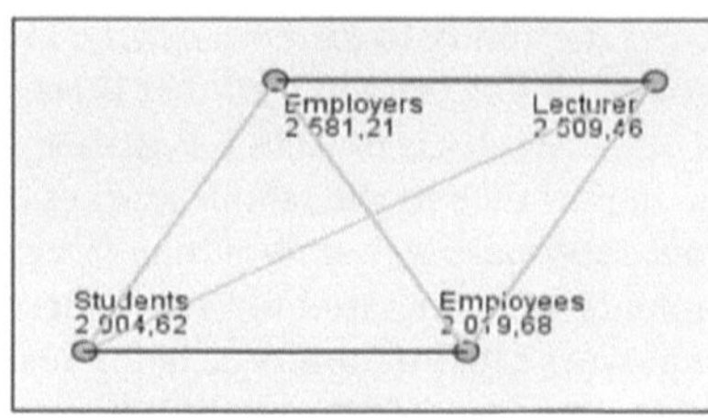

(d) Evaluate/self-evaluate the decisions/conclusions made

Fig. 40: *Evaluation skills block*

For the ability to *evaluate a situation on the basis of data/information*, a Kruskal-Wallis test showed that there was a significant difference between means (H=138.896; df=3; p<0.001). Post-hoc tests of pairwise comparisons showed that the importance in the labour market of the ability to *evaluate a situation on the basis of data/information* is evaluated similarly by the employees and the students, but compared to the teachers (p<0.001) and the employers (p<0.001), the employees rate this ability as being **less important**. Compared with the attitude of the teachers (p<0.01) and the employers (p<0.001), the students rate the ability to *evaluate a situation on the basis of data/information* as being **less important**. But between the teachers and the employers there is no statistically significant difference (Figure 40, c).

For the ability to *evaluate/self-evaluate the decisions/conclusions made*, a Kruskal-Wallis test showed that there was a significant difference between means (H=125.737; df=3; p<0.001). Post-hoc tests of pairwise comparisons showed that the importance in the labour market of the ability to *evaluate/self-evaluate the decisions/conclusions made* is evaluated similarly by the employees and the students, but compared to the teachers (p<0.001) and the employers (p<0.001), the employees rate this ability as being **less important**. Compared with the attitude of the teachers (p<0.01) and the employers (p<0.001), the students rate the ability to *evaluate/self-evaluate the decisions/conclusions made* as being **less important**. But between the teachers and the employers there is no statistically significant difference (Figure 40, d).

The employers and teachers were found to place more emphasis than the students and employees on the importance of all of the constituents of critical thinking for the modern labour market.

Attitudes towards critical thinking dispositions of importance in the modern labour market. It was found that the teachers (M=5.98), students (M=5.69) and employers (M=6.27) name fairness as the most important disposition in the modern labour market. The teachers (M=5.95), students (M=5.8) and employees (M=5.87) identify self-confidence as an important disposition in the modern labour market. Rightness is considered to be one of the most important dispositions in the labour market by the employees (M=5.9) and the employers (M=6.23).

In analysing the responses of the teachers, students, employers and employees, it was found that the employers were more likely than the teachers, students and employees to value the importance of the following dispositions in the modern labour market:

- impartiality, p<0.001 (mean rank, employer responses – 2624.41; employee responses – 2059.61; teacher responses – 2167.18; student responses – 1970.81);
- accuracy, p<0.001 (mean rank, employer responses – 2455.87; employee responses – 2076.11; teacher responses – 2317.94; student responses – 1992.56);
- fairness, p<0.001 (mean rank, employer responses – 2550.47; employee responses – 1955.43; teacher responses – 2250.28; student responses – 1936.77);
- caring for other people, p<0.001 (mean rank, employer responses – 2455.49; employee responses – 2126.66; teacher responses – 2250.28; student responses – 1961.87);
- self-confidence, p<0.003 (mean rank, employer responses – 2240.78; employee responses – 2106.24; teacher responses – 2227.92; student responses – 2036.63);
- flexibility, p<0.001 (mean rank, employer responses – 2360.78; employee responses – 2094.45; teacher responses – 2341.11; student responses – 1999.04);
- attentiveness, p<0.001 (mean rank, employer responses – 2307.90; employee responses – 2126.08; teacher responses – 2059.13; student responses – 2003.76);
- endurance, p<0.001 (mean rank, employer responses – 2248.28; employee responses – 2112.30; teacher responses – 2186.26; student responses – 2030.14);

- courage, $p<0.001$ (mean rank, employer responses – 2256.45; employee responses – 2140.57; teacher responses – 2149.31; student responses – 1993.37);
- perseverance, $p<0.001$ (mean rank, employer responses – 2319.34; employee responses – 2100.87; teacher responses – 2286.53; student responses – 2010.45);
- rightness, $p<0.001$ (mean rank, employer responses – 2468.12; employee responses – 2173.54; teacher responses – 2059.93; student responses – 1884.58).

Meanwhile, the teachers consider inquisitiveness to be a more important disposition in the modern labour market than the other groups of respondents do, $p<0.05$ (mean rank, teacher responses – 2279.29; employer responses – 2201.73; employee responses – 2067.18; student responses – 2097.08).

The students put more emphasis on the importance of the disposition of scepticism in the modern labour market than the teachers, employers and employees do, $p<0.001$ (mean rank, student responses – 2227.31; employer responses – 1997.57; employee responses – 2057.53; teacher responses – 1820.64).

In evaluating the importance of critical thinking dispositions in the modern labour market, it revealed that the representatives of both higher education and the labour market consider the most important critical thinking dispositions in the modern labour market to be self-confidence and fairness. The dispositions of open-mindedness, inquisitiveness and scepticism are considered by both groups to be of average importance in the modern labour market.

In evaluating the importance of critical thinking dispositions in the modern labour market within the group of higher education representatives, it was found that the more importance the teachers and students attach to specific critical thinking dispositions in the modern labour market, the more attention they give to their development in the study process. The opinion of the teachers and the students only differed on one critical thinking disposition: the teachers believe that the disposition of rightness is important in the modern labour market, but the students believe that this disposition is given less attention in the study process.

Within the group of labour market representatives, links emerged between the critical thinking dispositions valued by the employees and the dispositions that the employees expressed a need to improve. The employees consider self-confidence and rightness to be the most important critical thinking dispositions in the modern labour market, and express a need to improve precisely these critical thinking dispositions. The more the employees believe that these dispositions are important in the modern labour market, the more they emphasise the need to improve them. However, the opposite was true in the employer group. Even though the employers consider fairness, rightness and accuracy to be the most important critical thinking dispositions in the modern labour market, in evaluating the need to improve critical thinking dispositions in terms of their subordinates, they note the dispositions of flexibility and self-confidence.

Attitude regarding who is responsible for developing critical thinking. All four groups of respondents were found to agree that the person is responsible for developing his or her own critical thinking (teachers – $M=6.32$; students – $M=6.1$; employers – $M=6.18$; employees – $M=6.05$).

Statistically significant differences were found in analysing the responses of the teachers, students, employers and employees about who is responsible for developing a person's critical thinking. The teachers are more likely to agree with the statements that the development of critical thinking is the responsibility of:

the higher education institution, p<0.001 (mean rank, teacher responses – 2373.33, employer responses – 2314.88; employee responses – 2028.00, student responses – 2100.24);
the person him or herself, p<0.05 (mean rank, teacher responses – 2318.42, employer responses – 2140.58; employee responses – 2056.80, student responses – 2128.31).

Meanwhile, the employers were more likely than the teachers, students and employees to assign responsibility for developing a person's critical thinking to the organisation itself, p<0.001 (mean rank, employer responses – 2330.49, teacher responses – 2081.28; employee responses – 2083.69, student responses – 2050.05).

Attitude towards how higher education institutions prepare professionals for the modern labour market. Analysis of the research data revealed that the majority of the teachers (71.7 %), students (74.4 %) and employees (62.4 %) have a positive view of the preparation of professionals for the modern labour market at the country's higher education institutions. Meanwhile, only 44.5 % of the employers have a positive view of the preparation of higher education students for the modern labour market. Almost half of the employers who responded (46.8 %) do not have an opinion on this issue.

This means that both the higher education participants and the labour market participants have a positive view of the preparation of professionals for the modern labour market at the country's higher education institutions.

5. The Factorial Structure of Critical Thinking Skills Questionnaires

5.1 The strategy of confirmatory factor analysis

Confirmatory Factor Analysis using *Mplus* 8.4 with Maximum Likelihood Robust estimator was used to investigate the factorial structure of the two critical thinking skills questionnaires in student and teacher samples. The choice of Maximum Likelihood Robust estimator was based on the recommendations by Rhemtulla and colleagues (2012), which suggest the use of the estimator, when items have more than four response options and when response patterns are not heavily skewed or do not display a high degree of kurtosis. In our study, all critical thinking skills items had seven response options, with the average skewness of −0.619 (ranging from −0.895 to −0.458) and the average kurtosis of −0.085 (ranging from −0.458 to 0.792). This indicated the appropriateness of the Maximum Likelihood Robust estimator.

Considering that the Chi-square model fit statistic is sensitive to sample size (Kline, 2015), we used alternative indicators of model-data fit. In particular, we used the Root Mean Square Error of Approximation, Standardised Root Mean Square Residual, and the Comparative Fit Index, to assess model-data fit. Root Mean Square Error of Approximation and Standardised Root Mean Square Residual lower than 0.08 indicated an acceptable level of model-data fit. The Root Mean Square Error of Approximation and Standardised Root Mean Square Residual lower than 0.05 indicated a good fit. Comparative Fit Index higher than 0.90 indicated acceptable fit and Comparative Fit Index higher than 0.95 indicated good fit (Brown, 2015).

To evaluate the factorial structure of the critical thinking skills questionnaires, we tested a sequence of four theoretically plausible Confirmatory Factor Analysis models. The first (*unidimensional*) model was a single factor Confirmatory Factor Analysis model and tested a hypothesis that a single factor explains the variance and covariance of all questionnaire items. The second (*correlated factors*) model was a multiple-factor Confirmatory Factor Analysis model, which tested a hypothesis that items of the questionnaire represent eight distinct but correlated dimensions. The eight factors represented a set of distinct skills that were derived a priori, based on our theoretical speculations: decision-making, inference, explaining, analysis, self-regulation, argumentation, interpretation, and evaluation. The third (*higher-order*) model tested a hypothesis that there are eight distinct subordinate dimensions and a single superordinate and overreaching dimension. The superordinate dimension represents a shared variance of eight skill dimensions and specifies that the subordinate dimensions are uncorrelated, after considering the effect of the superordinate factor. The fourth and the last (*bi-factor*) model tested a hypothesis of the bi-factorial structure of the questionnaire. The key difference between the higher-order and bi-factor models is that the higher-order model includes an overreaching dimension that models the shared variance between different subdimensions, while the bi-factor model models the shared variance between the actual items (Brown, 2015). While a few bi-factor models exist, we used the orthogonal bi-factor model, meaning that a general factor and eight specific skill factors were uncorrelated with each other.

The more complex Confirmatory Factor Analysis models can be considered as nested in the simpler ones. Specifically, the correlated factors model is considered to be nested in a unidimensional model, the higher-order model is nested in a correlated-factors model, while the bi-factor model can be considered as nested in either a unidimensional or correlated-factors model (Brown, 2015). As these models are nested, they can be compared in terms of model-data fit. Consequently, to decide which model had a better representation of the correlation structure, we compared them using a "ΔCFI" criterion. Specifically, if one of the models had a Comparative Fit Index value greater than .01, it was considered to be superior in terms of data fit (Cheung and Rensvold, 2002).

Each of the four models was tested separately for student and teacher samples and separately for two different versions of the questionnaire: (a) critical thinking skills demanded in a labour market; (b) critical thinking skills mostly developed by academic staff. As such, four sets of models were tested. Considering that students and teachers received the same questionnaires, we also investigated if the measurement model parameters of the two measures were equivalent across students and teachers. That is, once the most likely factorial structure was chosen, we tested for *configural* (the presence of the same number of factors and correspondence between factors and indicators across groups), *metric* (equivalence of factor loadings), and *scalar* (equivalence of items' intercepts) measurement invariance, using the Multiple Group Confirmatory Factor Analysis, (Brown, 2015). These analyses were performed sequentially, beginning with configural, and progressing to scalar invariance (Dimitrov, 2010). Similarly, consecutive models (configural invariance, metric invariance, and scalar invariance) were compared using the "ΔCFI" criterion, for example, if newly added constraints (e.g., factor loading equality constraints) resulted in the decrease of Comparative Fit Index greater than 0.01, it indicated that a certain level of invariance (e.g., metric) does not hold (Cheung and Rensvold, 2002).

5.2 Factorial structure of the critical thinking skills questionnaire targeting critical thinking skills demanded in the labour market and its invariance in teacher and student samples.

In the teacher sample, the unidimensional model for the questionnaire targeting critical thinking skills demanded in the labour market had a rather poorer fit, which indicated that the covariance between the items cannot be attributed to a single factor. As such, this model was rejected. The correlated factors model, on the other hand, had an acceptable fit with the data. Compared to a unidimensional model, it was also clearly superior in terms of fit with data. However, the correlations between the factors were very high, that is, most of them exceeded 0.80 and some exceeded 0.90, indicating a very high degree of overlap between the eight factors. This result suggested the presence of a single overreaching common factor, which was modelled in the next two steps. The model-data fit of the higher-order model was also acceptable and not substantially different from that of the correlated factors model, suggesting that the shared variance of eight subfactors (skills) can be modelled as a single factor. However, the fourth bi-factor model had an even better fit with the data, and in terms of fit, it was also clearly better when compared to either a unidimensional model or a correlated factors model. This result suggested the superiority of the bi-factor model.

Similar results were obtained in the students' sample. The unidimensional model had a rather poor fit, suggesting that the presence of more than one factor, while the correlated factors model had a good fit with the data. The second-order and bi-factor models did not have a much better fit with data than the correlated factors model; however, both of these were not worse compared to the correlated-factors model. Yet, second-order and bi-factor models had a much better fit when compared to the unidimensional model. Considering the findings across the two samples, we decided that the bi-factor model had a better fit with the data and proceeded to test the invariance of this model across two groups.

The Multiple Group Confirmatory Factor Analysis using the combined (student and teacher) sample indicated that the bi-factor structure was invariant across the two groups. In particular, the configural invariance model, which did not impose any cross-group constraints and estimated a separate set of parameters in two groups, had a good fit with the data (Table 44). Metric invariance, which was tested by adding equality factor loading constraints across two groups, also did not result in a substantial decrease of model fit (ΔCFI was −0.005). This result indicated that factor loadings for the same measure in both groups were equivalent. The inclusion of intercept equality constraints, which was done to test for scalar invariance also did not have any effect on model-data fit (ΔCFI=0.000), indicating that item intercepts were also equivalent, which all together showed that the factor bi-factor structure of the critical thinking skills questionnaire targeting critical thinking skills demanded in the labour market was equivalent across the two samples. Table 36 summarises the findings of measurement invariance analysis.

Tab. 36: *Model fit statistics for the different Confirmatory Factor Analysis models for the critical thinking skills questionnaire targeting critical thinking skills demanded in the labour market (N=1664)*

	Model fit indices				
Model	χ^2	***df***	**RMSEA**	**SRMR**	**CFI**
Teachers' sample (n = 152)					
Unidimensional	927.65***	464	0.081	0.043	0.888
Correlated factors	748.07***	436	0.069	0.043	0.925
Higher-order	786.47***	456	0.069	0.044	0.920
Bifactor	653.91***	432	0.058	0.035	0.946
Students' sample (n = 1512)					
Unidimensional	5351.75***	464	0.083	0.042	0.854
Correlated factors	1739.58***	436	0.044	0.022	0.961
Higher-order	2133.38***	456	0.049	0.029	0.950
Bifactor	2063.32***	432	0.050	0.027	0.951
Combined sample (n = 1664)					
Configural invariance	2949.433***	864	0.054	0.028	0.951
Metric invariance	3192.812***	919	0.055	.038	0.946
Scalar invariance	3215.772***	942	0.054	0.039	0.946

*Notes. *** $p < 0.001$. χ^2 – model Chi-square; df – degrees of freedom; RMSEA – The Root Mean Square Error of Approximation; SRMR – Standardised Root Mean Square Residual; CFI – Comparative Fit Index.*

5.3 Factorial structure of the critical thinking skills questionnaire targeting critical thinking skills mostly developed by academic staff and its invariance in teacher and student samples

The unidimensional model for the critical thinking skills questionnaire targeting critical thinking skills mostly developed by academic staff in the teachers' sample had a very poor fit with the data. As such, we rejected it. The correlated factors model, on the other hand, also had a somewhat questionable fit. In particular, while the Root Mean Square Error of Approximation and Standardised Root Mean Square Residual suggested an acceptable fit of this model, the Comparative Fit Index was still somewhat lower than 0.90. The higher-order model, in terms of fit with data, was not substantially different from correlated factors models, again, suggesting the shared variance of eight subfactors can be modelled as a single factor. However, the fourth bi-factor model had a substantially better fit with the data when compared to both unidimensional and correlated factors models. Although the Comparative Fit Index value for a bi-factor model was still a bit lower than the desirable 0.90 value, the Root Mean Square Error of Approximation and Standardised Root Mean Square Residual values supported the model, which suggested that low Comparative Fit Index value could be attributed to a rather small sample of participants in the teachers' group.

The unidimensional model in a student sample had a bad fit and this result was well in-line with previous analysis. The three remaining models, however, showed a very good fit with the data. A comparison of the three (correlated factors, higher-order, and bi-factor) showed that the correlated factor model had the best fit with the data; however, the bi-factor model was not substantially worse than the correlated factors model. Considering the results of Confirmatory Factor Analysis in the teacher sample, as well as those obtained for the critical thinking skills questionnaire targeting critical thinking skills demanded in the labour market, we retained the bi-factor model. Table 37 summarises these results.

Tab. 37: *Model fit statistics for the different Confirmatory Factor Analysis models critical thinking skills questionnaire targeting critical thinking skills mostly developed by academic staff (N = 1664).*

	Model fit indices				
Model	χ^2	*df*	RMSEA	SRMR	CFI
Teachers' sample (n = 152)					
Unidimensional	1068.47***	464	0.093	0.080	0.734
Correlated factors	779.64***	436	0.072	0.071	0.849
Higher-order	805.84***	456	0.071	0.071	0.846
Bifactor	728.22***	432	0.067	0.063	0.869
Students' sample (n = 1512)					
Unidimensional	4443.29***	464	0.075	0.039	0.868
Correlated factors	1622.06***	436	0.042	0.023	0.961
Higher-order	1964.95***	456	0.047	0.029	0.950
Bifactor	1785.49***	432	0.046	0.025	0.955
Combined sample (n = 1664)					
Configural invariance	2654.621***	864	0.050	0.031	0.951
Metric invariance	2812.157***	919	0.050	0.041	0.948
Scalar invariance	2912.179***	942	0.050	0.042	0.946

Notes. *** $p < 0.001$. χ^2 – *model Chi-square; df – degrees of freedom; RMSEA – The Root Mean Square Error of Approximation; SRMR – Standardised Root Mean Square Residual; CFI – Comparative Fit Index.*

The Multiple Group Confirmatory Factor Analysis for this questionnaire using the combined student and teacher sample also indicated that the bi-factor structure was invariant across the two groups. In particular, the configural invariance model had a good fit with the data and supported the presence of the same number of factors in two samples. The inclusion of factor loading equality constraints for two groups also did not result in a substantial decrease of model fit (ΔCFI was −0.003) and neither did the inclusion of intercept equality constraints (ΔCFI=−0.002), indicating that item intercepts were also equivalent. In summary, results of Multiple Group Confirmatory Factor Analysis indicate that the factor bi-factor structure was also equivalent across the two samples. Standardised factor loadings for both, specific and general factors, were very similar across the two questionnaires. High general factor loadings in two critical thinking skills questionnaire versions indicated a presence of a very strong general factor, which accounted for a large proportion of item-response variances. The loadings of specific factors were weaker; however, in most cases, specific factors had at least one item that had a factor loading higher than the 0.30 threshold, which showed that some of the item variance can be attributed to specific skills.

The results suggest the perceived demand of critical thinking skills in the labour market and this perception correlates with the development of critical thinking skills in higher education (Table 38). This is the case for all critical thinking skills (decision-making; inference; interpretation; analysis; self-regulation; argumentation; interpretation; evaluation).

Tab. 38: *Standardised factor loadings obtained from the bi-factor model on the full sample for the two critical thinking skills questionnaires (N = 1664).*

Factor (skill)	**Item**	**Cthinking skills demand**		**Cthinking skills developed**	
		λ_s	λ_g	λ_s	λ_g
Decision-making	Make decisions independently	0.25	0.81	0.21	0.77
	Make decisions collegially	0.37	0.79	0.36	0.71
	Justify a decision made to others	0.30	0.80	0.42	0.74
	Make decisions according to the procedures established in the organisation	0.31	0.78	0.41	0.67
Inference	Summarise information	0.27	0.86	0.23	0.85
	Formulate evidence-based conclusions	0.36	0.86	0.30	0.84
	Formulate conclusions with regard to the context	0.35	0.84	0.33	0.82
	Formulate conclusions in anticipation of possible consequences	0.20	0.85	0.30	0.80
Explanation	Formulate questions for others	0.29	0.79	0.21	0.79
	Answer others' questions	0.33	0.82	0.27	0.81
	Explain an analysis carried out and the results obtained	0.22	0.86	0.25	0.81
	Explain the decision-making path	0.29	0.84	0.33	0.78
	Explain complex concepts	0.31	0.80	0.43	0.75
	Reveal the essence of a phenomenon	0.22	0.85	0.35	0.80
Analysis	Reveal connections between statements, facts, concepts	0.22	0.85	0.23	0.82
	Examine a situation from different points of view	0.31	0.85	0.29	0.83
	Find connections between the whole and its parts	0.37	0.84	0.38	082
	Collect data/information and link it to other data/sources	0.26	0.84	0.27	0.82

(continued)

Tab. 38: *Continued*

Factor (skill)	Item	Cthinking skills demand		Cthinking skills developed	
		λ_s	λ_g	λ_s	λ_g
Self-regulation	Know oneself	0.62	0.69	0.54	0.67
	Reflect (on one's thoughts, feelings, actions)	0.54	0.70	0.50	0.72
	Change according to the situation	0.48	0.74	0.35	0.72
Argumentation	Think based on facts/evidence	0.30	0.86	0.35	0.78
	Justify one's choices	0.36	0.86	0.40	0.82
	Base actions on reflection	0.27	0.82	0.27	0.78
Interpretation	Classify data/information	0.22	0.86	0.23	0.78
	Understand the content of data/information	0.28	0.87	0.25	0.84
	Convey data/information in one's own words	0.27	0.84	0.26	0.79
	Discern essential information from supplementary information	0.24	0.87	0.28	0.83
Evaluation	Evaluate data/information with regard to different opinions	0.23	0.83	0.18	0.78
	Evaluate data/information without prejudice	0.31	0.84	0.33	0.78
	Evaluate a situation on the basis of data/information	0.32	0.85	0.43	0.80
	Evaluate/self-evaluate the decisions/conclusions made	0.28	0.85	0.40	0.80

Notes. λ_s *– standardised loading on the specific factor;* λ_g *– standardised loading on the general factor. All loadings are statistically significant at* $p < .05$. *Cthinking skills demand – perceived demand of critical thinking skills in the labour market; critical thinking skills developed – mostly developed by academic staff. A factor loading is a correlation coefficient between each variable and each factor in a factor analysis. They are analogous to regression (slope) coefficients. The higher the loading, the closer the association of the item with the group of items that make up the factor. Loadings of less than 0,3 are generally not considered meaningful.*

It should be noted that when analysing decision-making skills, the sub-skills of *making decisions collectively* (λ=0.37) and *making decisions in accordance with organisation's procedures* (λ=0.31) are more highly valued in the labour market than the sub-skills of *making decisions independently* (λ=0.25) and *justifying the decision made* (λ=0.30). However, in education, the sub-skills of *justifying the decision made* (λ=0.42), *making decisions in accordance with the organisation's procedures* (λ=0.41) and *making decisions collectively* (λ=0.36) are given more emphasis.

The analysis of inference skill revealed that the sub-skills of *drawing evidence-based conclusions* (λ=0.36) and *drawing conclusions in consideration of the context* (λ=0.35) are more highly prioritised by teacher and students in the labour market than the sub-skills of *summarising information* (λ=0.27) and *drawing conclusions with anticipating potential consequences* (λ=0.20). However, the development of the sub-skill of *drawing conclusions in the context* (λ=0.33) is more emphasised than the other sub-skills in this group.

The analysis of the explaining skill showed that the sub-skills of *answering others' questions* (λ=0.33) and *explaining complex concepts* (λ=0.31) are given more priority in the labour market than the sub-skills of *formulating questions to others* (λ=0.29), *explaining the analysis carried out and the results* (λ=0.22), *explaining the decision-making process* (λ=0.33), and *revealing the essence of a phenomenon* (λ=0.22). In contrast, the sub-skills of *explaining the decision-making process* (λ=0.33), *explaining complex concepts* (λ=0.43), and *revealing the essence of a phenomenon* (λ=0.35) are more strongly emphasised in educational process than the other explanatory sub-skills.

When analysing analysis skills, sub-skills of *analysing the situation from different perspectives* (λ = 0.31) and *discovering connections between the whole and its parts* (λ = 0.37) are prioritised by teachers and students in the labour market more than sub-skills of *revealing connections between statements/facts/concepts* (λ = 0.22), *collecting data/information and linking it to other data/sources* (λ = 0.26). Meanwhile, the development of sub-skill of *discovering connections between the whole and its parts* (λ = 0.38) pays more attention than to other sub-skills of analytical skill: *revealing connections between statements/facts/concepts* (λ = 0.23), *analysing the situation from different perspectives* (λ = 0.29), *collecting data/information and linking it to other data/sources* (λ = 0.27).

It should be noted that all sub-skills of self-regulation skill (*knowing oneself* (λ = 0.62), *reflecting [one's thoughts, feelings, actions]* (λ = 0.54), *changing according to the situation* (λ = 0.48) are prioritised in the labour market. It has been found that more attention is paid to the development of all sub-skills.

In argumentation skill, the sub-skill of *reasoning about one's choices* (λ=0.36) is prioritised in the labour market more than the sub-skills of *thinking based on facts/evidence* (λ=0.30), *justification one's actions by reflection* (λ=0.27). Meanwhile, in educational process, the sub-skills of *thinking based on facts/evidence* (λ=0.35) and *reasoning about one's choices* (λ=0.40) are given more emphasis.

No statistically significant differences were found between the sub-skills of interpretation.

The analysis of evaluation skill revealed that the sub-skill of *assessing data/information without prejudice* (λ = 0.31), *assessing a situation based on data/information* (λ = 0.32) is prioritised by teachers and students in the labour market more than *assessing data/information based on different opinions* (λ = 0.23), *assessing the decisions made/conclusions* (λ = 0.28). It was found that in the educational process, more attention than to others is paid to these three sub-skills: *assessing data/information without prejudice* (λ = 0.33), *assessing a situation based on data/information* (λ = 0.43) and *assessing the decisions made*/conclusions (λ = 0.40).

This result also suggested that to model the effects of specific factors on outcome variables, complex variance decomposition techniques, such as structural equation modelling with latent variables, should be used.

5.4 Associations between critical thinking skills demanded in the labour market and critical thinking skills mostly developed by academic staff

To investigate the associations between critical thinking skills demanded in the labour market and critical thinking skills mostly developed by academic staff, we built and tested a Structural Equation Model. To construct this model, we first included two measurement models that were based on our previous analysis of the factorial structure of critical thinking skills questionnaires. In particular, we included a measurement model, which measured a general factor and eight specific factors measuring perceived critical thinking skill need in the labour market and then included a second one, which measured a general factor and eight specific factors measuring critical thinking skills developed by academic staff. To account for the likely residual associations between items measuring critical thinking skills demand in the labour market and items measuring critical thinking skills developed by academic staff, we included 32 residual correlations, for each pair of items. This model had a good fit with data (see Table 39, configural model).

Tab. 39: *Model fit statistics for the structural equation model linking the perceived demand for critical thinking skills in the labour market with critical thinking skills mostly developed by academic staff (N = 1664).*

	Model fit indices				
Model	χ^2	***df***	**RMSEA**	**SRMR**	**CFI**
Configural invariance	5645.20***	1775	0.036	0.026	0.953
Metric invariance	5749.05***	1830	0.036	0.029	0.952
Scalar invariance	5835.01***	1853	0.036	0.029	0.951
SEM model	5679.11***	1853	0.035	0.026	0.953

Notes. *** $p < 0.001$. χ^2 *– model Chi-square; df – degrees of freedom; RMSEA – The Root Mean Square Error of Approximation; SRMR – Standardised Root Mean Square Residual; CFI – Comparative Fit Index.*

To reduce the complexity and increase the parsimony of the Structural Equation Model, we tested if the factorial structure of perceived critical thinking skills demand in the labour market and critical thinking skills developed by academic structure questionnaires were equivalent, before proceeding to any further analysis. While these tests were not driven by strong theoretical justifications, we speculated that the two questionnaires may have a similar, if not identical factor structure, which, if found to be the case, could help reduce the number of free parameters in the model and provide more statistical power for the tests of model-data fit (Kline, 2015). The initial, configural invariance model, was the same model that we build in the first step, and as such, it had a good fit with data. The inclusion of factor loading equality constraints for two measures to test for metric invariance did not result in a substantial decrease in model fit (ΔCFI was −0.001). The inclusion of intercept equality constraints (ΔCFI = −0.001) to test for scalar invariance also did not produce any substantial decrease of model fit, indicating that factor loadings and item intercepts were equivalent across the questionnaire.

In the last step of our analysis, we respecified this model into a Structural Equation Model. In this model, each factor of critical thinking skills developed by academic staff was regressed on each factor of perceived critical thinking skill need in the labour market. Since this model had the same degrees of freedom, its fit was very similar to the scalar invariance model. Standardised slope parameter estimates from a Structural Equation Model linking perceived demand of critical thinking skills in the labour market with critical thinking skills mostly developed by academic staff are presented in Table 40.

Tab. 40: *Standardised slope parameter estimates from a Structural Equation Model linking perceived demand of critical thinking skills in the labour market with critical thinking skills mostly by academic staff (N = 1664).*

Predictor variables: Perceived critical thinking skills need in the labour market	**Outcome variables: Thinking skills developed by academic staff**								
	General factor	***Decision-making***	***Inference***	***Explaining***	***Analysis***	***Self-regulation***	***Argumentation***	***Interpretation***	***Evaluation***
General factor	0.43^{**}	0.21^{*}	0.38^{**}	0.26^{**}	0.24^{**}	0.11	0.27^{**}	0.27^{***}	0.24^{**}
Decision-making	0.01	0.01	0.09	0.01	0.00	0.07	0.23^{**}	0.17^{**}	0.20^{**}
Inference	0.24	0.03	0.10	0.04	0.17	0.19^{*}	0.28^{***}	0.36^{***}	0.30^{***}
Explanation	0.16^{*}	0.06	-0.13	0.18	0.04	0.02	0.04	0.11	0.02
Analysis	0.15^{**}	-0.19	-0.07	-0.02	0.26^{*}	0.05	0.13	0.33^{***}	0.35^{***}
Self-regulation	0.13^{*}	-0.05	-0.33^{***}	-0.09	-0.23	0.34^{***}	0.02	-0.20	-.007
Argumentation	-0.14	0 .05	-0.11	-0.09	-0.03	0.26^{**}	0.46^{***}	0.16^{*}	0.26^{***}
Interpretation	0.04	-0.12	-0.04	-0.11	0.09	-0.01	0.18	0.35^{***}	0.29^{***}
Evaluation	-0.11	0.02	0.02	-0.05	0.15	0.04	0.19	0.31^{***}	0.40^{***}
R^2	0.44	0.10	0.30	0.14	0.23	0.24	0.51	0.64	0.63

*Notes. * indicates a statistically significant parameter at $p < 0.05$; ** – $p < 0.01$; *** - $p < 0.001$. R^2 – determinacy coefficient, indicates the proportionate amount of variation in the outcome variable explained by predictor variables.*

Results of this analysis indicated the presence of some general and specific effects. Expectedly, the general factor of critical thinking skills developed by academic staff was most strongly predicted by the general factor of perceived critical thinking skills need in the labour market. However, with an exception of self-regulation, each specific dimension of critical thinking skills developed by academic staff was also positively predicted by the general factor of critical thinking skills need in the labour market. The remaining associations were somewhat more complex.

The general factor of critical thinking skills developed by academic staff was strengthened (positively predicted) by the perceived need for explaining, analyse, and self-regulation factors. Specific factors measuring decision-making and explaining skills development were not significantly predicted by any specific factors of perceived critical thinking skills need in the labour market. Interestingly, the specific factor of inference was negatively predicted by higher levels of the perceived need for self-regulation skills.

5.5 Factor structure of Attitudes Towards Critical Thinking Scale

Initially, Confirmatory Factor Analysis was used to investigate the factorial structure of the Attitudes Towards Critical Thinking Scale in student and teacher samples. We chose the Maximum Likelihood Robust estimator because all items of this scale had seven response options, with the average skewness of −0.382 (ranging from −0.648 to 0.028) and the average kurtosis of −0.148 (ranging from −0.012 to −1.123). Using the Confirmatory Factor Analysis approach, we first tested if a single factor explains the variance and covariance of all questionnaire items. However, Confirmatory Factor Analysis results suggested that a single factor model has a very poor fit with the data, in student (χ^2 = 987.69; df = 9; p < 0.001; RMSEA = 0.268, CFI = 0.490, SRMR = 0.150) and teacher sample was well (χ^2 = 27.67; df = 9, p = 0.001; RMSEA =0.117, CFI = 0.780, SRMR = 0.059).

Considering that the expected single-factor model was not supported, we turned to Exploratory Factor Analysis, which we also conducted using *Mplus 8.4* with Maximum Likelihood Robust estimator. Before proceeding to the analysis, the suitability of the data for Exploratory Factor Analysis was assessed by calculating the Kaiser-Meyer-Olkin (KMO) and Bartlett's test of sphericity, with *SPSS* 21. In both samples, the KMO value was close to or higher than 0.70, and Bartlett's test was significant (p < 0.001), supporting the factorability of the correlation matrix. Since the extracted factors were expected to be correlated, an oblique rotation strategy, that is, GEOMIN rotation, was used to interpret the factors (Sass and Schmitt, 2010).

To determine the optimal number of factors, we used a set of indicators. Considering that we used the maximum likelihood approach to analyse the factor structure (instead of Principal Axis Factoring or Principal Component Analysis), we also employed the Comparative Fit Index, the Root Mean Square Error of

Approximation, and the Standardised Root Mean Squared Residual, to investigate which factor solution has a good fit. In particular, the solutions with a different number of factors were compared with each other using these indices. We looked for solutions that had Root Mean Square Error of Approximation and Standardised Root Mean Squared Residual values lower than 0.08 and had Comparative Fit Index values higher than 0.90, as they indicated an acceptable solution (Brown, 2015). Besides, more in-line with a classical Exploratory Factor Analysis approach, we compared factor eigenvalues and considered the solutions that have factors with eigenvalues higher than one (Brown, 2015).

In both samples, one- to three-factor solutions were computed and compared, as those with more factors did not converge. Table 41 presents the results. In both samples, model fit statistics supported the two-factor solution. That is, in both samples, the one-factor solution did not show a good model-data fit in terms of Comparative Fit Index, Root Mean Square Error of Approximation, and Standardised Root Mean Squared Residual statistics. More so, the eigenvalue for a third factor was lower than one, showing that the third factor may not be meaningful. The two-factor solution, on the other hand, had a good fit with data and in both samples.

Tab. 41: *Results of Exploratory Factor Analyses: Model Fit Statistics.*

Number of factors	**Eigenvalues**	**Model fit statistics**					
		χ^2	*df*	n_{par}	**CFI**	**RMSEA**	**SRMR**
Teacher sample (n = 152)							
1	2.263	27.67	9	18	0.780	0.117	0.059
2	1.101	5.83	4	23	0.978	0.055	0.021
3	0.782	Did not converge					
Student sample (n = 1512)							
1	2.575	987.68	9	18	0.490	0.268	0.150
2	1.728	36.41	4	23	0.983	0.073	0.019
3	0.596	0.00	0	27	1.00	0.000	0.000

Note. χ^2 *– Chi-square test of model fit; df – degrees of freedom;* n_{par} *– the number of free parameters in the model; CFI – Comparative fit index; RMSEA – Root mean square error of approximation; SRMR – Standardised Root Mean Square Residual.*

Standardised loadings from a two-factor solution are presented in Table 42. While factor loadings had some similarities across two samples, some notable differences were also present.

Tab. 42: *Standardised factor loadings obtained from the exploratory factor analysis of perceived critical thinking scale in teacher and student samples*

Item	Teacher sample		Student sample	
	λ_1	λ_2	λ_1	λ_2
Critical thinking can be developed.	-0.40	0.17	-0.15	0.78
A person can think critically if he or she wants and tries to.	0.01	0.67	-0.01	0.71
A person's ability to think critically is unchanging.	0.80	0.00	0.84	0.01
Critical thinking only occurs when criticising.	0.53	0.01	0.90	-0.01
There are various ways to demonstrate critical thinking.	-0.17	0.37	0.10	0.69
Critical thinking is possible in every situation	-0.01	0.58	0.13	0.64

Notes. λ_1 *– standardised loading on the first factor;* λ_2 *– standardised loading on the second factor*

In particular, in both samples, items number three and four had clear and strong associations with one factor, while items two, five, and six had clear associations with the second factor. However, the first item on the scale had a different association with two factors across two samples. In the teacher sample, the first item loaded negatively on the first factor, while in the student sample, it loaded on the second factor. This result suggested that the factor structure of the scale was somewhat different across the two samples. It also suggested that items should be grouped differently for teachers and students. Despite this difference, the meaning of the factors across the two samples was rather similar. Considering the content of the items, we labelled the first as 'rigidity' and the second as 'elasticity'. Internal consistency of items belonging to the two factors was also sufficient. Chronbach's α coefficient was 0.60 for the rigidity factor in teacher and 0.86 in the student sample, while α coefficient was 0.58 for the elasticity factor in the teacher sample and 0.80 for the student sample.

5.6 Associations between rigidity and elasticity of critical thinking conception and teaching of critical thinking skills in teacher sample.

To investigate the associations between attitudes towards critical thinking and critical thinking skills mostly developed by academic staff, we built and tested a path model. The choice to employ path analysis with observed variables rather than structural equation modelling with latent variables was based on the fact that the teacher sample was rather small (structural equation modelling analysis requires medium or large samples). Considering that our measure of the teaching of critical thinking skills was represented by a bi-factor structure, using the previously discussed bi-factor Confirmatory Factor Analysis model, we estimated factor scores for the general and specific dimensions. In the path analytic model, the factor scores for each of these dimensions were used as outcome variables and the item-total scores of rigidity and elasticity of critical thinking were used as predictors of outcome variables. Considering this specification and the fact that no path constraints were introduced in our model, our path analytic model was completely saturated and had a perfect fit with data.

The standardised slope parameter estimates from a path model linking attitudes towards critical thinking with critical thinking skills mostly developed by academic staff are presented in Table 43.

Tab. 43: *Standardised slope parameter estimates from a path model linking attitudes towards critical thinking with critical thinking skills mostly developed by academic staff (N = 152)*

Predictor variables: Attitudes towards critical thinking	**Outcome variables: critical thinking skills developed by academic staff**								
	General factor	***Decision-making***	***Inference***	***Explaining***	***Analysis***	***Self-regulation***	***Argumentation***	***Interpretation***	***Evaluation***
The rigidity of critical thinking	-0.18*	0.01	0.07	0.06	-0.07	0.09	0.01	-0.19*	-0.12
The elasticity of critical thinking	0.23**	0.14	-0.10	0.02	0.11	0.08	0.03	-0.06	-0.07
R^2	0.07	0.02	<0.01	0.01	0.02	0.02	<0.01	0.04	0.02

*Notes. * indicates a statistically significant parameter at p < 0.05; ** – p < 0.01. R^2 – determinacy coefficient, indicates the proportionate amount of variation in the outcome variable explained by predictor variables.*

In general, one notable pattern of associations has emerged. The rigidity factor of critical thinking attitudes negatively predicted the general factor of critical thinking skills developed by academic staff, while the elasticity factor of critical thinking positively predicted this factor. What this finding shows that teachers who perceive the skills of critical thinking as something very rigid and inflexible tend to put less effort into developing skills related to critical thinking, while those who perceive the skills as critical thinking as something flexible and teachable, tend to put more effort in developing all skills related to critical thinking. Only one association emerged with specific factors. In particular, the rigidity of critical thinking also negatively predicted the teaching of interpretation skills.

5.7 Factorial structure of the questionnaire targeting dispositions of critical thinking mostly developed by academic staff and most demanded in the labour market

Considering that we did not have any *a priori* assumptions about the factor structure of a newly developed dispositions scale, the dimensionality (factor structure) of the scale was investigated using the Exploratory Factor Analysis, instead of the confirmatory one (Confirmatory Factor Analysis). In line with the previous analyses, Exploratory Factor Analysis was also conducted using *Mplus 8.4* with Maximum Likelihood Robust estimator. Again, the suitability of the data for Exploratory Factor Analysis was assessed by calculating the KMO test and Bartlett's test of sphericity. For each version of the scale (dispositions of critical thinking mostly developed by academic staff and dispositions of critical thinking demanded in the labour market) and in both samples (teacher and student), the KMO value was higher than 0.70, and Bartlett's test was significant ($p<0.001$), supporting the factorability of the correlation matrix. An oblique rotation strategy (GEOMIN) was used to interpret the factors.

The optimal number of factors was also determined using factor eigenvalues and a set of model-data fit indicators (we looked for solutions that had Root Mean Square Error of Approximation and Standardised Root Mean Square Residual values lower than 0.08 and had Comparative Fit Index values higher than 0.90, as they indicated an acceptable solution Comparative Fit Index, Root Mean Square Error of Approximation, and Standardised Root Mean Square Residual). While inspecting factor eigenvalues, we only considered solutions that have factors with eigenvalues higher than one. However, since in these analyses, the "eigenvalue > 1" criterion highly disagreed with model-data fit estimates, we also employed parallel analysis, to determine what level of eigenvalues can be considered as indicative of meaningful factors. Parallel analysis was conducted with 100 random data sets and the average eigenvalues from random data sets were compared to the eigenvalues computed with the study data. Study data factors with eigenvalues higher than those in parallel analyses were considered meaningful.

In both samples and for both versions of the questionnaire, one- to five-factor solutions were computed and compared, as those with more factors did not converge. Table 44 presents the results.

Tab. 44: *Results of Exploratory Factor Analyses for dispositions of critical thinking measure: Model Fit Statistics*

Number of factors	Eigenvalues	Model fit statistics					
		χ^2	*df*	n_{par}	CFI	RMSEA	SRMR
Dispositions of critical thinking mostly developed by academic staff/Teacher sample (n = 152)							
1	6.818	188.036	77	42	0.851	0.097	0.070
2	1.389	110.118	64	55	0.938	0.069	0.043
3	0.899	79.945	52	67	0.963	0.059	0.035
4	0.819	Did not converge					
5	0.730	315.176	31	88	0.619	0.246	0.021
Dispositions of critical thinking mostly developed by academic staff/Student sample (n = 1512)							
1	9.189	938.851	77	42	0.890	0.086	0.045
2	0.997	684.042	64	55	0.921	0.080	0.031
3	0.608	587.196	52	67	0.932	0.083	0.024
4	0.532	383.748	41	78	0.956	0.074	0.016
5	0.475	146.114	31	88	0.985	0.050	0.012
Dispositions of critical thinking mostly demanded in the labour market/Teacher sample (n = 152)							
1	8.540	268.423	77	42	0.832	0.128	0.071
2	1.292	104.933	64	55	0.964	0.065	0.032
3	0.915	61.392	52	67	0.992	0.034	0.023
4	0.591	77.749	41	78	0.968	0.077	0.020
5	0.458	44.595	31	88	0.988	0.054	0.014
Dispositions of critical thinking mostly demanded in the labour market/Student sample (n = 1512)							
1	8.551	1043.892	77	42	0.870	0.091	0.051
2	1.034	669.053	64	55	0.918	0.079	0.032
3	0.650	544.425	52	67	0.934	0.079	0.026
4	0.603	323.849	41	78	0.962	0.068	0.021
5	0.519	264.797	31	88	0.968	0.071	0.017

Note. χ^2 *– Chi-square test of model fit; df – degrees of freedom;* n_{par} *– the number of free parameters in the model; CFI – Comparative fit index; RMSEA – Root mean square error of approximation; SRMR – Standardised Root Mean Square Residual.*

Model fit statistics, for both versions of the questionnaire and across two samples, suggested solutions with more than one factor. However, model fit indices were not consistent across the four analyses. For dispositions of critical thinking mostly developed by academic staff scale, model fit indices (especially Root Mean Square Error of Approximation) suggested a three-factor solution in teacher and a five-factor solution in student samples. For dispositions of critical thinking mostly demanded in the labour market, indices suggested a three-factor solution in the teacher sample but did not indicate a good-fitting solution in the student sample. More so, the interpretability of the solutions suggested by model fit indices was very problematic. These solutions were characterised by multiple factor cross-loadings and factors with single or a few high-loading items. Consequently, we turned to a detailed inspection of eigenvalues.

Across the four analyses, the "eigenvalue > 1" criterion did not suggest solutions with more than two factors and in one case it suggested a one-factor solution. Parallel analysis, on the other hand, suggested that solutions with more than one factor were not meaningful. This result also suggested that the lack of model-data fit for one-factor solutions may not be attributed to the presence of multiple factors. Instead, it may be attributed to the presence of small residual correlations between items, which do not constitute substantial latent variables. To evaluate if this is the case, we also rand a set of supplementary single-factor Confirmatory Factor analyses, for both versions of the questionnaire and both samples. Single-factor Confirmatory Factor Analysis models (note that these had an identical fit as the single-factor Exploratory Factor Analysis models) and modification indices calculated for these models, suggested the presence of few minor residual correlations between some items of the scale, which explained the misfit of single-factor models. Summing up, we concluded that, across both samples and both versions of the questionnaire, items of the scale represent a single dimension.

Standardised loadings from Exploratory Factor analyses with a single-factor solution are presented in Table 45. Noteworthy, with one exception, all items of the scale had strong loadings on the main factor, that is, in almost every case, standardised factor loading was higher than 0.05, and only one item (scepticism) had a lower loading in some situations. Internal consistency of items belonging to the two factors was also sufficient.

Tab. 45: *Standardised factor loadings obtained in Exploratory Factor Analyses for dispositions of critical thinking measure*

Item no.	Item	Academic /teacher	Academic /student	Work / teacher	Work / student
1	Impartiality	0.58	0.73	0.75	0.69
2	Accuracy	0.64	0.80	0.85	0.79
3	Fairness	0.69	0.79	0.76	0.75
4	Caring for other people	0.65	0.81	0.75	0.78
5	Inquisitiveness	0.65	0.83	0.80	0.76
6	Self-confidence	0.73	0.85	0.81	0.70
7	Flexibility	0.70	0.86	0.81	0.83
8	Attentiveness	0.80	0.83	0.79	0.84
9	Endurance	0.67	0.82	0.78	0.83
10	Courage	0.70	0.84	0.81	0.82
11	Perseverance	0.66	0.85	0.86	0.79
12	Scepticism	0.30	0.47	0.39	0.60
13	Open-mindedness	0.70	0.77	0.66	0.73
14	Rightness	0.79	0.79	0.74	0.72
Cronbach's alpha		0.906	0.956	0.946	0.947

In summarising, analysis skills developed by academic staff were positively predicted by the perceived need for analysis skills, but not by any other. Self-regulation skills developed by academic staff were also predicted by the perceived need for self-regulation skills, yet it was also positively predicted by the perceived need for inference and argumentation skills. The focus on teaching argumentation skills was also positively predicted by the perceived need for argumentation skills, but it was also strengthened by the perceived need for decision-making and inference skills. The teaching of interpretation and evaluation skills had very similar patterns of significant predictors. Both dimensions developed by academic staff were positively predicted by the perceived need for decision-making, inference, analysis, argumentation, interpretation, and evaluation skills. Exploratory Factor Analysis identified that dispositions scale consisted from 14 dispositions represents a single dimension. It implies that critical thinking dispositions should be viewed as whole without breaking them down into separate elements.

Conclusions

The concept of critical thinking in higher education and the labour market is associated with a person's skills and dispositions. Critical thinking is seen as a process that depends on a person's skills, dispositions, values and beliefs. In both higher education and the labour market, critical thinking is considered to be a key competence, which manifests itself as the ability to make decisions based on real-life problems. The ability to make decisions and take action becomes one of the essential traits that employers expect from prospective employees, and teachers develop this skill. In evaluating the definition of critical thinking, the teachers and employers are more likely to emphasise the result of this process – the adoption of a reasoned and rational decision. This definition of critical thinking focuses on the understanding that in certain situations, no obviously right solution exists, so strong arguments are needed to make the right decision. Meanwhile, the students and the employees see the result in the very thought process, in which reflection on action and the ability to engage in impartial reasoning based on controlled, rational inference and decision-making play an important role.

In the context of both higher education and the labour market, the manifestation of critical thinking is associated with a person's efforts and desire, and opportunities to think critically in different situations. Critical thinking is manifested as a person's conscious choice to apply acquired knowledge and abilities in specific situations. Critical thinking means a person's active, purposeful and organised efforts to give meaning to his or her world by carefully examining his or her own thinking and that of others. Thus, in the context of higher education and the labour market, the manifestation of critical thinking is associated more with the personal context. Critical thinking is understood as a thought process that can be developed. However, there is another opinion among representatives of higher education and the labour market that critical thinking only occurs when criticising and that the ability to think critically is unchanging.

The higher education and labour market representatives consider inference skills to be the most important in the modern labour market. The ability to draw meaningful conclusions is recognised as a process of cognitive reasoning that, from the point of view of the employers and the teachers, is associated with summarising data-based information and anticipating consequences. In the opinion of the students and the employees, self-regulation skills are considered to be among the most important in the modern labour market; the employers and the teachers, however, believe that these skills are less important in the modern labour market. Interpretation skills are important for the employers and the teachers, when it is not enough to have knowledge or information alone, but the proper use of that knowledge and information in professional activities/studies is important when focusing on the applicability of knowledge and abilities. The critical thinking skills that are considered to be of average importance in the modern labour market are considered to be those at the interpersonal and social level, going beyond the individual's level of internal contemplation and seeking, in the broader context and taking different opinions into account, to analyse in detail and reasonably evaluate a situation/problem and make a rational solution.

From the point of view of the higher education and labour market representatives, the importance of developing critical thinking skills corresponds to the needs of the modern labour market, which are related to decision-making skills at the personal and interpersonal level. Higher education institutions strive to develop the abilities that are recognised in the labour market: inference, argumentation and interpretation skills. The students also note the importance of developing these skills. In the opinion of the employees and the students, the ability to know oneself and to reflect (on one's thoughts, feelings, actions), which is related to the personal level of critical thinking, are important skills in the modern labour market. However, it is the opinion of both groups of respondents that there is little recognition of the interpersonal and social level of the manifestation of critical thinking in the field of critical thinking skills.

In the context of higher education and the labour market, the dispositions of fairness, courage and perseverance are most valued in the modern labour market, while those of scepticism and open-mindedness are given as being of average importance. More attention is given in the study process to developing the critical thinking dispositions that the teachers and the students consider to be important in the modern labour market. The dispositions that the higher education and labour market representatives consider to be important are also the dispositions that need the most improvement/development. Various methods are used for the development of critical thinking skills and dispositions, most of which are focused on self-education. In terms of the critical thinking dispositions that need the most improvement, the higher education and labour market representatives identified flexibility, open-mindedness and accuracy.

Responsibility for developing critical thinking is delegated to the person and his or her desire or willingness to think critically. The willingness to think critically is associated with a thought process that depends on a person's dispositions, values and beliefs to think openly, making reasoned assumptions, and evaluating or weighing the persuasiveness of arguments. Responsibility for developing critical thinking is also delegated to the employee's organisation, and the less important factor in the development of critical thinking is considered by the higher education and the labour market representatives to be the role of the higher education institution.

The teachers' attitude to critical thinking and attitude to how they teach critical thinking are interrelated. Teachers who perceive the skills of critical thinking as something very rigid and inflexible tend to put less effort into developing the skills related to critical thinking, while those who perceive critical thinking as something flexible and teachable tend to put more effort in developing all skills related to critical thinking.

References

Aiken, L. R. (2002). *Psychological testing and assessment.* Boston: Allyn and Bacon.

Bilevičienė, T. & Jonušauskas, S. (2011). *Statistinių metodų taikymas rinkos tyrimuose [The application of statistical methods in market research.].* Vilnius: Mykolo Romerio universitetas.

Bitinas, B. (2006). *Edukologinis tyrimas: sistema ir procesas [Educational Research: The System and the Process].* Vilnius: Kronta.

Bitinas, B., Rupšienė, L. & Žydžiūnaitė, V. (2008). *Kokybinių tyrimų metodologija [Qualitative Research Methods].* Vilnius, Lithunia: Socialinių mokslų kolegija.

Brown, T. A. (2015). Confirmatory factor analysis for applied research, 2nd ed. New York, NY: Guilford Press.

Centre for quality assessment in higher education (n.d.). Aukštasis mokslas. [Higher education]. Retrieved from https://www.skvc.lt/default/lt/lietuvos-svietimo-sistema/aukstasis-mokslas.

Cheung, G. W. & Rensvold, R. B. (2002). Evaluating goodness-of-fit indexes for testing measurement invariance. *Structural Equation Modeling, 9*(2), 233–255. https://doi.org/10.1207/S15328007SEM0902_5.

Classificator of types of economic activity. (2007). Retrieved from https://e-seimas.lrs.lt/portal/legalAct/lt/TAD/TAIS.309099.

Creswell, J. W. & Creswell, J. D. (2021). *Research design: Qualitative, quantitative, and mixed methods approaches.* Newbury Park, CA: Sage Publishing.

Creswell, J. W. & Guetterman, T. C. (2019). *Educational research planning, conducting, and evaluating quantitative and qualitative research.* New York, NY: Pearson.

Davies, M. (2013). Critical thinking and the disciplines reconsidered. *Higher Education Research & Development, 32*(4), 529–544. doi:10.1080/07294360.2012.697878.

De Vaus, D. & de Vaus, D. (2013). *Surveys in social research.* New York, NY: Routledge.

Dimitrov, D. (2010). Testing for factorial invariance in the context of construct validation. *Measurement and Evaluation in Counseling and Development, 43*(2), 121–149. doi: 10.1177/0748175610373459.

Drost, E. A. (2011). Validity and reliability in social science research. *Education Research and Perspectives, 38*(1), 105.

Dwyer, C. P. (2017). *Critical thinking. Conceptual perspectives and practical guidelines.* Cambridge, England: Cambridge University Press.

Ennis, R. H. (1989). Critical thinking and subject specificity: Clarification and needed research. *Educational Researcher, 18*(3), 4–10. doi:10.3102/0013189X018003004.

Facione, P. A. (1990). *Critical Thinking: A Statement of Expert Consensus for Purposes of Educational Assessment and Instruction. Research findings and recommendations.* Fullerton, CA: California State University.

Halpern, D. F. (1998). Teaching critical thinking for transfer across domains. *American Psychologist, 53*(4), 449–455. doi:10.1037/0003-066X.53.4.449.

Hathcoat, J. D., Penn, J. D., Barnes, L. L. B. & Comer, J. C. (2016). A second dystopia in education: Validity issues in authentic assessment practices. *Research in Higher Education, 57*(7), 892–912. doi:10.1007/s11162-016-9407-1.

Jones, J. S. (2015). *Research ethics. Context and practice.* Newbury Park, CA: Sage Publishing.

Kardelis, K. (2016). *Mokslinių tyrimų metodologija ir metodai [Research methodology and methods].* Vilnius: Mokslo ir enciklopedijų leidybos centras.

Kline, R. B. (2015). *Principles and Practice of Structural Equation Modeling.* New York: Guilford Publications.

Kuhn, D. (1999). A developmental model of critical thinking. *Educational Researcher, 28*(2), 16–46. doi:10.3102/0013189X028002016.

McPeck, J. (1990). *Teaching critical thinking: Dialogue and dialectic.* New York, NY: Routledge.

Ministry of Social Security and Labour. (n.d.). Būtinasis stažas senatvės pensijai [Required seniority for old-age pension]. Retrieved from https://socmin.lrv.lt/lt/veiklos-sritys/socialinis-draudimas/socialinio-draudimo-ismokos/butinasis-stazas-senatves-pensijai.

Moore, T. (2011). Critical thinking and disciplinary thinking: A continuing debate. *Higher Education Research & Development, 30*(3), 261–274. doi:10.1080/07294360.2010.501328.

Official Statistics Portal. (2019). Statistical yearbook of Lithuania. Resident population. Retrieved from https://osp.stat.gov.lt/lietuvos-statistikos-metrastis/lsm-2019/gyventojai-ir-socialine-statistika/nuolatiniai-gyventojai.

Official Statistics Portal. (n.d.a). Statistics by themes. Retrieved from https://osp.stat.gov.lt/temines-lenteles7.

Official Statistics Portal. (n.d.b.). Resident population by sex and age at the beginning of the year. Retrieved from https://osp.stat.gov.lt/temines-lenteles7 https://osp.stat.gov.lt/statistiniu-rodikliu-analize?hash=a924b9a6-9877-4c14-9acd-e4b3ae7255ed#/.

Official Statistics Portal. (n.d.c.). Number of educational institutions, pupils, students and pedagogues. Retrieved from https://osp.stat.gov.lt/statistiniu-rodikliu-analize?hash=b331cbcd-c8ae-4560-b695-f7380924efcc#/.

Panter, A. T. & Sterba, S. K. (2011). *Handbook of ethics in quantitative methodology.* New York, NY: Routledge.

Park, Y. S., Konge, L. & Artino, A. R. (2020). The positivism paradigm of research. *Academic Medicine, 95*(5), 690-694. doi:10.1097/ACM.0000000000003093.

Phillips, D. C., Phillips, D. C. & Burbules, N. C. (2000). *Postpositivism and educational research.* Lanham, MD: Rowman & Littlefield.

Rhemtulla, M., Brosseau-Liard, P. É. & Savalei, V. (2012). When can categorical variables be treated as continuous? A comparison of robust continuous and categorical SEM estimation methods under suboptimal conditions. *Psychological Methods, 17,* 354–373. doi:10.1037/a0029315.

Rupšienė, L. & Rutkienė, A. (2016). *Edukacinis eksperimentas. [An educational experiment].* Klaipėda: Klaipėdos universiteto leidykla.

Salkind, N. J. (Ed.). (2010). *Encyclopedia of research design* (Vol. 1–0). Thousand Oaks, CA: Sage Publications.

Sass, D. A. & Schmitt, T. A. (2010). A comparative investigation of rotation criteria within exploratory factor analysis. *Multivariate behavioral research, 45*(1), 73–103. https://doi.org/10.1080/00273170903504810.

Sodra. (n.d.). Retrieved from https://www.sodra.lt/.

Tijūnėlienė, O. & Virbalienė, A. (2006). Anketos, pedagoginių reiškinių verifikavimo priemonės, psichologiniai konstravimo pamatai [Questionnaires, means of verification of pedagogical phenomena, psychological foundations of construction]. *Pedagogika, 82,* 91–100.

Tracy, S. J. (2019*). Qualitative research methods: Collecting evidence, crafting analysis, communicating impact,* 2nd ed. Hoboken, NJ: Wiley-Blackwell.

Vaitkevičius, R. & Saudargienė, A. (2006). *Statistika su SPSS psichologiniuose tyrimuose: mokomoji knyga [Statistics with SPSS.].* Kaunas: Vytauto Didžiojo universitetas.

Vaitkevičius, R. & Saudargienė, A. (2010). *Psichologinių tyrimų duomenų analizė: praktikos darbai [Analysis of psychological data.].* Kaunas: Vytauto Didžiojo universitetas.

Versli Lietuva. (2019). Verslumo tendencijos Lietuvoje 2019 m. pradžioje [Entrepreneurship trends in Lithuania in early 2019]. Retrieved from https://www.verslilietuva.lt/wp-content/uploads/2019/10/2019.09.30_verslumo_apzvalga.pdf.

Linking Critical Thinking Development in Higher Education and Demand in Labour Market

Abstract: The purpose of this chapter is to provide insights into the understanding, experience and manifestation of critical thinking in higher education and the labour market and to elucidate the links between the development of critical thinking in higher education and demand in the labour market. The qualitative research (phenomenographic) revealed the subjective conceptions and experiences of critical thinking among higher education teachers and students, as well as employers and employees. The conceptions and experiences of critical thinking of these research participants revealed not only differences, but also similarities. The quantitative research (survey) made it possible to distinguish the attitudes of all four groups towards the conceptions of critical thinking and establish the predominant ones, and to identify the importance of critical thinking skills and dispositions in the study process and the labour market. The qualitative and quantitative research results are highlighted in the context of other studies. At the end, summarising insights are presented about the links between the conception and manifestation of critical thinking in the study process and the labour market.

Keywords: teachers', students', employers' and employees' understanding of critical thinking, teaching and learning of critical thinking, encouragement and experience of critical thinking, ways of critical thinking improvement, responsibility for developing a person's critical thinking.

1. Insights about Critical Thinking in Study Process

1.1 How teachers and students understand critical thinking

In the qualitative research, the commonality of the conception of critical thinking of the teachers and the students is revealed through the experience of this phenomenon. Critical thinking is understood as a measure or instrument that helps make decisions in various situations and achieve the goals that have been set. The teachers and students give meaning to critical thinking in the area of practical activities –mostly the professional field. The practicality of critical thinking is related to the realisation of individual opportunities, evaluation of a situation, finding effective solutions that are the best for a particular situation, and the ability to justify one's opinion and present arguments and thus achieve a high level of professionalism. In this way, the cognitive skills of critical thinking are highlighted – to select, summarise and evaluate information, knowledge and situations, present them to others, look for and evaluate alternative solutions, and choose the best one. The quantitative research revealed cognitive skills and dispositions. Both the teachers and the students associate critical thinking skills with the ability to interpret and analyse, explain and evaluate, draw conclusions and adjust decisions based on them. In this regard, the results of qualitative and quantitative research are similar. Critical thinking is perceived as a valuable cognitive skill that leads to reasoned and reliable decisions.

However, critical thinking is valued not only as a skill, but also as a personal disposition. The qualitative research data revealed that both the teachers and the students understand critical thinking as the ability to think independently, the courage to question one's own opinions and decisions and those of others, and an empathic relationship with others. The significance of dispositions is also evident in the research results. A person's open-mindedness and inquisitiveness, analyticity and systematicity, trust in soundness of arguments and the pursuit of truth are listed as essential dispositions of critical thinking. The results of both studies suggest that dispositions are as important as cognitive skills (Healey, 2012; Mathias, 2015; Dwyer, 2017). It can, therefore, be argued that this partially refutes the opinion found in scientific literature that critical thinking is perceived more as a cognitive skill than as a disposition (Bassham, Irwin, Nardone and Wallace, 2013; Fahim and Masouleh, 2012). The data of the qualitative research clearly showed that the importance of dispositions is not merely a theoretical declaration – their value to the relationship with oneself and with others in various life and study space situations is also emphasised. The quantitative research data is in line with this attitude as well.

It should be noted that critical thinking is clearly linked to the pursuit of truth and justice. From the point of view of most scholars (Barnett, 2000; Rogoff, 2006; Brodin, 2007; Brookfield, 2012; Dunne, 2015; Danvers, 2016; Felix, 2016; Fisherman, 2017), this interpretation of the conception of critical thinking reveals the essence of criticality. It should be noted that teachers no longer associate criticality with criticism. The quantitative study found that the vast majority of teachers disagreed with the statement that critical thinking only occurs when criticising. This means that the understanding of critical thinking does not have any negative connotation, that is, it does not include criticising others. In the qualitative research data, this attitude was not observed at all. A slightly different attitude was detected among the students when analysing the quantitative research results. Some of the students, especially the younger ones, agree with the statement that critical thinking occurs only when criticising. However, in the qualitative research data, as in the case of the teachers, this attitude was not found among students.

The qualitative research findings reveal that the teachers underscore the necessity of the constant pursuit of truth, the need to remain true even in the most difficult situations, and the imperative of being honest with oneself and others. The pursuit of truth and justice is also pronounced in the quantitative research results. It is associated with the ability to question unsubstantiated assumptions and reasoning. In this respect, the research data highlight the ideas of researchers about critical thinking as honest and fair thinking (Paul and Elder, 2012), and as a person's open-mindedness and curiosity, pursuit of truth, and trust in soundness of arguments and evidence (Facione, Facione and Giancarlo, 2000).

Both the qualitative and quantitative research data highlighted critical thinking as the totality of intertwined and equally significant cognitive skills and dispositions. However, there are also significant differences. The teachers' conceptions of critical thinking revealed during the qualitative study were close to the ternary conception of the phenomenon put forward by Barnett (1997) of critical reason, critical being and critical action. The majority of the teachers and some of the students understand critical thinking as the ability to reason, and as being disposed to criticality, and as an action that combines knowledge, skills and dispositions. In their conceptions, all three components are tightly interconnected. The teachers' conceptions of critical thinking revealed during the quantitative study more closely reflect the consolidated attitude of experts to critical thinking (Facione, 1990). More than a third of the teachers and almost a quarter of the students who participated in the study treat critical thinking as the totality of a person's cognitive skills and dispositions.

The qualitative research findings testify that in most cases, both the teachers and the students perceive critical thinking as a significant skill expressed at the personal level. Critical thinking is considered as valuable as the value it provides for the development of cognitive powers in the personal and/or professional space. However, this attitude is not limited to the instrumental conception of critical thinking – it also reflects the traits of critical thinking as that of a growing and maturing person (Sigurðsson, 2017). This is especially pronounced in the attitudes of teachers found in the qualitative research results. They describe critical thinking as an instrument for 'self- and 'self-improving', meaning changing habits and modes of behaviour for one's own good and the good of others. This attitude is partly reflected in the quantitative research results as well. Some of the teachers agree with the statement that critical thinking is a strong human development thinking, while others agree with the statement that critical thinking helps to improve thinking and change habitual patterns of thinking.

It should be noted that the conception of critical thinking is highlighted less at the interpersonal and social levels than it is at the personal level. In the qualitative research, the interpersonal aspect in both study groups is revealed as the desire to better understand different perspectives and attitudes, and to find solutions that are right for yourself and others. In this way, the statements of other scholars (Jones, 2005; Ng'ambi and Johnston, 2006; Yang, 2008) about critical thinking as a collegial relationship, the open sharing of knowledge and abilities in a certain discipline, as well as the provision of help to others (Samson, 2016) are confirmed. The social significance of critical thinking is only reflected in the qualitative research in the attitudes of the teachers. They treat critical thinking as an important phenomenon of democratic society, and a sign of social progress and development. This opinion echoes statements of researchers (Boni-Aristizábal and Calabuig-Tormo; Raveendran and Chunawala, 2015; Schendel, 2016; Yang, 2008) about the interrelations between critical thinking and civic and democratic thinking. The social aspect of critical thinking was not found in the conceptions of the students. The interpersonal and social aspects are to some extent reflected in the quantitative research results. More than a tenth of the teachers and almost a fifth of the students who participated in the study associate critical thinking with the ability to reason, reflect and act critically for the good of oneself, others and society.

The results of both studies revealed that the essential difference between the teachers' and students' conception of critical thinking lies in the volume and depth of its content. The teachers' conceptions are much more spacious. The quantitative research results revealed that the teachers are much more likely than the students to agree with the statement that critical thinking is the totality of both skills and dispositions. The qualitative research findings revealed that the teachers' conceptions of critical thinking include not only cognitive skills, but also a wide field of dispositions and relationships – namely, the aspects of self-education and improvement, building an open relationship with the environment, critical thinking as a learning process, and critical thinking as creativity. An open relationship with the environment, as an integral part of the conception of critical thinking, is identified by the students as the ability to examine phenomena from different perspectives, but openness to the environment is not directly declared. The students, unlike the teachers, do not explicate the conception of critical thinking as learning to doubt, ask questions and test knowledge in the learning process. In the conceptions of the students, critical thinking is not a process of learning, but one of pressing problems and specific solutions. Such an applied approach to critical thinking is also found in studies done by other scholars (Lloyd and Bahr, 2010; Wangensteen, 2010). The students do not attribute signs of creativity to critical thinking either. From the students' point of view, creativity is partly expressed in the search for and adoption of independent, distinctive solutions, but the originality of the solutions is not emphasised. The teachers see links between critical thinking and creativity in the freedom to think and decide, to consider 'impossible' solutions, to look for unconventional, original ideas, and to create new rules and reality. This conception finds a direct match in the metaphorical description put forward by Paul and Elder (2008) of the links between critical thinking and creativity as two halves of the same apple.

Despite the differences in attitudes and nuances of the conception of critical thinking that emerged in both studies, it can be summarised that in the understanding of both the teachers and the students, critical thinking is a phenomenon that encompasses a person's cognitive skills and dispositions that have not only personal meaning but interpersonal and social meaning as well.

Neither the teachers nor the students have a clearly defined conception of the phenomenon that they are guided by in their practice. This situation can be treated in two ways. From the perspective of qualitative research, this is an obvious advantage. Authentic conceptions and experiences unconstrained by theoretical constructs enabled the researchers to look at critical thinking from a second order perspective and expand the content of theoretical constructs, revealing the nuances of the conception of the phenomenon under study. At the same time, the research participants also had the opportunity to formulate authentic conceptions stemming from their experience. However, in thinking about the effectiveness of the development of critical thinking, the lack of a conception and a clear teaching methodology can be seen as a shortcoming (Hassan and Madhum, 2007; LaPoint-O'Brien, 2013) and an obstacle to conveying the conception of critical thinking and its content to students (Duro, Elander, Maratos, Stupple and Aubeeluck, 2013).

1.2 The attitude of teachers and students to the development of critical thinking and how teachers teach and students learn critical thinking

The data of the quantitative research provide an opportunity to argue that teachers treat critical thinking as a competence that is developed and dynamic, which can manifest itself in a variety of situations. Meanwhile, the students' attitude towards critical thinking as a developed competence differed from the attitude of the teachers. While a significant proportion of the students agreed that critical thinking can be developed and demonstrated in a variety of ways and situations if efforts are made, some of the younger students were inclined to treat critical thinking more as a stable, unchanging competence.

Upon comparing the teaching experiences of the teachers and the learning experiences of the students, the qualitative research revealed several key aspects. The first is the unequal treatment of independent work. The teachers assign independent theoretical and practical tasks in order to develop students' thinking and deepen their understanding of the subject and their ability to look for solutions and evaluate their decisions. The teachers also use independent assignments to encourage students to actively participate in the learning process. So that they search for and process material themselves, understand what they have to look into more, and identify what they understand and what they do not; so that they acquire and strengthen their creative abilities, learn the tasks performed, and at the same time prepare for an independent professional path. This practice is revealed in the quantitative research as well. The teachers devote the most attention to developing independent decision-making skills. Meanwhile, the students emphasise not so much the aspect of independence as they do learning to make decisions according to certain procedures, rules or established order. However, it is the opposite in the qualitative research findings, where the students identify the aspect of independence as significant for the formation of their critical thinking. They point out that the teachers teaching to work independently, make decisions independently and solve problems presupposes free, independent thinking, which they treat as the height of person growth and the sense of their power to make changes. Thus, the students associate the element of independence not so much with analytical and procedural abilities as with their personal maturity. In this respect, the research data highlight the importance of specific, defined tasks described in scientific literature for the development of critical thinking in learners (Bensley, 2010; Heijltjes, 2015).

Another aspect that emerges from the comparison of the experiences of the teachers and the students is the strengthening of students' analytical powers. The data of the qualitative research testify that in order to improve students' analytical skills, teachers teach them to deeply analyse texts, carefully evaluate information, select and verify material, understand cause-effect relationships, distinguish the essence of phenomena, and link theory with practice. The latter aspect is also revealed in the quantitative research. However, certain nuances of differences also emerged. The quantitative research results show that the teachers mainly develop analytical powers by teaching to draw evidence-based conclusions, and to argue and interpret them by presenting them to others. Slightly less attention is given to analysis, perceiving it as teaching to analyse and select sources, link the totality of a phenomenon and its parts, and evaluate information in the context of different sources, discussing different attitudes towards the same phenomenon. It is interesting to note that according to the data of both studies, the teachers teach critical thinking by explaining, asking questions and expanding the content; however, teaching students to ask critical questions themselves is poorly reflected. The contextual development of critical thinking is revealed in the qualitative research. Teachers teach to analyse the study material in relation to the broader academic, professional and social context, and teach to look at the same phenomena from different perspectives. Teachers try to make students realise that the subject they are studying is part of a larger whole. The experience of students also testifies to this. They learn to analyse different approaches and take them into account when drawing conclusions and proposing solutions. Yet, for the students, this is more of an incentive to start taking an interest in the content being studied rather than to expand and develop their analytical skills, as the teachers claim. Context evaluation looks somewhat different in the quantitative research. This data show that in the study process, teachers devote much less attention to skills related to the analysis and evaluation of context and different perspectives. This marked difference could be explained by the fact that qualitative research opens up a much broader picture of the phenomenon under study and provides an opportunity to reveal its various aspects and nuances. Meanwhile, quantitative research only records the more or less frequently recurring meanings of experiences. In summary, it can be argued that the teaching and learning of critical thinking is clearly contextualised – experienced and undergone in a specific learning environment, situation or culture, or framed in the subject studied. Because according to McPeck (1981, p. 50), critical thinking always *manifests itself in connection with some identifiable activity or subject area and never is in isolation.* The way it is understood and experienced depends largely on these contextual circumstances, as well as on the personal qualities and experience of the teachers and students. In this respect, the research data highlight the ideas of Jones (2005), Danvers (2016; 2018), Mcnamara, Sweetman, Connors, Lofgren and Greene (2020) and many others about the need to put critical thinking in context. From the point of view of the researchers, the development of critical thinking can be ineffective if cultural, ethical, civic and intellectual peculiarities are not taken into account.

Another significant factor in the learning process is the teaching and assessment methods used by teachers. In the qualitative research, both groups listed independent work with different sources of literature and information, individual and collegial analysis of problems and cases, simulations, questioning and discussion. The latter method is especially valued by students. They pointed out that discussion allowed them to unleash their critical thinking skills of publicly presenting and justifying their opinion, discussing through argumentation, discovering more points of view and understanding that there is more than one truth, and daring to disagree with the dominant opinion in the group. In this respect, the research data coincide with the conclusions of other scholars (Abrami et al., 2015; Davies, Jindal-Snape, Collier, Digby, Hay and Howe, 2013; Halpern, 2014; Huang, Lindell, Jaffe and Sullivan, 2016) on the importance of discussion and debate for developing critical thinking. When talking about the benefits of discussion for learning, the teachers emphasised the benefits for both the students' personal maturity and the development of analytical skills. For students, meanwhile, discussion was important as an opportunity to dare to speak their mind and to express an independent opinion openly. The qualitative research data reveal a slightly different picture. Among the methods used, both the teachers and the students first singled out case analysis, and only then discussion. In this study, considerable attention is also given to original, atypical tasks that encourage students to use their heads and find a unique key for solving the problem. The teachers describe such non-standard tasks as thought-provoking, deep, complex and creative. Studies (Byrnes and Dunbar, 2004; Schendel, 2016) show that such unusual, experimental teaching methods are indeed effective in developing critical thinking skills. Students have to apply the acquired knowledge in new and ambiguous situations, and demonstrate deep thinking and researcher competences. Performing such atypical tasks is in part related to the evaluation of critical thinking. The teachers argue that it is these tasks that make it possible to understand whether the students are able to think critically. The students share this thinking and link these tasks to the revelation and development of critical thinking skills. Tasks of this nature are also reflected in the quantitative research findings, only they are not among the priority teaching and learning methods listed by the teachers or students.

The qualitative research data revealed another, rather unexpected way of teaching – teaching by personal example, that is, by the teachers expressing thoughts, declaring beliefs and values, and modelling behaviour. The teachers believe that this is the best way to demonstrate an equal and collegial relationship, raise the value of professional mastery, and develop the person. The students did not share this kind of teaching experience. The experience of teaching by personal example was also reflected in the quantitative research. Granted, both the students and the teachers say that this method of teaching is not used often. Personal example can indeed be an effective way to develop critical thinking. The teacher, as an authority, sets an example of what it means to learn critical thinking and how it can be learned, simultaneously emphasising the effectiveness of critical thinking (Wass, Harland and Mercer, 2011).

The qualitative research findings clearly testify that critical thinking is learned through active interaction between the teacher and student. The study revealed that the main actor in this interaction is the teacher. The teacher's active role is manifested in the organisation and implementation of teaching. The teacher tells, explains, shows, demonstrates, illustrates and asks. The students also talk about this active position of the teacher. The teacher asks students questions, assigns tasks and analyses problems together with students, and teaches them to select, interpret and evaluate the material being studied. The teacher is also a passive teacher of critical thinking. Passivity does not mean being absent – it just means a lower level of involvement. The teacher only organises learning –assigns tasks and monitors their performance, formulates questions and waits for answers, and organises group work, delegating the role of the teacher to the students. The students do not recognise such a teacher in their experience. Their teacher remains an active participant in the teaching and learning process, organising and jointly implementing learning tasks. There is no way to discern active interaction in the quantitative research. However, the research data clearly show that the teachers feel that they devote more attention to the development of critical thinking than the students do. This divide of opinions signals that teachers may not be fully aware of the students' experience, and that the teachers' learning objectives may not be entirely clear to the students. In this regard, the idea put forward by Davies (2015) – that in order to come to an understanding and achieve tangible results, defining and clearly communicating what critical thinking skills are to be developed and how is crucial – is very important. It is also important to understand that critical thinking is a process, and that developing it is time-consuming (Bezanilla, Fernández-Nogueira, Poblete and Galindo-Domínguez, 2019). In this study, neither the teachers nor the students emphasised time as a significant critical thinking factor in the teaching and learning process.

The qualitative research data provide an opportunity to distinguish between two types of teaching approaches: the infusion approach and the immersion approach (Ennis, 1985). The latter approach is more common. Teachers integrate critical thinking into the teaching of their subject, but do not formulate critical thinking as a learning objective and do not apply special learning strategies. Furthermore, they do not inform students that they are being taught to think critically. This conclusion stems from both analysis of the data and the direct statements of the teachers and students that they do not have a specific definition of the conception, a specific methodology, or a teaching plan. The teachers are not always sure if they are really developing critical thinking, and the students are not sure if they are really being taught critical thinking. These findings correlate with literature and research reviews conducted by researchers from other European countries (Promoting Critical Thinking in European Higher Education Institutions: towards an educational protocol, 2019), which testify to the not entirely systematic and deeply conscious development of critical thinking in higher education. The infusion approach is a more thought-over and planned, yet much less common way of teaching critical thinking. Teachers think over the content and methods of teaching, and purposefully select tasks that promote critical thinking. The readiness of teachers to apply different strategies and methods for developing critical thinking is crucial for effective teaching and learning (Genc, 2008; Lin, 2014; Sziarto, McCarthy and Padilla, 2014). However, the data from this study reveal only certain aspects of teacher preparation.

1.3 How teachers and students improve critical thinking

Analysis of the qualitative research data revealed the teachers' experiences in learning critical thinking. The teachers claim that they never had any special opportunities to learn what critical thinking is or how to teach critical thinking. They develop their critical thinking competences by independently studying literature (usually professional), observing the environment and people, and being in an intensive learning relationship with themselves or other people (usually colleagues). Organised learning is manifested in participation in conferences or training, when, during conversations and discussions, professional competence is improved, horizons are broadened, self-reflection is developed, and existing dispositions, knowledge and skills are rethought. However, they themselves consider this kind of learning critical thinking to be random and situational, but not targeted. The results of the quantitative research testify to similar ways of learning critical thinking. The teachers usually read books, engage in self-reflection, participate in seminars and conferences, analyse the environment and discuss with others. The teachers also emphasised the need to improve certain skills and dispositions. Among the most commonly cited were inference, decision-making, explanation and analytical skills, and the dispositions of courage and perseverance.

The need for teachers to develop critical thinking skills is linked to interpersonal relationships. They would like to improve the quality of decisions made collegially, and want to learn to better argue and justify their choices. Interestingly, instead of focusing on skills that receive less attention in real practice, such as analysis, evaluation, explanation and self-regulation, the teachers would like to improve the critical thinking skills that are most obvious in practice – inference, argumentation and interpretation. That is, they want to improve the skills that they already focus on. The qualitative research was not intended to ascertain the needs for improvement, and the context of the research data did not reveal any specific needs.

The students' quantitative research results revealed a rather vague picture of the improvement of critical thinking skills. The students improve their critical thinking in an irregular and random manner. Like the teachers, they also participate in seminars and conferences, reflect, read books, discuss, observe and analyse environmental phenomena. In general, critical thinking learning for both the students and the teachers can be termed as random self-education. These findings can neither be confirmed nor refuted by other research. How teachers learn critical thinking themselves and what the need is for the development of this competence was not found in scientific literature. Neither was any data found on how students develop their critical thinking skills outside of formal studies.

1.4 Who is responsible for developing critical thinking

The quantitative research results revealed that both the teachers and the students are inclined to pass responsibility for the development of critical thinking to the individual him or herself. The responsibility of the organisation where the individual works is stressed a bit less frequently. It is worth noting that the teachers and the students have different attitudes towards the role of the higher education institution. The teachers are more likely than the students to agree with the statement that the higher education institution must also take responsibility for developing critical thinking. The role of the higher education institution is also relevant in the preparation of future labour market participants. However, more than a quarter of the teachers and a fifth of the students who participated in the study do not have an opinion on the level and quality of preparation. There is also a small proportion of respondents in both groups who have a negative view of the role of the higher education institution in preparing specialists who are critical thinkers. These findings reaffirm the convictions of European researchers (Promoting Critical Thinking in European Higher Education Institutions: towards an educational protocol, 2019) that leaving the development of critical thinking to the sole responsibility of the individual is not allowed. It must be an integral part of higher education and research and the policy of the higher education institution. The higher education institution must take responsibility for developing critical thinking. The qualitative research did not address the question of responsibility for developing critical thinking, and no aspects of this question were reflected in the field of study.

1.5 Why critical thinking is important for the modern labour market

The quantitative research also sought to ascertain which critical thinking skills and dispositions the teachers and the students give priority to in the labour market. It was ascertained that inference, argumentation and interpretation skills are considered to be the most important. Decision-making, evaluation and analytical skills are considered to be of slightly less importance, and explanation and self-regulation skills are considered the least important. The importance of inference is related to the ability to anticipate possible consequences, formulate evidence-based conclusions, and summarise information. Argumentation is associated with the ability to think and reason your thinking based on facts, and interpretation is associated with the ability to discern basic information from secondary information. The importance of evaluation is manifested in drawing conclusions, making decisions that need to be made either collegially or independently, and adhering to the order and procedures established in an organisation. The importance of explanation is associated with the ability to explain the results obtained, reveal the essence of a phenomenon, and explain the decision-making path. The ability to explain complex concepts and the ability to formulate questions for others are considered to be of slightly less importance. For the modern labour market, it is also important to examine phenomena and situations on the basis of data from various sources, and find connections between the whole and its parts. Self-regulation manifests itself in the ability to change when needed, to know yourself better, and to reflect on your actions. It is important to note that these results correlate with the critical thinking skills that the teachers gave as being developed and in need of improvement. That is, the critical thinking skills developed by the teachers, and the skills that they feel a need to improve, and the skills that they think are most relevant to the labour market, are identified in the same order of priority.

The attitude of the students in highlighting critical thinking skills is slightly different from that of the teachers. Unlike the teachers, the students feel that self-regulation (self-knowledge reflection, the ability to change) is very important. However, they have a similar evaluation of the ability to argue, draw conclusions and make decisions. The students' attitude towards self-regulation, argumentation, inference and decision-making in the labour market correlate with the critical thinking skills that they prioritised in the study process.

When evaluating critical thinking dispositions, the teachers first noted fairness, flexibility, self-confidence and accuracy. The dispositions of scepticism, open-mindedness, caring for others, impartiality and inquisitiveness are considered the least important. It is interesting to note that inquisitiveness is more valued by older teachers than younger teachers. In specifying which dispositions they give the most attention to in the study process, the teachers also mentioned fairness and accuracy. From the point of view of the students, self-confidence, fairness, attentiveness, accuracy and flexibility are very important. Scepticism, open-mindedness, endurance, impartiality and inquisitiveness are least valued. The students, by prioritising the importance of self-confidence in the labour market, also point out that this disposition is given considerable attention at the higher education institution as well.

Thus, it can be argued that the attitudes of the teachers and the students towards what is being developed and what is important in the labour market coincide. What is prioritised among the skills and dispositions developed is also considered to be the most valuable in the context of the labour market.

The qualitative research did not ask about the importance of critical thinking for the labour market. However, critical thinking skills such as the ability to make choices and find the right solution in a variety of life situations, including professional ones, are very prominent in the experiences of both the teachers and the students. In this respect, the qualitative research findings coincide with the quantitative research results. However, in evaluating the importance of dispositions, that of inquisitiveness, exploration and not trusting a single truth was very pronounced in the teachers' qualitative research. It is associated not only with personal development and a deeper look at the material being studied, but also with benefits in professional life in pursuit of professional mastery. The students' experiences highlight open-mindedness to different attitudes and the ability to look from different perspectives, but this is not related to the future profession. The students see this as a sign of personal growth.

2. Insights about Critical Thinking in the Labour Market

2.1 How employers and employees understand critical thinking

In analysing the results of the qualitative research on how the employers and employees understand critical thinking, the similarities and differences in this understanding can be distinguished. First of all, a similarity in the employers' and employees' understanding of the conception of critical thinking is revealed in the qualitative research data by the fact that both the employees and the employers understand critical thinking as specific personal skills focused on the search for truth, and as specific personal dispositions reflecting the expression of courage in professional activities. Both groups of research participants understand critical thinking as thinking that is free of preconceptions. It is a thinking where when dealing with different situations, a person is not guided solely by his or her personal experience or attitude and does not succumb to environmental pressure. Organisational performance research emphasises that only employees who are critical thinkers are motivated to seek the truth (Ku and Ho, 2010) and detailed information, and to generate ideas from different perspectives without succumbing to environmental opinion (Jiang and Yang, 2015). The search for truth is defined as a kind of prosocial collective motivation that shows a person's inner desire to commit to improving the organisation objectively and honestly (Jiang, Gao and Yang, 2018).

It is this thinking that helps to reasonably evaluate a situation and make objective decisions. Another very distinct commonality of the conception identified in analysing the results of the qualitative research is that critical thinking is understood by both the employers and the employees as the ability to look at a situation from different perspectives, which makes it possible to discuss phenomena without bias. The understanding of critical thinking as questioning the absolute, indisputable truth, scepticism, and the desire not to become attached to subjective opinions was particularly pronounced in both study groups. Critical thinking is understood as a certain position based on doubt as to the existence of any reliable criterion of truth; it is understood not only as reasoned decision-making, but also as reasoned communication based on reasoning. An aspect of the conception of critical thinking that was common to both study groups was self-confidence in terms of expressing opinions and taking on challenges. Self-confidence is also manifested in the ability to act independently, freely generate ideas, make decisions, take responsibility and not be afraid to make mistakes.

Both study groups understand critical thinking as personal efforts to act professionally. This understanding signifies the importance of critical thinking at the personal level, which correlates with its importance at the interpersonal/

organisational level, where critical thinking is understood as the result of personal thinking recognised in the employee-employee, employee-group of employees and employee-employer relationship, giving particular attention to organisational results. According to Felix (2016), critical thinking helps a person to constantly improve not only for his or her own sake as a professional, but also for the sake of organisational change. Employees who are critical thinkers change the organisational culture and develop new ideas for the organisation's services/products and practices (Shahinpoor and Matt, 2007).

It should be noted that in both groups' understanding of critical thinking, the social dimension is the least pronounced. In the case of the employers, it only emerges when talking about making innovative decisions that guarantee a breakthrough in the organisation, and in the case of the employees – through giving meaning to operating results in creating social justice. Critically thinking people think for themselves and make decisions themselves, but their thinking and decisions are influenced by the living context, social reality and social relationships. Critical thinking comes from being in an intense relationship with another. It is as individual as it is communal and social (Brookfield, 2005). Critical thinking is what people do by communicating and interacting while engaging in certain activities. Critical thinking is not just a person's individual thinking activity (Kuhn, 2008, p. 13). Thus, critical thinking clearly has several dimensions: personal, interpersonal and communal/social. In the context of the lived world, all of these dimensions are naturally interrelated.

In analysing the results of the qualitative research on how the employers and employees understand critical thinking, certain variations in this understanding were also identified. In the employers' understanding, the expression of the dispositions of independence and self-confidence is more pronounced. Self-confidence creates the preconditions for taking initiative, generating innovative, unexpected, atypical solutions, and putting forth original proposals. Self-confidence enables an organisation to create added value (King and Kitchener, 2004). This aspect of critical thinking also unfolds as a reaction to a crisis situation when initiative is taken to act spontaneously but confidently. Meanwhile, the employees' conception of critical thinking highlights the importance of empathy, which manifests itself at the interpersonal and social levels as an emotional response to other people's experiences, encouraging them to help or change their situation in order to ensure social justice in society.

An essential finding of the qualitative research is that the employers and employees understand critical thinking not only as reasoning and declarative positions, but also as practical application in professional contexts. The results of the qualitative research reveal that critically thinking employees can be recognised not only from the statements that they make, but also from their actions, that is, how they use the knowledge available in their professional activities for the well-being and development of the organisation. The activities of critically thinking employees are based on specific knowledge, information and available experience, which is thought over and ultimately translates into action. The qualitative research findings reveal that the essence of critical thinking lies not only in finding the right answer, but also in the disposition to constantly look for it, reasonably doubt, and ask questions of oneself and the environment.

The results of the analysis of the understanding of critical thinking of both the employees and the employers reveal that in the labour market, critical thinking is understood more in line with Barnett's (1997) concept, which emphasises not only the importance of the thought process, but also the importance of applying the results of the thought process in action. Critical thinking should not be confined to the thought process. It is inseparable from the daily challenges of professional activities (Indrašienė et al., 2019).

In Barnett's (2000) conception of criticality, as awakeness of mind plays a special role. Awakeness of mind prevents employees from getting stuck in a routine and encourages them to constantly respond to the challenges posed by the changing environment. This disposition enables employees to look for the best solutions for themselves, their customers and the organisation (Indrašienė et al., 2019). According to Danvers (2016) and Segall and Gaudelli (2007), the essence of critical thinking is the ability to doubt the assumptions that our usual thinking is based on by asking meaningful questions in order to change the reality of the organisation.

Analysis of the quantitative research results revealed that the employers' and employees' conception of critical thinking is associated with certain personal skills and dispositions. Most of the employees and employers tended to agree with Facione's (1996) definition of critical thinking, which emphasised the totality of cognitive skills and dispositions. Analysis of the quantitative data revealed that the definition of critical thinking which focuses on the skills necessary to increase the effectiveness of an organisation is more acceptable to the employers than to the employees. The least acceptable definition of critical thinking for both the employers and the employees is the understanding that critical thinking is the improvement of a person's thinking by changing habitual patterns of thinking. The definition of critical thinking as the ability to reason, reflect and act critically for the good of oneself, others and society (Barnett, 1997) was more acceptable to the employers. It should be noted that both the employees and the employers view critical thinking as a person's abilities that can manifest themselves in a variety of professional situations.

It can be assumed that there is no established, unified conception of critical thinking in the labour market: each participant treats critical thinking differently. This is in line with the systematic literature review (Indrašienė et al., 2019). It was found that research is very rarely based on a particular conception, and that there is a great lack of research where a unique new conception is developed or constructed. On the other hand, there is very little research analysing critical thinking in organisational/labour market contexts. The analysis of the conception of critical thinking is more the subject of research in the field of education, including higher education.

2.2 The importance of critical thinking skills and dispositions in the labour market and the need for improvement

Analysis of the quantitative research results revealed a commonality in the attitudes of the employers and the employees about the development of critical thinking. It was found that in both groups, the prevailing opinion is that critical thinking is a developed competence, and its development depends on each person's desire and efforts. Devlin (2002) and Marton, Dall'Alba, Beaty (1993) note that the encouragement of others is crucial in the development process, but that the learner's own assumption of personal responsibility for learning is equally important. Personal responsibility is a component of metacognition, without which the development of improvement is impossible.

It was found that the employers and employees consider the most important critical thinking skills in the modern labour market to be those that belong to the group of inference skills: summarising information, formulating evidence-based conclusions with regard to the context, and anticipating possible consequences. It is important to note that these skills were also identified by employers as the ones that their employees most need to improve. The importance of critical thinking is highlighted when informed decisions need to be made decisively – employees need to be able to formulate convincing and appropriate conclusions by taking certain logical steps (Subramanian, 2020). This echoes the findings of other studies that critical thinking is a necessary skill in order to avoid mistakes due to overconfidence or bias (Davitch and Folker, 2017).

In the opinion of the employers, explanation skills (formulating and answering questions, explaining an analysis carried out and the results obtained, explaining the decision-making path, explaining complex conditions and revealing the essence of a phenomenon) and interpretation skills (classifying data/information, understanding their content, conveying data/information in own words, and discerning essential information from supplementary information) are also important in the labour market. Only employees with a set of critical thinking skills such as interpretation, analysis, evaluation, inference, explanation and self-regulation can explain their thinking and decision-making process (Facione, 2011).

Meanwhile, the employees consider the abilities in the group of self-regulation skills to be the most important in the labour market. In the opinion of the employees, the ability to know yourself and the ability to reflect (on your thoughts, feelings, actions) are the most important skills in the labour market. It is important to mention that, as the analysis of the quantitative research results revealed, the employees stressed much more strongly than the employers the need to improve self-regulation skills (know yourself; reflect on own thoughts, feelings, actions). So unlike the employers who evaluated the need of the employees working in their company to improve individual critical thinking skills, the employees placed particular emphasis on the need to improve their self-regulation skills. The importance of self-knowledge and reflection is emphasised (Wolcott, 2006; Andrews, 2007; Ruutmann, 2019) as a necessary precondition for the right decision. According to

Rogoff (2006), reflection must become part of the daily professional activities of each member of the organisation so that what is being sought in the activities of others can be applied in personal professional activities.

The employees also name argumentation skills (thinking based on facts/evidence, substantiating your choices, basing actions on contemplation and reflection) and decision-making skills (making decisions independently and collegially, substantiating the decision made, making decisions according to the procedures established in the organisation) as being equally important in the labour market. Analysis of the quantitative research results also revealed the opinion of the employers that it is important for their subordinates to improve the latter skills. This is in line with studies conducted by other researchers (Kreitzberg and Kreitzberg, 2011; Phan, 2011; AMA, 2012; Fung, 2014; Powley and Taylor, 2014; Penkauskienė, Railienė and Cruz, 2019), which reveal that the success of an organisation is determined by the ability of employees to respond quickly to changing situations and make reasoned, research-based decisions.

Analysis of the quantitative research results revealed that from the point of view of the employers and the employees, not only the aforementioned skills are important in the labour market – critical thinking dispositions are as well. Fairness, rightness, flexibility and self-confidence are valued. Meanwhile, scepticism, open-mindedness and inquisitiveness are valued the least. Analysis of the quantitative research results also revealed the attitude of the employers and the employees towards the need to improve critical thinking dispositions. In this case, a larger gap was found between the opinions of the two groups: compared to how the employers evaluated what critical thinking dispositions their direct subordinates should improve, the employees were more likely to express a need to develop courage, endurance, scepticism, self-confidence, perseverance, fairness, caring for other people and rightness.

Although open-mindedness is least valued by the employees and employers, it is noted in scientific literature that open-mindedness allows critical thinking to be 'corrected' (Lipman, 1988). Only an open-minded thinker is prepared to critically and continually evaluate his or her own attitude (Bermingham, 2015). It is open-mindedness that is seen as a precondition for scepticism. There is a notable connection between open-mindedness and self-reflection, as the former promotes the result of the latter. The same can be said for curiosity, another attitude that inspires reflection (Facione, 2013).

2.3 How employers encourage, and employees experience critical thinking

One of the key variations in analysing the employers' and employees' qualitative research results is that the employers emphasise the importance of promoting critical thinking in employees, but in the employees' critical thinking experiences, the role of the employer in promoting critical thinking is only revealed very episodically. The employees associate the experience of critical thinking in professional activities more with their own personal position and behaviour in action. On the other hand, the qualitative research data revealed certain similarities between how the employers promote and the employees experience critical thinking in professional activities. The qualitative research results revealed that as one of the forms of promoting critical thinking, the employers ask questions that encourage thinking about a specific situation, problem or solution. It should be noted that the employees emphasised the importance of questions without prioritising the source of the questions, but evaluating the added value of constantly asking questions in professional activities.

The qualitative research results revealed that in order to arouse critical thinking in employees, the employers give them challenges, as a kind of provocation. This promotes responsibility in employees and encourages them to delve deeper into the situation being analysed or the suggestions being made. The employees also emphasise the experience of critical thinking through a challenge, an exit from your personal comfort zone that forces you to think, act, do something differently than usual, and create a new experience. This is in line with the findings of other studies highlighting that critically minded employees become more involved in challenging activities by offering innovative alternatives to possible solutions (Jiang and Yang, 2015). Employees who are critical thinkers do not follow authority, and do not consider knowledge to be absolute. To confirm their decisions, require evidence and justification (King and Kitchener, 2004). According to Facione (1990), the ideal critical thinker is usually curious, open and honest in the face of personality.

In this context, both the employers and the employees associate the experience of critical thinking with delegated and assumed responsibility. Employers entrust employees with larger, more responsible projects which encourage the employees to not be afraid of making mistakes and to learn from their mistakes. It should be noted that both the employers and the employees give challenges the meaning of a growing experience: they encourage moving forward, looking for original solutions, and changing one's thinking. The research findings are in line with the results of studies conducted by other researchers which emphasise the ability of employees to respond quickly to changing situations and make decisions (Kreitzberg and Kreitzberg, 2011; AMA, 2012; Powley and Taylor, 2014; Penkauskienė, Railienė and Cruz, 2019). The research also shows that employees' critical thinking is positively related to change-oriented behaviours such as employees engaging in creative processes (Jiang and Yang, 2015), handling complex situations (Detert and Edmondson, 2011), and improving the organisation's performance (Facione, 1990; 2011).

Another aspect of the similarity of results is that critical thinking is experienced not only as professionally performed direct functions, but also as the employees' personal contribution to the development of the organisation and society. The experience of critical thinking is most pronounced from the personal aspect, which is found in all of the results, for both the employees and the employers. The employers place particular emphasis on this aspect, linking it to the success of the organisation and the creation of added value. Shahinpoor and Matt (2007) note that promoting critical thinking in employees has an impact on the organisation's operational efficiency and on strengthening employee loyalty to the organisation. Today's employee needs to be able to generate new ideas without being afraid to refute the old ones for the sake of the success of the organisation (Desai, Berger and Higgs 2016) and competitive advantage (Subramanian, 2020). In this context, research highlights the influence of critical thinking on the extent to which employees are involved in the creative process of developing and implementing innovation in an organisation (Natale and Ricci, 2006; Jing and Baiyin, 2015).

Researchers (Raveendran and Chunawala, 2015; Schendel, 2016; Boni-Aristizábal and Calabuig-Tormo, 2016; Sigurðsson, 2017) note that critical thinking is inseparable from civic participation, where everyone's involvement in solving social issues is crucial. However, in the qualitative research, the experience of critical thinking of both the employees and the employers is least manifested from the social aspect, that is, in the broader context beyond the boundaries of the particular organisation, where the activity contributes to the creation of value for society.

The qualitative research results revealed that employees who are critical thinkers tend to devote more effort and time to the search for truth by evaluating the reliability and validity of information, solutions and arguments. As the results of the employer study and other studies (Jiang and Yang, 2015) reveal, the role of managers in encouraging employee involvement is crucial in this process.

Employees experience critical thinking through the expression of a personal position, and employers promote this by creating a supportive environment, encouraging employee openness, allowing them to speak out, and demonstrating respect for the employees' opinions. On the other hand, employers create an environment conducive to critical thinking through organisational (regular meetings and discussions, which are recognised as part of the organisation's culture) or motivational (praise, encouragement, learning opportunities, financial reward) measures. Only by allowing employees to behave with dignity in the organisation do organisations acquire more productive and loyal employees, who create an environment conducive to critical thinking and learning (Shahinpoor and Matt, 2007).

Analysis of the quantitative research results revealed that the manifestation of critical thinking in professional activities is most associated by the employers with the employees' ability to react expeditiously to the situation at hand and responsibly make a reasoned decision, either independently or in interpersonal interaction. From the point of view of the employers, employees' critical thinking is also reflected in the ability to delve fully into a problem by using existing knowledge and looking for new knowledge. Hence, the manifestation of critical thinking in professional activities is most associated by the employers with decision-making abilities at the personal and interpersonal level. According to the employees, critical thinking is also strongly expressed in the context of information and knowledge management. This is in line with the results of a previous study (Indrašienė et al., 2021) emphasising that critical thinking can be interpreted in three ways: (1) as a precondition for knowledge management goals, (2) as a tool for knowledge management, and (3) as a condition for knowledge exchange. Critical thinking has been found to be one of the most important prerequisites for realising knowledge management goals. The process of knowledge sharing does not in itself create added value for the organisation. Only thought-out, evaluated and substantiated knowledge steers an organisation towards improvement. In this context, knowledge is not only one of the main resources of an organisation, but also the most important source of innovation. In the process of knowledge creation, critical thinking serves as a tool for knowledge management – critical thinking enables the creation of new knowledge through purposeful thinking and recruiting it for the benefit of the organisation. A difference came to light in the quantitative research between the attitudes of the employers and the employees towards the manifestation of critical thinking in professional activities: the employers emphasised much more strongly than the employees that critical thinking is manifested in collegial decision-making in crisis situations and in substantiated and motivated decisions. Meanwhile, the employees, differently from the employers, put more emphasis on critical thinking as the constant analysis of one's actions.

In summary, it can be stated that the quantitative research results are in line with the qualitative research results and suggest that in the context of the labour market, critical thinking manifests itself most at the personal and organisational levels – as a nurturing experience in challenging, provocative, atypical situations that require quick decisions.

2.4 Responsibility for developing a person's critical thinking

The quantitative research revealed that both study groups delegate responsibility for the development of critical thinking to the individual him or herself. To a lesser extent, responsibility for the development of critical thinking is assigned to the organisation where the person works and the higher education institution.

Analysis of the quantitative research results for both groups of respondents revealed that the majority of employees and employers have a positive view of the role of the higher education institution in preparing specialists for the modern labour market.

Scientific literature notes the role of higher education institutions in developing critical thinking skills, as higher education has a much broader mission than just preparing a person for a particular profession. Higher education is designed to prepare people to be active citizens who view life as a meaningful learning process, and whose thinking and behaviour are determined by ethical standards, personal and shared well-being and freedom (Franco, 2015). As higher education provides more tools for a person to be free, the inclusion of critical thinking development in studies becomes particularly relevant.

Critical thinking is also an important requirement for success as perceived by employers (Carnevale and Smith, 2013) and should therefore be at the forefront of higher education programmes. Critical thinking is one of the skills necessary for sustainable development as well (Rieckmann, 2012; Habets, Stoffers, Van der Heijden and Peters, 2020).

Conclusions

In both higher education studies and the labour market, critical thinking is understood as the totality of personal dispositions and valuable cognitive skills leading to reasoned and reliable decisions. Hence, this partially refutes the opinion found in scientific literature that critical thinking is perceived more as a cognitive skill, but not as a disposition.

There is no established, unified interpretation of the conception of critical thinking in higher education and the labour market. On the one hand, the diversity of conceptions reveals the complexity of the phenomenon itself, but on the other hand, it also signals a lack of agreement on what critical thinking is, and on how and why it is developed.

The understanding of critical thinking as well as how it is taught and learned in higher education and expressed in the labour market are contextualised – experienced and undergone in a specific learning or work environment, situation or culture. How it is understood and experienced basically depends on these contextual circumstances and the person's qualities and experience. It should be noted that the responsibility for developing critical thinking is largely delegated to the person him or herself. According to the research participants, how and at what level it is developed depends on each person's desire and efforts.

Critical thinking is considered to be an essential tool that helps find many practical solutions when operating in modern market conditions, which require a high level of competitiveness and efficiency. Critical thinking skills are also associated with solving new, unprecedented problems, managing the unexpected, and developing new ideas. Thus, the need to develop/improve critical thinking has a strong pragmatic orientation – to solve problems, make key decisions and direct one's activities towards improvement. Assessing critical thinking, especially in the context of the labour market, reveals a practical, consumerist attitude towards it. Critical thinking is seen as the abilities of members of an organisation to act in uncertain circumstances and solve various problems quickly in pursuit of economic performance and a competitive edge. All this is linked to technological progress and increasing competitiveness and economic advantage. However, in the context of higher education, critical thinking is also seen as something that nurtures personal growth, improves relations with the environment, and helps get to know others, social processes and world phenomena better.

Still, one of the most essential elements in both higher education and the labour market is the individual him or herself and mutual interaction, in which knowledge is cultivated and the horizons of thought are expanded. This interaction is based on an open, trust-based culture that brings clear benefits to each community, both tangible and intangible. Successful organisations are considered to be those that naturally and organically internalise personal knowledge and use it as a collectively accumulated asset. This means that the result of investing in the development of a person's critical thinking is a critically thinking community. Criticality is reflected as vigilance towards oneself and the environment, as constantly asking questions, and as self-reflection. Therefore, both in higher education and in the labour market, the critical thinking skills of each member must be strengthened so that later, they can build a sustainable society through individual social actions.

In both higher education studies and the labour market, critical thinking is most pronounced at the personal and interpersonal/organisational level as an experience that promotes personal growth in challenging, provocative, atypical situations, or when quick decisions are needed.

Critical thinking is least experienced at the social level, when acting not only for the good of oneself, but also for the good of others and society as a whole. The social aspect manifests itself as openness to the world, interest in the phenomena and processes taking place in it, and the desire to contribute to its improvement. In essence, all three levels – personal, interpersonal/organisational and social – are tangible and interconnected in the contexts of both higher education and the labour market, emphasising not only the person's intellectual growth, but also aspects of interpersonal interaction and acting for the progress of society.

References

Abrami, P., Bernard, R., Borokhovski, E., Waddington, D. I., Wade, C. A. & Persson, T. (2015). Strategies for teaching students to think critically: A meta-analysis. *Review of Educational Research, 85*(2), 275–314. doi:10.3102/0034654314551063.

AMA, (2010). Critical Skills Survey. Retrieved from https://docplayer.net/14250237-Ama-2010-critical-skills-survey.html.

AMA, (2012). Critical Skills Survey. Retrieved from https://docplayer.net/23395874-Critical-skills-survey.html.

Andrews, R. (2007). Argumentation, Critical Thinking and the Postgraduate Dissertation. *Educational Review, 59*(1), 1–18. doi:10.1080/00131910600796777.

Barnett, R. (1997). Higher education: A critical business. Oxford, England: OUP.

Barnett, R. (2000). *Realizing the University in an Age of Supercomplexity.* Buckingham, England: Society for Research into Higher Education and the Open University Press.

Bassham, G., Irwin, W., Nardone, H. & Wallace, J. M. (2013). *Critical thinking: A student's introduction*, 5th ed. New York, NY: McGraw-Hill.

Bensley, D. A., Crowe, D. S., Bernhardt, P., Buckner, C. & Allman, A. L. (2010). Teaching and assessing critical thinking skills for argument analysis in psychology. *Teaching of Psychology, 37*(2), 91–96. doi:10.1080/00986281003626656

Bermingham, M. (2015). Clearing up "Critical Thinking": Its Four Formidable Features. *Creative Education, 6*(4), 421–427. doi:10.4236/ce.2015.64042

Bezanilla, M. J., Fernández-Nogueira, D., Poblete, M. & Galindo-Domínguez, H. (2019). Methodologies for teaching-learning critical thinking in higher education: The teacher's view. *Thinking Skills and Creativity, 33*, 100584. doi:10.1016/j.tsc.2019.100584.

Boni-Aristizábal, A. &. Calabuig-Tormo, C. (2016). Enhancing pro-public-good professionalism in technical studies. *Higher Education: The International Journal of Higher Education Research, 71*(6), 791–804. doi:10.1007/s10734-015-9916-4.

Brodin, E. (2007). *Critical thinking in scholarship: Meanings, conditions and development*. Lund, Sweden: Lund University.

Brookfield, S. D. (2005). *The power of critical theory: Liberating adult learning and teaching*. San-Francisco, CA: Jossey-Bass.

Brookfield, S. D. (2012). *Teaching for critical thinking. Tools and techniques to help students question their assumptions*. San Francisco, CA: Jossey-Bass.

Byrnes, J. P. & Dunbar, K. N. (2014). The nature and development of critical-analytical thinking. *Educational Psychology Review, 26*, 477–493 doi:10.1007/s10648-014-9284-0

Carnevale, A. P. & Smith, N. (2013). Workplace basics: The skills employees need and employers want. *Human Resource Development International, 16*(5), 491–501. doi:10.1080/13678868.2013.821267.

Danvers, E. (2016). *Re-thinking criticality: Undergraduate students, critical thinking and higher education*. (Doctoral thesis, University of Sussex, Brighton, England). Retrieved from https://www.academia.edu/26213383/THESIS_Re_thinking_criticality_undergraduate_students_critical_thinking_and_higher_education.

Danvers, E. (2018). Who is the critical thinker in higher education? A feminist re-thinking. *Teaching in Higher Education, 23*(5), 548–562. doi:10.1080/13562517.2018.1454419.

Danvers, E. C. (2016). Criticality's affective entanglements: rethinking emotion and critical thinking in higher education. *Gender & Education, 28*(2), 282–297. doi:10.1080/09540253.2015.1115469.

Davies, D., Jindal-Snape, D., Collier, C., Digby, R., Hay, P. & Howe, A. (2013). Creative learning environments in education – A systematic literature review. *Thinking Skills and Creativity, 8*, 80–91. doi:10.1016/j.tsc.2012.07.004.

Davies, M. (2015). A model of critical thinking in higher education. In M. B. Paulsen (Ed.), *Higher Education: Handbook of Theory and Research* (pp. 41–88). Cham, Switzerland: Springer International Publishing.

Davitch, J. M. & Folker Jr., R. D. (2017). Operationalizing air force critical thinking. *Air & Space Power Journal, 31*(4), 62.

Desai, M. S., Berger, B. D. & Higgs, R. (2016). Critical thinking skills for business school graduates as demanded by employers: A strategic perspective and recommendations. *Academy of Educational Leadership Journal, 20*(1), 10–31.

Detert, J. & Edmondson, A. (2011). Implicit voice theories: Taken-for-granted rules of self-censorship at work. *Academy of Management Journal, 54*(3), 461–488. doi:10.5465/AMJ.2011.61967925.

Devlin, M. (2002). Taking responsibility for learning isn't everything: A case for developing tertiary students' conceptions of learning. *Teaching in Higher Education, 7*(2),125–138. doi:10.1080/13562510220124231.

Dune, G. (2015). Beyond critical thinking to critical being: Criticality in higher education and life. *International Journal of Education Research, 71*, 86–99. doi:10.1016/j.ijer.2015.03.003.

Duro, E., Elander, J., Maratos, F. A., Stupple, E. J. N. & Aubeeluck, A. (2013). In search of critical thinking in psychology: An exploration of student and lecturer understandings in higher education. *Psychology Learning and Teaching, 12*(3), 275–281. doi:10.2304/plat.2013.12.3.275.

Dwyer, C. P., Hogan, M. J., Harney, O. M. & Kavanagh, C. (2017). Facilitating a student-educator conceptual model of dispositions towards critical thinking through interactive management. *Educational Technology Research and Development, 65*(1), 47–73. doi:10.1007/s11423-014-9360-7.

Ennis, R. H. (1985). A logical basis for measuring critical thinking skills. *Educational Leadership, 43*(2), 44–48.

Facione, P. A. (1990). *Critical thinking: A statement of expert consensus for purposes of educational assessment and instruction. Research findings and recommendations.* Fullerton, CA: California State University.

Facione, P. A. (2011). *Critical thinking: What it is and why it counts.* Millbrae, CA: Measured Reasons.

Facione, P. (2013). Critical thinking: What it is and why it counts. California Academic Press. http://www.insightassessment.com/CT-Resources/Critical-Thinking-What-It-Is-and-Why-It-Counts.

Facione, P. A., Facione, N. C. & Giancarlo, C. A. (2000). The disposition toward critical thinking: Its character, measurement, and relationship to critical thinking skill. *Informal Logic, 20*(1), 61–84. doi:10.22329/il.v20i1.2254.

Fahim, M. & Masouleh, N. S. (2012). Critical thinking in higher education: A pedagogical look. *Theory and Practice in Language Studies, 2*(7). doi:10.4304/tpls.2.7.1370-1375.

Felix, S. M. C. (2016). *Fostering criticality within neoliberal higher education: a critical action research study with first year students in Kazakhstan.* (Doctoral thesis, University of Sussex, Brighton, England). Retrieved from https://sro.sussex.ac.uk/id/eprint/61301/.

Fisherman, D. (2017). *Everyday Criticality: Questioning, Expertise, and the Embodiment of Critical Judgment. (Doctoral dissertation,* Montclair State University, Montclair, NJ). Retrieved from https://digitalcommons.montclair.edu/etd/39/.

Franco, A. (2016). What do "Ode to Joy," the Nobel Peace Prize, umbrellas and cartoons have in common? Why critical thinking matters and how higher education moulds. *Higher Education for the Future, 3*(1), 108–124. doi:10.1177/2347631115610231.

Fung, D. (2014). The influence of ground rules on Chinese students' learning of critical thinking in group work: A cultural perspective. *Pedagogy, Culture & Society, 22*(3), 337–368. doi:10.1080/14681366.2014.899611.

Genc, S. Z. (2008). Critical thinking tendencies among teacher candidates. *Educational Sciences: Theory and Practice, 8*(1), 107–116.

Habets, O., Stoffers, J., Van der Heijden, B. & and Peters, P. (2020). Am I fit for tomorrow's labor market? The effect of graduates' skills development during higher education for the 21st century's labor market. *Sustainability, 12*(18). doi:10.3390/su12187746.

Halpern, D. F. (2014). *Thought and knowledge: An introduction to critical thinking*, 5th ed. New York, NY: Psychology Press.

Hassan, K. E. & Madhum, G. (2007). Validating the Watson Glaser critical thinking appraisal. *Higher Education: The International Journal of Higher Education and Educational Planning, 54*(3), 361–383. doi:10.1007/S10734-006-9002-Z.

Healey, R. R. (2012). The power of debate: Reflections on the potential of debates for engaging students in critical thinking about controversial geographical topics. *Journal of Geography in Higher Education, 36*(2), 239–257. doi:10.1080/03098265.2011.619522.

Huang, G. C., Lindell, D., Jaffe, L. E. & Sullivan A. M. (2016). A multi-site study of strategies to teach critical thinking: "why do you think that?" *Medical Education, 50*(2), 236–249. doi:10.1111/medu.12937.

Indrašienė, V., Jegelevičienė, V., Merfeldaitė, O., Penkauskienė, D., Pivorienė, J., Railienė, A., Sadauskas, J. & Valavičienė, N. (2019). What critical thinking and for what? *Social welfare: Interdisciplinary approach, 1*(9), 24–38. doi:10.21277/sw.v1i9.460.

Indrašienė, V., Jegelevičienė, V., Merfeldaitė, O., Penkauskienė, D., Pivorienė, J., Railienė, A., Sadauskas, J., Valavičienė, N. (2021). Linking critical thinking and knowledge management: A conceptual analysis. *Sustainability, 13*(3), 1476. doi:10.3390/su13031476.

Jiang, J., Gao, A. & Yang, B. (2018). Employees' critical thinking, leaders' inspirational motivation, and voice behavior: The mediating role of voice efficacy. *Journal of Personnel Psychology, 17*(1), 33–41. doi:10.1027/1866-5888/a000193.

Jiang, J. & Yang, B. (2015). Roles of creative process engagement and leader–member exchange in critical thinking and employee creativity. *Social Behavior and Personality: An international journal, 43*(7), 1217–1232. doi:10.2224/sbp.2015.43.7.1217.

Jones, A. (2005). Culture and context: Critical thinking and student learning in introductory macroeconomics. *Studies in Higher Education, 30*(3), 339–354. doi:10.1080/03075070500095788.

Jones, A. (2007). Multiplicities or manna from heaven? Critical thinking and the disciplinary context. *Australian Journal of Education, 51*(1), 84–103. https://doi.org/10.1177/000494410705100107.

King, P. M. & Kitchener, K. S. (2004). Reflective judgment: Theory and research on the development of epistemic assumptions through adulthood. *Educational Psychologist, 39*(1), 5–18. doi:10.1207/s15326985ep3901_2.

Kreitzberg, A. P. & Kreitzberg, C. B. (2011). The Business Case for Critical Thinking. Retrieved from https://intra.cbcs.usf.edu/common/file/HireABull/The%20Business%20Case%20for%20Critical%20Thinking.pdf.

Ku, K. Y. L. & Ho, I. T. (2010). Metacognitive strategies that enhance critical thinking. *Metacognition and Learning, 5*(3), 251–267. doi:10.1007/s11409-010-9060-6.

Kuhn, D. A. (2008). *Education for thinking*. Cambridge, CA: Harvard University Press.

LaPoint-O'Brien, T. (2013). Action Research: The Development of Critical Thinking Skills. Retrieved from https://eric.ed.gov/?id=ED540359.

Lin, S. (2014). Science and non-science undergraduate students' critical thinking and argumentation performance in reading a science news report. *International Journal of Science and Mathematics Education, 12*(5), 1023–1046. doi:10.1007/s10763-014-9524-2.

Lipman, M. (1988). Critical thinking—What can it be? *Educational Leadership, 46*, 38–44.

Lloyd, M. & Bahr, N. (2010). Thinking critically about critical thinking in higher education. *International Journal for the Scholarship of Teaching and Learning, 4*(2), 1–4. doi:10.20429/ijsotl.2010.040209.

Marton, F., Dall'Alba, G. & Beaty, E. (1993) Conceptions of learning. *International Journal of Educational Research, 19*, 277–300.

Mathias, J. (2015). Thinking like a social worker: Examining the meaning of critical thinking in social work. *Journal of Social Work Education, 51*(3), 457–474. doi:10.1080/10437797.2015.1043196.

Mcnamara, J., Sweetman, S., Connors, P., Lofgren, I. & Greene, G. (2020). Using interactive nutrition modules to increase critical thinking skills in college courses. *Journal of Nutrition Education and Behavior, 52*(4), 343–350. doi:10.1016/j.jneb.2019.06.007.

McPeck, J. E. (1981). *Critical thinking and education*. New York: St. Martin's Press.

Natale, S. & Ricci, F. (2006). Critical thinking in organizations. *Team Performance Management, 12*(7/8), 272–277. doi:10.1108/13527590610711822.

Ng'ambi, D. & Johnston, K. (2006). An ICT-mediated Constructivist Approach for increasing academic support and teaching critical thinking skills. *Journal of Educational Technology & Society, 9*(3), 244–253.

Paul, R. & Elder, L. (2008). *The thinker's guide to the nature of functions of critical and creative thinking.* CA: Foundation of Critical Thinking.

Paul, R. & Elder, L. (2012). *Critical thinking: Tools for taking charge of your learning and your life.* Boston, MA: Pearson.

Penkauskienė, D., Railienė, A. & Cruz, G. (2019). How is critical thinking valued by the labour market? Employer perspectives from different European countries. *Studies in Higher Education, 44*(5), 804–815. doi:10.1080/03075079.2019.1586323.

Phan, H. H. (2011). Deep processing strategies and critical thinking: Developmental trajectories. Using latent growth analyses. *Journal of Educational Research, 104*(4), 283–294. doi:10.1080/00220671003739382.

Powley, E., H. & Taylor, S. N. (2014). Pedagogical approaches to develop critical thinking and crisis leadership. *Journal of Management Education, 38*(4), 560–585. doi:10.1177/1052562913519081.

Promoting Critical Thinking in European Higher Education Institutions: Towards an educational protocol (2019). Eds. Dominguez, C. & R. Payan-Carreira. Universidade de Trás-os-Montes e Alto Douro.

Raveendran, A. & Chunawala, S. (2015). Values in science: Making sense of biology doctoral students' critical examination of a deterministic claim in a media article. *Science Education, 99*(4), 669–695. doi:10.1002/sce.21174.

Rieckmann, M. (2012). Future-oriented higher education: Which key competencies should be fostered through university teaching and learning? *Futures, 44*(2), 127–135. doi:10.1016/j.futures.2011.09.005.

Rogoff, I. (2006), "Smuggling" – An embodied criticality. Retrieved from https:// xenopraxis. net/r eadings/ rogoff_ smuggling. pdf

Rüütmann, T. (2019) Development of critical thinking and reflection. In M. Auer & T. Tsiatsos (Eds.), *The Challenges of the Digital Transformation in Education.* Cham, Switzerland: Springer.

Samson, P. L. (2016). Critical thinking in social work education: A research synthesis. *Journal of Social Work Education, 52*(2), 147–156. doi:10.1080/10437797.2016.1151270.

Schendel, R. (2016). Constructing departmental culture to support student development: Evidence from a case study in Rwanda. *Higher Education: The International Journal of Higher Education Research, 72*(4), 487–504. doi:10.1007/s10734-016-0036-6.

Segall, A. & Gaudelli, W. (2007). Reflecting socially on social issues in a social studies methods course. *Teaching Education, 18*(1), 77–92. doi:10.1080/10476210601151599.

Shahinpoor, N. & Matt, B. (2007). The power of one: Dissent and organizational life. *Journal of Business Ethics, 74*(1), 37–48. doi:10.1007/s10551-006-9218-y.

Sigurðsson, G. (2017). Transformative critique: What Confucianism can contribute to contemporary education. *Studies in Philosophy and Education, 36*(2), 131–146. doi:10.1007/s11217-015-9502-3.

Subramanian, K. R. (2020). Organizational aspirations and critical thinking of managers. *Journal of Advances in Social Science and Humanities, 6*(4), 1173–1182. doi:10.15520/jassh.v6i4.485.

Sziarto, K. M., McCarthy, L. & Padilla, N. L. (2014). Teaching critical thinking in world regional geography through stakeholder debate. *Journal of Geography in Higher Education, 38*(4), 557–570. doi:10.1080/03098265.2014.958658.

Wangensteen, S. (2010). *Newly graduated nurses´ perception of competence, critical thinking and research utilization.* (Doctoral dissertation, Karlstad University Studies, Karlstad, Sweden). Retrieved from http://www.diva-portal.org/smash/get/diva2:344929/FULLTEXT01.pdf.

Wass, R., Harland, T. & Mercer, A. (2011). Scaffolding critical thinking in the zone of proximal development. *Higher Education Research & Development, 30*(3), 317–328. doi:10.1080/07294360.2010.489237.

Wolcott, S. (2006). *College faculty handbook: Steps for better thinking. A classroom model for teaching, learning and assessing higher order thinking skills.* Bellevue, Washington: Wolcott Lynch Associates.

Yang, Y. C. (2008). A catalyst for teaching critical thinking in a large university class in Taiwan: Asynchronous online discussions with the facilitation of teaching assistants. *Educational Technology Research & Development, 56*(3), 241–264. doi:10.1007/s11423-007-9054-5.

Conclusions and Recommendations for Higher Education

Abstract: Higher education has a special role in the European Union, and its importance is accentuated by the growing demand for highly qualified people. High qualification is associated not only with specific professional knowledge and skills, but also with the ability to think independently and critically in resolving problems and making decisions. Higher education is perceived as being responsible both for preparing specialists for the labour market, and for fostering broad education, high morals and strong values. Future specialists are expected to be not only professionals in their field, but also responsible citizens – addressing global environmental and cultural ecology problems, managing smartly in a complex world overloaded with information and technological possibilities, finding ways to deal with the unknown through communication and cooperation, and persistently pursuing the well-being of all. In this context, higher education is becoming a very important tool for promoting personal development and social progress, which is unimaginable without educated, thinking, professional employees. They are the ones who are building an economy based on solid and constantly updated knowledge and ensuring the sustainable and harmonious development of society. The growing and changing demand for generic and professional competencies in the labour market requires higher education to constantly readapt to the current situation. And this also means reviewing and evaluating society's needs and emerging challenges, revising existing study programmes and creating new ones, rethinking practices for the preparation of specialists, and assessing the importance of the competencies being developed. The need for critical thinking is not only declared in many international and national documents – it is also obvious in real life. The value of a person who thinks and acts critically is evident in academic institutions, in work teams, and in public gatherings. These people usually become community leaders, authorities, desirable employees and critical friends in difficult life situations.

Keywords: problematic aspects and possible solutions, definition of critical thinking, multidimensionality of critical thinking, teaching and learning critical thinking, expression of critical thinking competence at the personal, interpersonal and social levels, the contextual nature of critical thinking, criticality.

Evidence of the need for critical thinking. In higher education, the commitment to developing critical thinking is reflected in the aspirations of the organisations, which are declared in missions and visions, study programme and course descriptions, and specific teaching and learning practices. In the strategic documents of higher education institutions, critical thinking is usually formulated as a long-term goal and a strategic direction, or it is a vision for the development and improvement of the organisation expressed in inaugural or other special speeches by the heads of the institutions. They usually mention the commitment to developing responsible citizens who are able to think freely and independently, and to preparing highly qualified specialists who are able to use and develop the most advanced technologies, and who are determined to value life as a meaningful learning process and to learn continuously over the course of it. It is a bit harder to discern and find such a commitment in the study programme and course descriptions. It is masked by standard wording arising from the specific requirements for programme descriptions. The limitations of their content do not create opportunities to establish the detailed expression of the critical thinking competency. The need for critical thinking and its realisation can be detected in real teaching/learning and practical work situations, by observing how it unfolds in people's thoughts, behaviours and actions. Practice is an excellent indicator of the realisation of the declared aspirations, established norms and defined rules.

Problematic aspects and possible solutions. This study provided an opportunity to look closely at and analyse how critical thinking is highlighted in scientific literature, study programme descriptions, and the attitudes and experiences of teachers, students, employers and employees. The research revealed several important problematic aspects that are highlighted here along with a proposed response.
The first aspect concerns the definition of the conception of critical thinking. The research results revealed that critical thinking is often treated as: (a) a self-evident phenomenon which does not require further explanation; (b) an ambiguous phenomenon with many different – and, in many cases, competing – meanings; (c) being defined by others and not requiring authentic interpretation and treatment.

The evidence for the first treatment lies in the analysis of the scientific articles and study programme descriptions, and in the insights of the experiences of the teachers and the students. Many of the authors of the scientific articles immediately set out to analyse critical thinking manifestations and practices, but either do not present what conception of critical thinking they are following in their article, or present a definition of critical thinking that is blurred. This creates the impression that the authors are guided by the conviction that the conception of critical thinking is self-evident, so no further explanation is needed. The study descriptions identify critical thinking skills and dispositions, but there is no way to understand what scientific approach to critical thinking the authors of the descriptions follow. It can be assumed that there are no clearly defined ones. Moreover, most of the teachers and students who participated in the empirical study revealed in their narratives that they do not have a clear treatment of the conception. During the qualitative research, the students said that critical thinking is considered to be a self-evident phenomenon that is understood similarly by everyone, and this is precisely why it is difficult to put into words.

The fact that critical thinking is treated as a multifaceted and multi-layered phenomenon is shown by both the results of the analysis of the scientific articles and study programme descriptions, and the results of the phenomenographic study and quantitative research. Critical thinking is perceived as deep, comprehensive and substantiated reasoning, as a reflexive disposition aimed at self-improvement, as an effective problem-solving tool, as a manifestation of creativity, and as a sign of civil society. In principle, all of the descriptions find reverberation in scientific literature and are in line with one or another treatment of the conception. Very often, critical thinking is equated not only with creativity and innovation, but also with tolerance of the unknown, crisis management, a wealth of knowledge and erudition. In order to provide targeted and scientifically based education, it is necessary for teachers to decide what scientific attitude and concept will be followed in the subject they are teaching. The diversity of conceptions and scientific approaches offers a wide range of options. There are sufficient examples illustrating the development of critical thinking based on specific scientific approaches and attitudes.

The evidence for the third treatment relates exclusively to the results of the analysis of the scientific articles – not a single article was found that formulated an authentic conception of critical thinking derived from the author's knowledge and experience. In almost all cases, the articles were based on already well-known authors and their theories, which were not further developed for authentic insights. A somewhat freer relationship with the phenomenon in question would open up its meaning even more, reveal the nuances of its features, supplement existing conceptions and theories, provide inspiration for new research, and at the same time form authentic conceptions of critical thinking.

In light of the arguments put forward, the following is proposed:

- Documents governing studies should go beyond declarations of the importance of critical thinking, and should clearly specify how critical thinking skills will be developed.
- In order to ensure that the development of critical thinking in students at institutions of higher education is a conscious, coherent and science-based process, it should first be agreed at the university, faculty or programme level what theoretical assumptions are and will be used as the basis for constructing the concept of critical thinking. What the extent and depth of the conception of critical thinking will be and, accordingly, what critical thinking skills will be developed, depend on this agreement.
- Study programmes should be constructed/updated/improved in accordance with the systematic attitude that critical thinking skills are to be developed in all study subjects, using teaching, study (learning) and assessment methods that promote critical thinking.
- Teachers should make it clear to students what is considered critical thinking, and how it manifests itself in the specific curriculum and/or professional field.
- Researchers should be encouraged, alongside their existing knowledge of critical thinking theories, to develop their own authentic theoretical insights and theoretical lines, and thus contribute to the development of theoretical thought in critical thinking.

The second aspect concerns the multidimensionality of critical thinking, that is, its components and the attitude towards this phenomenon as a personal quality, as a process, and as an end result. The research findings revealed that critical thinking is perceived as: (a) the totality of a person's cognitive skills and dispositions; (b) a process of thinking and learning; (c) a result manifested in solutions found to a problem, innovative products, or a change in the relationship with oneself, others or the environment.

Quantitative and qualitative analysis of the content of the study programme and course descriptions revealed that critical thinking tends to be conceptualised as a significant personal skill in a specific professional field or a generic competence that manifests itself in a social context. In the course descriptions, the conception of critical thinking is not detailed through the clarifying constituents of critical thinking, and is more often limited to the use of the concept of 'critical'. Analysis of the content of the study programme and course descriptions also revealed that three constituents of critical thinking are usually emphasised in the programmes: analysis, evaluation and interpretation. Less attention is given to critical thinking dispositions. Meanwhile, the results of the qualitative research and survey testify that, from the point of view of the representatives of both higher education and the labour market, critical thinking is the totality of dispositions and cognitive skills, and the former are sometimes considered even more significant than the latter. These findings contradict the results of the study description analysis, which suggest that cognitive abilities have superiority. It also serves as a counterweight of sorts to the prioritisation of critical thinking skills prevalent in scientific literature. Based on these findings, it can be assumed that what is actually considered valuable and significant is found in individual experiences, but not necessarily in the documents governing studies, and that what is analysed in scientific literature does not reflect the multifaceted nature of critical thinking.

The phenomenographic research participants do not have an unequivocal evaluation of critical thinking as a process either. From the point of view of the teachers, employers and employees, critical thinking is a process. For the teachers, it is a learning process in which the studied content and the essence of the phenomena are understood; questioning, doubting and checking is learned; and truth is searched for, solutions are discovered, and relationships are built. For the employers and the employees, it is a process in which problems are analysed, alternatives are evaluated, and decisions are made. In the experiences of the students, critical thinking is almost never reflected as a process of discovery, cognition, understanding and action. In the study programme descriptions, it was partly possible to discern the attitude to critical thinking as a learning process – mainly as learning to select information, analyse it, interpret it, evaluate it, and draw conclusions. In scientific literature, more space is devoted to analysing cognitive abilities being developed than to examining critical thinking processes.

Critical thinking as an end result is particularly pronounced in the experiences of the employers and employees. It manifests itself in specific professional problems that have been solved, and rational and sometimes extraordinary solutions and ideas. From the teachers' point of view, the result of critical thinking can be a problem solved, a task completed, a project created, a case analysis performed, or an idea proposed. The students have similar views. However, they place less emphasis on the value of critical thinking as an end result. In the study programme descriptions, the evaluation of critical thinking as an end result is rather insipid.

In light of the arguments put forward, the following is proposed:

- Critical thinking should be positioned as a synthesis of cognitive skills and dispositions, and this attitude should be followed in preparing and/or updating study programmes.
- During studies, sufficient time and attention should be devoted to recognising and experiencing critical thinking processes, and critical thinking should be evaluated as a learning process.
- During lectures and seminars, sufficient time and attention should be devoted to discussing the results of critical thinking and revealing their diversity and practical value.
- More attention should be devoted in research to studying critical thinking dispositions.

The third aspect concerns teaching and learning critical thinking. The research findings revealed that: (a) not all study subjects and programmes devote sufficient attention to the development of critical thinking; (b) teachers lack the knowledge and experience to teach critical thinking, and students lack an understanding of how and why they are taught critical thinking.

Analysis of the study descriptions revealed that critical thinking is not mentioned in all of the study programme and course descriptions that were examined. Critical thinking is most often mentioned in the aims and learning outcomes for programmes belonging to the Engineering Sciences group of study fields; critical thinking was identified slightly less often in the study field programmes in Social Sciences, Health Sciences and Life Sciences, and the least often in programmes belonging to the Mathematical Sciences and Veterinary Sciences groups of study fields. The analysis of scientific literature revealed that the development of critical thinking is given the most attention in Social Sciences, including Education Sciences, and a bit less in Science, Health, Technologies, Arts and Humanities.

The coherence and systematicity of the development of critical thinking can be judged from the review of scientific literature, from the analysis of study programme descriptions, and from the empirical research results. No examples were found in scientific literature illustrating how critical thinking is developed at the level of the entire institution or study programme. Nor were any examples found illustrating the development of critical thinking as a coherent process in the context of a particular subject being taught. The analysis of critical thinking study descriptions revealed its fragmentary representation in the context of study programmes. Critical thinking is usually listed as a goal and/or intended result, and only in very rare cases is it specified how it will be achieved, that is, what methods and means are planned to be used to develop and teach it. Also, the study descriptions do not reflect at all how evaluation is intended to be done, that is, what methods are planned to be used to assess critical thinking skills. It is the opposite in scientific literature, which has extensive examples of how – and using what ways, strategies and methods – critical thinking is taught in a specific subject, study programme or professional practice. However, there are relatively few publications that analyse and evaluate the effectiveness of strategies for developing critical thinking – what works and how, what doesn't work and why. During the qualitative research, both the teachers and the students shared a variety of examples of teaching and learning critical thinking. However, each group mentioned different things in terms of importance. For the students, independent work and atypical tasks were important. Meanwhile, the teachers emphasised situation/case analysis and collaborative learning. They also mentioned teaching by personal example, by modelling situations that require critical thinking, demonstrating critical thinking dispositions, and recognising the value of critical thinking. The students, however, did not present examples like this in their experiences. Neither group described critical thinking as purposefully planned and systematic teaching and learning. It should be noted that the students claim that they had never heard from teachers that their critical thinking was being developed in the study of a subject, or that teachers have such intentions. Therefore, only on the basis of their own understanding can they assume that teachers are developing it in some way. Thus, the development of critical thinking remains tacit – just implied and foreseeable. The fact that it is not stated testifies not only to a lack of knowing, but also to the absence of a conscious choice to develop it, assuming that it emerges on its own by teaching the content of a particular subject and developing professional skills.

The results of the qualitative and quantitative research revealed that the teachers have never participated in targeted training designed to develop critical thinking competencies. The teachers usually engage in self-education, reading professional literature, observing the environment and analysing events, participating in qualification development events, and discussing professional issues with colleagues. They claim that this is how they develop their critical thinking skills. In their free time, the students also read books and attend cultural events and, less frequently, seminars and conferences. Students are less likely than teachers to highlight the need to improve critical thinking competency. In the scientific literature that was examined, no examples were found analysing how teachers learn critical thinking or develop their critical thinking skills.

In light of the arguments put forward, the following is proposed:

- Course descriptions should not only declare developing the competency of critical thinking as a goal or intended result, but also provide student-centred active teaching/learning/study methods, enabling students to apply newly learned subjects and receive teacher feedback.
- After formulating or updating a programme's learning outcomes, the subject teachers must discuss together the study (learning) and assessment methods

that are planned to be used to encourage critical thinking in students. This would create conditions for maintaining the coherence of study (learning) and assessment methods and their systematic application by ensuring the conceptual links between the subject being studied and the development of critical thinking.

- At the beginning of the course, teachers should accurately define the learning outcomes that focus on the development of critical thinking in the learning process. The aim is to apply/develop innovative strategies for the evaluation and self-evaluation of critical thinking skills that could be used at both the personal and interpersonal level. Feedback processes should encourage critical thinking and enable students to learn not only from the comments of their teacher or peers, but also using meta-processes, for example, by thinking over and evaluating the learning process or outcomes.
- In order to develop critical thinking, it is important to encourage students to look for their own solutions by presenting global, integrated and complementary tasks and activities, providing a variety of learning opportunities, promoting collaboration, supplying a variety of teaching and learning materials, and giving students enough time to construct knowledge and relate it to real life.
- Teachers should be given incentive and the opportunity to improve their critical thinking development competencies through purposeful learning – by delving into scientific literature, participating in conferences and seminars on critical thinking, attending lectures given by more experienced colleagues, or organising professional discussions on critical thinking development issues.
- Teacher competence development programmes should be initiated and prepared which not only introduce the pedagogical and didactic aspects of the development of critical thinking, but also create conditions for applying this knowledge in practical teaching activities and reflecting and discussing in pursuit of the best results.
- Research should be focused on the analysis of critical thinking development in the widest possible range of study programme contexts.
- The systematic development of critical thinking should be studied, looking for links between programme regulations and study descriptions, real teaching and learning practices and the desired result.

The fourth aspect concerns the expression of critical thinking competency at the personal, interpersonal and social levels. The research findings revealed that: (a) the recognisability and value of critical thinking is usually limited to the individual; (b) the interpersonal expression of critical thinking is linked to the desire to understand others, usually in the context of joint activities; (c) the social significance of critical thinking is more declarative and is reflected in isolated phenomenographic research participant statements and course descriptions.

The analysis of both scientific literature and study programme descriptions revealed that critical thinking is usually treated as the strengthening of a person's cognitive powers, with unparalleled value to the person him or herself. The qualitative and quantitative research results are similar. Critical thinking is understood, experienced and undergone as a particular person's quality that is significant to the person him or herself – one which expands the horizons of personal knowledge, deepens understanding of the subject being studied, and develops professional abilities. In this way, the semblance of critical thinking as a self-serving, one-dimensional phenomenon is formed. However, there are different examples as well. The phenomenographic research results reveal the value of critical thinking for mutual relations. The interpersonal dimension of critical thinking is expressed in openness to other attitudes and experiences, recognition of variations and diversity, and fair and impartial treatment of others. However, this attitude is more often determined by necessity than by an overall humanistic approach. Understanding and accepting others is necessary for the purposes of joint studies or professional activities, the need to find a compromise or a solution to a problem. An existential humanistic attitude is reflected more as a declared aspiration than as an example of real practice. The social significance of critical thinking, such as taking an interest in world phenomena and studying them, examining current social problems, and being concerned about the progress of society, is also poorly reflected both in the statements of the phenomenographic research participant and in the course descriptions. There are striking individual examples, especially from the qualitative research, but this cannot be called a trend. In this respect, the phenomenographic research findings are similar to those of the course description analysis, which do not make it possible to substantiate statements made in official rhetoric about critical thinking as the development of learners' democratic values or civic powers, and the higher education institution – as taking responsibility for their fostering. Especially since, according to the quantitative research data, the responsibility for developing critical thinking is attributed to the person him or herself. Thus, a difference emerges between official declarations and people's individual opinions.

In light of the arguments put forward, the following is proposed:

- In order to ensure the relevance of study programmes, the various changes in the labour market should be studied and reflected in the curriculum.
- The study process should involve teaching and learning based on real-life simulations and should include work-based learning; specific examples should be used that illustrate how critical thinking can contribute to the well-being of others, solutions to current societal problems, and creation of the common good.
- Research should be focused on revealing the value of the interpersonal and social dimension of critical thinking.

The fifth aspect is related to the contextual nature of critical thinking. The research findings revealed that: (a) critical thinking is manifested and is recognisable in a specific context; (b) insufficient attention is given to revealing the context of critical thinking.

The qualitative and quantitative research provided an opportunity to highlight critical thinking as being manifested in a specific context, and a significant competence for a specific environment, situation, event and its participants. Students are taught to analyse and evaluate phenomena and events related to a specific professional situation or the subject being studied, and to explain their circumstances. The employers and employees provide examples of professional activities and describe specific circumstances and situations in which critical thinking manifests itself.

However, the analysis of scientific literature and the content analysis of the course descriptions revealed that insufficient attention is given to reflecting the context of critical thinking development. Most of the course descriptions declare the intended outcome – the manifestation of a person's critical thinking, without noting the context of its development. In scientific literature, considerable attention is given to depicting the tasks presented in lectures, describing the methods and tools used, and revealing the preparatory experimental work. However, there is far less analysis of the broader context of critical thinking – the prerequisites for the development of critical thinking, the conditions for maintaining it, as well as the concrete environment and specific circumstances. Little data was also found in scientific literature about the consequences of developing critical thinking. The qualitative research data hints at increased confidence among learners and bolder experimentation, and about independent decision-making among employees and courage to question unsubstantiated decisions made by others. However, these are more of short-term testimonials. No data is available on the long-term consequences of critical thinking.

In light of the arguments put forward, the following is proposed:

- The development of critical thinking should continue to be put in context as much as possible, disclosing its importance not only in the personal and professional field, but also in the broader context of community, country and world phenomena.
- Local, regional and societal issues should be included in study programmes, thus creating conditions for students' critical thinking skills to be manifested in a broader context. In other words, the development of students' abilities to apply theoretical knowledge in practice by analysing and solving real situations.
- Favourable and unfavourable contexts for critical thinking should be studied, revealing the prerequisites, conditions and circumstances for the development of critical thinking in higher education.
- The long-term consequences of developing critical thinking should be explored in order to ensure their longevity and sustainability.

The sixth aspect is related to criticality. The research findings revealed that: (a) criticality is considered to be at the heart of critical thinking; (b) insufficient attention is given to the development and fostering of criticality.

In the research findings, criticality is reflected as a careful and vigilant look at oneself and the environment, and as the constant questioning and rethinking of one's thoughts, decisions and actions and those of others. Criticality is also associated with truth and justice, which are considered to be not only ideals to be pursued, but also a necessary practice that manifests itself in day-to-day decisions. The aspect of criticality is very prominent in the qualitative research findings in the experiences of the teachers, employers and employees. It is not reflected in the students' experiences. Criticality was also found in isolated study programme and course descriptions. Analysis of their content revealed that criticality is directly related to the ideas of critical theory in certain specific arts programmes. Criticality is also analysed in scientific literature. Granted, in some publications it is given as an essential feature of critical thinking, while in others a distinct divide is made between criticality and critical thinking.

In light of the arguments put forward, the following is proposed:

- More attention should be given in the study process to the aspect of criticality, by teaching students self-analysis and self-reflection. Students should also be given the opportunity to make mistakes and correct themselves, constantly improve their work, and analyse various situations and phenomena related to issues of truth and justice not only in the professional context but also in the broader social context.
- Manifestations of criticality should be explored in more depth in various contexts of academic, professional and social life in order to reveal the uniqueness and value of the conception of critical thinking.

The study confirms that in the context of both higher education and the labour market, critical thinking is associated with a person's efforts and desire, and opportunities to think critically in different situations. Critical thinking manifests itself as a person's conscious choice and active, purposeful and organised efforts to apply his or her knowledge and abilities and take action in a specific situation to achieve the desired result. A critically thinking person must be able not only to analyse, research and think reflectively, but also to choose precisely this way of thinking.

Thus, critical thinking is a complex process that begins with the comprehension of information and ends with rethinking the decision made. And even though the need and aspiration to develop critical thinking is clearly stated in strategic educational documents, it has not become a systematic educational practice in institutions of higher education. This requires time, understanding and willingness. Only upon agreeing on what is considered critical thinking and what critical thinking skills and dispositions are most important in the context of the particular study programme, and recognising the development of critical thinking as a systematic process that all of the participants are responsible for the outcomes of, will the result be achieved. That is, the requirement of the modern labour market to prepare highly qualified specialists who are critical thinkers will be met.

In light of these results, we, as a team of researchers, express a deep conviction that critical thinking is an integral and necessary part of the life of the individual and society as a whole. Criticality is the quintessence of critical thinking and manifests itself in the totality of knowledge, attitudes, values, and skills in everyday and professional life. As educators, we strive to nurture criticality in our students throughout their lives. As researchers, we aim to notice significant details and nuances of the concept, but also want to be able to see the whole of the phenomenon, revealing its essence. And of course, be able to name it.

Summary

Critical thinking is an ability that is highlighted in strategic national documents, education and labour market research. Critical thinking is recognised as one of the tools for the formation and development of human and social capital, and an important global labour market competence. Critical thinking is used as a strong argument in developing missions of higher education institutions, implementing learning aims, and evaluating learning outcomes, staff abilities, organisational success and political decisions.

Critical thinking is often referred to as a higher education ideal – an aspiration which the efforts of the academic community must be directed toward. This aspiration is described as the ability of graduates to become critically thinking practitioners who are able to build a life and successfully collaborate with others in solving pressing problems, making important decisions, and contributing to the well-being of society as a whole. Researchers studying the conception and expression of critical thinking in higher education and/or the study process point to a certain discrepancy between the formulation of this ideal as an aspiration and its implementation in practice. This discrepancy could be explained by three interrelated reasons. First is the vagueness of the conception of critical thinking. It is either given many intertwined meanings (Sigurðsson, 2017) or it is reduced to a person's cognitive abilities, logical reasoning and the conclusions drawn from them, which testifies to an immature (Turner, 2005) and rather limited attitude (Walkner and Finney, 1999) towards the phenomenon of critical thinking. The second reason for the discrepancy is a lack of communication and cooperation at the higher education institution in efforts to develop critical thinking. If there is disagreement at the institutional level on what is considered critical thinking in a specifically defined context, it is unclear what critical thinking to teach and how to teach it (Noddings, 2017). There is risk of a real deviation between programme objectives, curriculum and its implementation, the goals of teachers, and the expectations of students. The lack of naming the phenomenon and highlighting its importance not only in official rhetoric, but also in real practice, makes mutual communication very difficult not only at the institutional level, but at other levels as well – education policy, education sciences and academic practice, and education and labour market institutions. This is the third reason for the discrepancy between critical thinking as an aspiration and its implementation. Discussions between university representatives (OECD, 2016) reveal that: (1) there is no clear agreement on the concept of 'critical thinking' – it is doubtful whether a consensus can be reached at all in the presence of cultural differences; (2) it is not clear how to evaluate critical thinking – it is feared that the evaluation of critical thinking will be limited to one or another existing instrument, and it is stressed that the assessment tools chosen must be appropriate for the specific context and needs; (3) higher education institutions devote insufficient attention to the development of this ability;

(4) teachers lack the knowledge and skills to develop critical thinking, so attention must be given to improving their pedagogical competencies.

Critical thinking has been more than just a part of academic rhetoric and educational practice for some time now. The voice of employers is increasingly being heard, calling for attention to be paid to the importance of critical thinking skills in the labour market, as well as in the rapidly changing world of information overload and change in general. Critical thinking is distinguished as one of the key 21st-century abilities of relevance in the labour market (Rave, Guerrero and Morales, 2020; Whiting, 2020). The importance of critical thinking is particularly evident in analysing and evaluating employee skills and organisational culture (Brown, 2011; World Economic Forum, 2018). It is thought that critical thinking, combined with skills such as collaboration, problem solving, leadership, creativity and self-discipline, will help employees function effectively in the organisation of today (Rethinking Education: Investing in skills for better socio-economic outcomes, 2014; European Union, 2018) and be competitive in the 21st-century labour market (Habets, Stoffers, Van der Heijden and Peters, 2020). The labour market is characterised by vagueness and rapid change, so new competencies, the application of technology, continuous market monitoring and a focus on change are a must. Studies show that employers have high expectations for critical thinking. According to employers, critical thinking: creates preconditions for a person to constantly improve for the sake of organisational change (Felix, 2016); encourages constant response to the challenges of the changing environment and enables employees to look for the best solutions for themselves, their customers and the organisation (Indrašienė et al., 2019); and enables employees to have self-confidence, as professionals, in dealing with difficult situations and raising questions in search of new, innovative solutions (Jiang, Gao and Yang, 2018). And not only so that employees can perform their direct functions well, but also so that they are able to raise substantiated, critical questions that lead to fair and better solutions, and know how to reflect on their own activities and those of others, correct mistakes, and grasp the importance of their personal contribution to the development of the organisation and society as a whole (Penkauskienė et al., 2019).

A World Economic Forum report (2020) emphasises that labour market demand may not be met due to the large gap between the manifestation of skills in practice and their declared development in the formal education system. The relevance of critical thinking skills in the labour market and education systems has become evident due to public social discourse. Researchers (Pithers and Soden, 2000; Burbach, Matkin and Fritz, 2004; Andrews and Higson, 2008) have long questioned the coherence between theory and practice in the development of critical thinking. The question is raised as to whether what is written in scientific literature about fostering and evaluating critical thinking is not just scientific wisdom without any real application (Facione, 2013), and whether existing assessment instruments are sufficient in practice (Davies, 2015; Macpherson and Owen, 2010; Schendel, 2016). This responds to the European Commission's Communication on European higher education in the world (2013) and the OECD recommendations (2015) on the need to review study programmes and teaching methods that develop young people's critical thinking in a more targeted and effective way so as to achieve sustainable learning outcomes that are applicable in practice. These convictions are also confirmed by research outcomes (Lai, 2011; Ennis, 2016; Arum and Roksa, 2011) arguing that the development of critical thinking at institutions of higher education does not have sufficient evidence of its successful application in practice, and that higher education institutions lack the effective programmes, teacher qualification and conducive academic environment needed to develop critical thinking (Abrami et al., 2015).

It is worth noting that in the empirical part of the monograph, the manifestation of critical thinking in higher education and the labour market first and foremost reflects the cultural context of the particular country: the study programmes analysed are that of Lithuanian institutions of higher education, and the qualitative and quantitative research participants are teachers and students at higher education institutions in Lithuania as well as employers and employees working at companies operating in Lithuania. However, the research findings are discussed in the context of international research. In order for Lithuania to remain competitive, the competencies of specialists developed in higher education studies must be relevant in the current and future labour market, which faces similar demand in terms of employee abilities in both Lithuania and other EU countries. There is a growing need for highly qualified professionals who are able to act and create quickly and efficiently in changing market situations, develop high value-added products, and implement innovations (Valavičienė, 2015). Therefore, the expectations of Lithuanian employers' correlate with the expectations of employers in other European countries (Penkauskienė, Railienė and Cruz, 2019). The importance of critical thinking skills also is noted in the National Progress Strategy 'Lithuania 2030' (2012), which states that imagination, creativity and critical thinking are considered important national resources. This strategy also points out that the current education system devotes insufficient attention to strengthening critical thinking skills in higher education.

The emphasis on critical thinking in international and national documents, the growing attention of global economic and labour organisations, the problem of defining the concept of critical thinking and the fragmented research all contributed to the idea of the 'Critical Thinking in Higher Education: The Study and Labour Market Perspective' research project. The objective of this project is to research the correspondence of higher education studies to the need for critical thinking expressed by the labour market. The totality of the study is reflected in the following problematic questions:

- What is considered critical thinking in the contexts of higher education and the labour market? What are the constituents of the conception of critical thinking?
- How is critical thinking understood (what real significance do higher education and labour market participants attach to it) and manifested in higher education studies and the labour market?

- What are the links between the development of critical thinking competence in higher education and the needs of the labour market?
- What should the development of critical thinking look like in higher education in order to reach an agreement on the educational significance and practical value of critical thinking?

The research methodology is based on the principle of triangulation, by combining different methods of data collection, analysis and interpretation, where the data complement each other and thus neutralise and reduce the deviation and errors that result from using only one research method. Taking advantage of the benefits of quantitative and qualitative research, the monograph presents four closely related studies: a systematic literature review, quantitative and qualitative content analyses of Lithuanian higher education study programme and course descriptions, a phenomenographic study of teachers, students, employers and employees, and a representative survey of these groups. All four studies followed research ethics rules, identified research limitations, and provided guidelines for further research. Efforts were also made to ensure the reliability and validity of the data in these studies.

The scientific/practical value of the monograph is based on the fact that:

- the conception of critical thinking is revealed through a systematic analysis of scientific literature published over the course of two decades;
- a detailed analysis of study programme and course descriptions in various study fields is carried out from the aspect of critical thinking development;
- the authentic attitudes of teachers, students, employers and employees towards critical thinking is revealed;
- the coherence of the development of critical thinking in higher education with the practical application of critical thinking skills in work activities is evaluated using mixed method research;
- the multifaceted approaches and methods of critical thinking research are highlighted.

The monograph consists of an introduction, six parts, conclusions and recommendations.

The purpose of the first chapter of the monograph *The Concept and Context of Critical Thinking in Higher Education and the Labour Market* is to reveal the relevance of critical thinking in the contexts of higher education and the labour market and to present the importance of defining the conception of critical thinking.

Based on the analysis of scientific literature and documents, it can be argued that the conception of critical thinking is constantly being reconsidered. This depends on the challenges of the period, the needs of the specific context, the scientific and research approach. The broad interpretation of the concept of critical thinking makes it difficult to come to an understanding and agree on what is really considered critical thinking. The need for a definition of the conception is obvious not only in order to understand one another, but also to coordinate actions. In terms of science – to substantiate research and to disseminate and communicate it in pursuit of the response of others, academic discussion and progress in science and society. In terms of education – to foster and improve critical thinking in the academic community. On the other hand, the very essence of critical thinking remains unchanged – the desire to understand what is right and what is not, and to know the truth or at least seek for cognition, despite different conceptions of truth and ways of exploring it. This is called criticality, no matter how it is understood and interpreted in various traditions. Criticality is defined as a person's ability to engage in quality thinking and a sign of the person's own worth. Critical thinking serves the improvement of the individual, interpersonal relationships and society.

The first two decades of the 21st century, the reality of which is characterised by an unprecedented rate of change in all areas of society, are also prompting higher education to change. The understanding that higher education must develop critical thinking stems from the recognition that individuals who think critically and reflectively are necessary to build and maintain the sustainability of societies. Starting with UNESCO's 2009 declaration, the development of critical thinking competencies in higher education has undergone major transformations. Even though inequalities between countries and regions exist not only because of political decisions in the education system, but also because of different cultural contexts in the broadest sense that may lead to the persistence of those inequalities, the introduction of critical thinking competence development into the higher education system still depends on the choice of the countries themselves. Research provides more and more knowledge about the various practices of developing critical thinking in higher education, which leads to more and more opportunities to become acquainted with the experience of foreign countries and their decisions and results, and to have more tools to build an effective critical thinking development system in higher education.

Thus, critical thinking is considered to be one of the key abilities of the 21st century for the well-being of the individual and society as a whole. It can be seen as an essential tool in the management of organisations, helping to find many practical solutions when operating in modern market conditions, which require a consistently high level of competitiveness and efficacy. Critical thinking enables employees to think creatively and independently, make decisions and conclusions, dynamically engage in productive and positive activities, and link theoretical subjects with practical situations. Investing in employees' critical thinking skills and motivating them to improve their critical thinking skills and dispositions and apply them in the day-to-day decisions of the organisation will, in the long run, lead to the creation of an organisation that thinks critically and applies knowledge management effectively. It is, therefore, expedient for an organisation to strengthen employee critical thinking skills, which will subsequently develop a competitive organisation through individual social actions.

The purpose of the second chapter of the monograph *Analysing the Concept of Critical Thinking in Higher Education: Systematic Literature Review* is to present, based on a systematic literature review, the dynamics of the concept of critical thinking in scientific publications from different periods in the context of higher education and to reveal the multidimensionality and comprehensiveness of critical thinking.

The selection process for the systematic literature review consisted of two stages: the selection of scientific journals and the selection of scientific articles. The scientific journals were selected from the Clarivate Analytics Journal Citation Reports database using two keywords: *education* and *educational.* During the selection, 342 journals meeting the criteria were found, which were then grouped according to four topics (Education & Educational Research; Education, Scientific Disciplines; Education, Special and Psychology, Educational) and quartiles (Q1–Q4). Sampling of the scientific articles within the selected journals was performed in the EBSCOhost database using the following selection criteria: ISSN of the particular journal, keyword *critical thinking* in the 'Subject terms' field, full text, 1997–2017 period, and English language. All 804 articles found were screened using the exclusion criteria, leaving 303 texts in the final list. The forms prepared by the researchers for data analysis made it possible to systematise the material obtained and perform a qualitative content analysis based on diachronic and synchronic approaches.

Following a diachronic analysis of the selected 1997–2017 publications, the following chronological features of the conceptualisation of critical thinking in higher education were found: the number of publications analysing critical thinking in higher education has been steadily increasing; they are more often based on empirical research than theoretical analysis; the empirical articles are based on quantitative or qualitative research methods, and mixed methods are only used in exceptional cases; critical thinking is more often analysed from a domain-specific rather than a domain-general perspective.

Synchronic analysis of the selected publications revealed that critical thinking is understood both as a transferable (general) competence and as a set of certain skills that manifest in a particular study area. There is no strict line between the definition of 'critical thinking as a domain-general skill' and 'critical thinking as a domain-specific skill'. Critical thinking goes beyond the borders of a particular discipline, enabling the person to think in broader contexts. The relatively small number of publications presenting one or another critical thinking intervention or strategy and the varying attention paid to their analysis make it impossible to draw deeper conclusions about the efficacy of critical thinking interventions. Interventions such as discussion, critical review, critical reflection, on-line discussions and case studies are most often mentioned in publications. The analysis of critical thinking is usually limited to the personal level focused on the targeted improvement of cognitive powers in order to achieve deeper knowledge and effective problem solving. The interpersonal aspect is reflected less in the publications, and is revealed in two ways: by learning with others and by contributing to the well-being of others. The social level of critical thinking emerges when revealing the essence of criticality, which is related to the ability to question assumptions by showing the tendency of knowledge and knowledge construction and raising important questions about the promotion of ideologies and the distribution of power and influence in society. This level also manifests itself in highlighting the mission of higher education, which is related not only to the provision of scientific knowledge, but also to learning to analyse more complex phenomena of public life – identity, truth, power – and to be determined to actively engage. In essence, the conceptualisation of critical thinking from a social perspective focuses not on what society is, but on what it should be. The main critical task posed to a person is learning to be human.

The purpose of the third chapter of the monograph *Critical Thinking as a Unique Competence: Evidence from Higher Education Studies* is to reveal the expression of critical thinking in higher education by analysing higher education study programme and course descriptions.

The analysis of all of the Lithuanian higher education study programme and course descriptions was performed using mixed methods, which included quantitative and qualitative methods of data collection, analysis and interpretation, and were based on the facilitation approach. The study consisted of four sequentially interrelated stages: analysis of 754 study programme descriptions, quantitative content analysis of the descriptions of 266 study programmes that mention the concept of critical thinking, quantitative content analysis of the seven study programme and course descriptions purposefully selected from various fields, and qualitative content analysis of the same seven study programme and course descriptions. Analysis of the quantitative data made it possible to examine how critical thinking is integrated into study programme and course descriptions at Lithuanian higher education institutions, and analysis of the qualitative data revealed the expression of the conception of critical thinking and the constituents of critical thinking.

The quantitative content analysis of the study programme descriptions revealed that the concept of critical thinking is mentioned in approximately one-third of the study programme descriptions. The highest frequency of the critical thinking concept was found in the Engineering Sciences, Life Sciences and Technology Sciences study field groups. The concept of critical thinking mentioned in the descriptions of the selected study programmes is expanded and detailed in almost all of the course descriptions. Critical thinking as a concept per se is more often mentioned in relation to generic competences than to subject-specific competences. Generic competencies stress the ability to evaluate, while subject-specific competences stress the ability to analyse.

Both the quantitative and qualitative analyses of the course descriptions revealed that critical thinking tends to be conceptualised as a skill, without specifying its nature – personal, professional (special), general or other. In most cases, critical thinking is highlighted as a significant personal skill in a particular professional field. It is also seen as a generic competence that unfolds in the broader – social – context. The significance of critical thinking for interpersonal relationships is poorly reflected. The revealed constituents of critical thinking are linked to the context of the specific subjects or presented in the abstract. Critical thinking is most commonly associated with creative, analytical, and reflexive thinking.

The purpose of the fourth chapter of the monograph *Critical Thinking in Study Process and Labour Market: Phenomenographic Study* is to reveal how teachers, students, employers and employees understand critical thinking, and how critical thinking manifests itself in the specific context of studies and the labour market.

Phenomenography was chosen as the main methodological approach to research aspects of the conception and constituents of critical thinking as perceived by representatives of higher education and the labour market. The study used purposeful sampling to select participants according to the principle of heterogeneity, that is, efforts were made to ensure that the participants in all four groups were of different age groups and genders, that the teachers and students were from different higher education institutions, study areas and subjects (teachers) or study fields and years of study (students), and that the employers and employees reflected a diversity of economic activities, sectors of activity, and management (employers) or professional (employees) experience. A total of 79 interviews were conducted with 18 teachers, 16 students, 28 employers and 17 employees. For the data collection, the semi-structured interview method was chosen, which ensured the clearness of purpose of the research, and provided flexibility to present the main and follow-up questions to the research participants, respond to the course of the actual interview, and focus on the relationship between the research participant and the research phenomenon rather than on the phenomenon itself. The analysis of qualitative data consisted of the following stages: repeated reading of the text, marking the parts of the text which were relevant to the interview questions, preparation of initial descriptions, grouping the data into categories based on similarities and differences, description of categories, distinction between dominant and non-dominant categories, assigning categories to dimensions/highlighting dimensions in relation to the categories, and creating a structural picture of the manifestation of the phenomenon in the outcome space. The study revealed the subjective conceptions and experiences of critical thinking among higher education teachers and students, employers and employees, as well as the differences and similarities in experiences.

The treatment of critical thinking by the students and the teachers is related both to action in the academic space, and to the general experience of the phenomenon in the personal and professional space. Both groups emphasise that they did not have a previously formed conception of critical thinking. The teachers pointed out that they do not have a special aim to teach critical thinking. Their teaching is an integral part of academic activities, in pursuit of a deeper understanding of the subject being studied, preparation for the profession, and the development of thinking and broadening one's outlook in general. It can, therefore, be argued that in their conception, critical thinking is associated with the development of both professional and generic competences.

Students and teachers understand critical thinking as the development of a person's cognitive abilities to select, compare, convey, interpret, evaluate and draw conclusions by working with the specific content of the subject being studied; a measure or instrument of a practical application – to solve a problem or find and apply a solution by modelling professional situations; a person's disposition to think independently, question the opinions and decisions of others without hesitation, and build an open, empathetic relationship with others.

The following differences between the teachers and the students in the understanding of critical thinking were identified: the teachers understand critical thinking as a holistic overall competence that provides the basis for the development of their own thinking as well as for the creation of a multifaceted, open relationship with the environment; the students perceive critical thinking in relation to the environment more narrowly – as the ability to reflect on phenomena from different perspectives; the teachers perceive critical thinking as a learning process – to know, understand, choose, evaluate; the students associate critical thinking more with the process of solving relevant problems; the teachers associate critical thinking with other phenomena – creativity, civil and democratic society; the students do not stress the connections between critical thinking and other phenomena.

The conception of critical thinking is revealed at the personal, interpersonal and social levels. Both the teachers and the students see the value of critical thinking for personal growth and professional development. In relation to other people, critical thinking is seen as an opportunity to improve one's thinking by studying and working together, as well as by solving relevant professional problems. In relation to society, critical thinking is seen as openness to change, progress, creative solutions and innovation. However, the latter aspect is only highlighted in the teachers' experiences.

Both the teaching and learning of critical thinking are exclusively related to deeper examination of the subject being studied, better knowledge acquisition, and the development of analytical skills. Comparison of the teachers' teaching experiences and the students' learning experiences reveals several key aspects common to both groups. First of all, critical thinking teaching and learning takes place in two ways: by organising joint activities, and by assigning independent tasks. The teacher takes an active role in teaching, explaining, demonstrating, and modelling. The students engage in the activities offered by the teacher. Passive teaching occurs when the teacher delegates learning responsibilities to the students, monitoring and coordinating the learning process, and the students engage in learning feeling the freedom to choose, decide, and create. The teachers use and the students recognise a wide range of methods for developing critical thinking: case and problem analysis, text analysis and evaluation, questioning, situation simulation, experimentation, and discussions.

Several differences in the teaching and learning experiences were also identified: the teachers value teaching through independent tasks in terms of personal empowerment, better immersion into the content being studied, and professional effectiveness, while the students tend to associate independent learning more with personal maturity and their recognition and evaluation as a person than with the development of abilities applicable in studies and professional life. The teachers claim to teach by personal example – sharing experience and scientific achievements – and clearly declare the values of openness to the truth, the pursuit of rightness, and the search for unique solutions and creativity. However, in their experiences, the students do not recognise the method of learning from the teacher's example.

The teachers also claim that no one taught them how to teach critical thinking. They develop their critical thinking competencies individually, through self-education – by reading, observing and analysing the environment – and collectively, during organised professional development training events – by listening to speeches and colleagues and discussing amongst themselves. The students also could not recall the teachers mentioning that they are specially teaching them critical thinking. The students' experiences reflected the learning of critical thinking in the usual lectures and practical classes organised by teachers. The students, like the teachers, associate the learning of critical thinking with a better understanding of the subject being studied, knowledge of the profession, deeper thinking, and the broadening of one's outlook.

The treatment of critical thinking by the employers and employees is inextricably linked to their daily professional activities. The conception of critical thinking is formed by contemplating an experience of the phenomenon and, conversely, the experience of critical thinking in the course of daily professional activities forms subjective conceptions of critical thinking.

The common components of the employers' and employees' understanding of critical thinking are revealed as individual abilities focused on the search for truth, and as courage in specific professional activities. It should be noted that both the employers and the employees understand critical thinking not only as cognitive abilities, but also as their expression in the course of daily professional activities. The practical applicability of this competence and the tangibility of concrete results are highlighted in both groups' understanding of subjective critical thinking. Both groups understand critical thinking as free thinking without preconceptions, when a person is not guided solely by his or her personal experience or attitude and does not succumb to environmental pressures. Critical thinking is interpreted as the ability to see and analyse a situation from different perspectives, anticipating and evaluating all possible risks. Both the employees and the employers note reasoned decision-making and communication of those arguments based on reasoning. Questioning the absolute, indisputable truth, healthy scepticism, the desire not to become attached to subjective opinions, and doubt as to the existence of any seemingly reliable criterion of truth are highlighted. In the understanding of both groups, critical thinking is associated with self-confidence and taking on the challenge of expressing an independent opinion, as well as with the ability to act independently and take responsibility without being afraid of making mistakes.

The identified variations in the understanding of the employers and employees are linked to certain features of critical thinking. In the employers' understanding of critical thinking, the manifestation of independence and self-confidence is more pronounced. These aspects of the employers' conception of critical thinking are revealed through the context of creating added value for the organisation. The employees' conception of critical thinking highlights the importance of empathy, which is revealed at the interpersonal and social levels as an emotional response to other people's experiences in order to help them or change their situation.

In summarising the experience of critical thinking among employees and employers in daily professional activities, commonalities were identified between how employers encourage critical thinking and how employees experience critical thinking. First is asking yourself and others questions – for employers, this is one of the forms of promoting critical thinking in employees, and for employees, it is a process that creates personal added value in professional activities. Second is presenting and accepting challenges – for employers, this is a provocation that stimulates critical thinking in employees, and for employees, it is a departure from their comfort zone. Challenges are given the meaning of a growing experience: they encourage you to move forward, look for original solutions, change your thinking, create new experiences. Third is delegated and assumed responsibility – for employers, this means encouraging employees to take on responsibility through increasing confidence in the employees and developing their responsibilities, and for employees, this means not being afraid to make mistakes and being able to learn from their mistakes. Fourth is the expression of personal position/opinion – both the employers and the employees consider this to be a sign of critical thinking. Critical opinion and personal position are expressed in a supportive environment, which in turn is described as motivating, applying adequate organisational measures. In this context, creating added value is also important – both the employers and the employees stress not only the creation of added value for the individual, but also the contribution to the development of the organisation and the well-being of society. Treating critical thinking as having multifaceted value is, therefore, the fifth connecting aspect in the opinion of the employers and the employees. The key variation that distinguishes the employers' and employees' experience of critical thinking is the promotion of critical thinking. The employers acknowledge that it is important to promote critical thinking in employees. Meanwhile, the employees do not underscore the role of the employer in promoting their critical thinking. They associate opportunities for the expression of critical thinking in professional activities more with their own dispositions and behaviour than with employer incentives.

The purpose of the fifth chapter of the monograph *Critical Thinking Competence in Study Process and Labour Market: A Quantitative Study* is to reveal how teachers, students, employers and employees define critical thinking, and what their attitude is towards the development of critical thinking skills and dispositions and their importance in the modern labour market.

In order to reveal the links between critical thinking in higher education and in the labour market, a quantitative study was conducted using the written survey method. The chosen data collection method made it possible to compare the opinions of the teachers and students, employers and employees, and to reveal the links between the study groups. In order for the sample to be representative of the entire statistical population, a multistage probability sampling method was used, by surveying four groups of respondents: teachers, students, employers and employees from all regions of Lithuania. A total of 152 teachers, 1.512 students, 528 employers and 2.012 employees participated in the research. In the questionnaire, all four groups were presented with blocks of questions about the perception of critical thinking, the importance of critical thinking skills, and the importance of critical thinking dispositions. Descriptive and inferential statistical methods were used for data analysis.

Analysis of the research data revealed that the conception of critical thinking in higher education and the labour market is associated with a person's skills and dispositions. Critical thinking is seen as a process that depends on a person's skills, dispositions, values and beliefs. In both higher education and the labour market, critical thinking is considered to be a key competence, which manifests itself as the ability to make decisions based on real-life problems. The ability to make decisions and take action becomes one of the essential traits that employers expect from prospective employees, and teachers develop this ability. In evaluating the definition of critical thinking, the teachers and employers are more inclined to emphasise the result of this process – the adoption of a reasoned and rational decision. This definition of critical thinking focuses on the understanding that in certain situations, no obviously right solution exists, so strong arguments are needed to make the right decision. Meanwhile, the students and the employees see the result in the very thought process, in which reflection on action and the ability to engage in impartial reasoning based on controlled, rational inference and decision-making play an important role.

In the context of both higher education and the labour market, the manifestation of critical thinking is associated with a person's efforts and desire, and opportunities to think critically in different situations. Critical thinking manifests itself as a person's conscious choice to apply acquired knowledge and abilities in a specific environment. Critical thinking means a person's active, purposeful and organised efforts to give meaning to his or her world by carefully examining his or her own thinking and that of others. Thus, in the context of higher education and the labour market, the manifestation of critical thinking is associated more with the personal context. It is important to note that critical thinking is perceived as a quality that can be trained. It is found and further developed in a dynamic process of thinking that is not finite in terms of human age and experience. However, there are also those who believe that the ability to think critically is unchanging, and is best expressed by criticising.

Inference is considered the most important ability in the modern labour market. This is what representatives of higher education and the labour market think. The ability to draw meaningful conclusions is recognised as a process of cognitive thinking that, from the point of view of the employers and the teachers, is associated with summarising data-based information and anticipating consequences. In the opinion of the students and the employees, self-regulation skills are considered to be among the most important in the modern labour market; the employers and the teachers, however, feel that these skills are less significant in the modern labour market. Interpretive skills are important for the employers and the teachers, because having knowledge or information alone is not enough. The proper use of that knowledge and information and application in professional activities and/or studies is essential. A clear priority is given to the use of inference for personal purposes. Interpersonal and social benefits are poorly reflected in this regard. The personal level is surpassed when the goal is to make a detailed analysis and substantiated evaluation of a situation/problem, and make a rational decision in a field wider than that of personal interests, taking different opinions into account.

From the point of view of the higher education and labour market representatives, the importance of developing critical thinking skills corresponds to the needs of the modern labour market, which are related to more than just inference. Higher education institutions strive to develop the abilities that are most frequently highlighted in the labour market: inference, argumentation and interpretation skills. The students also note the importance of developing these skills. In the opinion of the employees and the students, knowing yourself and reflecting (on your thoughts, feelings, actions), which is related to the expression of critical thinking at the personal level, is important in the modern labour market. Thus, the attitudes of both groups of research participants towards critical thinking as being more focused on personal cognitive abilities and relationships than interpersonal or social ones coincide.

The importance of critical thinking dispositions in the modern labour market is not questioned. Both the teachers and the students feel that considerable attention is devoted to their development in the study process. In the context of higher education and the labour market, the dispositions of fairness, courage and perseverance are most valued, while those of scepticism and open-mindedness are given as being the least important. The dispositions that the higher education and labour market representatives consider to be important are also ascribed to the dispositions that need further improvement/development. Various methods are used for the development of critical thinking skills and dispositions, most of which are focused on self-education. According to the representatives of higher education and the labour market, the dispositions of flexibility, open-mindedness and accuracy are the most in need of improvement and further fostering.

All of the groups of research participants believe that responsibility for developing critical thinking should be delegated to the person and his or her desire or willingness to think critically. The willingness to think critically is associated with a thought process that depends on a person's dispositions, values and beliefs to think openly, making substantiated assumptions, and evaluating or weighing the persuasiveness of arguments. To a certain extent, responsibility for developing critical thinking is also delegated to the employee's organisation, and the least significant factor in the development of critical thinking is considered by the higher education and the labour market representatives to be the role of the higher education institution.

The purpose of the sixth chapter of the monograph *Linking Critical Thinking Development in Higher Education and Demand in Labour Market* is to provide insights into the understanding, experience and expression of critical thinking in higher education and the labour market and to elucidate the links between the development of critical thinking in higher education and demand in the labour market.

Qualitative (phenomenographic) research revealed the subjective conceptions and experiences of critical thinking among higher education teachers and students, as well as employers and employees. The conceptions and experiences of critical thinking of these research participants revealed not only differences, but also similarities. Quantitative research (survey) made it possible to distinguish the attitudes of all four groups towards the conceptions of critical thinking and establish the predominant ones, and to identify the importance of critical thinking skills and dispositions in the study process and the labour market. In both higher education and the labour market, critical thinking is understood as the totality of personal dispositions and valuable cognitive abilities leading to reasoned, substantiated and reliable decisions. Hence, this partially refutes the opinion found in scientific literature that critical thinking is perceived more as a skill, but not as a disposition.

There is no established, unified explanation of the conception of critical thinking in higher education and the labour market. On the one hand, the diversity of conceptions reveals the complexity of the phenomenon itself, but on the other hand, it also signals a lack of agreement on what critical thinking is, and how and why it is developed.

The understanding of critical thinking as well as how it is taught and learned in higher education and expressed in the labour market are contextualised, that is, how it is experienced and undergone in a specific learning or work environment, situation or culture. How it is understood and experienced basically depends on these contextual circumstances and the person's qualities and experience. It should be noted that the responsibility for developing critical thinking is largely delegated to the person him or herself. According to the research participants, how and at what level it is developed depends on each person's desire and efforts.

Critical thinking is considered to be an essential tool that helps find many practical solutions when operating in modern market conditions, which require a high level of competitiveness and efficiency. Critical thinking skills are also associated with solving new, unprecedented problems, managing the unexpected, and developing new ideas. Thus, the need to develop, improve critical thinking has a strong pragmatic orientation – to solve problems, make key decisions and direct one's activities towards improvement. Evaluation of critical thinking, especially in the context of the labour market, reveals a practical, consumerist attitude to critical thinking. It is seen as the abilities of members of an organisation to act in uncertain circumstances and solve various problems quickly in pursuit of economic performance and a competitive edge. All this is linked to technological progress and increasing competitiveness and economic advantage. However, in the context of higher education, critical thinking is also seen as something that nurtures personal growth, improves relations with the environment, and helps get to know others, social processes and world phenomena better.

Still, one of the most essential elements in both higher education and the labour market is the individual him or herself and mutual interaction, in which knowing is cultivated and the horizons of thought are expanded. This interaction is based on an open, trust-based culture that brings clear benefits, both tangible and intangible, to each community. Successful organisations are considered to be those that naturally and organically internalise personal knowledge and use it as a collectively accumulated asset. This means that the result of investing in the development of a person's critical thinking is a critically thinking community. Criticality is reflected as vigilance towards yourself and the environment, as constant self-questioning, and as self-reflection. Therefore, both in higher education and in the labour market, the critical thinking skills of each member must be strengthened so that later, they can build a sustainable society through individual social actions.

In both higher education studies and the labour market, critical thinking is most pronounced at the personal and interpersonal/organisational level as an experience that promotes personal growth in challenging, provocative, atypical situations, or when quick decisions are needed.

Critical thinking is least experienced at the social level, when acting not only for the good of oneself, but also for the good of others and society as a whole. The social aspect manifests itself as openness to the world, interest in the phenomena and processes taking place in it, and the desire to contribute to its improvement. In essence, all three levels – personal, interpersonal/organisational and social – are tangible and interconnected in the contexts of both higher education and the labour market, stressing not only the person's intellectual growth, but also aspects of interpersonal interaction and acting for the progress of society.

The monograph ends with conclusions and recommendations for improving critical thinking competency and strengthening it in higher education.

The research conducted by the authors and presented in this monograph made it possible to take a careful look and analyse how critical thinking is highlighted in scientific literature, study programme descriptions, and the attitudes and experiences of teachers, students, employers and employees, and revealed several important problematic aspects.

The first aspect concerns the definition of the conception of critical thinking. The research findings revealed that critical thinking is often treated as: (a) a self-evident phenomenon which does not require further explanation; (b) an ambiguous phenomenon with many different – and, in many cases, competing – meanings; (c) being defined by others and not requiring authentic treatment.

The evidence for the first treatment lies in the analysis of the scientific articles and study programme descriptions, and in the summaries of the experiences of the teachers and the students. Many of the authors of the scientific articles immediately set out to analyse critical thinking manifestations and practices, but either do not present what conception of critical thinking they are following in their article, or present a definition of critical thinking that is blurred. This creates the impression that the authors are guided by the conviction that the conception of critical thinking is self-evident, so no further explanation is needed. The study descriptions identify critical thinking skills and dispositions, but there is no way to understand what scientific approach to critical thinking the authors of the descriptions follow. It can be assumed that there are no clearly defined ones. Moreover, most of the teachers and students who participated in the empirical study revealed in their accounts that they do not have a clear treatment of the conception. During the qualitative research, the students said that critical thinking is considered to be a self-evident phenomenon that is understood similarly by everyone, and this is precisely why it is difficult to put into words.

The fact that critical thinking is treated as a multifaceted and multi-layered phenomenon is shown by both the results of the analysis of the scientific articles and study programme descriptions, and the results of the phenomenographic study and quantitative survey. Critical thinking is perceived as deep, comprehensive and substantiated reasoning, as a reflexive disposition aimed at self-improvement, as an effective problem-solving tool, as a manifestation of creativity, and as a sign of civil society. In principle, all of the descriptions find reverberation in scientific literature and are in line with one or another conception. Very often, critical thinking is equated not only with creativity and innovation, but also with tolerance of the unknown, crisis management, a wealth of knowledge, and erudition. In order to provide targeted and scientifically based critical thinking education, it is necessary for teachers to decide what scientific attitude and concept will be followed in the subject they are teaching. The diversity of conceptions and scientific approaches offers a wide range of options. There are sufficient examples illustrating the development of critical thinking based on specific scientific approaches and attitudes.

The evidence for the third treatment relates exclusively to the results of the analysis of the scientific articles – not a single article was found where would the authentic conception of critical thinking derived from the author's knowledge and experience be formulated. In almost all cases, the articles were based on the main theorists of critical thinking, known authors and their theories, which were not further developed for authentic insights. A somewhat freer relationship with the phenomenon in question would open up its meaning even more, reveal the nuances of its features, supplement existing conceptions and theories, provide inspiration for new research, and at the same time form authentic conceptions of critical thinking.

In light of the arguments presented, the following is proposed:

- Documents governing studies should go beyond declarations of the importance of critical thinking, and should clearly specify how critical thinking will be developed.
- In order to ensure that the development of critical thinking in students at institutions of higher education is a conscious, coherent and science-based process, it should first be agreed at the university, faculty or programme level what theoretical assumptions are and will be used as the basis for constructing

the concept of critical thinking. What the content of the conception of critical thinking will be and, accordingly, what critical thinking skills, dispositions will be developed and by which methods, depend on this agreement.

- Study programmes should be prepared, updated and improved in accordance with the agreed conception of critical thinking and the systematic attitude that critical thinking has to be developed in all study subjects, using teaching, study (learning) and assessment methods that promote critical thinking.
- It should be clearly presented to students what is considered critical thinking, and how it manifests itself in the specific curriculum and/or professional field.
- Researchers should be encouraged, alongside their existing knowledge of critical thinking theories, to develop their own authentic theoretical insights and theoretical lines, and thus contribute to the development of theoretical thought in critical thinking.

The second problematic aspect concerns the multidimensionality of critical thinking, that is, its components and the attitude towards this phenomenon as a personal quality, as a process, and as an end result. The research findings revealed that critical thinking is perceived as: (a) the totality of a person's cognitive abilities and dispositions; (b) a process of thinking and learning; (c) a result manifested in solutions found to a problem, innovative products, or a change in the relationship with oneself, others or the environment.

Quantitative and qualitative analysis of the content of the study programme and course descriptions revealed that critical thinking tends to be conceptualised as a significant personal skill in a specific professional field or a generic competence that manifests itself in a social context. In the course descriptions, the conception of critical thinking is not detailed through the clarifying constituents of critical thinking, and is more often limited to the use of the concept of 'critical'. Analysis of the content of the study programme and course descriptions also revealed that three constituents of critical thinking skills are usually stressed in the programmes: analysis, evaluation and interpretation. Less attention is given to critical thinking dispositions. Meanwhile, the results of the qualitative research and questionnaire survey testify that, from the point of view of the representatives of both higher education and the labour market, critical thinking is the totality of dispositions and cognitive abilities, and the former are sometimes considered even more significant than the latter. These findings contradict the results of the study description analysis, which suggest that cognitive abilities have superiority. It also serves as a counterweight of sorts to the prioritisation of critical thinking skills prevalent in scientific literature. Based on these findings, we would assume that what is actually considered valuable and significant is found in individual experiences, but not necessarily in the documents governing studies, and that what is analysed in scientific literature does not reflect the multifaceted nature of critical thinking.

The phenomenographic research participants do not have an unequivocal evaluation of critical thinking as a process either. From the point of view of the teachers, employers and employees, critical thinking is a process. For the teachers, it is a learning process in which the studied content and the essence of the phenomena are understood; questioning, doubting and checking is learned; and truth is searched for, solutions are discovered, and relationships are built. For the employers and the employees, it is a process in which problems are analysed, alternatives are evaluated, and decisions are made. In the experiences of the students, critical thinking is almost never manifested as a process of discovery, cognition, understanding and action. In the study programme descriptions, it was partly possible to discern the attitude to critical thinking as a learning process – mainly as learning to select information, analyse it, interpret it, evaluate it, and draw conclusions. In scientific literature, more space is devoted to analysing cognitive abilities being developed than to examining critical thinking processes.

Critical thinking as an end result is particularly manifested in the experiences of the employers and employees. It manifests itself in specific professional problems that have been solved, and rational and sometimes extraordinary solutions and ideas. From the teachers' point of view, the result of critical thinking can be a problem solved, a task completed, a project created, a case analysis performed, or an idea proposed. The students have similar views. However, they place less emphasis on the value of critical thinking as an end result. In the study programme descriptions, the evaluation of critical thinking as an end result is rather negligible.

Based on the arguments put forward, the following is proposed:

- Critical thinking should be positioned as a synthesis of cognitive abilities and dispositions, and this attitude should be followed in preparing and/or updating study programmes.
- During studies, sufficient time and attention should be devoted to recognising and experiencing critical thinking processes, and critical thinking should be evaluated as a learning process.
- During lectures and seminars, sufficient time and attention should be devoted to discussing the results of critical thinking and revealing their diversity and practical value.
- More attention should be devoted in research to studying critical thinking dispositions.

The third aspect concerns critical thinking teaching and learning. The research findings revealed that: (a) not all study subjects and programmes devote sufficient attention to the development of critical thinking; (b) teachers lack the knowledge and experience to teach critical thinking, and students lack an understanding of how and why they are taught critical thinking.

Analysis of the study descriptions revealed that critical thinking is not mentioned in all of the study programmes and subject descriptions that were examined. Critical thinking is most often mentioned in the aims and learning outcomes for programmes belonging to the Engineering Sciences group of study fields; the expression of critical thinking was found slightly less often in the study field programmes in Social Sciences, Health Sciences and Life Sciences, and the least often in programmes belonging to the Mathematical Sciences and Veterinary Sciences groups of study fields. The analysis of scientific literature revealed that the development of critical thinking is given the most attention in Social Sciences, including Education Sciences, and a bit less in Science, Health, Technologies, Arts and Humanities.

The coherence and systematicity of the development of critical thinking can be judged from the review of scientific literature, from the analysis of study programme descriptions, and from the empirical research outcomes. No examples were found in scientific literature illustrating how critical thinking is developed at the level of the entire institution or study programme. Nor were any examples found illustrating the development of critical thinking as a coherent process in the context of a particular subject being taught. The analysis of critical thinking study descriptions revealed its fragmentary representation in the context of study programmes. Critical thinking is usually listed as a goal and/or intended result, and only in very rare cases is it specified how it will be achieved, that is, what methods and means are planned to be used to develop and teach it. Also, the study descriptions do not reflect at all how evaluation is intended to be done, that is, what methods are planned to be used to assess critical thinking skills. It is the opposite in scientific literature, which has extensive examples of how – using what ways, strategies and methods – critical thinking is taught in a specific subject, study programme or professional practice. However, there are relatively few publications that analyse and evaluate the effectiveness of strategies for developing critical thinking, that is, what works and how, what doesn't work and why. During the qualitative research, both the teachers and the students shared a variety of examples of teaching and learning critical thinking. However, each group stressed different things in terms of importance. For the students, independent work and atypical tasks were important. Meanwhile, the teachers stressed situation/case analysis and collaborative learning. They also mentioned teaching by personal example, by modelling situations that require critical thinking, demonstrating critical thinking dispositions, and recognising the value of critical thinking. The students, however, did not stress examples like this in their experiences. Neither group described critical thinking as purposefully planned and systematic teaching and learning. It should be noted that some of the students claim that they had never heard from teachers that their critical thinking was being developed in the study of a subject, or that teachers have such intentions. Therefore, only on the basis of their own understanding can they assume that teachers are developing it in some way. Thus, the development of critical thinking remains tacit – just implied and foreseeable. The fact that it is not stated testifies not only to a lack of knowing, but also to the absence of a conscious choice to develop it, assuming that it emerges on its own by teaching the content of a particular subject and developing professional skills.

The results of the qualitative and quantitative research revealed that the teachers have never participated in targeted training designed to develop critical thinking competencies. The teachers usually take an interest independently, reading professional literature, observing the environment and analysing events, participating in professional development events, and discussing professional issues with colleagues. They claim that this is how they develop their critical thinking skills. In their free time, the students also read books and attend cultural events and, less frequently, seminars and conferences. Students are less likely than teachers to highlight the need to improve critical thinking competency. In the scientific literature that was examined, no examples were found analysing how teachers learn critical thinking or develop their critical thinking skills.

Based on the arguments put forward, the following is proposed:

- Course descriptions should not only declare developing the competency of critical thinking as a goal or intended result, but also provide student-centred active teaching/learning/study methods, enabling students to apply newly learned subjects and receive teacher feedback.
- After formulating or updating a programme's learning outcomes, the subject teachers should discuss together the study (learning) and assessment methods that are planned to be used to encourage critical thinking in students. This would create conditions for maintaining the coherence of study (learning) and assessment methods and their systematic application by ensuring the conceptual links between the subject being studied and the development of critical thinking.
- At the beginning of the course, teachers should accurately define the learning outcomes that focus on the development of critical thinking in the learning process. The aim is to apply/develop innovative strategies for the evaluation and self-evaluation of critical thinking skills that could be used at both the personal and interpersonal level. Feedback processes should encourage critical thinking and enable students to learn not only from the comments of their teacher or peers, but also using meta-processes, for example, by thinking over and evaluating the learning process or outcomes.
- Teachers should think out and prepare tasks for students which prompt them to learn to look for solutions and work independently, encourage their cooperation, and link new knowledge with real life or real-life situations or problems.
- Teachers should be given incentive and the opportunity to improve their critical thinking development competencies through purposeful learning – by delving into scientific literature, participating in conferences and seminars on critical thinking, attending lectures given by more experienced colleagues, or organising professional discussions on critical thinking development issues.
- Teacher competence development programmes should be initiated and prepared which not only introduce the pedagogical and didactic aspects of the development of critical thinking, but also create conditions for applying this knowledge in practical teaching activities and reflecting and discussing in pursuit of the best results.
- Research should be focused on the analysis of critical thinking development in the widest possible range of study programme contexts.

- The systematic development of critical thinking should be studied, looking for links between programme regulations and study descriptions, real teaching and learning practices and the desired result.

The fourth aspect concerns the manifestation of critical thinking competence at the personal, interpersonal and social levels. The research findings revealed that: (a) the recognisability and value of critical thinking is usually limited to the individual; (b) the interpersonal expression of critical thinking is linked to the desire to understand others, usually in the context of joint activities; (c) the social significance of critical thinking is more declarative and is reflected in isolated phenomenographic research participant statements or course descriptions.

The analysis of both scientific literature and study programme descriptions revealed that critical thinking is usually treated as the strengthening of a person's cognitive powers, with unparalleled value to that person. The qualitative and quantitative research outcomes are similar. Critical thinking is understood, experienced and undergone as a particular person's quality that is significant to that person – one which expands the horizons of personal knowledge, deepens understanding of the subject being studied, and develops professional skills. In this way, the semblance of critical thinking as a self-serving, one-sided phenomenon is formed. However, there are different examples as well. The phenomenographic research outcomes reveal the value of critical thinking for mutual relations. The interpersonal dimension of critical thinking is expressed in openness to other attitudes and experiences, recognition of variations and diversity, and fair and impartial treatment of others. However, this attitude is more often determined by necessity than by an overall humanistic approach. Understanding and accepting others is necessary for the purposes of joint studies or professional activities, the need to find a compromise or a solution to a problem. An existential humanistic attitude is reflected more as a declared aspiration than as an example of real practice. The social significance of critical thinking, such as taking an interest in world phenomena and studying them, examining current social problems, and being concerned about the progress of society, is also poorly reflected both in the statements of the phenomenographic research participant and in the course descriptions. The qualitative research revealed striking cases, but they are isolated and do not form a trend. In this respect, the phenomenographic research findings are similar to those of the course description analysis, which do not make it possible to substantiate statements made in official rhetoric about critical thinking as the development of students' democratic values or civic powers, and about the higher education institution as taking responsibility for their fostering. Especially since, according to the quantitative research data, the responsibility for developing critical thinking is attributed to the person him or herself. Thus, a difference emerges between official declarations and people's individual opinions.

Based on the arguments put forward, the following is proposed:

- In order to ensure the relevance of study programmes, the various changes in the labour market should be studied and reflected in the curriculum.

- The study process should involve teaching and learning based on real-life simulations and should include work-based learning; specific examples should be used that illustrate how critical thinking can contribute to the well-being of others, solutions to current societal problems, and creation of the common good.
- Research should be focused on revealing the value of the interpersonal and social dimension of critical thinking.

The fifth aspect is related to the contextual nature of critical thinking. The research findings revealed that: (a) critical thinking is recognisable in a specific context; (b) insufficient attention is given to revealing the context of critical thinking.

The qualitative and quantitative research provided an opportunity to highlight critical thinking as being expressed in a specific context, and a significant competence for a specific environment, situation, event and its participants. Students are taught to analyse and evaluate phenomena and events related to a specific professional situation or the subject being studied, and to explain their circumstances.

The employers and employees provide examples of professional activities and describe specific circumstances and situations in which critical thinking manifests itself. However, the analysis of scientific literature and the content analysis of the course descriptions revealed that insufficient attention is given to reflecting the context of critical thinking development. Most of the course descriptions declare the intended outcome – the manifestation of a person's critical thinking, without noting the context of its development. In scientific literature, considerable attention is given to depicting the tasks presented in lectures, describing the methods and tools used, and revealing the preparatory experimental work. However, there is far less analysis of the broader context of critical thinking – the prerequisites for the development of critical thinking, the conditions for maintaining it, as well as the concrete environment and specific circumstances. Little data was also found in scientific literature about the consequences of developing critical thinking. The qualitative research data hints at increased confidence among learners and bolder experimentation, and about independent decision-making among employees and courage to question unsubstantiated decisions made by others. However, these are more of short-term testimonials. We do not have any data on the long-term consequences of critical thinking.

Based on the arguments put forward, the following is proposed:

- The development of critical thinking should continue to be embedded into context as much as possible, disclosing its importance not only in the personal and professional field, but also in the broader context of community, country and world phenomena.
- Local, regional and societal issues should be included in study programmes, thus creating conditions for students' critical thinking skills to be manifested in a broader context. In other words, the development of students' abilities to apply theoretical knowledge in practice by analysing and solving real situations or providing simulations.

- Favourable and unfavourable contexts for critical thinking should be studied, revealing the prerequisites, conditions and circumstances for the development of critical thinking in higher education.
- The long-term consequences of developing critical thinking should be explored and what ensures their longevity and sustainability should be examined.

The sixth aspect is related to criticality. The research findings revealed that: (a) criticality is considered to be at the heart of critical thinking; (b) insufficient attention is given to the development and fostering of criticality.

In the research findings, criticality is reflected as a careful and vigilant look at oneself and the environment, and as the constant questioning and rethinking of one's thoughts, decisions and actions and those of others. Criticality is also associated with truth and rightness, which are considered to be not only ideals to be pursued, but also a necessary practice that manifests itself in day-to-day decisions. The aspect of criticality is very prominent in the qualitative research findings in the experiences of the teachers, employers and employees. It is not reflected in the students' experiences. Criticality was also found in isolated study programme and course descriptions. Analysis of their content revealed that criticality is directly related to the ideas of critical theory in certain specific arts programmes. Criticality is also analysed in scientific literature. Granted, in some publications it is given as an essential feature of critical thinking, while in others a distinct divide is made between criticality and critical thinking.

Based on the arguments put forward, the following is proposed:

- More attention should be given in the study process to the aspect of criticality, by teaching students self-analysis and self-reflection. Students should also be given the opportunity to make mistakes and correct themselves, constantly improve their work, and analyse various situations and phenomena related to issues of truth and rightness not only in the professional context but also in the broader social context.
- Manifestations of criticality should be explored in more depth in various contexts of academic, professional and social life in order to reveal the uniqueness and value of the conception of critical thinking.

The study confirms that in the context of both higher education and the labour market, the manifestation of critical thinking is associated with a person's efforts and desire, and opportunities to think critically in different situations. Critical thinking manifests itself as a person's conscious choice and active, purposeful and organised efforts to apply his or her knowledge and abilities and take action in a specific situation to achieve the desired result. A critically thinking person must be able not only to analyse, research and think reflectively, but also to choose precisely this way of thinking.

Thus, critical thinking is a complex process that begins with the comprehension of information and ends with rethinking of the decision made. And even though the need and aspiration to develop critical thinking is clearly stated in strategic educational documents, it has not become a systematic educational practice in institutions of higher education. This requires time, understanding and willingness. Only upon agreeing on what is considered critical thinking and what critical thinking skills and dispositions are most important in the context of the particular study programme, and recognising the development of critical thinking as a systematic process that all of the participants are responsible for the outcomes of, will the result be achieved. That is, the requirement of the modern labour market to train highly qualified specialists who are critical thinkers will be met.

Zusammenfassung

Kritisches Denken ist die Fähigkeit, die in strategischen Dokumenten, im Bildungswesen und in Arbeitsmarktstudien der Länder aktualisiert wird. Es gilt als eines der Instrumente zur Bildung und Entwicklung von Human- und Sozialkapital als wichtige Kompetenz auf dem globalen Arbeitsmarkt. Kritisches Denken wird als wichtiges Argument bei der Schaffung der Missionen von Hochschuleinrichtungen, der Umsetzung von Studienzielen, der Bewertung von Studienergebnissen, den Fähigkeiten von Arbeitnehmern Personals und dem organisatorischen Erfolg sowie politischen Entscheidungen verwendet.

Kritisches Denken wird häufig als Ideal der Hochschulbildung identifiziert, als Ziel, auf das die Bemühungen der akademischen Gemeinschaft gerichtet werden müssen. Dieses Ziel wird als die Fähigkeit von Absolventen beschrieben, kritisch denkende Praktiker zu werden, ihr Leben zu gestalten, erfolgreich mit anderen zusammenzuarbeiten, um aktuelle Probleme zu lösen, wichtige Entscheidungen zu treffen und zum Wohl der gesamten Gesellschaft beizutragen. Forscher, die das Konzept und den Ausdruck des kritischen Denkens in der Hochschulbildung und/oder im Studienprozess untersuchen, weisen auf eine gewisse Diskrepanz zwischen der Formulierung dieses Ideals als Ziel und seiner praktischen Umsetzung hin. Eine solche Diskrepanz könnte mit drei untereinander zusammenhängenden Gründen erklärt werden. Erstens – mit der Unsicherheit des Konzepts des kritischen Denkens. Es hat viele miteinander verflochtene Bedeutungen (Sigurdsson, 2017) oder es wird auf die kognitiven Fähigkeiten einer Person, das logische Denken und die daraus abgeleiteten Schlussfolgerungen eingegrenzt, und dies zeugt von einem unreifen (Turner, 2005) und eher begrenzten Ansatz (Walkner und Finney, 1999) zum Phänomen des kritischen Denkens. Der zweite Grund für die Diskrepanz ist die mangelnde Kommunikation und Zusammenarbeit in der Hochschule, um kritisches Denken zu entwickeln. Wenn auf institutioneller Ebene Meinungsverschiedenheiten darüber bestehen, was als kritisches Denken in einem spezifisch definierten Kontext angesehen wird, ist nicht klar, welches kritische Denken zu lehren ist und wie zu lehren ist (Noddings, 2017). Es besteht die Gefahr einer echten Kluft zwischen den Programmzielen, dem Inhalt der Studienfächer und ihrer Umsetzung, den Zielen der Lehrkräfte und den Erwartungen der Studierenden. Die mangelnde Benennung des Phänomens, das seine Bedeutung nicht nur in der offiziellen Rhetorik, sondern auch in der realen Praxis verwirklicht, macht es sehr schwierig, nicht nur auf institutioneller Ebene, sondern auch auf anderen Ebenen – in der Bildungspolitik, Erziehungswissenschaft und in der akademischen Praxis, in den Institutionen der Bildung und des Arbeitsmarktes – zu kommunizieren. Dies ist der dritte Grund für die Diskrepanz zwischen kritischem Denken als Ziel und dessen Umsetzung. Diskussionen zwischen Hochschulvertretern (OECD, 2016) zeigen Folgendes: 1) Es gibt keine klare Einigung über die Definition von „kritischem Denken"; es ist fraglich, ob angesichts kultureller Unterschiede überhaupt eine allgemeine Einigung erzielt werden kann; 2) Es ist unklar, wie kritisches Denken zu bewerten ist; es werden Bedenken geäußert, dass die Bewertung des kritischen Denkens nicht auf das eine oder andere bestehende Instrument beschränkt sein sollte, und es wird betont, dass die ausgewählten Bewertungsinstrumente dem spezifischen Kontext und den Bedürfnissen angemessen sein sollten; 3) die Hochschulen schenken der Entwicklung dieser Fähigkeit zu wenig Aufmerksamkeit; 4) den Lehrkräften fehlen die Kenntnisse und Fähigkeiten, um kritisches Denken zu entwickeln, daher ist es notwendig, auf die Verbesserung ihrer pädagogischen Kompetenzen zu achten.

Kritisches Denken ist seit einiger Zeit nicht mehr nur ein Teil der akademischen Rhetorik und der Erziehungspraxis. Immer häufiger hört man die Stimme der Arbeitgeber, die fordert, dass auf die Wichtigkeit kritischer Denkfähigkeiten auf dem Arbeitsmarkt und allgemein in einer sich schnell verändernden Welt der Informationsüberflutung und des Informationswandels geachtet wird. Kritisches Denken wird als eine der für den Arbeitsmarkt relevanten Schlüsselkompetenzen des 21. Jahrhunderts betont (Rave, Guerrero und Morales, 2020; Whiting, 2020). Die Bedeutung des kritischen Denkens zeigt sich insbesondere in der Analyse und Bewertung der Fähigkeiten und der Organisationskultur von Arbeitnehmern (Brown, 2011; World Economic Forum, 2018). Es wird angenommen, dass kritisches Denken in Kombination mit Fähigkeiten wie Zusammenarbeit, Problemlösung, Führung, Kreativität und Selbstdisziplin Arbeitnehmern helfen wird, in der heutigen Organisation effektiv zu funktionieren (European Commission, 2014; Council of the European Union, 2018) und auf dem Arbeitsmarkt des 21. Jahrhunderts konkurrenzfähig zu sein (Habets, Stoffers, Van der Heijden und Peters, 2020). Der Arbeitsmarkt kennzeichnet sich durch Unsicherheit, rasche Veränderungen, die neue Kompetenzen erfordern, den Einsatz von Technologie, ständige Marktüberwachung und einen Fokus auf Veränderungen. Studien zeigen, dass Arbeitgeber hohe Erwartungen an kritisches Denken haben. Nach Einschätzung der Arbeitgeber schafft kritisches Denken die Voraussetzungen dafür, dass sich eine Person im Namen des organisatorischen Wandels ständig verbessert (Felix, 2016) fördert die ständige Reaktion auf die Herausforderungen des sich verändernden Umfelds und ermöglicht es den Arbeitnehmern, nach den besten Lösungen für sich selbst, ihre Kunden und die Organisation zu suchen (Indrašienė et al., 2019); ermöglicht es den Arbeitnehmern, als Fachkräfte Selbstvertrauen zu haben, schwierige Situationen zu lösen und auf der Suche nach neuen, innovativen Lösungen Fragen zu stellen (Jiang, Gao und Yang, 2018). Und dies nicht nur, um direkte Funktionen gut auszuführen, sondern auch um es den Arbeitnehmern zu ermöglichen, gültige, kritische Fragen zu stellen, die zu korrekten und besseren Lösungen führen, über ihre eigenen Handlungen und die Handlungen anderer nachzudenken und Fehler zu korrigieren, um die Bedeutung ihres persönlichen Beitrags zur Entwicklung der Organisation und der gesamten Gesellschaft zu verstehen (Penkauskienė, Railienė und Cruz, 2019).

Der Bericht des Weltwirtschaftsforums (2020) betont, dass die Bedürfnisse des Arbeitsmarktes aufgrund der erheblichen Kluft zwischen dem Ausdruck von Kompetenzen in der Praxis und ihrer erklärten Ausbildung im formalen Bildungssystem möglicherweise nicht umgesetzt werden können. Die Relevanz von Fähigkeiten des kritischen Denkens auf dem Arbeitsmarkt und in den Bildungssystemen ist aufgrund des öffentlichen sozialen Diskurses offensichtlich geworden. Wissenschaftler (Pithers und Soden, 2000; Burbach, Matkin und Fritz, 2004; Andrews und Higson, 2008) werfen schon seit langer Zeit die Frage nach der Kohärenz von Theorie und Praxis in der Erziehung zum kritischen Denken auf. Die Frage ist, ob das, was in der wissenschaftlichen Literatur über die Förderung und Einschätzung des kritischen Denkens geschrieben steht, nicht nur wissenschaftliche Weisheit ohne wirkliche Anwendung ist (Facione, 2013) und ob vorhandene Instrumente zur Einschätzung in der Praxis ausreichend sind (Davies, 2015; Macpherson und Owen, 2010; Schendel, 2016). Dies steht im Einklang mit der Mitteilung der Europäischen Kommission zur europäischen Hochschulbildung in der Welt (2013) und den Empfehlungen der OECD (2015) über die Notwendigkeit, Lehrpläne und Lehrmethoden zu überprüfen, die das kritische Denken junger Menschen gezielter und effektiver fördern, um nachhaltige, handlungsorientierte Lernergebnisse zu erzielen. Diese Bestimmungen werden durch die Ergebnisse von Studien bestätigt (Lai, 2011; Ennis, 2016; Arum und Roksa, 2011) die darauf hinweisen, dass die Entwicklung des kritischen Denkens an den Hochschulen keine ausreichenden Beweise für seine erfolgreiche Anwendung in der Praxis liefert; den Hochschulen fehlt es an wirksamen Programmen, der Qualifikation der Lehrkräfte und an einem günstigen akademischen Umfeld, um kritisches Denken zu entwickeln (Abrami et al., 2015).

Es ist erwähnenswert, dass im empirischen Teil der Monographie der Ausdruck des kritischen Denkens in der Hochschulbildung und auf dem Arbeitsmarkt in erster Linie den kulturellen Kontext eines bestimmten Landes widerspiegelt: Die Studienprogramme der litauischen Hochschulen werden analysiert, die Teilnehmer der qualitativen und quantitativen Studie sind in Litauen tätige Hochschullehrer und im Land Studierende sowie Arbeitgeber und Arbeitnehmer inländischer Unternehmen. Die Ergebnisse der Studie werden jedoch im Kontext/auf der Ebene der globalen Forschung diskutiert. Damit Litauen wettbewerbsfähig bleibt, müssen die Kompetenzen der im Hochschulbereich entwickelten Fachkompetenzen auf dem gegenwärtigen und zukünftigen Arbeitsmarkt relevant sein, auf dem ähnliche Anforderungen an die Fähigkeiten der Arbeitnehmer sowohl in Litauen als auch in anderen EU-Ländern bestehen. Es besteht ein wachsender Bedarf an hochqualifizierten Fachkräften, die in der Lage sind, in sich verändernden Marktsituationen schnell und effizient zu handeln, Produkte mit hoher Wertschöpfung zu schaffen und Innovationen umzusetzen (Valavičienė, 2015). Daher korrelieren die Erwartungen der litauischen Arbeitgeber mit den Erwartungen der Arbeitgeber in anderen Ländern Europas (Penkauskienė, Railienė und Cruz, 2019). Die Bedeutung von Fähigkeiten des kritischen Denkens wird in der staatlichen Fortschrittsstrategie „Litauen 2030“ (2012) erwähnt, in der es heißt, dass Vorstellungskraft, Kreativität und kritisches Denken als wichtige Ressourcen für ein Land angesehen werden. Andererseits weist diese Strategie darauf hin, dass das derzeitige Bildungssystem der Stärkung von Fähigkeiten des kritischen Denkens in der Hochschulbildung zu wenig Aufmerksamkeit schenkt.

Unter Berücksichtigung der Aktualisierung des kritischen Denkens in internationalen und nationalen Dokumenten, der wachsenden Aufmerksamkeit globaler Wirtschafts- und Arbeitsorganisationen, des Problems des kritischen Denkens und der fragmentierten Forschung, entstand die Idee zum Forschungsprojekts „Kritisches Denken in der Hochschulbildung: Studien- und Arbeitsmarktperspektive". Dieses Projekt zielt darauf ab, die Korrespondenz von Hochschulstudien auf den Bedarf für CT, ausgedrückt durch den Arbeitsmarkt, zu untersuchen. Die gesamte Studie drückt sich in folgenden problematischen Fragen aus:

- Was wird im Kontext der Hochschulbildung und des Arbeitsmarktes als kritisches Denken angesehen? Was sind die Komponenten (elements/constituents) des kritischen Denkens?
- Wie wird kritisches Denken verstanden (welche wahre Bedeutung hat es für Teilnehmer an der Hochschulbildung und am Arbeitsmarkt) und wie manifestiert es sich für im Hochschulstudium und auf dem Arbeitsmarkt?
- Welche Zusammenhänge bestehen zwischen der Entwicklung der Kompetenzen kritischen Denkens in der Hochschulbildung und den Bedürfnissen des Arbeitsmarktes?
- Wie sollte die Entwicklung des kritischen Denkens in der Hochschulbildung aussehen, um einen Konsens über die pädagogische Bedeutung und den praktischen Wert des kritischen Denkens zu erzielen?

Die Methodologie der Studie basiert auf dem Prinzip der Triangulation und kombiniert verschiedene Methoden der Datenerfassung, -analyse und -interpretation, wobei sich die Daten ergänzen und somit die Abweichungen und Fehler, die bei nur einer Forschungsmethode auftreten, neutralisieren und reduzieren. Unter Ausnutzung der Vorteile quantitativer und qualitativer Forschung präsentiert die Monographie vier eng verwandte Studien: systematische Analyse der wissenschaftlichen Literatur, quantitative und qualitative Inhaltsanalyse der litauischen Hochschulstudienprogramme und der Studienfachbeschreibungen, phänomenographische Studie von Lehrern, Schülern, Arbeitgebern und Arbeitnehmern sowie eine repräsentative Umfrage dieser Gruppen. Alle vier Studien wurden entwickelt, um die Zuverlässigkeit und Gültigkeit der Daten sicherzustellen, die Regeln der Forschungsethik einzuhalten, Forschungsbeschränkungen zu identifizieren und Richtlinien für die weitere Forschung bereitzustellen.

Der wissenschaftliche/praktische Wert der Monographie wird wie folgt begründet:

- Das Konzept des kritischen Denkens wird auf Grundlage einer systematischen Analyse von zwei Jahrzehnten wissenschaftlicher Literatur offenbart;
- es wurde eine detaillierte Analyse der Studienprogramme und Fachbeschreibungen verschiedener Bereiche im Hinblick auf die Entwicklung des kritischen Denkens durchgeführt;

- die authentische Haltung von Lehrern und Schülern, Arbeitgebern und Arbeitnehmern gegenüber kritischem Denken wurde offengelegt;
- die Kohärenz der Ausbildung zum kritischen Denken in der Hochschulbildung und der praktischen Anwendung der Fähigkeiten zum kritischen Denken bei Arbeitsaktivitäten unter Anwendung einer Studie mit gemischter Methode wurde bewertet;
- die vielfältigen Ansätze und Methoden der Forschung zum kritischen Denken werden hervorgehoben.

Die Monographie besteht aus einer Einleitung, sechs Teilen, Schlussfolgerungen und Empfehlungen.

Ziel des ersten Teils der Monographie *„Konzept und Kontext des kritischen Denkens in der Hochschulbildung und auf dem Arbeitsmarkt“* ist es, die Relevanz des kritischen Denkens in den Kontexten der Hochschulbildung und des Arbeitsmarktes sowie die Bedeutung der Definition des Konzepts des kritischen Denkens auf der Grundlage dieser Kriterien durch die Analyse wissenschaftliche Literatur und Dokumente aufzuzeigen.

Basierend auf der Analyse wissenschaftlicher Literatur und von Dokumenten kann festgestellt werden, dass das Konzept des kritischen Denkens ständig überprüft wird. Dies hängt von den Herausforderungen der Zeit, den Bedürfnissen des spezifischen Kontextes, dem wissenschaftlichen Ansatz und dem Zugang zu Forschung ab. Die breite Interpretation des Konzepts des kritischen Denkens macht es schwierig, sich zu verständigen und sich darüber zu einigen, was tatsächlich als kritisches Denken angesehen wird. Die Notwendigkeit einer Definition des Konzepts ist nicht nur offensichtlich, um sich gegenseitig zu verstehen, sondern auch um Handlungen zu koordinieren. Im wissenschaftlichen Sinne bedeutet dies, Forschung zu untermauern, zu verbreiten, zu kommunizieren, um die Reaktion anderer, akademische Diskussionen, wissenschaftlichen und gesellschaftlichen Fortschritt zu erzielen. Der Sinn von Bildung ist die Förderung und Verbesserung des kritischen Denkens in der akademischen Gemeinschaft. Andererseits bleibt das Wesen des kritischen Denkens unverändert – der Wunsch zu verstehen, was richtig ist und was nicht, die Wahrheit zu kennen oder zumindest Erkenntnis zu suchen, trotz unterschiedlicher Vorstellungen von Wahrheit und Möglichkeiten, sie zu erforschen. Dies nennt man Kritikalität, wie auch immer sie in verschiedenen Traditionen verstanden und interpretiert wird. Kritikalität wird als Merkmal des qualitativen Denkens einer Person und als Zeichen des eigenen Wertes der Person bezeichnet. Kritisches Denken dient der Entwicklung des Individuums, der zwischenmenschlichen Beziehungen und der Gesellschaft.

Die ersten zwei Jahrzehnte des 21. Jahrhunderts, deren Realität durch einen beispiellos rasenden Wandel in allen Bereichen der Gesellschaft gekennzeichnet ist, treiben auch den Wandel in der Hochschulbildung voran. Die Wahrnehmung, dass Hochschulbildung kritisches Denken fördern muss, beruht auf der Erkenntnis, dass kritische und reflektierte Menschen erforderlich sind, um die Nachhaltigkeit von Gesellschaften zu schaffen und aufrechtzuerhalten. Seit der Erklärung der

UNESCO im Jahr 2009 hat die Entwicklung von Kompetenzen des kritischen Denkens in der Hochschulbildung große Veränderungen erfahren. Zwar bestehen die Ungleichheiten zwischen Ländern und Regionen nicht nur aufgrund politischer Entscheidungen im Bildungssystem, sondern auch aufgrund unterschiedlicher kultureller Kontexte im weitesten Sinne, was dazu führen kann, dass diese Ungleichheiten fortbestehen, die Umsetzung der Kompetenzentwicklung für kritisches Denken im Hochschulsystem hängt jedoch von der Wahl der Länder selbst ab. Wissenschaftliche Studien bieten immer mehr Wissen über die verschiedenen Praktiken der Bildung für kritisches Denken in der Hochschulbildung, was zu immer mehr Möglichkeiten führt, sich über ausländische Erfahrungen, Lösungen und Ergebnisse zu informieren und über mehr Tools zu verfügen, um Ihr eigenes effektives System zur Entwicklung kritischen Denkens in der Hochschulbildung aufzubauen.

Kritisches Denken gilt daher als eine der wichtigsten Fähigkeiten des 21. Jahrhunderts für das Wohl des Einzelnen und der Gesellschaft insgesamt. Es kann als wesentliches Instrument für das Management von Organisationen angesehen werden, das dazu beiträgt, praktische Lösungen für die heutigen Marktbedingungen zu finden, die ein konstant hohes Maß an Wettbewerbsfähigkeit und Effizienz erfordern. Kritisches Denken ermöglicht es den Arbeitnehmern, kreativ und unabhängig zu denken, Entscheidungen und Schlussfolgerungen zu treffen, sich dynamisch an produktiven und positiven Aktivitäten zu beteiligen und theoretische Themen mit praktischen Situationen zu verknüpfen. Wenn in das kritische Denken der Arbeitnehmer investiert wird und sie motiviert werden, ihre Fähigkeiten und Einstellungen zum kritischen Denken zu verbessern und man sie in die täglichen Entscheidungen des Unternehmens einbezieht, werden Sie auf lange Sicht ein kritisches Denken und effektives Wissen entwickeln. Daher ist es für die Organisation zweckmäßig, die Fähigkeiten des kritischen Denkens der Arbeitnehmer zu stärken, die durch individuelles soziales Handeln eine wettbewerbsfähige Organisation schaffen.

Der zweite Teil der Monographie *„Analyse des Konzepts des kritischen Denkens in der Hochschulbildung: systematische Literaturübersicht“* hat folgendes Ziel: Auf Grundlage einer systematischen Analyse der wissenschaftlichen Literatur sollen die Dynamik des Konzepts des kritischen Denkens in wissenschaftlichen Publikationen verschiedener Epochen im Kontext der Hochschulbildung dargestellt und die Mehrdimensionalität und Vollständigkeit des kritischen Denkens aufgezeigt werden.

Das Auswahlverfahren für die Analyse systematischer wissenschaftlicher Literatur bestand aus zwei Phasen: der Auswahl wissenschaftlicher Zeitschriften und der Auswahl wissenschaftlicher Artikel. Die wissenschaftlichen Zeitschriften wurden aus der Datenbank Clarivate Analytics Journal Citation Reports unter Einsatz der zwei Schlüsselwörter *education* und *educational* ausgewählt. Bei der Auswahl wurden 342 Zeitschriften gefunden, die die Kriterien erfüllten und nach vier Themen (Bildung & Bildungsforschung, Bildung, wissenschaftliche Disziplinen, Bildung, speziell, Psychologie, Bildung) und Quartilen (Q1–Q4) gruppiert wurden. Die Auswahl wissenschaftlicher Artikel in diesen Zeitschriften erfolgte in der EBSCOhost-Datenbank anhand folgender Auswahlkriterien: ISSN der jeweiligen Zeitschrift; Stichwort *critical thinking* im Bereich der Fachbegriffe, Volltext, Zeitraum von 1997–2017, Englische Sprache. Alle 804 gefundenen Artikel wurden anhand von Ausschlusskriterien überprüft, wobei 303 Texte in der endgültigen Liste belassen wurden. Die von den Forschern entwickelten Formulare für die Datenanalyse ermöglichten es, das erhaltene Material zu systematisieren und eine qualitative Inhaltsanalyse auf der Grundlage diachroner und synchroner Ansätze durchzuführen.

Bei der diachronen Analyse ausgewählter Publikationen aus den Jahren 1997–2017 wurden folgende chronologische Merkmale der Konzeptualisierung des kritischen Denkens in der Hochschulbildung gefunden: Die Zahl der Veröffentlichungen, in denen kritisches Denken in der Hochschulbildung analysiert wird, hat stetig zugenommen; sie basieren häufiger auf empirischen Untersuchungen als auf theoretischen Analysen; empirische Artikel basieren auf quantitativer oder qualitativer Forschungsmethodik, nur in Ausnahmefällen wird eine gemischte Forschungsmethodik angewendet; kritisches Denken wird häufiger aus einer domänenspezifischen als aus einer domänenübergreifenden Perspektive analysiert.

Eine synchrone Analyse ausgewählter Publikationen ergab, dass kritisches Denken als übertragbare (allgemeine) Kompetenz und als eine Reihe bestimmter Fähigkeiten verstanden wird, die in einem konkreten Studienbereich auftreten. Es gibt keine strikte Grenze zwischen der Definition von „kritischem Denken als universelle Fähigkeit“ und „kritischem Denken als spezifische Fähigkeit“. Kritisches Denken geht über eine konkrete Disziplin hinaus und ermöglicht es einer Person, in breiteren Kontexten zu denken. Die relativ geringe Anzahl von Publikationen, in denen die eine oder andere Intervention/Strategie für kritisches Denken vorgestellt wird, und die ungleiche Berücksichtigung ihrer Analyse lassen keine tieferen Schlussfolgerungen über die Wirksamkeit der Anwendung von Interventionen für kritisches Denken zu. Interventionen wie Diskussion, kritische Überprüfung, kritische Reflexion, Online-Diskussion und Fallstudien werden in den Publikationen am häufigsten erwähnt. Die Analyse des kritischen Denkens beschränkt sich normalerweise auf die persönliche Ebene und konzentriert sich auf die gezielte Entwicklung kognitiver Kräfte, um tiefgründigere Erkenntnis und eine effektive Problemlösung zu erreichen. Der zwischenmenschliche Aspekt spiegelt sich weniger in Veröffentlichungen wider und wird auf zwei Arten offenbart: indem man von anderen lernt und zum Wohlbefinden anderer beiträgt. Die soziale Ebene des kritischen Denkens entsteht, indem das Wesen der Kritikalität offenbart wird, das mit der Fähigkeit zusammenhängt, Annahmen in Frage zu stellen, die Kontrastierung der Tendenziösität des Wissens und der Erkenntnis aufzuzeigen und wichtige Fragen zur Förderung von Ideologien, Machtverteilung und Einflussnahme in der Gesellschaft aufzuwerfen. Diese Ebene spiegelt sich auch in der Aktualisierung der Mission der Hochschulbildung wider, die nicht nur mit der Bereitstellung wissenschaftlicher Erkenntnisse im Zusammenhang steht, sondern auch mit dem Lernen, komplexere Phänomene des öffentlichen Lebens zu analysieren – Identität, Wahrheit, Macht und zu bestimmen aktiv beteiligt sein. Im Wesentlichen konzentriert sich die Konzeptualisierung des kritischen Denkens aus sozialer Sicht nicht darauf, wie die Gesellschaft ist, sondern darauf, wie sie sein sollte. Die wichtigste Aufgabe für einen Menschen ist das Lernen, menschlich zu sein.

Ziel des dritten Teils der Monographie *„Kritisches Denken als einzigartige Kompetenz: Evidenz aus Studien zur Hochschulbildung"* ist es, den Ausdruck des kritischen Denkens in der Hochschulbildung durch Analyse der Beschreibungen von Hochschulstudienprogrammen und Studienfächern aufzuzeigen.

Bei der Analyse aller Beschreibungen von Hochschulstudienprogrammen und Studienfachbeschreibungen im Land wurde eine gemischte Forschungsmethode, einschließlich quantitativer und qualitativer Methoden zur Datenerfassung, -analyse und -interpretation verwendet, und basierte auf dem Ansatz der Prozessbegleitung. Die Studie bestand aus vier aufeinander folgenden Phasen: Die Beschreibungen von 754 Studienprogrammen wurden analysiert; eine quantitative Inhaltsanalyse der Beschreibungen von 266 Studienprogrammen, in denen das Konzept des kritischen Denkens erwähnt wird, wurde durchgeführt; eine quantitative Inhaltsanalyse von 7 gezielt ausgewählten Studienprogrammen und Studienfachbeschreibungen verschiedener Studienbereiche sowie eine qualitative Inhaltsanalyse von Studienfachbeschreibungen derselben 7 Studienprogramme wurden durchgeführt. Die Analyse quantitativer Daten ermöglichte es zu untersuchen, wie kritisches Denken in die Beschreibungen von Studienprogrammen und Studienfächern litauischer Hochschulen integriert wird, und die Analyse qualitativer Daten enthüllte den Ausdruck des Konzepts des kritischen Denkens und der Komponenten des kritischen Denkens.

Die quantitative inhaltliche Analyse der Studienprogrammbeschreibungen ergab, dass das Konzept des kritischen Denkens in etwa einem Drittel der Studienprogrammbeschreibungen erwähnt wird. Die größte Anzahl des Begriffs kritisches Denken wurde in den Gruppen der Studienrichtungen Engineering sciences, Life sciences und Technology science gefunden. Der in den Beschreibungen ausgewählter Studiengänge erwähnte Begriff des kritischen Denkens wird in fast allen Beschreibungen der Studienfächer erweitert und detailliert beschrieben. Kritisches Denken als Begriff *per se* wird häufiger in Bezug auf allgemeine als auf fachliche Kompetenzen erwähnt. In den allgemeinen Kompetenzen wird die Fähigkeit zur Bewertung betont, und in den Fachkompetenzen wird die Fähigkeit zur Analyse akzentuiert.

Sowohl die quantitative als auch die qualitative Analyse der Beschreibungen der Studienfächer ergab, dass kritisches Denken eher als Fähigkeit konzipiert wird, ohne seine Natur zu spezifizieren – persönlich, beruflich (speziell), allgemein oder anderweitig. In den meisten Fällen wird kritisches Denken als eine bedeutende persönliche Fähigkeit in einem bestimmten Berufsfeld aktualisiert. Es wird auch als allgemeine Kompetenz angesehen, die sich in einem breiteren – gesellschaftlichen – Kontext entfaltet. Die Bedeutung des kritischen Denkens für zwischenmenschliche

Beziehungen wird kaum reflektiert. Die offenbarten Komponenten des kritischen Denkens beziehen sich auf den Kontext bestimmter Themen oder werden abstrakt dargestellt. Kritisches Denken wird am häufigsten mit kreativem, analytischem und reflexivem Denken assoziiert.

Ziel des vierten Teils der Monographie *„Kritisches Denken im Studienprozess und auf dem Arbeitsmarkt: eine phänomenographische Studie"* ist es aufzuzeigen, wie Lehrer, Schüler, Arbeitgeber und Arbeitnehmer kritisches Denken verstehen und wie sich kritisches Denken in einem spezifischen Studien- und Arbeitsmarktkontext manifestiert.

Die Phänomenographie wurde als methodischer Hauptansatz für die Erforschung des Konzepts des kritischen Denkens und seiner Komponenten in der Hochschulbildung und auf dem Arbeitsmarkt gewählt. Die Studie verwendete eine gezielte Auswahl von Teilnehmern auf der Grundlage des Prinzips der Heterogenität, d.h. mit dem Ziel, dass alle vier Gruppen unterschiedlichen Alters und Geschlechts sind; Lehrkräfte und Studierende repräsentieren verschiedene Hochschuleinrichtungen, Studienbereiche und unterrichtete Fächer (Lehrkräfte) oder Studienbereiche und Studienjahre (Studierende); Arbeitgeber und Arbeitnehmer spiegeln die Vielfalt der wirtschaftlichen Aktivitäten, Tätigkeitsbereiche, Management- (Arbeitgeber) oder Berufserfahrung (Arbeitnehmer) wider. Es wurden 79 Interviews mit 18 Dozenten, 16 Studierende, 28 Arbeitgebern und 17 Arbeitnehmern durchgeführt. Die für die Datenerfassung gewählte halbstrukturierte Interviewmethode, die den Fokus der Studie sicherstellte, bot Flexibilität, um den Studienteilnehmern grundlegende und konkretisierende Fragen zu stellen, auf das eigentliche Interview zu reagieren und sich nicht auf das Phänomen als solches zu konzentrieren, sondern auf die Beziehung zwischen dem Studienteilnehmer und dem Studienphänomen. Die Analyse der qualitativen Daten bestand aus folgenden Schritten: wiederholtes Lesen des Textes, Markieren des Textes auf der Suche nach Antworten auf Interviewfragen, Erstellung von Erstbeschreibungen, Gruppierung von Daten nach Ähnlichkeiten und Unterschieden in Kategorien, Beschreibung der Kategorien, Unterscheidung zwischen dominierenden und nicht dominierenden Kategorien, Zuweisen von Kategorien zu Dimensionen/ Hervorheben von Dimensionen in Bezug auf die Kategorien, Schaffung eines strukturellen Bildes des Ausdrucks des Phänomens – Ergebnisraum (outcome space). Die Studie enthüllte subjektive Konzepte und Erfahrungen des kritischen Denkens von Hochschullehrern und -studierende, Arbeitgebern und Arbeitnehmern, Unterschiede und Ähnlichkeiten in den Erfahrungen.

Die Behandlung des kritischen Denkens durch Studierende und Lehrkräfte hängt sowohl mit dem Funktionieren im akademischen Bereich als auch mit der allgemeinen Erfahrung des Phänomens im persönlichen und beruflichen Bereich zusammen. Vertreter beider Gruppen betonten, dass sie kein zuvor formuliertes Konzept des kritischen Denkens hätten. Die Hochschullehrer betonten, dass sie keinen besonderen Wunsch haben, kritisches Denken zu lehren. Ihr Unterricht ist ein wesentlicher Bestandteil der akademischen Aktivitäten, um ein tieferes

Verständnis des Studienfachs, der Vorbereitung auf den Beruf, der allgemeinen Entwicklung des Denkens und der Erweiterung des Horizonts zu erlangen. Daher kann argumentiert werden, dass kritisches Denken in deren Konzeption mit der Entwicklung sowohl beruflicher als auch allgemeiner Kompetenzen verbunden ist.

Studierende und Lehrkräfte verstehen kritisches Denken als die Entwicklung der kognitiven Fähigkeiten einer Person, indem sie mit dem spezifischen Inhalt des Studienfachs arbeiten – auswählen, vergleichen, vermitteln, interpretieren, bewerten, schlussfolgern; als Maßnahme oder ein Instrument zur praktischen Anwendung – ein Problem lösen, eine Lösung finden und sie anwenden, indem berufliche Situationen modelliert werden; als Einstellung einer Person, unabhängig zu denken, Meinungen und Entscheidungen anderer mutig in Frage zu stellen, eine offene, empathische Beziehung zu anderen aufzubauen.

Die folgenden Unterschiede im Verständnis des kritischen Denkens zwischen Hochschullehrern und Studierenden wurden festgestellt: Die Lehrkräfte verstehen kritisches Denken als eine ganzheitliche Gesamtkompetenz, die die Grundlage für die Entwicklung des eigenen Denkens und die Entwicklung einer facettenreichen offenen Beziehung zur Umwelt bildet; die Studierenden nehmen kritisches Denken in Bezug auf die Umwelt im engeren Sinne wahr – als die Fähigkeit, Phänomene im Lichte verschiedener Perspektiven zu reflektieren; die Lehrkräfte nehmen kritisches Denken als Lernprozess wahr – erkennen, verstehen, auswählen, bewerten; die Studierenden verbinden kritisches Denken mehr mit dem Problemlösungsprozess; die Lehrkräfte verbinden kritisches Denken mit anderen Phänomenen – Kreativität, zivildemokratische Gesellschaft; die Studierenden betonen nicht die Zusammenhänge zwischen kritischem Denken und anderen Phänomenen.

Das Konzept des kritischen Denkens wird auf persönlicher, zwischenmenschlicher und gesellschaftlicher Ebene offenbart. Sowohl Lehrkräfte als auch Studierende sehen den Wert des kritischen Denkens für das Persönlichkeitswachstum und die berufliche Entwicklung. Kritisches Denken wird im Verhältnis zu anderen Menschen als Chance gesehen, das eigene Denken zu verbessern, indem man lernt und zusammenarbeitet sowie relevante berufliche Probleme löst. In Bezug auf die Gesellschaft wird kritisches Denken als Offenheit für Veränderungen, Fortschritt, kreative Lösungen und Innovation angesehen. Letzterer Aspekt ist jedoch nur für die Erfahrung der Lehrkräfte relevant.

Sowohl das Lehren des kritischen Denkens als auch das Lernen beziehen sich ausschließlich auf die Vertiefung in das Studienfach, eine bessere Assimilation des Wissens und die Entwicklung analytischer Fähigkeiten. Ein Vergleich der Lehrerfahrungen der Lehrkräfte und der Lernerfahrungen der Studierenden zeigt mehrere Schlüsselaspekte, die beide Gruppen gemeinsam haben: Das Lehren und das Erlernen kritischen Denkens finden auf zwei Arten statt – durch Organisation gemeinsamer Aktivitäten und Zuweisung unabhängiger Aufgaben. Die Lehrkraft nimmt eine aktive Rolle im Unterricht ein – sie erklärt, demonstriert, modelliert. Die Studierenden nehmen an Aktivitäten teil, die von der Lehrkraft vorgeschlagen werden. Passiver Unterricht der Lehrkräfte manifestiert sich in der Übertragung von Lernverantwortlichkeiten auf die Studierenden – sie überwacht und koordiniert den Lernprozess, und die Studierenden lernen, indem sie frei wählen, entscheiden und kreieren. Lehrkräfte wenden eine breite Palette von Methoden zur Entwicklung des kritischen Denkens an und Studierende erkennen sie – Fall- und Problemanalyse, Textanalyse und -bewertung, Fragestellung, Situationssimulation, Experimentieren, Diskussionen.

Es zeigten sich auch verschiedene Unterschiede in den Lehr- und Lernerfahrungen: Die Lehrkräfte schätzen unabhängige, kritische Denkaufgaben sowohl für die persönliche Befähigung, für eine bessere Vertiefung der Studieninhalte als auch für die berufliche Effektivität. Die Studierenden hingegen verbinden selbstgesteuertes Lernen eher mit persönlicher Reife, ihrer Anerkennung und Wertschätzung als Person als mit der Entwicklung von Fähigkeiten, die im Studium und im Berufsleben anwendbar sind. Die Lehrkräfte behaupten, durch persönliches Vorbild zu lernen: Sie teilen Erfahrungen, wissenschaftliche Errungenschaften, erklären ihre Werte klar und deutlich – Offenheit für die Wahrheit, das Streben nach Gerechtigkeit, Kreativität, die Suche nach einzigartigen Lösungen. Die Studierenden erkennen jedoch in ihrer Erfahrung nicht, wie sie aus dem Vorbild eines Lehrers/einer Lehrerin lernen können.

Die Lehrkräfte sagten auch, dass niemand sie gelehrt hätte, wie man kritisches Denken lehrt. Kompetenzen des kritischen Denkens entwickeln sie individuell durch Selbstbildung: durch Lesen, Beobachten und Analysieren der Umgebung und gemeinsam während organisierter Veranstaltungen zur beruflichen Weiterentwicklung – bei Vorträgen, im Gespräch mit Kollegen und bei gegenseitigen Diskussionen. Die Studierenden konnten sich auch nicht erinnern, dass die Lehrkräfte sie speziell in kritischem Denken unterrichten würden. Die Erfahrungen der Studierenden spiegelten das Erlernen des kritischen Denkens in den Vorlesungen und Praxiskursen wider, die normalerweise von den Lehrkräften organisiert werden. Sowohl Studierende als auch Lehrkräfte verbinden das Erlernen des kritischen Denkens mit einem besseren Verständnis des Studienfachs, der Kenntnis des Berufs, tieferem Denken und Horizonterweiterung.

Die Behandlung des kritischen Denkens von Arbeitnehmern und Arbeitgebern ist untrennbar mit ihrer täglichen beruflichen Tätigkeit verbunden. Das Konzept des kritischen Denkens wird durch Reflexion über die Erfahrung eines Phänomens gebildet, und umgekehrt bildet die Erfahrung/das Erleben des kritischen Denkens in alltäglichen beruflichen Aktivitäten subjektive Konzepte des kritischen Denkens.

Die gemeinsamen Komponenten des Verständnisses von Arbeitgebern und Arbeitnehmern für kritisches Denken zeigen sich in individuellen Fähigkeiten, die auf die Suche nach der Wahrheit ausgerichtet sind, und im Mut zu bestimmten beruflichen Aktivitäten. Es ist zu beachten, dass sowohl Arbeitgeber als auch Arbeitnehmer kritisches Denken nicht nur als kognitive Fähigkeiten verstehen, sondern auch als Ausdruck ihrer täglichen beruflichen Tätigkeit. Die praktische Anwendbarkeit dieser Kompetenz und die Greifbarkeit konkreter Ergebnisse werden im Verständnis des subjektiven kritischen Denkens beider Gruppen aktualisiert. Beide Gruppen verstehen kritisches Denken als freies Denken ohne Vorurteile, wenn sie sich nicht nur an persönlichen Erfahrungen oder Einstellungen orientieren und keinem Druck von außen ausgesetzt sind. Kritisches Denken wird als die Fähigkeit interpretiert, eine Situation aus verschiedenen Perspektiven zu sehen und zu analysieren und alle möglichen Risiken zu antizipieren und zu bewerten. Sowohl Arbeitgeber als auch Arbeitnehmer nehmen eine argumentierte Entscheidungsfindung und eine begründete Übermittlung dieser Argumente zur Kenntnis. Es unterstreicht die Infragestellung der absoluten, unbestreitbaren Wahrheit, die gesunde Skepsis, den Wunsch, nicht an subjektive Meinungen gebunden zu sein, den Zweifel an der Existenz eines scheinbar verlässlichen Wahrheitskriteriums. Kritisches Denken im Verständnis beider Gruppen ist mit Selbstvertrauen und der Herausforderung verbunden, eine unabhängige Meinung zu vertreten, unabhängig zu handeln und Verantwortung zu übernehmen, ohne Angst vor Fehlern zu haben.

Die festgestellten Unterschiede im Verständnis von Arbeitnehmern und Arbeitgebern hängen mit bestimmten Merkmalen des kritischen Denkens zusammen. Das Verständnis der Arbeitgeber für kritisches Denken zeigt mehr Autonomie und Selbstvertrauen. Diese Aspekte der kritischen Denkkonzepte der Arbeitgeber werden im Zusammenhang mit der Schaffung von Mehrwert für das Unternehmen aufgezeigt. Die Bedeutung von Empathie zeigt sich im Konzept des kritischen Denkens der Arbeitnehmer, das auf zwischenmenschlicher und gesellschaftlicher Ebene als emotionale Reaktion auf die Erfahrungen anderer Menschen offenbart wird, um ihnen zu helfen oder ihre Situation zu ändern.

Wir haben die Erfahrungen mit kritischem Denken von Arbeitnehmern und Arbeitgebern in alltäglichen beruflichen Situationen zusammengefasst und Gemeinsamkeiten zwischen der Förderung von Arbeitgebern und der Erfahrung kritischen Denkens seitens der Arbeitnehmer festgestellt. Erstens – das Stellen von Fragen an sich und andere: Für Arbeitgeber ist dies eine der Formen der Förderung des kritischen Denkens von Arbeitnehmern, und für Arbeitnehmer ist es ein Prozess, der einen persönlichen Mehrwert bei beruflichen Aktivitäten schafft. Zweitens – das Stellen und Akzeptieren von Herausforderungen: Für Arbeitgeber ist es eine Provokation, die die Arbeitnehmer zum kritischen Denken anregt, und für die Arbeitnehmer ist es ein Heraustreten aus der Komfortzone. Herausforderungen wird ein Sinn wachsender Erfahrung gegeben: Sie ermutigen voranzukommen, nach originellen Lösungen zu suchen, das Denken zu ändern und neue Erfahrungen zu schaffen. Drittens – delegierte und übernommene Verantwortung: Für Arbeitgeber ist es die Förderung der Verantwortung der Arbeitnehmer durch Steigerung des Vertrauens in den Arbeitnehmer sowie die Entwicklung seiner Verantwortung, und für die Arbeitnehmer ist es die Angst vor Fehlern und die Fähigkeit, aus den eigenen Fehlern zu lernen. Viertens – Ausdruck des persönlichen Standpunktes/der persönlichen Meinung: Dies wird sowohl für Arbeitgeber als auch für Arbeitnehmer als Zeichen kritischen Denkens angesehen. Eine Kritische Meinung, eine persönliche Position wird in einem unterstützenden Umfeld zum Ausdruck gebracht, das wiederum als motivierend beschrieben wird, indem angemessene organisatorische Maßnahmen angewendet werden. In diesem Zusammenhang ist auch die Schaffung von Mehrwert wichtig.

Sowohl Arbeitgeber als auch Arbeitnehmer betonen nicht nur die Schaffung eines Mehrwerts für den Einzelnen, sondern auch den Beitrag zur Entwicklung der Organisation und zum Wohl der Gesellschaft. Kritisches Denken als vielschichtig zu betrachten ist somit der fünfte Aspekt, der die Ansichten des Arbeitgebers und der Arbeitnehmer verbindet. Ein wesentlicher Unterschied, der das kritische Denken von Arbeitgebern und Arbeitnehmern auszeichnet, ist die Förderung des kritischen Denkens. Die Arbeitgeber erkennen an, wie wichtig es ist, das kritische Denken der Arbeitnehmer zu fördern. Die Mitarbeiter betonen die Rolle des Arbeitgebers bei der Förderung ihres kritischen Denkens nicht. Sie verbinden die Möglichkeiten, kritisches Denken in beruflichen Tätigkeiten zum Ausdruck zu bringen, eher mit den eigenen persönlichen Einstellungen und Verhaltensweisen als mit den Anreizen des Arbeitgebers.

Ziel des fünften Teils der Monographie *„Ausprägung der Kompetenz zum kritischen Denken im Studienprozess und auf dem Arbeitsmarkt: eine quantitative Studie“* ist es aufzuzeigen, wie Lehrkräfte, Studierende, Arbeitgeber und Arbeitnehmer kritisches Denken definieren und welchen Standpunkt sie zur Entwicklung und Bedeutung der Fähigkeiten und Dispositionen des kritischen Denkens im Arbeitsmarkt der Gegenwart haben.

Um die Zusammenhänge zwischen kritischem Denken in der Hochschulbildung und dem Arbeitsmarkt aufzudecken, wurde eine quantitative Studie unter Verwendung einer schriftlichen Erhebungsmethode durchgeführt. Die gewählte Datenerhebungsmethode ermöglichte es, die Meinungen von Lehrern und Schülern, Arbeitgebern und Arbeitnehmern zu vergleichen und die Verbindungen zwischen den Forschungsgruppen aufzudecken. Um die Stichprobe repräsentativ für die gesamte Bevölkerung zu machen, wurde eine probabilistische mehrstufige Stichprobenmethode angewendet. Es wurden vier Personengruppen befragt: Lehrkräfte, Studierende, Arbeitgeber und Arbeitnehmer aus allen Regionen Litauens. An der Studie nahmen teil: 152 Hochschullehrer*innen, 1512 Studierende, 528 Arbeitgeber und 2012 Arbeitnehmer. Bei allen vier Gruppen enthielt der Fragebogen Fragenblöcke zur Wahrnehmung von kritischem Denken, zur Bedeutung von Fähigkeiten zum kritischen Denken und zur Bedeutung von Dispositionen für kritisches Denken. Für die Datenanalyse wurden deskriptive und inferentielle statistische Methoden verwendet.

Die Analyse der Daten ergab, dass das Konzept des kritischen Denkens in der Hochschulbildung und auf dem Arbeitsmarkt mit den Fähigkeiten und Einstellungen einer Person zusammenhängt. Kritisches Denken wird als ein Prozess angesehen, der von den Fähigkeiten, Einstellungen, Werten und Überzeugungen einer Person abhängig ist. Kritisches Denken sowohl in der Hochschulbildung als auch auf dem Arbeitsmarkt wird als Schlüsselkompetenz angesehen, die sich in der Fähigkeit äußert, Entscheidungen auf der Grundlage realer Probleme zu treffen. Die Fähigkeit, Entscheidungen zu treffen und Maßnahmen zu ergreifen, wird zu einem der wesentlichen Merkmale, die Arbeitgeber von zukünftigen Arbeitnehmern erwarten, und Lehrer entwickeln diese Fähigkeit. Bei der Beurteilung der Beschreibung des kritischen Denkens betonen Lehrer und

Arbeitgeber eher das Ergebnis dieses Prozesses – das Treffen einer begründeten und rationalen Entscheidung. Eine solche Beschreibung des kritischen Denkens konzentriert sich auf das Verständnis, dass es in bestimmten Situationen keine eindeutig richtige Lösung gibt. Daher sind starke Argumente erforderlich, um die richtige Entscheidung zu treffen. Studierende und Arbeitnehmer sehen hingegen das Ergebnis im Denkprozess selbst, in dem die Reflexion über das Handeln, die Fähigkeit zu unparteiischem Denken auf der Grundlage kontrollierter rationaler Schlussfolgerungen und Entscheidungsfindung eine wichtige Rolle spielen.

Der Ausdruck des kritischen Denkens sowohl im Kontext der Hochschulbildung als auch des Arbeitsmarktes hängt mit den Bemühungen und der Bereitschaft und den Möglichkeiten einer Person zusammen, in verschiedenen Situationen kritisch zu denken. Kritisches Denken manifestiert sich in der bewussten Wahl, erworbenes Wissen und Fähigkeiten in einer bestimmten Umgebung anzuwenden. Kritisches Denken bedeutet eine aktive, zielgerichtete und organisierte Anstrengung einer Person, ihre Welt zu verstehen, indem sie ihr eigenes Denken und das Denken anderer sorgfältig untersucht. Im Kontext der Hochschulbildung und des Arbeitsmarktes ist der Ausdruck kritischen Denkens daher eher mit dem persönlichen Kontext verbunden. Es ist wichtig zu beachten, dass kritisches Denken als erlernbares Merkmal wahrgenommen wird. Es entsteht in einem dynamischen Denkprozess und wird weiterentwickelt. Dieser Prozess ist in Bezug auf Alter und Erfahrung des Menschen nicht endlich. Es gibt jedoch auch diejenigen, die glauben, dass die Fähigkeit, kritisch zu denken, unveränderlich ist und sich am besten in Kritik ausdrückt.

Die Formulierung von Schlussfolgerungen wird als die wichtigste Fähigkeit auf dem modernen Arbeitsmarkt angesehen. Dies ist auch die Ansicht der Vertreter aus Hochschulbildung und Arbeitsmarkt. Die Fähigkeit, aussagekräftige Schlussfolgerungen zu ziehen, wird als ein Prozess des kognitiven Denkens anerkannt, der aus Sicht von Arbeitgebern und Lehrkräften mit der Zusammenfassung datenbasierter Informationen und der Antizipation von Konsequenzen verbunden ist. Nach Ansicht von Studierenden und Arbeitnehmern sind Selbstregulierungsfähigkeiten eine der wichtigsten Fähigkeiten auf dem modernen Arbeitsmarkt, die aber aus Sicht von Arbeitgebern und Lehrkräften auf dem Arbeitsmarkt der Gegenwart als weniger bedeutsam angesehen werden. Interpretationsfähigkeiten sind für Arbeitgeber und Lehrkräfte wichtig, da es nicht ausreicht, nur über Wissen oder Informationen zu verfügen. Eine angemessene Verwendung und Anwendbarkeit dieses Wissens und dieser Informationen in beruflichen Tätigkeiten und/oder Studien ist erforderlich. Offensichtliche Priorität hat die Verwendung der Formulierung von Schlussfolgerungen für persönliche Zwecke. Zwischenmenschliche und gesellschaftliche Vorteile spiegeln sich in dieser Hinsicht kaum wider. Die persönliche Ebene wird überschritten, wenn das Ziel darin besteht, die Situation/das Problem im Detail zu analysieren und eine rationale Entscheidung in einem breiteren Bereich als den persönlichen Interessen unter Berücksichtigung unterschiedlicher Meinungen zu treffen.

Die Bedeutung der Entwicklung kritischer Denkfähigkeiten aus Sicht der Hochschul- und Arbeitsmarktvertreter entspricht den Bedürfnissen des modernen Arbeitsmarktes, die nicht nur mit Schlussfolgerungen verbunden sind. Hochschuleinrichtungen bemühen sich, die Fähigkeiten zu entwickeln, die auf dem Arbeitsmarkt am relevantesten sind: Formulierung von Schlussfolgerungen, Argumentation und Interpretation. Die Bedeutung der Entwicklung dieser Fähigkeiten wird auch von den Studierenden festgestellt. Laut Arbeitnehmern und Studierenden ist es auf dem modernen Arbeitsmarkt wichtig, sich selbst zu kennen und zu reflektieren (seine Gedanken, Gefühle, Handlungen), was mit dem Ausdruck kritischen Denkens auf persönlicher Ebene im Zusammenhang steht. Daher stimmen die Standpunkte beider Gruppen von Studienteilnehmern zu kritischem Denken, das sich eher auf persönliche kognitive als auf zwischenmenschliche oder gesellschaftliche Fähigkeiten und Beziehungen konzentriert, überein.

Die Bedeutung der Dispositionen kritischen Denkens auf dem modernen Arbeitsmarkt wird nicht in Frage gestellt. Aus Sicht von Lehrkräften und Studierenden wird ihrer Ausbildung im Studienprozess viel Aufmerksamkeit geschenkt. Im Kontext der Hochschulbildung und des Arbeitsmarktes sind die Dispositionen von Ehrlichkeit, Mut und Beharrlichkeit am wichtigsten, während die Dispositionen von Skepsis und Offenheit am wenigsten wichtig sind. Die Dispositionen, deren Bedeutung von den Vertretern der Hochschulbildung und des Arbeitsmarktes zum Ausdruck gebracht wird, können auch den Dispositionen zugeschrieben werden, die weiter verbessert und weiterentwickelt werden sollten. Verschiedene Methoden werden verwendet, um Fähigkeiten und Dispositionen für kritisches Denken zu entwickeln. Diese konzentrieren sich hauptsächlich auf die Selbstbildung einer Person. Nach Ansicht von Vertretern der Hochschulbildung und des Arbeitsmarktes sind die Dispositionen für Flexibilität, Offenheit und Genauigkeit am dringendsten zu verbessern und weiter zu fördern.

Aus Sicht aller Gruppen der Studienteilnehmer muss die Verantwortung für die Entwicklung des kritischen Denkens an die Person und ihren Wunsch oder ihre Neigung zum kritischen Denken delegiert werden. Die Bereitschaft, kritisch zu denken, ist mit einem Denkprozess verbunden, der von den Einstellungen, Werten und Überzeugungen einer Person abhängt, offen zu denken, vernünftige Annahmen zu treffen und die Überzeugungskraft von Argumenten zu bewerten oder abzuwägen. Bis zu einem gewissen Grad wird die Verantwortung für die Entwicklung des kritischen Denkens auch an die Arbeitnehmerorganisation delegiert. Die Vertreter der Hochschuleinrichtungen und des Arbeitsmarktes betrachten die Rolle der Hochschuleinrichtungen als den am wenigsten bedeutenden Faktor für die Entwicklung des kritischen Denkens.

Ziel des sechsten Teils der Monographie *„Beziehungen zwischen der Entwicklung des kritischen Denkens in der Hochschulbildung und dessen Bedarf auf dem Arbeitsmarkt"* ist es, Einblicke in das Verständnis, die Erfahrung und den Ausdruck des kritischen Denkens in der Hochschulbildung und auf dem Arbeitsmarkt zu geben und die Zusammenhänge zwischen der Entwicklung des kritischen Denkens in der Hochschulbildung und dessen Bedarf auf dem Arbeitsmarkt genauer zu beleuchten.

Die qualitative (phänomenographische) Studie ergab subjektive Konzepte und Erfahrungen des kritischen Denkens von Hochschullehrern, Studierenden, Arbeitnehmern und Arbeitgebern. In den kritischen Denkkonzepten und Erfahrungen dieser Studienteilnehmer zeigten sich nicht nur Unterschiede, sondern auch Ähnlichkeiten. Die quantitative Studie (Umfrage) ermöglichte es, die Standpunkte aller vier Gruppen zu den Konzepten des kritischen Denkens zu unterscheiden, die vorherrschenden zu identifizieren und die Bedeutung der Fähigkeiten des kritischen Denkens und der Dispositionen im Studienprozess sowie auf dem Arbeitsmarkt zu identifizieren. Sowohl in der Hochschulbildung als auch auf dem Arbeitsmarkt wird kritisches Denken als eine Reihe wertvoller kognitiver Fähigkeiten verstanden, die zu argumentierten, begründeten und verlässlichen Entscheidungen führen, sowie als eine Reihe persönlicher Dispositionen. Somit wird die in der wissenschaftlichen Literatur im Umlauf befindliche Ansicht, dass kritisches Denken eher als kognitive Fähigkeit denn als Disposition wahrgenommen wird, teilweise widerlegt.

Es gibt keine etablierte einheitliche Interpretation des Konzepts des kritischen Denkens in der Hochschulbildung und auf dem Arbeitsmarkt. Die Vielfalt der Konzepte zeigt einerseits die Komplexität des Phänomens selbst, signalisiert andererseits aber auch die mangelnde Übereinkunft darüber, welches kritische Denken entwickelt wird und in weshalb es entwickelt wird.

Das Verständnis, die Lehre und das Lernen von kritischem Denken in der Hochschulbildung und der Ausdruck auf dem Arbeitsmarkt wird kontextualisiert – es wird in einem bestimmten Lern- oder Arbeitsumfeld, einer bestimmten Situation, einer bestimmten Kultur erlebt bzw. gelebt. Wie es verstanden und erlebt wird, hängt weitgehend von diesen kontextuellen Umständen, persönlichen Merkmalen und Erfahrungen ab. Es ist zu beachten, dass die Verantwortung für die Entwicklung des kritischen Denkens weitgehend dem Einzelnen übertragen wird. Nach Einschätzung der Studienteilnehmer ist es abhängig vom Wunsch und von der Anstrengung jeder Person abhängig, wie und auf welcher Ebene es entwickelt wird.

Kritisches Denken wird als wesentliches Instrument zur Entdeckung vieler praktischer Lösungen für den Betrieb in einem modernen Umfeld angesehen, das ein hohes Maß an Wettbewerbsfähigkeit und Effizienz erfordert. Die Fähigkeiten des kritischen Denkens stehen auch mit der Lösung neuer, beispielloser Probleme, dem Umgang mit Überraschungen und mit der Schaffung neuer Ideen im Zusammenhang. Das Bedürfnis nach Entwicklung/Verbesserung des kritischen Denkens ist daher stark pragmatisch ausgerichtet – auf Problemlösung, Treffen wesentlicher Entscheidungen und Ausrichtung der eignen Aktivitäten auf Verbesserungen. Bei der Einschätzung kritischen Denkens, vor allem im Zusammenhang mit dem Arbeitsmarkt zeigt sich der praktische, konsumorientierte Standpunkt zum kritischen Denken. Es wird als die Fähigkeit von Mitgliedern einer Organisation angesehen, unter unsicheren Umständen zu handeln, eine

Vielzahl von Problemen schnell und effizient zu lösen, Kosteneffizienz und Wettbewerbsvorteile zu erzielen. All dies ist mit technologischem Fortschritt, zunehmender Wettbewerbsfähigkeit und wachsendem wirtschaftlichem Vorteil verbunden. Im Kontext der Hochschulbildung wird kritisches Denken jedoch auch als Förderung einer Person, Verbesserung der Beziehungen zur Umwelt und Unterstützung beim besseren Kennenlernen anderer, sozialer Prozesse und Weltphänomene angesehen.

Eines der wichtigsten Elemente sowohl in der Hochschulbildung als auch auf dem Arbeitsmarkt ist jedoch das Individuum und die Interaktionen, in denen Wissen gefördert und Denkhorizonte erweitert werden. Diese Interaktionen basieren auf einer offenen, vertrauensvollen Kultur, die jeder Gemeinschaft klare Vorteile bringt, sowohl materielle als auch immaterielle. Erfolgreiche Gemeinschaften sind solche, die auf natürliche Weise persönliches Wissen organisch verinnerlichen und es als gemeinsames Gut nutzen. Dies bedeutet, dass das Ergebnis einer Investition in die Entwicklung des kritischen Denkens einer Person eine kritisch denkende Gemeinschaft ist. Die Kritik spiegelt sich in Wachsamkeit gegenüber sich selbst und der Umwelt wider, als ständige Selbstbefragung und als Selbstreflexion. Daher ist es sowohl in der Hochschulbildung als auch auf dem Arbeitsmarkt notwendig, die Fähigkeit des kritischen Denkens jedes Mitglieds zu stärken, das später durch individuelle soziale Handlungen eine nachhaltige Gesellschaft schafft.

Sowohl in der Hochschulbildung als auch auf dem Arbeitsmarkt ist kritisches Denken auf persönlicher und zwischenmenschlicher/organisatorischer Ebene am ausgeprägtesten als Erfahrung, die das persönliche Wachstum in herausfordernden, provokativen atypischen Situationen fördert oder in Situationen, wo schnelle Entscheidungen erforderlich sind.

Am wenigsten wird kritisches Denken auf gesellschaftlicher Ebene erlebt, wenn nicht nur zum eigenen Wohl, sondern auch zum Wohl anderer und der Gesellschaft insgesamt gehandelt wird. Der gesellschaftliche Aspekt manifestiert sich in Offenheit gegenüber der Welt, Interesse an den darin stattfindenden Phänomenen und Prozessen und dem Wunsch, zu ihrer Verbesserung beizutragen. Im Wesentlichen sind alle drei Ebenen – die persönliche, zwischenmenschliche/organisatorisch und die gesellschaftliche – sowohl im Hochschul- als auch im Arbeitsmarktkontext greifbar und miteinander verbunden, wobei nicht nur das individuelle intellektuelle Wachstum, sondern auch Aspekte der zwischenmenschlichen Interaktion und des Handelns für den gesellschaftlichen Fortschritt hervorgehoben werden.

Die Monographie schließt mit Schlussfolgerungen und Empfehlungen für die Entwicklung und Festigung der Kompetenz für kritisches Denken in der Hochschulbildung.

Die von den Autoren in dieser Monographie vorgestellten Forschungsergebnisse ermöglichten eine sorgfältige Untersuchung und Analyse der Aktualisierung des kritischen Denkens in der wissenschaftlichen Literatur, der Beschreibungen der Studienprogramme, der Standpunkte und Erfahrungen von Lehrkräften und Studierenden, Arbeitgebern und Arbeitnehmern und enthüllten mehrere wichtige problematische Aspekte.

Der *erste Aspekt* steht im Zusammenhang mit der Definition des Konzepts des kritischen Denkens. Die Ergebnisse der Studien haben ergeben, dass kritisches Denken häufig wie folgt behandelt wird: a) als selbstverständliches Phänomen, das keiner weiteren Erklärung bedarf; b) als mehrdeutiges Phänomen mit vielen verschiedenen und oft konkurrierenden Bedeutungen; c) als von anderen definiert und ohne erforderliche authentische Behandlung.

Die Beweise für die erste Behandlung liegen in der Analyse der wissenschaftlichen Artikel und der Beschreibungen der Studienprogramme sowie in den Zusammenfassungen der Erfahrungen von Lehrkräften und Studierenden. Ein nicht unerheblicher Teil der Autoren wissenschaftlicher Artikel machen sich sofort daran, die Manifestationen und Praktiken des kritischen Denkens zu analysieren, stellen jedoch nicht vor, welchem Konzept des kritischen Denkens sie in ihrem Artikel folgen, oder die Definition des vorgestellten kritischen Denkens ist undeutlich (blurred). Es entsteht der Eindruck, dass die Autoren der Vorstellung folgen, das Konzept des kritischen Denkens sei selbstverständlich, so dass keine weitere Erklärung erforderlich ist. Studienbeschreibungen bezeichnen Fähigkeiten und Dispositionen für kritisches Denken, aber es ist nicht möglich zu verstehen, welche wissenschaftlichen Ansätze für kritisches Denken von den Autoren der Beschreibungen verfolgt werden. Es kann davon ausgegangen werden, dass auch keine klar definierten existieren. Darüber hinaus zeigten die meisten Lehrkräfte und Studierenden, die an der empirischen Studie teilgenommen haben, dass sie in ihren Erzählungen keine klare konzeptionelle Auslegung hatten. In der qualitativen Studie sagten die Studierenden, dass kritisches Denken als ein Phänomen an sich betrachtet und von allen ähnlich verstanden wird, und deshalb sei es schwierig, es zu benennen.

Die Ergebnisse der Analyse der wissenschaftlichen Artikel und der Beschreibungen der Studienprogramme sowie die Ergebnisse der phänomenographischen Studie sowie die quantitativen Erhebungen zeigen, dass kritisches Denken als vielseitiges und vielschichtiges Phänomen behandelt wird. Kritisches Denken wird sowohl als tiefes, umfassendes und begründetes Denken als auch als reflexive persönliche Einstellung zur Selbstverbesserung, als wirksames Instrument zur Problemlösung, als Manifestation von Kreativität und als Merkmal der Zivilgesellschaft wahrgenommen. Im Wesentlichen finden alle Beschreibungen ein Echo in der wissenschaftlichen Literatur und reagieren auf die eine oder andere Behandlung des Konzepts. Sehr oft wird kritisches Denken nicht nur mit Kreativität, Innovation, sondern auch mit Toleranz gegenüber Unbekanntem, Krisenmanagement, einem großen Wissensschatz und Rechenschaftspflicht gleichgesetzt. Um zielgerichtetes und wissenschaftlich fundiertes kritisches Denken zu entwickeln, müssen die Lehrkräfte entscheiden, welcher wissenschaftliche Ansatz und welches wissenschaftliche Konzept in dem von ihnen unterrichteten Fach verfolgt werden. Die Vielfalt der Konzepte und wissenschaftlichen Ansätze bietet eine breite Auswahl von Möglichkeiten. Es gibt genügend Beispiele, um die Entwicklung des kritischen Denkens auf der Grundlage spezifischer wissenschaftlicher Ansätze und Standpunkte zu veranschaulichen.

Die Nachweise für die dritte Behandlung bezieht sich ausschließlich auf die Ergebnisse der Analyse wissenschaftlicher Artikel: Artikel, die ein authentisches Konzept des kritischen Denkens formulieren, das aus dem Wissen und der Erfahrung des Autors abgeleitet wurde, tauchten nicht auf. In fast allen Fällen berufen sich die Autoren auf die Haupttheoretiker des kritischen Denkens, bekannte Autoren, auf ihre Theorien, die im Streben nach authentischen Einsichten nicht weiterentwickelt wurden. Eine etwas freiere Beziehung zu dem behandelten Phänomen würde seine Bedeutung ausweiten, die Nuancen von Merkmalen aufdecken, bestehende Konzepte und Theorien ergänzen, Inspiration für neue Studien liefern und gleichzeitig authentische Konzepte des kritischen Denkens bilden.

In Anbetracht der vorgebrachten Argumente wird Folgendes vorgeschlagen:

- Die regulierenden Studiendokumente sollten sich nicht auf Erklärungen zur Bedeutung des kritischen Denkens beschränken, sondern klar darlegen, wie die Fähigkeiten des kritischen Denkens entwickelt werden.
- Um die Entwicklung des kritischen Denkens bei Hochschulstudenten zu einem bewussten, konsistenten und wissenschaftlich fundierten Prozess zu machen, muss auf Universitäts-, Fakultäts- oder Programmebene zunächst eine Vereinbarung zu den theoretischen Annahmen, auf denen das Konzept des kritischen Denkens beruht oder aufgebaut wird, getroffen werden. Es hängt von dieser Vereinbarung ab, wie der Inhalt des Konzepts des kritischen Denkens aussehen wird und welche Fähigkeiten und Methoden für das kritische Denken dementsprechend entwickelt werden.
- Die Entwicklung, Aktualisierung und Verbesserung von Studienprogrammen muss gemäß dem vereinbarten Konzept des kritischen Denkens und des systematischen Ansatzes, dass die Fähigkeiten zum kritischen Denken in allen Studienfächern entwickelt werden, vorgenommen werden, unter Anwendung von Lehr-, Studien- (Lern-) und Bewertungsmethoden, die kritisches Denken fördern.
- Den Studierenden muss klar präsentiert werden, was als kritisches Denken angesehen wird und wie es sich in einem bestimmten Studieninhalt und/oder Berufsfeld manifestiert.
- Forscher und Wissenschaftler müssen ermutigt werden, neben der Kenntnis bestehender Theorien des kritischen Denkens ihre eigenen authentischen theoretischen Einsichten zu entwickeln, ihre eigenen theoretischen Linien zu entwickeln und so zur Entwicklung des theoretischen Gedankens im kritischen Denken beizutragen.

Der *zweite problematische Aspekt* betrifft die Vielschichtigkeit des kritischen Denkens, d.h. seine Komponenten und den Standpunkt zu diesem Phänomen als Merkmal einer Person, als Prozess und als Endergebnis. Die Forschungsergebnisse haben gezeigt, dass kritisches Denken wie folgt wahrgenommen wird: a) als Gesamtheit der kognitiven Fähigkeiten und Dispositionen einer Person; b) als Prozess des Denkens und Lernens; c) als Ergebnis der gefundenen Lösungen, der innovativen Produkte, der Veränderung der Beziehung zu sich selbst, anderen und der Umwelt.

Basierend auf der quantitativen und qualitativen Analyse des Textinhalts von Studienprogrammen und Fachbeschreibungen wird deutlich, dass kritisches Denken tendenziell als bedeutende persönliche Fähigkeit in einem bestimmten Berufsfeld oder als allgemeine Kompetenz in einem gesellschaftlichen Kontext konzipiert wird. In den Beschreibungen der Studienprogramme wird das Konzept des kritischen Denkens nicht durch die klärenden Komponenten des kritischen Denkens detailliert beschrieben, sondern beschränkt sich häufiger auf die Verwendung des Begriffs „kritisch". Die inhaltliche Textanalyse der Studienprogramme und -fächer ergab auch, dass die Programme in der Regel drei Komponenten des kritischen Denkens hervorheben: Analyse, Bewertung und Interpretation. Den Dispositionen des kritischen Denkens wird wenig Beachtung geschenkt. Die Ergebnisse der qualitativen Studie und des Fragebogens belegen dagegen, dass kritisches Denken sowohl aus Sicht der Hochschuleinrichtungen als auch des Arbeitsmarktes eine Reihe kognitiver Fähigkeiten und Dispositionen ist, und letztere werden manchmal als noch bedeutender angesehen als kognitive Fähigkeiten. Diese Ergebnisse widersprechen den Ergebnissen der Analyse der Studienbeschreibungen, die auf eine Vorherrschaft der kognitiven Fähigkeiten hinweisen. Dies dient auch als eine Art Gegengewicht zur Priorisierung der Fähigkeiten des kritischen Denkens, die in der wissenschaftlichen Literatur vorherrschen. Basierend auf diesen Erkenntnissen würden wir annehmen, dass das, was tatsächlich als wertvoll und bedeutsam angesehen wird, in individuellen Erfahrungen zu finden ist, aber nicht unbedingt in den Dokumenten, die das Studium regeln, und was in der wissenschaftlichen Literatur analysiert wird, spiegelt nicht die Vielschichtigkeit des kritischen Denkens wider.

Kritisches Denken als Prozess wird auch von den Teilnehmern an der phänomenographischen Studie nicht eindeutig bewertet. Aus Sicht von Lehrkräften, Arbeitgebern und Arbeitnehmern ist kritisches Denken ein Prozess. Für Lehrkräfte ist es ein Lernprozess, in dem die Essenz der untersuchten Inhalte und Phänomene verstanden wird; die Studierenden lernen zu hinterfragen, zu zweifeln und zu prüfen; sie suchen nach der Wahrheit, finden Lösungen und bauen Beziehungen auf. Für Arbeitgeber und Arbeitnehmer ist dies ein Prozess, bei dem Probleme analysiert, Alternativen bewertet und Entscheidungen getroffen werden. In den Erfahrungen der Studierenden tritt kritisches Denken als Prozess der Entdeckung, Erkenntnis, des Verstehens und Handelns kaum hervor. In den Beschreibungen der Studienprogramme war es teilweise möglich, den Ansatz des kritischen Denkens als Lernprozess zu betrachten – hauptsächlich als Lernvorgang, Informationen auszuwählen, zu analysieren, zu interpretieren, zu bewerten und Schlussfolgerungen zu ziehen. In der wissenschaftlichen Literatur wird der Analyse der entwickelten kognitiven Fähigkeiten mehr Raum gewidmet als der Analyse kritischer Denkprozesse.

Kritisches Denken als Endergebnis zeigt sich besonders in den Erfahrungen von Arbeitgebern und Arbeitnehmern. Es äußert sich in gelösten spezifischen beruflichen Problemen, rationalen und manchmal in außergewöhnlichen Lösungen und Ideen. Aus Sicht der Lehrkräfte können die Ergebnisse des kritischen Denkens als gelöste Aufgabe, abgeschlossene Aufgabe, erstelltes Projekt, durchgeführte Fallanalyse und vorgeschlagene Idee betrachtet werden. Ähnlich sehen das auch die Studierenden. Nur betonen sie den Wert des kritischen Denkens als Endergebnis weniger. In den Beschreibungen der Studiengänge ist die Bewertung des kritischen Denkens als Endergebnis eher vage.

In Anbetracht der vorgebrachten Argumente wird Folgendes vorgeschlagen:

- Kritisches Denken sollte als Synthese kognitiver Fähigkeiten und Dispositionen positioniert werden und dieser Ansatz sollte bei der Entwicklung und/oder Aktualisierung von Studienprogrammen verfolgen werden;
- während des Studiums sollte ausreichend Zeit und Aufmerksamkeit für die Erkenntnis und die Erfahrung kritischer Denkprozesse verwendet werden; kritisches Denken sollte als Lernprozess bewertet werden;
- während der Vorlesungen und Seminare sollte genügend Zeit und Aufmerksamkeit gewidmet werden, um die Ergebnisse des kritischen Denkens zu diskutieren und ihre Vielfalt und ihren praktischen Wert aufzuzeigen;
- wissenschaftliche Studien sollten sich mehr auf die Erforschung kritischer Denkweisen konzentrieren.

Der *dritte Aspekt* steht im Zusammenhang mit dem Lehren und Lernen von kritischem Denken. Die Ergebnisse der Studie zeigten, dass: a) nicht alle Themen und Programme der Entwicklung des kritischen Denkens ausreichende Aufmerksamkeit widmen; b) den Lehrkräften fehlt das Wissen und die Erfahrung, um kritisches Denken zu vermitteln, und den Studierenden fehlt das Verständnis dafür, wie und warum ihnen kritisches Denken beigebracht wird.

Die Analyse der Studienbeschreibungen ergab, dass kritisches Denken nicht in allen untersuchten Studien- und Fachbeschreibungen erwähnt wird. Die größte Anzahl von Programmen, deren Zweck und Ziele das kritische Denken erwähnen, gehört zur Gruppe der Ingenieurwissenschaften, etwas seltener wurde der Ausdruck des kritischen Denkens in den Programmen der Sozial-, Gesundheits-, Biowissenschaften gefunden, und der kleinste Anteil zeigte sich in der Mathematik und den Veterinärwissenschaften. Die Analyse der wissenschaftlichen Literatur ergab, dass sich die Entwicklung des kritischen Denkens auf die Sozialwissenschaften einschließlich der Bildung und in etwas geringerem Maße auf das Studium der Naturwissenschaften, Gesundheit, Technologien, Künste und Geisteswissenschaften konzentriert.

Die Kohärenz und Systematik der Entwicklung des kritischen Denkens kann sowohl anhand einer Überprüfung der wissenschaftlichen Literatur als auch anhand der Analyse der Beschreibungen der Studienprogramme und anhand der Ergebnisse empirischer Forschung beurteilt werden. In der wissenschaftlichen Literatur gibt es keine Beispiele dafür, wie kritisches Denken auf der Ebene einer gesamten Institution oder eines gesamten Studienprogramms entwickelt wird. Wir konnten auch keine Beispiele finden, die die Entwicklung des kritischen Denkens als kohärenten Prozess im Kontext eines bestimmten unterrichteten Fachs veranschaulichen. Die Analyse der Studienbeschreibungen des kritischen Denkens zeigte ihre fragmentarische Darstellung im Kontext der Studienprogramme. Kritisches Denken wird normalerweise als Ziel und/oder zu erreichendes Ergebnis bezeichnet, und nur in sehr seltenen Fällen wird angegeben, wie es erreicht wird, d.h. welche Methoden und Mittel dazu bestimmt sind, es zu vermitteln und zu lehren. Außerdem spiegeln die Studienbeschreibungen überhaupt nicht wider, wie sie bewertet werden sollen, d.h. welche Methoden zur Bewertung der Fähigkeiten kritischen Denkens vorgesehen sind. In der wissenschaftlichen Literatur bietet sich ein gegensätzliches Bild: Es gibt viele Beispiele dafür, wie, auf welche Weise, mit welchen Strategien und Methoden kritisches Denken in einem bestimmten Fach, Studienprogramm oder einer bestimmten beruflichen Praxis vermittelt wird. Es gibt jedoch zu wenige Publikationen, in denen die Wirksamkeit kritischer Denkstrategien analysiert und bewertet wird – was funktioniert und wie, was nicht funktioniert und warum. Sowohl Lehrkräfte als auch Studierende teilten während der qualitativen Studie verschiedene Beispiele für das Lehren und Lernen von kritischem Denken. Aber jede Gruppe betonte unterschiedliche Dinge in Bezug auf die Wichtigkeit. Für Studierende waren selbstständige Arbeit und untypische Aufgaben wichtig. Die Lehrkräfte betonten die Situations- und Fallanalyse sowie das kollaborative Lernen. Sie erwähnten auch, anhand persönlicher Vorbilder zu lernen – Situationen zu modellieren, die kritisches Denken erfordern, die Einstellungen des kritischen Denkens demonstrieren und den Wert des kritischen Denkens erkennen. Die Studierenden haben solche Beispiele in ihren Erfahrungen nicht hervorgehoben. Weder die einen noch die anderen, identifizierten kritisches Denken als zielgerichtet geplantes und systematisches Lehren und Lernen. Es sollte beachtet werden, dass einige Studierende nach eigener Ansicht noch nie von Lehrkräften gehört haben, dass ihr kritisches Denken beim Studium eines Fachs gefördert wird oder dass die Lehrkräfte solche Absichten haben. Daher können sie nur aus ihrem Verständnis schließen, dass Lehrkräfte es auf irgendeine Weise vermitteln. Somit bleibt die Entwicklung des kritischen Denkens still und nur implizit vorhersehbar. Seine Unhörbarkeit zeugt nicht nur von einem Mangel an Wissen, sondern auch von einem Mangel an bewusster Entscheidung, es zu fördern. Es wird vermutet, dass es beim Lehren des Inhalts eines konkreten Faches, beim Entwickeln besonderer Fähigkeiten quasi selbst entsteht.

Die Ergebnisse der qualitativen und quantitativen Studie zeigten, dass Lehrkräfte nie an gezielten Schulungen zur Entwicklung von Kompetenzen des kritischen Denkens teilgenommen haben. Die Lehrkräfte interessieren sich normalerweise für sich selbst – sie lesen Fachliteratur, beobachten die Umgebung und analysieren Ereignisse, nehmen an Veranstaltungen zur beruflichen Weiterentwicklung teil und diskutieren berufliche Fragen mit Kollegen. Auf diese Weise behaupten sie, auch Fähigkeiten zum kritischen Denken zu entwickeln. In ihrer Freizeit lesen die Studierenden auch Bücher, besuchen kulturelle Veranstaltungen, etwas seltener Seminare und Konferenzen. Die Studierenden betonen seltener als die Lehrkräfte die Notwendigkeit, die Kompetenz für kritisches Denken zu verbessern. In der analysierten wissenschaftlichen Literatur gab es keine Beispiele für die Vermittlung kritischen Denkens oder die Entwicklung kritischer Denkfähigkeiten von Lehrkräften.

In Anbetracht der vorgebrachten Argumente wird Folgendes vorgeschlagen:

- In der Beschreibung des Studienfachs sollten nicht nur die Entwicklung kritischer Denkkompetenz als Ziel oder erreichbares Ergebnis deklarieren, sondern auch aktive Lehr-/ Studienmethoden ins Auge gefasst werden, bei denen die Studierenden im Mittelpunkt stehen und die es den Studierenden ermöglichen, neu erlernte Dinge anzuwenden und Feedback der Lehrkraft zu erhalten;
- nach der Formulierung oder Aktualisierung der Studienergebnisse des Programms müssen die Fachlehrer die geplanten Studien- (Lern-) und Bewertungsmethoden gemeinsam diskutieren, um das kritische Denken der Studierenden zu fördern. Dies würde Bedingungen schaffen, um die Kohärenz der Studien- (Lern-) und Bewertungsmethoden sowie den systematischen Charakter ihrer Anwendung aufrechtzuerhalten, indem die konzeptionellen Beziehungen zwischen dem untersuchten Fach und der Entwicklung des kritischen Denkens sichergestellt werden;
- Lehrkräfte sollten zu Beginn des Kurses die Lernergebnisse, die sich auf die Entwicklung des kritischen Denkens im Studienprozess konzentrieren, genau definieren. Es ist erstrebenswert, innovative Strategien zur Bewertung und Selbstbewertung kritischer Denkfähigkeiten anzuwenden/zu entwickeln, die sowohl auf persönlicher als auch auf zwischenmenschlicher Ebene Anwendung finden können. Feedback-Prozesse sollten kritisches Denken fördern und es den Schülern ermöglichen, nicht nur aus dem Feedback von Lehrkräften oder Kollegen zu lernen, sondern auch durch Metaprozesse wie Reflexion und Bewertung des Lernprozesses oder der Lernergebnisse;
- Die Lehrkräfte sollten über entsprechende Aufgaben nachdenken und sie für die Studierenden vorbereiten, in denen sie lernen, nach Lösungen zu suchen und unabhängig zu arbeiten, ihre Zusammenarbeit würde gefördert und neues Wissen würde sich auf Situationen oder Probleme im realen Leben beziehen.
- Lehrkräfte sollten einen Anreiz und die Möglichkeit erhalten, ihre Bildungskompetenzen für kritisches Denken durch gezieltes Lernen zu verbessern – durch Vertiefung in wissenschaftliche Literatur, Teilnahme an Konferenzen und Seminaren zum Thema kritisches Denken, Teilnahme an Vorträgen erfahrener Kollegen, Organisation professioneller Diskussionen zur Bildung für kritisches Denken.
- Es sollten Programme zur Verbesserung der Kompetenzen von Lehrkräften initiiert und vorbereitet werden, die nicht nur die pädagogischen und didaktischen Aspekte der Entwicklung des kritischen Denkens einführen, sondern auch Bedingungen schaffen, um dieses Wissen in praktischen Unterrichtsaktivitäten anzuwenden und im Streben nach dem besten Ergebnis zu reflektieren und zu diskutieren;

- die Forschung sollte auf die Analyse der Entwicklung des kritischen Denkens in den unterschiedlichsten Kontexten von Studienprogrammen konzentrieret werden;
- die systematische Entwicklung des kritischen Denkens sollte untersucht werden, indem nach Zusammenhängen zwischen Programmbestimmungen und Studienbeschreibungen, realen Lehr- und Lernpraktiken und dem anvisierten Ergebnis gesucht wird.

Der *vierte Aspekt* steht im Zusammenhang mit dem Ausdruck der Kompetenz kritischen Denkens auf persönlicher, zwischenmenschlicher und gesellschaftlicher Ebene. Die Ergebnisse der Studie zeigten, dass: a) die Erkennbarkeit und der Wert des kritischen Denkens normalerweise auf den Einzelnen beschränkt sind; b) der zwischenmenschliche Ausdruck kritischen Denkens mit dem Wunsch verbunden ist, den anderen zu verstehen, und dies meistens im Kontext gemeinsamen Handelns; c) die soziale Bedeutung des kritischen Denkens aussagekräftiger ist und sich in den einzelnen Aussagen der Teilnehmer an der phänomenographischen Studie oder in den Beschreibungen der Studienprogramme widerspiegelt.

Eine Analyse sowohl der wissenschaftlichen Literatur als auch der Beschreibungen von Studienprogrammen hat ergeben, dass kritisches Denken häufig als Stärkung der kognitiven Kräfte einer Person mit beispiellosem Wert für die Person selbst behandelt wird. Die Ergebnisse der qualitativen und quantitativen Forschung sind ähnlich. Kritisches Denken wird als ein Merkmal einer bestimmten Person verstanden und erlebt, das für sie/ ihn von Bedeutung ist. Es erweitert den Horizont des persönlichen Wissens, vertieft das Verständnis des Studienfachs und entwickelt berufliche Fähigkeiten. Auf diese Weise wird die Sichtbarkeit des kritischen Denkens als eigennütziges, einseitiges Phänomen geschaffen. Es gibt jedoch auch andere Beispiele. Die Ergebnisse der phänomenographischen Studie zeigen den Wert des kritischen Denkens für zwischenmenschliche Beziehungen. Die zwischenmenschliche Dimension des kritischen Denkens drückt sich in der Offenheit für andere Ansichten und Erfahrungen, in der Anerkennung von Unterschieden und Vielfalt sowie in der fairen und unparteiischen Behandlung anderer aus. Ein solcher Ansatz wird jedoch häufiger von der Notwendigkeit als von einer ganzheitlichen humanistischen Haltung bestimmt. Das Verstehen und Akzeptieren des anderen ist aufgrund der Ziele des gemeinsamen Studiums oder der beruflichen Tätigkeit, der Notwendigkeit, einen Kompromiss zu finden und für die Lösung des Problems erforderlich. Der existenzielle humanistische Ansatz spiegelt sich eher als erklärtes Streben denn als Beispiel für echte Praxis wider. Die soziale Bedeutung des kritischen Denkens, wie das Interesse an und die Erforschung von Weltphänomenen, die Analyse aktueller sozialer Probleme, die Sorge um den Fortschritt der Gesellschaft, spiegelt sich auch in den Aussagen der Teilnehmer an der phänomenographischen Studie und in den Beschreibungen der Studienfächer nur gering wider. Die qualitative Studie hat signifikante Fälle ergeben, die jedoch isoliert sind und keine Trends abbilden. In dieser Hinsicht ähneln die Ergebnisse der phänomenographischen Studie den Ergebnissen der

Analyse der Beschreibungen der Studienfächer, die es nicht ermöglichen, Aussagen in offizieller Rhetorik über kritisches Denken als Entwicklung der demokratischen Werte oder bürgerlichen Kräfte der Studierenden und über die Hochschule als verantwortliche Institution für die Pflege dieser Werte zu untermauern. Darüber hinaus wird nach den Daten der quantitativen Forschung die Verantwortung für die Entwicklung des kritischen Denkens der Person selbst zugeschrieben. Somit gibt es einen Unterschied zwischen offiziellen Erklärungen und den Meinungen von Einzelpersonen.

In Anbetracht der vorgebrachten Argumente wird Folgendes vorgeschlagen:

- die Relevanz von Studienprogrammen zu untersuchen, verschiedene Veränderungen auf dem Arbeitsmarkt zu erforschen und sie im Studieninhalt widerzuspiegeln;
- Lehren und Lernen auf der Grundlage realer Simulationen im Studienprozess anzuwenden, um das Lernen am Arbeitsplatz einzubeziehen; spezifische Beispiele zu verwenden, die veranschaulichen, wie kritisches Denken zum Wohlbefinden anderer, zu Lösungen für aktuelle gesellschaftliche Probleme und zur Schaffung des Gemeinwohls beitragen kann;
- die Forschung darauf zu konzentrieren, den Wert der zwischenmenschlichen und gesellschaftlichen Dimension des kritischen Denkens aufzudecken.

Der *fünfte Aspekt* betrifft die Kontextualität des kritischen Denkens. Die Ergebnisse der Studie zeigten: a) Kritisches Denken wird in einem bestimmten Kontext ausgedrückt und erkennbar; b) Es wird nicht ausreichend darauf geachtet, den Kontext des kritischen Denkens aufzudecken.

Qualitative und quantitative Studien boten die Möglichkeit, kritisches Denken in einem bestimmten Kontext und als signifikante Kompetenz für ein bestimmtes Umfeld, eine bestimmte Situation, ein bestimmtes Ereignis und seine Teilnehmer zu aktualisieren. Die Studierenden lernen, Phänomene und Ereignisse in Bezug auf eine bestimmte berufliche Situation sowie das Studienfach zu analysieren, zu bewerten und ihre Umstände zu erklären.

Arbeitgeber und Arbeitnehmer geben Beispiele für berufliche Aktivitäten, beschreiben spezifische Umstände und Situationen, in denen kritisches Denken auftritt.

Die Analyse der wissenschaftlichen Literatur und die Analyse des Inhalts der Beschreibung der Studienfächer ergaben jedoch, dass der Berücksichtigung des Kontextes der Entwicklung des kritischen Denkens nicht genügend Aufmerksamkeit gewidmet wird. Die meisten Beschreibungen von Studienfächern bringen das erwartete Ergebnis – die Manifestation des kritischen Denkens einer Person, ohne den Kontext ihrer Ausbildung festzuhalten. In der wissenschaftlichen Literatur wird viel Wert darauf gelegt, die in den Vorlesungen vorgestellten Aufgaben darzustellen, die angewandten Methoden und Werkzeuge zu beschreiben und die vorbereitenden experimentellen Arbeiten aufzudecken. Der breitere Kontext des kritischen Denkens – die Voraussetzungen für die Entwicklung des kritischen Denkens, die Bedingungen für dessen Unterstützung, das konkrete

Umfeld und die spezifischen Umstände – wird jedoch viel weniger analysiert. In der wissenschaftlichen Literatur gibt es auch wenig Daten zu den Auswirkungen der Entwicklung des kritischen Denkens. Die Daten der qualitativen Studie geben Hinweise auf das gesteigerte Vertrauen der Studierenden, auf mutige Experimente, auf die von Arbeitnehmern unabhängig getroffenen Entscheidungen und den Mut, unvernünftige Entscheidungen anderer in Frage zu stellen. Dies sind jedoch eher kurzfristige Zeugnisse. Uns stehen keine Daten über die langfristigen Folgen des kritischen Denkens zur Verfügung.

In Anbetracht der vorgebrachten Argumente wird Folgendes vorgeschlagen:

- Die Entwicklung des kritischen Denkens sollte so weit wie möglich weiterentwickelt werden und seine Bedeutung sollte nicht nur im persönlichen und beruflichen Bereich, sondern auch im weiteren Kontext von Phänomenen der Gemeinschaft, des Landes und der Welt eröffnet werden;
- in die Studienprogramme sollten lokale, regionale und gesellschaftliche Themen einbezogen werden, wodurch Bedingungen für den Ausdruck der Fähigkeiten des kritischen Denkens der Studierenden in einem breiteren Kontext geschaffen werden. Mit anderen Worten sollen die Fähigkeiten der Schüler, theoretisches Wissen in der Praxis anzuwenden, entwickelt werden, wobei reale Situationen analysiert und gelöst oder Simulationen bereitgestellt werden;
- den günstigen und ungünstigen Kontext für kritisches Denken zu untersuchen und die Voraussetzungen, Bedingungen und Umstände für die Entwicklung des kritischen Denkens in der Hochschulbildung aufzudecken;
- die langfristigen Konsequenzen der Entwicklung des kritischen Denkens zu untersuchen, was deren Langlebigkeit und Nachhaltigkeit gewährleistet.

Der *sechste Aspekt* hat mit der Kritikalität zu tun. Die Ergebnisse der Studie zeigten: a) Kritikalität wird als Kern des kritischen Denkens angesehen; b) der Entwicklung und Aufrechterhaltung des kritischen Denkens wird nicht genügend Aufmerksamkeit gewidmet.

In den Ergebnissen der Studie spiegelt sich Kritikalität in einem sorgfältigen und wachsamen Blick auf sich selbst und die Umwelt wider, als ständiges Hinterfragen und Überdenken der eigenen Gedanken, Entscheidungen und Handlungen. Die Kritikalität steht auch mit Wahrheit und Gerechtigkeit im Zusammenhang – zwei Begriffen, die nicht nur als die zu verfolgenden Ideale angesehen werden, sondern auch als die notwendigen Praktiken, die sich in alltäglichen Entscheidungen ergeben. Der Aspekt der Kritikalität wird in den Ergebnissen der qualitativen Studie – in den Erfahrungen von Lehrern, Arbeitgebern und Arbeitnehmern – sehr deutlich. Er spiegelt sich nicht in den Erfahrungen der Studenten wider. Kritikalität wurde auch in einzelnen Beschreibungen von Studienprogrammen oder Studienfächern gefunden. Die Analyse ihres Inhalts ergab, dass Kritikalität in bestimmten spezifischen Kunstprogrammen in direktem Zusammenhang mit den Ideen der kritischen Theorie steht. Die Kritikalität wird auch in der wissenschaftlichen Literatur analysiert. Zwar wird sie an einer Stelle als wesentliches Merkmal des kritischen Denkens bezeichnet, an anderer Stelle wird jedoch klar zwischen ihr und dem kritischen Denken unterschieden.

In Anbetracht der vorgebrachten Argumente wird Folgendes vorgeschlagen:

- Im Studienprozess sollte dem Aspekt der Kritikalität mehr Aufmerksamkeit geschenkt, den Studierenden sollten Selbstanalyse und Selbstreflexion beigebracht und die Möglichkeit geboten werden, Fehler zu machen und sich selbst zu korrigieren, ihre Arbeit ständig zu verbessern, verschiedene Situationen und Phänomene in Bezug auf Wahrheit und Gerechtigkeit nicht nur im beruflichen, sondern auch in einem breiteren gesellschaftlichen Kontext zu analysieren;
- die Manifestationen der Kritikalität in verschiedenen Kontexten des Studiums, des beruflichen und sozialen Lebens sollten eingehender untersuchen werden, um die Einzigartigkeit und den Wert des Konzepts des kritischen Denkens aufzuzeigen.

Die durchgeführte Studie lässt die Feststellung zu, dass der Ausdruck des kritischen Denkens sowohl im Kontext der Hochschulbildung als auch im Kontext des Arbeitsmarktes mit den Bemühungen und der Bereitschaft und den Möglichkeiten einer Person zusammenhängt, in verschiedenen Situationen kritisch zu denken. Kritisches Denken äußert sich in der bewussten Wahl einer Person und der aktiven, zielgerichteten und organisierten Anstrengung, ihr Wissen, ihre Fähigkeiten anzuwenden und in einer bestimmten Situation zu handeln, um das gewünschte Ergebnis zu erzielen. Ein kritisch denkender Mensch muss nicht nur in der Lage sein, reflektiert zu denken, zu recherchieren und zu analysieren, sondern auch eine solche Denkweise zu wählen.

Kritisches Denken ist daher ein komplexer Prozess, der mit der Wahrnehmung von Informationen beginnt und mit der Reflexion über die getroffene Entscheidung endet. Und obwohl die Notwendigkeit und das Streben nach der Entwicklung des kritischen Denkens in strategischen Bildungsdokumenten klar zum Ausdruck kommt, ist es nicht zu einer systematischen Bildungspraxis in der Hochschulbildung geworden. Dafür braucht es sowohl Zeit als auch Verständnis und Einstellung. Nur wenn man sich darüber einig ist, was als kritisches Denken angesehen wird, welche Fähigkeiten und Dispositionen für kritisches Denken im Kontext eines bestimmten Studienprogramms für die Entwicklung des kritischen Denkens als systematischer Prozess, für dessen Ergebnisse alle Prozessteilnehmer Verantwortung tragen, am wichtigsten sind, dann wird das Ergebnis erreicht. Das heißt, die Anforderung des modernen Arbeitsmarktes, einen kritisch denkenden, hochqualifizierten Spezialisten auszubilden, werden erfüllt.

List of Tables

List of Figures

ERZIEHUNGSKONZEPTIONEN UND PRAXIS

Herausgeben von Gerd-Bodo von Carlsburg

Band 1 Barbara Hellinge / Manfred Jourdan / Hubertus Maier-Hein: Kleine Pädagogik der Antike. 1984.

Band 2 Siegfried Prell: Handlungsorientierte Schulbegleitforschung. Anleitung, Durchführung und Evaluation. 1984.

Band 3 Gerd-Bodo Reinert: Leitbild Gesamtschule versus Gymnasium? Eine Problemskizze. 1984.

Band 4 Ingeborg Wagner: Aufmerksamkeitsförderung im Unterricht. Hilfen durch Lehrertraining. 1984.

Band 5 Peter Struck: Pädagogische Bindungen. Zur Optimierung von Lehrerverhalten im Schulalltag. 1984.

Band 6 Wolfgang Sehringer (Hrsg.): Lernwelten und Instruktionsformen. 1986.

Band 7 Gerd-Bodo Reinert (Hrsg.): Kindgemäße Erziehung. 1986.

Band 8 Heinrich Walther: Testament eines Schulleiters. 1986.

Band 9 Gerd-Bodo Reinert / Rainer Dieterich (Hrsg.): Theorie und Wirklichkeit – Studien zum Lehrerhandeln zwischen Unterrichtstheorie und Alltagsroutine. 1987.

Band 10 Jörg Petersen / Gerhard Priesemann: Einführung in die Unterrichtswissenschaft. Teil 1: Sprache und Anschauung. 2., überarb. Aufl. 1992.

Band 11 Jörg Petersen / Gerhard Priesemann: Einführung in die Unterrichtswissenschaft. Teil 2: Handlung und Erkenntnis. 1992.

Band 12 Wolfgang Hammer: Schulverwaltung im Spannungsfeld von Pädagogik und Gesellschaft. 1988.

Band 13 Werner Jünger: Schulunlust. Messung – Genese – Intervention. 1988.

Band 14 Jörg Petersen / Gerhard Priesemann: Unterricht als regelgeleiteter Handlungszusammenhang. Ein Beitrag zur Verständigung über Unterricht. 1988.

Band 15 Wolf-Dieter Hasenclever (Hrsg.): Pädagogik und Psychoanalyse. Marienauer Symposion zum 100. Geburtstag Gertrud Bondys. 1990.

Band 16 Jörg Petersen / Gerd-Bodo Reinert / Erwin Stephan: Betrifft: Hausaufgaben. Ein Überblick über die didaktische Diskussion für Elternhaus und Schule. 1990.

Band 17 Rudolf G. Büttner / Gerd-Bodo Reinert (Hrsg.): Schule und Identität im Wandel. Biographien und Begebenheiten aus dem Schulalltag zum Thema Identitätsentwicklung. 1991.

Band 18 Eva Maria Waibel: Von der Suchtprävention zur Gesundheitsförderung in der Schule. Der lange Weg der kleinen Schritte. 3. Aufl. 1994.

Band 19 Heike Biermann: Chancengerechtigkeit in der Grundschule – Anspruch und Wirklichkeit. 1992.

Band 20 Wolf-Dieter Hasenclever (Hrsg.): Reformpädagogik heute: Wege der Erziehung zum ökologischen Humanismus. 2. Marienauer Symposion zum 100. Geburtstag von Max Bondy. 1993. 2., durchges. Aufl. 1998.

Band 21 Bernd Arnold: Medienerziehung und moralische Entwicklung von Kindern. Eine medienpädagogische Untersuchung zur Moral im Fernsehen am Beispiel einer Serie für Kinder im Umfeld der Werbung. 1993.

Band 22 Dimitrios Chatzidimou: Hausaufgaben konkret. Eine empirische Untersuchung an deutschen und griechischen Schulen der Sekundarstufen. 1994.

Band 23 Klaus Knauer: Diagnostik im pädagogischen Prozeß. Eine didaktisch-diagnostische Handreichung für den Fachlehrer. 1994.

Band 24 Jörg Petersen / Gerd-Bodo Reinert (Hrsg.): Lehren und Lernen im Umfeld neuer Technologien. Reflexionen vor Ort. 1994.

Band 25 Stefanie Voigt: Biologisch-pädagogisches Denken in der Theorie. 1994.

Band 26 Stefanie Voigt: Biologisch-pädagogisches Denken in der Praxis. 1994.

Band 27 Reinhard Fatke / Horst Scarbath: Pioniere Psychoanalytischer Pädagogik. 1995.

Band 28 Rudolf G. Büttner / Gerd-Bodo Reinert (Hrsg.): Naturschutz in Theorie und Praxis. Mit Beispielen zum Tier-, Landschafts- und Gewässerschutz. 1995.

Band 29 Dimitrios Chatzidimou / Eleni Taratori: Hausaufgaben. Einstellungen deutscher und griechischer Lehrer. 1995.

Band 30 Bernd Weyh: Vernunft und Verstehen: Hans-Georg Gadamers anthropologische Hermeneutikkonzeption. 1995.

Band 31 Helmut Arndt / Henner Müller-Holtz (Hrsg.): Schulerfahrungen – Lebenserfahrungen. Anspruch und Wirklichkeit von Bildung und Erziehung heute. Reformpädagogik auf dem Prüfstand. 2. Aufl. 1996.

Band 32 Karlheinz Biller: Bildung erwerben in Unterricht, Schule und Familie. Begründung – Bausteine – Beispiele. 1996.

Band 33 Ruth Allgäuer: Evaluation macht uns stark! Zur Unverzichtbarkeit von Praxisforschung im schulischen Alltag. 1997. 2., durchges. Aufl. 1998.

Band 34 Christel Senges: Das Symbol des Drachen als Ausdruck einer Konfliktgestaltung in der Sandspieltherapie. Ergebnisse aus einer Praxis für analytische Psychotherapie von Kindern und Jugendlichen. 1998.

Band 35 Achim Dehnert: Untersuchung der Selbstmodelle von Managern. 1997.

Band 36 Shen-Keng Yang: Comparison, Understanding and Teacher Education in International Perspective. Edited and introduced by Gerhard W. Schnaitmann. 1998.

Band 37 Johann Amos Comenius: Allverbesserung (Panorthosia). Eingeleitet, übersetzt und erläutert von Franz Hofmann. 1998.

Band 38 Edeltrud Ditter-Stolz: Zeitgenössische Musik nach 1945 im Musikunterricht der Sekundarstufe I. 1999.

Band 39 Manfred Luketic: Elektrotechnische Lernsoftware für den Technikunterricht an Hauptschulen. 1999.

Band 40 Gerhard Baltes / Brigitta Eckert: Differente Bildungsorte in systemischer Vernetzung. Eine Antwort auf das Problem der funktionellen Differenzierung in der Kooperation zwischen Jugendarbeit und Schule. 1999.

Band 41 Roswit Strittmatter: Soziales Lernen. Ein Förderkonzept für sehbehinderte Schüler. 1999.

Band 42 Thomas H. Häcker: Widerstände in Lehr-Lern-Prozessen. Eine explorative Studie zur pädagogischen Weiterbildung von Lehrkräften. 1999.

Band 43 Sabine Andresen / Bärbel Schön (Hrsg.): Lehrerbildung für morgen. Wissenschaftlicher Nachwuchs stellt sich vor. 1999.

Band 44 Ernst Begemann: Lernen verstehen – Verstehen lernen. Zeitgemäße Einsichten für Lehrer und Eltern. Mit Beiträgen von Heinrich Bauersfeld. 2000.

Band 45 Günter Ramachers: Das intrapersonale Todeskonzept als Teil sozialer Wirklichkeit. 2000.

Band 46 Christoph Dönges: Lebensweltliche Erfahrung statt empirischer Enteignung. Grenzen und Alternativen empirischer Konzepte in der (Sonder-)Pädagogik. 2000.

Band 47 Michael Luley: Eine kleine Geschichte des deutschen Schulbaus. Vom späten 18. Jahrhundert bis zur Gegenwart. 2000.

Band 48 Helmut Arndt / Henner Müller-Holtz (Hrsg.): Herausforderungen an die Pädagogik aufgrund des gegenwärtigen gesellschaftlichen Wandels. Bildung und Erziehung am Beginn des 3. Jahrtausends. 2000.

Band 49 Johann Amos Comenius: Allermahnung (Pannuthesia). Eingeleitet, übersetzt und erläutert von Franz Hofmann. 2001.

Band 50 Hans-Peter Spittler-Massolle: Blindheit und blindenpädagogischer Blick. Der *Brief über die Blinden zum Gebrauch für die Sehenden* von Denis Diderot und seine Bedeutung für den Begriff von Blindheit. 2001.

Band 51 Eva Rass: Kindliches Erleben bei Wahrnehmungsproblemen. Möglichkeiten einer selbst- psychologisch ausgerichteten Pädagogik und Psychotherapie bei sublimen und unerkannten Schwächen in der sensorischen Integration. 2002.

Band 52 Bruno Hamann: Neue Herausforderungen für eine zeitgemäße und zukunftsorientierte Schule. Unter Mitarbeit von Birgitta Hamann. 2002.

Band 53 Johann Amos Comenius: Allerleuchtung (Panaugia). Eingeleitet, übersetzt und erläutert von Franz Hofmann. 2002.

Band 54 Bernd Sixtus: Alasdair MacIntyres Tugendenlehre von *After Virtue* als Beitrag zum Disput über universalistische Erziehungsziele. 2002.

Band 55 Elke Wagner: Sehbehinderung und Soziale Kompetenz. Entwicklung und Erprobung eines Konzeptes. 2003.

Band 56 Jutta Rymarczyk / Helga Haudeck: *In Search of The Active Learner.* Untersuchungen zu Fremdsprachenunterricht, bilingualen und inter- disziplinären Kontexten. 2003.

Band 57 Gerhard W. Schnaitmann: Forschungsmethoden in der Erziehungswissenschaft. Zum Verhältnis von qualitativen und quantitativen Methoden in der Lernforschung an einem Beispiel der Lernstrategienforschung. 2004.

Band 58 Bernd Schwarz / Thomas Eckert (Hrsg.): Erziehung und Bildung nach TIMSS und PISA. 2004.

Band 59 Werner Sacher / Alban Schraut (Hrsg.): Volkserzieher in dürftiger Zeit. Studien über Leben und Wirken Eduard Sprangers. 2004.

Band 60 Dorothee Dahl: Interdisziplinär geprägte Symbolik in der visuellen Kommunikation. Tendenzen therapeutisch-kunstpädagogischer Unterrichts- modelle vor dem Hintergrund multimedialer Zeitstrukturen. 2005.

Band 61 Gerd-Bodo von Carlsburg / Marian Heitger (Hrsg.): Der Lehrer – ein (un)möglicher Beruf. 2005.

Band 62 Bruno Hamann: Pädagogische Anthropologie. Theorien – Modelle – Strukturen. Eine Einführung. 4., überarbeitete und ergänzte Auflage. 2005.

Band 63 Airi Liimets: Bestimmung des lernenden Menschen auf dem Wege der Reflexion über den Lernstil. 2005.

Band 64 Cornelia Matz: Vorbilder in den Medien. Ihre Wirkungen und Folgen für Heranwachsende. 2005.

Band 65 Birgitta Hamann: Grundfragen der Literaturdidaktik und zentrale Aspekte des Deutschunterrichts. 2005.

Band 66 Ralph Olsen / Hans-Bernhard Petermann / Jutta Rymarczyk (Hrsg.): Intertextualität und Bildung – didaktische und fachliche Perspektiven. 2006.

Band 67 Bruno Hamann: Bildungssystem und Lehrerbildung im Fokus aktueller Diskussionen. Bestandsaufnahme und Perspektiven. 2006.

Band 68 Ingeborg Seitz: Heterogenität als Chance. Lehrerprofessionalität im Wandel. 2007.

Band 69 Margret Ruep / Gustav Keller: Schulevaluation. Grundlagen, Methoden, Wirksamkeit. 2007.

Band 70 Harald Schweizer: Krach oder Grammatik? Streitschrift für einen revidierten Sprachunterricht. Kritik und Vorschläge. 2008.

Band 71 Martina Becker / Gerd-Bodo von Carlsburg / Helmut Wehr (Hrsg.): Seelische Gesundheit und gelungenes Leben. Perspektiven der Humanistischen Psychologie und Humanistischen Pädagogik. Ein Handbuch. 2008.

Band 72 Sigvard Clasen: Bildung im Licht von Beschäftigung und Wachstum. Wohin bewegt sich Deutschland? 2009.

Band 73 Gerd-Bodo von Carlsburg: Enkulturation und Bildung. Fundament sozialer Kompetenz. 2009.

Band 74 Hermann-Josef Wilbert: Musikunterricht im Rückblick. Eine alternative Musikdidaktik. 2009.

Band 75 Britta Klopsch: Fremdevaluation im Rahmen der Qualitätsentwicklung und -sicherung. Eine Evaluation der Qualifizierung baden-württembergischer Fremdevaluatorinnen und Fremdevaluatoren. 2009.

Band 76 Leonard Wehr: Partizipatorisches Marketing privater Hochschulen. Corporate Identity als Ziel von Bildungsmarketing. 2011.

Band 77 Konstantinos D. Chatzidimou: Microteaching als erlebnis- und handlungsorientierte Methode im Rahmen der Lehrerausbildung und der Didaktik. Eine theoretische und empirische Untersuchung. 2012.

Band 78 Miriam Lange: Befähigen, befähigt werden, sich befähigen – Eine Auseinandersetzung mit dem Capability Approach. 2014.

Band 79 Eva Rass (Hrsg.): Comenius: Seiner Zeit weit voraus...! Die Entdeckung der Kindheit als grundlegende Entwicklungsphase. 2014.

Band 80 Cornelia Frech-Becker: Disziplin durch Bildung – ein vergessener Zusammenhang. Eine historisch-systematische Untersuchung aus antinomischer Perspektive als Grundlage für ein bildungstheoretisches Verständnis des Disziplinproblems. 2015.

Band 81 Rüdiger Funiok / Harald Schöndorf (Hrsg.): Ignatius von Loyola und die Pädagogik der Jesuiten. Ein Modell für Schule und Persönlichkeitsbildung. 2017.

Band 82 Lara Rodríguez Sieweke (ed.): Learning Scenarios for Social and Cultural Change. *Bildung* Through Academic Teaching. 2017.

Band 83 Fred Maurer: Leseförderung durch Kriminalliteratur. Deutschdidaktische Annäherungen an ein verkanntes und vernachlässigtes Genre. 2019.

Band 84 Otilia Clipa / Erica Cîmpan: Social-Emotional Competences of Preschoolers. The Impact of Outdoor Educational Activities. 2020.

Band 85 Mariana Sirotová / Veronika Michvocíková /Marián Host'ovecký: Serious Games in University Education of Future Teachers. 2021.

Band 86 Valdonė Indrašienė/ Violeta Jegelevičienė / Odeta Merfeldaitė / Daiva Penkauskienė / Jolanta Pivorienė /Asta Railienė / Justinas Sadauskas / Natalija Valavičienė: Critical Thinking in Higher Education and Labour Market. 2021.

www.peterlang.com

www.ingramcontent.com/pod-product-compliance
Ingram Content Group UK Ltd.
Pitfield, Milton Keynes, MK11 3LW, UK
UKHW041824100926
8556IPUK00002B/8

9 783631 833704